HOW TO HYPNOTIZE YOURSELF & OTHERS

BY RACHEL COPELAN, Ph. D.

WINGS BOOKS

New York • Avenel, New Jersey

This publication is designed to provide accurate and authoritative
information in regard to the subject matter covered. It is sold with
the understanding that the publisher is not engaged in rendering
legal, accounting, or other professional service. If legal advice or
other assistance is required, the services of a competent professional
person should be sought. *From a Declaration of Principles jointly
adopted by a Committee of the American Bar Association and a
Committee of Publishers.*

This 1995 edition is published by Wings Books,
a division of Random House Value Publishing, Inc.,
40 Engelhard Avenue, Avenel, New Jersey 07001,
by arrangement with Lifetime Books, Inc.,
Hollywood, Florida, 33020.

Wings Books and colophon are trademarks
of Random House Value Publishing, Inc.

Random House
New York • Toronto • London • Sydney • Auckland
http://www.randomhouse.com/

Printed and bound in the United States of America

Library of Congress Cataloging-in-Publication Data

Copelan, Rachel.
How to hypnotize yourself and others.

Originally published: New York : F. Fell Publishers, c1981.
1. Hypnotism—Therapeutic use. 2. Autogenic training.
I. Title.
RC495.C66   1983   615.8'512   83—18775

ISBN: 0-517-42806-7

20 19 18 17 16 15 14 13 12 11

Contents

CONTENTS

Preface

We are living in a decade where more and more people are searching for alternative answers to the conventional ways of solving problems. In the 1990's the trend is toward self exploration and self-help to prevent the many evils that result from the over-stressed lives most of us live.

The best method of relaxing the body and keeping the emotions elevated is through the proven process of hypnosis. When all else fails, when pills and potions leave side effects more detrimental than the original ailment, intelligent people reach inward to the source of the disturbance.

Hypnosis is at last coming into its own after centuries of being dismissed as theatrical magic or the practice of "quacks." Ignorance and superstition have combined to create a veil of mystery obscuring the nature and benefits of this valuable technique. In the past few years, millions of people have seen examples of hypnotic phenomena on prime-time television. There is a tremendous popular curiosity about them and very few books to answer the need. Those books that are available are mainly written for professionals working in the fields of psychology and medicine. The few books that have been written for the layman tend to be limited to the uses and techniques of a decade ago.

The purpose of this book is to acquaint both the beginner and professional with most up-to-date methods and uses of hypnosis. With simplified techniques that anyone can quickly learn, it is possible to harness a dynamo of mental energy more productive than any oil well in the Middle East. If you are like most of us, you will use only ten percent of your brain's capacity in your lifetime. Imagine the potential for good if we could learn how to tap some part of the remaining ninety percent! WELL, WE CAN! Hypnosis is not only effective as a key to the mind, it can also help to direct the mind's energy to alter our concepts and sensations.

During hypnosis, applied suggestion causes changes to take place in the message system that leads from the brain through the spinal cord, and on through countless branches of nerves, large and small, short and long. The twitch of an eye, the motion of a finger, a puff on a cigarette, the lifting of a beer bottle, all are controllable through hypnotic thought. Nerve responses are complex and multitudinous, yet respond to simple reconditioning techniques when receptivity is established during induced hypnosis. Pain, pleasure, boredom, and joy are all reactions to a passing thought. For this reason, thoughts sometimes will enslave an individual and the power of his mind will turn against him, magnifying his problems instead of helping him solve them. Hypnosis is the facilitator that helps you to tap the brain's resources and efficiently use its energy in a most positive, controlled manner.

Hypnosis is the wedge with which we can enter and stretch the mind to enhance the human potential for personal and professional growth. There is no other single therapeutic technique that holds out so many possibilities for exploration.

Part One
For Beginners

Habits and Hidden Hypnosis

We have all been secretly hypnotized. Yes *you* probably have, too, unless you are one of those rare individuals who has never watched a television program. Most people drift into a common, everyday trance when they gaze into the light of the TV tube. Indirect hypnosis manipulates the minds of millions of unsuspecting viewers everyday. Surreptitiously, subliminal persuasion leaves its mark upon the collective subconscious. Ideas implanted by commercials affect the health and behavior of all of us. We eat, drink, dress, and make love based on what we see and hear. Television has the power to lull the mind into a state of exaggerated suggestibility, opening it up to behavior control from the outside.

Billions of dollars are spent each year in the United States to push products we could live better without. Intelligence not withstanding, we allow ourselves to be coerced into consuming products dumb animals would run from: sleep inducers, fat reducers, uppers, downers, pain killers for every part of the body. TV, in fact, can train the brain to anticipate pain even when you feel fine.

Advertisers are well aware of the basic principles of hypnosis: (1) Relaxation, (2) Concentration, and (3) Suggestion. It's simple. As we sit relaxed and concentrate on the light, we absorb the suggestions directed at us. During such periods we are extremely vulnerable because we enter a hypnotic state of consciousness (Alpha). Have you noticed how often a commercial is repeated? This is another principle of hypnosis. Repetition enforces suggestion and finally engraves the behavior into the reflexes of the nervous system. The dictionary defines habit this way: "An act or practice so frequently repeated as to become relatively fixed in character and almost automatic in performance."

Every moment of the day and night, newspapers, billboards, radio announcers, and television commercials are implanting harmful habits deeply into the mind. Inevitably, *we become outer-directed instead of inner-protected.*

The average person spends fifteen years of his life immobilized, gazing at the television tube with childlike faith in what he is told. Periodically, every few minutes, day after day, specially-trained voices, ringing with sincerity, assure us that their pills and potions are *the* panaceas. Some people become so convinced by this colossal put-on that they buy things they never heard of.

Surveys estimate that U.S. pharmaceutical companies spend billions of dollars each year to promote over-the-counter drugs. Headache soothers, nerve smoothers, uppers, downers, sleep inducers, and weight reducers are incessantly pushed on the unwary consumer. We are psychologically tricked by motivational researchers, social scientists, and psychological consultants to lose control of our appetites. Substances we could live longer without, such as alcohol, cigarettes, and fattening foods, come to seem indispensable.

Why do we deliberately do harm to our health?

Obviously, one's instinct for self-preservation becomes confused by the steady bombardment of the ad men. Our senses are assaulted by psychological devices which our conscious minds cannot detect, secret in-depth language is used to subconsciously stimulate our tastes, and the result is that bad habits are implanted and reinforced without our suspecting it.

Eventually, masses of people are convinced problems have easy, superficial solutions. The persuaders evoke more than physical appetite. They also appeal to the emotions: fears of rejection, guilt, and loneliness. Instead of helping us to use our innate abilities to cope with the challenge of daily living, the media has been converting the human mind into catatonic dough. To some extent, most of us have fallen prey to the huckster's pitch, letting ourselves be channeled into unthinking habits custom-built to serve industry's motive to make a profit even if the product promotes death.

If the advertising media doesn't get to you, you may become influenced by the bad habits of the people around you. Only the rare, self-aware person manages to remain untouched by the behavior of others. For most, it's easier to succumb to the lure of the piper who sings, "Dance to the tune or become a social misfit." Rather than be ostracized, we fall into step—team players for free enterprise.

Eventually the indoctrination becomes ingrained as the victim begins to react with neurotic compulsion. This weakening of will leads to behavior even more harmful than the original stimuli promoted. Milder drugs escalate to stronger dosages. The alcoholic's "one drink" may graduate into "one bottle," the pot smoker's one joint into dependency. Addiction is reinforced as addicts are accepted into some of the highest social circles, where being "spaced out" is the "in thing." Try attending a party where most people are smoking pot. Refuse to participate and you may be treated like a "square" and not invited back. Yet, unless we are able to reject being programmed, we face not only the prospect of dehumanization, but also "moronization" as we come to behave more and more like brainless robots.

YOU CAN BREAK THE SPELL

Fortunately, the human brain is able to change. Learn to think for yourself! Habits are adjustable. Behavior is malleable. Areas of the mind marred by years of unhealthy thinking can become areas of growth and improvement through the utilization of positive programming. We can outgrow learned limitations and achieve the highest degree of innate potential.

Hypnosis helps in focusing on the inner reality of who you really are and what you want from life. Moreover, hypnosis is dynamically helpful in achieving those ends. You don't have to remain a cooperative puppet assisting in your own demise. You can stand on your own feet, take over your own controls and snip the strings of manipulation by others.

Self-enhancement requires systematic *deconditioning*, followed by *reconditioning*. Habits tend to cling like the tentacles of an octopus unless you are determined to free yourself from their grasp. The process is mental and it helps to know that, where your behavior is concerned, the most powerful mind involved is your own.

FROM THE WOMB TO THE TOMB

From the moment a baby is born, society's molding begins. The infant leaves its mother's womb and becomes a separate individual. Soon he is the recipient of suggested behavior that influences all of his future habits. He experiences sensations, which are stored in his memory bank. As he hears and feels, impressions that result form images for future reference.

It is interesting to note that children are in a trance state about fifty percent of their waking time. Their sponge like vulnerability explains their superior ability to absorb and retain information.

From the womb to the tomb, a persistent contest for control prevails between the "other world" and one's inner world of intelligence. Most of us allow the outside to take over the inside and so we travel from birth to old age, acquiring one habit after another. Some habits are, of course, useful and necessary, while others are so dreadfully addictive and destructive they lead to illness and premature death. If some of your habits disturb you, consider yourself normal, for we are all creatures of habit. Like a soft bed, habits are easy to get into and hard to get out of.

Once our power over the selection and rejection of habits has vanished, desire surpasses logic because the user has lost his ability to evaluate objectively. From the richest to the poorest, everyone is hooked to at least one bad habit. Fact is, most of us have more than one. A network of harmful behavior takes over as one habit interlaces with another. Finally, a destructive lifestyle evolves.

Overeating	Uppers	Cocaine
Smoking	Downers	Negative Thinking
Alcohol	Marijuana	

Some people, collecting bad habits like a hobby, are burdened with all of these. Combinations are limitless and uniquely individual. Periodically, the routinized person may attempt to alter his fixed conduct. He may give up cigarettes, but in most cases he drifts back. If able to stay off cigarettes, he may substitute fattening food or alcohol. Instead of smoking himself to death, he's eating or drinking himself to death. And it matters little to the undertaker which bad habit did him in.

IMITATION IS A POWERFUL FORCE

We know that human social conduct is reinforced through emulation. Your senses feed your habits. The input to habit comes from *sensory perception*. Our thoughts and actions respond to:

What we see	What we smell
What we hear	What we touch
What we taste	

The human mind works like a computer, absorbing information through the senses. Reactions are fed back to the muscles, nerves and reflexes.

As a child grows, he learns that certain words evoke specific responses. Throughout the rest of his life, each word he hears, each sight he sees, every event his senses absorb elicits images and reactions. This response is called output.

Your mind is constantly concerned with input and output.

For example, the word "animal" might bring to mind a positive or negative image, depending upon previously acquired impressions. To a child once frightened by an angry dog, it would present a negative image, while to another child it might recall a pleasant memory of a playful pet.

Reflexes are trained to behave in a ritualized pattern by the process of image-recall. Our brain is constantly flashing images for our consideration. Not only old images, but those we pick up from our immediate environment. This is why it's important to develop the ability to sort out the wanted from the unwanted impressions.

HOW SUGGESTION WORKS

We have noted that television is a prime example of mass suggestion. These days, a person cannot hang out the laundry without worrying about "Tattle-tale gray," "Ring-around-the-collar," and so on.

Fears of acid-indigestion, cancer, and heart attack bombard the television viewer as he sits transfixed, open-mouthed and blank-minded. The more a person absorbs, the more he suspects something must be wrong with him. Many psychologists believe worrisome commercials can cause the very problem the announcer warns against. No wonder people are confused.

Take, for example, Mrs. Gullible. Mrs. Gullible watches television night and day. She begins to imagine she has every ailment described. Before long, filled with anxiety, she makes an appointment to see a doctor for a checkup.

By the time Mrs. Gullible arrives in the doctor's office, she is a bundle of nerves, expecting bad news. After a thorough examination, the doctor assures her that there is nothing physically wrong with her. But Mrs. Gullible won't take no for an answer. The power of television suggestion has left its mark in her mind.

"Look me over again, doctor," she persists. "I must have a lump somewhere.

Her complaints continue. Headaches, backaches, sleeplessness, anxiety. As a result, not only has she been conned into buying useless products, but she harbors a fear that no matter what the doctor says, something must be wrong. She travels from doctor to doctor in search of one who will confirm her fears. As long as Mrs. Gullible persists in her negative expectations, she may eventually develop a symptomatic ailment. *This syndrome is responsible for a great number of psychosomatic illnesses.*

Hypochondriacs are people who, like Mrs. Gullible, have fallen into the habit of imagining ailments that exist only in their fantasies. These people are highly suggestible because of their impressionable imaginations.

Scrutinize your own behavior. Do your negative habits override your positive ones? Are you propelled by a force over which you have no control? Keep in mind problems are not solved by pills, puffs of smoke, sniffs of powder, or chocolate cream pie. Problems can only be solved by facing them squarely and by taking the proper action to eradicate them. Hold a mirror up to the innermost workings of your mind. You may find some of your thinking habits just to be someone else's, implanted while you were least suspecting it.

The first step against bad conditioning is *deconditioning*, which erases the old imprint so you can start with a clean slate. The next step is *reconditioning*, which imprints new and better thoughts for healthier behavior. Hypnosis accomplishes this through retraining the reflexes.

A conditioned reflex can be defined as a reflex which is activated by a new signal as the result of new connections being formed within the brain. It exists in every person, is produced by repetition, and will tend to deteriorate unless regularly reinforced. (This last characteristic can be useful or detrimental.) The conditioned reflex is involved in the development of athletic skills, too. *Thought initiates specific movement.*

THE CONDITIONED REFLEX

The conditioned reflex is at the root of every habit pattern. This is the automatic response that makes you get out of bed in the morning, walk to the bathroom, wash your face, brush your teeth, dress, eat breakfast, go to work, and follow you usual routine.

We are products of our environment. Every experience we have leaves a mark on the cortex of the brain. This works in very much the same way as a tape recorder does. Like a recorder, imprints are played and replayed. Each time an experience is repeated, the markings on the cortex of the brain are strengthened. Repeating a habit makes this engraving penetrate deeper.

Dr. Ivan P. Pavlov was a Russian physiologist. He received the Nobel prize for physiology and medicine in 1904 for his outstanding contribution in tracing patterns of human behavior based on laboratory research with animals. He was the first authority on the development of conditioned reflexes. In his experiments with dogs, he not only discovered how habits originate, but what makes them repetitive.

Using the following test, Dr. Pavlov discovered a reflexive habit could be firmly established in a dog. He would ring a bell and then offer the dog food. After this procedure had been repeated several times, whenever Dr. Pavlov rang the bell the dog would salivate in eager anticipation. Eventually the dog began to salivate if he heard the bell ring *even when he was not hungry.* The bell had become a signal to the brain which started the flow of digestive juices. In other words, the brain told the glands, "Secrete! Food's coming," even after the dog's belly was full.

How does the Pavlov experiment with a dog compare to human behavior?

PEOPLE ARE ALSO TRAINED ANIMALS

Human beings respond to stimuli in very much the same way as animals. In spite of their superior intelligence, sensory signals set off reflexive behavior.

For example, take the plight of Rosemary Jones. Rosemary weighs two hundred and sixty pounds. Whenever she passes a bakery window, her mouth begins to water. Her body doesn't need the calories, yet she "can't help herself."

"Should I or shouldn't I?" she agonizes. "Oh, just this one last time," she tells herself. "One more cream puff won't make that much difference.

The moment she swallows, Rosemary wishes she hadn't.

" Oh, why did I do it?" she scolds herself. "It doesn't make sense I'll never do such a stupid thing again," she promises and means to keep her promise, too. She does, until the next temptation Like Pavlov's dog, her salivary glands responded to her senses even when there was no hunger. Just as the experimental dog reacts, so do we when the bell in our mind rings.

The mere mention of the word "food" will tickle the palate of a habitual overeater, even if he's already stuffed. Drinkers of alcohol, cigarette smokers, and drug addicts behave in the same programmed way, responding to signals like trained animals in a circus act.

Bob T., one of my clients, said, "Every time the telephone rings, I automatically reach for a cigarette, even if I've just finished one." He paused and smiled sadly. "Even if it's not my telephone."

Another habit-hooked client, Harry P., described himself as "totally dependent on one martini to pick me up before dinner and a couple afterward to settle me down for the evening."

Habit-addicts associate their habit with emotional satisfaction. Thus, when feeling signs of distress, they reach for a pacifier.

Dr. Pavlov not only demonstrated that habits become entrenched by repetition; he also discovered something else.

CONDITIONING IS STRONGER AND FASTER WHEN THE EMOTIONS ARE INVOLVED.

Whenever Pavlov's laboratory dogs were irritable or anxious, they reacted with increased tensions and salivated more. Keep in mind that appetite is often not based on hunger or real need, but rather on emotions because emotions spur physical reactions.

HOW EMOTIONS AND HABITS INTERRELATE

Dr. Pavlov proved that a conditioned reflex (habit) could be established even from *just one input if strong emotion is present*. Because this is true, traumatic shocks can bring on reflexive behavior which may last a lifetime. The following example illustrates how this principle works both for a man and an animal:

A new mailman approaches a house. The dog living on the premises barks. The inexperienced mailman kicks the dog. The dog becomes frightened and snaps at the mailman's trousers.

The conflict persists as long as the mailman and the dog continue to react to each other with fear, and the habit extends beyond this particular situation. The mailman reacts with fear when he sees *any* dog and the dog barks at *every* mailman.

Let's see how this sort of automatic reaction applies to people in the ways they relate to each other. A woman molested by a man when she was a child may forever after tremble with fear at the advances of *all* men. Her automatic withdrawal may keep her from marrying, raising a family, and enjoying male-female intimacy.

The same may hold true for men who have had a disturbing experience with a woman early in life. Have you ever heard a man say: "All women are alike!" Such a person is reacting with conditioned emotions.

A black man may have been treated badly by a particular white employer, yet suppressed his hatred in order to keep his job. The power of that suppressed hatred can cause him to later react with strong distrust and hatred toward every white man who reminds him of his earlier boss.

The problem of reacting automatically and without logic has significance beyond the distrust it can create between two individuals. Conditioning affects entire nations and races. There are people who dislike all Jews, all Blacks, all Catholics, all Protestants, all Russians, even if they have known only one person in that category.

The habit of prejudice can become a barrier between people on many levels, involving even such simple things as physique or hair color. Some people cannot stand redheads; others, short people; others, tall people, or fat people, or thin people. Most habit reactions of a prejudicial nature have their root in some emotional experience of the past.

HABITS CAN BE BROKEN

Every human being comes into this world equipped with the necessary mental machinery to adjust to the harsh conditions of life and change them. This is not difficult if the desire is strong enough. When a person is motivated to change, he can do so. The hypnotic process is similar to the one which gave him the habit in the first place. Instead, however, absorbing of negative, harmful suggestions in the relaxed, receptive state, he uses positive, helpful ones and reverses the effect.

The most encouraging characteristic of a habit pattern is that the repetitive activity can be interrupted when the mind is turned to other interests. Hypnosis causes a break in the continuity of a habit, thereby acting as a wedge to weaken its hold on the mind. This is the key that can help change a harmful habit into a helpful one, because if the interruption can happen once, it can happen again and again.

PERSONALITY AND HABIT PATTERNS

Habits not only affect the body, but form the foundation of one's personality and character. People who chain-smoke or bite their nails are saying something about how they relate to life. Physical habits are merely ripples on the surface. Deep in the mind's riverbed, stress rocks and shocks the psyche. Emotional responses tend to become habitual. For example, some people, if given a choice between reacting with a smile or a frown, will invariably frown. Who decides whether you will feel happy or unhappy? Only you. Happiness is a habit. Abraham Lincoln said, "People are just about as happy as they make up their minds to be."

The point is, some people look at life with cheerful expectations while others expect everything to go wrong. Those anticipating the worst get what they're looking for. They also reinforce a very prevalent personality habit: self defeat. The habitual "loser" reveals his feelings about himself in his "body language." He may glue his eyes to the ground and walk with rounded shoulders or his body in a slump. If he would lift his head, arch his chest, and draw in his abdominal muscles, he would not only look like a winner, but reflect a winning personality.

Physical habits are the flip side of the way we feel toward ourselves. Emotional habits color not only the surface personality, but the deeper character as well. People are habitually depressed, habitually evasive, habitually late, habitually disorganized, habitually dishonest. The list is endless. Each individual combination of physical and emotional habits shapes you into the particular person you are.

Remember, hypnosis doesn't just take away your habits. Rather, it is a tested method for exchanging bad habits for good ones. It trains you how to maintain a relaxed body and tranquil mind, prerequisites for a strong and attractive personality.

The "wish to fail" is also a habit. People fall into the habit of unconsciously handling their affairs improperly. By so doing, they subconsciously make sure not to succeed.

Disaster-prone people fall into an automatic pattern in which they are always expecting failure. And every negative thought, no matter how fleeting, carries an anticipation of defeat.

The habit of negativism can actually turn some people into serious neurotics, according to a recent news release. Headed "Bad Habits That Drive You Crazy," it quotes Dr. Joseph Wolpe: "Neuroses are emotional bad habits. A neurosis results from a fearful response to things or situations which offer no real threat. Therapists now use their knowledge of learning processes to weaken and eliminate these bad habits. At the same time, they teach patients how to respond reasonably to a situation.

WINNERS AND LOSERS

There are winners and there are losers. I'm not talking about betting on a horse. I'm talking about betting on yourself. You can't control the horse's mood, but you can control your own.

Negative people tend to put off making decisions. This traps them into another bad habit: procrastination. One of the worst human failings is resistance to facing up to responsibility. We push unpleasant tasks into the background, waiting for "some other time," postponing while hoping the problem will simply disappear. For some procrastinators, tomorrow never comes. Days, months, and years may go by and they don't "get to it." Before they realize, their lives have passed by and they haven't fulfilled their dreams.

One interesting aspect of personality is that other people notice our failings more and sooner than we do. Traits can become so imbedded we do things automatically without knowing it. Routinized be havior is a giveaway to others as to what is going on in the deeper mind. For example, a salesman who wants to project confidence yet nervously interrupts his client is revealing rather than concealing his insecurity.

A self-proclaimed "loser," Gregory R., complained of his inability to close a sale. "I never seem to get the breaks," he said. "Other men have good luck. They get ahead of me and I'm always left behind. I don't understand why I'm so unlucky."

Do You Believe It's Really Luck that Makes a Person Succeed?
Or Is It His Pattern of Thinking

Gregory had not yet learned the sales power of his own mind. Eventually, he learned to apply self-hypnosis to change his self-image from low to high. The result was remarkable. Once he had lifted his self-esteem, his life took a turn for the better. Confident behavior invites and paves the way for success. Gregory also found he had to eliminate additional habits which had grown out of his self-denigrating attitude.

Here are the personality habits which interfered with Gregory's sales success. This was his "formula for failure."

The Procrastination Habit

Gregory was a chronic putter-offer. Slow to make decisions, fearful of making mistakes. He allowed things to slide. Bills piled up. Down to his last clean shirt in the drawer. Phone calls remained unanswered. Visits to his dentist postponed.

Gregory lived in a world of disorder and neglect. His life was swamped with unfinished business. But putting things off was only *one* of his problems. He also had:

The Fear of Success Habit

This is a common hang-up affecting millions of people. Because with success once attained, one must live up to its responsibilities. In order to avoid success, he postponed and developed:

The Self-Pity Habit

This is a pattern of thinking that habitual losers suffer from and that perpetuates their defeatist behavior, which eventually carries over into most areas of their lives.

The Alcoholism Habit

In Gregory's case, this led him straight to the nearest saloon where alcohol was used as a cop-out. And of course, then he had another habit to cope with.

HABITS HAVE ROOTS

Most of us are like Gregory. We develop a complex of physical and emotional habits which "branch out" from the "main trunk" of our daily behavior. While habits are sprouting, we may not notice them. Eventually they force themselves on our consciousness and we are amazed at their overpowering strength.

Sources of compulsive conduct can be traced back. Once you discover and uncover the "soil" and the "roots" of your "tree of behavior," you will better understand the "blossoming" that occurs on the surface. When the problem becomes clear, and you face up, you are ready for the next steps: how to dig it out, snip it off, reseed, replant, and grow healthy and meaningful habits.

Some capricious behavior stems from imitation. We tend to fall into a reaction pattern through parental indoctrination. Well-meaning parents, filled with love and "do-goodness," often train their children to follow in their footsteps. "Step into my shoes," says Dad hopefully, even if the shoes are uncomfortable; living through one's children is a bad parental habit. How often do we hear, "I've been teaching Junior how to run the button business since he was fourteen years old. Someday when I'm ready to retire to Florida, he'll take over for me and build it bigger and bigger."

While listening to this spiel year in and year out, Junior is secretly hating buttons. What Senior does not realize is: his shoe may not fit Junior's foot. Junior might prefer to be a ball player, an astronaut, or a rock musician. Torn between loyalty to parents and a desire to stand on one's own feet causes resentment and anger which becomes self-destructive.

Oral compulsiveness, such as eating, drinking, and smoking, can often be traced to early experiences. Habits feed on childhood memories, which are linked to emotions. The earliest moments of life can play a part. When a baby is loved and treated in a consistently warm and understanding way, he has stronger resistance to negative behavior in adult life.

Unless we use the mind's capacity for erasing past influences, we may remain forever linked to behavior suited to the infantile needs of childhood. An understanding of the nature of personality comes when we examine the attributes a child assumes as he or she matures. During the first six years of life, we develop:

1. Trust in or distrust for other people.
2. A general sense of self-confidence or self-doubt.
3. Initiative to try or fear of failure.
4. Sexual identity or gender confusion.
5. Friendliness toward or alienation from others.
6. Creative expression or destructiveness.

These habit patterns are more or less integrated into an individual's personality for life. However, one is never too old to improve, in spite of a bad beginning.

In reconditioning behavior that stems from negative early influences, the skilled hypnotherapist will regress the subject to early memories and use the information for reprogramming.

The most important influence upon a child's early development comes from parents, who set the standards for behavior. Parents' habits register on the minds of the tiniest children. Attitudes and actions are transmitted from the mature to the immature along with assorted information and misinformation. Brooding about what their parents did and didn't do causes many people to spend the best part of their lives on the psychiatrist's couch rehashing and regretting early happenings. Focusing on the past can downgrade the future, and therapy often fails because to dwell on misfortune and mistakes only reinforces their continuance.

One of the outstanding achievements of the therapeutic trance is its ability to wipe out traumatic memories. The subject finds upon awakening that his modes of functioning, both mental and physical, have been altered for the better. With the help of the hypnotherapist, a kind of subtle brainwashing takes place. The troubled person finds that his attitudes have switched from anxiety about the past to enthusiasm for the present and the future. Best of all, this occurs without striving, in a state of serene, positive anticipation.

Hypnosis not only utilizes positive suggestions, but also makes use of a very important aspect of suggestion, *the art of forgetting*. Under hypnotic and posthypnotic suggestion you learn to forget as deliberately and easily as you learn to remember or choose to forget. With out realizing what we are doing, some of us cling to memories as a self-punishing device because we are too guilt-ridden to allow ourselves the pleasure that comes with being guilt-free. Useless memories which limit happiness should be obliterated to make room in the subconscious for useful ones.

In cases of extreme emotional disturbances such as those resulting from rape, child abuse, fires, accidents or torture, a skilled hypnotist can perform techniques of amnesias and wipe out the memory entirely. When used for behavior modification, hypnotherapy erases habitual flashbacks to old images at the same time it lowers the tension level.

HOW THE NERVOUS SYSTEM WORKS

The human nervous system is composed of the brain, the spinal cord, and a network of nerves that branch out through the body. The nerves extend from head to toe, and information about every habit you have follows the route from the brain to the area of the body concerned. All bodily activities are thus controlled. This communication goes on day and night, whether you are awake or asleep. In lower animals, the feedback is instinctual. In human beings, however, emotions enter into the process as well as conscious thoughts. This is why so many people are troubled by problems other animals don't have.

The maze of nerves that forms the network of sensory input decides which information to pass on to the brain, unless there is interference by the intellect. Most people, however, are slaves to automatic nervous reaction. They react like robots to suggestions to chain-smoke, overeat, overdrink, etc.

Anyone can train himself to break the pattern and reverse the process. When conscious intelligence tells the nervous system what to accept and what to reject, we can become masters of our habits. In addition to the involuntary function of the brain, the area known as the cerebral cortex is largely responsible for decision making. Hypnosis can be used to help the cortex to function better and, thus, to make better decisions. The cortex is taught to desensitize the nerves dependent upon harmful substances such as nicotine, alcohol, or other drugs. Actions and habit responses will reflect negative conditioning until the nervous relay syndrome is deliberately changed on a subconscious level.

IT'S ALL IN YOUR HEAD

Nothing that man's brain has invented can compare with the brain itself. If man were to build a computer to do the work of one human brain, the computer would have to be as enormous as the Empire State Building and a lot more complicated. When we consider the size of the human brain, it is amazing to realize that this one organ accounts for the activity of the voluntary and involuntary systems of the body as well as consciousness, thought, perception, and creativity.

The specialized compartments of the brain each has a particular job to do in servicing the body and the thinking processes of the mind. They not only govern the involuntary internal organs, such as those that make up the digestive, circulatory, reproductive and respiratory systems; they also direct every single physical motion, down to the flicker of an eyelash. In addition, *every automatic habit and personal idiosyncrasy originates there.*

Since man first developed his ability to question, he has searched in awe for the answers to the mysteries which surround him. Man has used his intelligence to project far out into his environment, to the point where now he can study even faraway galaxies. Yet the greatest of all mysteries is not in outer space but in the inner space of our skulls. Inside the bony cave of the human head lies the real riddle of the universe, where about a trillion brain cells altogether weighing only about 3 to 3 1/2 lbs., control memory, imagination, communication, health, and happiness.

Hypnosis has been practiced for centuries under various names but didn't know how the altered state was accomplished. It was generally thought that the practioner had some special power. Now we know that it is the subject who actually brings about the changes with the practioner's guidance. The changes take place from the inside rather than outside. In the last decade brain scientists have broken the mystery of how the hypnotic process is triggered by the brain. Three new concepts have immerged.

1. NEUROPEPTIDES—This natural chemical is known to effect such basic functions as sleep, tension, appetite, drug and tobacco addiction, learning, sex and pleasure. Peptides are produced by the endocrine and nervous system and are found in Endorphins.

2. ENDORPHINS—This term refers to opiates manufactured by the brain. Hypnotic therapy tends to release this morphine-like substance and brings about changes in breathing, depression, aleviation of pain in dental work as well as arthritis and other painful conditions.

3. RIGHT /LEFT BRAIN—This concept explores research dealing with the theory of hemispheric specialization of the brain. This concept points to the right side of the thinking brain as the source of creative thinking and imagination. Visualizations, sensory stimulation and dreams are just a few of the services that the right side of the brain performs. The left side specializes in logical and linear thinking as well as conducting the practical business of translating the right-brain images into physical mani festations.

THE HYPNOTIC CONNECTION

The link between the right-brain imagery and the left-brain activity is a tubular structure called the Corpus Callosum. This passageway houses a mass of nerve fibers. These conductors carry messages from the right side to the left. The messages are autosuggesting or hetero-suggestions which travels from the positive image visualized on the right side of the brain to the left side to be actualized.

We have discovered that the neurons in the nervous system are the chemical transmitters of messages from brain to body. Everything is controlled, from the heartbeat and motor abilities to sensory perception and emotional responses. Thoughts and emotions are then transmitted to a special area of the brain which sorts it out.

The cerebral cortex is the brain's analyzer, acting as a receiving station for information fed to it by the nervous system. There are billions of interconnecting nerves that act together to produce individual habit patterns. These nerves are dictated to by the cortex, which receives thought in the form of suggestion from sight, sound, or any combination of the senses. The cortex then transforms the idea of feeling into bodily action. Sometimes it's harmful, sometimes helpful, depending upon attitude and the degree of stress associated with the thought. When stress or troubled emotions accompany a thought to the cortex, the resulting tension interferes with the positive functioning of this part of your brain.

TENSION REINFORCES COMPULSIVE HABITS

Most bad habits have one basic thing in common: they flow stronger in the soil of nervous tension.

What causes the vast majority of modern-day people to be so tense?

It seems that man's brain has created more than his nervous system can handle. The increased competitive tempo of the machine age is contrary to nature's need for mental recuperation through tranquillity and physical relaxation.

Too many people are caught up in the pursuit of wealth. In their enthusiasm, they lose sight of other values. They find that the part by which happiness enters in has died within them. Having spent their lives heaping up colossal piles of treasure, they suddenly discover they have built their pyramids in a joyless desert.

In their haste to accumulate possessions, they forget "you can't take it with you." There are no pockets on shrouds and I've never seen a Brink's money van following a hearse to the cemetery. Trying too hard to succeed materially not only increases tension, but can lower life expectancy.

Relaxed people, on the other hand, are not only more flexible in their outlook, they are better able to take in stride the stress that upsets tense people. Instead of allowing every event to fill them with anxiety, they relax, shrug off problems and accept challenges as part of life. Pressures can push you up and help you grow if you're looking in the right direction—upward instead of downward.

WHATEVER YOU PROJECT—YOU BECOME

No one is immune to worry, regardless of color, age, sex, or economic status. The poor man worries about where his next meal is coming from. The rich man gets ulcers over his next million. A wealthy industrialist complained, "If only I didn't have so many responsibilities maintaining my fortune!" This man's blood pressure goes up and down with the stock market report.

Once tension takes over the habit pattern, we respond automatically without conscious thinking. More and more miserable, we find ourselves caught in a nervous whirlpool which pulls us down.

Tension starts in the brain as a reaction to stress. The impulses which the brain receives in the form of suggestion (or sensory input) pass through the body by way of the spinal column.

The spine encases the spinal cord, which passes bundles of nerves through the openings in the vertebrae. These nerve bundles separate into countless long, thin fibers that connect the brain to every part of the body.

Your nervous system is as vital to your health as an electrical system is to the proper functioning of an industry. Sensations are flashed to the brain and immediately a reaction takes place in some part of the anatomy. They are more than five hundred muscles attached to the various parts of the body. When a muscle receives a message from the brain, the muscle impulsively shortens and contracts, thereby causing pressure on the nerves that pass through it.

Should there be no release of this contraction, the excess tension remains in the muscles surrounding the nerve fibers. This prolonged contraction is at the base of nervousness. Therapists refer to this condition as "residual tension." Dr. Hans Selye, father of the theory of psychosomatic illness, believes that unresolved areas of tension within the body eventually lead to the breakdown of healthy functioning and thus are the fore runners of disease. However, not all tension is bad. Some is essential to survival. A certain amount of tension supplies the alertness which is essential for an emergency.

The trouble comes when a person is tense most of the time whether he is threatened or not. Instead of tension functioning as an emergency measure, it accumulates from hour to hour and day to day without release. Living under pressure all the time eventually overwhelms the nervous system.

DON'T OVERBURDEN YOURSELF

If you place too many burdens upon yourself, you will surely add tension. Learn to set priorities. Select one project at a time on which to focus your attention.

If you are in a constant state of rushing to meet responsibilities, you will find people very eager to load you with them.

X Treating every crisis as a calamity also adds tension. Take care of the most essential problem and don't look for new ones.

If you try to cram too much into any one day, you will add to your tension.

If your boss has been giving you a hard time, talk it out with him, instead of holding it in. Explain how you feel without losing your temper or your job. Chances are he will respect you for it. In general, to end inner tensions, face up to the facts which are upsetting you. Worrying about a problem without taking positive action only prolongs the problem.

Improvement in one's condition must come through accepting reality and exercising the art of the possible. Sometimes that means compromise, adaptiveness and flexibility. This is what it takes to be the kind of easygoing, outgoing, relaxed person who thinks in a creative and productive way.

Without the satisfaction of total living, tension mounts. The resulting physical breakdown from unresolved tension can cause serious damage. When you hear someone say, "My stomach is tied up in knots," this is a simple indication of how tension might lead to a physical problem like an ulcer.

Hypertension and high cholesterol are additional ways in which our body chemistry reacts to excessive stress. Investigators explain that our adaptive mechanism becomes weakened under prolonged nervous anxiety. Doctors who specialize in psychosomatic ailments recognize tension as the great masquerader. Hundreds of physical and mental disorders can be traced back to this source.

How Does Hypnosis Deal with Tension?

From the very first session, subjects report a deep feeling of relaxation throughout their muscles and nerves. This pleasant feeling remains for from three to five days depending upon the depth of the trance and suggestibility of subject.

Can Anyone Be Hypnotized?

Anyone who wishes to be can be, with the possible exception of morons and babies, since they do not know what the hypnotist is attempting to do and can not concentrate upon his voice. Various reports on hypnotizability, based on controlled research, indicate that, of those tested, 95 percent are influenced to some degree. Of these, 20 percent reach a medium trance and 10 percent a deep or somnambulistic trance level. The rest responded with a lighter trance but were able to increase depth after one to three repetitions of hypnotic induction.

Personally, I believe just about anyone can be helped through hypnosis. Who can say that the five percent were not hypnotizable until every hypnotist has given up on them? I have hypnotized many people who were told they could not be hypnotized. Factors such as motivation, personal rapport between therapist and subject, and physical surroundings all contribute to, or detract from, hypnotizability.

How Does the Hypnotist Work?

The art of inducting the hypnotic trance begins with putting the subject at ease. Physical comfort evokes relaxed feelings. The chair or couch is important, the temperature of the room, light, and outside sound must all be taken into account so that distractions can be minimized. The therapist begins by exploring the subject's motivation and expectations. It is important that the hypnotherapist remove misconceptions and fear of the trance by explaining that it is a natural state of mind and body. The first session establishes confidence and rapport. Subsequent sessions reinforce suggestions based on personal programming.

Does the Hypnotist Become Emotionally Involved?

Yes. To this degree: the subject, or troubled person, reacts more positively to genuine interest and concern. I have found that an element of
love is the strongest factor in the therapeutic situation. This is a detached kind of love. Personal attachments are avoided because in the
final stage of hypnotherapy control is turned over to the subject through
the teaching of self-hypnosis.

How Does Hypnotherapy Differ from Stage Hypnosis?

The hypnotherapist shares many of the views of other psychotherapists
concerning the dynamics of unconscious processes. An appreciation of
the subject's responses and needs are uppermost in the mind of a good
hypnotherapist. The hypnotherapist is not a showman. We do not use
verbal magic to impose anything alien upon the subject. There is no
mysterious manipulation or possession of the subject by the hypnotist.
The skilled therapist is involved in helping the subject to use his or her
own latent mental powers.

How about Self-Hypnosis? Does it Work Just as Well?

Sometimes even better. An important aspect of self-hypnosis is that the
skill is with you twenty-four hours a day and wherever you happen to
be. Thousands of people have trained themselves using the simple methods described in this book. Some people with serious problems need an
instructor to set up a suitable program for them. Once this is established,
self-hypnosis is carried on by the subject in real-life situations on a day-
to-day basis. The role of the hypnotist is that of a teacher, activating and
developing what is already inside the person rather than imposing foreign suggestions from the outside.

Self-Hypnosis:
The Deepest Meditation

Cicero, the Roman orator said, "A happy life begins with tranquility of mind." Sounds simple, doesn't it? Yet this quest has confounded sages through the ages. For a special few, meditation has proven to be the answer. Although practiced throughout human history in many remote regions of the world, it still remains an esoteric art. This book is dedicated to exploring the mysteries of your mind and how you can master those mysteries with hypnosis.

There are still witch doctors in the Amazon jungle and Yogis in Indian temples who believe they have a God-given gift that makes them different from other human beings. The truth is, we all possess the ability to perform mental magic, but few know how to put the power to use. Almost anyone can master mind-control techniques and turn himself on to unlimited self-enrichment.

The fundamental difference between meditation and self-hypnosis is that whereas meditation helps one to detach from problems, *hypnosis zeros into the problem, examines its causes, finds a solution, and then eliminates the problem.* The secret of hypnosis is focused concentration excluding all outside interference. Self-hypnosis is more than inner-dwelling. It is also inner-direction and self-protection. Its use of carefully constructed personal programming with regard to specific goals is another aspect of hypnosis that lifts it above mere contemplation or reflection.

Many of the meditative forms used by modern-day practitioners draw their techniques from ancient Eastern religions. The object of Eastern meditation is spiritual detachment from one's environment. Characteristic of meditation is a vague, drifting-away quality that puts the subject out of touch with responsibility. Both traditional meditation and hypnosis relieve unbearable pressures and enhance one's ability to cope. They both feel pleasant, are useful in relieving tension, and provide a temporary escape from reality. However, when reality returns with its pressures and problems, hypnosis has tuned the mind in instead of out.

People who have had some experience with meditation, whether it is TM or yoga, find it easier to attain hypnosis because one level of meditation leads to the other. Meditation takes you from the wide-awake state of mind called *beta* to an altered state called *alpha*. *Alpha* then leads to the *theta*, which is hypnosis. When a person becomes proficient at using self-hypnosis he can easily drift into *delta*, otherwise known as sleep.

Self-hypnosis, also called autohypnosis, is a state of heightened suggestibility wherein personal programming can be directed to and accepted by the subconscious mind. The untapped reservoir of intelligence is brought to the surface and almost anything is possible. Well-trained practitioners sometimes can match the success of professionals in alleviating their own behavioral problems. Self-hypnosis also reduces stress and promotes a stronger personality.

Most people learn how to induce self-hypnosis by first being hypnotized by a professional. However, this is not always necessary if the person is willing to practice regularly with the techniques described in this chapter. If you have had some experience with meditation or yoga breathing methods, self-hypnosis will be easy for you to achieve. It is the scientific application of planned positive autosuggestion during the meditative state that brings about the desired results. Without a concise, practical program, meditation remains a method of "spacing-out" instead of "spacing-in" where the power of change resides.

Autohypnosis is the spotlight which brings enlightenment to the darkest corners of despair. You can use it to set fire to old habits and clear the field for better ones. Once you eliminate negative thinking and faulty self-imagery you will find a resurgence of submerged creativity. Each time you reach into the limitless well of your potential you will uncover and discover personal treasure.

HOW DOES HYPNOSIS FEEL?

To begin with, hypnosis is not sleep. When we are asleep, we are largely unconscious, with our conscious minds inactive. During sleep, the subconscious mind as well as the conscious mind is inaccessible to the "input" of suggestion. Hypnosis, rather, feels like suspended animation. The body sleeps while the mind is totally aware and receptive to ideas. There is a profound feeling of relaxation through every nerve and muscle of the body. This physical contentment is combined with a feeling of blissfulness.

The self-hypnotic trance is a planned extension of an everyday experience. Most of us spend a part of our waking lives in trances of varying levels. Everyone slips into an altered state of consciousness at least twice a day: just before fully awakening in the morning and just before falling asleep at night. During these times our senses are detached from outside influence. We may also drift into hypnosis during periods of reflection when our thoughts are concentrated inwardly. It happens to some people when they listen to music or watch television. The difference between haphazard self-induced hypnosis and planned, scientific self-hypnosis is the result. Characteristic of the latter state is a sense of purpose. You allow nothing else to enter the creative, curative space. During accidental hypnosis you remain the same; during planned self-hypnosis remarkable improvements take place.

In exploring the interior world of your mind and its links to your body, you begin to see and feel beauty within yourself and learn how to reach out to the wonders of the world around you. People have said the state of hypnosis has brought with it a new idea of space, a feeling of airiness, and a sense of timelessness. Others have said, "I feel a new freedom, not only physically in a sense of weightlessness, but also emotionally free from feelings of worry or concern. Anything seems possible." Another member of the self-hypnosis class explained her feelings this way: "There is a total disembodiment. I float up and away from the surface of this planet to a new and unexplored dimension." A number of other people have described the experience as one of "birth or rebirth" or "as if I am starting life all over again." For some, the feeling is even spiritual: "My soul feels immortal, eternal. My inner space merges with the vastness of outer space."

Yet none of these expressions may convey what the feeling is like when it happens to you. Like falling in love, it's hard to describe, but you'll know when it happens. At the beginning, the hypnotic trance may come in brief flashes. Those flashes will last longer as you practice. The novice knows that he has properly locked on when the sensation is one of almost, but not quite, falling asleep—that moment just before drifting into an altered state of consciousness.

Once you learn to recognize the feeling of self-hypnosis, you will train yourself to prolong and deepen the trance. The deeper you go, the stronger your ability to improve will grow. However, even in a very light state of meditation, which we call "hypnoidal," positive suggestion is very effective. What people may lack in depth they can compensate for in the manner in which they apply the principle of positive autosuggestion.

Hypnoidal, or light, self-hypnosis is characterized by some disassociation from tension and negativism. This can sometimes occur without our realizing it, as when we listen to music, watch TV, or are being entertained by a speaker or comedian. Day dreaming is another example of self-hypnosis. When we find ourselves fantasizing while staring off into space, reading a book or watching a movie, there is a tendency toward light autohypnosis. The state develops from concentration of thought and relaxation of body.

The main difference between self-induced hypnosis and that which is induced by a professional practitioner is the depth of trance. While some few people can bring about a deep level of self-hypnosis most need the help of a professional for deep-seated problems such as phobias and psychogenic disturbances.

There are five component parts to self-hypnosis:

1. Motivation   4. Imagination
2. Relaxation   5. Autosuggestion
3. Concentration

Voltaire said, "When I can do what I want to do, there is my liberty for me." There can be no freedom to enjoy life when a person's mind is chained to obsolete behavior. The self-induced trance, properly utilized, is a powerful force which liberates the body, mind, and emotions. Instead of being at the mercy of a controller, you become your own controller.

Self-hypnosis is based on the premise that you can explore formally unexplored areas of thinking and guide yourself away from constricting problems linked to the past. Self-examination leads to re-evaluation and then to eradication. Each of us is equipped with deeper areas of brainpower capable of decision making and profound logic. During hypnosis, you enter into that center of high intelligence andfind new awareness which endows your life with deeper meaning.

You will develop an ability to concentrate on a given subject and exclude the troublesome flashbacks. Later, in a waking state, you will find yourself resisting the flow of that old behavior you want to get rid of. You will learn to sort out what mental material is important to you. One of the wonders of the mind is its faculty to absorb and assimilate information constantly. Events, attitudes, every new happening is tucked away for future reference. This elasticity gives the mind not only an almost unlimited ability to store up impressions, but also the flexibility to alter concepts, thereby expanding personal development.

Problem solving begins with a strong emotional desire for a change. Without motivation, self-hypnosis will not work. One would be better off visiting a professional hypnotist for conventional hypnotherapy. Even in cases where hetero-hypnosis (induction by another person) is used, lack of motivation forms a barrier against the acceptance of positive suggestion. The will to improve is basically essential to the process.

Some people overcome obstacles, others are overcome by obstacles. Which kind of person are you? If you tend to be negative, take heart, for happiness can be learned. Anyone with normal intelligence can unlearn defeating attitudes and learn more winning ones. The process begins when you *make up your mind to change your mind.* Slow starters become self-starters through hypnosis. You can learn to discipline your thoughts and discuss emotional lethargy as a tiresome burden.

Directional drive provides a reason for awakening in the morning with enthusiastic exuberance. Instead of being satisfied with mediocrity, we begin to see possibilities for improvement. People with drive don't wait for their ship to come in. They row out to meet it.

SPURS TO MOTIVATE YOURSELF

Do Small Tasks Well

Add enthusiasm to routine chores. Small things become larger in importance when you do a special job. Live by Émile Coué's slogan, "Every day in some small way, I do things better and better." As you develop skill in doing little things you will be strengthening your capabilities. Every positive happening is a link to larger successes.

Seek New Interests

Look for a missing ingredient in your life. Is there something you've always wanted to do but didn't get around to? Seek out and explore new activities. Study new courses. Look into the activity of worthy organizations. Add new interesting people to your circle of friends. Examine your own hidden talents.

Allow Yourself to Feel

Become more involved with all of your senses. Listen to the sounds around you and to what people are really saying to you. Observe the world with the wondering eyes of a child. Stop to breathe in not only the scent of flowers, but the fresh air that accompanies the birth of each new day. Feel the loving sensation of touching and being touched. Enjoy life.

Communicate with Others

Become more involved with other people. Too many people suffer from "spectatoritis." Life's bystanders bore not only others but themselves. Look. Listen. Feel. Touch. And smile frequently. Enrich your personality by exchanging points of view with others. Be assertive as well as attentive to the other person's side of an issue.

List Your Good Qualities

Many people who lack drive underrate their capabilities and talents. If you can see yourself as having possibilities for success in any field of endeavor, your motivation will be increased. The quality of self-worth is basically essential to any achievement, because if we feel worthless, we also feel undeserving.

Live Life with Purposefulness

Everyone needs goals and a plan to achieve those goals. Whether the goals are for improving your inner environment or the outer environment, you have to have a program. PLAN THE WORK AND WORK THE PLAN. Without a guide or a roadmap, how can we ever reach a destination?

YOU CAN'T GO WRONG IF YOUR GOALS ARE RIGHT

The smallest goal achieved is better than the largest unfulfilled dream. Be practical about your goals. Striving for the unattainable is the surest road to failure. Expand to your highest potential while at the same time accept your limitations. For instance, many writers dream of writing the great American novel, but few come close. For every book like Dostoevsky's *Crime and Punishment*, millions of lesser books are quickly forgotten. However, this doesn't mean people of lesser talent should not create. Rather, success is measured by how closely your abilities are matched by the effort you put forth. Goals should be fitted directly to one's potential. If you develop a passionate interst in something greater than what you are involved in at this moment, you may find that your petty problems diminish, your mind becomes clearer, and your emotions become more stable. The first ground rule in setting a goal is self-confidence. Proceed on the assumption that success will come in stages. It's easier to reach the top of a mountain if you follow the sloping path that circles around it, than it is trying to climb directly up the steep side.

How to Begin Your Changeover?

First, write down the things you believe will make your life happier and healthier. By writing down your thoughts, you will immediately have a clearer idea of the changes that need to be made. Next, give one problem priority. If you attempt too much at one time, the task may seem overwhelming. When the mind is cluttered, it's difficult to get started.

To encourage yourself to get started, select one small immediate task that will help in solving the problem. Taking action triggers energy for the next step. At the end of the day review your achievement. Then ask yourself, "What can I do next?"

Organize. Organize your thoughts. Organize your actions. Indecision and procrastination deter us, keep us dangling in limbo. We make progress by moving in a definite direction, not by debating, arguing, or rolling around in circles. Once you have a plan, the next step is to let the plan have you—your mind, your heart, your energy, and your confidence. Your goal is the rope to hang on to as you move forward. A goal is not only the rope but the hope.

Fears, self-doubts, susceptibility to bad habits all diminish and can vanish when one gets caught up in striving for a good goal. Throughout time, the finest achievements of mankind have been accomplished through good planning. We may not all be world leaders, but for *your* life there is no greater leader than yourself. Aldous Huxley puts it simply, "There's only one corner of this universe you can be sure of improving and that's your own self."

Once you have gained control over some of the negative factors in your behavior, it's important that you use self-hypnosis to "stay clean." Repeat your positive autosuggestions several times a day in addition to periods of meditation. And tell yourself, "I am determined to stay clean of harmful habit and I am building better ones."

Think positively at an times. Never say, "How will I do it? "Instead say, "How about doing it this way?" *See the problem as temporary, the solution as permanent.*

Self-hypnosis acts as the magic lantern of your mind, highlighting buried strengths and ferreting out causes of problems long forgotten. During periods of self-hypnotic meditation you learn to master your mind so that constructive decisions can be reached. In short, self-hypnosis brings awareness.

There are numerous spin-off benefits. Your personality will take on new poise and serenity. Many people become more orderly and organize their personal and professional lives. On a physical plane, psychosomatic symptoms such as headaches, nervous stomach, insomnia, and sexual dysfunction will automatically lessen. This improvement can be directly traced to the relaxed state that follows a session of self-hypnosis. Self-hypnosis will change your life in every way—physically, mentally, and even spiritually. Ordinary living becomes extraordinary.

DEVISE YOUR OWN PERSONAL PROGRAM

Since the time of the caveman, both thinkers and doers have done their thinking first and their doing later. Creative people are only as great as the size of their thinking. Successful ones see beyond petty problems to the larger canvas of life. A personalized plan helps you conquer the obstacle course and leap over the hurdles.

One's own destructive habits are the greatest obstacles to personal success. However, take heart, for much can be done by following the steps described here.

As Mark Twain said, "A habit cannot be tossed out of the window; it must be coaxed down the stairs—step at a time." While some personality problems can be changed quickly with hypnosis, bad habits must be diligently worked on because they cling tenaciously. The steps from Motivation to Actualization comprise a system that works in many

areas, as you will learn. However, self-hypnosis is not an instant formula for perfection. The pursuit of perfection is doomed to failure.
Nobody can become perfect, but, with persistence, you can expect to
elevate your way of life and make a new world for yourself. That it can
be done is attested to by outstanding people throughout the world.

Without a plan for success, we fall prey to all sorts of destructive
environmental pressure. Pent-up human potential turns into frustration
and morbidity. One of my students bemoaned the fact that he was
getting nowhere in his job. A commercial artist, Paul Z. had many
creative ideas, but was relegated to tedious work such as setting up
lettering on layout ads. He possessed the talent, but not the motivation
to push himself forward toward a more rewarding position. Others with
less ability but more confidence were giving him orders and receiving
almost twice his salary. "I know I'm capable of much more but I don't
have the will power to do anything about it." Paul griped as he plodded
along. "It's not just the money. It's the idea of not living up to my
artistic potential. I just can't make aggressive demands other people do.
Maybe I feel rejection, I'm not sure."

Fortunately, something unexpected happened to fire Paul's motivation. He had been living with Dorothy, whom he loved, but had not
married with the excuse he could not afford the financial responsibility.
One day she revealed that she was pregnant. Paul was delighted and
hugged Dorothy as they laughed and cried together. Now Paul had the
magical emotion—*motivation*. He knew he'd need a larger income to
face his new responsibilities. Money was the carrot dangling before his
nose. Paul spoke to his boss, persuading him to look at some ideas on a
layout for a newly acquired account.

Before long Paul was working in a private office with his name on
the door and a secretary to do his routine work. By the time Junior had
arrived, Paul's salary had almost doubled and he was on his way up the
ladder. Thus, sometimes circumstances alone can provide the motivation
to succeed. Responsibilities to others help many people wipe out fears
and apprehension.

While we know that, under the stimulus and spur of intense emotion
and desire to please a loved one, one's reserves of will may be tapped,
we can also develop motivation by a "self-reward system." The desire
to succeed is in direct proportion to the expected reward, whether mon-
etary or emotional. Sometimes the reward is a greater actualization of
the self.

List your unused talents on a piece of paper so that you can study yourself. Seeing your capabilities clearly stated will help to inspire you to reach outward and upward.

Arnold F. was an alcoholic who had been fired from a succession of jobs. "What are some of the nice things people have said about you?" I asked him. He couldn't think of one until he was hypnotized. Then he wrote:

> "I make friends easily. I have a pleasant voice. They say I have a sense of humor. I'm a neat dresser. I'm a good sport, spend easily. Women say I'm attractive."

Without doubt Arnold was all of the things he described *when he was sober.* However, after a few too many drinks, he became belligerent, his voice raucous, his personality offensive, and his clothes sloppy. And women certainly did not find him attractive then.

It was important for Arnold to examine the underlying reason for his drinking. We were able to discover the origin of his problem by using Regression, and Automatic Writing, techniques described elsewhere in this book. Once armed with this knowledge, he realized that his job was serving as a constant source of temptation. As an executive in a large import firm, he often took buyers to lunches where social drinking was expected of him. Finally, he asked for a transfer to another branch of the company and has been sticking to a program of non-drinking with the help of self-hypnosis ever since.

An honest appraisal of one's routinized behavior is valuable in order to become aware of why we do things. Negative habits are strengthened by self-deception. We often hear people say:

"Cigarettes steady my nerves." Truth is cigarettes are injurious to the nervous system and to the rest of the body.

"Alcohol helps me unwind." Truth is alcohol can unwind you until you fall apart. For some people one jigger wrecks their equilibrium.

"A little dessert sweetens my stomach." Truth is too many sweets can cause health problems, including diabetes, obesity, and hypoglycemia.

"Marijuana turns me on sexually." Truth is persistent use of pot can not only lower the sex drive, but might also cause hormonal changes.

Failure to look at themselves realistically causes addicted people to remain trapped in limbo, powerless to break the grip of self-defeating habits. The most difficult part of correction lies in identifying the problems and then taking responsibility for them. We tend to blame others for the way we behave. "If my wife didn't bug me, I wouldn't drink so much." That's a classic one. Or: "I don't want to insult the hostess, so I eat the dessert." Only by taking responsibility can we gain control.

RELAXATION AND CONCENTRATION

Meditation and self-hypnosis both require complete physical relaxation. Only then is the mind free to do its magic. With training, it takes five to twenty minutes to reach a tension-free state.

Begin by selecting a place conducive to privacy, one where you will not be disturbed by friends or the ringing of the phone. The process works best when you can return to the same place time after time. Using the same setting repeatedly has a reassuring, comforting effect. Stretch out on a bed, lounging chair, or even the floor—whichever suits you best. The familiarity of the position you relax in also helps your nervous system to let go.

Loosen any restrictive clothing which might limit your deep breathing. Unbutton buttons. Unhook hooks. Unfasten belts, girdles, brassieres. Remove your shoes and socks. Take off glasses, jewelry, and anything else which might interfere with relaxation. Now that you have settled into a comfortable position, empty your mind of any precise thinking. Let it wander. Let problems wait for another time. Luxuriate in the sweet peace of doing nothing. Savor the sense of just being.

If your body is resistant, the following technique will help. It's called *muscle-tensing*. Contract the large muscle groups: in the thighs, buttocks, stomach, and upper arms. Grip them tightly as you think, "Tense up! Tighter!" Then command muscle-release by thinking, "Let go! Completely!" Feel your body go limp and heavy. Next, think of your body as disjointed, like a big, loose rag doll sprawled on a soft pillow.

Now focus your eyes somewhere above eye level. Feel your eyelids grow heavy, but hold off closing until you count backwards from ten to zero. When you reach zero, close your eyelids slowly as you say to yourself, "There is nothing to see on the outside and so much to experience on the inside." Now your resting eyes send a message of restfulness to the mind and the mind transfers the restfulness to the rest of the body.

Focus on Diaphragmatic Breathing

Slowly breathe in to the count of five and breathe out to the count of five. You should be lying or sitting faceup with one hand resting on your diaphragm so that you can monitor your breathing rhythms. The regular vibrations of your respiratory system will lull you into deeper relaxation. When you inhale, your tummy should rise because the diaphragm acts like a bellows opening the chest cavity enabling you to draw in your full capacity of oxygen. One third of the oxygen we breathe goes directly to the brain. This helps us not only to feel relaxed but also drift closer to a sleeplike state. When you exhale the tummy recedes and all muscles tend to relax even more. Throughout the only motion is the slow, easy rise and fall of your tummy. The relaxed pulmonary sensations soothe the heart and all of the internal organs of your body. Feel yourself become part of the ebb and flow of energy that moves all life on this earth. Be aware that you share the air with everyone.

Get Ready to Relax Completely

Now that your eyes are closed and you're breathing smoothly and regularly, you will release the tension in your muscles, nerves, and blood vessels. Stress causes muscles to go into spasms that grip the nerves and vessels. This reduces circulation of blood to other areas of the body and can lead to pain and disease. Disease exits in relation to the absence of ease. Fortunately, we are all capable of increasing easiness. Let's begin. Make a suggestion to your body to "let go all over." We start with the scalp and progressively suggest "a heavy, loose, limp feeling into each area of the body."

The following relaxation routine can be recorded on a cassette player and played back for easy memorization. However, if you have experienced meditation, you are probably familiar with feeling relaxed and drifting into "your level."

PROGRESSIVE DIFFERENTIAL RELAXATION

"My scalp feels loose, limp, and relaxed. My forehead is smooth, serene like a newborn baby. My eyelids are very heavy, deeply at rest.

All the little nerves and muscles around my eyes are totally relaxed."
THINK THE THOUGHT AND YOU WILL FEEL THE FEELING.
Proceed down through every muscle of your body.

"My cheeks are soft and smooth. The hinges of my jaw are slightly
parted, loose, and limp. Lips barely touching. Teeth are apart. Tongue
resting in lower part of my mouth. Tongue feels soft, limp. My neck
feels very open and extremely relaxed. Shoulders so heavy. Arms heavy
. . . loose, limp. Deeply, completely free of tension. My entire torso is
heavy and relaxed. My hips are very heavy, the buttocks seem to melt
their heaviness into the surface which is supporting me. A pleasurable
feeling flows down through my legs and into my toes."

If an area of your body is especially tense or feels stressful, dwell
on that area a little longer. For example, let's consider the back. Many
people suffer pain in areas of the back, and if you do not give that spot
particular differential relaxation suggestion, the discomfort will interfere with the depth of meditation and decrease the benefit derived
from self-therapy. To relax the back thoroughly, try this subliminal
patter:

"I am going to count down the vertebrae in my spine from 33 to 0.
33 . . . 32 . . . 31 . . . 29 . . . 28 . . . 27 . . . 26 . . . 25 . . . 24 . . . 23
. . . 22 . . . 21 . . . 20 . . . all the way to 0." As you count backwards,
visualize your entire back as twice as wide and twice as long as you
would ordinarily. When you finish counting, say: "My back feels so
wide and long, so very open. Lots of room for the nerves, the muscles,
and the vertebrae to float around aimlessly in the wide open spaces of
my back. All tension is gone and will not return." LET YOUR
THOUGHTS RETURN TO THE ENTIRE BODY.

"Now my entire body feels pleasantly limp . . . from the inside of
my bones to the outside of my skin . . . I feel no tension . . . free of all
pressure, just a loose, limp, heavy sense of well-being."

Let your mind surrender to this sublime restfulness as you just hang
loose. When your body is completely at ease, your mind begins to clear
away its trivia and debris. Within moments, you will be aware of a
revitalizing glow which will permeate your entire physical and mental
self. When this sensation of super-elation rises to its height, you will
drift closer to the ultimate source of your own life-giving energy. This
serene state marks the threshold of *alpha*, a mental state particularly
receptive to positive suggestion. *Alpha* will lead you into *theta*, a mental
state wherein the life forces of your body will be recharged, rejuve-
nated, and energized. At this time, a glow of exultation will flow through

every nerve and fiber of your being and you will experience rebirth, not only in mind and body, but in your spirit as well.

Direct your awareness toward specific areas of your body. You may detect fine vibrations, a tingling sensation, perhaps a feeling of warmth. You can select any area for special attention. Let a healing feeling of well-being penetrate that exact spot. Get in touch with the vibrations of your breathing and imagine an opening about the size of a quarter directly in the center of the problem area. As you exhale, picture a thin, misty stream of air coming out of the opening and say to yourself, "With this breath I release all tension and stress from this area. I will now enter a deeper, healthier state of mind"

If your problem were a headache, for example, you would imagine an opening at either side of your temples and see the head ache evaporating as you exhale the stress out of the openings.

CONCENTRATING YOUR MENTAL ENERGY

Before you can concentrate your mind on goals and self-enrichment, you must clear the mind's passageways. Once you are relaxed, suspend conscious thinking. Postpone decisions and judgments to another, more suitable time. Now that your body is making no demands on your mind, be aware of "peace of mind." If an unwanted, undesirable thought tries to push its way in, push it out again. This is your time of tranquillity. Don't allow any intrusions.

To help yourself mentally relax, think of a restful scene: a day in the country or at the beach, or perhaps a time when you were fishing or swinging in a hammock, free of all worries. Here is my favorite patter for mental relaxation: (If possible, record it and listen with eyes closed).

"I see myself walking in the country on a beautiful summer day, just the right temperature. A gentle breeze sways the branches of the trees and somewhere a bird is singing. The look and sound of nature empties my mind of all problems. Old memories float away from my center. I feel free. I picture myself looking younger, healthier. I see before me two tall trees and a hammock hung between the trees. I stretch out in the hammock and watch the clouds in the sky. Puffs and fluffs of clouds drift and shift, changing their shapes and then disappearing. The sky is blue and a little airplane is writing a message. The message says, 'PEACE OF MIND.' " As you concentrate on the message, see it now dimmer and dimmer and vanish completely.

At this stage of your induction into self-hypnosis, you will feel an intimate sense of togetherness within yourself. The difference between concentration in a waking state and in the hypnoidal state is as follows: During ordinary concentration, the mind focuses on an object or problem from the outside, whereas, during hypnosis, the mind is inverted and thoroughly thinks through a problem from the inside. There occurs not only transcendence of mind over body, but the deliberate exclusion of any intruding outside influence. Hypnoidal concentration bring into focus untapped intelligence capable of penetrating the reasons and causes of troublesome behavior. Complete absorption digs out the truth of your problems. In order to benefit the most from the power of hypnosis, use this period to sort out your problems, stresses, and worries:

1. Focus your thinking upon the *troubles you cannot control.*
2. *Accept the above conditions* as beyond your influence.
3. Concentrate on the negative factors *over which you have control.*
4. Think of *possible solutions* to those stress factors.

Many people waste their mental energies trying to control conditions which are really out of their control. The advanced illness of a loved one. Accidents. Taxes. The hostility around the world. If you cannot solve a problem, let it go. Narrow down your responsibilities. Set realistic goals, select one, and give it priority. Concentrating your mental and emotional powers on attainable goals will give you the spirit you need to propel yourself to reach your destination.

Inevitably, disturbing thoughts of past conflicts will try to enter into your concentration. There is a resistance factor we must overcome. When unwholesome thoughts rear their ugly heads, dispel them by going even deeper into your concentration on positive solutions. The correct way to conquer negativism is to turn your focus as quickly as possible to the opposite idea. Eventually, *negativism dies through sheer neglect.* And then, problems which once appeared complex and insurmountable dissolve under the concentrated focus of your deeper intelligence.

Concentration clears the muddled mind and opens the door to the infinite creative reservoir that all of us possess and so few of us ever tap.

Concentrated introspection awakens the creative imagination. Hidden talents remain buried unless we focus energy into them. A painter becomes a better painter by shutting out of his thoughts everything

except the vision he wants to place on the canvas. A poet or musician can only create when he has channeled his thinking directly to the center of his creation, blocking out all else. Tension is the opposite of concentrated relaxation, and the stressed person cannot reach the deeper areas of his abilities. The mystique of psychic improvement comes from the selective, exclusive direction of the mind's forces.

The pensive mind generates *theta* vibrations of creativity. This flow of energy provides a piercing insight into the heart of the subject concentrated upon and is the secret of creative genius. When hypnotic concentration is used in conjunction with a personal plan for creative improvement, dramatic reversals of behavior are possible. I know of a heroin addict whose whole life was devoted to aimless wanderings about New York City, during which he committed petty robberies to support his habit. After learning how to hypnotize himself and develop his creativity, he discovered he had talent for painting. At the time, he was hospitalized for drug withdrawal and had a lot a time on his hands. I arranged for him to receive art materials and soon he changed from a pathetic, addicted person into a vibrant, confident one. This person, who was previously unable to concentrate for even a few moments, is now painting for long hours and earning a living from it. Upon visiting his studio, I was amused to find him concentrating so deeply on his work that he did not hear while I entered and strolled around for quite some time. He explained, "When I paint I go into such deep concentration, I reach *alpha* even with my eyes open. When I practice self-hypnosis, I only have to close my eyes and I immediately drift into *theta*."

History is filled with stories of great discoveries which occurred during periods of deep concentration. After people had given up on a problem, they found the answer when they least expected it while daydreaming or drifting into slumber. Elusive solutions do not respond to forced concentration in a waking state because we *tend to try too hard*. How ever, when we concentrate our mental powers during a period of meditation, we open latent mental powers which oftimes surprise us.

Major advances in human progress have taken place when creative geniuses least expected it, while they were catnapping or in a detached state of mind. They variously described their mental condition at times of revelation as, "daytime reverie," "in a world of my own," "withdrawn into my private thoughts," "snoozing," "spaced out." The story goes that Henry Ford once hired an efficiency expert to evaluate his company. After several weeks, the expert reported back to Mr. Ford. His appraisal was extremely favorable except for one flaw.

"It's that man down the hall," complained the efficiency expert. When I go by his office, I see him leaning back with his feet on the desk; taking a snooze. He's wasting your money, Mr. Ford."

"Oh, that man," answered Mr Ford. "Once he got an idea that saved us millions of dollars. At the time, his feet were planted right where they are now.

Mavericks and dreamers are sometimes the genuine geniuses of our times. Freedom from the usual limitations of deadlines allows them to innovate during periods of deep concentrated relaxation.

What inventive minds have in common is the ability to withdraw from outside communication into an inner communication. By so doing, they gain insight and a special kind of wisdom that leads to great achievement. The roster of famous people who have changed the course of history by using some form of mental programming, which we now know as self-hypnosis, covers every field of accomplislment.

In world affairs, there was Napoleon Bonaparte, Winston Churchill, Franklin Delano Roosevelt, and Mahatma Gandhi, to mention just a few. Among artists, Leonardo da Vinci and Pablo Picasso described in their writings how they visualized a painting long before they did the actual work. Da Vinci's inventions often came to him while daydreaming. Many of the world's most outstanding musical composers created while in a trancelike reverie. Works by Brahms, Beethoven, Mozart, Puccini, and Wagner have endured for years giving deep pleasure to millions of people. All of these composers used some variation of self-hypnosis. A modern-day composer explained, "I go into my shell and listen to my music before I set it down on paper. Creative work is preconceived."

Inventors tell us their products were preconceived during periods of relaxation and concentration akin to autohypnosis. Thomas A. Edison often mentioned, "My ideas leaped out of my dreams." He was famous for his daily catnaps during which time there was a pad and pencil beside his bed. When an idea came to him, he would immediately jot it down for future development. Sometimes Edison would meditate on unresolved problems while fishing. One day, as he pondered the problems caused by a rubber shortage, he drifted into his subconscious and came up with a solution. In a flash of insight, he thought of crossbreeding the goldenrod, a hybrid rubber-producing plant, with a simple plant. The miracle plant which resulted contained fourteen percent rubber, enabling the United States to produce a synthetic material necessary in winning World War II.

Let's go back a little further into our history. Elias Howe, while working on the first model of the sewing machine, was stumped by the problem of threading a machine-driven needle whose point reached into the shuttle. One evening, as he drifted into a light slumber, he had a vision of a harpoon with a rope threaded near its point. This triggered the invention of an effective machine needle and changed the course of the entire textile industry.

Albert Einstein was among the many other scientists who took time to ponder and sleep on a problem in order to form the essence of a revolutionary new theory. His contribution to our understanding of relativity was made in this manner.

The molecular formula for benzene, which became the foundation of twentieth-century organic chemistry, was also revealed in a dream to the English scientist Michael Faraday. The list goes on and on. What did these successful people have in common?

They possessed strong motivation, a desire to succeed.

They were aware of what they wanted to accomplish.

They used relaxation deliberately and concentrated deeply during periods of meditation.

They also knew how to use their imaginations in a creative manner.

They had to be positive thinkers, applying the principle of autosuggestion to find solutions.

You don't have to be a genius to apply the same principles to your own life and goals. Remember, a well-conceived personal program can turn any course of events from failure to success. The steps described herein were developed over a period of many years of extensive experimenting and experiencing. The system works for others. It can certainly work for you, too.

Expect that for a few sessions you will simply be daydreaming or in a light state of meditation. It takes repetition to drift into the hypnotic, therapeutic trance level. Keep practicing; the results are worth the effort.

Self-hypnosis has been successfully used to correct, prevent, or alleviate a wide range of bad habits as well as to move people's lives in better directions. The steps of self-hypnosis are workable tools. But the best tools cannot be effective without human effort. The more dedicated you are, the more dramatic the benefits you'll derive.

Behind all remission of harmful behavior or illness lies faith in a system. For some people, the system might be the one used by their psychiatrist or surgeon. Believing only in external forces, however, limits improvement. Turning over the responsibility entirely to someone else just makes you part of *their* system. The system that works best is your own inside-yourself-system. That's where the real power is.

Life is made up of the things that happen to you from the outside, called *input*, combined with the way you react to that input, which is called *output*. The inner system that you develop is called personal programming. And the best inner system for successful *personal programming* is self-hypnosis. While there are people who can improve and elevate themselves without consciously being aware of an inner system, they are in the minority and their success is merely accidental.

Through self-hypnosis, you will find that your success is inner-directed, goal-oriented, and cannot fail. In order to discover how an organized plan can work for you, *decide what it is you want*. When you know, then you can write the script to live your life. Tell yourself, "I am author of my own world and only I can change it. It is not always the situation in which I find myself, but rather the perspective that I choose to take that's most important, and that perspective will always be a positive one."

Imagination and Autosuggestion

The basic principle of role-playing from childhood on is that people become what they pretend to be. Imagery exerts its control within the consciousness of each of us, usually without our being aware of it. Mental pictures flash incessantly on a subliminal level of perception. Insidious images can chain you to outmoded habits and emotional reactions which do not serve your best interests.

How do you see yourself? Before you can improve your self-image, you must examine the one you have. Your imagination will help you unsnarl the knots of tension resulting from past role-playing. Instead of being restricted to illusions of a lesser self, you will unravel the cord of past conditioning and build a new identity based on the reality of your full potential. Hypnosis structures the images for you. Once a person is freed from haunting visions of the past, new, self-fulfilling dreams lead to a better life.

Images are the maps which direct us to a new destination. It's more important to see where you're going, because you have already seen where you've been. (That's why your eyes are in the front and not in the back of your head.) Unfortunately, many people cling to hurts and hardships linked to the past. What is *your* view of your earlier life? Do you see it in the far distance . . . or very close? Too many people are unable to live in the present because the past has burdened them with unhappy memories. Instead of assuming responsibility, they blame others for victimizing them. Decide what you want in life and take the responsibility to work toward that goal. Imagination will make the trip a pleasant one.

"You've got to have a dream if you want a dream to come true," goes the lyric from "South Pacific." Your dream must be more than inspiring, it must also be feasible. Fantasy can only become reality when your intelligence believes in the practicability of your vision.

"To accomplish great things, we must not only act but also dream, not only plan but also believe," said Anatole France. An achiever must be a believer—in himself. Underachievers see themselves as less capable than they are. Their concept of self is limited to the meagerness of their dreams. We are limited only by our own reluctance to believe in our own capabilities. Yet, even mediocre people have slumbering aspirations held captive by humdrum thinking. Imagination directs all human actions. Your vision of yourself can make you a star, an also-ran or a never-will-be. Your mind is the engineer and its "imagineering" creates the blueprint for your life.

Once you are able to envision success-oriented goals, your anticipation of the future will become a strong driving force. "Possibility thinking" will eliminate vacillation from your belief system. Positive expectations will produce assertive enthusiasm, which is the spark of success. See your images vividly; the stronger the picture, the stronger your emotions will be stirred. When you are able to conjure up the new image, tell yourself, "I can, I will, and I must achieve my goals." Imagination coupled with self-confidence inevitably brings realization.

SEVEN VISIONS TO A BETTER LIFE

Once you are completely relaxed and have drifted into a concentrated state of meditation, imagine you are watching a preview on a TV or movie screen.

You will play all roles in *The Theatre of Your Mind:* you are the director, the actor, and the audience.

Set the scene; create the situation suitable to your needs. Visualize your future as you wish it to be.

Vision One: Improved Health

Consider this vision as something to do until the doctor comes, or if he has declared, "Nothing can be done. You have to live with it": see yourself standing in front of a full-length three-way mirror. From every angle you look ten to twenty years younger and in perfect health. See the happy expression on your face, confident and free of anxiety. Imagine a blue light which we shall call *the healing energy* focused on the troubled area, a strong searchlight piercing through to the mysterious source of the illness and wiping it out . . . completely and deeply. Look into the mirror and repeat to yourself ten times, "I am healthy and normal. All traces of my old problem have vanished and will not return." The more you know about your ailment, the more effective the visualization will be. If an organ of your body is impaired, learn as much as you can about the physiology of that organ. If your blood chemistry has gone awry, question your doctor about it. Become knowledgeable. The more authentic your image, the more dramatic the results.

Dr. Carl Simonton, known for his work with visual imagery in treating cancer patients, tells of the case of a man with an advanced malignancy in his throat. The patient was taught to enter *alpha* and visualize a war taking place between his white blood cells and the cancer cells. The defending white cells were seen as the conquerors, destroying the cancer cells and freeing the victim. This visualization proved effective in combatting the malignancy.

Vision Two: Ego Building

The person with low self-esteem often got that way by seeing himself as less than real. To compensate, make your fantasy *better* than reality. Picture yourself at an elegant testimonial dinner in which you are the guest of honor. Imagine the music playing as you enter the large spacious dining room. Lots of flowers. Everyone dressed formally. Imagine people on the dias arising and saying great things about you. See yourself receiving an important award. If you were an actor, you'd see an Oscar. A writer or scholar envisions the Pulitzer or Nobel prize. In addition to the prominent people praising you, see members of your family and various people from your past, including anyone who has been less than kind to you. Then see yourself taking over the speaker's platform and delivering a speech about your aims in life. Finally, picture the audience standing up to give you a rousing ovation. As the image fades, see the most important people clustered around you to shake your hand and pat you on the back.

Daryl T. was a struggling musician who worked at a menial job during the day and practiced his guitar evenings and weekends. He often said, "I play for myself. Other people do not want to spend money on my kind of music. Besides, I'm not really that good." After training himself in visualization, he finally boosted his confidence and began to play professionally. He also learned to visualize improvements at each performance. This creative rehearsal improved his skill to such an extent he is now sought after.

Vision Three: To Achieve Goals

To achieve goals you must first picture in your mind exactly what you want to accomplish in life. Meditate upon your choices. Then select the one that feels the most emotionally gratifying. Decide where you want to be five years from now. Consider the means of reaching your destination. As you visualize the mental screen, list your short-term and long-term goals. Act out the various scenes and options that might present themselves. In your mental picture, confront the different possibilities and consequences of success. Imagine conversations with experts in your field of endeavor. Ask questions and receive meaningful answers. See yourself pursuing your goals. Notice how assertive your attitude is, how well you look, and the affirmative responses of people you come in contact with.

"I'm always rushing around and never seem to get anywhere," a woman complained to me. She was an outstanding actress who spent most of her time going to auditions and being rejected. Through self-hypnosis and positive imagery, she discovered that what was missing from her aspiration was proper training. She planned the work and then worked the plan. Her immediate goal was to improve her appearance, so she lost weight and bought a new wardrobe. Next, she took additional training in voice and stage presence. Visualizing herself as a winner made it happen. She is now appearing in a smash Broadway musical.

Vision Four: Personal Relationships

Improving communication with a spouse or lover sometimes takes more than conscious effort. You can share a relaxing, inspiring fantasy and ease a great deal of stress out of a relationship. Meditate together while holding hands. Picture yourselves sailing away on a cruise ship to faraway corners of the earth. Make love in exotic hideaways. Sail around the Hawaiian Islands. Bask in the sun on some deserted beach. Rehearse a deeper kind of intimacy between you; gain insight into each other.

Very often, failing relationships can be traced to minor misunder standings. Use periods of contemplation to review conversations that lead to anger or frustration. Preview improved dialogue and notice the difference in response. Envision yourself deeply loved and desired. Flights of fancy have no bounds when it comes to romance. They can make an endearing relationship out of one that was merely endured.

In addition to intimate communication, use your imagination to enhance the manner in which you relate to co-workers and friends. See a closer understanding develop between yourself and others. During your reverie, be completely honest. Air your gripes and grievances. Ventilate buried angers. Explain yourself to this imaginary friend and accept his opinions and suggestions. As tension subsides, express your appreciation and ask to hear his side of the argument. Listen and learn about the other's deeper feelings.

Paul M. complained that his co-workers didn't like him. "I don't know why, but every time I walk into a room, they stop talking as though they had been saying things about me." But there's no need to wonder when you can use your imagination. Paul learned to conjure up the troublesome scene. He imagined he was hidden in a closet and eavesdropped on their conversation. True, they were discussing him. But not in the manner he suspected. Quite the contrary. What they were saying was, "Paul is so unfriendly. He behaves as if he thinks he's better than other people." Paul's imagination brought him closer to reality.

Vision Five: Personality Problems

Select a character trait or personality problem that you would like to improve. If you have several, as most of us do, give the most urgent one top priority and focus your meditation upon it. If it is shyness, for example, you begin by building a situation in which you behave in an assertive, self-confident way. Reverse your responses from acting withdrawn to acting boldly. See yourself behaving dramatically different. Originate a new personality, with magnetic charisma attractive to the most exciting people. Remember that all reality was once a figment of someone's imagination.

Consider the problem of *procrastination*. Most of us are guilty of it at one time or another. Some people procrastinate until they are too old to do anything about their dreams. Don't be guilty of waiting too long. While meditating, picture yourself as doing the chore or taking the trip you've been putting off. See yourself enjoying the activity. Involve positive emotional satisfaction in your dreaming. Once you see yourself performing tasks which you have avoided, you will have a sense of having broken the ice. Doing the real job will then be so much easier because you will have eliminated the pitfalls and interferences.

Another personality problem is jealousy. Extreme possessiveness can ruin an otherwise close relationship. Jealous people have an active imagination in reverse. They imagine their loved one as being unfaithful even when fidelity exists. Instead of confronting the partner and causing dissention, here's what one woman imagined: "I see my husband, who is a traveling salesman, relaxing and reading in his room. When I see him having dinner out of town, I picture him with male friends telling them about his wonderful wife and how he looks forward to coming home." In the past, she had visions of his cavorting around with women, and when he returned from a trip, instead of enjoying their time together, they quarreled. With the help of positive mental imagery, their relationship improved to such an extent that, the last I heard, he had invited her along on one of his business trips.

Vision Six: Fears and Phobias

Many unfounded fears and anxieties are caused by imagining disasters that never occur. The list is endless. From A for Agoraphobia (fear of crowds), to Z for Zoophobia (fear of animals), it seems everybody is afraid of something. Many people have irrational fears which limit their daily existence. Fear of riding an elevator is a classic example. Fear of flying is another.

To overcome fear, face it! Confront in your mind whatever frightens you. Instead of letting your thoughts run away from the phobia, focus your concentrated energy right into the anxiety. Suppose, for instance, you have a dreaded fear of high places. Begin your play-acting by seeing yourself climbing up three steps on a short ladder. Next time you meditate, visualize yourself at the top of a tall staircase looking down. Each time you confront your fear, act more boldly, as you take yourself higher and higher. Finally, picture yourself looking down from a window in the Empire State Building or some other skyscraper. Add to the vision a close-up of your face, relaxed and smiling without any sign of discomfort.

Jimmy K. had been frightened by a dog when he was six years old. At the age of eighteen, Jimmy was still terrified of animals. To cure himself of this fear, Jimmy was trained to see himself first petting a very small puppy who was on a leash. In a subsequent session, the dog grew a little larger. Each time he worked with the image, the dog matured, until Jimmy pictured himself feeding a large dog and taking him for a walk on a leash. Finally, he envisioned himself rolling in the grass with a dog who loved him.

IMAGINATION AND AUTOSUGGESTION

Vision Seven: Bad Habits

Whether the bad habit is nail-biting, heroin, or chocolate cream pie, bad habits often become cruel masters, robbing us of our freedom of choice. To regain your liberty, you must study the prison you have constructed for yourself. What are the bars holding you in? Each individual has a distinctive style of behavior, with qualities both good and bad. Somewhere in that configuration is the need for redesigning the inner diagram. Constructive fantasy alters perception. The dependent person who once saw himself trapped in a prison of habits begins to envision possibilities of escaping from his bonds.

Here's a case of a woman who's biggest problem was her mouth: Katherine M. suffered from a number of compulsive oral habits, one linked to the other. If she wasn't chewing, she was puffing a cigarette or drinking alcohol. Apathy and indulgence had turned her from an attractive young woman weighing 120 pounds to a despondent, rotund matron who weighed 220. In a letter to me, she described herself as "a sloppy pig." When I met her, I knew why. Her clothing was too tight, and the fat bulged in layers around her body. Her once lovely hair was dishevelled and her teeth discolored from smoking.

"I can't help myself," she moaned in self pity. "I have no control." Obviously, she needed control, but more than that Katherine needed a new self-image. After trained to reach her center of control through self-hypnosis, Katherine created a corrective illusion which brought her excellent results. She is now back to 120 pounds and looks just fine.

THE IMPROVED IMAGE

Katherine visualized a movie screen with the title, *The New Katherine M.* She saw herself on the screen slim and well-groomed, she was surrounded by a group of admirers congratulating her on a job well done. While others were behaving like gluttons—overeating, guzzling booze, fouling the air with smoke—Katherine remained serene, aloof. She saw herself smiling with a bright "toothpaste-ad-smile." She scanned her body, noticing the improvements: flat stomach, fingers free of stains. Each time Katherine meditated on her self-image, she added something new. She saw herself with a special man who showed special interest in her. She saw herself succeeding in relationships, something which had been impossible for her before. She began to know and understand the emotions which churned inside of her, the desires and needs which had been unfulfilled. Her improved image

d. Her improved image was with her at all times, carried
nosis to the waking state.

AUTOSUGGESTION FOR REPROGRAMMING

"We possess within us a force of incalculable power, which if we direct
in a wise manner, gives us mastery of ourselves. It permits us not only
to escape from physical and mental ills, but also to live in relative
happiness."

So wrote Dr. Émile Coué of France over a half century ago in his
book *The Coué Method.* Dr. Coué, exponent of the theory of autosuggestion, achieved his successful results long before the theory of psychosomatic medicine became popular. Not only did he cure various
illnesses, but converted despondent people into happy, fulfilled ones.
Through his method of positive thinking, Dr. Coué transformed the lives
of millions of people and started a long trend of books on using the mind
for positive improvement. Many modern movements of the mind, like
Silva Mind Control and E.S.T. have drawn basic concepts from Dr.
Coué's work.

Émile Coué's method is based on two factors:

1. Where willpower and imagination come into conflict, the power
of imagination will always win out. This is so because the will
comes from the periphery of the mind and imagination reaches into
its core.

2. Imagination can be trained and expanded more readily than will-
power, which is more elusive. Willpower needs to be forced emotionally
and thereby increases stress. Imagination is free-flowing and diminishes
stress.

Autosuggestion creates a new kind of reality when it is combined with imagination, a reality that is different and better than before,
free of past echoes. Unfortunately, most people are oblivious to the
workings of their unconscious minds. What you know consciously represents only about one-tenth of the iceberg. With self-hypnosis, it will
be easy for you to probe into the other nine-tenths buried beneath the
surface.

Dr. Émile Coué said "When you wish to do something reasonable, or
when you have a duty to perform, always think it's easy. *Make the words
"difficult," "impossible," and "I cannot" disappear from your vocabulary.*
Tell yourself "I can, I will, I must."

By considering anything easy, it becomes easier for you, though the act might seem difficult to others. You perform quickly and well, and without fatigue since no willpower on your part need be applied. Whereas, if you had considered the task difficult, it would have become so because you would have failed to believe in yourself.

When you know how to direct positive thoughts, they work as a benevolent kind of brainwashing.

The conditioned reflex which produced the harmful behavior is removed once a more appropriate idea is accepted by the subconscious. Suggestions need not be verbalized. Silent thoughts are also "self-suggestions," influencing us to move in a determined direction.

Stop and consider: what are the silent suggestions you are now giving yourself? Your mind constantly turns your thoughts into bodily reaction. You will see dramatic evidence of this when you learn to direct your brain power to serve your best interests instead of the other way around. Be prepared to see a phenomenal change for the better. Emphasizing possibilities of success instead of failure starts the changeover. Positive conditioning works the same way that negative conditioning does, except *in reverse*. Patiently hammering away at a bad habit will not only eliminate it, but clear the site for one which will serve you better.

Once you see improvement, however slight, encourage yourself by affirmation. Self-praise helps build self-confidence. Nothing is as powerful as your own voice. Ego-strengthening is needed to compensate for the downgrading most people are subjected to during the growing-up years.

DECONDITION YOUR BEHAVIOR

Habits are projections of the roots that once nurtured us. How about your habits? What sort of soil nourished them? When you become aware that the behavior that suited you in childhood is no longer suitable for you as an adult, you will be on your way to deconditioning yourself.

Awareness clears space in the mind for a new set of habits. It's like cleaning out an old closet that's accumulated junk. During hypnotic meditation, you take a long hard look inside your space, spend enough time to understand, and then proceed to the positive reconstruction.

Once the slate is washed clean, the creative mind has unlimited freedom to plan a new life-style.

RECONDITION YOUR LIFE

Positive programming is implanted through carefully selected suggestions which reverse signals to the reflexes. Suggestions are reconditioning phrases. When they are repeated over and over again, they repute your actions into a new groove. The degree to which you improve depends on how willing you are to change. Motivation and level of self-esteem influence the rate of success.

ATTITUDE AFFECTS LIFE'S ALTITUDE

How high or low you feel is a reflection of how strong or weak your self-image is. The purpose of self-suggestion is to make the most of the best and the least of the worst of your natural attributes. When you tell yourself *I can't*, chances are *you won't*. On the other hand, if you tell yourself, *I can* and *I will*, you stand a much better chance of reaching your objective, since thoughts predetermine action.

A common stumbling block to self-realization is anticipation of failure. When one secretly expects to lose, confidence takes a back seat. One of my clients, Stanley R., talked to me about his past. "I can still hear the unkind criticism I received from my parents as a boy."

Every time Stanley allowed the past to influence him, he reinforced his problem. "My family said I was clumsy. Badly coordinated. Being the youngest in a large family, their evaluation of me seemed accurate. How could a ten-year-old boy know they were judging me by adult standards?"

With autosuggestion under self-hypnosis, Stanley programmed himself to step away from the past and see himself in the present. He trained himself to play golf, tennis, and the piano. This so-called "clumsy, badly coordinated" child had matured sufficiently and stopped listening to voices from his past. He was able to talk to himself like a winner.

The lesson to be learned from Stanley: *Stop listening* to other voices from faraway rooms. Nobody knows you better than yourself. Take charge, reclaim your mind. This process is called counter-hypnosis because it is a correction of bad hypnosis inflicted upon us by others. We replace outside mental manipulation with mental self-control.

YOU ALWAYS HAVE A CHOICE

We are all bombarded with things other people would like us to do. However, we don't have to say yes. We can also say no or, better, we can use two significant words: *I prefer.* The meaning is obvious. Preferring gives you not only choice, but control and mastery over events. Use these two words to start your program of autosuggestion for behavioral improvement:

I prefer not to smoke. I prefer to be healthy.
I prefer not to overeat. I prefer a youthful body.
I prefer not to be an alcoholic. I prefer to think clearly.
I prefer to sleep through the night and awaken refreshed.

Exercising your preferences will make you a more assertive person and more highly regarded by all who come in contact with you. If you don't make choices, others less interested in your welfare will make the choices for you.

Words have power. Especially the words you use to describe yourself, to yourself as well as to others. Your choice of vocabulary can not only make or break behavior patterns, but make or break your life. Certain four letter words, for instance, carry with them automatic stigma and hostility, no matter how casual the intent. On the other hand, four letter words like *love, life, good,* and *fine* can heal and help.

Mark Twain said, "The difference between the right word and the almost right word is the difference between lightning and the lightning bug." In formulating autosuggestions, the right choice of words can accelerate improvement and the wrong choice retard growth. Some words are very special. They can bring about a sense of elation, instill pleasurable feeling, and inspire great confidence.

Using the proper words, it is possible to overcome many major obstacles in your life as well as expand your scope of accomplishment. I have put together a list of ten words with positive power. They pack a strong vibrational wallop on the subconscious mind. If they suit you, use them. If not, create your own.

SERENITY	ECSTASY	SUCCESS
CONFIDENCE	LOVE	GLOWING
ENERGY	POWER	CREATIVE
HEALTH		

POSITIVE THINKING FROM A TO Z

Here is an interesting list of positive words created by a member of my class. Grover T. was a salesman and had excellent results not only in improving his self-image but in increasing his income. He combines the blackboard technique with "alphabet suggestions." In this manner, he not only deepens his trance level but programs himself at the same time. While under hypnosis, imagine yourself writing and erasing the alphabet from A to Z as you focus on each corresponding thought.

A. AWARENESS AND ACTION
B. BETTER BUSINESS
C. CALM, CONFIDENT
D. DISCIPLINE, DRIVE
E. ENTHUSIASM, ENERGY
F. FEELING FINE
G. GREAT GOALS
H. HEALTHY, HAPPY
I. INCREASE INCOME
J. JOG JOYFULLY
K. KEEP KEEN
L. LONGER LIFE
M. MIND MASTERY

N. NO NERVOUSNESS
O. OVERCOME OBSTACLES
P. POSITIVE PROGRESS
Q. QUALITY 'S QUANTITY
R. REMARKABLE RESULTS
S. SENSATIONAL SUCCESS
T. TRANQUIL THOUGHTS
U. UNIFY, UNDERSTAND
V. VIM & VIGOR
W. WEALTH WITHOUT WORRY
X. XCITING XPERIENCE
Y. YOUNGER & YOUNGER
Z. ZIP, ZEST, ZENITH

Begin by finding one word that has especially good vibrations for you. Even one uplifting word can do wonders for you. Repeat it again and again as you meditate upon it. Remember, repetition caused the negative traits to become entrenched, so reversing the procedure will help positive traits gain a foothold. Build groups of words and short sentences. Reprogramming requires choosing words and thoughts that have strong emotional conviction. Once you have found them, never let them go. Use them over and over again, while you are day-dreaming, meditating, or using hypnosis.

When awake, sometimes say your positive autosuggestions out loud. Look into a mirror when you awaken in the morning and just before bedtime, look into your own eyes. Tell it to yourself until the words slip off your tongue without effort. Recite them slowly, passively with anticipation of realization.

Most people assume thoughts are involuntary and that they cannot help thinking what they think. Nothing is further from the truth. Even the most obsessive thinking can be restrained and retrained. Do you minimize your capabilities or attributes? Most people do, mistakenly believing that modesty is respected. Unfortunately, many people go to extremes and behave in a humble fashion. By so doing, they fall prey to manipulation by others who think little of them.

Where does self-limiting behavior come from? It draws from an inner source of self-destruction. Self-putdowns are born inside the troubled mind. Even more detrimental than talking to others in this way is the silent conversation people carry on within themselves. Have you ever silently thought, "How could I be so stupid?" or "I look too fat," "too thin," "too tall," "too short," . . . etc . . . etc. Everyone has. When you find yourself resorting to such attitudes, use the *cancel-out* technique. Say to yourself, "Stop! Cancel out!" or "Cease, desist, I've had enough of that!" "Quit that garbage! Get lost!"

The cancel-out technique can be used silently or verbalized. You will find it useful in correcting habits such as overweight, smoking, and insomnia, as well as in behavior modification in personal relationships. Once you have mastered this method, you will find yourself automatically responding to negativism with authoritative positivism. Then you can simplify the command using only one word repeated several times: "Cancel!" or "Stop!"

After giving yourself the command, say to yourself, "You will, instead, accept this positive suggestion. . . ."And then you proceed to feed to yourself your own suggestion, which will contradict the negative thought or activity.

Below are a few autosuggestions which have proved useful to others. You can create more specific ones to deal directly with your own problems:

I am free of fear and feel more confident.
Whatever happens, I will not lose my temper.
I value myself and will behave with pride.
I will stick to the diet and lose weight. -
Smoking is for sick people. I quit.
I am master of my fate, captain of my soul.
All pain is going and soon will be gone.

FORMULATE A SURVIVAL SYSTEM

The key to maximizing your way of life is having a method to counter-act the destructive forces that face all of us. The method must be based on an overview of yourself and your own attitude toward your mind and body. See yourself as uniquely special, very worthy, with everything you need to survive and overcome all problems. Think in terms of what you can do, not what you cannot do. From a cold to cancer, you've got what it takes to overcome. Others have done so and so can you. From the top of your head to the tip of your toes, be aware constantly of a *healing-feeling* drifting and shifting to every area of concern.

Almost everyone has to give up some bad behavior. Explore your own behavior. Are you addicted to any substance that you should elimi-nate? Before you can develop a system to elevate yourself, you must understand where you have been. Make a list of your bad habits and unwanted behavior. Become aware of what you do, what you say, and what you think. When under hypnosis, you will discover even more as you probe the subterranean regions of your mind. With concentrated thought, you will see clearly the pattern which triggers repetition of your behavior. Once you recognize the "signal," you are one step closer to removing the triggering device which sets off routine habit. Once you have interfered with the regularity of the habit, you have also weakened its hold on you. Once the cycle of *thought-trigger-reflex* is broken, deconditioning can begin. The habit is now neutralized and ready to be wiped out by *signal reversal.*

Any time you feel the urge to repeat an old action that is detrimen-tal to you, that very urge will be the signal to do the opposite. For example, the urge to smoke becomes retranslated as the signal to fill your lungs with fresh air. Cravings to self-destruct become cravings to self-construct. Here is the basic formula for reversing your signals:

Whenever I Think I am Going to ....
                                                            (Old habit)
That Will Be My Signal to Instead ....
                                                            (New habit)

If, for example, smoking is your bad habit complete the formula this way: "Whenever I think of smoking, that will be my signal to instead take three deep breaths."

If you are overweight, your signal reversal might be: "Whenever I think of eating something I shouldn't, the thought will signal me to pull in my stomach and stick to the diet.

Signal reversal is not only effective for changing bad habits into better ones; it works equally well for personality problems. Over a period of time, students have submitted various examples of signal reversal that have worked well for them. Here are a few. Perhaps one will suit your personality. If not, I am sure you will create a more suitable one.

> *The Unwanted Behavior:* Shyness
> *The Formula:* "Whenever I Feel Shy and Tend to Back Away,
>   I Will, Instead, Smile and Extend My Hand in
>   Friendship."

The formula can trigger specific action or can be generalized.

> *The Unwanted Behavior:* Worry
> *The Formula:* "Whenever I Begin to Worry Needlessly, I Will,
>   Instead, Think of a Solution and Do Something
>   about It."

Some of the problems that lend themselves to this technique are jealousy, obsessive guilt, possessiveness, perfectionism, indecision, and phobias. These are but a few. The list is endless and extends to every area of human conflict, mental, emotional, and physical. Try creating a formula for transforming negative personal relationships into positive ones. Are you enjoying a fulfilling love relationship? If so, you can make it better. If not, tap your highest intelligence and find out why you are denying yourself this ultimate pleasure. Then formulate your programming to correct the situation. It might be worded this way:

> *Whenever I Think of Myself as Lonely and Loveless, That will Be a Signal for Me to Affirm All My Good Qualities and Project Loving Feelings Toward Others.*

Some people alienate others by their introverted personalities. A young woman troubled by increasingly frequent periods of depression used this wording: *"Whenever I Feel Miserable and Low. That Is the Signal for Me to List My Good Qualities and Raise My Spirits Higher and Higher."*

Regular practice of this technique assures you that every negative thought triggers the opposite reaction. Create your formula while meditating in self-hypnosis. Reinforce it while in a waking state as often as possible. Be vigilant. At the first sign of the slightest negative feeling, put your foot down firmly. Let your mind know you are free of the old enslavement and will not be lured back.

The best habit you can cultivate is diligent practice. Set aside at least one half hour for hypnotic meditation each day. Stick with it until you succeed. Thomas A. Edison said, "Our greatest weakness lies in giving up too soon. The most certain way to succeed is to try just one more time." Faithful adherence to the technique will not only change your mind, but your body and the course of your life.

In addition to periods of self-hypnosis with positive autosuggestion, repeat your formula the last thing at night and the first thing in the morning. At these times, your mind is less resistant and reconditioning is most effective. Make a habit of reviewing your accomplishments. Praise yourself for showing improvement. Self-approval is the greatest boost to motivation. Success breeds more success and, once recognized, positive forces within you multiply to complete the total changeover.

From time to time, review your personal program and progress. If you reach some of your short-term goals, set new ones. Persist. Stick to your goals. The ultimate freedom will be well worth the effort. Confucius had something to say about everything and this topic is no exception. "In all things," he said, "success depends upon previous preparation, and without such preparation, there is sure to be failure." Your program is your previous preparation.

HOW TO BRING YOURSELF OUT OF HYPNOSIS

After taking yourself into autohypnosis and repeating your autosuggestions at least ten times, you may be ready to come out of the trance. Keep in mind that you are at no time in danger of staying "under." You would simply drift from hypnosis into sleep and awaken in a few minutes. Whether you are hypnotized by a professional or do it yourself, you are always in control and can awaken at will, just as you have awakened many times from a light nap.

After hypnosis, you will feel refreshed and new. Your mind will be sharp and clear, but your body and emotions will be free of the old trouble some tensions. To wake up feeling just great, count from 1 to 10 using positive reinforcement with each count. As you count up, feel your spirits rising.

>*One* . . . Getting ready to wake up now, feeling fine.
>*Two* . . . My mind is clear and keen, raring to go.
>*Three* . . . I am cheerful and happy, eager to face the day.
>*Four* . . . My body feels rested, refreshed, lots of energy.
>*Five* . . . This was a successful session with positive results.
>*Six* . . . Next time I will go even deeper with better results.
>*Seven, Eight, Nine, Ten* . . . Wide awake, feeling wonderful!!

Remember, all skills require time and effort to acquire. I suggest that you *place the special verbalized material on a tape and memorize the techniques.* This will be equivalent to having a professional train you in the art of self-induction, you will be able to look to yourself for answers and corrections in many areas. However, in no instance should a lay person attempt to use self-hypnosis to try to cure a serious illness without first consulting a qualified physician. Self-hypnosis is primarily an adjunct to the medical profession, not a substitute for medical expertise. Those with a serious mental or emotional problem will require the assistance of a trained psychotherapist or hypnotherapist. There is no danger in using self-hypnosis in such cases; it simply will not work for the seriously disturbed, who need to be guided into the areas of mental concentration where improvements originate. Mentally disturbed people tend to wander during meditation, and a skilled therapist knows how to bring them into focus. If you are in need of a professional person, contact your local medical or psychological associations.

Eating, Smoking, Drugs and Insomnia

Too many square meals make people rounder and lonelier. America's number one negative habit is overeating. Too many people use food as a replacement for emotional needs such as love and security. The tragedy of food obsession is that obesity tends to further alienate people from others. A cloak of excess flesh does not shield against emotional hurt. Fat cannot cushion blows to delicate egos.

"I've been humiliated by my husband," explained Florence. "He used to take me to his college reunion and always acted proud of me. But this year, Ronnie said he wouldn't attend because he was ashamed to be seen with me."

She paused, dabbed her eyes and unconsciously popped a sweet into her mouth. "I'm so fat," she moaned. "I've gained at least ten pounds a year since we've been married. From a size twelve, I've gone to size twenty and a half. But, Miss Copelan," Florence appealed to me, "if Ronnie really and truly loved me, wouldn't he accept me fat and all?"

In fact, Ronnie couldn't accept his wife's obesity. He had married an attractive, slender girl and now he was embarrassed for his friends to see the shape she was in.

Needless to say, despite all arguments, they did not attend the college reunion. But, to Ronnie's delight, Florence responded positively to hypnotic suggestion. She was placed on a limit of 1200 calories as post hypnotic suggestion. The following year, they attended the reunion in high style. Florence wore a size twelve dress and Ronnie beamed proudly at her side. She is a fine example of the use of professional hypnosis combined with self-hypnosis which she practices every night when she goes to bed.

However, more than Florence's weight had bothered Ronnie. Slimmed down, she reflected the new happiness and contentment in her marriage. When she was overweight, her appearance indicated her emotional insecurity. Ronnie felt her emotions reflected upon him as a husband. They also worked out problems which related to their sexual relationship. You will read the sexual implications in a future chapter.

HUNGER VERSUS APPETITE

Too many people confuse hunger with appetite. Appetite is a habit. Hunger is a real need. The two are not the same.

Appetite is provoked by suggestion while hunger is the message we receive when we need nourishment. Proper diet is essential to provide the elements necessary for the body to renew tissue and keep the organs functioning as nature intended.

Compulsive eaters strain their will power and by-pass mind power. In other words, they consciously struggle to deny appetite instead of correcting the mental programming which causes them to crave unnecessary calories. The body only does what the mind tells it to do.

In order to help overcome the "stuffing" habit, hypnosis begins by teaching the subconscious how to think about food. Overeaters need a bit of brainwashing to clear away conditioned habits.

An overweight teenager, Elsie, told me, "My family used to call me 'the human garbage can.' I always cleaned up everybody's leftovers. When I was a little kid, they thought it was cute. But after I grew up they began to ridicule me.

Hypnosis helped Elsie change her self-image. She had to learn to respect her body and accept healthier living habits.

If you do not already know about calories, a balanced diet, and the importance of vitamins, take a lesson from Elsie, who is now a happy size seven and strolls down the beach wearing a polka-dot bikini.

Get into the habit of a healthy program of nutrition. As Elsie learned, eating a small amount of food doesn't guarantee weight loss.

CALORIES DO COUNT

To lose one pound of fat, you must burn up approximately 3000 calories through physical activity. If a person eliminates 1000 calories a day, he can lose approximately two pounds a week. Most people require less calories than they are accustomed to eating. Once Elsie discovers the power of her mind, she began losing weight in a most natural way, without conscious effort or struggle.

Fundamentals of Weight Reduction:

1. Take in less energy in the form of food than your body uses. Reduce carbohydrates to the barest minimum. Increase proteins to the maximum.

2. Exercise your body at every opportunity. Never sit when you can stand, never ride when you can walk. Stretch and bend every time you can.

People Who Stay Slim Obey the Following Rules:

1. They postpone eating as often as possible.
2. They are selective about what they eat.
3. They chew slowly before swallowing.

If you obey all of the precepts above, you will not only grow slim, but remain slim. The most desirable weight for anyone is the weight at which a person looks and feels best. Height, bone structure and muscular development must all be taken into account.

FACE UP TO FACTS

What has been your maximum weight? _____
Your minimum weight as an adult? _____
How much weight would you like to lose? _____
You can lose from three to five pounds a week through hypnosis, depending upon your physical structure. How many pounds do you think you would be comfortable losing each week?_____
Now divide that number into your first figure and see how many weeks it will take you to lose the total amount. Set your target date.____
Now you have a goal to reach. Your computerlike mind has picked up the message you have just written and will find a way to make the wishful thinking reality. Autosuggestion will communicate this motivation to your body reflexes.
Remember that a great incentive to losing weight is that favorite dress or suit you have hidden away in the closet because it's too small to wear.

SMOKERS ARE SELF-POLLUTERS

The United States Health Department reports that smokers tend to die five to ten years before nonsmokers. That's a pretty good reason to quit, right? Still, tobacco addicts cling to the self-destructive habit.

I heard a hostess tell her guest recently, "Sit down, John, relax and have a smoke."

She may as well have said, "Sit down, John, and have a stroke."

Smoking can be just as injurious to the heart as to the lungs. Actually, when a person lights up a cigarette, he does not relax. Sitting down is relaxing, not the smoke. Smoking increases tension. If you've ever watched a person puff away on a cigarette as if his life depended on it, you would see he is far from relaxed.

One of the most difficult aspects of breaking the smoking habit is its tendency to accompany another activity that is relaxing. For example, during coffee breaks or after dinner, a smoker will often light up a cigarette. Coffee breaks are supposed to be a time for relief from stress. But for many people, they represent time to reinforce bad habits. For the overweight person, the doughnut that goes with the coffee just adds to the surplus poundage.

A good idea during coffee breaks would be to change over to exercise or relaxation breaks. Many large corporations recognize the importance of this need to stimulate employees, and have set aside space and equipment for this purpose.

But those employees not fortunate enough to work in a place where special facilities are available can always just find a chair during their "break" and do self-hypnosis to improve their positive programming.

THE EVIDENCE IS OVERWHELMING

Every day new evidence appears linking smoking to more diseases. The secretary of the U.S. Department of Health recently stated in an A.P. news story, "Cigarette smoking continues to be confirmed as a serious health hazard, one which is unquestionably the cause of much unnecessary disease and death."

Consider this. Even the mildest filter tip cigarette speeds up the heartbeat, upsets circulation and limits oxygen to the lungs.

What happens when you quit smoking?
1. You will breathe easier.
2. Your circulation will improve.
3. You will feel less tired and nervous.
4. Your sense of smell will improve.
5. Your cough will lessen or disappear.
6. Your heart and lungs will strengthen.
7. And because you stop with hypnosis, you will never drift back to
it again. How is this possible? Because negative suggestion is removed
and positive suggestion takes over.

HOW MUCH SMOKING IS HARMFUL?

How many times should a man strike his wife?
    How many times should a boy kick a dog?
    Even one cigarette is one too many for most people. Remember the
first time you tried a cigarette, how sick it made you feel? That was the
time to quit.
    A good rule about what is healthy and what is unhealthy is to ask
yourself, would I offer this to a child? If your answer is no, it is also
unhealthy for you, at any age.
    A 35-year-old movie director, Frank, R., came to see me to help
him stop smoking. He confessed that he smoked from three to four
packs a day.
    "It's my job," Frank alibied. "I'm under constant tension. Every-
one bugs me for something all day long. A cigarette calms my nerves."
    I noticed Frank's hands. They were trembling. His nerves were far
from calm. He looked down at his quivering fingers, sheepishly embarrassed.
    "This is nothing. You should see how I shake when I'm not smok-
ing," he quipped.
    "Are you trying to tell me that smoking four packs of cigarettes a
day helps your nervous system?" I asked.
    "Guess I'm trying to cop out," he answered. "The fact is, I came
to see you hoping to be helped through hypnosis. I can't go on this way
much longer. Honestly, it's become serious. I wake up at night coughing
up black phlegm. I've had to give up playing tennis because I get too
winded. I'm constantly tired and know I must be a perfect target for
cancer. My brother already has it. I've tried everything and so far
nothing works."

Frank took time out to cough. Then he continued. "I've thrown away six cartons of cigarettes; six times I've quit—but I always drift back."

Frank did quit smoking with hypnotherapy six years ago and has not drifted back. He is just one of millions of smokers who have been permanently reconditioned through hypnotic techniques.

CAN THE SMOKER REGAIN HIS HEALTH?

Smoking destroys living tissue. When a person coughs, struggling to breathe, the lining of his respiratory system becomes sticky, coated with an ugly, grey chemical substance. This sludge blocks the passages, eventually resulting in lung infection and sometimes even a collapsed lung. After a person has given up smoking for several years, this sludge is eliminated by the natural processes of the body. After ten years, his life expectancy can even match that of abstainers. These statistics are based on reports from the American Cancer Society's massive survey of a million men and women.

One way to cut down on smoking is to learn how to breathe correctly. Some people lose their desire to smoke once they learn how to breathe the way nature intended, with full lung capacity. The average person is a shallow breather using only about 20% of his lungs for breathing. On the other hand, smokers who inhale bring the fumes down to the unused 80 percent of their lungs. This action momentarily provides them with a contented feeling. However, once they finish their cigarettes, their breathing becomes shallow once again.

When people breathe with 100 percent of their lungs, they not only get a satisfied feeling; they also get sufficient oxygen to rejuvenate body cells and to sustain perfect health.

Practice the following self-hypnosis exercise several times a day for five to ten minutes.

1. Sit upright without having your spine touch the back of the chair.

2. Place your hands loosely on top of your thighs. Space your feet about 10 inches apart.

3. Close your eyes and focus on the rhythms of your breathing.

4. Breathe in and out quickly and rhythmically through your nose. Do this a dozen times. You may cough and spit up phlegm. This is helpful for cleaning the trachea.

5. Place your right hand on your lower diaphragm. Monitor the movement of your lungs as they fill with oxygen.

6. Breathe in and out in twelve slow, deep rhythmic breaths. Inhale to the count of five, then pause and exhale to the count of five. This will cleanse the lower areas of your lungs.

FACE THE FACTS

Ask Yourself:

1. How much do I smoke? _____
2. When do I reach for a cigarette? _____
3. Does tension make me smoke more? _____
4. Do I smoke during the night? _____
5. Do I smoke with my meals? _____

After you answer the above questions and have conscious awareness, be assured that you can cut down on your smoking or quit entirely, if you really choose to do it. Once you face facts, use the following autosuggestion to enforce your determination to quit.

Repeat the following five times each:

1. I have quit smoking forever.
2. No one can coax me into taking a cigarette.
3. When someone offers me one, I will answer, "Thanks, but I do not smoke anymore."

Here are some additional tips on cutting down.

1. Smoke half of a cigarette. The tobacco itself acts as a partial filter. The last half is the worst, loaded with tar and nicotine.
2. Limit yourself. No more than eight cigarettes a day.
3. Use the low tar variety with a filter tip since king-size contains more nicotine and tar.
4. Reduce inhaling. Smoke irritates the bronchial membranes.
5. Keep a record. Mark down each time you have an urge to smoke. When you resist giving in, give yourself a star. Experiments show people who keep track of what they are doing decrease negative habits.

DRUGS, ALCOHOL, AND HYPNOSIS

Alice H., 37 years of age, was an alcoholic. She had tried psychoanalysis for about five years without success. While she was under the care of several physicians, medications of every sort were tested and discarded. Alice was divorced and the mother of three small children who had been taken from her by the court and placed with the father. The children's father, Mark, was also alcoholic. Mark had, in fact, taught Alice to drink and then accused her of being an unfit mother. Since Mark held the purse strings and had political connections, he managed to keep the children, allowing the mother only occasional visitation rights.

Alice then drank even more heavily. Depressed and dazed about the entire situation, she finally met an understanding young man, Jonathan, who sympathized and went to great lengths to help her. Jonathan stood by her during her worst bouts with the bottle. He supplied funds enabling Alice to undergo analysis and receive all known medical treatment. Finally, when everything else failed (as is so often the case) hypnosis was used.

Alice was serious about overcoming her problem, "the quicker the better." The time wasted and the trouble created by her problem drinking finally got to her. "My children are growing up without knowing their mother," she said unhappily. The love of Jonathan was also an incentive to pull herself together. She didn't just want to cut down or be a social drinker; she wanted to stop drinking completely.

Alice became a willing and eager subject, anxious to lick her problem. With strong motivation and determination, she was able to overcome the habit and become a sensible person again. The reasons which caused her to drink came to the surface and were noted by the hypnotherapist.

Alice had read a book on hypnosis which described the various techniques and presented case histories of the subjects. Her parents were arrogant, which caused her to dislike and resent an authoritative hypnotic approach. She preferred to be corrected and reasoned with in a soft, permissive manner. The hypnotist asked Alice to help in programming her feelings of aversion to alcohol. Alice made a list, and restructured her thoughts. She then entered into a medium trance during the very first session and was given autosuggestions for aversion to alcoholic beverages. During this state of relaxed receptivity, the suggestions of complete and lasting aversion to alcohol were allowed to penetrate. Because the suggestions increased the depth of her concentration, she demonstrated to the therapist the sincerity of her motivations. *The resistant subject who is not properly motivated will tend to lose depth the moment therapeutic suggestions are applied.*

Alice did not take another drink after her first session. Instead, she was encouraged to find new interests. She went back to work and was able to keep a job for the first time. Jonathan was still supportive. He encouraged her and kept her away from "bad company." Soon Alice herself was able to take charge of their social engagements. She discovered that she could even sit with an occasional drinking group and sip ginger ale or water and it didn't bother her.

One month later, Alice visited my office to report her aversion for alcohol had become so deep and complete that when she went for a massage, the alcohol used for the rub made her nauseous.

WHEN DOES A DRINKER BECOME AN ALCOHOLIC?

The social drinker can stop drinking anytime he or she wants to, or whenever circumstances compel them to, but the compulsive alcoholic cannot control his urge. He continues to drink until he loses self-control and self-respect.

Not every drinker becomes an alcoholic. Some people learn to hold their liquor. They can stop whenever they want to stop. Others go to the other extreme and lose total control of their intake.

George S. was such a man. He consumed at least half a quart of alcoholic beverages every day. Cocktails before dinner, beer or wine with his meal, and the familiar nightcap before bedtime. He was brought to see me by his teenage son, Michael.

"We never realized my father drank until one night when he came home sober and we noticed the difference," Michael said.

George S. interrupted, "I wouldn't be here now if it wasn't for my liver. The doctor warned me I'll have to go to the hospital unless I quit drinking right away."

A twenty year old habit is not easy to give up. George was a chronic alcoholic, who lacked discipline and energy. His eating habits were poor and his sex life, nil. For George, it was a case of developing an entirely new kind of program for living. With the help of an audio cassette tape which he played several times a day, and ten sessions of hypnosis, George S. finally learned to control his weakness.

DRUG ADDICTION

The habit monster has many claws. In addition to the widespread problems of overeating, smoking, and drinking, millions are plagued by the drug habit.

The World Health Organization states: "Drug addiction is a state of periodic and chronic intoxication detrimental to the individual and to society, produced by the repeated consumption of a drug (natural or synthetic). Characteristics of addiction include:

1. An overpowering desire to continue use.
2. An emotional drive to obtain it by any means.
3. A tendency to increase the dose as the drug lessens its powers.
4. A psychological and sometimes physical dependence."

This definition includes all three types of drugs: those prescribed by doctors, those sold over the counter legally, and those pushed on the street illegally.

Drugs more popularly addictive are the opiates such as heroin, opium, cocaine, and marijuana. The barbituates and amphetamines, which are often medically prescribed, may be added to this list.

A person who is aware of his habits and honestly wishes to get rid of them can learn how to get high on life. We have all the natural resources, providing we learn how to use them.

To begin with, an optimistic approach is needed in order to cope with the ordinary and extraordinary problems which confront us. This means leaning to take life as it comes, and learning to accept the consequences.

Through hypnosis, mental attitudes become more optimistic. We discover within ourselves the "makings" of a better way of life. Hypnosis holds the key to many a seemingly locked door. The greatest treasure in the world is the inner peace and tranquillity which comes from knowing that normal health, both emotional and physical, is within the mind's reach. Naturally induced hypnotic "high" feeling never wears off, but remains with you through all adversity.

SPECIAL BONUS—A GOOD NIGHT'S SLEEP

If you are like most people, there have been nights when you toss and turn, restless and exhausted. The harder you strive and strain for sleep,

the more wide awake you become. One of the great bonuses of practicing self-hypnosis is that you will never be troubled by insomnia again.
Self-hypnosis is the gateway to regular nighttime slumber, and once you
train yourself to relax deeply, you will be able to simply slip over the
boundary into a restful night's sleep.

Everyone needs a good night's sleep. Our century's pace of living
has become so intense, the human mind is overstimulated by the time
evening arrives. People in perpetual motion have problems unwinding
the tautness of their mental and physical springs. Falling asleep has
become a lost art for man and sends millions of people to doctors for
relief. Often relief is elusive because medication does not erase the root
cause of insomnia. Only a relaxed body and a tranquil mind can do that.

Doctors, as well as the patients themselves, are sometimes guilty of
the overuse of sleeping pills, many of which are sold over the counter
without a doctor's prescription. These are called "sedative or medicative
hypnotics." Isn't it strange that we use drugs to create a hypnotic effect
when hypnosis itself is so simple to learn and so harmless to use? This
is another example of how we have been brainwashed to behave contrary to our natural instincts. You are equipped with everything you need
to decelerate rapid daytime tempos and slow down the pulses of your
body. Your best sleep medicine is always prevention. It is possible to
stop insomnia before it starts through the manner in which you handle
your daily routine of living. It is important not to overreact to routine
pressures.

HOW MUCH SLEEP DO WE NEED?

Everybody needs regular sleep, but not everybody needs the same amount
of regular sleep. What constitutes a full night's sleep for one may equal
a catnap for another. There are many myths and fallacies about sleep.
One is that we all require eight hours per night. A short sleep differs
from insomnia. Some people awaken fully rested with as little as four or
five hours of profound slumber. Others wake up tired unless they have
nine or ten.

The long accepted dictum that everybody needs eight hours falls
flat by the wayside when you consider Thomas Edison and Albert
Einstein, who slept only four or five hours a night and accomplished so
much. Yet everyone needs a certain amount of sleep. When they don't
get their required amount, panic may set in. Headaches, backaches, or a

dragged-out feeling may result the next day. A pall of anxiety hangs over the insomniac when he keeps trying and fails to sleep.

If a person lives to age 75, for example, chances are he'll spend one third of his life sleeping. Whether that third will make the other two thirds meaningful, depends upon how well he revitalizes himself during sleeping hours. As one grows older, he requires less sleep. A baby sleeps on and off around the clock; an adult usually sleeps between six and eight hours. There is evidence that men sleep longer than women, extroverts longer than introverts, fat people longer than thin people, and worriers longer than relaxers.

HINTS FOR A GOOD NIGHT'S SLEEP

Prepare yourself for sleep before retiring. Don't take worries to bed with you. Tell yourself that you can't do anything about them till morning, anyway.

Instead of ignoring disturbing noises such as rattling windows and creaking doors, get up and eliminate them.

Avoid late night television, arguments, eating, and drinking, because all these stimulate the body and mind.

Relax your muscles completely by stretching your legs and arms fully. Tense, then relax. Repeat a few times.

Give your bed your full weight. Yield into the surface supporting you. Let tension melt away.

Breathe deeply and regularly, allowing each breath to drift you deeper into drowsiness. Then close your eyes slowly. You are now entering the state of *alpha* which is the threshold for self-hypnosis. Stop worrying. Self-hypnosis automatically leads into sleep unless you deliberately wake yourself up.

Visualize yourself stretched out on a hammock, swaying in the breeze from side to side. Or floating in a boat on a serene lake. Counting is also helpful. Instead of counting sheep in the usual way, count backwards from one hundred to zero. You may fall asleep before you have finished counting.

If not, visualize a blackboard. You are holding chalk in one hand and an eraser in the other. Mentally draw a large circle on the blackboard.

Fill the circle with a large X.

Erase the X with your free hand, starting at the center. Erase carefully so as not to erase the circle.

Now write the word SLEEP inside the circle. Write it slowly and deliberately. Erase it and go deeper.

Repeat this until you feel yourself drifting off.

ANOTHER SLEEP INDUCER

Write the number 100 within a circle.

Erase it and take a deep breath, then exhale.

Next, write number 99. Erase it mentally. Breathe and exhale.

Continue down from 100 to 0 on a descending scale.

Feel yourself going deeper and deeper into a state of drowsiness until you drift into sleep.

When you awaken in the morning, the first thought to come into your mind will be: "Every day in every way I feel better and better. When I go to sleep tonight, I will sleep all night and awaken feeling fresh and relaxed."

In seventeen years as an active hypnotherapist, I have never failed to cure sleeplessness, whether the condition was acute or chronic or both. This is because hypnosis itself is the threshold of sleep. It guides the brain from *beta* to *alpha*—then to *theta* and, finally, *delta*, which is sleep.

Acute insomniacs are helped a great deal by using a pretapped hypnosis session which they listen to just prior to falling asleep. The subject is instructed to place the recorder next to the bed and turn the volume down low. After several nights, slumber is inevitable.

Self-hypnosis works for those who are mildly stressed and have occasional problems with insomnia. However, for more deeply rooted sleep disorders that have existed over a long period, the help of a professional may be necessary for one or two sessions.

Part Two
Advanced Techniques

Hypnosis in Professional Practice

After a two-hundred-year struggle for recognition, hypnosis has evolved into a valuable, respectable adjunct to medicine and psychology. Its therapeutic values are applauded by serious-minded scientists. Clinical and experimental research into hypnotic phenomena is now going on in every civilized country. Courses in the subject are being offered by professionals in leading universities, not only in the United States but in many countries behind the Iron Curtain. In the Soviet Union, hypnosis is used routinely for presurgery and postsurgery to eliminate complications and to accelerate the healing process.

Although hypnosis has been only slowly gaining acceptance in the United States among the more conservative physicians, on September 18, 1958, the Council on Mental Health of the American Medical Association recommended instruction in hypnosis be included in the curriculum of medical schools. Since then, many physicians have familiarized themselves with its therapeutic uses. Thousands either practice hypnosis themselves or employ the services of a lay hypnotist. Physicians of all kinds, from plastic surgeons to podiatrists, find it useful both in clinical work and diagnostic analysis. Those with the necessary acumen can use hypnotic methodologies to further the art of healing in hundreds of ways. You owe it to yourself to add this valuable modality to your professional armamentarium.

What makes hypnosis work? To understand the nature of hypnosis, you must realize the patient is not treated by hypnosis, itself. Rather, *he is treated while in the hypnotic state.* Hypnosis catalyzes the curative process. The therapeutic trance is a combination of physical relaxation and mental concentration conducive to the acceptance of suggestion. When positive suggestions for healing are verbalized by the physician or therapist, they register on the subconscious mind and result in an improved condition.

The degree of success is based upon how much *faith* the subject has, not only in his own ability to heal himself, but more important, in the ability of his physician to help him do so. The physician, even before he begins to hypnotize, has an enormous power as a figure of authority. This is equally true of the law enforcement officer, the clergyman, and the politician, all of whom use some form of hypnosis in their work. Authoritative suggestion is easily translated into absolute commands by the subject's receptive mind.

One of the most important aspects of hypnosis for the professional is the added cooperation one receives from the subject because of the removal of resistance. In areas where pain and discomfort are factors that interfere with treatment, hypnosis is especially useful. Dentists have been using it for years. One that I know uses these words: "As soon as you hear the sound of the drill, it will be a signal for you to relax and feel no pain." This is basically the technique of signal reversal and be used in every field of healing.

Patients often appear suffering from the residual affects of accidents or other body trauma that occurred previously in their lives. This chronic pain that has not responded to conventional medical treatment may stem from the memory that remains in the nerves and muscles of the particular area. Without the use of the mental processes the physician may never be able to treat the problem. With hypnosis, you can bring about post trauma release and free the patient from years of unnecessary agony.

During hypnotherapy it is not uncommon to witness a fascinating phenomena take place. You see a ripple of release occur in the area focused upon. The body tends to readjust itself as the points of pain are released. This does not always happen in the first session. The patient must be conditioned to reach his or her most profound level of hypnotic relaxation. When this takes place other useful physical improvements are possible.

Researchers at the Menninger Foundation also reported remarkable results in eliminating the distress of headache pain. Through hypnosis, some patients were trained to tell their hearts to pump less blood into their heads, thus reducing the agony of migraine headaches. The patients were told while in trance to visualize their hands, then to concentrate on their hands becoming warmer and warmer. They were told that as their hands grew warmer, the blood was draining from their heads into their hands, thus relieving the pain and pressure of the headache. A wide variety of experiments has proven the merit of hypnotherapy. At the University of Colorado Medical Center, psychologists report that mind-body therapy cured chronic pain in patients who had suffered for many years, tried everything else, and failed to find anything that worked. The list of such positive results grows longer every day.

Dr. Neal E. Miller of Rockefeller University, working with a team of medical researchers, has demonstrated that involuntary bodily functions such as blood pressure maintenance, heartbeat and even the control of cholesterol levels can be beneficially affected in some patients through mental persuasion. In my own personal experience as a clinical hypnotist engaged in experiments on cholesterol, I was finally able, after one hour of self-hypnosis to lower my cholesterol level almost 100 points. This test was verified with blood specimens taken every hour for 9 hours. When stress was applied, the cholesterol level went up, and when hypnosis was induced the cholesterol level want down. The next day, the test showed that my cholesterol level was about 40 points lower than the highest reading, but not as low as during the trance state.

This experience convinced me of the efficacy of hypnotherapy as a means of stress-management. It also reaffirmed my belief in the need for expanding research in this area. While work is going on in some university medical schools, including Columbia, Harvard, and the University of Pennsylvania, much still remains to be done. A great deal of the current work involves theory and technique. However, theory without sufficient application is as powerless as practice uninformed by theory is blind. This book has been written as a pragmatic guide to help fuse theory with practical application.

When professionals have applied hypnosis, the results have delighted them. Both orthodontists and opticians (particularly in the fitting of contact lenses) have successfully used hypnotic suggestion. And in psychotherapy, the use of hypnosis has increased 100 percent in the last decade. Hypnoanalysis releases subconscious material through dream interpretation and word association as well as the standard methods do. The therapist guides the subject into *alpha*, which is meditation, and then deeper into *theta*, which is hypnosis.

HYPNOSIS AND BRAINWAVES

In the last few years there have been a number of newspaper articles written extolling the wonders of brain-wave therapy. "Feature articles in the New York Times, the Wall Street journal and scores of medical papers and periodicals inform us of the amazing discovery that the brain has the ability to change its vibrations and affect not only behavior, but even the involuntary workings of our internal organs. Traditionally, science has categorically divided bodily function into two types: voluntary or involuntary—controlled or automatic. This rigid dichotomy appears to be dissolving in the light of new knowledge.

HOW BRAIN WAVES ARE CLASSIFIED

1. Beta Waves

The *beta* state is one of physical alertness, with mind and emotions responsive to the senses. Most of our waking time is spent in this state, which is associated with tension and striving. While in *beta*, one experiences a sense of being controlled by time and space.

2. Alpha Waves

This is the area of mind which brings increased creativity and physical relaxation. Not only is the level of stress reduced but many people enter a light or hypnoidal trance called meditation. At this level, there is a slowing down of brain and body pulsation.

3. Theta Waves

Theta is the portal for entering nighttime sleep. We all pass through *theta* twice a day: when we fall asleep and when we awaken in the morning. With hypnosis, we maintain *theta* for as long as the session lasts. At this level, behavior can be modified.

4. Delta Waves

Delta is profound sleep. There is a further slowing down of mental vibrations. While in *delta*, we dream and sort out our mental and physical machinery. This is a period of regeneration and cell renewal, and, without sufficient *delta* sleep, one can suffer from sleep deprivation. More study of this state is needed.

STAGES OF HYPNOSIS

There are six levels of hypnosis. Some people drift from one level to another during a single session. Others may reach one stage and never allow themselves to go any deeper. In most cases, the subject will reach a medium level of hypnosis after two or three sessions and return to that depth during all future therapy. As long as the results are favorable, the depth reached is unimportant.

Stage 1: Hypnoidal

A feeling of physical lethargy. Heavy muscles and relaxed nerves. Thoughts tend to wander. Drowsiness.

Stage 2: Light Hypnosis

Muscular response to suggestion. Eyes roll back. Subject reacts to suggestion of arm rigidity ("stiff and rigid as a bar of steel"). Mind is concentrated on suggestions.

Stage 3: Medium Hypnosis

Subject deeply relaxed, cannot rise from chair or bed unless told to do so. Subject will not speak except by suggestion.

Stage 4: Deep Hypnosis

There may be partial amnesia upon awakening. Analgesia can be suggested as well as increased sensory awareness. Posthypnotic suggestion works well.

Stage 5: Somnambulism

Complete amnesia and anesthesia is possible. Positive hallucinations. Regression to childhood. Progression to future events.

Stage 6: Profound Somnambulism

In addition to the above, subject is capable of negative hallucination, i.e., removal of recorded information such as previous brainwashing. Posthypnotic suggestions are carried out as commands.

The first three stages, from hypnoidal through medium trance, are called *mensic*. During these levels, the subject will remember everything the hypnotist has said. Many will doubt they were hypnotized. Through the first three stages, habit correction and behavior modification takes place. With the last three stages, from deep hypnosis to profound somnambulism, the subject will not remember what was said while under hypnosis. These deeper stages are useful in areas such as surgery, childbirth, dentistry, and the correction of criminal behavior such as rape. However, about 80% of the time, hypnosis is used for modifying behavior such as smoking, obesity, and insomnia, or the lowering of pain thresholds—all of which may be done using the first three stages of hypnosis. Deep hypnosis is not necessary in these cases.

PREPARING THE SUBJECT

After a brief conversation to prepare the subject for induction procedure, a series of tests will be applied to determine the degree of response to be expected from a particular subject. Here's one way to prepare and relax the patient in order to eliminate anxiety.

HYPNOTIST: "Tell me what you think hypnosis is like. What do you expect to feel when you are hypnotized?"

PATIENT: "I guess it's like falling asleep even if you don't want to. Maybe like losing consciousness . . . I'm a little afraid of someone else controlling me."

HYPNOTIST: "Well, it's not exactly like falling asleep. Hypnosis isn't sleep. It's physical relaxation and mental concentration. You will never be unconscious. Just the opposite. You will be aware of everything that goes on. All you have to do is cooperate and concentrate on the things you want to have happen. It's simply a matter of the hypnotist and the subject working together so this very pleasant state of awareness can be brought about to help you. Hypnosis is deep meditation and is very natural. I will show you how it works and soon you will enjoy the feeling very much."

TESTING FOR SUSCEPTIBILITY

Tests reveal to the hypnosis operator whether the person he will be working with is *passive-submissive* or *challenging-dominant*. This determines his choice of techniques and the emotional quality of voice in verbalizing suggestions. Testing is also the beginning of establishing rapport and places the operator in control of the therapeutic relationship. There are two methods of hypnotizing which you adapt to suit the personality of the subject.

1. Authoritarian

The hypnotist makes direct suggestions indicating that something will occur. Speak slowly and distinctly as to a child. Use this approach for the passive type.

2. Permissive

Use a softer tone of voice. Tell the subject to imagine, think, picture, and visualize. Use this approach for the dominant type.

The dominant type is less able to accept orders. Therefore, he must be won over to trust you, so don't come on too strong. The submissive type is used to take orders so you might get right to the subject at hand. Be direct. Say, "I want you to do exactly as I say, for your own good." Be strong and assertive in your choice of words and your gestures as well as in your tone of voice when dealing with the submissive individual.

Proper utilization of the trance state hangs on the delicate thread of a trusting interpersonal relationship between the subject and the practitioner. This is gradually established during the process of hypnotic conditioning and will improve with time. Developing this empathetic relationship is difficult for some therapists whose background has trained them in a cool clinical approach. If so, they will be limited in being able to help the person in need. Oriental hypnotists overcome this difficulty by meditating along *with* their subject. The Master regards the power of hypnosis to be greatly influenced by his own mental attitudes. After viewing some of the remarkable results produced by yogi hypnotists, it might prove interesting to test some of their methods.

The big difference between Oriental methods of hypnotism and the Western methods is that the latter make the use of verbal suggestion primary, whereas Eastern Masters project their own inner images upon the subject. Oriental hypnosis employs only authoritarian techniques that are shrouded with a great deal of mysticism and religious belief.

CHEVREUL'S PENDULUM TEST

The Chevreul Pendulum, named after a French doctor, is constructed from an object like a small crystal ball tied to the end of a chain or string. The subject is told to hold the string while the weight hangs at eye level. The pendulum is used both for testing and for induction. It also has a fascination for most people, because they are completely in control of its action. In view of this factor, the technique differs radically from other aids to exterior concentration and stimulation. There is a biofeedback reaction from the central nervous system into the fingers which hold the string. Impress upon the subject that his inner mind is in complete control of its outer motion. He is influencing the swing through internal energy. On the other hand, a rotating hypnosis disc or a flashing light has an entirely exterior influence upon the subject.

Have the subject sit in a comfortable chair. Suggest relaxation. Now place the string in his hand so that raising the center of the pendant is slightly above his eye level. Steady the ball with your hand.

Begin by saying, "Hold this pendulum so that the light strikes it. Keep staring at it and listen to my voice. I want you to think of it as going around and around in a circle. Just think of it going around clockwise . . . around and around . . . going faster and faster . . . around and around . . . and now, think of it stopping. When it stops, think of it going in the opposite direction, counter-clockwise . . . around and around, that's it . . . faster now, around and around. Stop the pendulum with your thoughts. Now think of it going from left to right, back and forth . . . back and forth . . . right to left and left to right. That's wonderful. You've got the idea.

"Now, direct the pendulum to swing in the other direction from me to you, you to me . . . now, in this direction, it's going back and forth, moving faster now . . . swinging wider and wider . . . back and forth. Keep concentrating in any direction you choose, all by yourself, by your own thoughts . . . moving, faster and faster. . . ."

The receptive subject will indicate by the movement of the pendulum just how responsive he is to suggestion. If the pendulum does not swing freely in the directions of suggestions, the test will indicate some degree of resistance.

THE FALL-BACK TEST

HYPNOTIST: "Stand over here, your toes and heels together and relax. That's it." Run your hands down the arms lightly and continue. "Look up at that spot and listen to my voice. Now, as I place my hands beside your face and begin to draw them back, you will feel yourself falling back; you will fall back and I will catch you." Begin pulling your hands back. You may flutter your fingers at the sides of the head where they can be seen out of the comers of the eyes. "Continue falling back, falling, falling back." As the subject falls backward, catch him or her by the shoulders and say, "Good, you see, you concentrate very well." If the subject does not respond, don't indicate your disappointment, but act as though the response was just what you expected. Proceed with the next susceptibility test or waking suggestion. Remember, even with these beginning suggestions, you are actually applying hypnotic persuasion.

HAND CLASP

"Clasp your hands together and gaze at this knuckle (indicate), now listen to me. I want you to picture your hands as gripping together like steel bands . . . tighter and tighter . . . think tight and now visualize your hands as sticking together like glue . . . sticking like glue and now they are stuck, stuck together so tight you cannot pull them apart . . . when I count to 3, I want you to try to pull them apart but you can't, they are stuck . . . 1, 2, 3 . . . try but you cannot . . . stop trying and they will come apart easily."

VARIATION—HAND CLASP

Say, "Stand over there and relax. Put your hands out before you like this." Demonstrate by extending your own arms straight from the shoulders, clasping your hands together. Then instruct, "Clasp your hands together as I am doing. Now turn your palms outward toward me like this (demonstrate). Close your eyes and listen carefully. Raise your arms up, up straight over your head. That's right, until your palms are facing the ceiling. And now, with your hands in this position, they are stuck together like bands of steel . . . now they are stuck tight . . . stuck tight together . . . so very tight you cannot pull them apart . . . stuck tight . . . when I count to 3, I want you to try to separate them, *but you cannot* . . . 1, 2, 3 . . . try, but *you cannot* separate them . . . stuck tight. Now stop trying. Lower your arms and your hands will come apart easily. Open your hands and relax."

Explain to the subject that it is impossible to think two things at the same time. Illustrate this fact by the following exercise.

Have the subject either stand or sit. Say, "Extend one arm and clench your fist. Now think, 'my fist is clenched tight . . . clenched tight, very tight . . . so very tight.' Think 'it's clenched so tight I cannot open it.' When I count to 3, you will try, but you will be unable to open it . . . it's stuck tight . . . very tight . . . 1, 2, 3. Try, but you cannot." If he opens his hand, explain that he simply could not think 'I can' and 'I cannot' at the same time. I often use this test as an explanation of how to cooperate by concentrating on the idea hypnosis will work. Point out that he must think one thing or the other, he *cannot* think both that it's stuck and *not* stuck at the same time. This puts him on the spot.

ARMS RISING AND FALLING TEST

As in the application of the other exercises, have the subject stand in a relaxed position. Say, "Stand over there facing me and relax. Raise your arms straight out, like this, palms facing each other (demonstrate). Turn your right palm up toward the ceiling. Make a fist of your left hand, thumb extended, arm extended toward the ceiling. Good. Now close your eyes and make a mental image of your hands in this position. Listen to my voice as I instruct you. Imagine I am placing a very heavy book on your right palm that is weighing your hand down, and getting heavier and heavier. And now I want you to imagine I am tying a balloon to the thumb of your left hand. Feel your hand becoming lighter and lighter as the balloon pulls your left hand up . . . up . . . higher and higher, feeling lighter and lighter.

"Now your left arm is rising while the right hand is falling. Now imagine I'm placing another very heavy book on your right hand. Think of it as getting heavier and heavier, dropping down, so heavy. And feel the left hand rising higher and higher. Now open your eyes and look at your hands."

If there is no reaction, you can assume at this point that the subject is not suggestible. If the hands do separate about one third of the way, it indicates a *light* trance subject. Half way up, a *medium* trance subject. When the hands separate all of the way, with the left hand overhead and the right hand pointed down, this indicates a *deep* trance subject.

This is often referred to as *the yardstick test*. The subject is usually amazed when the hands separate markedly, since he is not really conscious of where his hands are moment by moment. If he responds very well, compliment him on his concentration and vivid imagination. If the response is disappointing, pass it off until further testing is done. Don't ever tell a subject you are disappointed. Let him think he did what was expected.

You might give the subject a choice of word pictures, like a very heavy book, a heavy weight, a stone, an extra balloon tied to the wrist, a puff of wind pushing it up, or a string tied to the ceiling and pulling it up. This test is frequently applied at the beginning. If the response to any test isn't promising, consider your subject might feel shy at the start of his therapy and try the test again next time he visits.

The Induction Process

Induction is composed of two parts:

External Focus. The subject is told to look at a stationary object, such as a pen, pencil, glass ball, candle, or spot on the wall. Or a moving object, such as a flashing light, whirling disc, etc. After suggestions for heaviness of the eyelids, the subject is told to close his eyes at the count of 5 or 10 (or any number).

Once the eyes are closed, the subject enters into the second phase of the induction procedure.

Internal Focus. The subject is told to concentrate on inner body awareness, relaxation and deep breathing. The process can be varied by the use of sounds such as music, bell, gong, or metronome.

Hypnotist says, "When you hear the sound of the bell, you will close your eyes and go into hypnosis with the sound of my voice. Your legs are growing heavy, very heavy. Your arms are growing heavy, very heavy. Your entire body is growing heavy, very heavy. You are going deep, deep asleep." (Repeat)

INDUCTION WITH FINGER METHOD

This is suitable for the person who reacts favorably to previous testing. "With your eyes closed, I place my finger on your forehead. Now turn your eyes inward and upward, as I run my finger to the top of your head. Follow my finger with your eyes. Now with my finger up here, continue to look at it and try to open your eyes. You will be amazed to find that you cannot. (Do not let him try too long. Now begin to slowly rotate his head and you will induce the trance.) Your legs are heavy, your arms are heavy, your entire body is heavy, you are deep, deep asleep and you cannot open your eyes. You are deep, deep asleep, legs heavy, arms heavy, body heavy, deep asleep, can't open your eyes; try, you cannot, try hard, you cannot open them . . . stop trying, stop trying, deep, deep asleep. (Stop rotating his head and proceed with the session.)

INDUCTION BY FIXATING ON SPOT

The hypnotist says, "Pick a spot on the ceiling and gaze at it. Keep on looking at the spot and listen to my voice. Relax as you stare at the spot. Feel yourself relaxing all over . . . deeper and deeper. As you keep staring at the spot, your eyes will become very heavy and drowsy. Your entire body is becoming heavier and heavier . . . your arms, heavy . . . limp and relaxed . . . legs limp and heavy and relaxed . . . feet are becoming relaxed . . . relaxed all over.

"As you keep staring at the spot, your eyes may begin to tear, to blink . . . you are getting drowsy . . . heavy . . . sleepy . . . a wonderful feeling, warmth and relaxation flowing all through your body as you relax more deeply than ever before . . . your eyes blinking . . . tearing . . . they feel like closing . . . closing soon. When they dose, you will fall into a deep, restful sleep . . . deep . . . sound asleep . . . the sound of my voice makes you sleepier and sleepier . . . you are going to fall into a pleasant state of relaxation . . . eyes will close soon . . . think of sleep . . . it is getting harder and harder . . . for you to focus your eyes . . . they are Closing. . . ."

Once you have completed the external focus, you tell the subject to internalize. "Keep on going deeper . . . as I count backward from 5 to 0, you will keep going deeper and deeper . . . asleep . . . hear my voice as you let go and allow yourself to drift deeper and deeper. You will not awaken till I tell you to . . . the sound of my voice will send you deeper . . . you want to go deeper. Let go all over . . . feeling wonderfully relaxed as you go deep inside of yourself."

At this point, you may place your hands over the subject's eyes or raise one of his arms and let it drop. Continue to deepen hypnosis through pyramiding suggestions and repetition of hypnotic phrases.

BLINKER METHOD FOR EYE CLOSURE

This is an alternative method for closing the eyes to begin hypnotic induction. Eye closure is produced by steadily gazing at some point or object of fixation while the hypnotist suggests: "Eyelids growing heavier." The hypnotist then counts, having the subject open and close his eyelids on alternate counts as follows. "I am now going to begin counting. I want you to open and close your eyes with the count. I will count from 1 to 20. By the time I reach 20, or before, your eyes will be so heavy, they will stay closed and you will fall into sound sleep. One, your eyes are open, 2, close your eyes, 3, open, 4, close. Your eyes are becoming heavier with each closing. Five, open, 6, close, getting drowsy, sleepy. Very heavy. Seven, 8 . . . getting heavier . . . your eyelids are so heavy . . . you are trying but they do not want to open . . . soon you will be able to keep them closed . . . 9, 10. Eyes heavy, drowsy, sleepy. Eleven, 12. Heavier and heavier, very heavy now. Thirteen, 14, eyes so heavy, so sleepy, pleasantly drowsy. Fifteen, 16. Eyelids so sleepy going into a deep, pleasant sleep soon. Seventeen, 18. Eyelids so heavy and drowsy. Nineteen, barely opening. Twenty. Deep asleep. Now you can let them stay closed."

Eye catalepsy can be produced at this point in many cases, followed by rapid deepening and further challenges for testing of hypnotic depth. This is advisable only with subjects who have shown remarkable suggestibility in the waking suggestion stage.

RAPID INDUCTION TECHNIQUES

Standing Induction. Apply this technique for quick induction of very susceptible subjects—those who have responded well to testing or have been previously hypnotized. Place your hands on his shoulders, look into his eyes and, as you gently sway his shoulders from side to side, say something like this:

"Look into my eyes and relax . . . you are going into deep sleep . . . deep sleep . . . your eyes are closing now . . . you are going deep asleep . . . deep asleep . . . your eyes are closed now . . . *deep asleep* . . . deeper and deeper asleep as I guide you into this chair, you will go still deeper . . . everything will take you deeper. Now you are seated comfortably. Listen to my voice and you will feel yourself letting go and going much . . . much deeper asleep."

This can make a very dramatic presentation in front of a group of people when you have been careful to select the right subject. If a particular technique does not seem to be working, switch to another method. Calmly continue to deepen the trance. Once eye closure is accomplished, keep your composure and keep your voice steady.

ARM CATALEPSY

Demonstrate with a suggestible subject in the way explained above. Then, with an air of complete confidence, raise his arm, extend it straight out and say, "As I raise your arm, it will become stiff and rigid . . . as stiff and rigid as a bar of steel, so rigid . . . you cannot lower it, no matter how hard you try . . . try . . . you try . . . hard . . . you cannot . . . stop trying . . . and now go deep asleep . . . deep asleep . . . now you can lower your arm, and as you do so, you fall deeper asleep . . . much deeper . . . my voice takes you deeper . . . going much deeper now . . . take a deep breath and go deeper . . . inhale . . . that's good . . . exhale now and go deeper." Continue induction with the usual methods. Any of the susceptibility tests can be transferred into induction techniques. This takes advantage of the surprise element. Quick methods are excellent for demonstration purposes. They help to increase susceptibility in prospective subjects who are watching the presentation.

TRANSFERRING A TEST INTO HYPNOSIS

After the Hand Clasp Test which we described previously, say, "Now your hands are stuck tight . . . tight together . . . you cannot pull them apart . . . try, but you cannot . . . stop trying! Go deep asleep . . . deep, sound sleep. Going deeper and deeper. Now, when I try to pull your hands apart, they will loosen up and come apart easily. As they do, I want you to fall into an even deeper sleep. The deeper you go, the stronger your improvements will show."

Some people are so hypnotizable you will be able to achieve instantaneous hypnosis. Experience will help you recognize such easy subjects. Those who are eager to respond to such commands as, "your hands are stuck together," etc., without analyzing them, can be inducted rapidly and it would be a waste of your professional time to use prolonged methodology.

Transferring a test into a trance within a few minutes is feasible with about 20 percent of your patients. You will be able to recognize such a subject not only by strong responses to testing, but he may also appear a bit dazed, with a confused facial expression. The subject may also speak in a muted voice and be somewhat unstable on his feet. If so, all that may be necessary for induction is to: (1) gaze at the subject, (2) point to his eyes, and (3) command, "sleep!" This works especially well where there is a particular readiness to be helped, such as in a patient being prepared for surgery.

HEAD ROTATION METHOD

First say, "Close your eyes as I count to three and snap my fingers." After snapping your fingers, place one hand on his forehead, the other at the back of his head. Slowly rotate his head as you say: "Deep asleep now. Arms heavy, legs heavy. Deep, sound asleep quickly." Then roll the head in the opposite direction and say, "As I rotate your head the other way, I want you to go twice as deep, twice as deep . . . to do yourself twice as much good." Withdraw your hands. As the head falls forward onto his chest, continue to pyramid suggestions to go deeper and deeper. Keep in mind that the responsive subject is eager to be helped quickly. The very fact that you are an authoritative figure speeds induction.

But if such methods are used while the person is resistant, then only failure will result. Once the subject fails to be hypnotized, he becomes increasingly difficult. All techniques, therefore, for inducing "instantaneous or rapid induction" must be applied logically, taking into account all factors. The apparent suggestibility of the subject, the prestige of the operator, whether or not the person has been previously hypnotized, and other factors may influence success.

Direct Gaze

"As you gaze into my eyes, you will feel very sleepy, your eyes will close . . . close your eyes now and go deep asleep." Passes of the hand can be made around the eyes, the fingers can touch the eyelids. You may also cup your hands over the subject's eyes to suggest deepening the trance. Remember to keep your gaze fixated.

Two Pointed Fingers

Close the thumb, ring and little finger, pointing the middle and first finger directly at the eyes, separated like a V. Say, "Your eyes will close as I bring my fingers closer and closer to your eyes . . . let your eyes close now and go deep asleep."

Finger Pressure On Nerve Points

Gaze directly at subject's eyes as you place the thumb of one hand on his forehead and the thumb of the other at the back of the head. Press and say, "As I press these two areas, you will feel yourself falling into a deep . . . deep sleep. Your eyes are closing now . . . deep asleep." The head may be moved forward or downward covering the eyes.

Spiral Hypno-Disk

When using a hypno-disk as a fixation point, give the following suggestions for eye closurers: "Keep your eyes fastened on the center of the wheel . . . as you watch it . . . notice that it vibrates . . . the white circles become more prominent, then the black circles become prominent. The circles seem to fade into the distance and you begin to feel as if you are being drawn into the circle . . . your breathing is deep and regular . . . you are getting drowsy, very drowsy . . . soon you will be asleep, very deep asleep. . . ."

Counting backward, say, "As I count backward from 5 to 1, your eyes will close and you will fall into a deep hypnotic sleep . . . 5, 4, 3, 2, 1 . . . deep asleep." You may also have a longer countdown if the individual seems a little tense.

Arm Catalepsy

Approach the subject confidently as you raise his arm up and extend it straight out from the shoulder, saying, "Your arm is stiff and rigid . . . as rigid as a bar of steel. You can't bend it . . . try, but you can't . . . as you try, your eyes will close . . . closed . . . deep asleep. Now your arm will relax and, as it falls down, you will go even deeper asleep."

Touch, Sight, Sound

Hand the subject an object to hold. It might be a coin, a glass ball, or a pen. Say, "As you hold this object, your hand will close over it tightly . . . the feel of the object in your hand is making you very sleepy and, as you look at it and listen to my voice, you are getting very sleepy . . . eyes closing now, deep asleep . . . your hand is closed tight on the object . . . you cannot open your hand . . . try, but you cannot . . . stop trying and go deeper asleep."

Placebo

Hold a bottle of water with a spray attached. Direct subject's gaze toward fixation point and as you begin to spray the harmless liquid on the back of his neck, say, "As I spray this liquid on your neck, it will relax you so you will fall into a deep sleep . . . your eyes are sleepy . . . very sleepy . . . the liquid is relaxing you . . . eyes closed now . . . deeper and deeper asleep." The liquid spray can be used as a deepening technique and also for the removal of psychosomatic pain.

SHORT INDUCTIONS FOR BUSY PROFESSIONALS

Transferring tests into hypnotic induction is sometimes referred to as *"The Surprise Technique."* You say, "Close your eyes and sleep!" The subject is startled by a direct command, and the mind tends to become passive, momentarily, and when suggested, "Arms heavy, legs heavy," the subject obeys because he doesn't have time to think. He is caught unawares. The critical faculties of the mind are bypassed in a moment of passivity. This will be discussed further in the section dealing with overcoming resistance.

Focus On Light. After seating the patient comfortably, suggest relaxation. Have patient look at any light used in medical examination and suggest: "Relax, look at this light. Relax all over. Listen to my voice and let yourself go. Very loose, comfortable. As you gaze at the light, your eyes are growing pleasantly drowsy and heavy. Let go of all tension, relax more and more. Eyes growing heavier and heavier, drowsy and heavy. Closing now, you are going into a deep, deep state of relaxation. Deeper and deeper into relaxation. Listen to my voice and go deeper. Nothing bothering you, feeling very well, so relaxed. Your eyes so heavy, arms heavy, relaxed all over. Deep asleep now." Proceed in the usual manner to deepen hypnosis and utilize the therapeutic state for necessary purposes. Medical examination in which instruments, i.e., eye charts, etc., are used can employ this technique. The patient is taken off-guard so that he does not have time to think or analyze suggestions of the doctor to the effect that changes are taking place. Nothing is said about what is going to take place, as customary in standard induction techniques. The patient is caught off-guard and goes along with the suggestions.

USING SOUND

Metronomes. A metronome with a slow beat can be a great assist to the hypnotist. You may produce eye closure by saying, "Listen to my voice and let my voice relax you completely. Listen and you will hear a gentle ticking, a beat of the metronome. As you listen to the beat of the metronome, the sound will take you deeper . . . deeper and deeper . . . the beat of the metronome is sending you into hypnosis . . . every beat sends you deeper into sleep . . . it says to you . . . deep . . . asleep . . . deep . . . asleep . . . each beat is lulling you deeper and deeper."

Air Conditioners or Fans. "With your eyes closed, listen to my voice and follow what I say . . . begin to concentrate on the soft, whirring sound of the air conditioner . . . the monotonous drone will lull you deeper and deeper asleep . . . the purring sound of the motor sends you deeper . . . much deeper now . . . ever deeper asleep."

Music or Music Boxes. Music can be helpful. It should be soft, slow preferably, with strings. Organs are also effective. Music should be muted in the background, never loud or close by. Say, "As you listen to the soft music, it will keep on helping you go deeper. The music is soothing, very smoothing to the nerves, lulling you deeper and deeper asleep."

Tape Recordings or Records. This is another means of relaxing anxious patients who are in the waiting room, especially at the dentist's office. Such a devise can come in handy during group hypnosis while the operator moves around and speaks softly to individual subjects. Tape recorders are also useful for developing both autohypnosis and general state of relaxation. This gives the overworked operant a rest.

Listening to Breathing. Another way to use sound for induction and also as a deepening technique is to say, "Listen to the sound of your breathing. Breathe more deeply and slowly. As the air comes in, think of it as cool and refreshing, and as you hear the sound of the air being exhaled, let that sound signal you to go into hypnosis. Each breath that you breathe will take you deeper. Listen to your breathing and go deeper."

DEEPENING TECHNIQUES

There are numerous methods for deepening hypnosis, once the subject is relaxed and cooperating. The most effective techniques create an inner change in the state of one's mind, an awareness of the altered consciousness. This is referred to as "deepening through realization." Basic techniques for deepening are:

1. Realization through awareness.
2. Pyramiding of suggestions.
3. Reinduction within the same trance.
4. Endogenic hypnosis suggesting mind/body contact.
5. Picture visualization. Use of blackboard, mirror, etc.
6. Sensorimotor reactions. Hand levitation, rigid catalepsy.
7. Pressures, passes, and stroking.
8. The Hammock, Tunnel, and Canoe techniques.
9. Shock or confusion techniques.
10. Drugs, such as Sodium Amytal, Sodium Pentothal, and Trilene.

DEEPENING THROUGH REALIZATION
AND PYRAMIDING HYPNOSIS

Deepening hypnosis must be approached from a very different point of view than *overcoming resistance*. True, in overcoming resistance most of the deepening techniques are employed, but the psychology involved is radically different. During the routine procedure of hypnotic conditioning, the average subject who wants to be hypnotized will follow the suggestions of the operator. When he is told, "Everything takes you deeper . . . go . . . deeper," *he accepts the idea that the things the hypnotist says are true*. The refractory subject, however, will analyze everything, argue with himself as to why it isn't working, and not even realize he is doing it. When the subject fails to respond to the usual deepening techniques, he then becomes a refractory subject, and the approach must be adjusted to the individual situation.

After the initial induction technique, the subject fixates his eyes and soon eye closure takes place. Begin pyramiding hypnosis in the following manner: "Deep . . . deep asleep . . . going deeper. Now count backward from 100 to 0. And with every count, go deeper, counting and going deeper with every count . . . if you lose count, just pick up wherever you think you left off, it doesn't matter. Just keep on counting and going deeper. When you reach 0, raise the index finger of your right hand to indicate you have reached 0 and have taken yourself down deeper." When finger rises, proceed:

"Good, now I want you to picture yourself strolling in the park on a lovely summer day. As you walk along, feeling so peaceful, so related, you see two large trees and a hammock swinging between them. Go to the hammock, let your body sink into it, relaxing more and more . . . the sun is shining down, warm and pleasant. The hammock is swinging back and forth, back and forth, taking you deeper, and deeper asleep. As you lie here, relaxing, going deeper and deeper, you visualize a blackboard before you . . . you take a piece of chalk and draw a large square on the blackboard and trace it around clockwise three times, around and around, and this takes you deeper. And now, in the other direction, around and around, and this takes you much deeper.

"Now you erase the square and begin writing and erasing the alphabet all the way from A to Z and each letter you write and erase takes you deeper. Now you write A. See it vividly in your mind's eye and as you erase the letter A, go deeper. Now write B . . . and erase it . . . keep on writing and erasing, writing and erasing. Each letter takes you deeper. If you lose your place, just pick up wherever you think you left off. It doesn't matter. Keep on writing and erasing and going deeper with each letter. Raise the index finger of your right hand when you reach Z . . . good . . . and now, as I count back from 5 to 0, you will go deeper . . . everything I say takes you deeper . . . 5, 4, 3, 2, 1, 0 . . . deeper and deeper asleep to do yourself the most good."

HAND LEVITATION

"Concentrate on your right hand . . . soon, you will feel your right hand becoming light, as light as a feather. Your fingers begin to twitch. Your hand will begin to rise, getting lighter and lighter . . . so very light as though you had a balloon tied to the wrist, pulling it upward, up, up . . . your hand is growing lighter and lighter rising up, higher and higher . . . higher . . . so very light, always lighter . . . soon it will float up and touch your face. When it does, you will fall into a deeper state of hypnosis. Deeper and deeper now . . . very deep . . . touching soon . . . and when your hand touches your face, you will feel yourself falling into a deep, deep sleep.

"Touching now and going deeper . . . much deeper . . . as I press your shoulders, you will go deeper . . . deeper . . . as I stroke your forehead, go deeper. And now, visualize yourself walking in the country again, beside a lovely lake . . . clear and beautiful. There's a boat drawn up beside the shore, the boatman beckons you to get in and take a ride. You climb in, sink down into the soft cushions, trailing your fingers in the water. The sun is shining down, warm and pleasant . . . the water is warm on your fingers. As the boat glides along, you are trailing your fingers in the water, so relaxing, while going more deeply asleep . . . deeper and deeper . . . and now, the boat has drifted into the shade, and here as you trail your fingers in the water, it is icy cold . . . very cold . . . you can hardly hold your hand in the water . . . you will be glad when the boat goes into the sun again.

"Now it has, and the water is warm in the sun. As the boat glides along, you are going more deeply and deeply asleep. . . ."

TUNNEL TECHNIQUE

" . . . the boat is drifting into a tunnel . . . a lovely grotto, like the Blue Grotto in Capri . . . there's a soft blue light here and you are relaxing more and more. You see beautiful paintings on the wall . . . lovely paintings in soft colors and you hear soft music in the background, your favorite melody. Beautiful soft music like a lullaby, lulling you more and more deeply asleep. And now the boat comes out into the bright sunshine again and as the boat drifts along the shore, you see lovely flowers . . . fragrant, lovely flowers smelling sweet. And now you come back to shore where you climb out and walk up a grassy hill and there's an apple tree . . . you see some lovely red apples and pick one, take a bite of the apple . . . it's sweet and tasty, very good."

Picture visualization routines such as the blackboard, canoe, and tunnel techniques include images incorporating the five senses. The subject "sees" the boat and pictures on the walls, "feels" the temperature of the water—hot and cold, hears music, smells flowers, and tastes fruit.

ANOTHER SENSORIMOTOR METHOD

Hand levitation deepens through sensorimotor reaction. There are several other similar exercises. Another is *the revolving hands method.* Take the subject's hands and set them in motion. Revolve them around each other as you say, "Now your hands are revolving round and round,

going round and round, making circles. And it has become automatic . . .
they keep revolving . . . around and around . . . automatically, they keep
going, round and round, faster and faster. It's impossible for you to stop
them. They keep going around and around as you go deeper and deeper.
Try, but you cannot stop. Your hands keep on turning, and you keep on
going deeper . . . deeper and deeper. Now your hands start turning in the
opposite direction, going round and round . . . faster . . . round and
round. And you keep going deeper, still deeper as your hands keep on
going round. Now, you can't stop them. They are turning round automatically. Try to stop them but you cannot . . . stop trying and go
deeper.

"Relax your hands now and as they drop back in your lap, you go
much deeper . . . deeper and deeper . . . everything takes you deeper."

The induction employs counting, picture visualization, sensorimotor
reactions, hand levitation, and revolving hands, as well as the tunnel and
canoe techniques. Realization of hypnosis is increased by hand levitation and the revolving hands with challenge to stop. Through the subject's
awareness of a change in consciousness, deepening takes place. *The
challenges are important for establishing the awareness of hypnosis in
the subject.*

PRESSURE AND PASSES

The passing of hands over the subject without actually touching him
was widely used in ancient times, but has gone out of vogue with
modern scientific hypnosis methods such as biofeedback. However, if
the subject believes passes or other contacts will deepen his hypnotic
state, he will tend to respond in the manner suggested by the operator.
Passes are made down the arms, chest, and shoulders, while suggestions
are made to go into a deep sleep. When the subject's eyes are closed, the
passes should be made between the subject's eyes and the source of
light in the room. Downward passes are generally used when putting the
subject under hypnosis and upward passes when awakening him. A
countdown while making downward passes will strengthen the induction and a count upward while awakening also works well.

Pressures are made on the subject's shoulders with accompanying
suggestions for cooperation in inducing hypnosis as well as going deeper
on command. The operator simply places his hands on both shoulders,
or only on one shoulder and then bears down lightly, while whispering
in the subject's ear, "Deep asleep!" Repeat several times to reinforce.

Passes over the forehead are executed by using the two forefingers which move from the bridge of the subject's nose out to the temples. When you reach the temples, exert a slight pressure, and then release your fingers. Repeat several times. This has a soothing and relaxing effect on the subject and is recommended for patients with eye problems or headaches.

It is very important to let the subject know in advance when you are going to make physical contact, no matter how slight. Say, "In a moment I will make passes over your forehead and this will take you deeper," or "I am going to press your fingernail and when you feel my touch, this will be a signal to go deeper and never bite your nails again." Pressing the fingernails is also used to reinforce any kind of suggestion. It has a double purpose, to deepen and also to implant suggestions.

CONFUSION AND SHOCK TECHNIQUE

Take advantage of the surprise element by making suggestions which confuse the subject. An example is to have the subject concentrate on the finger method and then transfer it into an induction. "As I place my finger between your eyes, roll your eyes up, following my finger. As your eyes roll up, close your lids and relax. With your eyes in this position, your eyes are stuck tight . . . try to open them, but you can't."

The operator places one hand across the subject's forehead, the other at the back of the neck. Rotate the head as you say, "Arms heavy, legs heavy, deep asleep . . . deeper and deeper asleep. Begin counting backwards from 20 to 0, each count taking you deeper and deeper."

DEEPENING BY COUNTING

Have the subject count to himself silently backward from 20 to 0 while you count aloud from 0 to 20. Have him concentrate first on one part of his body, then another—right hand, left shoulder, left hand, the top of his head, take a deep breath, hold his breath while he counts backward from 5 to 0 and you count aloud from 0 to 5. Awaken him quickly without warning and then immediately put him under again.

Reinduction during the same session catches the resistant subject by surprise and often proves the solution to his inner fears of hypnosis. Repeat several times that each time he drifts into the hypnotic state, he will go deeper than before. When you awaken him between inductions say, "Deep asleep—again . . . much deeper than before." Reinduct swiftly, allowing him only enough time to open his eyes and make some slight movement. Do not arouse him completely.

Stress in an authoritative voice that he "must go deeper than before" as you repeat the counting technique. An interesting variation on traditional counting methods is the following. "I am going to begin counting in a different way. As I count backwards you will go more deeply asleep and when I count forward, you will awaken a little with each count. Now go deeper as I count from 10 to 0 . . . 10 deeper . . . 9 deeper . . . 8 deeper . . . etc." When you get to 0, reverse the counting this way: "Now you will awaken just a little . . . 1 . . . 2 . . . 3 . . . now deeper again . . . much deeper than the last time . . . 10 deeper . . . 9 deeper . . . 8 deeper . . . etc." Repeat this routine several times. And then switch the signals. "When I count forward you will go deeper and when I count backward you will awaken. . . ."

Because you reverse the signals, the subject becomes confused and finds himself concentrating more than he would ordinarily. This switch also makes him feel the contrast in state of consciousness from going deeper to awakening. This produces a greater realization of the part he is playing in his own therapy.

Counting techniques can be varied in many ways. You can involve the subject by having him count silently to himself as you count out loud. Tell him to count by fives or twos as an alternate to simple counting. The length of the countdown can be from 1,000 to 0 or from 5 to 0. This depends on the length of the hypnosis session and the need of the particular individual.

Combining counting with breathing for deepening is also very effective. Say, "Count off ten deep breaths and take yourself deeper with each breath." You can also combine counting, breathing, and giving suggestion, "As you count off ten breaths, tell yourself 'I feel full and satisfied with the minimum of food.'"

POSTHYPNOTIC SUGGESTION

A good reaction carried out after the conclusion of the hypnotic session is referred to as a posthypnotic phenomenon. Stimulus for the improved activity comes from the suggestion which the hypnotherapist gave to the subject. The phrasing of the posthypnotic suggestion should be carefully worked out with the subject before induction. In this way the subject is

taught to accept responsibility for the degree of his response to
therapy.

Bizarre suggestions that changes rational thinking should be avoided.
Here is an example. Albert T., 54 years of age, complained of impotence which had troubled him for six years. I asked what sort of suggestions he would like to receive once he was hypnotized.

"Tell me I will be able to perform like a superstud. Like I did when
I was nineteen," he insisted.

I offered the wording used by people with similar problems: "healthy
and normal sexual function."

"Oh, no. That's too mild," he persisted. Suggest that I perform like
a superstud. Make it real strong." I followed his instructions, word for
word.

That night, when the moment of truth arrived, poor Albert was
embarrassed. He couldn't believe his own suggestions because the idea
seemed too ridiculous to him. Fortunately, at his second session, he
worked out believable suggestions. "Each time I have sexual intercourse, I will show improvement. I am healthy and normal and soon
will function with full power and vigor."

During the next visit, he reported a definite change for the better.
After eight sessions of hypnotherapy, Albert felt he could carry on with
just self-hypnosis and an occasional booster session.

Accepting suggestion involves a personal belief system. Therefore,
directives to the subconscious must be realistic and thoroughly understood. Only then will posthypnotic activity replace unwanted behavior.
Suggestions must be keyed to the real needs and desires of the subject
so that his emotional drive will be stirred. With proper motivation, a
posthypnotic suggestion may last days or even years. Sometimes it lasts
forever, like the posthypnotic suggestion, "Never touch a cigarette for
the rest of your life," or "You will never gain back a single pound that
you lost."

Posthypnotic suggestion in such cases is reinforced during periods
of meditation or keen awareness.

For people who have special difficulty in managing stress, weekly
hypnotherapy sessions are encouraged as a preventive measure against
the build-up of tension. Posthypnotic suggestions are worded to help
them remain relaxed under trying conditions. "No matter what happens
in the family or on the job, you will stay calm and think of positive
solutions."

Many professionals feel that the depth of trance at the time of
administering posthypnotic suggestion is critical. This is not necessarily

so. While a deep level of trance is always helpful in establishing response to hypnotic suggestion, a light trance can also work if the posthypnotic suggestions are repeated many times. Keep in mind that the light trance subject can become a deeper subject the next time. Therefore, give him a posthypnotic suggestion as follows. "The next time you go into hypnosis you will go twice as deep, to do yourself twice as much good."

Posthypnotic suggestion is most effective when tied in with an everyday activity, especially when the activity is as natural as breathing. "Each time you take a breath you will feel full and satisfied and will postpone eating until the proper time. Each breath will satisfy you as if you have just eaten."

For the person working on an improved figure, try this, "Each time you pass a mirror, you will remember to stand up straight, pull in your stomach and hold your head up proudly."

For the alcoholic, it might be, "Anytime you see another person drinking you will remember that you cannot handle alcohol and that you prefer to remain sober. You will have a nonalcoholic beverage, instead."

Posthypnotic behavior modification sometimes works well with aversion techniques. For example, a subject who wants to stop smoking might be told, "If you *buy* a pack of cigarettes, you will have an uneasy feeling in your stomach. If you *light* one, a sense of nausea. If you *inhale*, the nausea will become increasingly worse. You will have to put it out, or it will cause you to throw up." Before employing aversion techniques, discuss it with your subject. He may decide to cooperate rather than anticipate a unpleasant reaction.

Some people are very happy with aversion suggestions. I remember a woman who was strongly allergic to chocolate. "Please tell me it will smell and taste like feces . . . like dog poo." She was adamant and I complied and the results were outstanding. She lost the urge for chocolate after just one session.

Take the time to talk it over. Get to know the subject. What is just right for one individual may be just terrible for the next one.

Another important application of posthypnotic suggestion is in transferring control to the subject. This is done toward the end of each session, before wake-up and at the termination of the therapy. The object of transference is to enable him to provoke the phenomenon in himself by himself. In a case of insomnia you might say, "Each night when you go to bed, tell yourself, "Sleep through the night. Wake up rested in the morning! Giving yourself suggestions will work just as forcefully as when I give them to you."

AWAKENING THE HYPNOTIZED SUBJECT

No one has ever failed to awaken from hypnosis, even when the operator has performed inexpertly. The problem for the beginner is to induce hypnosis. Awakening is the easiest part. If the operator should drop dead, which is highly unlikely, or leave the room without instructing the subject when to awaken, the subject would simply wake up. This would happen naturally, of his own free will, without a suggestion to do so.

Some subjects will awaken by themselves the moment the hypnotist stops talking. These are the light subjects. There are also some somnambulist subjects who will take a short nap, if you let them. This could last from five minutes to a half hour, depending on how deep they have drifted and how tired they were when they arrived.

Inform the subject when it is almost time to awaken. Say, "In a little while it will be time to wake up. You will feel as if you have slept for several nighttime hours. Rested and refreshed. However, this session will not interfere with your sleep tonight. You will sleep especially well." Most hypnotists are counting to arouse the subject. It is wise to combine the wake-up with positive suggestions of well-being.

"When you hear the number 10 (or 5 or 3), you will wake up feeling better than you have ever felt before.

> *One.* "Get ready to wake up now, feeling just fine."
> *Two.* "Your mind is clear and keen. Memory perfect."
> *Three.* "Looking forward to a pleasant evening (day, week)."
> *Four.* "Cheerful, happy, confident with positive outlook."
> *Five.* "You will follow through on all of your suggestions.
> *Six. Give Him His Top Priority Posthypnotic Suggestion.*
> *Seven.* "Repeat . . . Eight . . . Repeat . . . Nine . . . Repeat."
> *Ten.* "Wide awake now! Feeling great!"

For the person who has reached only a light state of hypnosis, a count of 3 is usually sufficient. "When I count to 3 you will awaken feeling fine. *One.* "You are ready to awaken."
> *Two.* "You are beginning to awaken."
> *Three.* "You are wide awake now."

If the eyes are slow to open you may snap your fingers or clap your hands for emphasis, but this is usually unnecessary. If you are doing a demonstration it might add a bit of pizzazz to clap your hands. This is also one way to gain the attention of an audience that may have become drowsy.

There are some subjects who are reluctant to give up the pleasant euphoric feeling of the trance. When a subject regularly drifts into *delta*-deep sleep, he may be doing so to avoid the acceptance of posthypnotic suggestion. In such rare cases, tap his fingertips as you give the wake-up suggestions and raise the volume of your voice. When you speak faster and more loudly, you spur the brainwaves back to the *beta* rhythm.

How to Overcome Resistance

Occasionally a person may seem willing to cooperate and yet unconsciously resist the process. Usually, this is due to two causes. On one hand, some fear may stem from misconceptions about hypnosis, resulting in a high level of nervous tension. Begin by overcoming obstacles to relaxation. Is the light in the room soft enough? Is the temperature comfortable? Is there a chair or couch suitable for reclining? Is a visit to the bathroom necessary? Are there any unpleasant noises such as the ringing telephones? And—most important—does the subject have subconscious fears that must be eliminated?

On the other hand, a latent fear of losing control and revealing hidden secrets may exist. This may surface in the form of trying too hard instead of relaxing and letting the hypnotic feeling happen. A tense, over anxious person often makes this mistake and the hypnotist must find a way to overcome any interference.

During the initial interview, ask your subject what experience he has had with hypnosis. Often people have seen stage hypnotists demonstrate with highly suggestible subjects who are commanded to perform embarrassing acts. They may expect magic or, conversely, believe they are bad subjects because once they did not go "under the spell" of the stage hypnotist.

"I'm too strong-willed to be hypnotized," said one prospective subject.

Others, having witnessed stage hypnosis, will expect one session to correct a lifetime of problems. Anticipation of results, whether negative or positive, has a great deal to do, not only with the initial induction, but with future results from continued therapy for habit correction.

REEVALUATE YOUR METHODS

One approach to helping the refractory subject is to observe how he reacts to different testing techniques—permissive or authoritarian. Test him again, executing several permissive and then several authoritarian techniques. Notice the difference in response. A classic example of improper application of technique follows:

The subject is passive, eager with eyes wide, dazed and trusting. This subject is already partially under self-hypnosis, is already motivated and expecting to be put under. Here the operator should work quickly. In such a case, there is no need for long, drawn-out, progressive relaxation methods. If you use slow, permissive, lullaby-type of voice, he will not respond favorably because he expected to go deep asleep immediately. The subject's expectations should be fulfilled by the therapist. That is why it is important to interview the patient and ask what his previous experience has been in this area. Ask him, "What do you expect will happen?" Based on the answer you receive, plus the results from the testing, you will have your answer about whether to employ authoritative or permissive methodology.

When a subject declares, "I cannot be hypnotized. My mind is too strong," respond affirmatively, "That's fine. The stronger your mind is, the greater will be the results from hypnosis. We will use your mental power to make it work." Then explain the role of self-hypnosis in every induction. For this person, the permissive approach will work better because he is on guard against being controlled. Once he is convinced that he is always in command of his therapy, he will take pride in taking himself deeper. Underneath his reluctance is usually fear of other people, so speak softly, slowly and "suggest" rather than "command."

You must suit the technique to the subject. The rapid induction style that works wonders for the docile, agreeable person, would, on the other hand, encounter resistance in the strong-minded questioning type who does not like to take "bossy" orders. Here you should apply as lower, permissive, gentle method to gain trust. Make him feel "it happens because *he* wants it." In this way, the subject senses he is in control and he will cooperate.

With the white-collar or intellectual type of individual, it helps to discuss various methods and give the subject a choice. One may like the elevator routine (described below), while another fears and hates elevators. And so with other exercises, such as counting, hand levitation, etc. Some people have little imagination, cannot imagine a balloon tied to the wrist or any of the picture visualization methods, but counting holds their attention. An accountant, for example, relates to numbers; an artist relates to visualization.

Repeated reinduction brings realization of an altered state of consciousness. First, hypnotize the subject to a light or medium level and say, "Each time you go into hypnosis, you go deeper. That's the way it works—deeper and deeper each time . . . wake up now." The operator snaps fingers or claps hands. *Give No Warning.* This action brings with it the realization of a difference in consciousness because of its suddenness.

Then say, *with authority,* "Deep asleep again, deeper than ever, go deeper this time, deeper each time." Continue rapidly with deepening techniques. Awaken the subject. Then, reinduce the trance state once more. State clearly and repeatedly, "Each time you go into hypnosis, you go deeper. Each time you wake up, you will be ready to go back even deeper. That's the way hypnosis really works. Now get ready to go much deeper."

Reinduction (going in and out of hypnosis) within the same session and at successive sessions deepens the trance level. This should be explained in the beginning and restated from time to time. Rapid awakening and reinduction will break stubborn resistance markedly. The subject is compelled to admit something is happening because he notices changes in his state of consciousness from awake to drowsiness. Another form of reinduction within the same trance is accomplished by a simple method. Say, "Now I am going to count in a special way. When I count backward, you go deeper. When I count forward, you awaken a little more. Then, when I resume counting backward, you go much deeper. First, I will count from 10 to 0, and with each backward count, you go deeper . . . 10, deeper . . . 9, deeper . . . deeper and deeper . . . very deep now . . . 6, deeper . . . deeper . . . 5 . . . deeper . . . 4 . . . much deeper . . . 3 . . . deeper . . . 2 . . . much deeper now . . . 1, 0 . . . very deep . . . and now, waking up a little . . . 1 . . . a little more . . . 2 . . . waking up more . . . 3 . . . a little more . . . 4 . . . more still . . . 5, 6, 7, 8, 9, 10 *awaken* . . . now deeper . . . 10 . . . asleep . . . 9, 8, 7, 6, 5, 4, 3, 2, 1 . . . deeper asleep. . . ."

Suggest the subject take up the count himself and deepen his own trance, counting forward and backward. This gives the timid subject a sense of security when he realizes he is participating in the process of self-hypnotic conditioning. This exercise is the beginning of self-hypnosis. Few hypnotists know about this method or realize how much can be accomplished with subject participation. Because it is rather confusing, it requires concentration. The greatest value is the deepening and reawakening procedure which brings the realization of a change of consciousness. This is sometimes referred to as "the confusion technique" because the subject is not permitted time to analyze and intellectualize what is going on with his subliminal thought processes.

APPROACH TO NEW TECHNIQUES

For the difficult subject, a change of scene is often helpful. Another room, chair or couch. Lights dimmed low. If he is fearful, lights turned up. Make the next session decidedly different from the first one—if past results were inadequate. If you haven't used any special effects before, such as flickering lights, or a hypno-disc machine, do so now. Combine them with various body-awareness techniques for pyramiding hypnosis to a deeper state. Most subjects tend to get tired and bored when gazing at an exterior point of fixation such as a light or hypno-disc, which helps speed induction.

THE AUXILIARY HYPNOTIST

Testing and induction phases are conducted as usual. At a given point, the hypnotist calls upon the auxiliary hypnotist to verify the progress being made. Sometimes no progress is evident. However, when such a discussion indicates that there is progress, it invariably implants the *suggestion* of cooperation. Hypnotist #1 says, "He is going deeper, his breathing is slowing up remarkably, he's relaxing wonderfully, isn't he?" Hypnotist #2 confirms this in a positive tone of voice, expressing amazement at the rapid progress of the subject and commending him for his ability to respond. The purpose is to get the subject to think *with the hypnotist and nothing else*. When he thinks "deep sleep" to the exclusion of all other thoughts, he will indeed feel like drifting into a deep sleep.

THE PLACEBO TECHNIQUE

The placebo is sometimes given to a patient by a medical hypnotist in the form of innocuous pills which have no real curative value except in the patient's mind. Such a medication can be given with a suggestion it will cause the subject to go into a deep trance. Pressures with the fingers on nerve points and "passes" are used much the same way. They work because the subject expects them to work. Various "hypnotic areas" can be pressed with suggestions: "As I press your temples, you will feel yourself going deeper. Pressing on these areas causes you to go much deeper." The temples and back of the neck are special points for pressure. Liquid can be sprayed on the back of the neck, giving a cool feeling, at the same time suggesting that the subject go deeper into hypnosis.

CAROTID ARTERY PRESSURES

This method for "instant" hypnotic induction is often overrated, misunderstood and dangerous. Pressing arteries can cause serious damage, even death. Nonetheless, some uninformed hypnotists use this method. Pressure on the carotid sinus causes instant collapse, and sometimes the subject can be manipulated into hypnosis and respond to suggestions. But it has never been proven that this condition is hypnosis. This state, bordering on semi-consciousness, is usually brief. The technique involves a morbid delusion of ego on the part of the practitioner and should be forbidden by law.

GROUP HYPNOSIS

The group setting can provide an ideal way of reassuring the fearful subject. Seeing others who have derived benefits from hypnosis will help the newcomer. Begin the session by asking the experienced members for progress reports. The recounting of positive results will stimulate the beginner's interest and his desire to get into the swing of therapy. Select a good subject and demonstrate hypnotic phenomena such as hand levitation, or rigid arm catalepsy. After demonstrating with one subject, place the entire group under hypnosis using customary techniques. Handling a slow subject in this way works well and prepares him for private sessions with better results.

CONFUSION TECHNIQUES

Recalcitrant subjects often respond to unusual methods that catch them unaware. In producing the various responses such as eye closure, arms rising and falling, clenched hands, hand levitation, etc., rapid suggestions for contradictory actions are made casually, as if by mistake. Reverse suggestion of "the left hand light, the right hand heavy," to the opposite.

Example (hand levitation): "Your left hand is heavy, as heavy as lead, while your right hand is light and floating up . . . your left hand is very light, floating up fast . . . your right hand is heavy . . . both hands are stuck. You can't lift them . . . now they are both floating up . . . now take a deep breath. Your left hand is heavy, as heavy as lead . . . your right hand is light, getting lighter and lighter . . . take another deep breath. Inhale. Exhale. And go deeper asleep. . . ." After a time, resume levitation until response is adequate. The subject will then be glad to return to a consistent pattern of suggestion.

A second example (arms rising and falling): "Your right arm is heavy, it has a heavy book on it, it's falling. And your left arm has a balloon tied to the wrist. It's floating up. Now your right arm feels very light, floating up like a feather on a breeze. Now your left arm feels heavy and is falling down fast, heavier and heavier. Take a deep breath and hold it . . . exhale. Now both arms are rigid."

"Now relax them and go deeper. Your right arm is getting heavier and heavier. Falling . . . your left arm rising . . . the right is falling, the left is rising."

A third example (multiple confusion technique): "Stand over here, put your toes and heels together. Close your eyes and take a deep breath. Hold it as long as you can. Now exhale and take another deep breath and hold it as long as you can. Exhale." The hypnotist stands behind the subject, takes hold of his shoulders, and starts rotating him in a circle, keeping up an emphatic string of contradictory suggestions. Then awaken him without warning time after time, saying, "Deeper each time I awaken you."

"Going to sleep soon, but first, take a deep breath—hold it. Exhale again. Inhale. Hold it. Exhale . . . close your eyes. Start counting aloud backward from 100. Raise your arms straight out. Your right arm is heavy. It has a heavy book on it, forcing it down. There is a balloon tied to your left thumb, pulling it up . . . up. Keep on counting . . . going deep asleep. Take another deep breath. Keep on counting. Your left arm rising up . . . higher and higher. . . . Your right hand rising now, your left arm falling . . . getting heavier and heavier . . . keep on counting . . . deep asleep now. Each time deeper than the time before . . . losing count. Almost unable to count. Wake up. Open your eyes. Now close them again and go deeper. Deeper each time . . . begin counting again . . . legs beginning to grow limp . . . forgetting the count. Hardly able to count. Drop into this chair and go into a deep sleep."

Rapid awakening and reinduction is in itself very effective for deepening the trance. You can, in addition to the reinduction method, combine several confusion techniques. Once you have accomplished disassociation through the postural sway, suggest heavy rhythmic breathing in tempo to the swaying, "As you sway breathe in slowly and deeply; as you sway in the opposite direction, exhale and go deeper."

Giving many commands in rapid succession is especially confusing to the analytical person. This approach gives him no opportunity to rationalize. Taken off guard, he becomes overwhelmed by the rapid change from one directive to another. The rapid induction and reawakening, plus commands to concentrate on breathing and swaying, soon become too much to think about. When he hears the final command, "Now close your eyes and go into a deep sleep," he welcomes the release from having to concentrate on changing suggestions and drops into a trance level without further resistance.

Before bringing such a subject out of hypnosis, instruct him as follows: "The next time you need to be hypnotized, it will be much easier. Now that you have discovered how pleasant it can be, you will look forward to the experience. All resistance is now gone. You now realize that you have always had inner control and could wake up on your own if you wanted to. You choose to be hypnotized for your own good and, therefore, next time you will cooperate much more."

At the next session, begin by telling him, "Last time you did very well, but this time you will do even better. Each time you are hypnotized, it will be easier and easier and will do you more and more good." This time he will respond to a standard technique more readily. After induction suggest, "Now I want you to go as deep as you did last time by cooperating in this way. Count backwards silently, from 10 to 0, and as you do so, take yourself just as deep as you were before."

You have now involved the subject in helping you hypnotize him.

NARCO-HYPNOSIS: LAST RESORT

In the hands of a skilled medical hypnotist, drugs may prove useful in helping a patient whose resistance stems from phobia or extreme lack of motivation. While it is always best to produce trance naturally and with the patient's cooperation, there are cases where physical or emotional trauma makes concentration impossible. In such cases, drugs such as Sodium Amytol and Sodium Pentothal have been applied with speedy results. However, to avoid dependence on drugs during future inductions, the patient should be told, "In the future, you will be able to enter the hypnotic state when told to do so. You will simply remember how good it feels and be able to return to the pleasant trance level without the future use of drugs."

The proper time to implant this suggestion is before administering the drug, while the patient is still in a conscious state. There is a tendency, in using narco-hypnosis, to overdose. When the dosage is heavy, the subject will tend to drift too deeply into slumber and lose suggestibility. Remember hypnosis is *theta*, the threshold to sleep. Going too deep takes one into *delta*, where suggestibility is lost.

When skillfully and sparingly utilized, results with drugs can be remarkable in saving time and uncovering, as in psychotherapy, deeply buried traumatic material. In cases of drug or alcohol addiction, narco-hypnosis is often indicated because there is a basic reluctance to cooperate in overcoming the addiction. Because such subjects are accustomed to being dependent on a substance outside of their own power, a drug can prove temporarily useful.

During wartime, narco-hypnosis has often been widely used to extract information from captured enemy troops. Espionage and counter-espionage forces also employ this method because of its speed. It has also been used to get weary soldiers back into action. Hypnosis tends to lower the stress, enabling the soldier to temporarily overcome environmental pressure. Practitioners should be aware that there is a difference between trance induction and trance utilization. Realizing the trance to be a period of receptivity, suggestions must be formulated that will be adhered to by the subject in a waking state. Stress reactions must be unlearned under hypnosis and better reactions learned. Carefully formulated suggestions evoke cooperation and promote the fulfillment of the patient's potential.

In psychoanalysis, there have been positive reports of the application of Trilene (Trichlorethylene), a drug used as an inhalant for deepening hypnosis. Spontaneous abreaction of traumatic memory frequently occurs even without specific suggestion or age regression techniques. Trilene is simple to use and, in the hands of a professional, harmless. It leaves no unpleasant aftereffects. The response is fast and brief unless the drug is used repeatedly. While less effective in catalyzing induction than Sodium Pentothal and Sodium Amytol, its benefits as an adjunct to hypnosis for memory recall should be noted.

It has been my experience that using drugs rarely induce hypnosis without the added skill of techniques such as progressive relaxation and suggestion. What can be said for drugs is that they may be of help to some medical people in reducing the time of induction. Their effect is to facilitate cooperation in patients with musculoskeletal tensions of an extreme nature. In cases where patients are not motivated to accept suggestion, narcotics are of little value.

HOW TO USE DRUGS FOR HYPNOSIS

Physicians who frequently use hypnosis inform me that some of the tranquilizing agents can be helpful in decreasing central automatic reactivity and in maintaining a receptive cortical pattern. Meprobamate preparations and phenobarbital may facilitate cooperation in patients with unusual nervous tension problems. Sodium Amytol or Pentobarbital are used intravenously, while Trilene may be administered by inhalation.

When a drug is used intravenously, it is injected into the median basilic vein in the antecubital fossa. Dosage will very, three to fourteen grains in distilled water, 10 cc or more. The less, the better, keeping in mind always that the real success of all hypnotic technique depends mainly upon the strength of the relationship between hypnotist and subject. From a practical viewpoint, the most important consideration is not so much which technique brings the subject into the hypnotic state, but rather how to administer the therapy once the receptive state is reached.

In addition to their medical application, sometimes drugs will be used to induce a hypnotic state in order to learn information during a criminal investigation. Where the subject is overly tense and has difficulty relaxing enough to be hypnotized, a drug can sometimes be used effectively (with the person's permission). Sodium Pentothal is sometimes referred to as *the truth serum*. Used properly, it will loosen resistance and bring back forgotten material buried away because of stress. It is not used for interrogating criminals, but rather in working with cooperative witnesses.

The procedure works as follows: after the drug is administered by a qualified person, the physician instructs the subject to count backward from 100. The person's voice will begin to falter, and finally he will stop counting altogether and slump over. His jaw drops; relaxation of muscles to the extent that they become limp is noticeable. Suggestion will produce effective results in some subjects, but not all. Some will merely drift to sleep before the suggestions can work. After sleep, the patient remembers nothing. Others retain enough consciousness to remain in a trance level. At this point, it is wise for the hypnotist to suggest strongly that, hereafter, the subject will go into a deep hypnotic trance without drugs anytime the hypnotist suggests sleep.

Curiously, most subjects swear they were not hypnotized, but simply "knocked out," because their own sense of control was side-stepped by the narcotic. However, if induced a few minutes later, the subject will immediately go into a deep trance and phenomena can be reproduced. This method is extremely efficient. The only value of drugs lies in their effect on the following inductions, which has brought the subject's own state of mind about naturally.

THE USE OF TRILENE (TRICHLORETHYLENE)

Dampen a swab of cotton with Trilene and hold it over the subject's nose while giving hypnotic induction suggestions. Have the subject inhale the fumes and suggest he concentrate on going deeper. Inhalation of Trilene deepens hypnosis rapidly and produces abreaction of traumatic incidents. The degree of realism is extreme and the relief afterward is marked. Suggest that the inhalation of "this pleasant aroma will help you in every way. This is a natural substance, very beneficial in every way."

Explain in advance of administering the drug: "Trilene is a mild anesthetic used in minor surgical cases. Continued use is not recommended though it is harmless and non-habit forming." This method is often used in Great Britain and the Scandinavian countries as an aid to psychotherapy. Some of the results have been remarkable.

When using such drugs as Sodium Pentothal, suggestions of going deeper next time without drugs should be applied at the deepest trance level. Use "signal technique" such as "when I say deep asleep and count backward from 5 to 1, you will go even deeper than you are now. Any time that I say . . . 3 . . . you will go deeper than you are now . . . deeper each time."

EMOTIONAL RAPPORT

Popular misconceptions about hypnosis stem from fear of passing control over to the hypnotist and anxiety about not coming out of the hypnotic state. Operationally, hypnosis produces best results when favorable mental communication is established between hypnotist and subject. Acceptance of the operator require emotional rapport because most uninitiated subjects are inclined to be fearful and doubtful. Therefore, the professional must inspire confidence and project a genuine desire to help. Emotional warmth is more likely to work in trance induction than dependence upon technique alone.

While teaching hypnosis to both the lay person and professionals, I have noticed how the application and utilization varies from one practitioner to another. The presence of trust is as important to the success of the hypnotist as it is to that of any other healer. Many people are not suited to the practice of professional hypnosis because of personality limitations. No matter how well they may master methods and techniques, little can be accomplished without the ability to establish empathetic contact with the subject.

In order for the brain to accelerate healing, one must first reach the trance level. Intelligence in other areas has no bearing on the ability to benefit from suggestion. Suspicion and resistance are the most serious deterrents, for they create anxiety, which in turn militates against the relaxation of the mind essential to begin the hypnosis process.

Cooperation on the part of the subject is necessary since *no one can be hypnotized against his will.* Therefore, the professional should be less authoritarian and more sympathetic in his attitude. Hypnosis is not a battle of wills between hypnotist and subject. Rather, it is a situation in which the two must work together harmoniously with the best interests of the patient in mind.

The emotions play a strong part in the learning process and, for this reason, we begin suggestion by evoking pleasant emotions in the subject. This can be quite rewarding. Many hypnotic subjects experience deep emotional reactions during early stages of induction. A blissful expression floods the face as stresses melt away. Suggestions given at this time are very effective.

The sensitive hypnotist who is capable of sufficient insight into the personality and needs of his subject can use this open emotional readiness to put the suggestions through skillfully. This is proper use of hypnosis. Freud speaks of "distributions of mental energy." To combine the proper distribution of both mental and emotional energy seems logical. The patient learns to redistribute emotional energies into better channels from negative to positive. This channeling can be dramatically effective, and actually inspire hope where none existed before.

In emotional states, the hypnotist with insight will sense the right moment for implanting suggestions strengthened by the psychic fusion of hypnotist and subject. Whether we speak of the state of hypnosis as regression or as transference, fusion occurs and should be fully utilized to meet the needs of the hypnotized subject. Many subjects who go through the induction stage into medium and deep trance will show a tendency to behave as though fast asleep and seem devoid of emotion. Don't be fooled. The muscles in the face may be flaccid and free of tension, but the mind is alert and feelings can be very sensitive.

FUSION OF BOTH PERSONALITIES

After the initial stages of induction, the subject senses the personality of the hypnotist *whose tone of voice and choice of words convey his sincerity.* With adequate prehypnotic insight, early indications of emotion in the subject can be advantageous. While in this state of heightened self-observation, the subject's inner feelings are aroused through the subjective sense of oneness. He can then be directed to sense his ability in self-mastery and to find new ways to enhance himself.

Freud and Breuer originally held that effective discharge of intense feeling was associated with traumatic events, and that hypnosis becomes a purge of sorts for the patient. When the subject, or patient, is reached on a feeling level, he becomes intensely involved in his own therapy, thereby advancing more rapidly. Sharing the emotional experience with the hypnotist will often produce a speedy curative effect. This varies according to the relationship between the subject and the hypnotist.

Frequently, we find it advantageous to have a subject abreact in order to wipe out negative memories. The degree of suffering will then decrease and he will invariably become indifferent to the trauma in his past. Pointing out each time that the subject has "come through it all" will reassure him considerably. New content can be added, both for abreaction and for ego strengthening.

Direct the subject's abreaction of pleasurable events before the end of the session. This will aid in ego strengthening and build confidence. Positive awakening has a strong posthypnotic effect.

ANXIETY NEUROSIS

Here is an induction technique which is useful in eliminating fears and anxieties. Tell your subject: "Picture yourself descending in an elevator.

It's a local elevator, stopping at each floor. Each floor takes you deeper. Feel the car stopping, going deeper all of the time, a feeling of falling down very pleasantly, ever deeper. As the car keeps on going down, you begin to feel a pleasant, safe feeling of descending into a warm, comfortable state of peace and relaxation. All anxiety and tension leave you as you keep on feeling yourself drifting down in the car, deeper and deeper asleep. As you keep repeating to yourself, with the motion of the elevator going down, 'deep, deep, peaceful sleep, everything just fine, feeling happy and well, because I choose to feel that way and know there is every reason for me to feel well and happy, happy, safe and at peace, as the elevator drops down, floor by floor, it is taking me deeper, feeling better and better, secure, safe, contented, and this will last . . . feeling better and better as I feel the elevator descending, floor by floor, almost all the way down now, deeper and deeper into serenity, peace and well-being."

There is one situation where the descending elevator would be the improper technique to use for anxiety, and that is when the fear is one of elevators themselves. In such a case, have the subject imagine instead that he is on an open escalator and "going deeper into better, more secure mental and emotional feeling."

Unusual and Specialized Techniques

Although the major emphasis should be on perfecting a simple induction procedure, once you master a solid foundation, you may wish to expand your abilities into more sophisticated channels. In addition to the standard methods, there are manifold ancillary methods developed by professionals in their practical day-to-day work. This chapter will guide you in the management of the following advanced techniques:

Age Regression

You will guide the subject backward into the warehouse of memories. Used to uncover hidden material and for other recall.

Time Progression

A preview of coming events. Take a look into future possibilities. Used in surgery rehearsals and in self-imagery.

Automatic Writing

A dependable method to tap the subconscious for information. Bypasses the ego and the armor which resists opening up.

Group Hynotherapy

How to conduct hypnosis with a group of people who have various problems. Group regression and progression.

Prolonged Trance Therapy

When all else fails, the subject is kept under hypnosis for several hours or even days. Used in drug addiction cases.

Indirect Hypnosis

Inducing hypnosis without the knowledge of the subject requires a special skill. Suggested for medical use only.

The above methodology can be adapted to a great variety of individual problems. When used appropriately, the results may astound not only the subject but the operator. It is wise to master one technique at a time, although many of them work very well in combination. For example, *age regression* combined with *time progression*, in the same session, would be useful in examining past emotional problems and then taking a look into the future to see how things could be better. They work well together as a negative and positive visualization.

AGE REGRESSION AND TIME PROGRESSION

"Life can be understood looking backward, but must be lived forward," wrote the Danish philosopher, Kierkegaard. Hypnosis gives us a backward look and a forward one, and also *gives us foresight rather than hindsight.*

Age regression under hypnosis can be accomplished in one of two ways: (1) through recall of past events, names, numbers, the subject taps information recorded in the brain or (2) through recall and revisualization, the subject relives the past through "flashbacks." The trained hypnotherapist produces regression easily because all this information, both technical and visual, has been recorded in detail by the brain.

Age regression uncovers reflections from another time without the original emotional trauma. Imagination plus awareness arouses clarity in the brain instead of the old confusion. We are able to observe obsolete emotional patterns and realize that certain old feelings are not suited to new situations. Insight protects us from the past anxieties and projects us into a higher plane as subjectivity gives way to objectivity and an overview of past problems.

Accepting past images without reverting to old patterns of sensitivity involves an attitude of detachment. People who remain linked to old memories perpetually lament "what might have been" instead of considering "what can be" right now. Hypnosis can help illuminate not only the event, but the feelings behind the event. Through hypnosis, behavioral patterns become loosened and dislodged from old ways of thinking.

Clearing out obsolete thoughts is not always easy. They stick like glue, like undesirable tenants who refuse to vacate. Sometimes we need to become adamant, assertive, and serve them with an eviction notice. Habitual thinking forms well-worn paths which become engraved into the brain after much travel along the same route. Through age regression and time projection, one can not only assess past events, but leave them behind and move into the future. Once the mind awakens, old images become obscured and obstructed by new ideas which grow quickly.

PRODUCING AGE REGRESSION

Looking back into one's childhood and earlier years is quite harmless if handled with expertise. For the beginner, I suggest short regressions until you develop the skill. Take the subject back just a few years the first time, and then increase the regression each time you conduct a session.

Here's how it works. The hypnotist directs a dream toward a period of the subject's childhood, going back year by year. Before attempting regression, the hypnotist should have some knowledge and understanding of the subject's personality, and his past, particularly his early experiences. A factor vital to success is the trust the subject has in the therapist. He must be convinced beyond a doubt that his well-being is the most important consideration in the hypnotic situation. At no time should he feel anything but safe, protected, and benefited. The process of regression should be unhurried. If the subject appears emotionally disturbed as he recalls traumatic events, the therapist should not bring him out of hypnosis, but should handle the anxiety then and there. Use the trance level to pacify the subject. Distress will pass quickly with your kindly assurance that the past is finished and no longer threatening.

Before beginning age regression, it is advisable to have the subject write his name or draw a simple picture, i.e., an animal, house, or person. This test is used after regression for comparison of age differential. Regression is then brought about, one day at a time, one year at a time, depending upon the individual case and how long ago the trauma was inflicted. Give your subject time for the remembrances to come forth.

For example, if the subject is about 25 years of age, and you wish to regress him to age 7, take him back to "24, 23, 20, 18, 15, 12, 10, 9, 7." You can skip years, especially if the person is presently much older. (Otherwise, the session would be unnecessarily lengthy.) We tend to remember events by stages of our lives rather than by dates.

Always allow time for each phase to make its impression on the mind before moving back to a younger age. When you ask the person to answer questions, notice how the voice changes, whether the facial expressions are of a younger age. Call attention to birthdays, Christmas, and school terms as specifically as possible. Ask where he is, what he is doing. Give him sufficient time to deepen the trance before beginning regression. If he answers quickly in his natural voice, he may not be reliving the experience, but simply remembering. If he is recalling information, he will say, "I *was* in school" rather than "I am *now* in school." If he is merely remembering, he may mention the teacher's name, "My teacher's name *was* Miss Jones."

However, true regression places him in the midst of the incident and he will say, "I *am* in the first grade. My teacher *is* Miss Jones. She *is* teaching us to write." You will then know that this is a true regression. Should you regress him back to a very young age, he will be unable to speak, but will make noises, and cry or gurgle like a baby. When this occurs, it's best if you have established a nonverbal signal such as lifting a finger.

In cases of age regression to childhood, people who did not speak English until they were older may respond in a foreign language. This is also a sign of an actual regression. In all cases, have a nonverbal communication like a finger movement or movement of a foot to signify "yes" or "no" to questions you may ask of the subject.

Now, reluctant subjects will play a game, role playing instead of revivification. They will act out whatever they believe the therapist requires. This may be a way of avoiding traumatic memories. In such cases, the hypnotist may encounter resistance. This is best handled by slowing down the rate of regression and stopping at a time close to the incident. Later you may gradually return to the desired age. Suggestions given should be well thought out in advance and discussed. Sometimes automatic writing (described elsewhere) can be less painful than verbalizing. This method is speedy and very revealing, and works well in light hypnosis as well as at deeper levels. Several examples are given under *automatic writing*.

EXAMPLES OF REGRESSION

Frank H., 24 years old, was anxious and depressed. He had a fear of subways and of meeting people, and was claustrophobic. Frank had been medically discharged from the armed services. Diagnosed as schizophrenic, he had tried the usual therapies, including psychoanalysis, with no improvement. Responding to hypnotic suggestion well after three sessions he developed a deep trance. He was regressed gradually to age ten, at which time he recalled violent scenes between his mother and father as well as trouble in school, fear of adults, and hiding in the closet from his father.

At another time, Frank was regressed to age three and spoke in Spanish, which was the language spoken in his home. His voice was a babyish whine, scarcely intelligible, as he described a scene between his mother and father. A violent argument and physical fight took place. Frightened, he ran into the bathroom and hid in the tub. When he tried to come out of the bathroom, the door was stuck. The room grew dark and when he finally got the door open and emerged into the hallway, his uncle was there. He was even more afraid of his uncle than of his father. His uncle chased him down the dark hall. It was suggested he would remember the incident and be able to discuss it fully without pain because, after all, he had survived.

Frank recalled everything and spoke freely. "Isn't it silly to let such a thing upset you for so many years?" he commented. "Look what a big guy I grew up to be, six feet tall and afraid of shadows and quarreling people. How could anyone be so foolish?"

Frank responded to therapy very rapidly after regression. He found a job and eventually married a lovely young woman.

TIME PROGRESSION

Both hypnotic age regression and time progression involve a reorientation from one's perception of space-time. Progression refers to the artificial hallucination of events of the future. Once a person gains awareness from retrospection, he is better able to deal, not only with his present, but with his future. Instead of restricting his thinking to the way he has been, hypnosis helps him see himself as he could be—as he should be. Visionaries are those who can free their imagination and build a dream to strive for. Imagined situations can later be transferred into real-life situations. Time or age progression projects your thoughts into an unknown space and time—a year from now, five years, ten years—or it might be just a few days or hours. An actress might use the technique to visualize herself on opening night getting a standing ovation. A salesman could use time progression to rehearse his sales pitch and see himself writing a huge order.

During hypnosis, the person hallucinates positive improvements, tests himself in new situations, and tries on the garb of a successful person. While he may still retain his chronological age, he takes a look into the way things might be and develops "possibility thinking." Keep in mind that although some people can be *re*gressed easily because they are merely tuning into recorded information, *pro*gression involves use of the imagination, and the ability to visualize future events not yet experienced. In many cases, confidence in personal fulfillment has not been "programmed" into him by his past experience. His self-image may be weaker than his capabilities warrant. The successful use of "time progression" is based upon the trilogy, *conceive, believe, and achieve.* Each concept is equally important. One may conceive, but without belief, achievement is impossible. Imagining positive events tends to raise positive anticipation, which in turn fires the motivational drive to carry one through to a goal.

A good example is the following case history of a young woman, Jody L., who wanted plastic surgery in order to correct a birth defect. She feared the operation and kept postponing surgery. Under progression, she was told: "See yourself standing in front of a mirror. The nurse has just removed the bandages and you see yourself looking perfectly beautiful. Healed without a trace of scars. You are very pleased at the good results. There are no bruises—no black and blue marks. No redness, no swelling. People are standing around you complimenting you. See yourself clearly. See and you will be what you see."

There is infinite possibility in using imagination in particular situations, depending upon the individual. A skilled therapist facilitates the subject's receptivity to his own inner associations with positive images and integrates this response into action. We do not force moods or feelings, but rather encourage the built-in mechanisms already existing inside all of us. Because belief systems vary, it's well to inquire whether or not the person you are working with is religious, believes in nature, or "cosmic power." Effectiveness can be increased by activating the morals and beliefs already existing in the person.

Dr. William Kroger in his book, *Clinical and Experimental Hypnosis* cites a case history in which progression convinced a subject he should not undergo surgery. While under deep hypnosis, an apprehensive and tense individual who came for consultation on the advisability of having a vasectomy, was told that the surgery had already been performed, and that it was now five years later. He was told to think and feel the emotions and sensations of a man who had had a vasectomy. The doctor then asked him, "How have you been feeling since you were sterilized?" He replied, "Oh, Doctor, I haven't had a good night's sleep since my operation. It's made me very tense and nervous. This isn't the time for me."

After dehypnotization, he was advised to postpone surgery until certain meaningful and deeply repressed material could be worked out with a psychologist. Afterward, he was ultimately able to accept the consequences of the proposed surgery. He was also able to achieve greater personality integration because of the insight he gained under hypnotherapy.

In a similar way, rehearsals of surgery, childbirth, dental work, and other procedures which might involve apprehension on the part of the patient are useful in the elimination of anxieties. A lively imagination plus positive anticipation combine to prepare the subject for the best possible results. Surgical rehearsals are a certain antidote to the jitters that so many patients complain of prior to the operation. I use a technique called *The Yes or No Technique*. Here is the verbalization: "Picture two screens, like T.V. or movie screens. One shows a sign reading *yes* and the other a sign reading *no*. On the YES screen see yourself having had the operation. Everything has worked out just fine. The results were even better than you expected. Now take a look at the other screen. You have decided against the operation. What are the consequences? Take a look at your two choices—*yes* or *no*. Which one makes more sense to you? This preview will help you make up your mind. The decision will be the best one at this time.

UNCOVERING AND DISCOVERING SECRETS

Many people bury the most important information deep inside the subliminal caverns of their minds. Take the case of Kenneth R., a business executive, married and extremely conservative. His aim in life had always been to be successful, yet no matter how much he earned, Kenneth always considered himself a failure. By the time he discovered hypnotherapy, he had already had two nervous breakdowns. The first occurred when he was still a college student. Anxious and worried about living up to the expectations of his parents, he was filled with so much fear that his life became unbearable and he attempted suicide. His second breakdown occurred following a business disaster when he had to declare a bankruptcy. Kenneth was in his middle forties at this time and was institutionalized for his breakdown. Upon his release, he began seven years of psychoanalysis that he said did not resolve his feelings of depression. Many medications were tried with no appreciable success. Finally, someone suggested hypnosis.

Kenneth was a resistant subject from the start, having lost all faith in therapy. After four weeks that included four one-hour office sessions and the use of a cassette self-training tape that he played at home three times a day, Kenneth entered a light hypnoidal state. His case is important because there is the tendency among hypnotists to give up too soon and label a difficult subject as "nonhypnotizable." With persistence, almost every human being can be helped to some degree by hypnosis.

Although Kenneth was not a deep subject, we were able to produce some regression to a time before he had his first breakdown. He was handed the pad and pen for automatic writing.

"Write down, just as thought occurs to you, anything that may explain whatever is bothering you."

AUTOMATIC WRITING

Automatic writing is one of the most fascinating and valuable tools of hypnosis. Yet few hypnotherapists utilize this phenomenon. Many of them are under the misconception that automatic writing requires the deepest stage of hypnosis, somnambulism. This is far from the truth. Automatic writing even occurs at nonhypnotic levels such as "doodling" while a person is distracted on the telephone. Non associated scribbling is often filled with symbolic images and can reveal a great deal about the "doodler."

Material produced in this manner may reveal trauma buried under many layers of self-deception. Automatic writing brings out the truth, and, when combined with hypnosis, offers a method of uncovering information vital to a patient's recovery. Sometimes the subject chooses to draw pictures rather than write words. Sometimes the revelations come forth as disjointed syllables which need to be interpreted later. In any case, important, helpful insight will be forthcoming no matter whether you are working with a deep or light subject.

I have found it useful to work with a large artist's sketch pad and a felt-tip pen. The large pad is appropriate because many people tend to write much larger than normal when hypnotized. Perhaps this is because they "open up" more or revert to a more childish manner of scrawling. The writing is done with closed eyes, and the larger surface assures the operator that the results will be legible. A soft-tipped pen is needed because when in a trance state most people feel very light-handed and if you use a pencil or ordinary pen you may not be able to read the material.

Regression is often used prior to automatic writing. The subject is first inducted to as deep a level as possible. This usually requires two sessions. He is then guided to a particular time or event.

The trance depth necessary for producing automatic writing and regression is largely a matter of opinion, depending on the degree or rapport between operator and subject. Take time to explain how it works. Confidence and self-assurance help a great deal. Begin by showing examples of other people's writings under hypnosis. Explain: "Mary worked out her problems so much faster after she wrote these words. John found the right kind of job through the symbols in this drawing."

VERBALIZATION FOR AUTOMATIC WRITING

After locating the time or event about which the subject is to write, you bring about a sense of disassociation in his writing hand. (Be sure to check before induction whether your subject is right-handed or left-handed.) "As I stroke your hand, you will begin to feel it becoming numb, losing all feeling. Your hand feels light and detached from the rest of your body. Your hand is being controlled by a nerve which goes directly to your brain where the hidden information is stored. You no longer have conscious control of your hand. Your brain is feeding memories directly to your hand. Your hand has the information and is able to write it down easily. Even if the information was once painful, it doesn't bother your hand. Your hand has no emotions; it is automatic like a robot hand. Your robot hand gets the information from the computer brain and writes it down on the paper. Your hand will write only the truth. You will not think or question what is being written. Start writing answers when you hear my question."

At this point you direct the subject's mind to the area of trauma and ask short questions such as: "Where are you?" and "How do you feel?" Allow sufficient time for the subject to think and write. As the subject is writing, suggest: "After hypnosis is terminated, you will understand and be able to interpret what you have written." Repeat this several times.

After the session, the written material is evaluated. The subject is questioned about what he really meant when he wrote the information. Sometimes the words will be symbolic of deeper meaning. Very often the words will be abbreviated or transferred into symbolic shapes or objects such as a star, box, or other geometric design. A great deal of time is saved by this direct technique.

AUTOMATIC DRAWING AND DOODLING

In some cases, automatic drawing or doodling has certain advantages. For instance, where a language barrier exists or there is regression to an age before the subject learned to write, you might say, "Draw me a picture of how your father looked at the time," or, "Just let the pen doodle anything it wants to do." The results are often surprising. In the case of Alvin H., his childhood experience had been so painful he had difficulty recalling that period in his life. When he was told, "Do a cartoon strip representing the four worst things that happened to you," he portrayed himself as a dog being beaten by his father. Alvin was not an artist. The sketches were executed crudely, but the content was very powerful. At first he explained the dog this way: "My father would not let me have a dog. I was afraid if I brought one home he would beat it." Then he corrected himself: "No . . . the dog is really me. I was treated like a dog by my father, who had a terrible temper."

Interpretation of the results in automatic writing and drawing depends on an established, trusting relationship between therapist and subject. Rather than assuming you have the answers, it is best to ask the subject, "What do these writings mean to you?" When handled properly, the after-talks help to clarify not only events but hidden attitudes.

THE "AS-IF" OR SUBSTITUTION METHOD

When normal techniques of automatic writing or doodling fail to elicit the necessary communication—when the paper remains blank—try this. Suggest that the subject is merely an observer, examining a person with problems. Tell him: "Write down on the paper what is wrong with this person. You know him better than anybody else does. Look inside his head and see what he is thinking and write it down." Tell him he is an assistant to the therapist and is investigating the problem. "Allow your hand to write out a report on this person. You want to help him because he is really a nice person who needs help."

Virgil T. at 14 years of age, was having trouble in school. Although he had a high I.Q., he was noncooperative and a poor student. Virgil had a history of smoking, drinking, and drug abuse. His parents had forced him to come for a session in hypnosis. He stubbornly refused to communicate. When I attempted automatic writing, the only time his hand moved was to draw small circles . . . zeros . . . Virgil was trying to tell me something.

The substitution method worked like a charm. I suggested, "Write 'as-if' you are an observer investigating a boy with problems in school. Let your hand write about what causes this boy's trouble." Virgil readily responded with the following:" . . . trusted . . . he wants to be trusted . . . he is afraid . . . teacher insults him too much . . . he's cutting classes. . . ."

After the session, he opened up to the therapist and explained that his father was old-fashioned, and that he could not turn to him for advice. The father was invited to attend the next therapy session, and frankness and openness developed between father and son. This case history is an example of how communication can be increased through automatic writing rather than having the subject speak under hypnosis. In some cases, speaking rouses the subject and brings on feelings of resistance.

AUTOMATIC WRITING AS A TECHNIQUE IN THERAPY

Peter was a 38 year-old man who had been an alcoholic for sixteen years. He had failed to receive help in psychoanalysis. Alcoholics Anonymous didn't appeal to him. Shock treatments, faith healing, medication, and all kinds of other cures were tried to no avail. Peter was no puny nipper; he was a three-bottle-a-day man and it didn't matter to him what brand or type of liquor he imbibed.

Peter was a difficult subject. Hypnosis, with and without Pentothal, had been tried by a medical hypnotist but without success. After ten sessions of hypnosis using automatic writing, he was finally developed into a good subject. When Peter was asked to recall a time when he was 16 years of age, he wrote: "It's closing in, closing in, the street is closing in." What he had been referring to he did not recall, but rather spoke more freely about his other problem, which centered around a travelling phobia which kept him from going more than a block from his house. He had had several epileptic seizures, beginning at age ten, and he feared being overcome by a seizure in public and so stayed home most of the time. His fear would cause acute panic in him.

At his next session, Peter was hypnotized and he was regressed to age ten. He was asked to write about what happened at that age that had upset him. He wrote: "I stole money from mama's handbag. I am running . . . running . . . she is closing in." This time he recalled the original experience as well as the feeling of terror which had overcome him. He cried throughout the one-hour session, but remained at a deep trance level. We were able to reconstruct his entire neurotic behavioral pattern later in a private counseling session.

As a small child, he had occasionally stolen small sums of money from his mother's handbag whenever he felt rejected or unloved. Later he would suffer pangs of guilt and fear of punishment should his thievery be discovered. One day after being scolded by his mother for problems in school, he took the largest amount so far, a dollar bill. Afterward, Peter was running down a dark, narrow street when he was suddenly overcome by extreme anxiety and had his first seizure. His mother never confronted him with the fact that she knew he was stealing. Had she done so, the disturbance in his personality may not have become so deeply engrained into his nervous system. Perhaps she felt it would "just go away in time." It didn't. Peter became worse.

After his first seizure, he developed agoraphobia, fear of leaving the confines of his house. He would not step off his front porch. This lasted until he was an adult. In fact, his first hypnotic session was conducted in his home because of his phobia about travel. At the first session, he was trained to expect to leave for just one hour, so that he could visit the hypnotist's office. After being cured of agoraphobia through hypnosis, he tried many other therapies to no avail and later returned to hypnotherapy to overcome his addiction to alcohol. Finally, Peter learned self-hypnosis, which he now practices every day, and he has remained in good mental and physical health ever since.

One problem Peter was unable to resolve was his distaste for work. During hypnosis, he would awaken from a profound trance if he were told he'd feel well enough to find a job. In this case, Peter is a classic example of the fact that a hypnotist cannot always force a subject to accept a new image.

Jason R., 26 years old, suffered from primary impotence. Though he was physically healthy in every respect, he could not remember ever having an erection. He explained that in spite of his inability to function, he often felt strong sexual desire for intercourse with women but inevitably would end up masturbating with a flaccid penis. This had been his practice since adolescence. While he had intense sensation in the penis, the flow of circulation was psychologically shut off. Jason was referred to me by his urologist, who explained that he could find no evidence of any organic disturbance.

After three conditioning sessions, he reached sufficient trance depth for regression techniques to be employed. Jason was regressed to the age of 9, at which point he raised his hand as a signal to me that some information was forthcoming. I placed a large writing pad on his lap and a felt-tip pen in his hand, and Jason wrote in a childish, 9-year-old scroll:

"I am taking a shower. Dad is shaving at the sink, or maybe brushing his teeth. I say, 'Dad, come over here. I want to show you something.' He comes over and I point to my penis, which is hard. I ask him, 'How come it does that?' Dad laughs and says, 'Throw some cold water on it and it will go away.' Dad gets the glass of water from the sink and pours it over my penis and the erection goes away. Then dad goes into the kitchen and tells my mother and they both have a good laugh. I wonder what's so funny about me. Something must be wrong because they hush up as soon as I come out of the bathroom."

Once the original trauma was isolated, Jason's therapy proved very effective in removing the repressive block interfering with his sexual response. Many of the other techniques described in this book were also used, with excellent results. After six sessions, Jason awakened one morning with an erection and soon after was able to transfer this ability to lovemaking during the evening hours. He has since married.

GROUP OR MASS HYPNOSIS

Because people are generally more susceptible after witnessing an induction performed with someone else, follow this procedure:

1. *Test for suggestibility* using any of the methods described earlier. The *Hand Rising and Falling* test is the one I prefer.

2. *Select the most responsive* subject (or subjects) to use for a demonstration in front of the rest of the group.

3. *Demonstrate an induction* with the suggestible subject(s). One of the speedier inductions will be sufficient to prove the point.

4. *Proceed With Group Induction* following the simple instructions which follow. The technique works with ten to ten hundred, easily.

Demonstrations are useful in convincing skeptics in the group that the phenomenon of hypnosis is for real. However, in working with a large group (hundreds or thousands), there will always be a percentage who will not allow themselves to be hypnotized. They will watch with a fascinated expression as the rest of the audience goes into trance. This does not indicate that they are less hypnotizable, but rather that they are not ready at this moment in time to cooperate in the induction. It is wise to say to a large group, "Those of you who would prefer to watch may do so. However, if at any time your eyes should grow tired, just close them and join the group and relax with us."

Stage hypnotists often follow the procedure outlined here. They rely on selecting the most agreeable subjects in the audience and after demonstration proceed with a routine similar to the following:

"I want every one of you to take a deep breath, breathe in, in, in, in, *hold it, hold it.* O.K. Now exhale. Let it all out. . . . Now, in a few moments I am going to ask all of you to close your eyes, and after you have closed your eyes, I am going to have you take five deep breath. . . . After you have taken five deep breaths, you will hold the *fifth breath,* while I count backwards, 5, 4, 3, 2, 1, . . . When I reach 1, you will be deep asleep and will not be able to open your eyes. Remember now, you will hold the *fifth breath,* while I count backwards 5, 4, 3, 2, 1 and then *deep asleep.* . . . Now, all of you close your eyes. Good. . . . Now:

Number One: "Breathe in, in, in, hold it . . . hold it
. . . exhale . . . exhale."
Two: In, in, in, in, and out, out, out, relax deeply."
Three: *"Breathing in all the way in, now exhale out, out."*
Four: "In, in, in, and out, out, out."
Five: *Take a really deep breath, hold it, hold it. Five, Four, Three, Two, One, Exhale Completely!!*
Deep . . . Deep . . . Asleep . . . You Will Remain Deep, Deep Asleep Until I Awaken You . . . You Will Find This Experience Restful and Self-Enriching. The Deeper You Go, the Greater the Benefit to You. Now, Get Ready to Relax From the Top of Your Head to the Tips of Your Toes."

You now proceed with deepening techniques such as progressive relaxation, countdowns, etc. Group or mass hypnosis is no more difficult than individual hypnosis. The routines are the same after you eliminate the original resistance by demonstrating with a highly suggestible subject. Group hypnotherapy is a marvelous aid in handling juvenile behavior modification, improving study habits in classrooms, in drug rehabilitation, obesity, insomnia, and in pain clinics. Hypnosis in a group is also a practical solution for preventing mental illness because it is lower in cost than individual therapy and eases the practitioner's case load.

Group hypnosis dates back all the way to the Egyptians. Many ancient people performed group rituals which were hypnotic in nature. Mass chanting and hypnotic meditation to the steady beat of drums was widely accepted as part of the religious healing arts. Healing with the mind predates medical practice and is still used in many primitive societies with some surprising results.

Just as the healer in ancient times, the hypnotist moves among the group, touching each subject's shoulder and whispering individual suggestions into each subject's ear. The suggestions begin as soon as the entire group has reached at least a light-to-medium trance level. Then the operator goes to each individual and reads from the card the subject is holding. (Experience has taught me not to depend on memory in giving suggestions to a large group.) Each person is told in advance to write their suggestions on a card and hold the card as they are inducted into the trance. As you approach each subject, you are verbalizing as follows: "Now as I speak to each of you and touch you upon the shoulder, you will go deeper. The rest of you will use the sound of my voice to go deeper." When the problem is one which the subject is shy about, such as sexual dysfunction, the suggestion is whispered directly and very softly into the individual's ear to respect his privacy. However, when the suggestion can benefit everyone and is of a general nature such as improved learning or better sleep, it is spoken in a moderate voice.

Some disturbances are universal, and group suggestions will often include Confidence Building, Improved Self-Image, Better Organization, Healthier Personal Habits, Serenity, Faith, Cheerfulness, Tolerance, Freedom from Fear, Decisiveness, Setting Goals, Independence, and Financial Success.

In addition to building better inner images, the group approach is ideal for positive brainwashing that rids the mind of unwanted, obsessively negative images such as Confusion, Procrastination, Anger and Hostility, Indecision, Guilt, Nervous Tension, Pains, and Irritability.

The average length of time needed for good results is from 1 1/2 to 3 hours. When working with individuals, you will need from forty minutes to an hour to achieve proper depth of trance level.

GROUP RESPONSE IN AUTOMATIC WRITING

The following events transpired at a hypnotherapy group session. Ten people participated, both male and female, aged 21 to 43. The subjects had been previously conditioned in private sessions to reach medium and deep trance levels. The object of the group was to train them in memory and recall so that when automatic writing took place they would be ready. There were four group sessions in which regression and automatic writing were utilized.

First Session. While under hypnosis they were told (collectively) that they were to recall a time at which they were first made aware of their particular problem. They would then focus on the circumstances and people connected with the original cause of the problem. The technique for regression was as follows:

"As I count backwards from 43 years of age, see yourself growing younger with each count. Those of you who are younger than 43, join into the countdown when you hear the number representing your age." I counted down to 21, the age of the youngest member of the group, and then continued the regression, "21, 20, 19, 18, (and so on)." They were told to signal when they remembered a traumatic incident by raising a forefinger. I then placed a writing pad and pen in each person's hand. When everyone had pad and pen, I instructed them to write their names. Most of them wrote in large childish script or printed.

Second Session. After repeating the above procedure, seven out of the ten began writing meaningful information. Of the remaining three, two were still insufficiently deep and the third sat with her eyes closed weeping and unable to communicate. Examples of the positive writing follow:

Alice B., age 30, was an asthmatic and hoped hypnosis would lessen the severity of her attacks. She wrote part of a sonnet by Shakespeare which expressed the death wish. One word stood out clearly: "suffocation."

Margie V., age 21, weighed 85 lbs., although she was 5 foot, 6 inches tall. Her condition, known as anorexia nervosa, began when she was 19 years of age and a newlywed. She weighed 125 lbs. when she married, having been on a diet when she originally weighed 135. Margie did not write words; she doodled. The drawings resembled sticks. Some of the sticks were assembled into people. Her later writings were to the point.

Albert M., 31, was embarrassed when he revealed that his problem was enuresis (bed wetting). He had rarely had a dry night since he was an infant. Traditional approaches had been tried with no results. He was an excellent subject. "The house is too cold," he wrote. He explained later that as a child he had lived near Buffalo and in a house with little heat in the winter. He had become conditioned to sleep through urination rather than get up to go to the toilet in the cold.

There were less interesting responses from the remaining members during this session. Two of them had routine overweight problems.

Third session. There were now eight people in the group. The young woman who had been unable to communicate was referred to a psychiatrist for analysis. One of the other people decided he was unable to work in group and returned to private sessions. Alice B., the asthmatic, wrote profusely of her first attack, blaming her mother for not allowing her to date her first boyfriend. She released a tremendous amount of hostility. Margie V. revealed she was trying to turn her young husband's sexual drive down because he "comes on too strong. Now he's afraid to touch me." She smiled as she wrote this.

Hank D., a homosexual, had been unable to write anything at the first session. Now he wrote, "I feel healthy and normal this was. As a child, I knew I was different." He later told the group that he visualized himself as bisexual even as a very small child. He had had a vision of himself as a person with breasts and a penis.

Fourth Session. By this final group session in automatic writing, all eight people had mastered the art and were doing self-analysis with supervision. One of the group members who had not demonstrated any particular ability to visualize said that he had regressed all the way back to a previous life. Victor W. wrote, "Rough sea. I am going down. Dead. Year, 1807." He described to the group a scene that contained a pirate ship and himself as assistant to the ship's cook. This rather amused me, because in the many years of practicing hypnotherapy, I have listened to hundreds of reports of reincarnation as a result of hypnotic induction. However, most of the reports are of past lives as prominent people. Queens, kings, presidents are the most popular, making one wonder how much of the report is hallucination and wishful thinking. In Victor's case, however, seeing himself merely as an assistant to the cook gave his story some sense of authenticity. While there is no way to prove reincarnation, those of us who have worked with hypnosis for many years do not rule out the possibility, since there have been similar writings reported by hypnotists in various parts of the world.

This group was also taught techniques of self-hypnosis that they used to good advantage in many different ways. I asked them each to

write to me several months after working in the group so that I could list
the improvements they made. Here is a list of the ways in which
hypnosis and self-hypnosis improved the lives of these ten people:

"Learning French for a trip to Paris."
"Helped me learn how to dance."
"Sleep better than I did before."
"My sex life has improved. More stamina."
"Overcame biting my nails and snoring."
"Keep my temper under control much better."
"Get along better with my co-workers."
"Hypnosis worked for painless dental work."
"Lost some more weight. Don't eat sweets."

PROLONGED TRANCE THERAPY

Extending the length of the therapeutic trance to several hours or even
days can be extremely useful in breaking entrenched behavioral patterns. Dramatic short-term recovery is possible in many situations, e.g.,
lowering stress where there is excitation from shock, aiding the drug
addict and alcoholic during the withdrawal period, and improving cases
of extreme obesity where eating patterns must be radically altered in a
short period of time.

The subject is hypnotized to a suitable level and told he will not
awaken until instructed to do so. "You are going to relax and 'sleep it
off.' When you wake up much later, you will feel as if you have had a
full night's sleep. Only this time you will wake up without your old
problem. You will wake up as if you are reborn—new person without the
old problem." During the interview, he is instructed on how to cooperate to help himself in the procedure. He is told that the longer he stays
in trance, the better he will feel; the further he goes into hypnosis, the
further he will go forward correcting his problem.

Proper suggestions are discussed with the subject. He is then told to
start a long count (1,000 or 500 down to 0), each count to take him
deeper and deeper. While the subject is silently counting to himself, the
operator proceeds with progressive body relaxation. This is done very
slowly, with long pauses and lapses in the voice so that the subject will
become accustomed to periods when he keeps himself under by counting. Prolonged trance works best with a preconditioned subject who has

been trained to enter a medium to deep level. Otherwise the subject will keep coming out and the effect will be lessened. Keep in mind that after an hour or two, he can open his eyes and still remain in hypnosis. This will be necessary for periods of eating and going to the bathroom. However, the eyes are only opened intermittently and never except when the hypnotist gives the command.

In cases where the hypnotic trance is prolonged for many hours or days, an auxiliary hypnotist is advisable. Tapes and records will also prove useful. You can prerecord some of the countdown routines and various deepening techniques to use when you need to take a break from the program. It is best not to leave the patient listening to tapes longer than fifteen minutes at a time, as there may be a tendency to lose some depth. Human contact is far more effective in achieving results, because the subject senses the emotional rapport and concern of the operator. The duration of the therapy varies according to the condition of the subject.

Time distortion plays a vital role in the degree of recovery, as a few case histories will demonstrate.

George Z. suffered from a combination of several serious problems. Not the least of these was a serious drug addiction that had kept him in a state of extreme apathy for almost five years. As a war veteran, he was transferred from one hospital to another. All treatment, both medical and psychological failed to help him overcome his total lack of self-esteem. In addition to his drug dependency, he also had violent episodes and been arrested for assault with a dangerous weapon on three separate occasions. His last arrest was for threatening his mother with bodily harm if she did not provide him with money for his drug habit. His mother contacted the hypnotherapist during a period when her son was out on bond:

"There is so little time for him to be helped. Soon he will be sentenced and put away. Can you do something quickly while he's available for treatment?" Prolonged trance therapy was decided upon as a means for accelerating his improvement. George responded immediately to this suggestion: "Space out. Just like you do when you are high on drugs. Only this time, we are working with nature to cure you of all need for the junk. You will come out clean and free of the habit. Are you willing for this to happen to you?"

He readily agreed. George loved to be hypnotized. He felt relief in turning his problem over to someone else, even if it was only for several hours. George was kept under for ten hours with the help of two hypnotists and several recordings. Music was also used in the background. In selecting music, pick something that is soft, slow, and sounds like a lullaby. Lyrics are contraindicated because they draw mental concentration away from the suggestions. Because of the long duration of this therapy, we recorded his personalized suggestions and played them when we needed a voice rest.

George progressed into the induction rapidly by the use of "awakening and reinduction techniques." Because this was his first experience with hypnosis, all sorts of methods were employed. Standard as well as specialized methods kept taking him deeper at each induction. He remained in the trance state during the entire time, which included his brief breaks to eat, stretch, and wash up. Here is the verbalization given just before a break.

"When you hear the count of 3, you will open your eyes and remain in hypnosis. You will do exactly as you are told until you are instructed to close your eyes once again. You are permitted, upon opening your eyes, to walk immediately to the bathroom and then return to your chair where you will be fed some nourishment. When you finish your food, you will immediately be told to close your eyes and go deep asleep. Now get ready to open your eyes and remain in hypnosis. One, 2, 3, eyes open . . . stay under. Go to the bathroom and come back."

When George was reinducted, he immediately slipped into the deepest level of hypnosis. It was firmly suggested that he would feel healthy and strong and disgusted with all drugs, and that he would become a helper in the drug rehabilitation movement to assist young people to avoid all the suffering he had been through. After the fourth induction, he signaled with his forefinger that he agreed to this suggestion.

When George was finally awakened at the end of the ten-hour period, he was amazed that it was already dark out. We had started the therapy at 10 A.M. and, by 8 P.M., the auxiliary therapist and I were feeling a bit exhausted. George, however, felt chipper and filled with energy. He could not believe that ten hours had passed. It seemed to him that the passage of time had been accelerated, condensed into just an hour or so. His memory of the experience was vague, but his attitude had clearly changed. It touched us emotionally to see him put his arms around his mother, who had come to see that he got home alright. At that moment it seemed impossible to imagine that just a few short months before he had made a threat on her life. Such is the nature of the mind distortion which accompanies the abuse of drugs.

When George completed his jail sentence, he visited the therapy center where he had received his prolonged hypnotherapy. He joined a group therapy session which was in progress at the time. In addition to participating in group sessions, he now goes out with a woman, works part-time, and is a volunteer in a teenage drug rehabilitation center.

When some people suffer the shock of an accident, the trauma may remain with them for a long time. Charlene T. was a stewardess who had the misfortune to be working on an airliner which crashed upon landing, killing dozens of people. Charlene was deeply depressed and complained of persistent nightmares about the crash. In addition, she was terrified of flying and because this was her means of livelihood, she had been out of work for two years.

"I've got to snap out of it and get back to work soon," she confided. "My bank account is running dry. Please do what you can to speed it up."

Charlene was a preconditioned subject. She had attended both group and private sessions. One hypnotist was used, with a cassette tape during rest periods. The following techniques proved successful: regression back before the accident, progression forward to a happy, safe career, and signal reversal from negative thoughts to positive ones. We also used the *directed dream technique* to wash the nightmares out of her memory.

Another case of prolonged sleep therapy is that of Elise R., age 34. Problems: mental confusion, which rendered her unable to concentrate on her work, and compulsive eating. Though Elise knew every diet, she could not stick to one more than a few days. She had been through six years of analysis. After several sessions of hypnosis, she was still unable to control her emotional eating habits.

One day, while under hypnosis, another client arrived early and I escorted him into an adjoining room. I instructed Elise meanwhile to listen to my voice and keep going deeper, even though she might not fully understand my words.

"You will not care to listen," I told her, "but the sound of my voice will take you deeper, no matter what I am saying to the other person. You will not awaken till I place my hand on your shoulder and say, "Wake up now." Elise was told to keep implanting the positive suggestions that she would have no desire for fattening foods and would eat only the minimum amount. At the termination of the one-hour session she seemed much deeper than ever before, though I had not addressed myself to her directly. She was indirectly keeping herself in hypnosis using the distant sound of my voice. Elise remained under hypnosis for four hours by this method. I repeated the technique four times, and she was finally able to conquer her compulsion and to work out her other disturbing problems as well. Eighteen months later, her recovery seemed complete.

Benson T., age 26. His problems included a fear of meeting new people, anxiety regarding work, and claustrophobia. Benson was discharged from the army and listed as disturbed. Many diagnoses had been made regarding his case. He was called schizophrenic, paranoic, and a lobotomy had been recommended by army medics.

After three sessions utilizing regression and automatic writing, Benson was placed in prolonged trance in the same manner as Elise. Tape recordings were employed as a supplement to live suggestions. He remained in trance from three to six hours daily for five days. At the end of that time, Benson was strongly motivated to find suitable employment. Since, he has gotten married and has persevered in the same job for more than a year. Now is free of anxiety, gets along with people, and is so well-adjusted that he is considering raising a family.

Anne B., age 35, was terrified of dental work. She required six prolonged hypnotic sessions, lasting four hours each. In addition, she had ten sessions in group hypnosis. The results were very positive. She developed great self-confidence and learned how to administer self-anesthesia through autohypnosis. At this writing, Anne, a recent bride, tells me that she will transfer her knowledge of local anesthesia to painless childbirth, if and when she becomes pregnant.

INDIRECT HYPNOTIC INDUCTION

It is possible to induce the hypnotic state in very susceptible subjects without their awareness. Some dentists use this approach on children by telling them, "When you hear the drill, close your eyes and make believe you are watching your favorite T.V. show. Any time I tell you to wash your mouth, you will do so and then close your eyes and go back to watching your favorite show." All doctors are strategically in a good position to practice indirect hypnosis without the problem of resistance because they often represent to the patient an authority whose opinion is not to be questioned.

Indirect hypnosis should only be used in cases where overt induction will raise fears and anxiety that would interfere with the treatment. If the hypnotist wants to induce the hypnotic state without discussing it with the subject, he must avoid words typically associated with hypnotic induction. Words such as "sleepy or drowsy" can be circumvented substituting "relaxation," "concentration," or "meditation." Many clinics use hypnosis techniques under the guise of *behavior modification.* There are dentists, doctors, and psychiatrists who use substitute terms in cases where a patient might be afraid of hypnosis. The patient might be told he is being "sedated" or that the physician intends to use "psychosomatic induction," or "narcosynthesis."

The basic principle of disguised hypnosis is based on a common misconception that hypnosis is synonymous with nighttime sleep. The prospective subject assumes he will become drowsy, fall asleep, be unable to hear the operator, and will not remember anything when he awakens. This is only true of a small percentage of highly susceptible subjects. In about seven out of ten cases, the subject remembers easily. The truth is that hypnosis is more similar to the wakening state than it is to nighttime sleep. The main difference is that, under hypnosis, the subject is highly suggestible and tends to be agreeable to the commands of the operator. This same suggestibility can be achieved without direct reference to the term, "hypnosis."

APPLYING THE INDIRECT METHOD

The success of the induction lies in studiously avoiding words that may have a disturbing meaning to the subject. Prepare the induction by eliminating any stress factors, making sure the subject is as comfortable as possible. Begin the induction by using one of the standard tests for suggestibility such as the *arms raising and falling test.* Call the test, for example, *power of imagination.* You can use this test both in group and with individual inductions. Conduct the test with the subject standing facing you as you demonstrate. After the test, tell the subject, "You have a fine imagination. Now we are going to relax and use your imagination to get rid of fatigue and emotional irritations." For some subjects, you merely have to tell them you are going to teach them "meditation," and they will proceed to induct themselves without any reluctance.

Suggest eye closure by saying, "You will be able to use your power of imagination much better with your eyes closed. Close your eyes so that you avoid the interference of other images." From this point on, you can advance to other procedures being careful to substitute other words for "deep sleep" and hypnotic terms such as "suggestion." Substitute expressions such as "pleasant tranquillity," "emotional serenity," "free-flowing feeling," and "spiritually uplifting" work well as deepening phraseology. Instead of "suggestion," talk about "improved self-image."

An alternate disguised technique is to refer to the experience as "*alpha* mind-control," telling the subject he will learn to control his own mind. Another substitute term is "natural biofeedback technique." After all, what's in a name? It's the results that count!

The Trained Brain
Eliminates Pain

Hypnosis is effective as a medical adjunct both as an analgesic and an anesthetic. Hypnotic suggestion alters the way messages of pain are perceived, processed, transmitted, and interpreted by the brain and central nervous system. From the temporary, localized pain, experienced at the dentist's to the chronic pain of cancer patients, hypnosis offers new hope in alleviating suffering.

Headaches, backaches, arthritis, rheumatism, angina pectoris, sciatica, menstrual cramps, labor pains, and accident injuries are but a few of the numerous ailments which respond to the methods described in this book. For more and more people, hypnosis has proven to be a boon in lowering the threshold of pain and lessening the need for drugs.

How does hypnotism work as a painkiller? Let's consider migraine headaches. The classic migraine patient complains of painful throbbing around the head and eyes. Visual distortion—spots or an aura of flashing lights—are also often cited. Vascular disturbance inflicts its misery by dilating the blood vessels around the head. This stretching of the blood vessels creates a pounding sensation that causes severe pain. Under hypnosis, the patient is told to visualize himself relaxing and to see the congestion in his head drain away into other areas of the body. "Picture your hands turning rosy red as the blood moves from your head into your hands."

Jean C., age 45, complained of headaches for ten years. Every known means of relief had failed. Doctors pronounced Jean organically healthy, except for "nervousness." Under deep hypnotic trance, probing failed to reveal any underlying cause of her migraine problem other than stress. She was hypnotized seven times in bi-weekly sessions and given suggestions of relaxation and general well-being. Jean was told her headaches had no valid cause, but were simply habits which were correctable. Her first session brought some relief but then she complained of a headache before her second session. She almost gave up therapy because she expected to be relieved instantaneously after the first session. A friend of hers experienced speedier results, which had led her to believe that one session would be sufficient. She didn't realize that people vary in their ability to respond and that what is suitable for one may not be adequate for another.

Jean came for the third session and afterward felt much better, so she continued for the full treatment, which lasted twelve sessions. She persisted in studying hypnosis after her headaches were completely eliminated to improve her memory and recall. Highly impressed and pleased with the results, Jean decided to return to professional writing, which she had given up several years prior when the headaches had disabled her.

Writing gave Jean renewed feelings about life. "Without some creative activity, my life was just one big headache," she said. "Now everything is opening up. I feel life has no problems, only challenges."

THE BRAIN MANUFACTURES IT'S OWN PAINKILLER

Scientists have long been aware that the brain is the center of pain perception. They are learning more every day. Among the newest information is the knowledge that the brain gives forth a morphinelike chemical responsible for the lessening of pain. Imagine, an incredibly potent painkiller available to everyone, able to relieve the most excruciating pain, with no harmful side effects. Best of all, there is no fear of possible addiction, and your brain's chemistry is with you at all times. This natural substance is two hundred times as powerful as morphine. It is called *dynorphin*, one of a family of exciting brain chemicals called *endorphins*. These chemicals are a major part of the body's defenses. Evidence suggests hypnosis releases endorphins from the brain during trance.

Although endorphins are still under investigation, we know they are part of a collection of approximately fifteen brain chemicals called peptides. Many others probably are lying dormant, awaiting discovery. The secretion of these chemicals is believed to profoundly affect our emotions and behavior. This may explain the general feelings of well-being experienced by the person who meditates or uses hypnosis regularly.

Some people produce more natural painkiller and, therefore, have a lower threshold of pain than those who inhibit the flow of this vital substance in themselves. Expectations of suffering seem to affect the degree to which we lessen or increase our own discomfort. The discovery of the brain's narcotic manufacture raises hopes that we can diminish the use of the addictive painkillers that have entrapped so many people. Neuroscientists discovered this new information in their search for the mechanism by which drugs such as heroin and morphine produce a state of euphoria and deaden pain, thereby causing addiction.

Scientists suspect these natural narcotics attach themselves to certain areas of the brain, producing a chemical reaction with positive results. Hypnotherapists believe that, with successful application of the principles of hypnosis, the brain can be trained to produce extra secretions of painkiller without added stimulation by drugs.

HOW TO PRODUCE ANESTHESIA

Strategies for controlling pain vary to a great extent, depending upon the individual. If the person is highly hypnotizable, the operant may decide to use one of the speedier methods. Here's one that works well: ask the patient to visualize a local anesthetic being injected directly into the painful area. Then say: "The pain is becoming less and less. You have now been anesthetized. Numbness is taking over." This procedure is especially useful in dentistry. Here the dentist tells the patient to open his mouth and close his eyes. Dentist, after tapping the gum: "I have just injected Novocaine into the right side of your mouth. Your jaw is becoming completely numb. This numbness will become even stronger when you hear the sound of the drill. Nothing will interfere with the nerves becoming number and number. When I count backward from 10 to 0, the pain will be gone."

When the drilling is finished, the doctor will say: "The nerves in your face will now return to normal. When I count from 1 to 5 and say, 'wide awake,' you will open your eyes and there will be no aftereffects of discomfort."

A pill or ointment may be suggested as a substitute for the injection. Another technique: "Imagine the nerves that lead into the area controlled by switches in your brain. See your hand turn the switch and the pain is turned off."

It is a truism that pain is perceived in the mind and central nervous system, rather than in the skin or muscles at the exact site of the problem. Conclusive proof of this is illustrated by the phenomenon of the "phantom limbs." The Phantom Limb Syndrome is a bizarre complication that sometimes occurs following surgical amputation. The patient feels sensation in a part of the body that no longer exists. A surgeon described his patient's reaction after amputating his left leg at the knee:

"I feel a painful tingling in my foot," the patient said. "It feels as it's still there." He complained of calf muscles aching. This reaction is explained as a conditioned reflex based upon a mental image. The thought of his injured limb produced the pain. In return, the pain then reproduced an image of the missing part. Anticipation is a fundamental part of cognition. Anticipating depends upon previous experiences that are stored in the memory warehouse. As a result of expectation, pain and body image become linked together in an automatic reflex.

Treatment consists of teaching the patient self-hypnosis. He is taught to relinquish his unreal memory of the limb and to use self-imagery as an aid in adjusting to reality. Hypnosis is also used in such cases to train the patient to relax and comfortably accept the prophylactic replacement. Hypnosis also facilitates cooperation before surgery. It can be employed to promote better sleep, bed rest, and stimulate appetite and general recovery after surgery.

The sensitive physician knows you do not limit treatment merely to parts of the body, but attend to the emotions as well. Hypnotic suggestion is invaluable in altering the patient's outlook on his misfortune, encouraging cheerfulness and expectations of improvement.

HELP FOR THE CANCER PATIENT

There are many ways in which the cancer patient can be helped through hypnosis. To begin with, it helps in controlling emotional depression, and building confidence in recovery. Patients report relief of the nausea resulting from radiation treatment and chemotherapy. In addition, where surgery is indicated, hypnosis lessens the need for anesthesia. In many cases, cancer patients treated with hypnosis get enough relief from pain that their need for narcotic drug is substantially reduced.

Dr. Frank Lawlis and his wife, Dr. Jeanne Achterberg, of the University of Texas Health Science Center in Dallas, studied the results of mental imagery on ninety cancer patients and reported that, in the large majority of cases, the mental visualization of healing aided recovery. The researchers teach patients to envision their internal disease process and then to picture the forces of their bodies overcoming the disease.

They stress the importance of the patient's understanding how the body functions in both a healthy and diseased state. To sharpen their imaginations, Dr. Lawlis guides his patients through individualized relaxation exercises. In some especially difficult cases, he uses his self-hypnotic system in conjunction with drugs and other medical treatment.

A victim of cancer, who claims to have achieved complete remission, described his visualization this way: "I imagine I am surrounding the cancer cells with white light and then I talk to them mentally as you would to troublesome people. I tell the cells they must stop their activity and go somewhere else. They are unwanted."

This subject believed he could influence his own healing, and perhaps his strong belief had a positive reaction. This phenomenon appears to have enough validity to provide an avenue for future exploration in the same way religious healing now commands the interest of researchers. In all areas of healing, a self-helping attitude on the part of the patient brings hope and can certainly do no harm.

Some years ago a group of hypnotists volunteered their services to terminally ill cancer patients at the Memorial Hospital in New York City. They reported that some of the patients who had not been able to move their limbs because of pain and weakness responded so well to hypnotic suggestion they were able to get out of bed, dress, and see a movie in the hospital theater. While they were beyond complete healing, their last few months were made more bearable by the regular visits of the therapists who trained them to use self-hypnotic suggestion to lessen the pain and discomfort of their condition. For many terminally ill people who have grown immune to the effect of pain-killers, hypnosis offers relief as a last resort measure.

In some hospitals in Europe tapes are used for terminally ill people to ease their suffering during the last few months. Joyce Slone, a psychiatric nurse who practices hypnosis, reported that such is the practice at The Institute of Suggestology in Yugoslavia, where patients can tune in on healing or reconditioning tapes while they are convalescing. The doctors there claim regression of serious diseases based on mental reconditioning.

THE PAIN OF DENTISTRY

The use of hypnosis as an adjunct to the practice of dentistry is no longer controversial. Trained hypnodontists are now making full use of

HOW TO HYPNOTIZE YOURSELF

its many benefits. The skilled hypnodontist carefully applies the techniques, encouraging hypnosis where practical while, at the same time, employing traditional methods.

The bravest person among us may shudder at the thought of a trip to the dentist's chair. For this kind of patient, dentists find hypnosis a valuable tool in making the experience less fearful as well as less painful. Hypnotic anesthesia has made dentistry possible for many who heretofore were unable to submit themselves to the needed treatment. Not only do the techniques cause treatment to be tolerable for the patient; the dentist is also relieved of undue strain in handling difficult patients.

The value of a psychosomatic approach as an integral phase of dental practice has been proven not only to lessen the pain of drilling, but also effective in allied work such as orthodontistry, periodontistry and other special areas. There is more to hypnosis than merely putting the patient "to sleep" and performing on a numb subject. Drugs could do that. Hypnosis is used in a more important way—to relax the person emotionally, thereby eliminating stress and apprehensions. Hypnodontists cite a special advantage over injecting anesthetic. There are no side effects such as numbness and mood changes, which often accompany the use of drugs. Also, self-hypnosis can be taught to difficult patients who can self-administer autosuggestions in the few minutes prior to treatment, while they are in the waiting room.

Where children are concerned this is especially important, because a pleasant experience conditions the child to future visits without the usual fussing. This can make the difference between a healthy mouth and a lifetime of dental problems. Dentists have told me that the more squeamish the patient, the easier he is to hypnotize. The stronger the distaste for dental work, the stronger the motivation to avoid pain and discomfort. Therefore, the patient opts to cooperate as an escape.

The science of hypnodontia has spread to such an extant that a special organization exists, The American Society of Psychosomatic Dentistry. This is an association of ethically minded dentists who have been trained and certified to apply hypnosis in dentistry. The members recognize the psychological reactions of each individual in relation to his treatment. The dental application of hypnosis was begun early in the year 1948, many years before the American Medical Association recognized hypnosis as a valid medical adjunct, by a group of dentists in the northwest, working under the leadership of pioneer Thomas O. Burgess, Ph.D, a clinical psychologist often referred to as the "father of dental hypnosis." The organization is now national in scope and publishes the

Journal of The American Society of Psychosomatic Dentistry. The mystic confusion surrounding hypnosis has worn away and now this scientific phenomenon is applauded for its many successes.

RELIEF FROM CHRONIC BACKACHE

Many sufferers of back ailments tend to be fatalistic about their problem. "The doctor said I just have to live with it," is an expression we often hear. This sort of mental reinforcement makes it difficult to convince the troubled person that a cure is possible. Negative thinkers have sensitized themselves to endure needless mental and physical anguish. Some are driven to the edge of suicide due to the excruciating pain affecting not only a specific nerve, but their entire nervous system.

Dr. William S. Kroger, in his book, *Clinical And Experimental Hypnosis*, says: "There is an 'organ language' which the body uses to voice its protest. The choice of the organ system is determined by the focal area in which the conflict occurs."

Thus, expressions such as, "carrying a load on my back," "get off my back," "pain in the ass," and "pain in the neck" all become an emotional base for localizing discomfort, which indeed may lead to pain. The more the negative expression is verbalized, the greater its power as a conditioning force. We are all influenced by choice of words and the emotional-physical impact which they deliver.

Relieving pain of psychosomatic origin begins by helping the afflicted person gain awareness of his unconscious habit of emotional reinforcement. Dr. Kroger recommends using both posthypnotic suggestion as well as teaching the patient self-hypnosis and autosuggestion. Pain removal by a hypnotherapist always requires the patient's permission, because symptom removal may cause the unaware individual to shift the symptom to another area.

After standard induction to as deep a trance level as possible, mobility is suggested in the following way. The patient is told to move the pain from its entrenched position. "See it shifting . . . drifting . . . up and down . . . then to the front . . . up through the respiratory system and, finally, breathe it out with the next outgoing breath. Expel the pain out of the body completely . . . never let it return . . ."

Some therapists suggest: "Visualize the pain as a blue mist. Picture an opening in the area of pain and, as you exhale, see the blue mist exiting out of the opening in the troubled spot." Instant removal of pain is possible, providing the subject is medium to somnambulistic. The hypnotist places his hand directly on the painful area and says, "My hand is a sponge . . . ready to soak up all your pain. You will give it to me and I will throw it away because you don't need it. Now as I count from 1 to 3, the pain is gone. . . one. . . going . . . two . . . going . . . three, take a deep breath and blow it out . . . release the pain permanently . . . three . . . going . . . going . . . all gone!"

ANOTHER VISUALIZATION

"Picture your back as twice as wide as you normally think of it . . . also twice as long. Get the feeling of wide, open spaces . . . lots of space for the muscles, nerves, shoulder blades, and vertebrae to float around in . . . wide open back . . . feel the spaciousness. Now imagine the nerves in your back branching out of the spine in knots."

The patient sees his pain in knots. Then he is told to visualize the knots unraveling, the muscles opening up no longer gripping the nerves. After he awakens, he feels free of pain. The suffering person must then be taught how to use self-hypnosis to remove the pain should it return another time.

In cases of arthritis, one of the most common sources of human agony, pain often disappears during the very first hypnosis session because arthritic pain is to a great extent a result of tension, and when the muscles are relaxed during hypnosis the pain is definitely eased. To aid in the remission of any illness, the patient is trained to envision his internal organs fighting the disease. He learns to see images of his body having overcome the ailment. The images do not have to be medically factual, as long as they are believable to the subject. Imagination is stronger than reality when belief and hope are present.

CHILDBIRTH

Patients who have experienced hypnotic anesthesia for childbirth are unanimous in their approval. Hypnosis and the use of self-hypnosis are fast assuming a dignified position in the area of obstetrics. By using these methods, a large percentage of pregnancies can be carried through the early stages of delivery without the use of sedation or anesthesia. However, in the second stage, some degree of medical analgesia is sometimes resorted to, depending upon the individual case.

Women are becoming cognizant of methods to control and relieve pelvic pain that do not depend upon noxious drugs and other such agents. Hypnosis may not ever supplant drug anesthesia; however, it can serve as an important supplement to methods already in use. There are a variety of reasons why a pregnant woman may elect to use hypnoanesthesia rather than drugs. Very often fear is the greatest motivator.

"I am terribly afraid of the pain of childbirth," said Clara Z. "When I discovered I was pregnant, I was terrified. I felt I couldn't go through with the birth. I heard about drugs they could give me, but that made me even more frightened of being unconscious. Then a friend told me about a hypnotist who helps people get rid of fears of things like flying and elevators. So I went to see him."

One of the things that convinced this young woman to use hypnosis for her delivery was that with it she could be conscious and involved in the birth process. Her anesthesia was administered by a trained hypnotist. However, many women learn the art of self-hypnosis and lessen their own pain by managing labor in a more relaxed way. The patient who chooses hypnoanesthesia must be trained in advance of delivery in the physician's office. It works best if she attends a series of sessions which act as rehearsals for the eventual birthing experience. Hypnosis works to eliminate the discomfort of labor, but does not impair the sensations and pleasant emotions of the experience. Free of pain and anxiety, the mother is fully aware and can enjoy her baby's first cry. Instead of pain, she feels the contractions merely as a tensing of the abdominal muscles.

Rhythmic breathing is an important part of this training process. Among the suggestions given are the following: "Breathe deeply as you were trained to do in your practice sessions. Concentrate on the rhythms of your breathing, the rising and falling of the lower diaphragm. As you feel a muscular contraction of labor, begin to pant in short breaths. Count the number of short breaths that you take between each contraction."

Focusing the patient's attention away from the pain and directing her thoughts into counting and breathing tend to lessen anxiety, and the sensation of pain becomes diminished. Hypnosis also reduces anxiety, speeding up the time between each stage of labor. Many obstetricians use hypnosis as the sole anesthesia in most of their cases. Dr. James A. Hall of the University of Texas Health Sciences Center in Dallas says, "Hypnosis can be coordinated with labor so that the beginning of each contraction is a signal for the patient to relax deeper into a hypnotic trance. The end of each contraction leads her to come out of the hypnotic state and communicate with her physician."

In other words, contractions and depth of hypnosis are harmonized by this method. An important postnatal hypnotic suggestion is for accelerated healing and the return to normal activity as quickly as possible and without complications. It has been found that, through the use of hypnosis and self-hypnosis, the usual moaning and crying of women in labor has been eliminated.

MENSTRUAL PAIN

Doctors tell us there is no valid explanation why some women have cramps and others don't. Sometimes doctors will tell a young woman, "Your condition might improve after you've had a baby," which isn't very practical to the single woman or the sixteen-year-old who may be suffering every month with her period. There are many prescriptions and over-the-counter painkillers that claim to offer relief from menstrual pain. However, some of these products can be dangerous, as witnessed by the fact that the Federal Drug Administration has banned several of them.

Self-hypnosis is especially effective and more practical than going to a hypnotist every month in order to prevent the recurrence of menstrual cramps. In fact, a woman can avoid the onset of cramps by giving herself the autosuggestion that she will have a normal, natural flow without discomfort.

"Glove anesthesia," which involves the focusing on numbness in the hand, works remarkably well with menstrual cramps. The person simply places the hand which has been anesthetized over the pelvic area and concentrates on transference of numbness to that area. One young woman who studied self-hypnosis with me created the following fantasy which works very well for her in removing pain from any part of her body:

"The first thing I do is relax and go into my space, my "center"— then I imagine myself shrinking into a tiny little nurse and I visualize myself inside my own body locating the source of the pain. I see it as a warm, red area. I then imagine myself placing an icepack on the pain and cooling it off."

Her visualization was simply a matter of mind over matter. I have since described the technique to other people suffering from internal pain, and they have reported back with positive results. Testimonials to the therapeutic effectiveness of self-hypnosis have become commonplace.

Skin Reflects Inner Emotions

The psychosomatic etiology of such skin disorders as eczema, alopecia areata, dermatitis, warts, psoriasis, and pruritus has long been established. Silently, spontaneously, our skin reveals inner feelings we would sometimes rather conceal. The condition of the epidermis reflects the underlying mental mood because skin and nerves are closely connected by sensitive, responsive tissue.

Because of this link, hypnotic suggestion has been able to produce various sensory effects upon the skin, such as blisters, numbness, and sensations of extreme heat or cold. The nervous system is capable of directing emotional force to concentrated areas or organs of reception. This may be why vast numbers of young people are troubled by skin eruptions at a time when they are very vulnerable to emotional upset. Just when the facial appearance is of greatest concern, the emotions reflect negative inner images. Acne is one of the most distressing skin reactions influenced by psychosomatic factors. Because at times the emotions can trigger or perpetuate this ailment, dermatologists often send people to a psychologist or hypnotist for a combined cure, mental and physical.

Many psychologists believe acne may be aggravated by a sense of in security about the approaching responsibilities of maturity. Thus, sometimes emotional adjustment proves to be more effective than medication. Hypnosis can be very helpful in creating greater awareness of this kind of problem in the patient. There have also been cases of acne clearing up quickly with the aid of a hypnotist who suggests aversion to picking at the lesions: "Any time you can think of picking at your face, you will visualize an ugly scar and stop instantly. You will then see your face becoming clearer and clearer."

One of the remarkable uses of hypnosis is in alleviating the distress of itching. Irritated thinking increased the itching feeling.

Because so many skin disorders are psychosomatic in origin they are therefore changeable. Deep neuromuscular relaxation, combined with suggestions given during the therapeutic trance, often brings speedy results. I have seen skin lesions heal before my eyes within a one-hour period of hypnosis. One of the techniques employed in the correction of acne and other skin disorders is the "mirror technique." Seeing oneself free of the unwanted ailment spurs the imagination to carry out the envisioned improvement.

Mental messages move quickly through the nerve passageways. Imagination tends to set off a physical response. We all have experienced skin reactions to our emotional feelings. Fear may cause "goose pimples" and body hairs to stand on end. Embarrassment may create a rosy blush for some, and an uncomfortable flush for others. Anxiety increases perspiration and stress often aggravates skin itching.

In cases of chronic itching in which there is no apparent physical cause, repeated verbalization aimed at symptom removal helps a great deal. Tell the hypnotized subject, "Your skin feels smooth and comfortable. See it looking perfectly clear without blemishes. Remember you have no reason to scratch. There is no itching . . . just a smooth comfortable feeling."

Suggest that the fingers are becoming very heavy, like lead, and therefore unable to scratch even if thoughts of itching do occur. Once you stop the person from picking on himself, remarkable improvement will occur in cases of psoriasis, eczema, hives, and acne. When the mind accepts a more positive attitude, physical reactions become self-protective rather than self-destructive.

EMBARRASSMENT TRIGGERS BLUSHING

The blush has long been the province of the poet, associated with the charm of innocence. Shakespeare loved the blush. Henry V, while pressing his courtship on Katherine, pleads, "Most fair Katherine, will you have me? Put off your maiden blushes . . . ." And Desdemona's father describes her ". . . of spirit so still and quiet that her motion blushed at herself."

Webster's Dictionary is clear on the subject of the emotional link involved: "Blushing . . . a reddening of the face, especially from shame, modesty, or confusion." Blushing is more than a physical reaction of blood rushing to the face. It is psychological. We blush when the inner self is unexpectedly touched by a thought which unearths a secret feeling we have tried to keep hidden. Regardless of emotional stimuli, blushing may be attractive at 14, but a nuisance at 40—especially for a man in our macho society. When young people are unable to resolve problems of stress, they become older people with hang-ups which are really hangovers from the past.

Leonard R. was a sales promoter for a cosmetics firm. Public speaking was not easy for Leonard. Throughout his youth, he had fought shyness. He diligently took all the prescribed courses, and read all the advertised books. Still, whenever he delivered a promotional spiel to an audience, he sweated profusely and his face grew red. His colleagues became accustomed to his flushes. He was always described as the man with "the ruddy complexion." Everyone seemed to accept Leonard's red face except Leonard.

"How can I stop this stupid blushing?" he asked at this first therapy session.

"A good place to start is to find out the original cause—the situation that triggered your uncomfortable feelings."

Under my guidance, he regressed and discovered the cause of his problem. Each time he made a misstatement about his product or exaggerated its worth, a sense of guilt, which he associated with lying during childhood, brought about the blushing. Regressing further into his past, Leonard remembered that, even as a small child, his mother would say, "I can always tell when Leonard is lying. God paints his face red so everyone will know."

Leonard was finally able to laugh at this recollection from his childhood. "What a silly reason for blushing during a sales promotion!"

Awareness opened his mind to the uselessness of his outgrown psychosomatic symptom of guilt. What is suitable as a reaction in childhood is seldom fitting for the mature person. Most of the problems of immaturity are due to situations where people are grown up physically, but are still thinking and feeling as children.

HIVES AND REPRESSED ANGER

Ramona L., a 42 year-old grade school teacher, broke out in huge, red welts whenever she repressed her anger. Explaining that her condition worsened whenever she felt aggravated by her students, Ramona showed the beginnings of insight into her condition. For many years, however, she had been convinced the hives resulted from food allergies.

"I used to think it was tomatoes, potatoes, strawberries, or cucumbers. I went on a rigid diet. Still, nothing helped. I even tried psychoanalysis—five years with no luck. Finally, my medical doctor suggested I call you for hypnosis."

At her first session, Ramona mentioned her addiction to tranquilizers. "It's the only way I can tolerate the wild brats I teach." In addition to the hives, her doctor suggested she be taken off tranquilizers and instructed to stick to a sensible low-calorie diet that he provided. During the middle of her third session, Ramona reached a deep trance level and we explored the source of her aggravation. To tap the warehouse of her recorded early memories, I suggested:

"Visualize the time and the situation that first caused the welts to appear. Who are you with? What is happening? Concentrate on your feelings and notice how your skin reacts."

As I spoke, I watched her arms closely. Within minutes, angry welts flared up. Though Ramona was in a deep trance, a look of amazement spread over her face. At this point, I reversed the image. "Now picture yourself completely healed. You are strolling in the country with a pleasant breeze caressing your clear skin. You look good and you feel so relaxed. Your skin is perfect."

Serenity melted the muscles of her face. I stared at her arms and said, "The welts are growing paler and smaller. The skin on your arms as well as your entire body will soon be perfect . . . the welts are growing smaller and paler . . . smaller and paler. . . ."

The hives vanished even faster than they had appeared. I discovered that Ramona was able to turn her hives on and off by focusing her mental power on a negative or positive visual image.

The impact of what had happened under hypnosis convinced Ramona she had control over her body's reactions. Now, whenever an annoying situation occurs, instead of feeling anger, she knows how to reverse her disturbing emotions. She is conditioned to smile, take three deep breaths, and think of a solution to the problem.

Two years have passed since Ramona's last visit to my office. She has been practicing self-hypnosis and autosuggestion as described elsewhere in this book. During her last telephone call, she informed me, "I have been using self-hypnosis to control my weight, improve my sleeping habits, and reduce my tensions. Also, I have been able to discontinue using tranquilizers and medication for the hives. I don't let anger get under my skin anymore," she said, (which demonstrates the high level of her awareness), "I just let it all roll off my back!"

ECZEMA AND ANXIETY

Nick D., a 29-year-old waiter, suffered from recurring eczema for eight years. Whenever the rash appeared on his hands, his employer asked him to stay home until the condition cleared up. If you are thinking maybe Nick didn't like his job, you are right. But he never dreamed there was a connection between his resentment at being in "the servant business and his breaking out in a rash. His frustrated desire to do something more suitable to his talents and ego resulted in eczema.

Nick tended to be absent-minded, often forgetting part of a customer's order. Misplacing objects in the kitchen caused the chef great annoyance and Nick was often chastised. He soon decided to study electronics in the evening. He didn't do very well as a student, finding it difficult to concentrate even though it meant getting away from being a waiter.

When I questioned him, he described himself as lacking the self-confidence to succeed at something new. "And besides," he rationalized, "I need the money I earn as a waiter to live on." Nick was trained to give himself the following autosuggestions through self-hypnosis:

"I will enjoy my work and remain relaxed. My hands will stay clear . . . no more eczema. Excellent memory . . . both as a waiter and for studies."

After four sessions of hypnosis and daily self-hypnosis with the use of a tape, Nick reported a diminishing of the eczema and an outstanding improvement in his memory. About this time, his uncle opened a restaurant and Nick became the manager, a position of authority which he enjoyed immensely. His eczema has disappeared completely.

PSORIASIS AND REJECTION

One of the most interesting case histories is that of Marcella B., a 27-year-old recreation worker in a day nursery. Though it was a hot summer day, she wore a scarf around her head, a blouse with long sleeves, and slacks to cover the lesions on her legs. Only her crusty eyebrows revealed the extent of her condition. Marcella rolled up her trouser legs and took off the bandana to show me, and said, "I've had psoriasis all my life. I've tried everything. Even psychological counselling hasn't helped me. I don't have much faith in anything. I don't think anything can help. Frankly, I'm trying hypnosis only as a last resort."

She explained with tear-filled eyes how parents of children where she worked asked her whether psoriasis was contagious. The only positive factor, she explained, was that during times when she was very relaxed the condition seemed to clear slightly.

Suggestions of relaxation, confidence, and faith were given Marcella. Although she was a resistant subject, after five or six sessions she finally reached a level deep enough for subliminal communication. I worked with her for six months, one one-hour session a week. At home, she listened to a tape recorder of positive suggestion twice a day in between her sessions with me. We were encouraged during periods when the psoriasis would completely clear up, then disappointed when the condition returned when we least expected it.

We decided to tap the deeper recesses of her mind for the earliest manifestation of the disorder. Age regression was used, followed by automatic writing.

Marcella's memory uncovered important material. Here is her story as revealed under hypnosis:

"I am 5 years old. I am at a summer camp with lots of other kids. We are in the recreation building. The boys and girls are playing a game. All the little girls put one shoe in a pile. Then the boys come in, choose one shoe, and try to match it to the right girl wearing the other shoe. Bobby got my shoe. He said, 'Oh, no, not her. I don't want her for a partner. She's too fat and ugly.'"

When Marcella came out of trance, I asked, "Do you think you were fat and ugly as a child?"

"Not really. Actually, I was a cute, little, chubby girl. But Bobby hurt my feelings and I cried hysterically. No one could console me. My parents had to take me home from the camp. I brooded about his remark for years afterward, feeling rejected. I still cry when I think about it."

"What has this to do with your psoriasis?"

"I still think of myself as fat and ugly, and feel unworthy of the attention of a nice looking guy. My bad skin keeps everyone away from me." Had she ever dated, I wondered?

"I never went out with boys in high school or college. They all shunned me, even the girls did. I had very few friends."

"How do *you* evaluate yourself?" I asked, "Say, on a scale from 1 to 10."

"At the bottom of the list—zero. I'm afraid to even look into the mirror. What I see disgusts me. I remember when I lived back home with my parents, every time I took a bath and saw my body in the mirror I had a crying fit all night."

Marcella was, in reality, a beautiful young woman. Her features were regular and delicate. Her full smile revealed perfect sparkling teeth. Though her scalp was covered with crust, her hair was thick and luxurious. Her figure was full, shapely and well-proportioned. She hid her body under loose, old-fashioned, homely clothing, anything to discourage the attention of men. Only her shoes were new and bright—perhaps a holdover from her experience as a child in summer camp.

I remember the joyful day when Marcella reported that her elbows and lower arms had completely cleared. She came in with her arms exposed in a revealing blouse. Her scalp had begun to clear. She admitted the positive results of hypnotic suggestion and within two weeks all the scales fell off. We were elated. However, a dramatic setback occurred that left Marcella feeling devastated.

She had visited her parents' home in Jersey to show them her remarkable recovery. Lo and behold, upon awakening and looking into the old bathroom mirror, she regressed back to her old memories, and noticed signs of redness returning to her legs and arms. At that moment, Marcella gained a deep awareness of the power of self-imagery. She left her parents' home feeling depressed, but felt better after discussing the connection between her emotions and her skin problem. Fortunately, she was able to remove the lesions once again through hypnosis. Six years have passed and Marcella is free of psoriasis.

REMOVAL OF WARTS

Reports from other hypnotists corroborate my own findings that 60 to 70 percent of warts cases respond positively to suggestive therapy. The deeper the hypnotic trance, the sooner one sees good results.

At 17, Mark T. had six warts on his right hand and several on his buttocks. His mother had come to me for help in solving a weight problem. During her last visit, she said, "I wonder if you can help my son. He broke out in warts when he was about 13. He may not tell you, but he also has warts on his buttocks close to the anal opening. The warts appeared soon after he was molested by a pervert while playing in the schoolyard." This case proved to be one of the strongest convincers that warts, like other skin blemishes, are closely linked to emotion and imagination. Mark was hypnotized three times and suggestions were made that the warts would diminish, then disappear and never return. His warts became smaller after the very first session. They were all gone by the third. Two years later, I called Mark to check and he reported the warts had not reappeared.

Josephine B. called me on the phone to complain she had developed warts on her hands and knees as a result of watching television. While at first this may appear preposterous, further questioning disclosed she had been watching a daytime serial sponsored by a wart remedy company. Repetitive suggestions during the commercials relating to the ugliness of warts had a reverse effect. She assumed the problem instead of the cure.

Because her warts were mentally induced, a learned condition, once Josephine relaxed she was able to unlearn the condition. After five hypnotic sessions, all the warts had dissolved. She still watches her favorite T.V. show, but knows enough about indirect hypnosis to protect herself from the harmful suggestions. Every time she sees the commercial, she tells herself, "This is not meant for me. I don't have warts and I don't want them."

The most unusual and fascinating case involving warts is that of Janie, a beautiful 16-year-old girl. Shy, lacking self-confidence, Janie behaved like a 12-year-old rather than like the young lady she was. The first time I saw her she was wearing a tee-shirt with a picture of a frog painted on it. Her habitual pose was with her head hung low, and her hands crossed and tucked into her armpits. Upon examining her hands, I saw the worst case of warts I had ever seen. They covered her fingers, wrists, and reached up toward her elbows. The right hand and arm were considerably worse than the left.

Fortunately, Janie proved to be an excellent subject, intelligent and cooperative. The first session showed slight improvement. At the second session, I decided to dig out the source of the problem. Age regression was used with verbal response.

"Why do you wear a frog on your shirt?" I asked.

"Because I love frogs. I think they're cute."

I took her back year by year, having established a signal so that when I mentioned the year when she first got the warts, she would raise her finger and then speak. Regressing to 8 years of age, Janie said, "I am playing with a frog and he just wee-weed on my hands. Everybody tells me I will get warts."

"Why do you still like frogs?" I asked.

Janie spoke in a baby voice, "I have a book and it tells how a frog turns into a prince if you treat it good."

When Janie came out of hypnosis, we talked about her relationship with boys. She was very immature for a sixteen-year-old and frightened about sex. The warts were one way of holding back her maturity. But, most important, she clung to the warts as a way of identifying herself with her imaginary prince. "I used to think that when a cute guy who looked like a prince came along, he'd recognize me by my warts and know I like frogs. I know it sounds silly but that's the way I used to feel."

Janie not only got rid of the warts, but also her misconception that life was based on fairy tales. Now she can understand herself, and her feelings toward the opposite sex much better.

GROUP THERAPY AND WARTS

Several adults who were attending group hypnosis for other purposes such as weight reduction and smoking also had warts and skin blemishes. Warts disappeared after multiple suggestions that related to the group's overall program. While some warts took longer to diminish and required reinforcement at home through self-hypnosis, all warts and skin blemishes vanished eventually.

There are numerous cases of warts being removed through suggestion without using hypnosis. As a child, an elderly aunt told me, "Prick the largest wart with a pin and then hide the pin where no one can find it." I did this and three warts disappeared miraculously overnight. Perhaps this was the beginning of my staunch belief in the power of suggestion. I know now that what the mind gives, it can also take away. My aunt had indirectly hypnotized me as a child, preconditioning me to expect good results. A dependable law of the mind is that anticipation brings its own reflection. *Conceive, believe, and you will achieve.*

SKIN STIGMATA—PASSION AND PUNISHMENT

The term *stigmata* is derived from the early Greek language and originally referred to the branding with hot irons of captured or fugitive slaves. After the crucifixion of Christ, the term stigmata took on a special meaning. Religious writers describe stigmata as the reproduction of the wounds that Christ suffered on the cross upon the body of a worshipper. Many of the authenticated cases involve saints, monks, nuns, and other ascetics. The most famous case of stigmata is that of St. Francis of Assisi. When he died in 1226, his followers examined his body and were amazed to discover that, in addition to the wounds, he bore fleshy formations that looked like nails. The *miracle* of St. Francis had great impact and after his death there was a dramatic increase in the number of reported cases of stigmata. Are stigmata caused by a miracle or by man's imagination?

Even the church leadership is beginning to wonder. The Catholic World Dictionary warns, ". . . care must be taken that the stigmata are real and due to genuine holiness and not self-deception or the result of mental suggestion." One thing seems certain; other kinds of symptoms may be seen for some time prior to the appearance of the overt wounds. All stigmatized people on record give evidence of mental and emotional anguish before the actual physical demonstration takes place. The unresolved question is this: if stigmata are regarded as a miracle, why is it that an hysterical emotional condition is a necessary prerequisite for the onset of the phenomenon?

It is also interesting to note that the nature of the wounds varies from one individual to another. Depending on the person's visual conception, the shape of the punctures might be square, round or oblong. There may be a great deal of pain and/or bleeding—or none at all. An explanation for the wide variability may be found in the fact that in many cases the stigmatists tend to reproduce the kinds of wounds found on a particular crucifix which they have seen. There have also been cases where stigmata appear and disappear during repetition of passionate prayers. *The conditioning effect of prayer is akin to autosuggestion and the state of meditative contemplation is similar to self-hypnosis.* These factors point to a strong possibility that stigmata may be psychosomatic in origin.

Stigmata are not confined to the Christian religion alone. Dr. Von Arnhard, a writer on religious history, speaks of frequent stigmata found among Moslem ascetics who immerse themselves in the sacred contemplation of the life of Mohammed. These stigmatics respond to their inner images and emotional stress by reflecting the wounds suffered by Mohammed during the battle for the spread of his faith. Instances of spontaneous stigmata among other religious sects have also been reported. The case that I will now describe is that of a modern young Jewish man of 24 who strongly identified with the agony of Christ.

I met Joseph during my most recent visit to London, when I was teaching self-hypnosis to a group of young people as an alternative to drug addiction. One of the students referred to him as "a Jesus freak." He called himself Joseph St. John, and considered himself a Latter-day saint. Joseph was tall, thin, and looked much older than his years because of the expression of pain etched into the lines of his face. A long, white robe reached to the tops of the sandals that covered his bony feet. His hair flowed down his back, as did his beard over his chest. Joseph could have stepped into a Cecil B. DeMille epic and played the part of Jesus without the help of a speck of makeup. As he stood facing me, he fingered a heavy, baroque cross, which hung from a chain around his waist.

A teenage girl, Lynn, had spoken to me about Joseph the night before. Now they both stood there—she, embarrassed; he, distrustful. She explained, Joseph and I live together. Although we love each other and sleep in the same bed, our relationship is just spiritual. Joseph is sexless. There have been times when I try to arouse him, but he turns away from me. He claims he is celibate because of his religious feelings, but I know something physical is worrying him. He gets terrible pains in his sex organs. Once when he started to warm up to me, he actually went into convulsions of agony. His hands even swelled up one time when he gave me a massage."

I asked Joseph if he had been to see a medical doctor and he assured me that he had had a complete physical examination and the doctor told him there was no organic cause for his pain. At my urging, Joseph had his doctor call me, and in the course of the conversation, he suggested I try hypnosis. I knew that in order for hypnosis to prove effective, Joseph would have to relinquish his need to suffer, that he would have to free himself of the guilt-punishment syndrome. And, most important, he would have to give up his identification with Christ's suffering on the cross.

Joseph responded well to testing for suggestibility and concentration and proved to be an excellent subject for hypnosis. After four sessions, the swelling in his hands was noticeably diminished and the genital pain had lessened. However, he and I both knew that there was a deeper cause of his distress. With his doctor's permission, I decided it would be helpful to regress him to the first time he felt genital pain in order to alleviate triggering his painful flare-ups.

Since my time in London was limited, I arranged to see Joseph every day for one hour. By the second week, he was ready to turn his inner telescope backward into time. We arranged for him to signal me when I mentioned the age where the problem started. When I counted back to 13, he raised his hand. I placed a large writing pad in his lap and handed him a pen.

"Write whatever comes to mind. Tell the truth. The truth will set you free of pain. Explain how your problem got started." With eyes closed and deep in hypnotic trance he wrote: My real name is Joseph P. I live in Great Neck, Long Island. I am in my 13th year and my parents are upset. I am supposed to be confirmed and have my Bar Mitzvah, but I was never circumcised because I was a sickly baby and that's why they put it off. Now my mother tells me I have to have my tonsils out, but while I'm unconscious the doctor circumcises me instead.

While he wrote, I repeated in a monotone: "You are healthy. You are normal. There is no reason for pain; therefore, you feel no pain."

He paused at one point and drew a cross and wrote under it: "My mother crucified me and castrated me."

I questioned him about the redness and swelling of his hands.

He answered, "Before I was circumcised, I masturbated. My mother used to make remarks about my dirtying the sheets."

"When did you start to identify with Christ?"

"While I was still in the United States. I told my parents I had renounced the Jewish religion. I felt my real religion was to admit my pain to be the pain Jesus suffered for mankind."

"Why are you celibate?"

"I have given up the love of flesh for the love of God."

"What kind of a person were you before you identified with Christ, when you were Joseph P.?"

"An honor student in art college. I had a one-man exhibition a gallery at the age of 16."

I suggested he had two choices: He could continue to suffer pain in a life of celibacy without a woman's love and other fulfillment, or he could give up his painful, martyred self-image and live life as Joseph P., a young, talented artist. Joseph finally decided to forfeit the pain. After almost two months of daily hypnotherapy during which time he also listened to conditioning tapes at home, he finally made the changeover. I often wonder how much of human sexual dysfunction originates from self-denial and stigmatic punishment.

One happy day, Joseph arrived at my hotel and I hardly knew him. He wore a plaid shirt and leans instead of his usual religious costume. His hair and beard were neatly trimmed. Not only had his facial expression changed, but even his voice was different. His girl-friend, Lynn, was with him. They brought me gifts and a painting Joseph had done to express his feeling after his first sexual experience without pain. At this moment the picture hangs over my typewriter. It is filled with both religious and sexual symbols, proof that the two are often intertwined.

I have since learned that Joseph and his girlfriend, Lynn, are back in the United States and that he has made contact with his parents. It is hoped that a greater awareness and closer communication has developed among them all.

Sexual Dysfunction and Hypnosis

Larry S., 33, had a high sex drive and a low self-image. While women aroused him to the point of frenzy, he always ended up feeling frustrated. Fearing criticism, ridicule, and ultimate rejection, he resorted to masturbation to the exclusion of female companionship.

When Nancy came to work in his office, Larry, a bookkeeper, had difficulty keeping his mind on any figures other than Nancy's. Still, he lacked the courage to ask her for a date. Instead, after staring at her all day, he'd return to his apartment at night and give in to his only sexual release, thereby satisfying himself. Having become conditioned to the sensation of his own hand, on the rare occasions when Larry had attempted sex with a woman, his overanxiety caused him to lose control. Even so, he decided to try one more time.

One day, he mustered his courage and asked Nancy, "How about having dinner with me tonight?"

"I'd love to," she said, wondering what had taken him so long.

They spent an enjoyable evening together, until the moment of truth came. Nancy, being a warm-blooded girl, invited Larry to her apartment. As the elevator went up, his libido went down. He wondered and worried: "Will I be able to follow through? Will I be able to hold an erection long enough to satisfy her?" In wondering and worrying, Larry predicted his own downfall. Of course he did not perform adequately. All self-predictions come true. It is impossible to succeed if you expect to fail.

UNDERSTANDING HUMAN SEXUALITY

Sexual fulfillment is composed of an interweave of emotional, mental and physical responses—in that order. On this, most experts agree. Psychological factors precede physical manifestations. Therefore, it is only natural that hypnosis should play an increasingly positive role in the correction of such problems through mental persuasion. The inability to function seldom begins in the flesh but rather in the flash of images in the mind. The "fantasy of failure" takes over.

We perceive our bodies in three ways
1. What we are taught in childhood
2. What we imagine through fantasy
3. What we feel through our senses

Too often, we have been conditioned to view our sexual flesh as less than perfect. Because of this we have to use corrective imagery and sensory awakening to restore proper feeling and function. Hypnosis trains the patient to change his inner view and explore his real feeling. Negative memories, no matter how distant in the past, tend to lower pleasurable sensation because of the extreme vulnerability of sexual tissue to thought. In no area of human function is response to thought so immediate.

It is the responsibility of the therapist to teach the subject how to convert negative repressive images into positive, releasing ones. After training the subject to overcome his or her inadequacies, self-hypnosis should be taught, so that the subject can remain in control at all times. Suggestions and techniques are then applied during actual sexual experiences.

The variety of psychogenic sexual disorders which respond to hypnotic suggestion include:

Male Problems	*Female Problems*
Premature ejaculation	Disinterest, analgesia
Inability to get an erection	Clitoral exclusivity
Fetishes (fur, leather, etc.)	Inability to reach orgasm
Fear of penetration of vagina	Fear of pregnancy

In addition to the problems peculiar to gender, there are also some that affect both men and women. Both need to develop better sexual communication in order to prolong and intensify the pleasurable experience of intercourse.

SEX PROBLEMS WHICH AFFECT BOTH GENDERS

Overactive or Underactive Sex Drive
Inhibition, Anxiety, Sense of Guilt
Fixation on (or Rejection of) Masturbation
Disgust and Aversion to Oral Sex
Compulsive Promiscuity, Absence of Emotion
Latent Homosexual Desires, Transvestism

First, it should be noted that both men and women have problems functioning sexually sometimes. It usually happens when the mind interferes, thinking in ways that cause feelings of insecurity. When a man is trying too hard to impress a woman with his prowess, or a woman is worrying about her looks or whether she will become pregnant, the mind shuts off feeling.

I would like to draw an analogy between the state of consciousness experienced during sex and that which occurs during hypnosis itself. In both instances, there is an intensity of mental concentration combined with physical relaxation. When either is missing in lovemaking or in meditation, we remain in *beta*, which interferes with the free flow of fantasy. And without fantasy we cannot exclude environmental intrusions.

It is also important to know that there are physical factors that can cause sexual dysfunction. These include diabetes, obesity, drinking, and the use of assorted drugs prescribed for high blood pressure and depression. The most common cause of sexual problems, however, is psychological: the expectation of failure. The pianist who thinks about his fingers too much finds that by the time of the concert he has stiffened up. The skater who worries about falling takes an unplanned slide.

Some people silently tell themselves, "I can't." But inside every "I can't" person is an "I can." Too many people give up on themselves in despair.

LACK OF SEXUAL CONFIDENCE

Charles K. arrived late for his appointment and apologized profusely. He explained that he felt great embarrassment in discussing his sexual problem with a woman therapist. Why then, I wondered, had he chosen me?

"I figure that if I can talk about it with you, maybe it will help me get over being so nervous with other women." His face was flushed and his hands were restless. Charles responded to routine questions haltingly, as if he was carefully considering his answers before taking a chance on offending me. I asked about his childhood.

"What I remember as most painful is being teased and ridiculed about my nose, the way it sticks out at a funny angle."

Charles turned to show me his profile. I thought to myself, "A little pointed, but so what? Doesn't look too unusual. . . ." Out loud, I said, "Your nose seems to suit your face. It may have seemed too large when you were a child, but obviously you grew up to fit the nose. After all, nobody's perfect. A bit of difference makes each of us distinctive and more interesting."

He was not placated. "My father used to call me anteater! And my sister nicknamed me 'frankfurter nose.' Some of my close friends still call me Frank instead of Charles. I know my family didn't mean to be cruel, but by the time I was fifteen I had a bad inferiority complex. I was convinced girls were laughing at my nose every time I heard someone giggle."

Charles nervously avoided answering direct questions about his sexual difficulties. Finally, in answer to my direct question, "How has your nose affected your sex life?" Charles lowered his eyes and said, "Well, I'm 28 years old and I'm still afraid to ask a girl to go out with me. I'm especially worried about talking to strange women. Even when I know them, like I do my sister's friends, I still feel they might say something nasty about the way I look."

As mentioned above, therapists often find that hang-ups are really hangovers from past negative conditioning. Hang-ups, like hangovers, can be eliminated by removing the source of the problem. Just as negative self-images are learned, so can they be unlearned and a better sense of self established. I explained to Charles that before he could feel confident about a woman liking him, he would have to begin by liking himself. He had two choices as far as his nose was concerned: he could learn to live with it or have some plastic surgery. Under hypnosis he wrote, "Love me. Love my nose." Charles was developing a sense of awareness. He began to realize that a sense of self-worth doesn't depend on the size of one's nose or the size of one's penis or the size of one's breasts. Rather, it stems from how you feel about each part of yourself, and whether you accept or reject the total image.

A similar case of low self-esteem was that of Iris D., a beautiful young woman who was self-conscious about her breasts. Although she had worked professionally as a high-fashion model, her experiences in intimate relationships had convinced her:

"I'm just not sexy. I'm a turn-off. Men have told me that I'm built like a boy. Sure, the faggy clothes designers love my body, but the guy I want tells me to get implants."

Iris didn't get silicone implants. She decided to get a new boy friend who likes her just the way she is.

After many years of working as a sex therapist using hypnotic methods to help my clients, I have heard every kind of cop-out for sexual malfunction.

"I'm losing my hair. Women like men with hair." Nonsense. Some of the world's greatest lovers have been hairless or balding.

"My teeth are crooked. I have a lousy smile." So what? Good-looking teeth are often made by a dentist. There are many balding, crooked-toothed people with pointed noses who have good sex and enjoy living. They simply see themselves as worthy of a loving relationship.

FEMALE ORGASM

Sadie S., 26, though married five years, had never reached orgasm. Before long, both Sadie and her marriage deteriorated. Her husband, Alex, began to stay out late with the "boys." When she confronted him, he complained, "It's your fault. It's that you don't have any interest in sex. You should go talk to your doctor about it."

Sadie took his advice and her gynecologist proposed hypnosis when he could discover no organic reason for her disinterest in sexual intercourse. After ten sessions of private hypnotherapy, she finally achieved the ability to respond to the point of climax. Her marriage is now stabilized, and instead of going out with the boys, Alex invites the boys to his home to meet his wife, who has a new attitude not only about her sexual self but also about her own appearance.

Sadie was so delighted with the results she sent her sister, Rose, who had similar problems, to me. Rose complained that sex was an ordeal. She not only could not reach an orgasm, but felt pain upon penetration. I explained that this was a result of her tension and not because of the size of her vagina.

"I guess that's true because I gave birth four times and one of my babies weighed almost ten pounds."

In probing into the reasons both Sadie and her sister Rose resisted sexual pleasure, we discovered that their upbringing had inhibited their normal reflexes. They were unable to "lean back, relax, and enjoy it." However, now that her sister Sadie had achieved orgasm, Rose was already ready for good results. And because positive expectations bring their own rewards, results were speedier with Rose. After just four sessions, she reported improvement to the point of clitoral orgasm and was still practicing her posthypnotic suggestions for total orgasm.

Here are the suggestions which worked well for the sisters Sadie and Rose: "Relax and allow pleasant feelings to flow. Sex is healthy and proper. Nothing to be ashamed of. More and more sensation with each sexual experience. Easy orgasm without straining. Better each time." They were instructed while under hypnotic trance to practice self-hypnosis regularly, especially before sexual intercourse, as a means of preparing the mind and the nervous system for a pleasant experience.

AVOIDANCE OF SEX

One of the most common difficulties underlying sexual inadequacy in both male and female are feelings of fatigue, sometimes real, sometimes imagined. We have heard the proverbial jokes about woman who are perpetually tired or complain of a headache. These days, this kind of an excuse is equally common among men. Weariness often has a common origin—fear of failure to satisfy or be satisfied. Some people become mentally exhausted just thinking about sex. Behind the exhaustion is the concept of sex being a burden rather than a source of joy.

In the case of nonresponsive women, fear of sex may be complex. Fear of pain, penetration, and pregnancy head the list. There are also fears relating to attractiveness and possible rejection because of imperfections such as small breasts. Some women are so embarrassed by overt sexuality that they suppress sensual urges and live their lives with tremendous amounts of residual tension, which ultimately results in a variety of physical ailments. Pelvic congestion is not peculiar to the female. Behind a man's complaint of feeling too tired may also lie a repression of fears.

One of the great fears which plague men is the fear of failure to perform adequately, which for many means the inability to get an erection or to sustain the erection long enough to satisfy his mate.

Without confronting and correcting the problem, many couples develop a hidden hostility toward each other which spreads into the rest of their life. Intercourse for them becomes a battle rather than an exhilarating experience of love.

OVERWEIGHT AND SEXUAL INHIBITION

Remember Florence, the overweight wife? Her real problem wasn't her appetite; underneath her constant gorging lay a deeper sense of emptiness. She felt unloved and unlovable. The cold fact was that she couldn't warm up to her husband's sexual advance. While he complained of her "frigidity," she complained of his lack of emotional feeling for her. Meanwhile, her disappointed husband kept struggling and failing to sexually arouse her. Florence was far from frigid. Her sexual potential for pleasure was simply lying dormant, waiting to be awakened.

Florence had fallen into a pattern familiar to many overweight women, one of accommodating without participating. Lack of spontaneity and sensuous involvement turns women into spectators, detached from their own antics. Sometimes sex amuses them, but more often it bores them. As bystanders, they become strangers to themselves and their sexual needs. Florence was one of these women, afraid of partaking in the exchange of pleasurable feeling. A sense of unworthiness because of her weight stood between her and the intimacy she so badly needed. She continued to suffer from self-perpetuating, psychic masochism, unable to surrender to pleasurable sexual sensation.

Florence had fallen into the habit of being totally inactive, both during foreplay and intercourse. "I would just lay there and let him do his thing." Later Florence would learn that inactivity suppresses sexual feeling, while active involvement spurs orgasmic sensation. She would discover through hypnotherapy that sex is more than physical. Later she would learn to correlate sensual and emotional pleasure, but now Florence was like a young, innocent child. She longed to be pleased, but was unable to permit herself to relax and enjoy intimacy. She used her obesity as a shield of armor to keep her from becoming really close to her husband. Invariably, after a disappointing sexual experience, she would steal out of bed, and quickly and quietly devour everything she could find that was edible.

"Once I ate a whole loaf of bread and two jars of peanut butter at one sitting," she confessed, "and I wasn't even hungry that night."

After Florence lost the excess weight, she also lost her sexual inhibitions. Her hunger for food was transferred into a hunger for sexual/ emotional closeness. Her center of pleasure had moved from oral gratification to the sexual gratification of maturity. As she became more confident in her body, she developed stronger sexual feeling and, after several months of therapy, finally reported that she was able to achieve orgasm. "I can enjoy sex in any position. I'm not ashamed to get on top, which used to upset me because I felt so enormous."

However, improvement didn't just happen. Florence worked at it diligently. Most people find that when they lose some weight, even five or ten pounds, there is a definite improvement in their sexual energy. While all fat people do not necessarily have a sexual problem, over-weight definitely interferes with mobility and the sexual self-image. The middleage spread doesn't just happen to women. A man spreads, too. When he does, straining for intercourse with an overtaxed, sometimes overfull stomach can strain the heart, and cause other serious physical problems.

THE INADEQUATE MALE

Tolstoy said, "Man survives earthquakes, epidemics, the horrors of disease and all the agonies of the soul, but for all time his most torment-ing tragedy has been, is, and will be—the tragedy of the bedroom.

Sexual deprivation and malfunction are habits that are learned. As such, they can be unlearned, and self-fulfilling habits can replace them. Some people go through their lives without sexual fulfillment because their relationships with others is fraught with nervous tension and ex-pectations of defeat.

The need for self-actualization is basic and, without a satisfying sex life, one is never totally fulfilled emotionally or physically.

Take the case of Murray A. Murray was 43 years old and a wid-ower. He married young, and his only child, a daughter, was 21. She soon left home and became a wife. Murray, a successful businessman, traveled all over the world, then returned to his palatial home alone. This was difficult for Murray because he did not enjoy being a loner. Women interested him, but though he made attempts at attracting them, it was more talk than action. His conversations never culminated in pillow-talk. When a woman hinted at sex, or showed too much warmth, Murray cooled off. He made excuses to avoid sex, pleading he had to leave for an appointment, promising to call again. But he never kept his promises. Though sexually inclined and sexually deprived, he fled the confrontation. Why was Murray avoiding a successful relationship with a woman?

Murray was short, stout, and insecure. Alongside his bulging wallet dangled a miniscule penis. Afraid he could not satisfy a woman, he wasn't going to take the chance of being humiliated and rejected. When it came right down to it, Murray felt he'd never make the grade, so why even attempt it and be insulted?

When Murray came to me for help, he admitted he hadn't been to bed with a woman for six years, ever since his wife had died. "Life is passing me by," he complained. "Without sex, I don't feel like a man." Murray was miserable, unhappy, lonely. After six months of reconditioning, Murray's confidence increased. During a group session, he began to notice Marion. Marion had the bad habit of being too aggressive toward men. Luckily, Murray needed some of her outgoing personality in order to balance his lack of confidence.

One night, Marion sought him out after the group therapy session. She invited him to a party and taught him to dance. She drew him out, humored him and, before long, they were attuned to one another. Marion saw substance in Murray, recognized qualities she liked in a man, and his money wasn't bad, either. With kindness, gentleness, and patience, she bolstered his ego and built his confidence. His insecurities dissolved in her warmth, and Murray became a total person again. It is interesting to note that the small size of Murray's penis turned out to be an asset. Marion's reason for hypnotherapy was vaginismus, which made penetration difficult.

ACCEPTING RESPONSIBILITY FOR SEXUAL HANG-UPS

Blaming others is a surefire way to hang on to hang-ups. Only by admitting a problem exists and accepting responsibility for it can the remake job be done. Positive suggestion under hypnosis is a powerful tool for reshaping sexual reflexes. Hypnosis brings mind-control through thought-patrol. With it, you can lift your libido as high and as wide as your imagination will allow. Sexual satisfaction is self-cultivated, but for some the link between expectation and experience has never been established. Such people need to be taught by the therapist that the most erotic part of their sexual apparatus is the mind.

The mind has greater power than all the drug, alcohol, and marijuana in the world. Those who learn mind-mastery over their bodies can reach unimagined heights of ecstasy. The basic reason that hypnosis has proved to be so dramatically useful in solving sexual problems is that both hypnosis and sexual intercourse take place in an altered state of consciousness called *alpha-theta*. Sexual foreplay requires the same level of concentrated thought as the hyponoidal trance. Sexual intercourse leading to orgasm requires a depth of focused attention similar to that required for a deep hypnotic trance. Because of this correlation, when you train the brain to enter hypnosis, you are also preparing the subject to function better sexually.

For the man who lacks sustaining power and the woman who has difficulty reaching a climax, the effects of hypnosis seem miraculous. It is the difference between chance and choice. You can choose to improve upon mediocre sex and raise fulfillment to a new dimension. If the man is too fast, hypnosis slows him down. If the woman is too slow, hypnosis speeds her up.

Some people fall into the self-defeating trap of blaming their sexual problems on their mates. Janet F., attractive and intelligent, complained about her husband, "He is warped. His sexual desires are brutal, unnatural."

Janet had undergone five years of psychotherapy with some slight improvement. However, she still suffered from anxiety, was confused, and unable to cope with a marital relationship. After questioning her in some detail about her husband's sexual behavior, I discovered that his so-called "brutal, unnatural desires" were for oral stimulation. She felt oral sex was degrading and an indication that her husband looked down upon her.

"He treats me like I'm a hooker or some bimbo he picked up in a bar. He uses four letter words and that turns me off. I want to be talked to with respect."

After conditioning Janet to a deep level of hypnosis, she revealed an insecure childhood with parents who were not only cold to each other but indifferent and insulting to her.

"They were always telling me I would never amount to anything. They said I was stupid. When I would dress up for a date they would say 'you have too much makeup on. You look like a hooker.' My father once said, 'you're a bum just like your mother.' He would accuse me of chasing men, call me worthless, sinful."

Janet, like so many other young people, carried out her parents' negative prophecy. When she was 17, she ran away from home and found a job in a massage parlor. After a period of drug use and prostitution, she broke away and landed a job in a department store as a sales clerk. It was here that she met her future husband whom she married on her twenty-first birthday. Now, after five years and the birth of a son, the marriage was falling apart and so was Janet.

After six sessions, she reached a somnambulistic level and was regressed. The following exchange occurred:

Hypnotist: "You are going back in time. You are now 26 . . . going back further . . . now 25 . . . feeling fine as you go back in time . . . 24, everything very clear, 23 . . . further back, 20 . . . you are getting there . . . 18 . . . you are there 17 . . . now, concentrate . . . tell me where are you and what are you doing?"

Janet became very agitated. This was the year when she had run away from home. Tears ran down her cheeks, although her body remained perfectly still. She was crying while in trance. I considered bringing her out of trance, but decided instead to comfort her at the level she was in. I softly stroked her shoulder and whispered that this would all soon be gone and everything would be wonderful, without problems. Then suggestions were made that she would be able to re-experience leaving home without being unduly upset emotionally.

"See your past as if you were watching a T.V. show with a flash-back that is interesting but not disturbing." Reassured, she became calm and was guided into a deeper stage of revivification. She began to speak out loud at my suggestion.

"I've made up my face like a slut, the way they always say I am. Too much lipstick and mascara and my hair is puffed up. Tight sweater to show my bust. Tight skirt to show my rear end. A man named Tom is waiting down the street. He's going to give me a job in a massage parlor. So what . . . everybody says I'm bad anyway."

When Janet was aroused from the trance, suggestions were given that she would view the regression as a valuable experience in clarifying her past and bringing her an awareness of the causes behind her present behavior. She was greatly relieved, saying, "Well, I understand what was wrong with my parents now. They were using me because of their own hang-ups. And I also understand what I'm so uptight about my husband wanting oral sex. It reminds me of a time in my life I would like to forget."

Janet and her husband had several sessions of joint marital counseling with me. During this time, I taught them self-hypnosis techniques for mutually satisfactory sexual intercourse.

SEX OFFENDERS

According to official reports one out of every six children is periodically sexually molested. This figure does not include the vast numbers of unreported incidences.

Almost every day the media shocks us with new cases of child molestation. Is this a phenomenon of our troubled times or has this problem always existed? If we accept the scientific fact that every human act has a root and reason, we must assume that sexual child abuse happened in the past and is handed down from one generation to the next. The following case illustrates how this chain reaction works.

Derek, a thirty-five-year-old pool maintenance man described his problem as "a compulsion to play with small children." He was eager to convince me that he had never acted out his fantasy. "I work around pools and see these cute little kids in their bathing suits, sometimes nude, and it turns me on. I want to pick them up and fondle them but I resist the urge." Under questioning he described how he masturbated while thinking about the children. Although he protested his innocence, he did agree to submit to hypnosis so that he might discover the cause of his obsessiveness. After several sessions he was able to achieve a sonambulist state in which I could induce a directed dream. I suggested that he was able to speak and answer my questions and he did so without restraint.

In a trance level he revealed what he had consciously concealed— even from himself. He had been arrested in his early twenties for sexually abusing his step-children. (When a subject reaches this ultra-depth, they tend to tell the whole truth in spite of themselves, because fears of retribution are set aside.) This revelation led to my inviting his ex-wife to his next therapy session which proved to be a turning point in his recovery. She described him as "acting like a baby, very dependent and wimpy." She also said that he had an inordinate passion for playing with her breasts and suckling on them even when sex was not involved. What she was describing was a man who had remained fixated in his infantile stage of development. What did this have to do with his urge to fondle children? Hypnotic exploration provided the answer to this question that has confounded so many investigators.

After the initial induction procedure, the technique of 'age regression' was employed. His ability to recollect events in his childhood filled in the missing gaps. Here is his verbatim response while under a deep trance level:

"My mother told me she wanted to throw me out the window because I cried too much. She didn't want to breast feed me. My father drank and finally left us when I was 3 yrs old. My mother had a boyfriend who brought toys and played with my private parts while he masturbated. I looked forward to the attention. Then he split with my mother and I missed him."

Adults who enjoy sex-play with children frequently have been denied sufficient demonstrative affection. They carry with them a residual need for sensual body contact. In the normal child this skin to skin affirmation of love is supplied by the mother in infancy during nursing, bathing and play-time.

When the rejected child becomes an adult, the repressed yearning is still there. However, now the roles are reversed. The physically grown man is still a child emotionally and tries to fill the gap of child-adult affection.

Derek and I agreed that his greatest need was to become mature and to see himself as a worthy, valuable person.

After six months of weekly hypnotherapy sessions, Derek has been de-conditioned (brain-washed, as he calls it) from his inappropriate, anti-social behavior toward children. He is presently involved with a woman who seems right for him. She is very attentive and affectionate and accepts him as a person who needs more demonstrative love than most other people.

In cases of antisocial sexual behavior such as child abuse, incest, and rape, hypnosis holds out new hope of eliminating the problem at its source. There have been reports by state corrections officials in Connecticut who have been treating sex offenders with hypnotism combined with electric shock treatment. Because shock techniques are considered controversial, they are only used in extreme cases. However, to date, the results have been extremely positive, without any detrimental side effects. Commissioner of Prisons John R. Manson was quoted as saying: "Not one of the many convicts treated in the state program has so far been recharged with repeating further sex offenses." The program was set up for hardened sexual offenders with records of repeated attacks upon children.

When asked to describe the hypnosis-shock program, state officials said that only volunteers participated. The inmates were first hypnotized and then given suggestions of negative aversion in relation to sexual thoughts about children. They were then given positive suggestions to respond to thoughts about mature women. They were shown slides of nude women and children. When they watched the slides of women, the voice of the hypnotists suggested normal response and feelings of arousal in the future under the proper circumstances. However, when a child's picture was flashed on the screen, the convicts received an electric shock in the genital area. The shock was startling and unpleasant but not so severe enough to do physical damage.

The inmates were then hypnotized again, both in private and in group, and put through an imaginary sexual experience with a child. During the visualization, fear and horror were evoked and emotions of shame, guilt and disgrace were emphasized. The process was repeated until the inmate could no longer associate sexual pleasure with children because his reflexes had been reversed.

Hypnotherapy is also used to trace events back to the original root of the problem. Regression to childhood may be employed and, in several cases, the therapist has discovered that similar offenses had been committed against the prisoner when he was a child. A mental cleansing procedure takes place along with reeducation aimed toward desensitizing the molester away from children. He is then sensitized to respond normally to mature females when he leaves the prison.

Once the disturbed person learns hypnotic principles, he begins to avoid the feedback of unwanted reflexes. Eventually the convicts are taught how to do self-hypnosis and eliminate the troublesome signals permanently. The conditioned patterns which caused the difficulty in the first place are replaced by a better frame of reference.

HYPNOSIS FREES ACCUSED

In Philadelphia, a witness under hypnosis corroborated clues leading to the arrest of a 36-year-old plumber suspected of being the "jogging rapist." William Cray was charged with seven counts of rape and ten attempted rapes. Police say Gray jogged up to young girls, asked them the time, and then assaulted them. After an extended period of searching, police were unable to track down the suspect. Then one day, a woman walking a dog heard a 16-year-old girl scream. She then saw a man jump over a hedge and flee in a car. After being hypnotized, the witness was able to fill in a precise description of the man, what he was wearing, and the car in which he fled.

A major problem facing attorneys today is that people can't remember what they have seen and become emotionally disturbed when questioned. Defense Attorney Douglas Combs, who practices in Kansas City, described how a poorly educated Mexican-American, Jesse Flores, was cleared of rape and murder charges through hypnotic techniques. Attorney Combs stated the client was charged in the death of Margarita Haro, a 17-year-old girl. "The evidence was overwhelming, a defense attorney's nightmare."

The state alleged that the teenager, an acquaintance of Flores, drove off with Flores after an argument with her mother, who opposed the relationship. Three days later, Margarita's body was found in a roadside ditch. An autopsy showed she died of a skull fracture. Flores claimed he didn't kill the girl. He was very nervous and spoke with difficulty. Much of what he said was incoherent, rambling, and emotional. His attempts to explain made him appear guilty. Combs enlisted a clinical psychologist who used hypnosis to interview Flores in his jail cell. The psychologist recorded the interview on video tape so it could be studied by the attorneys.

"At the conclusion, we had the missing details we needed to reconstruct what really happened," said Combs. "It turned out there was no commission of a crime." The girl had fallen or jumped from Flores' car. Flores stopped and found the girl was breathing. He then placed her in his car, intending to take her home to her mother. On the way, be realized she was bleeding and he removed some of her clothing to see how badly she was injured. Flores then panicked and, afraid of facing the girl's mother, left the girl and ran off. When the District Attorney viewed the tape, he ordered a polygraph test which backed up the statements Flores had made under hypnosis. The judge then dismissed all charges against Flores and he was freed.

HOMOSEXUAL TO HETEROSEXUAL AND VICE VERSA

According to the Masters and Johnson survey and the Kinsey Report, there are more heterosexuals repressing homosexuality than the other way around. Sexual confusion and misconception mirrors the confused world around us. Most homosexuals prefer their choice of life-style and have no intention of changing. There are some isolated cases, however, in which a homosexual may decide to become a heterosexual. Contrary to popular misconception, this is entirely possible through hypnotherapy. The following case, while not typical of homosexuals in general, illustrates the power of the mind in determining the nature of one individual's sexual activity.

Hollis G., an actor, 28 years of age, wanted to give up his homosexual life-style, "settle down, marry, and have children." He appeared sincere and well-motivated, and in the initial stages of therapy quickly gained insight into the origin of his sexual behavior. He didn't believe he was born to be homosexual. In fact, he was one of the rare homosexuals who felt uncomfortable as a nonconformist.

After six months of biweekly sessions, Hollis developed an aversion

for all sex and remained celibate for several months. Then, for a period
of weeks he lived a bisexual life-style which culminated in the woman
winning out, and he settled down for six months in a devoted heterosexual relationship. He reported his success to me and told me of his
plans for marriage. His behavior at this point indicated a complete
reversal in sexual activity. An excellent subject, Hollis produced remarkable examples of automatic drawing and self-directed dreams. There
was recurring theme in his dreams and fantasies that indicated a highly
critical attitude toward his intended wife. In speaking of her in a conscious state, his reports were glowing; however, after periods of self-
hypnosis he would report that he was troubled by anger, only toward his
fiancee, but also toward his mother and sister. One day, while in trance,
he spontaneously regressed to the age of seven. When he came out of
the trance he told his story.

"At the age of seven, I had a close friendship with the boy next
door. We really loved each other." Hollis became very emotional as he
recalled his childhood feelings. "His name was Wally and we used to
play around sexually. Nothing much. Just touching and measuring our
penises to see who was bigger. My sister was watching us from the
closet where she deliberately hid. She told my mother, who banished
Wally from the house. I was never allowed to speak to him again."

In spite of the anger Hollis felt toward his sister and mother, he gained
a great deal of awareness from the recall of this experience. He was
most determined to break with his homosexual past and marry his fiancee. Hollis persisted until he finally believed that his homosexual behavior was symptomatic of a deeply rooted neurosis that could be traced
to his early relationship with his sister and mother. Because he believed
this to be true, it was true for him. He believed that his was an acquired
behavior resulting from psychological rather than physical causes. Added
to this was a strong religious need to be accepted by his church members.

Hollis and his girl were married in a church wedding and soon after
she became pregnant. At last report, they had been married for four
years and were doing well.

HYPNOTHERAPY FOR SEX PROBLEMS

DIFFERENTIAL RELAXATION

Instead of using the standard progressive relaxation technique, (from the
top of the head to the tips of the toes), begin by suggesting that the

subject focus his or her awareness upon the pelvic area. "Imagine a powerful magnetic force shining over the pelvic area into the flesh of your genitals. All negative stress will be converted into positive energy and stored in your sexual center for future use." Now proceed to relax the subject from his or her toes up to the magnetic force that is transmuting the negative current into positive sexual power. Next, start at the scalp and carry the energy down to the pelvic area: "The magnet is drawing all the tension from every part of your body and changing it to super sexual energy." Repeat the exercise several times.

SPECIAL BREATHING TECHNIQUE

Instead of the usual "with each breath you drift deeper and deeper," here is a sexual breathing exercise borrowed from ancient yoga technique. It is called *the magic cycle*. Suggest: "As you breathe in, imagine that you have a tube that carries oxygen and energy down through the center of your body into the pelvic cavity. As you exhale the air, visualize a misty stream of warm air coming out of the opening of your sexual organ (penis, or vagina). As you breathe in this important life force (*Prana*), you are breathing in sexual power for (control, orgasm, a stronger erection, etc.). As you breathe out, you are expelling all your problems, tension, and stress. Visualize a stream of refreshing cool air flowing into your nostrils, warming up inside your body, and drifting out of your sexual opening, warm, moist, and very pleasant. With each breath your sexual confidence and ability grows stronger and stronger."

A DEEPENING TECHNIQUE

In addition to standard routines, such as countdowns, the following method combines deepening with autosuggestion: "The deeper you go into self-hypnosis, the stronger your sexual improvement will grow. Tell the subject to repeat to himself silently, as you speak out loud, the above suggestion, changing it to first person, "The deeper *I* go into self-hypnosis, the stronger *my* sexual improvement will grow." Combine "hetero-hypnosis" and self-hypnosis with the following technique, "As I count backward from 50 to 0, you count forward from 0 to 50. This will take you much deeper. *Both your counting and mine will double your sexual improvement.*"

FANTASY AND SELF-IMAGE

The subject's normal, healthy body image may be eclipsed due to repetitive sexual failure. You will get good results by training the subject to improve his or her inner self-image. "See yourself standing nude in front of a full length mirror, looking good and feeling healthy and happy. Look into your eyes and tell yourself you are attractive, normal, and improving with every experience." The suggestions may vary according to the specific problem. Another very effective technique is: "Imagine you are sitting in a movie theater where a very erotic film is to be shown. You are the star, the director, the writer, and the audience. Picture yourself behaving without your old problem. You are naturally virile and responsive. You have no guilt, no embarrassment. After you have successfully completed the best sexual experience of your life, take a bow. You were great. Hear the applause. Tell yourself, 'I have everything it takes to turn that rehearsal into the real thing.' And next time, you will do even better. Each time you will improve."

TAILOR-MADE SUGGESTIONS

Suggestion, when believed and accepted by the patient's subconscious, becomes internalized. Therefore, the suggestions should be formulated with the subject before induction. Posthypnotic suggestion is carried forward by the patient into the next sexual encounter. Phrase the suggestion in the first person and tell the subject to mentally repeat the phrase as you speak out loud. For men it might be: "I can restore full potency and have long-lasting control." Or, "I am sexually confident. What the mind caused, the mind can cure. "I will regain my youthful virility. Sex is right at any age." Keep the suggestions short and to the point. For women, try these: "I am sexually normal. I have everything it takes to reach orgasm." "I enjoy sex without guilt or embarrassment. I will experiment freely. "I enjoy the feeling of the penis. There is no pain, no anxiety!." Train your subject to practice positive autosuggestion at all times. Clearing the mind of negative anticipation requires affirmative reinforcement before, during, and after sexual intercourse.

SENSORY AWAKENING

Sensuality can be markedly increased. Orgastic sensation can be intensified by internalizing images and suggestion. Every picture and every thought has an inner message of its own. Inhibiting blocks can be dissolved and pleasure heightened. Because people use only a speck of their sensory potential, expect outstanding results in this area. Suggest: "All of your senses will harmonize in intensifying pleasure and creating better function. Your sense of sight. Your sense of hearing. Your sense of smell. Your sense of taste and touch. All will combine to make each experience more fulfilling in every way: mentally, emotionally, physically and spiritually. You will feel pleasure more and more deeply and completely."

TRAINING THE SEX MUSCLES

Thoughts cause a chain reaction as every idea sparks an emotion, which, in turn, reacts on a particular muscle of the body. Thoughts of pain, such as those that occur to the fearful, nonorgastic woman, can cause vaginismus, a tightening of the sphincter muscles, and prevent penile penetration. Other women lack muscle tone, which is an obstacle to their reaching orgasm and decreases sensation for the male. Men, also, need to learn how to train their sex muscles. For premature ejaculation, muscle flexing increases staying power. Hypnotic training increases staying power. Hypnotic training accelerates this important control. When your subject is in medium or deep trance, suggest: "Tense your sexual muscles as if you are holding in the urge to urinate. Focus on keeping this contraction until you count to 5. Contract the muscles as you breathe in. As you exhale, relax the muscles, counting from 5 to 0, slowly." Then tell your patient to rest while he counts to 10. Repeat the training several times, then explain: "Feel as if you are drawing together extra circulation and sexual energy. You have frontal muscles, anal muscles, and muscles at the base of the penis or inside the vagina. Flexing this group of muscles will bring you greater tone and control."

REGRESSION WITH AUTOMATIC WRITING

The hypnoanalyst may find it necessary to uncover the root of the problem in order to clarify the patient's understanding of why the dysfunction exists. The process requires a medium to deep trance level and usually involves four to six conditioning sessions. Regress year by year, "You are now 25, 24, 23, 22, etc." Go slowly, taking enough time for the subject to visualize himself in a sexual embrace. Suggest: "When you come to a situation which negatively affected your function, raise the forefinger of your right hand, and I will give you a pen and pad, and you will explain how your problem originated."

Hypnosis Meets New Challenges

The use of hypnosis is rapidly spreading into areas long considered out of bounds. Once looked upon as a parlor stunt and then only reluctantly accepted by the medical and psychological professions, today its use is widespread among all sorts of respected people. Hypnotic practice is widely used not only in hospitals and psychiatric clinics, but in jails, in the courtrooms, in sports, in the schoolroom, and even inside churches and synagogues. Judges, lawyers, and police officers have come to recognize hypnosis to be an excellent investigative tool, a reliable aid in memory recall and rehabilitation of criminals. Proponents cite case after case in which information gained through hypnosis led to the solution of difficult criminal cases.

The Chowchilla, California kidnapping case may be the best known example. Under hypnotic induction, a school bus driver recalled a license number that led police to the kidnappers who had abducted a busload of schoolchildren. Extremely useful in piecing together the forgotten information that helped to convict the kidnappers, hypnosis was also used as psychotherapy for some of the children, who were greatly disturbed by the experience. There are no limits to the variety of ways in which this fast growing art can be utilized.

An increasing awareness exists among sports figures that self-images improved during hypnotic trance can make the difference between being a winner and an also-ran. Hypnosis can also produce increased concentration and communication inside the classroom and makes the work of a teacher much easier. Inside prisons, psychologists are using it as an aid in retraining prisoners to become socially useful citizens. Specialized methods are employed as a wedge with which to enter and understand the criminal mind, and as a means by which changes and solutions can be discovered.

CRIME AND LAW ENFORCEMENT

Judicial attitudes regarding the use of hypnosis to obtain evidence are mixed. Certain states have yet to admit information gained in this manner. However, it wasn't too long ago that presently accepted forms of evidence such as fingerprinting, breathalizers, ballistics, and handwriting exemplars were undergoing the same kind of critical scrutiny. Now, even mechanically produced evidence from lie-detection machines is commonplace in criminal trials an over the country.

Tapping the unknown areas of the subconscious still worries some diehards and conservatives. However, many agencies (including the FBI) find that hypnotic investigation fills a void, solving the problem of how to get people to remember what they've forgotten. Modern day investigators point to the stunning success with what they term, "a new weapon—hypnotism." In fact, law officers are cracking open some of the most baffling of their previously unsolved cases. Hypnosis has become a boon to the overworked and understaffed police departments in many urban areas.

In New York City, the police department has appointed its own official hypnotist, and his success in solving difficult criminal cases has won him nationwide acclaim. Hypnosis has proven to be the magic key for unlocking the frightened minds of the countless witnesses who have blocked out important details after viewing a disturbing crime. The information is there, but the confused person cannot recall it when tension gets in the way.

Sgt. Charles Diggett, the New York Police Department's official hypnotist since 1976, declared, "Our subconscious minds automatically bury the painful parts of the experience. Otherwise we'd never be able to get over it." Sgt. Diggett has been called in to help solve 113 cases since the program was officially introduced. New information turned up in 62 percent of the cases, directly resulting in arrests. In the case of a young man whose uncle was shot, the teenage boy's description under hypnosis was so detailed that the homicide detectives realized he knew the suspect personally. After hypno-induction, the teenager was easily able to select the man's picture from mug shots.

In Los Angeles, both the Police Department and the FBI are using hypnosis with equally startling success. Lt. Dan Cooke of the Los Angeles Police Department stated: "We have ten lieutenants who have been specially trained as hypno-investigators. They are employed extensively in many of our cases and are loaned to other cities throughout the state." Dr. Martin Reiser, Director of Behavioral Science Services of the L.A.P.D., is also Director of a fast-growing organization called *Law Enforcement Hypnosis Institute*, where he trains investigators from all over the country in the use of special hypnosis techniques such as time regression and revivication.

Dr. Reiser tells of a small boy who saw his father murdered and hastily scribbled the license number of the fleeing killer's car. "The boy had transposed two digits and was unable to report the number correctly. Under hypnosis, he remembered the license and an arrest was made." Dr. Reiser says that hypnosis produced information in nearly 80 percent of the 350 cases in which it was used. "More and more agencies want to get people trained because hypnosis works and is very cost-effective."

The FBI seems to agree. "It is a magnificent way of interviewing and relaxing a person to tell what they have witnessed," said Special Agent Supervisor, Dr. Patrick Mullany, Senior Psychologist at the FBI Academy in Quantico, Virginia. "We have four special agents who are licensed, certified hypno-investigators, and believe it is a valid way of getting information."

Lt. Harry Haines, Chief of Detectives in Concord, California, also uses hypnosis with excellent results. He commented, "People give better, more vivid descriptions than they can under a normal fully conscious state." He also made the following important point: "Hypnosis is only used on witnesses and victims. We never use it on suspects. Obviously, you would not hypnotize somebody into making a confession. And, of course, we only hypnotize witnesses with their full consent."

Can an accused murderer be convicted by "memory-jogged testimony?" Here's a case in point. Mrs. Dyanne Quaglino was struck and killed by a car that sped away without stopping. A witness and tire tracks led police of Sánta Barbara, California to the car that was involved. Later, they traced the car to Myron Jenson, who had sold the questionable vehicle to another person several months prior to the accident. But to whom? They found the man's name, but Jenson could not remember what the man looked like. Detectives showed him a picture of their murder suspect, the dead woman's husband. Jenson was at first confused. He said the photo seemed to ring a bell, but he wasn't positive. After hypnosis, he was sure. Jenson's testimony was the crucial element in Mr. Quaglino's conviction on a charge of first degree murder.

Here's a reverse application of police hypnosis. Weekly hypnotic trances are helping a group of sheriff's deputies to relax from the everyday pressure of being cops. A hypnotist conducts "tension relaxation sessions" with the Lee County Sheriff's Department of Fort Myers, Florida. In a typical session, hypnotist Robert C. Ward instructed twenty-five hypnotized deputies to "feel relaxation flowing through your face, shoulders and body." He explained, "One of the side benefits is that police are able to leave their jobs behind them and go home to be a good father and husband rather than a tense police officer who might be irritable and take it out on the family. It also helps them ward off headaches, ulcers, and premature aging—all caused by tension."

One deputy reported, "I'm generally more energetic and pleasant to be around after hypnosis. I feel more like getting back to the job and tackling problems, and also sleep more peacefully."

JUDGE HYPNOTIZES DEFENDANTS

Judges are also becoming involved in applying hypnotic techniques. Here is one judge who uses it to set criminals on the right path. Judge F. E. Robertson of Grant County, Washington, reported in a newspaper story: "I must have hypnotized 34,000 defendants over the past 25 years." Judge Robertson has helped people overcome emotional difficulties, drinking problems, and even physical ailments.

He recalled one of his most difficult cases: "A young boy with criminal tendencies was sent to me by authorities who asked me to try to keep him from getting into trouble again. After some hypnosis therapy, the boy never was in trouble with the law again. Instead of becoming a criminal, he went on to become one of the best wrestlers this state ever produced."

Some prisons around the country are beginning to install rehabilitation programs which include self-hypnosis classes. At San Quentin prison in California, a woman hypnotist, Jeanne West, has conducted classes in self-hypnosis for inmates, with outstanding results. These classes are biweekly and last for four hours with thirty to forty men attending. The inmates have learned how to relax, adjust to the food (which had caused problems), and to utilize their time to better advantage. They learned self-anesthesia for dentistry and surgery. Two members of the class are studying for the ministry. Another is a teacher's aide. Others have become active in community programs. Several have blossomed into creative writers, poets, and painters. One inmate has married and is working in the family business. All the men have the highest praise for hypnosis and say it changed their self-image for the better, giving them more confidence and self-assurance. They also have stopped blaming others for their predicament and are able to accept responsibility for their misfortunes.

The program at San Quentin received a great deal of positive publicity all around the world. The British Broadcasting Corporation interviewed the hypnotist and prison-classmates via Telstar.

Although hypnosis has been previously employed in correctional institutes in lecture format, this was the first time anywhere that self-hypnosis was taught in classes on a regularly scheduled basis. The governor of California attended the graduating class and expressed his praise for the remarkable results. Let's hope it spreads to institutions all over the world.

SPECIAL TECHNIQUES IN CRIMINAL INVESTIGATION

Before information can be obtained from a witness, victim, or offender, a trusting relationship has to be established between the hypnotizer and the hypnotized. This requires breaking down barriers of anxiety which are always present and interfere with the gathering of information. Relaxed, pleasant conversation should always precede induction techniques. Once induction is accomplished, the subject should be tested for depth of trance. If the level is merely hypnoidal or light, very little real information will be obtained. Another session may be necessary in order to achieve sufficient depth for meaningful interrogation.

Questions should be formulated in advance, so they are concise and require the minimum in the way of an answer. Preparation is important as confusion on the part of the questioner will also confuse the hypnotized person. Time and age regression are employed after basic questioning in order to bring about revivification, which goes deeper than direct answers.

The operator asks the person to go back to the time and place where the incident occurred and to relive the experience. This may tend to be traumatic, so tell the subject: "You are merely an observer. This will not upset you in any way. You are merely watching a flash-back as in a movie. You feel no emotional involvement." The question is often asked of me: "Can the person fake hypnosis? Can a subject lie?" The answer is the same as that given to questions about polygraph machines. No—not if the operator is experienced, submits the subject to testing, and double checks the results. It requires adequate training and consistent practice to acquire the necessary skill and expertise.

CLERGYMEN ARE NOW USING HYPNOSIS

Until lately, hypnosis has been feared and condemned by the clergy, who have usually been poorly informed about this vital therapy. A book circulated among church people, *Diabolical Religion of Darkness* by Jess Pedigo, asks: "Are you aware that demons have admitted Satan as the source of power behind hypnotism?" In still another book, *Angels of Light* by Herbert E. Freeman, hypnosis is grouped with ESP, Ouija boards, cults, psychics, clairvoyants, astrologers, mediums, seers, and fortune tellers. The book's premise is that power derived from only two sources—God or Satan—and concludes that because none of the above can be associated with God, they therefore must be directed by Satan. The book ignores biblical teaching, which tells us all healing power is derived from God, that He created man a creature of choice with the ability to choose between good and evil. When we examine what is happening to all religious sects today, it is obvious that some new attitudes are sorely needed.

Surveys point to the fact that most people have turned away from traditional religion. Seventy percent of the Catholics, 75 percent of the Protestants, and 80 percent of the Jews in the U.S. no longer attend regular religious services. In a recent inquiry conducted by Father Edmund Nadolny, a priest, the question was asked, "Why are people staying away from church?"

Using radio, television and the news media, he reached over five million people. Based on twenty thousand replies, the main reason was indicated to be that people felt their clergyman church to be out of touch with present day problems.

Fortunately, we are now experiencing a remarkable change in the attitude of some theologians, who are beginning to apply techniques of hypnosis in many important ways in order to help members of the congregation. The Rev. Francis R. Duffy is an example of how to combine ministry with "power-of-mind" techniques. A native of Philadelphia, Father Duffy became interested in hypnosis in 1962 when he was chairman of the Social Sciences department at Duquesne University in Pittsburgh. His interest was triggered by his concern for students who tended to do well until confronted by examinations.

Father Duffy, 63 years of age, has used hypnosis, not only in pastoral counseling, but also for emotional, mental, and physical problems. He has helped over 2000 persons of an ages throughout the nation to kick the smoking habit, and overcome stuttering, fingernail biting, enuresis (bed-wetting), obesity, and shyness.

"Every now and then," Father Duffy said, "somebody suggests that I, as a priest, am doing something reprehensible by practicing hypnosis. My answer is that two popes long ago authorized twilight sleep, which is deep relaxation reached through hypnosis, for women during childbirth, and that authorization still remains.

At Parks College of Aeronautical Technology, Rev. J. J. Higgins, a Jesuit priest, uses hypnosis to help students overcome exam jitters. Father Higgins has employed this technique for more than seventeen years with about one sixth of the college's 600 students and in the process has had some spectacular results. Father Higgins has the blessing of his Jesuit superiors.

MENTAL ATTITUDE AND SPORTS

Can a hypnotist help your game? Can you visualize yourself coming in with a par for 18 holes, whipping your toughest tennis rival, and getting one strike after another at the bowling alley?

Sports-minded hypnotists say that if you can "conceive and believe, you can also achieve." Your body will do anything you ask it to do as long as your request is reasonable. All physical activity is mental in origin. Professionals are the first ones to admit this. Leading professionals in many sports say it may be as much as 80 percent mental. Hypnosis can give both top professionals and rank amateurs an extra edge. Hypnosis spurs the potential to make anyone more than mediocre.

Stage hypnosis has fostered misconceptions. Many people have come to believe that to have success with hypnosis, a deep trance is required. That's the stuff that comes from old Bela Lugosi movies. Self-hypnotic tennis or golf is relaxed concentration and has nothing to do with a deep trance. In sports, hypnosis trains the participant to have total, acute awareness. Most of all, it magnifies positive expectations.

The athlete not only brings his racket or his club into competition, he also brings his personality. Winning becomes not just beating the other fellow, but feeling like a winner inside. Many coaches of football, baseball, or basketball teams talk to their players about "psyching up." The self-hypnotic factor can make the difference between being the victor and being the victim in a competitive match.

George Foster of the Cincinnati Reds hit more home runs than anyone else in the major leagues for a period of time. Hypnosis turned out to be his secret assistant. Whenever George was troubled, he concentrated at the plate, and went into his special self-hypnosis routine.

His hypnotist, Dr. Robert Bernstein from Indianapolis, trained him to live up to his highest batting potential.

"George had a problem concentrating, which caused him to hesitate when he was at bat. He needed to talk to someone outside the baseball team about this problem. George was hypnotized to have mental awareness at all times. He can be compared with a pianist who becomes too involved thinking about the individual movements of his fingers on the keyboard rather than relaxing and playing instinctively. George simply needed a mental nudge to get back on track."

It required only a short session to put George Foster's batting average back on the beam. His batteries recharged, he forged ahead to win.

A United Press International report from England tells us about Gary Player's victory in the British Open Golf Tournament by four strokes. Gary says, "By using self-hypnosis, I put myself in a state of perfect concentration out there and was confident all the way." Carol Semple won the British Women's Open Championship to become the first American in twenty-five years to win two successive titles. "I suffer from nerves in the big matches," she says. "I have a cassette tape I play to prepare myself. I listen to the reassuring voice telling me how to relax, concentrate, and play a round of winning golf. "Miss Semple, hugging her trophy, gives thanks to her hypnosis cassette tape.

A Hollywood, Florida hypnotist, Cheryl Weisberg, describes her sessions with a group of women tennis players: "I had them lay down in a dark room while teaching them progressive relaxation exercises. Once the body is relaxed, you can be sure the mind follows. When you reach that point, we build a channel of communication between the subconscious mind and the physical movements of the body. Once he or she develops the knack," Miss Weisberg says, "a tennis player can induce self-hypnosis in just three minutes." She suggests such an interlude once a day, especially before a match.

Former San Francisco quarterback, John Brodie, goes into hypnosis and imagines in slow motion the enemy defensive line. This gives him the opportunity to study responses carefully in order to enhance his own performance.

Gary Rees of the University of Miami Swimming Team is also a booster of hypnosis. He specializes in long-distance events in which swimmers are often weakened by fatigue from lactic acid build-up. Under hypnosis, visual imagery becomes the antidote to fatigue. Rees imagines how his muscles look under a magnifying glass. "I see the lactic acid as milk or thick cream running over my muscles, which I picture as a red cobblestone street. I then envision a magical spray counteracting the lactic acid, washing it away like a mist."

An added problem for the long-distance swimmer involves sucking in wind. Rees says he used visualization to make every breath count more for energy. "I imagine my lungs so enlarged they fill my entire body. I see oxygen as a white cloud filling up my whole hollow self ... my body reacts as if I have all the oxygen and air I need because every breath is magnified by my mind."

GAMBLING—LOSERS BECOME WINNERS

Do you want better odds at the casino? Here's a tip from professional gamblers who say, "Psyche yourself up!" Good winning streaks depend upon good mental attitude as well as on luck. The difference between being a constant loser or a consistent winner is the degree of concentration you bring to the game. Hypnosis increases one's ability to focus attention upon what is happening at the moment. It strengthens retention, and improves memory and recall of numbers, cards, and rules of the game.

Certain games are easier to beat than others. Mechanical devices such as slot machines and wheels of fortune are not responsive to mental power because of computer programming. Chance rather than choice is the determining factor. Therefore, play the machines long enough and you're bound to be a loser. However, with the heightened awareness derived from hypnosis, you can dramatically improve your chances at blackjack, baccarat, and the crap table.

Learn the subtleties of the game you wish to conquer, but don't be fooled into thinking you can alter the system which favors the house. True, you may be able to influence the percentage of winning, but not the built-in odds against you. The most important tip from the professionals who use self-hypnosis is, "Know when to quit." A message of insight, or psychic hunch, will be delivered at the right moment when you have trained yourself with autohypnosis.

It may sound a bit wild, but reports indicate hypnosis can make you a better horseplayer. Masters of self-hypnosis do not lose their shirts at the race track because they are less likely to be reckless. Most players, when on a losing streak, become desperate and take unnecessary risks in order to recoup. Trying too bard to win becomes a negative force while a calm, self-confident attitude helps one win. The law of averages proves that the more frequently a person bets, the greater his chances of losing. Therefore, bets should be well-calculated. Apparently, professional horseplayers are successful because they have studied their subject well, and the acquired knowledge leads them to make only spot plays based on information rather than emotion. They never risk money on a horse unless the horse has a better than even shot at winning.

How does this relate to hypnosis? While hypnosis cannot give you knowledge about a given sport, it can unlock latent, subconscious talent, releasing hunches based on information. Having applied self-hypnosis, you are in complete control of your feelings while at the track, so if your horse loses one day, you don't panic, and still have confidence in the same horse next time. Regardless of the odds, the professional will bet until the horse wins again. Self-hypnotized players do not become overexcited by winning or terribly depressed by defeat. A calm, businesslike attitude is usually maintained. The horseplayer's only concern is the amount of profit he can make by betting. According to studies conducted by psychologists, confidence and positive anticipation bring about a higher percentage of victories.

THE COMPULSIVE GAMBLER

An epidemic of gambling, both legal and illegal, is sweeping the country. In addition to gambling conducted by privately owned enterprises, many states have set up lotteries to boost their dwindling coffers. At least forty-four states are involved in some form of legalized gambling, from casinos and bingo to jai alai and lotteries. Television game shows add to the indoctrination. Reports indicate over half of the United States population is engaged in some form of gambling. The states are to blame for much of this increase although they excuse themselves by pointing out that gambling is a dependable source of revenue. This situation has brought about a surge in the number of compulsive gamblers in the U.S., which is now estimated to be between six and nine million.

There is a correlation between the urge to gamble and other problems such as sexual madequacy. Here's why. The gambler tends to believe he can compensate for feeling like a loser in one area by being a winner at another game. Gambling gives him the semblance of a thrill, the excitement and glamour which is missing from his life. For the person suffering from sexual dysfunction, gambling may be a substitute in that it provides a nervous build-up of tension and anticipation followed by a quasi-orgastic release when he wins or loses.

In the end, compulsive gambling proves to be a form of self-punishment just as being a chronic loser at sexual-social relationships does.

A TYPICAL CASE HISTORY

Clifford P. chewed the stub of a cigar while he agonized over his compulsive need to gamble. "The more I lose, the more I find reason to go back and play again. I'll bet on anything: horses, sports, whether it will rain. I even bet against myself . . . whether I'll put on my left or right sock first."

Clifford readily admitted he was sexually impotent at times. "If I have to choose between making it at the game tables or making it with a woman, I'd rather shoot craps."

He told about the time a friend in Las Vegas had introduced him to a beautiful showgirl. After buying her a few drinks, he found himself in bed with her. He had walked out of a poker game, rather than admit to his friend that he was less interested in sex than poker. Now here he was, unable to get an erection with one of the most beautiful young women in Vegas.

"Please don't tell my friend," he pleaded. "Let me go back to the game, and I'll send you a nice present."

I asked Clifford why gambling was so important. "I trip out on gambling," he explained. "I fantasize about being a really big winner. I imagine myself going off on a fantastic vacation, first class . . . building a monument to my parents . . . or a hospital in their name." Meanwhile, in reality his gambling had already cost him his business, his marriage, and the respect of his children.

Clifford was ready to be helped through hypnosis. We not only eliminated his urge to gamble, but corrected the basic source of his insecurity—his sexual inadequacy.

Louis T. was so compulsive a gambler, all he had to do was see a picture of a horse and he'd rush to the track to place a bet. Outside of holding back the barest amount of money for existence, Louis gambled most of his earnings away. No amount of logic could convince him to quit.

One day he confided to a friend: "I don't have money for rent, for food, or for medicine. I haven't eaten a square meal in three days. I'm desperate."

"Louis, do you mean to tell me you're stone broke? Not even betting money?"

"Oh, I got betting money, but I don't have money for rent. . . ."

Here is the self-hypnosis routine which helped Louis overcome gambling. Under hypnosis, he would deliberately imagine the following scene: "I am arriving in Las Vegas with a big sack of money, *one million dollars*. I see myself entering the gambling casino, moving from table to table, and holding onto my sack of money without betting a cent."

Louis was training his brain to resist temptation. "I picture myself leaving the casino, going to my room and counting my money. Hooray! I'm a winner! I didn't lose a cent. Then I reward myself. I see myself going out on the town, spending the money on more satisfying things. I see myself wearing a new outfit, driving a custom-made car, escorting a beautiful girl, living it up, and having a great time, like a winner, instead of being depressed, like a loser."

TEACHING AND LEARNING DISABILITY

We are all aware that students complain about anxiety associated with testing and examinations, and the fear of failure contributes to the shutting down of mental responses. On the other hand, hypnosis speeds up the learning process and acts as a stabilizer for the emotionally insecure student. Pinpoint concentration helps us to assimilate, retain, and recall information. This can make the difference between success and failure in any learning experience.

Self-hypnosis is helping novices in police academy work. Postal workers are memorizing schemes. Nurses use it in their training. Actors in learning scripts. Musicians in perfecting scores. Salesmen in practicing their pitch. Even politicians can sound believable through self-hypnosis. Any one can build confidence and assertiveness and project a more pleasing personality.

Teaching through hypnosis is done in three stages:

1. Before hypnotic induction, the material is read. The teacher makes sure it is understood. Questions are answered.

2. The students are then related into a suggestible hypnotic state.

While hypnotized, information is repeated and reinforced with autosuggestion.

3. After coming out of hypnosis, the student follows post hypnotic suggestions of retention and recall. It is wise to include suggestions of improved study habits and stronger motivation to succeed.

LEARNING LANGUAGES

Hypnosis has long been recognized as a valuable aid in the learning of languages. Hypnosis can also be employed in recalling a language once spoken and forgotten with the passage of time. Lost or buried knowledge can be dredged up from the recesses of the mind and reactivated. Many language courses are now beginning to feature accelerated learning through the use of hypnotic techniques.

A friend, Clarisse T., who teaches Spanish in a community college, invited me to participate in her class to determine if hypnosis would be useful in speeding up the learning process. She was concerned with increasing class attentiveness as well as their ability to recall the material and use it in every day conversation.

We began our experiment with a lesson by Clarisse in the proper pronunciation of Spanish vowel and consonant sounds. I then hypnotized the group using basic induction methods, beginning with progressive body relaxation and positive suggestion, and ending with post-hypnotic suggestion. Most people drifted into a light to medium trance, which is sufficient for learning a language.

Clarisse proceeded to read out loud from the Spanish textbook. She asked each student to repeat certain key words after hearing them pronounced correctly. They responded in unison in monotonous sing-song voices, indicating that they had drifted deep enough to bypass emotional response and work with the rational higher mind. The first group session lasted two hours; one hour was devoted to inducing trance and the other hour was used for study and memorization.

However, at the second session, all five subjects relaxed into a suitable trance level within twenty minutes, and the rest of the time was; devoted to learning the language. Results were impressive. Suggestions of hyperacuity and hypermnesia were implanted into the subconscious to work posthypnotically.

Upon awakening, the group was tested for retention of the material covered in the session. Each student reviewed what he had learned and, by so doing, contributed to the general knowledge and progress of the group.

Clarisse and I were pleased to discover the length of learning time was reduced by two thirds. Upon further experimentation, I have since learned it is not only the depth of trance that brings positive results, but motivation and expectation. Thus, if a student believes he is a poor hypnotic subject, results will be better if he concentrates on the suggestions instead of forcing depth of hypnosis. As a result of this work, *all students learned a minimum of 200 words per session without difficulty,* regardless of trance depth.

Allison R. was especially well-motivated, eager to learn Spanish quickly so she would be able to speak the language better on her visit to Mexico. Allison amazed the group by being able to gather a working vocabulary of 3000 words within five two-hour sessions. Two factors contributed to her success:

Allison was strongly motivated, looking forward to kindling a romance with a young man she had met in Mexico on her last trip. At that time, she could not speak any Spanish. Now her romantic feelings spurred her to be able to communicate with him. The other positive factor was the hypnotic training she had received for weight reduction some months prior to her language studies. Once a person has been conditioned to hypnosis, he can always be reinducted if he so desires.

Barry H. and John H. were brothers, aged 23 and 21, struggling to achieve passing grades in the first and second year of college. They came to my office together to share the session. Both complained of difficulties in concentrating in class and on their homework. Barry, the older brother, described himself as a procrastinator, "I put off till tomorrow what I should do today." John worked diligently, but believed he was less intelligent than Barry. Being two years younger than his brother, John never seemed able to live up to his older brother's level.

They shared one thing: severe apprehension about tests and a fear of flunking out of college. On the positive side, both young men were strongly motivated to improve, and cooperated with hypnotic techniques. They were agreeable and flexible, and after an eight-week course in self-hypnosis during which they came for two hours each week, their memories improved as well as their powers of concentration and their self-confidence. They were ultimately delighted to earn excellent records, rising from C averages to B-plus and A.

In addition to bettering their study habits, Barry's and John's program of improvement included cutting down on watching television and curtailing the use of cigarettes, marijuana, and alcohol.

Jerry B., age 14, looked younger due to his short stature and childish facial expression. He was failing in a parochial school that he bitterly hated. He seethed with rage as he described real or imagined abuse by his teachers. His antagonism had increased to the point where he was unable to study at all. Jerry missed classes periodically and turned in blank pages instead of homework. His mother managed to get him to come to me for therapy on the threat of sending him to reform school. Jerry confessed he had destroyed his report card rather than have his father punish him for poor marks. I noticed Jerry's fingernails were bitten down to the raw skin.

"What seems to be the problem, Jerry?" "I hate this school," he said. They are too strict and the teacher insults me in front of the class. She said I was not only short in body, but short in brains. I stayed out of school for five days."

Nothing his parents could say diminished his anger until they agreed that he could transfer to another school at the end of the semester. Meantime, Jerry joined a six-week hypnosis course twice a week in which he learned to concentrate with renewed interest on his school work. His mother says he is now doing fine in the public school, working hard to catch up to the level of his peers. The hypnosis group in which he participated consisted mostly of adults. Discovering that adults had problems gave him an awareness that people are more alike than different. The older members of the group encouraged him to keep trying and cited problems of their own teenage years. Jerry took great pride in living up to the expectations of the group and was not a disappointment to them.

THE CASE OF UNEQUAL TWIN BROTHERS

Chuck H., ten years old, was in the third grade and considered a poor student. His twin brother, Clark, was in the fifth grade and doing well. Chuck had failed to get passing grades in his second and third term. His confidence was shattered from constantly being compared to his brother. His comprehension and memory were low. Two preliminary sessions were necessary to develop the trance state, which was medium. At his third session, this conversation took place. I asked, "How was your school work this past week?" "I brought my test papers to show you," Chuck said. "I'm doing a lot better. You told me I would be able to concentrate and now I'm able to understand the teacher most of the time."

"That's fine, Chuck. Today you're going to write down the suggestions you want to improve by. Now that you know hypnosis works, we
can proceed to accomplish much more." I handed Chuck a pencil and
pad, and without the hesitation or confusion that bothered him at the
first session he wrote: "First, I want to learn faster, catch up to my
brother. Second, better concentration and remember my work. Third, be
good at doing the times tables and long division."

I proceeded: "Chuck, just lean back and relax all over. Now you
know how to relax easily so close your eyes and let your muscles feel
loose. Think about your arms getting very heavy. . . pleasantly heavy.
Your legs heavy . . . relaxing all over . . . as I count from 5 to 1, let
yourself go deeper with each count. Just give in and let it happen.

"Now concentrate on your right hand . . . soon you will feel your
hand getting lighter and lighter . . . it feels tingly as you concentrate on
it. Just keep listening to my voice, concentrate on the meaning of all of
the suggestions I am about to give you. There's lots of time . . . no
pressure . . . repeat each suggestion I give you 10 times. Count the
suggestions off on your fingers . . . First suggestion . . . 'I will learn
faster, catch up to my brother.'" I paused and watched his fingertips
count off ten repetitions. Each of his three suggestions were implanted
in the same way.

I continued. "It is becoming easier and easier for you to relax and
concentrate on every word I say to help you . . . you are learning to use
your bright and intelligent mind . . . better and better. (Praise accelerates
results, especially when working with children.) Now I am going to
press your fingertips gently, and this will take you deeper and deeper
because you want to go deeper and deeper to learn faster and faster.
Each time you study with this method, you will learn to follow positive
suggestions. As your studies improve, you will love your schoolwork
more and more. You will help yourself grow up to be a fine man with an
excellent education. Your schoolwork is becoming very interesting . . .
everyday more and more interesting.

"Now as I count backward from 20 to 0, you will go deeper, much
deeper into trance, concentrate on the count and feel so deeply relaxed
and comfortable. Twenty, 19, 18, 1, 16, 15, 14, 13, 12, 11, 10, 9, 8, 7,
6, 5, 4, 3, 2, 1. Much deeper. Listen closely, with all of your concentration, and repeat the next suggestion, and accept it fully.

"Learning fast . . . repeat this suggestion, pressing your fingers
down, one at a time . . . the little finger of your right hand . . . learning
fast . . . each time you repeat it, it makes a more lasting impression in
your mind . . . and you let yourself go deeper . . . learning fast."

Each suggestion is repeated, with a few deepening techniques between suggestions. It helps children to repeat the suggestions aloud. Some verbalize inaudibly, forming the words with the throat, lips, and tongue.

Speaking while in trance has a tendency to cause some subjects to lose depth, especially in the lighter stages. This should be left to the discretion of the hypnotic operator. After all of the ideas have been implanted, further suggestions of well-being and confidence in the method working are instilled. The subject is then awakened.

After the trance state is suitably developed, whether medium, deep, or somnambulistic, the subject can open his eyes without awakening when told to do so, and can read and memorize rapidly. The subject matter can be read by the hypnotist or the student can be instructed to open his eyes and read himself. Suggestions of hyperacuity and hypermnesia will result in speeded-up learning.

Sometimes a bad self-image contributes negatively to scholastic attitudes. Susan T. was 17 and 40 pounds overweight. Though of normal intelligence, she was failing in Algebra, History, and Latin. Her poor study habits included eating junk food and watching television while supposedly doing her homework. Obviously, both eating and watching T.V. are distractions from the concentration necessary to memorize homework. Susan complained of a lack of incentive. She just did not care about learning. Her mind was involved with her appearance and with feelings of social rejection.

I decided to include suggestions on weight loss and appetite control. After losing the first 5 pounds, she began to apply herself to her studies. At last report she was 15 pounds lighter and had received an A on an algebra test.

Howard M., 16, had a history of playing hookey. On two occasions, he had run away from home when pressured to attend school regularly. As a result, he was a poor reader, sullen toward his parents, and generally had no direction or goals in his life.

"What do you really want to do?" I questioned while he was under hypnosis. He mumbled something about a guitar.

Upon awakening, Howard revealed that he had asked for music lessons from his father at the age of 13 and had been refused. I arranged a deal between him and his parents. He would have the money to rent a guitar and take lessons for a limited period of time, provided he applied his energies to his schoolwork. After six months of doing well in his music and other work, his parents bought Howard his own guitar and the difference in his attitude toward school, and his parents, changed considerably.

LEARNING DISABILITIES

It is important for parents to be alert in spotting learning problems as early as possible, the best time being before the child enters school. However, one should not necessarily see a developmental difference between one child and another as serious. A single symptom of slow learning could merely represent a temporary quirk. What may appear to be slow for one child may be normal for another.

If parents perceive marked slowness in a child's responses and learning development, they should bring their concern to the attention of a pediatrician who understands the variances of mental and emotional development in children. When in doubt, do not transfer your anxieties to the child, because worry about normalcy simply compounds the problem. Children with learning disabilities, even those who are mentally retarded, are often good subjects for hypnotherapy. High intelligence is not a requisite for hypnotizability. Most children with problems are uneducated, rather than unable to *be* educated. Many have simply not been taught to learn and study properly. Hypnosis teaches them how to tap their unexplored assets. The results are often immediate.

Concerned parents can contact The Association For Children with Learning Disabilities (ACLD). They have 750 chapters across the country and can guide you to the proper kind of assistance. Information is available on diagnostic clinics, special school programs for children and parents, professional counseling, hypnotherapists, and so forth.

A brief description of some of the learning disabilities which respond to hypnotic suggestion follows:

Ataxia. Abnormal (meaning below average) muscular control of various parts of the body. The absence of orderliness. This can be worsened by emotional stress, causing lack of coordination between thoughts and feelings.

Dyslexia. Inability to read printed or written words with understanding. Often associated with impairment of comprehension and too much pressure to learn. Hypnotherapy lessens the stress.

Dysgraphia. Difficulty with writing. Lack of coordination among mind, eye, and hand. Often linked to the child who cannot write spontaneously, but can copy from printed material.

Dyscalculia. Inability to grasp mathematical concepts with normal teaching. Sometimes improvement is speedy when an alternative method, such as hypnotic visualization, is taught.

Hyperkinesis. Abnormally increased motor activity; constant movement without apparent purpose. Can also refer to excessive verbal responses—fast rambling speech and constantly interrupting.

Hypokinesis. Abnormally quiescent state, unresponsive, tendency to withdraw, inattentive to stimuli. Low energy and disinterest in surrounding activity. Stimulation of nerve centers through suggestion.

Perceptually Handicapped. Inability to recognize or to become aware of certain words, objects, and other data through the senses (sight, hearing, touch, taste, and smell). Sensory awareness used.

Strephosymbolia. The reversal of symbols as in reading and writing. (Was for saw, for example.) Revolving screen is visualized under hypnosis.

NERVOUS CHILDREN HAVE SCHOOL PROBLEMS

Sometimes children are classified as having learning disabilities when, in fact, they are unable to concentrate because of stress and anxiety. The trance is a state of relaxed learning without the intervention of pressure or coercion. Fortunately, most children respond favorably to hypnotic suggestion because they are less critical of the procedure. Even emotionally retarded and brain-damaged children can improve, because hypnosis increases alertness and builds belief in oneself. Children who are hypnotized learn from three to five times faster and with less effort than they would normally. Proof of new learning must always lie in results, as you will note in the following case history.

Reginald S. was 12 years old and several years behind his age group in reading and arithmetic. His problem was first diagnosed when he was seven as *strephosymbolia*. In addition to his reading and arithmetic problem, Reginald stuttered, a clear sign of the nervous tension he was suffering. As the only child of college-educated parents, he felt especially pressured to succeed scholastically. After several months of hypnotic training to help him relax physically and emotionally, he learned to compensate for his visual limitations and is now a top student. To assure his continued improvement, Reginald was given the posthypnotic suggestion that his mother or father would be able to place him in a trance by the key word *improve*. This is best in cases where the parent-child relationship is a good one. Even then, suggestions should be written out and accepted by the child in advance. This approach engenders trust—not only that the hypnotist who develops trance in the first place is sincere, but also that the parent will not take advantage and slip in suggestions against the child's wishes. In other words, the child is given a feeling of security.

SPEECH PROBLEMS

Speech disturbances often begin when children have school problems. When Don started stuttering at 5, his folks said, "He'll outgrow it." At 20, Don still stuttered after eight years of analysis and three speech therapists. Working toward a career as an architect, Don knew stuttering would limit his advancement. He was especially nervous in the presence of authority figures such as parents, teachers, and prospective employers.

Socially, Don was also inhibited. Although unusually handsome and well-dressed, he had never dated. Stuttering became worse around girls. His only attempt at sex was with a prostitute with whom he could not function because of nervousness.

Fortunately, Don proved to be a cooperative subject, as is the case with many stutterers. I found his breathing to be spasmodic and irregular. Under hypnosis, therefore, Don was trained to breathe fully from the diaphragm, to let his voice flow smoothly with the exhalation of air. One's pattern of breathing is always an indication to the therapist of underlying tension. Shallow, spasmodic breathing is associated with fear and anxiety, while deeper diaphragmatic breathing is characteristic of greater harmony of the internal rhythms of the body.

Stutterers must first master the art of smooth, controlled breathing, and hypnosis is extremely effective in this regard.

Since stuttering is a manifestation of deeply rooted tension, we worked out a complete relaxation and reconditioning program. The suggestions given to him under hypnosis included the following:

"I will remain relaxed under all circumstances. Increase confidence, poise, be at ease with women. Breathe deeply and speak slowly and freely. Every time I speak, I sound better and better."

By the second week, Don's friends began noticing he was more at ease. He slowed down—taking time to think and breathe before speaking.

At his third session, Don discussed the possible reason for his problem, mentioning that his father and mother had divorced when he was a small child. However, he was unable to recall any specific traumatic incidents which might have contributed to his distress.

During the fifth session, I suggested *automatic writing* as an uncovering technique to find the reason for his problem. When he was in as deep a state as be could achieve, I set a large writing pad on his lap and placed a felt tip pen in his hand, directed the automatic writing as follows:

"What happened to cause you to stutter? Let your hand write the answer. Your hand will write. Your subconscious mind knows the answer and wants to help you. Soon your pen will begin to move . . . now . . . it is moving . . . begin to write . . . what caused you to stutter in the first place? Continue to write until the truth reveals itself. This will give you insight and understanding . . . think back to the first time that you stuttered . . . make believe it's happening right now . . . who are you with?"

Don wrote slowly in small cramped letters, hardly legible. When the pen fell from his hand, I knew there was no more material forth-coming at that time. One of the words Don wrote was "*wore*."

"What does this unfinished sentence mean? 'My mother. . . *wore*?'" Upon awakening, Don was amazed. He recalled a violent scene he had witnessed at the age of 5. His mother had returned late one night and his father started an angry argument. At one point, he struck his mother and Don awakened hearing her scream. He heard his father call his mother "whore." However, in writing the word, Don had left out the letter "h" in an attempt to conceal the shocking truth from himself. As a small child, he had not realized the meaning of the word, but the violence had shattered his sense of security. For years after the incident, he suffered from nightmares, and became fearful and submissive in his behavior. It was at this time that he remembers stuttering for the first time.

After his revelation, Don seemed better able to relax. Even his speech was more relaxed. It is now two years later, and he speaks clearly and without difficulty. Don continues to use self-hypnosis to improve his learning habits and to remain relaxed and confident when dating women.

Glossary
Additional Uses for Hypnosis

The following list is compiled from my own files and the case histories of other professional hypnotherapists and physicians. Also included are some of the uses reported by students using self-hypnosis.

ABORTION. Deep subjects with optimum body control report spontaneous abortion. Also valuable in diminishing bleeding after abortion.

ABRASIONS. Bruises and sores are soothed and encouraged to heal with positive suggestion under hypnosis and/or self-hypnosis.

ABREACTION. A technique used in psychoanalysis by which forgotten thoughts are brought forward to conscious awareness and relived.

ABSENT-MINDEDNESS. The tendency to be occupied with one's own thoughts to the exclusion of outside events. Withdrawn and forgetful.

ACCIDENT-PRONE. Liability toward involvement in mishaps causing pain or injury. Largely due to mental-emotional states of confusion.

ACCOUNTING. Rapid calculations as well as greater efficiency. Attention to detail and ability to ignore outside distractions.

ACNE. Adolescent skin eruptions respond favorably to hypnotherapy because of stress factor. Anxiety is lessened, self-image improved.

ACTING. Memorizing lines and cues. Poise. Accept difficult direction. Feel the part. Become the character. Improve timing.

ACUMEN IN BUSINESS. Efficient planning. Organize bills and paper work. Discipline yourself to work. Originality of ideas.

ADAPTATION. The ability to adjust to altered living conditions. New location, climate, job, change of vocation. Marriage—divorce.

ADVERTISING. Set up better work schedules. Creativity in promotion. Increase sales. Meet deadlines. Insight in making deals.

AGING. The reduction of stress and emotional anxiety retards the aging process. Also, increases stamina and resistance to illness.

AGORAPHOBIA. An abnormal fear of being in open spaces. Anxiety about leaving home or being in unfamiliar surroundings.

AIDS. Aquired Immune Deficiency Syndrome. Behavior modification helps in prevention as well as control of symptons.

AIRPLANE TRAVEL. For crew, alertness at the controls. For fearful passengers, confidence, relaxation, sleep throughout trip.

ALCOHOLISM. Affecting over 50 million Americans, even 12-year-olds. Hypnosis brings about permanent cure in weeks or months.

ALLERGIES. Overreaction to substances such as pollen, dust, and animal fur resulting in inflammation of nasal passages reduced and soothed.

AMNESIA. In cases of lost memory or identity, hypnosis helps in recall of names, numbers, and places. Used for finding lost documents.

ANALGESIA. Pain relief. Produced by developing localized insensibility. Analgesia can be retained by postsuggestion. Helps arthritis, bursitis.

ANESTHESIA. Loss of sensation is accomplished in order to permit painless dentistry and surgery. Hypnotist often assists during operations.

ANGER. This seething, destructive emotion can be channeled into positive, constructive energy with increased inner direction.

ANIMAL TRAINING. Quick thinking, patience, an attitude of alertness and courage. Transferred to the animal by trainer's inner control.

ANOREXIA. Total lack of appetite results in severe emaciation. A hysterical condition, extremely responsive to hypno-suggestion.

ANXIETY. A malady which plagues most of us at some time in life. This emotional sensation is changeable. Causes rooted out.

ARCHITECTURE. Using techniques of visualization, the architect pictures a completed project and is better able to carry out his work.

ARTHRITIS. Pain control is extremely valuable as well as developing greater dexterity in stiff calcified joints of the body and hand.

ART WORK. Painting and drawing abilities are enhanced. Sharper sense of color and form surfaces. An unblocking of higher talents.

ASTHMA. Breathing difficulty is lessened by relaxing chest muscles and improving the respiratory system's rhythms. Reduces anxiety.

ASTRAPHOBIA. Fear of thunderstorms has limited outdoor travel for many people. Original cause wiped out of memory bank.

ATHLETICS. Through positive suggestion and imagination, ballplayers, runners, and other sportsmen perform to highest potential.

AUTOMATIC WRITING. An uncovering technique where subject answers questions put to him by a hypnotist to recall memory of past events.

AUTOMOBILE TRAVEL. Car sickness is lessened. Fear of driving overcome. Alertness at wheel and in traffic increased markedly.

AWARENESS. The ultra-depth meditative level of hypnosis puts one in touch with one's higher intelligence. Know the inside of your mind.

BARTENDING. Memory, concentration, attention to details, getting along with people without necessarily drinking. Sympathizing easily.

BEAUTY. Your mind can preserve your good looks on the outside through improved self-image from inside. Better sleep, relaxation improves appearance.

BEHAVIOR MODIFICATION. Hypnosis speeds the changeover from negative to positive attitudes and activities. Removes hang-ups.

BLADDER CONTROL. Upon medical referral, the sensation of needing to urinate can be removed from the habit reflexes assuming no illness present.

BLEEDING. To lessen loss of blood during surgery and after accidents. Also for menstrual hemorrhaging and patients with hemophilia.

BLOOD PRESSURE. Testing before and during HYPNOSIS proves that a moderate depth lowers blood pressure 10 to 25 points.

BLUSHING. The rush of blood to the face is triggered by thoughts of embarrassment. Hypnotic reconditioning is extremely effective.

BOATING. Many have overcome fear of water and developed better balance. Freedom from seasickness and nausea. Improve confidence for sailing.

BOREDOM. The person who is listless, living in a rut without enthusiasm can be trained to program fun into his life. Increase interest in hobbies.

BOWLING. Posthypnotic suggestion brings great coordination. Bowler pictures himself delivering the strike just as ball leaves hand.

BRAINWASHING. Hypnosis is used to wipe out painful memories. For fresh outlook on life. Useful for victims in rape cases and child abuse.

BREAST DEVELOPMENT. Medical hypnotists report effective response by increasing circulation. Remove negative mental limitations.

BREATHING PROBLEMS. Rhythms of breathing can be corrected in a trance-state. Respiratory diseases react positively and quickly.

BRIDGE PLAYING. The ability to remember cards which have been played. A remarkable increase in concentration gained. Win more games.

BRONCHITIS. Hypnosis tends to open up the breathing passage-ways and release accumulated phlegm in the bronchial tubes.

BRUXISM. Describing the clenching and grinding of the teeth. This disturbance most often occurs during the night and is due to stress.

BULIMIA. A psychological disturbance resulting in an insatiable appetite for food. The patient eats constantly and anything available.

BURSITIS. Medical practioners find that chronic pain in shoulders and elsewhere can be somewhat ameliorated through hypnotic suggestions.

CANCER. Hypnotherapists are sometimes called in by attending physicians to relieve terminal pain where the patient resists conventional drugs.

CHARLEY HORSE. Muscle spasms quickly respond to the ultra-deep relaxation which takes place under hypnotic trance. Useful for athletes.

CHEMISTRY. Students find their memories improve for learning formulas. Professional chemists also use hypnosis for creative laboratory work.

CHERAPHOBIA. Fear of gaiety, loud laughter, or boisterous behavior that results in depression and anxiety. Sometimes found among the elderly.

CHILD ABUSE. A growing problem often resulting from discord between parents who have lost their ability to cope. Hypnosis brings rationality.

CHILDBIRTH. Pain during labor can be entirely eliminated and childbirth can become a pleasurable experience rather than a fearful one. A boon.

CHILD, GIFTED. For the bright child, hypnosis offers the possibility of unlimited expansion of latent creativity. Self-hypnotic techniques used.

CHILD, SUBNORMAL. The child who is dull or less than average finds new areas of growth within the untapped potential. Sensorimotor exercises.

CHINOPHOBIA. Fear of the snow. Snowflakes terrify when they touch the skin of people with this problem. Desensitization is employed in trance.

CHIROPRACTIC ADJUSTMENT. Hypnosis is used to relax overly tense patients. The doctor combines his skill with suggestions for improvement.

CLAIRVOYANCE. "Psychic" ractitioners report greater insight and occult abilities by entering a hypnotic trance level.

CLAUSTROPHOBIA. Fear of confined spaces such as closets, elevators, and rooms without windows. One of the most common of phobias. Correctible.

CLIMACTERIUM, MALE. Thought of as analogous to the menopause in females. Fatigue, decreased sexual drive, irritability, etc. Responsive to hypnosis.

CLUMSINESS. An unconscious ineptitude which prevents the patient from performing certain acts. Poise and skill are increased through images.

COLDS. Immunity to colds is improved through proper breathing and adherence to health rules. Resistance is increased through positive suggestion.

COLITIS. Because bowel problems are intensified by tension, the affect of self-hypnosis training brings strong relief.

COLOR BLINDNESS. Some cases of color blindness have responded to posthypnotic suggestion. Incorrect teaching often limits self-confidence.

COMEDIANS. Professional comics, like actors, use self-hypnosis to memorize lines and to keep their spirits high in difficult times.

COMPULSION. Repetitive motor action even though the subject wishes to change. Such as alcoholism, overeating, and smoking—all can be moderated.

CONCENTRATION. This is the first step in the induction process and is the very first beneficial result of self-hypnosis.

CONFIDENCE. Self-image is enhanced, especially confidence. One develops greater sense of worthiness and other values, such as persistence.

CONSTIPATION. The sphincter muscles are trained to relax and elimination becomes easy. Strain and hemorroidal pain are greatly minimized.

CONSTRUCTION WORKERS. The need for balance, alertness, and courage. Fear of heights, tunnels, sewers, and electrical currents are areas we have helped.

CONTACT LENSES. People learn to wear contact lenses with comfort, reduce strain and excess tearing. A great aid to the ophtholmologist.

CONTRACEPTION. Self-hypnosis has been found helpful in reducing the tendency of body to reject diaphragms and intrauterine devices.

CONVALESCENCE. The calming influence of the meditative practice of hypnosis and self-hypnosis reduces patient restlessness, aids in recovery.

COUGHING. Nonorganic throat irritations can be removed. Constant cleaning of the throat is often due to nervous anxiety.

COURAGE. Facing the harsh realities of life takes mental-moral strength. Following through without faltering is made easier through hypnosis.

CREATIVITY. Free the hidden abilities in any and all creative areas—painting, sculpture, dance, interior decorating, writing, music, etc.

CRIME. Hypnosis is used in prisons to correct underlying antisocial attitudes. Also to discover motives and hidden information.

DANCING. Learn steps easily, develop timing, grace and rhythm. For professionals—overcome stage fright. Greater poise.

DEATH. Coping, calming with the inevitability of death is a difficulty made easier when the mind is trained to enter the ALPHA STATE.

DENTISTRY. A popular practice in the removal of pain, especially in cases where Novocaine cannot be used. No fear of needles—quick healing.

DENTURES. Artificial dentures more easily accepted. Settle into the gums quickly and soon begin to work as one's own teeth. Gums heal faster.

DEPRESSION. Psychologists and analysts report remarkable results with hypnotic techniques as alternative or addition to drug therapy.

DERMATOLOGY. Most skin disturbances are emotionally connected. When all else fails hypnosis often turns the tide toward healing.

DETOXIFICATION. Self pollution from smoking, drugs, alcohol or bad diet is alleviated by the contact between mind and body.

DIABETES. An aid for the diabetic in sticking to his diet. In some cases, detected early, remission of the illness has been reported.

DIARRHEA. Chronic nervous bowel behavior becomes subliminal until the deeper mind is contacted to re-condition the reflexes.

DIETING. For people on a salt-restricted, cholesterol, carbohydrate diet, self-hypnosis is a boon, bringing control of appetite.

DIRECTED DREAM. An aid to unblocking fears and anxieties. Administered under professional direction can also be used for self-understanding.

DISCIPLINE. Hypnosis spurs the urge to do what needs to be done with decisiveness and determination. Eliminate excuses and cop-outs.

DRUG DEPENDENCY. Correct the basic insecurities which lead to drug addiction. A high euphoric feeling under hypnosis makes drugs unnecessary.

DYSMENORRHEA. Menstrual pains and cramps can be alleviated. This is done with approval of the physician after thorough medical examination.

DYSPHONIA. A relatively common disorder which appears as hoarseness. For no apparent reason, the voice becomes higher or lower than usual.

EATING. You can develop an aversion to unhealthy foods or beverages. Learn the ability to control urges and keep the proper weight level.

EDUCATION. Examinations and tests become easier. Assimilating knowledge for a better career, greater self-respect and increased income.

ELECTROLYSIS. The removal of unwanted hair from the face and other parts of the body can be accomplished without pain under hypnosis.

ELEVATORS. Fear of elevators affects many people and, fortunately, is corrected with ease by a trained hypnotist. Desensitization techniques.

EMOTIONAL CONTROL. Hypnosis increases insight to the reasons we have emotional highs and lows and acts to stablize.

EMPHYZEMA. Like bronchitis and asthma, this respiratory condition can not only be minimized but often brought under control.

ENERGY. Stamina is sometimes more mental than physical. Quick energy is suggested. "One hour's rest shall equal five or six."

ENTHUSIASM. Joyfulness in relation to work and people. The power of the mind can inject a sense of high expectation of good happenings.

ENURESIS. Bedwetting, a common problem affecting young children. Often remains into teens. Hypnosis helps when all else fails.

ESPIONAGE. The secret material codes and messages are memorized on a subliminal level to be recalled later under hypnosis. Used world-wide.

EXERCISE. The discipline to exercise regularly becomes automatic. Using self-hypnosis, one is unaware of the exertion. Results quickened.

EYESTRAIN. Nerves and muscles around the eyes relax. Circulation increases. Train yourself to come out of the trance with clearer vision.

EXORCISM. Practice of removing unwanted spirit beings. Hypnotists have been employed under supervision of priest, minister, or psychiatrist.

FAINTING. Momentary loss of consciousness, swooning or lightheadiness comes from loss of circulation to the brain. Hypnosis encourages bloodflow.

FAITH. People who lose belief in themselves can be opened up to trust and anticipation of positive happenings. Believing helps in receiving.

FAITH HEALING. The scientific process of the healing is through the subjects own mental faculties. Belief creates change.

FASTING. For religious or health purposes, anyone can be conditioned to fast for a day or several days, depending upon the situation.

FEARS OF ALL KINDS. Fire, darkness, snakes, spiders, shadows, thunder. All respond to some degree to positive suggestion in a trance.

FEEDBACK. Reinforcement from mind to body reflexes. Hypnosis functions to strengthen inner programming to modify behavior quickly.

FERTILITY. In cases where the inability to bear children is psychological rather than organic, a reversal of attitude often brings about pregnancy.

FETISHES. Those who are dependent upon an object to function sexually can be deprogrammed, then reprogrammed in order to function normally.

FEVER. Body temperature may be elevated or lowered by hypnotic means in cases where problem is psychogenic rather than organic.

FLAGELLATION. The art of whipping as a sexual excitement. Often a manifestation of sadomasochism. Correctable if motivated.

FLATULENCE. Passing wind can be controlled with subconscious conditioning. Even in cases where there is a digestive problem. The mind can postpone.

FLYING. A popular solution to the fear of flight, hypnosis has been used by thousands. Therapy consists of sleeping through trip pleasantly.

FORENSIC HYPNOSIS. An aid to lawyers in uncovering the truth. Forgotten information, dates, names and places recalled.

FORGETFULNESS. A memory disturbance often associated with emotionally charged situations. Desire to avoid pain of the past.

FRIGIDITY. A term denoting lack of female sexual response. Difficulty in reaching orgasm. Hypnosis proves it is mental instead of physical.

GAGGING. Difficulty in swallowing pills is often habit rather than organic interference. The throat can be opened to receive medication.

GAMBLING. Compulsive habits, having been learned, can be unlearned. Suggestions for a more constructive way of life are instilled.

GENDER IDENTITY. The behavior and appearance of masculinity or femininity can be strengthened. Orientation toward assigned role sometimes accomplished.

GERIATRICS. The handling of elderly patients is simplified by the use of positive suggestion. Appetite improves as well as disposition.

GOALS. The setting of short-term and long-term goals is an important aspect of hypnotic programming. We can all benefit by planning ahead.

GOLF. Players report increased stamina, greater concentration, elimination of slicing and raising of the head. Scores improve remarkably.

GOOSE FLESH. The contraction of the small muscles surrounding hair follicles occurs during fright or extreme cold. The mind modifies.

GROWTH. Exceptionally effective in the psychological sense. Also, useful physically for undersized children and teenagers.

G-SPOT. Women report that under self-hypnosis they can identify the vaginal area and intensify internal orgasmic feeling.

GUILT FEELINGS. Realization that one has done wrong often exaggerated. Associated with lowered self-esteem and need for self-punishment.

GYNECOLOGY. The physician finds hypnotic suggestion an important aid in relaxing the nervous patient in order to carry out examination.

GYNEPHOBIA. A morbid fear of contact with a woman's body often stems from early negative experience. Regression to source brings awareness.

HABITS. Repetitive behavior becomes entrenched in the subconscious. Get into your subconscious and exchange bad habits for good ones.

HAIR GROWTH. Reports indicate that self-hypnosis, diligently applied, can retard loss of hair. In some cases, even regrowth has been noted.

HALLUCINATIONS. Imagined or false sense of perception (often found among mentally disturbed) can be helped in a receptive subject.

HANDICAPPED. No matter the disability, the power of the mind can provide a hopeful attitude and the confidence to improve.

HANDWRITING. Correcting problems in writing is made easier by using subliminal suggestions and visualization techniques.

HEADACHES. Even severe migraine appears to respond in varying degrees to hypnotic suggestion and deep relaxation. Throbbing ceases.

HEADBANGING. Commonly observed during temper tantrums in small children. Best time for induction is before bedtime.

HEALING. Psychosomatic ailments especially show improvement with ultra-depth techniques. Faith healers often use hypnotic methods.

HEARING. Some nonorganic problems have been recorded as highly responsive to hypnosis. Also used to develop tolerance to hearing aids.

HEARTBURN. Chronic digestive discomfort is lessened by relaxing the sphincter muscles which surround the esophogus.

HICCUPS. The spasms which persistently rock the diaphragm. When all else seems to fail, hypnosis often brings instantaneous results.

HOARDING. The practice of collecting objects of a particular kind that have no practical use. Usually a sign of emotional disturbance, need for love.

HOMOSEXUALITY. Transference to heterosexual relationships has been successful in many cases where the motivation has been strong.

HYDROPHOBIA. Fear of water is often encountered in the day-to-day work of hypnotists. Anyone can become a fearless swimmer with help.

HYPERACTIVITY. Excessive muscular activity, often refers to disturbed childhood behavior. Short attention span, relaxation helps.

HYPERSEXUALITY. Greatly increased sexual activity beyond one's physical needs. Persistent repetition of the sex act, yet never achieving orgasm.

HYPNODRAMA. A useful technique in which the subject cybernetically re-enacts past problems or relationships and discovers solutions.

HYPOCHONDRIA. The person who consistently fears imagined illnesses can use his imaginative powers to eliminate anxieties and face reality.

HYPERESTHESIA. Increased sensitivity to touch, sometimes excruciating. Seen in hysterics who overact to physical stimuli. Tolerance.

HYPERTENSION. High blood pressure responds favorably to hypnosis under medical and clinical supervision. Self-hypnosis self monitors.

HYPERVENTILATION. Because this condition is stress-related, the introduction of hypnotic breathing techniques brings relief.

HYSTERECTOMY. Pre-operative suggestion for emotional and physical recovery accelerates the post operative stages of healing.

HYSTERICS. An extremely emotional state resulting in abnormal sensations, fits of laughter, or convulsive crying. Hypnosis soothes and reassures.

IDEALIZATION. Overestimation of the love-object, which often leads to disappointment and depression. Object is exalted in the mind. Unreality.

IDENTITY CRISIS. Loss of the sense of person and social continuity. Inability to adapt to new role in society. Strong need to change personality.

IDEOGAMY. Inability to have sexual intercourse with any woman except one's wife or some individual woman. Situational impotence results.

ILLITERACY. Concentration and learning ability is maximized, as well as recall of information for reading and writing.

IMAGE IMPROVEMENT. Self-analysis under hypnotic guidance leads to a more realistic self-evaluation. You can see yourself at your best.

IMPOTENCE. Most cases of impotence are mental rather than physical. Therefore, mental persuasion can revive male's sexual drive.

IMPULSIVENESS. Sudden action without forethought or rational judgment often leads to mistakes. Preventing rash decisions becomes automatic.

INFERIORITY COMPLEX. Feeling of inadequacy in relation to others and the world are changeable. Self-worth takes over. Image improves.

INHIBITIONS. Conditioned attitudes which limit one's level of fulfillment can be altered. Useful in areas of sexuality and personality.

INCOMPATIBILITY. Marriage counselors find harmony and understanding often results from a joint hypnosis session including husband and wife.

INFECTIONS. Slow healing and low immune response can be strengthened by a dedicated program of positive suggestion.

INJECTIONS. The needle need not hurt at all. Learn simple self-hynosis method of affecting local anesthesia to any area of your body.

INTERCOURSE. Sexual interaction improves through removal of resistances and the control of sensation. Corrects psychosomatic disturbances.

INSECURITY. Irrational feelings of unprotectedness and helplessness vanish when a strong sense of independence and self-esteem is developed.

INSIGHT. Getting to know the "inner you" through repeated sessions with meditative self-hypnosis. Brings wide-range and penetrating awareness.

INTROVERSION. Common personality disturbance where the person's attention is morbidly turned inward limiting interaction with others.

INVALIDISM. The mental state of a patient who, though free of physical illness, imagines himself sick and refuses to accept healthy living.

IRRITABILITY. The testy individual who is easily disturbed by petty annoyances can be trained to remain calm and reason with logic.

ISOLATION. Fear or aversion to making contact with other people or groups. Self-inflicted loneliness can be replaced with friendliness.

ITCHING. Uncontrollable scratching, often with no organic cause, resulting from nervousness or habit. Self-hypnosis smooths and soothes.

JEALOUSY. The insecurity which underlies envious feelings about another person are lessened. Insight and understanding improve with self esteem.

JET LAG. Plane travel can turn one's day into night. Equilibrium and balance is re-established quickly. Adjustment to new time schedule.

JOCKEYS. For extra stamina when feelings of exhaustion begin. Improve timing of trot and pacing. Think like a winner. Patience and energy.

JOGGING. Long distance joggers often "psyche" themselves up to reach higher goals of acheivment. Persistance is improved.

JOVIALITY. Put your most cheerful face forward. Getting out of the doldrums is easy with inner suggestion. Relate to others openly with warmth.

JUDGMENT. Think things through to logical conclusion. Recognize true relationship of ideas. Avoid snap judgments. See other point of view.

JUVENILE DELINQUENCY. Group hypnosis works wonders for young people in trouble. Hypnosis presents alternatives to anti-social behavior.

KICK-OFF. Football players report posthypnotic suggestion can increase distance and accuracy. Mental rehearsal during hypnosis builds power.

KLEPTOMANIA. Compulsive stealing because of emotional needs. Hypnosis can reveal reasons for behavior through regression and automatic writing.

LANGUAGE. The time involved in learning a new language is cut to about one-third. Recall improves. Learn to think in new language.

LARYNGITIS. Inflammation of the larynx can be lessened with focused healing. Trance-level meditation speeds return of voice.

LAZINESS. Indolence, aversion to work. Habitual resistance gives way to repetitive suggestion for improved motivation.

LEADERSHIP. Organizational and political leaders use the dynamics of mind-power to build a following. Helps in public speaking, TV, etc.

LEARNING HABITS. Students find that self hypnosis can make their study time more effective. Helps in passing exams.

LEISURE. Program your leisure time to make the most of every moment. Develop the ability to relax quickly while on vacation. Plan your trip.

LESIONS. Wounds from injuries or surgery heal faster with hypnotic suggestion. We have also noticed less pain and signs of scarring.

LETHARGY. The listless person who feels drowsy or dull needs the psychic lift in spirits and energy only his mental energy can give him.

LIMPING. In cases of labored, jerky movements when walking, imagery helps if lameness has not completely atrophied the muscles from disuse.

LISPING. Like shuttering and stammering, speech impediments show remarkable improvement with the help of a skilled practitioner of hypnosis.

LONGEVITY. Regular sessions of relaxation, coupled with positive suggestion to improve health, adds up to extra years without ailments.

LOVABILITY. For those who have difficulty in relating to others, hypnosis brings added charisma and empathy.

LOVE. The ability to express affection and to receive pleasure from others—ability to gratify oneself as well as others.

LYING. The habitual fabricator often is unaware of his deeply rooted habit. With guidance and training he learns to face realities of life.

MALINGERING. Simulation of symptoms of illness or injury with intent to deceive. For some people this can become an escape from reality.

MANNERS. Improve the behavior of the young. Politeness, consideration in cases of unruliness, or need for group training as in schools.

MARIJUANA. Dependency on pot for euphoric feeling is replaced with natural tranquillity and mind-control over physical/emotional self.

MARITAL DISCORD. Marriage counselors use hypnosis to bring couples closer. Communication established under joint hypnotic induction.

MARKSMANSHIP. Self-hypnosis sharpens visual concentration. Steadier nerves and muscles increase coordination for greater accuracy.

MASOCHISM. A person who enjoys inflicting pain and discomfort upon himself, as well as encouraging another to mistrust him—self-hate.

MASSAGE. Hypnotic suggestion when combined with stroking and muscle manipulation expands benefits of deep relaxation. Learn technique easily.

MASTURBATION. Excessive self-stimulation resulting in psychological dependency and exclusion of other forms of intercourse. Controlled.

MATHEMATICS. Greater insight and understanding of basic principles. Numerical formulas absorbed quickly under concentrated meditation.

MEDICATION. The administration of medicines, swallowing of pills becomes easier with a cooperative patient. Many nurses use indirect hypnosis.

MEMORY. The mental faculty of retaining information for immediate recall becomes enhanced with the improved concentration which results.

MENOPAUSE. The discomfort of "change of life" which many women experience as hot flashes and dizziness is often more mental than physical.

MENTAL HEALTH. As a preventive measure, hypnosis has no rival, because it is based on developing a positive outlook on all issues.

METAPHYSICS. Psychics employ hypnotic techniques to enhance extra sensory perception and study parapsychological phenomena.

MIGRAINE HEADACHES. The tensions which bring on severe pain are dispersed. Diminishes throbbing at temples. Used in many clinics.

MODELS. Very useful for maintaining posture in both fashion work as well as artists' models. Also, to maintain weight. Build confidence.

MONEY MAKING. Increasing one's income comes with the organization of mind and time. Plan a positive program of action.

MOTIVATION. This is the deciding factor between success and failure. Post-hypnotic suggestion spurs energy to reach goals.

MOURNING. When sorrow and lamentation exceeds the normal mourning period, a hypnotist can divert attention toward other pursuits.

MUSCLE CRAMPS. "Charley horse" or other spastic muscle pains respond to the relaxing methods of hypnosis. Nerves "let go."

MUSIC. Perception of sound is sensitized and amplified. Subtler nuances of melody more easily recognized in music appreciation.

MYSOPHOBIA. Unnatural anxiety about dirt, germs, and infections. People so troubled tend to wash their hands too often or wear gloves.

NAGGING. Like other troublesome habits, this one lends itself to the deconditioning process of hypnotic suggestion. Awareness increases.

NARCISSISM. An exaggerated opinion of oneself, usually a reaction to low self-esteem. Demonstrated by constantly looking in the mirror.

NAIL BITING (or picking). A simple problem to overcome. Often a few sessions with a professional hypnotist is all that is required.

NAUSEA. Stomach distress can be alleviated if psychogenic. In cases of extreme obesity, practitioner may suggest nausea to curb appetite.

NEATNESS. Both youngsters and adults who tend to be careless and slovenly learn how to organize their belongings and improve appearance.

NECROPHILIA. A sexual perversion, real or fantasy, in which the love object must be dead in order for the disturbed person to become aroused.

NECROPHOBIA. An unreasonable terror of being in the presence of a dead person. Manifested in dread of photos of coffins, attending funerals, etc.

NEGATIVISM. A conditioning of thinking which plagues many. One goes against own best interests. Positivism replaces old attitudes quickly.

NEURESTHENIA. A nervous disorder; general decline in mental and physical energy characterized by symptoms of fatigue, aches, pains, and depression.

NERVOUSINESS. Emotional stress and anxiety respond quickly and easily. Remarkable results are witnessed after the very first session.

NIGHT-EATING. The syndrome of nighttime nibbling even when not hungry is very common. Often people wake up in middle of night for an unnecessary snack.

NIGHTMARES. Terrifying dreams can be lessened by self-hypnosis exercises before falling asleep. In many cases, pleasant dreams can be suggested.

NIGHT-WALKING. Somnambulistic strolling can be dangerous. Autosuggestions before bedtime very helpful to eliminate this compulsion.

NOISINESS. Sensitivity to sound, even when so moderate as to go unnoticed by others can seriously disturb the ultra-sensitive. Desensitization used.

NOSE BLEEDS. Stress factor is often responsible for difficulty in conquering chronic and persistent nose-bleeding. Hypnotists report success.

NURSING. Nurses find the techniques of relaxation and positive suggestion aid in healing. Also recommended for nursing mothers. Improves milk.

NYCTOPHOBIA. Abnormal fear of nighttime or darkness. Shadows seem to move like monsters. Usually associated with traumatized young children.

NYMPHOMALNIA. Used to describe a woman with uncontrollable, insatiable sexual desires. Denoting frequency of desire rather than complete fulfillment.

OBEDIENCE. Hypnosis is sometimes employed in classroom situations where turmoil and unruly behavior interferes with the welfare of the group.

OBESITY. Lose weight without hunger pangs. Weight loss is steady and remains off permanently as new eating habits are established.

OBSESSIONS. Are emotional impulses that persistently force themselves into one's consciousness. Thoughts can be rechannelled.

OBSTACLES. Blocks and interferences to successful living can be overcome. With persistent autosuggestion under self-hypnosis, careers blossom.

OBSTETRICS. Treatment of women before, during and after childbirth. Obstetrician uses hypnosis to eliminate pain during delivery.

OCCULT. Mediums and psychics use the hypnotic trance to tap their cosmic "sixth sense." Reports of astral projection and other psychic phenomena.

OCCUPATIONAL APTITUDE. New approaches and added possibilities open up. Abilities, skills, and talents long hidden reveal themselves.

OPHIDIOPHOBIA. Fear of snakes can be so obsessive as to extend even to words and pictures as well as the letter S. Hypnosis desensitizes.

OPPORTUNITY. Recognizing opportunity when it knocks takes perception and positive anticipation. Insight and planning through meditation.

OPTOMETRY. Hypnosis is a boon to doctors in fitting glasses and contact lenses. Toleration of lenses becomes easier and adjustment time is shorter.

OPTIMISM. Positive thinking increases immediately because hypnosis is based on the concept, "make the most of the best, the least of the worst."

ORAL COMPULSION. Overeating, nail biting, smoking, alcoholism, thumb sucking, constant munching. All respond to proper suggestion.

ORGANIZATION. Work out logical plans, and learn to tie up loose ends. Neatness, accuracy enhanced. Tap your subconscious to work out a plan.

ORGASM. Sexual inhibition which retards development of feeling during intercourse. For both men and women greater control becomes natural.

ORTHODONTICS. The prevention and correction of irregular teeth. Practitioners find hypnotic suggestion helps patients tolerate braces.

OVERDOSE. Hypnotists have been called in to bring about vomiting in cases of poisoning or drug abuse. Hypnosis also helps in keeping alert.

PAIN CONTROL. In cases where continuance of drugs is harmful, hypnosis can be used to remove sensation of pain and lower its threshold.

PANAPHOBIA. A sense of panic which might be related to almost anything. The anxiety-ridden victim remains alienated from others and stays indoors.

PARAPSYCHOLOGY. Mediums and others involved in the occult often use the hypnotic trance to expand their awareness and concentration.

PASSIVITY. Nonassertiveness causes many people to live a limited life. Hypnosis builds confidence and bolsters ego to behave more assertively.

PATENCE. A great virtue of happy living is waiting serenely for things to happen. Learning to be tolerant of others comes with inner peace.

PERCEPTION. Open your sensory system to keener awareness through sight, hearing, touch, smell and taste. Sensitize input and learn control.

PERSPIRATION. Unusual sweating, often a sign of inner stress. Sweaty palms reveal anxieties raging within. Easily corrected through hypnosis.

PESSIMISM. Because the basic premise of hypnosis is to "think positively" inevitably the practitioner becomes uplifted in his mental outlook.

PHOTOGRAPHY. Knowledge of hypnotic techniques (with approval of subject) helps in getting more relaxed poses and best facial expression.

PHOBIAS. The variety of phobias seem endless. Dust, wind, forests, birds, caves, heights, ocean, cracks in the sidewalk, etc., etc.

PHYSIOTHERAPY. Hypnosis is a dependable aid to the therapist who is retraining patients to use their muscles to function better. Aids walking.

PIANO PLAYING. Finger dexterity is improved. Memory becomes sharper. Regular practice can become a joy rather than a chore. Opens creativity.

PILOTS. In order to stay alert and attentive under all circumstances, pilots use self-hypnosis for energy stimulation. Excellent for students.

POETRY. Under meditation, listening to the still, small voice of inspiration produces elevated inner thoughts and beautiful concepts.

POISE. Inner confidence and calm attitude shines through, bringing an aura of regal pride. Useful for actors, lecturers, and politicians.

POSTURE. Slouching is bad body language. Train your body to sit stand, and walk in a balanced, erect way. Visual imagery and muscle training.

PREMATURE EJACULATION. A sexual disorder which troubles many men. Dramatic improvement becomes evident after just a few hypnotic sessions.

PREVENTION OF ILLNESS. Hypnosis reinforces good health habits and strengthens the will-power to improve lifestyle.

PROCRASTINATION. Getting on with the tasks which need doing, rather than putting them off. Taking immediate action is programmed subconsciously.

PROMPTNESS. Some people are late for every appointment, to the annoyance of others. Punctuality can be trained into the reflexes with quick results.

PSORIASIS. Many professional hypnotists report great improvement in patients referred by doctors. Some cases of dramatic remission.

PSYCHOSOMATIC AILMENTS. Science has accepted that the mind can make one ill. Therefore, reversing the action, the mind can also help one improve.

PSYCHOTHERAPY. Hypnosis allows the doctor to open his patient to reveal hidden problems under a detached transcendent state of being.

PYROMANIA. Morbid impulse to set fire to things. Often culminates in the actual act of setting fires. Analysis under hypnosis reveals reasons.

PYROPHOBIA. Terrifying fear of fire. Victims often complain of recurring nightmares of being burned. Sometimes associated with religion.

QUALIFYING. In sports, auditions, job interviews, those employing self-hypnosis have greater confidence and stronger positive expectations.

QUEASINESS. Uneasiness and discomfort such as nausea or dizziness. Sometimes used to denote a troubled or guilty conscience.

QUERULENCE. Suspicious and unreasonable, touchy, easily dissatisfied, complaining of ill-treatment without cause. A personality disturbance.

QUIBBLING. Argumentative for the sake of arguing. Nit-picking. Such a person uses ambiguous or irrelevant language to evade a definitive point.

QUOTIENT, INTELLIGENCE. The ratio of a subject's intelligence (determined by tests) compared to average for his age group. Hypnosis removes blocks.

RACIAL RELATIONS. Hypnosis found to bring greater tolerance and acceptance during periods of racial strife. Used in group therapy sessions.

RACING. The mind makes the difference in contests of speed such as running, driving, sailing. Self-hypnosis can decide if you're a winner or not.

RADIOLOGY. Radiologists report that hypnosis facilitates diagnostic procedures. Eliminates anxieties and relaxes intestinal tensions.

RAPE. Hypnosis is imployed to great advantage for both rehabilitating the victim as well as in treating the sexual offender to understand his act.

READING SKILLS. For slow learners where remedial work is indicated, reading skill is accelerated through the help of a professional.

RECONDITIONING. Hypnotic techniques prove useful in restoring normalcy to damaged body reflexes, mental attitudes and emotional stability.

REGRESSION. A valuable tool in psychoanalytical work with disturbed people. A return in memory to earlier behavior to understand and correct.

REHABILITATION. Hypnosis used in conjunction with medication. Vocational retraining to achieve maximum psychosocial adjustment. Speeds recovery.

REJUVENATION. Mitigates pathological symptoms of old age. Good results with sexual impotence in men. Restores a more youthful appearance in women.

RELAXATION. Relief from body tension is almost immediate as progressive body relaxation is the first step toward hypnotic induction.

RESPIRATION. In cases of breathing difficulty such as emphysema and asthma, hypnosis relaxes the chest muscles, restores normal rhythms.

RHEUMATISM. A painful disorder of joints or extremities or back. A medical referral required to hypnotist who lessens pain and stiffness.

RHINOPLASTY. Plastic surgeon of the nose is often painful with swelling and difficulty in breathing. Bruises diminished.

SADISM. Describing people whose sexual pleasure depends on pain, or cruelty. Humiliating another person also a personality problem.

SALESMANSHIP. The ability to convince others to buy one's product increased by direct eye-to-eye contact and persuasive tone of voice.

SCULPTURE. Greater feeling for form and design. Dexterity of hands and strength of media control. Originality of composition enhanced.

SEASICKNESS. The rocking motion of rough seas can be easily ignored under posthypnotic suggestion. Nausea and anxiety diminished.

SEIZURES. At the first warning of a peti-mal seizure, rapid induction and positive suggestion helps to diminish the distress.

SELF-IMAGE. Get to like yourself through deeper insight. Learn to see your best attributes. Live up to your highest potential. Succeed.

SENILITY. Characteristic manifestations of old age can be retarded with the early application of antiaging hypnotic techniques.

SEXUALITY. Overcome unsureness in relation to intimacy. Build confidence and assertiveness. Experience sexual fulfillment in every way.

SHORTHAND. Lean the symbols under concentrated meditation. Self-hypnosis makes assimilation of learning quicker and recall often complete.

SHYNESS. Socially inept people learn to become more outgoing, able to meet new people without embarrassment. Develop better communication.

SINGERS. Dry throat and tense vocal cords are relaxed. Pitch may be improved and range of sound extended. Volume and resonance increased.

SKIN RASHES. Dermatologists often send patients with nonspecific skin problems to hypnotherapists to explore for possible psychogenic causes.

SMOKING. Many lives have been saved by removing the desire. Thousands of clinics are using hypnotic-type methods to help people quit smoking.

SNEEZING. Uncontrollable spasms of sneezing have been brought under restraint when every other method has failed. Hypnosis interrupts reflex.

SNORING. Self-suggestion under autohypnosis applied just before falling asleep will alleviate this problem. Posthypnosis lasts through the night.

SOMNAMBULISM. Deepest trance level of hypnosis where there is no memory when awakened. Also observed in sleepwalkers without hypnotic trance.

SOMNILOQUY. Talking in one's sleep may not only disturb one's bedmate, but cause problems for erring husbands. Subject rouses before speaking.

SPACE TRAVEL. Astronauts as well as regular pilots find techniques of hypnotic time distortion useful in tolerating stress. Fortitude.

SPEEDREADING. Concentration and mental focus is increased. Outside distractions are transcended. Retention and comprehension improved.

STAGE-FRIGHT. Performers, politicians and lecturers rise above fear of facing an audience. Stage presence projected. Poise, charisma.

STUDY HABITS. Organization and determination to succeed on a higher level. Improves concentration and reduces anxiety about examinations.

STUTTERING. Spasmodic gripping of the vocal cords is relieved. Many children have shown remarkable control in just a few weeks of hypnosis.

SUICIDE. Those despondent souls on the verge of ending their lives can be deterred by hypnosis until proper analysis corrects the cause.

SURGERY. Your mind can bring about analgesia and anesthesia. Freedom from fear. Minimizes bleeding. Accelerates healing and recovery.

SWIMMING. Olympic champions tell us that self-hypnosis makes the difference between mediocrity and winning the meet. Improves timing and rhythm.

TACHYPHAGIA. Compulsive food grabbing and eating rapidly without regard for taste or hunger. Often found in deteriorating schizophrenics.

TALENT. Natural untapped abilities and aptitudes are discovered by reaching into the deeper areas of mind. Visualization of work completed.

TARDINESS. People who are habitually late for appointments, who dawdle or behave in a sluggish manner can be aided and trained for promptness.

TEACHING. Imparting knowledge takes patience and tolerance. Instructors use both self-hypnosis for themselves and "hetero-" for students.

TEAMWORK. In collegiate sports, group hypnosis has proven most effective. Even the "peptalk" before a game is a form of indirect hypnotic suggestion.

TELEPATHY. The exchange of thoughts or images. This faculty can be expanded under hypnotic training. Bypass conscious thoughts of limitation.

TEMPER TANTRUM. An angry, explosive state of mind can be brought back to reason. Tolerance induced. Irritability reduced. Control instilled.

TENSION. The stress and strain of everyday living troubles all of us. The immediate effect of hypnotic system is profound relaxation.

TENNIS. Learn how great your abilities are with inner tennis. Using visual images you train your mind to control your muscle reflexes.

TERMINAL ILLNESS. Helping the patient to minimize pain and

emotional anxieties toward the end of life. Inner calm and acceptance of death.

TOOTHACHES. Until one is able to visit the dentist, hypnosis removes pain and discomfort. Some practitioners affect total anesthesia.

TRANSCENDENTAL MEDITATION. A highly lauded Indian technique is in reality a medium level of self-hypnosis, in which one rises above stress.

TRICHOTILLOMANIA. A morbid tendency to pull one's own hair. Often associated with anxiety-prone young children as well as adults.

TRISKAIDEKAPHOBIA. Fear of the number thirteen manifests itself in various restricting ways, such as fear of the thirteenth of each month.

TWITCHING. Involuntary spasms of muscles cause jerking movements of the face or parts of the body. Dramatic results through relaxing nerves.

TYPEWRITING. Develop speed and minimize errors through increasing your concentration and finger dexterity. Muscle reflexes become automatic.

ULCERS. Medically described as psychophysiologic in origin, this disorder of the digestive tract can be cleared up with suggestion.

UNCOMFORTABLE. The common state of uneasiness due to new or distressful circumstances can be corrected because hypnosis tranquilizes.

UNDERACHIEVING. Failure to succeed or perform up to one's ability is often based on low self-esteem. Image improved through mirror technique.

UNDERSTANDING. Comprehension can be expanded as one taps the deeper areas of inner intelligence. The power of abstract thinking enhanced.

UNREALITY. The escapist has difficulty in coping with practical problems. Under hypnotherapy reality is visualized as less threatening.

UROPHILIA. A pathological, inordinate interest in urine and urination. Often in relation to sexual preferences and perversity. Correctible.

VAGINA DENTATA. A morbid fantasy that the female vagina has teeth. Vaginal opening equated with a devouring mouth. Employ desensitization.

VAGINISMUS. Pain during intercourse is brought about by spasms of the internal sphincter muscles. Self-hypnosis loosens the tensions.

VANDALISM. A hostile compulsion to destroy the property of

others. The underlying anger is uncovered and brought under control through hypnosis.

VASECTOMY. Surgical contraception for males is made more comfortable. Freedom from pain or anxiety as accelerated healing takes place.

VERBIGERATE. To repeat the same word or phrase over and over again. Often this deeply rooted habit is subconscious and needs trance level.

VERTIGO. A sensation of dizziness, a whirling in the head, feelings of imbalance are usually symptoms of aggravated stress. Hypnosis works.

VIRILITY. Manly vigor can be greatly enhanced. Sexual performance improves and mental concentration takes over control of genitals.

VISION. Many people report improved sight in cases where the problem is stress-related rather than organic or genetic in origin.

VITALITY. When energy is at a low ebb, your mind can bring you at burst of renewed power. Vibrant added stamina can result.

VOCABULARY. Extending one's capacity to use words correctly, add new words to enrich one's speech and communicate with other people.

VOCATIONAL APTITUDE. Tapping the warehouse of talents and skills to improve income and pleasure in working. Hidden abilities surface.

VOICE. You can improve the sound of your voice. Loud, soft, harshness. Speaking too fast or too slow. Getting rid of unwanted accents.

VOMITING. In cases of intestinal distress or food poisoning, vomiting can be brought about by suggestion under hypnosis with medical aid.

VOYEURISM. Inordinate desire to spy on members of the opposite sex for sexual gratification. Regression to source provides relief.

WANDERLUST. The compulsion to rove about and travel without regard to circumstances which demand staying in one place. Inner peace.

WARTS. Many hypnotists are reporting excellent results in the removal of warts and other skin growths. Check with physician first.

WEAKNESS. Lack of physical strength is often based on mental attitude. Feelings of exhaustion must first be checked by a doctor.

WEALTH. Most millionaires have adopted a mental method in visualization. They see their goals as easily obtainable and forge ahead.

WEATHER ACCLIMATION. An ability to adjust to changes in weather. Extreme heat or freezing weather can be made less stressful.

WEIGHT. The stabilization of weight can be attained for the under weight as well as the overweight. Fluctuation brought under control.

WHEEZING. Difficulty in inhaling and exhaling causes some people to emit a whistling sound such as that associated with asthma. Ameliorated.

WILL-POWER. Self-bypnosis brings the ability to use inner mental persuasion to achieve control over one's disturbing behavior patterns.

WISDOM. Enhance your inner potential for deep creative meditation. Ancient gurus and seers have established prayer and meditation for this.

WITHDRAWAL SYMPTOMS. Chills, excessive sneezing, cramps, vomiting, and muscular twitching an respond favorably to suggestion under hypnosis.

XENOPHOBIA. An unreasonable fear and/or hatred of foreigners or strangers. To a lesser degree discomfort of anything new or unusual.

X-RAY TECHNICIANS. To quiet patients and gain their co-operation. Used indirectly, on a light trance level, for holding positions.

YAWNING. Uncontrollable, repetitive yawning can be both embarrassing and irritating. Your habit reflexes can be reconditioned to resist.

YOUTHFULNESS. A feeling of enthusiasm and freshness is more mental than physical. Therefore try mental persuasion and see the change.

ZEST. Motivational energy to set practical goals and reach them without wasting time. The listless person finds new meaning to life.

ZOOLAGNIA. Sexual attraction to animals, sometimes unconscious as in extreme adoration of pets to the exclusion of human sexual relations.

ZOOPHOBLA. Fear of all animals no matter how small or tame. Usually associated with trauma in childhood. Banish with regression to source.

WITNESS AGAINST THE BEAST

To
David Erdman

WITNESS AGAINST
THE BEAST

*William Blake and
the Moral Law*

E. P. THOMPSON

'Christ died as an Unbeliever'
WILLIAM BLAKE

The New Press, New York

Published in the United States by The New Press, New York
Distributed by W. W. Norton & Company, Inc.
500 Fifth Avenue, New York, NY 10110

Library of Congress cataloging in publication data

Thompson, E. P. (Edward Palmer), 1924–
Witness against the beast: William Blake and the moral law / by
E. P. Thompson
p. cm.
ISBN 1 56584 058 5
1. Blake, William, 1757–1827 – Political and social views.
2. Dissenters, Religious – England – History – 18th century.
3. Radicalism – England – History – 18th century.   4. Blake, William,
1757–1827 – Religion.   5. Blake, William, 1757–1827 – Ethics.
6. Ethics, Modern – 18th century.   7. Radicalism in literature.
8. Ethics in literature.   I. Title.
PR4148.P6T47   1993b
821'.7 – dc20   92–50819 CIP

First edition

Published simultaneously with Cambridge University Press,
Cambridge, England

Established in 1990 as a major alternative to the large,
commercial publishing houses, The New Press is the first
full-scale nonprofit American book publisher outside of
the university presses. The Press is operated editorially in
the public interest, rather than for private gain; it is
committed to publishing in innovative ways works of
educational, cultural, and community value, which despite
their intellectual merits might not normally be
"commercially" viable. The New Press's editorial offices
are located at the City University of New York.

Printed in the United States of America

10 9 8 7 6 5 4 3 2 1

Contents

Contents

Illustrations

(Between pages 106 and 107. All pictures are by William Blake.)

1 *Eve Tempted by the Serpent.* Tempera, painted for Thomas Butts, c.1799–1800 (courtesy of the Victoria & Albert Museum)
2 *Satan Exulting over Eve.* Pencil, pen and black ink and watercolour over colour print, 1795 (courtesy of the J. Paul Getty Museum)
3 *The Temptation and Fall of Eve*, from Nine Illustrations to *Paradise Lost.* Pen and watercolour on paper, 1808 (gift by subscription; courtesy of Museum of Fine Arts, Boston)
4 *Job's Evil Dreams*, Plate 11 of *Illustrations to the Book of Job*, 1821 (courtesy of the Pierpont Morgan Library, New York)
5 *Moses Erecting the Brazen Serpent.* Pen and watercolour on paper, c.1805 (purchased 1890; courtesy of Museum of Fine Arts, Boston)
6 Title page to *Europe*, 1794 (copy G; courtesy of the Pierpont Morgan Library, New York. PML 77235)
7 *Elohim Creating Adam.* Colour print finished in pen, from the Thomas Butts Collection, 1795 (courtesy of the Tate Gallery)
8 *Michael Foretells the Crucifixion*, from Nine Illustrations to *Paradise Lost.* Pen and watercolour on paper, 1808 (gift by subscription; courtesy of Museum of Fine Arts, Boston)
9 *The Nativity.* Tempera on copper, from the Thomas Butts Collection, c.1799 (courtesy of the Philadelphia Museum of Art, Gift of Mrs William T. Tonner)
10 'The Garden of Love', from *Songs of Experience*, 1794 (King's College, Cambridge. Print supplied by the Syndics of Cambridge University Library)
11 'London', from *Songs of Experience*, c.1794 (King's College, Cambridge. Print supplied by the Syndics of Cambridge University Library)

vii

Preface

This study has its origin in the Alexander Lectures delivered in the University of Toronto in 1978. I am very much remiss in delaying publication for so long, and I offer my apologies to the University. (The demands of the peace movement and, subsequently, illness contributed to the delay.) Although this text has greatly expanded from the Lectures, the book still carries their shape: that is, in Lecture 1 I somehow covered the themes in Part I of this book, and in Lectures 2 and 3 the themes in Part II. I must once again thank the University for its encouragement and hospitality.

I have had generous help from many persons: from Jean Barsley (formerly Mrs Noakes); from John and Susan Beattie and their family for their hospitality while I was in Toronto; from G.E. Bentley Jr, Katy Ellsworth, James Epstein, Michael Ferber, Heather Glen, P.M. Grams, J.F.C. Harrison, Christopher Hill, Peter Lineham, Günther Lottes, Iain McCalman, Hans Medick, Jon Mee, A.J. Morley, the late Philip Noakes, Morton D. Paley, Michael Phillips, Mary Thale, Sir Keith Thomas, Malcolm Thomas and John Walsh. Eveline King has transformed my untidy manuscript into accomplished typing. Dorothy Thompson, once more, has given me every kind of support.

I have dedicated the book to David Erdman, the great Blake scholar, even though the dedication may prove to be an embarrassment to him, since (as I know) he disagrees with several of my suggestions. He is the most generous and helpful scholar that I have known, and we have had rich exchanges – rich at least on his part – over the past thirty years. In 1968 we jointly taught a graduate course on Blake at New York University, and I have been warmly entertained by David and his wife, Virginia, at their house on Long Island. It has been a privilege to work alongside such a superb authority on the Romantics.

I also owe thanks to the libraries and institutions which I used during my research. These included the British Library, the Public Record Office, Westminster Library, the Bodleian, Birmingham University Library and Dr Williams's Library. Particular thanks must go to the Librarian and staff at the premises of the Swedenborg Society, who assisted me in many enquiries and who enabled me to consult Conference papers and Minutes, although they knew that I was not a receiver. My critical account of the early years of the Church is poor repayment, although accounts no less critical are endorsed in subsequent Swedenborgian scholarship. I must also thank Manchester University, whose award of a Simon Senior Fellowship in 1988–9 enabled me to catch up on my research, and to those graduate seminars (at Brown University, Dartmouth College, Queen's University, Ontario, and at Rutgers) which discussed these ideas with me and contributed their own thoughts. And my very warm thanks go to those who have, from time to time, given me material assistance to pursue my research: W.H. and Carol Terry, Mr and Mrs Kenneth F. Montgomery, James and Virginia Newmyer, and the Newby Trust.

My thanks must also go to those institutions which have given permission to me to reproduce pictures. (They are listed in the List of illustrations.) The chapter on 'London' is a slightly modified version of the same in *Interpreting Blake*, ed. Michael Phillips (Cambridge, 1978).

I use few abbreviations, and these are obvious ones. The exceptions are: in text and notes E stands for *The Poetry and Prose of William Blake* (New York, 1965), ed. David Erdman, with commentary by Harold Bloom. N refers to *The Notebook of William Blake*, ed. David Erdman (Oxford, 1973).

Introduction

I should explain at once what kind of a book this, and why I have been foolhardy enough to add yet one more volume to the overfull shelves of studies of William Blake. And, first of all, what this book is not. This is not another introduction to the poet and his works: excellent ones already exist. Nor is this a general interpretive study of William Blake as a whole, of his life, his writing, his art, his mythology, his thought. I will not even attempt a close engagement with the very substantial output of expert Blake studies in the past half-century. So that what I offer in this book must be, in some sense, a view from outside the world of Blake scholarship.

Can such a view be of any value? This will be for readers to judge. But I have been emboldened by a growing conviction that there are problems inside the world of Blake scholarship which might helpfully be commented upon by a historian from without. For while the scholarship advances, I am not certain that agreement about the man, or his ideas, or even about individual poems, advances in step. On the one hand, we have a multitude of individual studies, each adding some minute particulars to the sum. On the other hand, the intelligent reader, coming new to Blake, faces real difficulties in understanding what this sum may be. For there are now a great many William Blakes on offer, and while some of these are very much more convincing than others, most of them have some plausibility. Northrop Frye remarked many years ago that 'it has been said of Boehme that his books are like a picnic to which the author brings the words and the reader the meaning'. This remark, Frye continues, 'may have been intended as a sneer at Boehme, but it is an exact description of all works of literary art without exception'.

This has always seemed to me to be a wise comment; and yet it is a partial one, and one that leaves me uneasy. For there are so many picnics going on today – each one of them licensed by some words of Blake – and in so many different places. In 1965 Harold Bloom was able to write, with his customary confidence, that Blake 'was not an antiquarian, a mystic, an occultist or theosophist, and not much of a scholar of any writings beyond the Bible and other poetry insofar as it resembled the Bible'. I think that his judgement is more or less right, if we use the term 'scholar' in a modern, academic sense. And yet, both before and after that judgement, we have seen the publication of volumes, of some scholarly weight, to show Blake the neo-Platonist, the mason and illuminist, the profound initiate in hermetic learning, the proto-Marxist, the euhemerist, the Druid . . . And if more cautious scholars avoid such direct identifications, they offer us instead William Blake as a syncretic polymath – a man aware of all these positions and traditions, as well as others, moving freely through some remarkably well-stocked library, replete with ancient, Eastern, Hebrew and arcane, as well as modern, sources, and combining elements from all of these at will.

A historian has one difficulty with this. Blake's library – which by some accounts must have been costly and immense – has never been identified. I will return to this point, since I think we may be able to surmise one or two curious libraries, as well as his own private collection, to which he had access (see pp. 41–3). But even as we ask this mundane question (which library?), we are forced to ask ulterior questions. Who was Blake? Where do we place him in the intellectual and social life of London between 1780 and 1820? What particular traditions were at work within his mind? I have written this book in the hope that a historian's view, in this matter of placing, may prove to be helpful.

The problem today is to bring all of Frye's 'picnic parties' together. By all means let each of us bring our own meanings, but let us at least picnic in the same place. It is a curious consequence of the abundant Blake scholarship of the past few years that this has actually become more difficult than it used to be. Over a hundred years ago there was some consensus as to what kind of a man Blake was; the oral traditions and records resumed in Alexander Gilchrist's first major biography (1863) gave us a confident picture of a 'visionary', eccentric genius of robust 'Jacobinical' convictions. This placing was refined, but not substantially challenged, in Mona Wilson's *Life* of 1927; it was given a nudge to the 'Left' by Jacob Bronowski (*A Man without a Mask*, 1944), who perhaps over-stated the artisanal situation of Blake as an engraver; and this over-statement has been redressed by the learned studies, over a lifetime, of Sir Geoffrey Keynes, and of David Erdman, G.E. Bentley and many others, who have clearly identified Blake's familiarity with the community of London's artists.

Erdman's major study (*Blake: Prophet against Empire*, 1954, revised editions, 1965, 1969 and 1977) succeeded also in placing Blake's thought within the political and cultural context of his times. On the directly political themes I have (no doubt to the surprise of some readers) little to add. In my own placing of Blake I have learned very much from Erdman and I am greatly in his debt. All that his reconstruction of Blake lacks, in my view, is the thrust of a particular intellectual tradition: antinomianism. In brief, it is Blake's unique notation of Christian belief, and not his 'Jacobin' political sympathies, which still stands in need of examination. Despite Jon Mee's recent recovery of many possible contemporary influences upon Blake (*Dangerous Enthusiasm*, 1992) this still remains true.

This is not to say that the matter has gone unnoticed. As long ago as 1958 A.L. Morton published *The Everlasting Gospel: A Study in the Sources of William Blake*, and these insights were much enlarged in *The World of the Ranters* (1970) and by Christopher Hill in *The World Turned Upside Down* (1972). My debt to these scholars will be evident. But while Morton showed many suggestive parallels between 'Ranter' rhetoric and imagery and those of Blake, he could not identify any vectors between the 1650s and Blake's time. I cannot say that I have found with certainty any such vectors, but I have searched somewhat further, and I have also attended more closely to antinomian beliefs and their possible situation in the eighteenth-century intellectual culture. (If any readers are uncertain as to the meanings of antinomianism I must beg them to be patient: these will be explained.)

Despite every precaution, we have a continuing difficulty in our approach to Blake, which derives from our tendency to make overly academic assumptions as to his learning and mode of thought. It takes a large effort to rid ourselves of these assumptions, because they lie at an inaccessible level within our own intellectual culture – indeed, they belong to the very institutions and disciplines with which we construct that culture. That is, we tend to find that a man is either 'educated' or 'uneducated', or is educated to certain levels (within a relatively homogeneous hierarchy of attainments); and this education involves submission to certain institutionally defined disciplines, with their own hierarchies of accomplishment and authority.

Blake's mind was formed within a very different intellectual tradition. In the nineteenth century we sometimes call this, a little patronisingly, the tradition of the autodidact. This calls to mind the radical or Chartist journalist, lecturer or poet, attaining by his own efforts to a knowledge of 'the classics'. This is not right for Blake. For a great deal of the most notable intellectual energies of the eighteenth century lay outside of formal academic channelling. This was manifestly so in the natural sciences and in the *praxis* of the early industrial revolution; and it was equally so in important areas of theology and of political thought.

The formal, classical intellectual culture (which I will call 'the polite culture'), whose summits were attained at Oxford and Cambridge, was offered to only a small elite, and was, in theory, further limited by the need for students and fellows to conform to the doctrinal orthodoxy of the Church of England. Much of the (strongly intellectual) traditions of Dissent lay outside these doors. But alternative centres of intellectual culture can be seen not only at the level of such institutions as the Dissenting Academies. They exist also in stubborn minority traditions of many kinds.

Not only political and economic history can be seen as 'the propaganda of the victors': this is true also of intellectual history. Looking back from the nineteenth century, the victors appeared to be rationalism, political economy, utilitarianism, science, liberalism. And tracing the ancestry of these victors, it was possible to see eighteenth-century thought as the progression of 'enlightenment', sometimes working its way out through the churches, as rational Dissent passed through unitarianism to deism. It is only recently that historians have attended more closely to very vigorous alternative – and sometimes explicitly *counter*-enlightenment – impulses: the Rosicrucians, Philadelphians, Behmenists: or the elaborate theological and scientific theories of the Hutchinsonians, who were polemically anti-Newtonian, and who had both academic exponents and a more humble visionary following. In London in the 1780s – and, indeed, in Western Europe very generally – there was something like an explosion of anti-rationalism, taking the forms of illuminism, masonic rituals, animal magnetism, millenarian speculation, astrology (and even a small revival in alchemy), and of mystic and Swedenborgian circles.

Alternative intellectual traditions existed also – and especially in London – at the level of family traditions, and obscure intellectual currents surfacing, submerging and then surfacing again in little periodicals, or in chapels which fractured into several petty chapels, which invited new ministers or gathered around new voices, which knit up ideas and unravelled them and knit them up again throughout the eighteenth century. And we have to learn to see the minds of these men and women, formed in these kinds of collisions and voluntary associations, with more humility than patronage. Out of such an 'education', of informal traditions and collisions, came many original minds: Franklin, Paine, Wollstone-craft, Bewick, Cobbett, Thomas Spence, Robert Owen. And it is in this kind of tradition that we must place Blake.

In this tradition experience is laid directly alongside learning, and the two test each other. There is nothing of our present academic specialisation: thought may be borrowed, like imagery, from any source available. There is, in this tradition, a strong, and sometimes an excessive, self-confidence. And there is an insistent impulse towards individual system-building: the authority of the Church, demystified in the seventeenth century, had not yet been replaced by the authority of an academic hierarchy or of public 'experts'. In Blake's dissenting London of the 1780s and 1790s this impulse was at its height. Men and women did not only join the groups on offer, the Church of the New Jerusalem, the Universalists, the Muggletonians, the followers of William Huntington and of Richard Brothers (the self-proclaimed 'nephew' of the Almighty), they argued amidst these groups, they fractured them, took a point from one and a point from another, conceived their own heresies, and all the time struggled to define their own sense of system.

Of course, this has been recognised, and for a long time, by Blake scholars. I do not mean to read a lesson to those many scholars who have already done so much to place Blake's work in context. But historians have not yet done as much as might be done to help them, by recovering the obscure traditions of London Dissent, and in the absence of this work there is an ever-present tendency for criticism to slide into a de-contextual history of ideas.

And for this there might seem to be a licence afforded by Frederick
Tatham, a friend of William and Catherine Blake in their last
years, and an early biographer. Writing in 1832, Tatham said: 'His
mental acquirements were incredible, he had read almost every
thing in whatsoever language, which language he always taught
himself.' And more than thirty years later he repeated this claim:
Blake 'had a most consummate knowledge of all the great writers
in all languages . . . I have possessed books well thumbed and
dirtied by his graving hands, in Latin, Greek, Hebrew, French and
Italian, besides a large collection of works of the mystical writers,
Jacob Behmen, Swedenborg, and others.'

But if we set out to read 'almost everything in whatsoever language' we may end up, not with Blake, but with an academic
exercise. And from 'all the great writers in all languages' we are
at liberty to make our own selective construction of Blake's 'tradition', a construction which will actually distract us from William
Blake. If I must name names, then let me name Miss Kathleen
Raine, although her work (*Blake and Tradition*, 1968) is only one of
the most formidable of other works which offer to place Blake
in relation to Behmenist, hermetic, neo-Platonist and Kabbalistic
thought. In Raine's notion of 'the tradition' we are pointed towards
Porphyry or Proclus or Thomas Taylor (the neo-Platonist contemporary of Blake), and often suggestions are made which are helpful
and sometimes probable. But although Raine stands at an obtuse
angle to the reigning academicism, her notion of 'tradition' remains
academic to the core. Why is this so?

It is partly because we have become habituated to reading in
an academic way. Our books are not 'thumbed by graving hands'.
We learn of an influence, we are directed to a book or to a 'reputable' intellectual tradition, we set this book beside that book, we
compare and cross-refer. But Blake had a different way of reading.
He would look into a book with a directness which we might find
to be naïve or unbearable, challenging each one of its arguments
against his own experience and his own 'system'. This is at once
apparent from his surviving annotations – to Lavater, Swedenborg,
Berkeley, Bacon, Bishop Watson or Thornton.

He took each author (even the Old Testament prophets) as his
equal, or as something less. And he acknowledged as between
them, no received judgements as to their worth, no hierarchy of
accepted 'reputability'. For Blake, a neighbour, or a fellow-reader

of a periodical, or his friend and patron, Thomas Butts, were quite as likely to hold opinions of central importance as was any man of recognised learning. Certainly, his reading was extensive; nothing should astonish us; and whatever libraries he used, he entered some odd and unfamiliar corners.

My own answer to the problem of what guided his reading will become apparent in this book. But, in brief, I suppose that his learning was both more eccentric and more eclectic – even, at times, more shallow – than is sometimes suggested. It was eccentric, in the sense that he did have some access to an almost-underground tradition of mystic and antinomian tracts, some of these derived from the seventeenth century. Eclectic (and sometimes casual or shallow), in the sense that, whereas some scholars have found in him a profound student of comparative religion and myth, I think it possible that Blake's imagination was sufficiently supplied with images of ancient and alien religious rites and beliefs from readily available secondary sources, such as William Hurd's popular compendium, *A New Universal History of the Religious Rites, Ceremonies, and Customs of the Whole World* (1788) – a work which employed a number of his fellow-engravers. And even when we enter firmer territory, such as the acknowledged Swedenborgian influence upon Blake, I will attempt to show that certain of Blake's ideas owed less to a reading of Swedenborg's writings than to an obscure little magazine published from a barber's shop in Hoxton, or to his reactions to some execrable hymns written by a zealous Swedenborgian minister, Joseph Proud. Or, when he wrestled with deist thought, I will suggest that he was less influenced by acknowledged thinkers of the Enlightenment than by Volney's *Ruins of Empire*, which the cognoscenti of the London Corresponding Society – master craftsmen, shopkeepers, engravers, hosiers, printers – carried around with them in their pockets. And, finally, when he denounced the Tree of Mystery, he certainly operated within a wide field of intellectual reference; but he was also stung to fury by a certain Robert Hindmarsh, who was introducing ceremonial forms and priestly ordinances into the nascent Church of the New Jerusalem.

Ideas happen in this kind of way. But they happen most of all in this kind of way within the tradition which Blake inhabited and extended. We must confront Miss Raine's notion of 'the tradition' and ask *which* tradition? The answer should not come to rest in a

simple either/or, as in Robert Redfield's notion of a 'great' (or
polite) and a 'little' (or popular) tradition of culture. Blake inhabited both of these at will. But he took with him, into both of them,
a mind and sensibility formed within a different, and a particular,
tradition again: a particular current within bourgeois (and, often,
artisan) Dissent. Much of Raine's 'tradition' appears, at first sight,
to say some of the things that Blake is saying, but it is saying them
in a different way. It is genteel, other-worldly, elusive, whereas
Blake – whether in poetic or in visual image – has a certain lit-
eralness of expression, robustness and concretion. Again, Raine's
'tradition', except where it draws upon Boehme, lacks altogether
the radical edge or bite of Blake's expression. And (Boehme again
excepted) it lacks the conscious posture of hostility to the polite
learning of the Schools, *including* the polite neo-Platonist or hermetic speculations of gentry and professional men.

This is a point of importance. I will not delay to document it
now. Any reader of Blake knows that it is so, and this book will
keep an eye upon that point. Blake's hostility to academicism is
often expressed with superb vigour, and very often within the
field – the visual arts – to which he might be said, in a contemporary sense, to have submitted to an orthodox training: turn, for
example, to his annotations to Sir Joshua Reynolds. At times this
hostility to academicism and to polite learning assumes the tones
of class war:

Rouze up O Young Men of the New Age! set your foreheads against the
ignorant Hirelings! For we have Hirelings in the Camp, the Court & the
University: who would if they could, for ever depress Mental & prolong
Corporeal War. Painters! on you I call! Sculptors! Architects! . . . believe
Christ & his Apostles that there is a Class of Men whose whole delight
is in Destroying. We do not want either Greek or Roman Models if we
are but just & true to our own Imaginations, those Worlds of Eternity in
which we shall live for ever; in Jesus our Lord. (E94)

This is not only a war of the Imagination against the artifice and
fashion of the polite culture; it is also a war of faith against a class
of destroyers, and of the patronised practitioners of the creative
arts against the hirelings of camp, court and university who are
their patrons. This conscious posture of hostility to the polite culture, this radical stance, is not some quaint but inessential extra,
added on to his tradition. It *is* his tradition, it defines his stance,
it directs and colours his judgement. At times in his later years (as

in passages of his 'Descriptive Catalogue' (1809) or in his unpublished 'Public Address' on his painting of the Canterbury Pilgrims
(*c.*1810), this stance becomes wilful and plainly cantankerous.

I have tried to explain the intention, and also the limitations, of
this book. This is not, I repeat, an introduction to William Blake,
nor a general interpretive study. Nor is it, in the sense of adding
'background' or social and political context, a sketch of the 'historical' Blake. It is an intervention of a different kind. I am pursuing
an enquiry into the structure of Blake's thought and the character
of his sensibility.

My object is to identify, once again, Blake's tradition, his particular situation within it, and the repeated evidences, motifs and
nodal points of conflict, which indicate his stance and the way his
mind meets the world. To do this involves some historical recovery,
and attention to sources external to Blake – sources which, very
often, he may not have been aware of himself. For it is necessary
to define, first of all, an obscure antinomian tradition; and then to
define Blake's very unusual, and probably' unique, position within
it. And we cannot understand, or shuffle around, Blake's ideas
until we have defined these in relation to contrary or adjacent
ideas. For example, we will be in no position to judge, with Donald
Davie in *A Gathered Church*, whether Blake's religious insights were
or were not 'beneath contempt' unless we have understood something of the doctrines of justification by faith, imputed righteousness and atonement, as they were understood by certain of his
contemporaries, and as they were revised, or rejected, by him.

Very certainly, Blake's ideas undergo important changes, but
even so he returns to certain elementary affirmations and constant
preoccupations. I have indicated these places, from every part of
his work, as evidence of the continuity of this structure but not in
order to suggest consistency in his conclusions. My central study
is more strictly limited, and falls chiefly within the years 1788
and 1794. This enables me to approach three themes. First, the
antinomian tradition, the possible ways in which it could have
been received by Blake, and his own unique notations. This is the
theme of Part I. Second, the moment of the founding of the Church
of the New Jerusalem, and Blake's situation within the controversies surrounding this. Third, the moment of confluence of antinomian and of 'Jacobinical' and deist influences, and the continuing

argument to which this confluence gave rise in Blake's mind and art. These are the themes of Part II.

These three moments, in my view, give us an understanding of Blake: they show us who he was. By 1794 the structure of his ideas has been laid down, and we have in our hand the clues which lead forward to the later writings. But if I succeed in identifying this structure, I by no means wish to reduce all that Blake wrote or thought to this structure. From this antinomian/deist argument there is a radiation, an exploration outwards, some of which is ambivalent, much of which I do not understand, and none of which I wish to enclose or to bring back to these primary elements.

Finally, a word of encouragement to any readers who have been attracted to Blake but who feel themselves to be beginners. They are welcome on board and I hope that they will enjoy the voyage. I have tried to explain myself as I go along: indeed, readers already learned in Blake studies (whom I welcome aboard with more trepidation) may be impatient at the care with which I explain antinomianism or Jacob Boehme. But I cannot overcome all difficulties and I must assume at times a greater familiarity with Blake's writings than beginners may have. They are urged to have an edition of Blake's complete poems beside them and to explore it as an antidote to me. For the rest Part I of this book is concerned in the main with the transmission of certain highly unorthodox or heretical Christian ideas from the mid-seventeenth century to Blake's time, and it is not closely concerned with Blake himself, although an eye is kept upon possible parallels in his own thought, tropes and visual images. It is necesary only to know that Blake was born in 1757 into a hosier's family with (it is probable) a strong radical anti-Court tradition, served his apprenticeship as an engraver, studied (and exhibited) at the Royal Academy, published his first collection, *Poetical Sketches*, in 1783, formed friendships with several notable artists, including John Flaxman and Henry Fuseli, but left little other evidence of his vigorous interior life or beliefs until 1788, on the eve of the French Revolution. His exciting output then, in his early thirties, between 1788 and 1794, which included the *Songs of Innocence and Experience* and *The Marriage of Heaven and Hell*, entitles him in the view of one historian (A.L. Morton) to be known as England's last and greatest antinomian. That is the place which I started from and in 1968 I gave an early lecture on Blake at Columbia University (in New York City), at a time of excitement when some sort of campus revolution against the Moral Law was going on, and I startled the audience by acclaiming William Blake as 'the founder of the obscure sect to which I myself belong, the Muggletonian Marxists'. Instantly I found that many fellow-sectaries were in the room. As the years have gone by I have become less certain of both parts of the combination. But that is still the general area in which this book falls. In a brief introduction to Part II I try to explain myself further.

PART I

Inheritance

CHAPTER I

Works or faith?

> When Christians unto Carnal Men give ear,
> Out of their way they go, and pay for't dear;
> For Master *Worldly Wiseman* can but shew
> A Saint the way to Bondage and to Wo.

In this verse, John Bunyan sought to enforce the lesson of Christian's first severe temptation in *Pilgrim's Progress*. After crossing the *Slough of Despond*, Christian had met with Mr Worldly Wiseman, who dwelt in the town of *Carnal Policy*. Mr Wiseman was full of good advice, and he told Christian that 'in yonder Village (the Village is named *Morality*) there dwells a Gentleman whose name is *Legality*, a very judicious man'. *Legality* could certainly help Christian to lift the burden from his shoulders, and if the old gentleman was not at home, then certainly the 'pretty young man', his son, 'whose name is *Civility*', would be able to do it as well as his father. And then, Mr Worldly Wiseman urged, Christian could send for his wife and children and settle in the village of *Morality*: 'there thou shalt live by honest neighbours, in credit and good fashion'.

The temptation was so severe that Christian succumbed to it. He turned aside from the straight and narrow path to the wicket-gate of faith, and set off for *Legality*'s house, which stood on a high and threatening hill. Beneath this hill he might well have perished, had not *Evangelist* come up with him again. *Evangelist* turned Christian back into the path, rebuking him ('the just shall live by the faith . . . be not faithless, but believing'), and instructing him as to the abhorrent creed of Mr Worldly Wiseman: 'he savoureth only the doctrine of this world (therefore he always goes to the Town of *Morality* to church)' and 'he loveth that doctrine best, for it

Note: The place of publication in the works cited is London, unless otherwise stated.

3

saveth him from the Cross'. As for *Legality*, he is 'the Son of the Bond-woman', and 'she with her children are in bondage':

This *Legality* therefore is not able to set thee free from thy Burden. No man was as yet ever rid of his Burden by him; no, nor ever is like to be: ye cannot be justified by the Works of the Law; for by the deeds of the Law no man living can be rid of his Burden: therefore, Mr *Worldly Wiseman* is an alien, and Mr *Legality* a cheat; and for his son *Civility*, notwithstanding his simpering looks, he is but an hypocrite and cannot help thee. . .

At this, *Evangelist* called aloud to the Heavens for confirmation, and words and fire came out of the mountain under which they stood, declaring: '*As many as are of the works of the Law are under the curse. . .*'

So Christian set out on a journey which was to take him from the seventeenth century to the eighteenth century and beyond, and through the hearts of hundreds of thousands of readers. But the twentieth-century reader has more difficulty in understanding the severity of this temptation. Why did Christian not just stop, and put his burden down? Or, if the reading is somewhat less crass, then certain tones of social or class conflict are noted: the humble dissenting Christian is tempted by the forms and compromises of carnal policy, and of the Established Church – but why should the doctrines of Morality be at odds with the gospel of the Cross, and, if the straight and narrow path of faith has nothing to do with Legality, or Morality, or Works, then how is it marked out and to what gate does it lead? I think it very probable that the eyes of many readers today traverse such passages in a benevolent haze of suspended attention.

I will argue, however, that such passages demand our full response. Their implications may be very radical indeed. In this episode, Bunyan is marking out a path which leads directly to antinomian conclusions, and which takes us, equally directly, into the structure of Blake's thought. We will not delay now to enquire how far John Bunyan endorsed these conclusions, or how far he hedged around his antinomian premises with doctrinal reservations.[1] We will note only that this episode of temptation carries us into a characteristic diagram of oppositions:

---

[1] In fact Bunyan was strongly critical of antinomianism, perhaps the more so because his own doctrines 'often skirted' it: see Christopher Hill, *A Turbulent, Seditious and Factious People: John Bunyan and his Church, 1628–1688* (Oxford, 1988), chapter 17, and p. 86.

Works	*versus*	Faith
Morality		The Cross
Legality		The Gospel of Forgiveness of Sins
Bondage		Freedom

And, if the path of *Legality* be taken, then it leads on to formalism, carnal policy, opportunism and, finally, to mere simpering *Civility*.

I will also argue that the doctrine of justification by faith, in its antinomian inflexion, was one of the most radical and potentially subversive of the vectors which carried the ideas of seventeenth-century Levellers and Ranters through to the next century. Since I can hear a scandalised snort from the Marxist–structuralist corner, I must ask the less committed readers to excuse me for a moment while I chastise my more brutish comrades. What (they are asking in that corner) can this odd-looking doctrine of justification by faith have to do with enlightenment and rigorous rationality? Surely it is no more than one more form of indulgent self-mystification within the otiose religiosity which was the sole inheritance of the English Revolution? And, if we are to make allowance for this religiose ideological formation, surely it is equally clear that the only socially effective Christian doctrine capable of motivating a radical practice must have rested upon a doctrine of Works – a zealous and this-worldly emphasis upon affirmative moral actions?

The answer is that there are persons and places for which this last proposition is valid. But that, for much of the eighteenth century, the doctrine of justification by faith was – and was seen to be – the more 'dangerous' heresy. And this was because it could – although it need not – challenge very radically the authority of the ruling ideology and the cultural hegemony of Church, Schools, Law and even of 'common-sense' Morality. In its essence it was exactly that: *anti*-hegemonic. It displaced the authority of institutions and of received worldly wisdom with that of the individual's inner light – faith, conscience, personal understanding of the scriptures or (for Blake) 'the Poetic Genius' – and allowed to the individual a stubborn scepticism in the face of the established culture, a fortitude in the face of its seductions or persecutions sufficient to support Christian in the face of the State or of polite learning. This fortitude need not necessarily be accompanied by evangelistic zeal or affirmative social action; it might equally well be defensive, and protect the quietism of a private faith, or the introverted spiritual pride of a petty sect. But it could also nourish (and protect) a more active faith which rested upon a confidence in spiritual 'freedom', liberated from the 'bondage' of Morality and Legality.

That the language of Christian's temptation continues with undiminished vigour may be seen if we traverse abruptly across more than one hundred years, from *Pilgrim's Progress* (1678) to London in the 1790s. One of the large, self-appointed noises in plebeian London at that time was William Huntington, S.S. The 'S.S.' stood for 'Sinner Saved'. Born in 1745 in a labourer's family (he was proud to proclaim that he had once been a coal-heaver), Huntington had come, by way of a small Baptist congregation in Thames Ditton and an Independent church in Woking, to London in 1782. Here he ministered at first to Baptists, but, by the 1790s, he was his own evangelist and prophet, ministering throughout the decade from Providence Chapel, Great Titchfield Street.[2] There came from his pen, throughout the 1790s, a torrent of pamphlets, sermons, admonitions and expostulations, of a loud and windy nature.

The wind blew from an antinomian quarter – indeed, from much the same quarter as exemplified by Christian's temptation by Mr Worldly Wiseman. In the 1780s he was warning his congregation lest '*legality* . . . entangle and govern their consciences'. In contrast to mere 'workmongers', the Saved must know that 'the Saviour's laws are written within us'.[3] In the early 1790s the antinomian wind blew most fiercely, and Huntington's rhetoric moved through the familiar oppositions between ceremonial, formal law, and established forms on the one hand (all these were 'a yoke of bondage') and faith and free grace on the other.

We may sample the rhetoric from *The Child of Liberty in Legal Bondage* (1794). Huntington, a self-called evangelist, decried 'legal preachers, who handle the law unlawfully . . . While they entangle the sheep of Christ, themselves are nothing but *thorns and briars.*' Established religious forms were no more than 'the old vail of the

---

[2] Ebenezer Hooper, *The Celebrated Coalheaver, or Reminiscences of the Reverend William Huntington, S.S.* (1871); Thomas Wright, *Life of William Huntington, S.S.* (1909). See also Jon Mee, 'Is there an Antinomian in the House: William Blake and the After-Life of a Heresy' in S. Clarke and D. Worrall (eds.), *Historicizing Blake* (forthcoming); and *Dangerous Enthusiasm: William Blake and the Culture of Radicalism in the 1790s* (Oxford, 1992), pp. 62–5.

[3] William Huntington, *A Sermon on the Dimensions of Eternal Love* (1784), pp. 5, 9.

law, under which the gospel is hid'. Faith must always take priority to form. When not illustrated by faith–

The law, when reflected on the mind of man, is *blackness and darkness*, and the spirit of it is darkness, fear, bondage, wrath, death, and furious jealousy still.

This, and much more of the same kind, between 1792 and 1795, when the winds of political liberty blew strongly in London. Huntington himself was no political reformer: he was a High Tory and an admirer of Pitt. But his flock was strongly disposed towards the reforming cause, and he had great difficulty in governing it: 'there was a knot of young wise men among us, who were great readers and admirers of Tom Paine. . .' These clamoured against his discourses in the House of God, but fortunately six of them soon exposed themselves by becoming given up to the sin of adultery. Presumably their partners in sin were found among those women who–

Young and old, are breathing out *slaughter* against the ruling powers. Tom Paine and Satan have stuffed their heads full of politics.[4]

In 1795 Huntington had great difficulty in holding back his flock from running after Richard Brothers, the most notable of the millenarial prophets of the New Jerusalem, while others of his flock seceded towards Winchester and the Universalists.[5] Some of his following (he implies) were, during the general repression of reformers in the mid-1790s, 'bereaved of their houses and goods', became emigrants, were imprisoned, transported or even hanged.[6] Others–

Who had some sound notions of the gospel, and some good views, and who were capable of sound speech which could not be condemned, were given up to the devil and Tom Paine, that they even sucked in the rebellion, blasphemy, and carnal logic of that man. . .

[4] William Huntington, *A Watchword and Warning from the Walls of Zion* (1798), pp. 76, 2–3. Huntington thought the women 'had better guide the houses, teach their children to read, and take in a little plain work'.
[5] Huntington attacked Richard Brothers in *The Lying Prophet Examined* (1795), Elhanan Winchester and the Universalists in *Discoveries and Cautions from the Streets of Zion* (1798) and elsewhere. Jon Mee, 'Is there an Antinomian in the House', discusses the breach between Huntington and Garnet Terry, who adopted more radical positions, somewhat closer to Blake.
[6] William Huntington, *Discoveries and Cautions from the Streets of Zion* (1798). These allegations probably testify to Huntington's monomania.

Others promised themselves 'from week to week French liberty by the Sword of France and by the destruction of their own country'.[7] As if to outbid the Painites and the millenarial prophets, Huntington bent the boughs of his rhetoric low with the imagery of the New Jerusalem:

Coming to God with the judge of all under his teaching, and to Jesus, the mediator of the new covenant by faith, and to the saints in heartfelt love and affection, is coming to the heavenly Jerusalem; for all believers *are fellow-citizens with the saints, and of the household of God.* To let Jerusalem come into our mind, in the language of the New Testament, is *to love one another...*

For those who had received this gospel, 'Gospel Jerusalem is now with us.'[8]

Huntington is an unimportant figure and he is scarcely relevant to my theme. What relevance he has lies in his *un*importance. With his flock pulled hither and thither, to Paine, to Brothers, to the Universalists, to the ultra-Jacobins, he is like evangelising flotsam floating upon the culture of radical Dissent. But he can keep afloat only by inflating his raft with the rhetoric which blows all around him. We approach too often the 'mind of the age' through the language of the rational or humanist Enlightenment: through Paley, Priestley, Price, Wedgwood, Erasmus Darwin or through genteel Behmenists. But stick your foot, or your library ticket, into the sea of pamphlets and sermons of Dissent and of Methodist breakaways, and we are back in 'the Tradition' indeed; but the tradition is that of seventeenth-century Anabaptists and Ranters, of Ezra and Isaiah, of John Bunyan, of the New Jerusalem, of watchwords from the walls of Zion, of the Land of Beulah, of ancient prophecies, of blood on the walls of palaces, lambs entangled in thorns and briar and of 'the old vail of the law, under which the gospel is hid'.

It is, of course, a rhetoric very much closer to the language of Blake than is the rhetoric of the Enlightenment. Inattention to this Londonish rhetoric has led us to see Blake as a more isolated figure than he was. But while it brings us very close to Blake's language and imagery, the fit is not exact; and when we shift our attention from the vocabulary to the structure of ideas, then the gap becomes manifest.

---

[7] *Ibid.*, pp. 14–15.   [8] *A Watchword and Warning from the Walls of Zion*, pp. 64–5.

The fit between the ideas of Huntington and of Blake is suggested by the title (but not the contents) of a tract of 1792: *The
Moral Law not Injured by the Everlasting Gospel*. These terms were
perfectly familiar to the disputatious London Dissenter of that
time. But if Blake had written such a tract, then its title would
have been, not reversed, but inverted: *The Everlasting Gospel Injured
by the Moral Law*. It is not only that Blake stands within the antinomian tradition. He stands at a precise, if obscure, point within it,
and his writings contain the purest, most lucid and most persuasive
statements that issued from that tradition in any voice and at any
time: 'The Gospel is Forgiveness of Sins & has No Moral Precepts
these belong to Plato & Seneca & Nero', or:

> When Satan first the black bow bent
> And the Moral Law from the Gospel rent
> He forgd the Law into a Sword
> And spilld the blood of mercys Lord. (E200)

The difficulty of such statements (if any remains) arises only if we
try to tease their meanings into something else. If we take them to
mean exactly what they say – that the Moral Law is the direct
antagonist of the Gospel of Mercy – then they may present problems to us, but they have the simplicity of stone.

A precise, if obscure point within the antinomian tradition . . .
I will attempt a reconstruction of this tradition, and consider the
ways in which it may have been extended to Blake. I have no
unexpected disclosures to offer. I must commence with conjectures,
and conclude with some firmer evidence, out of which further conjectures will arise.

CHAPTER 2

Antinomianisms

'Antinomian' was, in the eighteenth century, as often a term of abuse as of precision. The orthodox hurled the accusation of Anti-nomianism at their opponents, very much as, in other times and places, accusations might be hurled of heresy, anarchism, terrorism or libertinism. And the objects of such abuse often turn out to be innocent of any such subversive intentions. They may be (as in Wesley's *Journals*) members of the flock who neglect attendances and who pride themselves too far on their own purity of heart; or, with some writers, a stern theological eye may fall upon a humble fornicator for whom the pursuit of a *doctrine* has never entered his thoughts. The term 'αντί νομος means, after all, *against the law*; and most men and women may, at one time or another, fall under that imputation.

I do not mean to search back into antiquity for the origin of this heresy. I am more concerned with a cluster of ideas present in late eighteenth-century England, and with their derivation from seventeenth-century sources. In this tradition antinomian doctrine was founded most commonly upon passages in St Paul's epistles to the Romans and to the Galatians. These passages, which origin-ated in St Paul's polemics against the slavish observance of Jewish ceremonial and ritual regulations, were taken to have a very much wider significance. The Mosaic Law was seen, not only in its ceremonial edicts but also in its moral commandments, to be the necessary rules of government imposed upon a faithless and unre-generate people:

The law was our schoolmaster to bring us unto Christ, that we might be justified by faith.

But after that faith is come, we are no longer under a schoolmaster. (Galatians 3. 24–5)

Christ, by his sacrifice upon the Cross, in fulfilment of God's ancient covenant with man, 'hath redeemed us from the curse of the law' (Galatians 3. 13). Thereafter it is not by 'the works of the law' but by 'the hearing of faith' that believers may be justified (Galatians 2 and 3, *passim*). Believers within the church 'are become dead to the law by the body of Christ' (Romans 7. 4), they are 'delivered from the law' (Romans 7. 6):

There is therefore now no condemnation to them which are in Christ Jesus, who walk not after the flesh, but after the Spirit.

For the law of the Spirit of life in Christ Jesus hath made me free from the law of sin and death. . . (Romans 8. 1 and 2)

This is not all that St Paul said, nor is it without ambiguity. But such passages as these were commonly taken as texts by Puritan divines who inclined towards antinomian tenets. Thus James Barry, whose sermons were reprinted by William Huntington, cited such texts and concluded: 'There remains, now, no condemnation in force against that man or woman who believes in the Son of God.'

Neither did the Son of God flinch or shrink in the contest, till he had vanquished and overcome the condemning power of the law; leaving it, and all the other enemies of his elect, nailed to the cross; having, by his death on the cross, put to death the damnatory sentence of God's righteous law against God's elect. . .[1]

This is close also to Michael's doctrine in Book XII of *Paradise Lost*: 'Law can discover sin, but not remove. . .'

> So Law appears imperfect, and but giv'n
> With purpose to resign them in full time
> Up to a better Cov'nant. . .

Christ, by his sacrifice, fulfilled the old Mosaic Law, delivered mankind from its curse, and–

> . . . to the Cross he nailes thy Enemies,
> The Law that is against thee, and the sins
> Of all mankinde, with him there crucifi'd,
> Never to hurt them more who rightly trust
> In this his satisfaction. . .

[1] James Barry, *The Only Refuge of a Troubled Soul in Times of Affliction . . . or the Mystery of the Apple Tree* (two sermons revised and published by W. Huntington, 2nd edn, 1802), p. 80.

Henceforward those who are justified by faith (but not by 'legal
works') enter upon a state of grace, subject to no laws save 'what
the Spirit within/ Shall on the heart engrave'.[2] Thus those two
markedly antinomian divines, James Barry and Milton's Michael.
But neither would have *acknowledged* themselves to be such. Indeed,
Barry actually complained:

If we preach up justification by the alone righteousness of the Son of
God, freely imputed by God's act of free and Sovereign Grace, without
any thing of the sinner's own qualifications joined, as con-causes therewith; then we are accounted Antinomians, we preach Free Grace, Free
Grace. . .[3]

If we situate ourselves in the late eighteenth century, then we
may distinguish between three positions which were described as –
and which sometimes were accepted by their professors as – antinomian. The first is inseparable from Calvinist or determinist presup-
positions. Indeed, it may be the doctrine of election taken to its
own *reductio ad absurdam*; or, in its social expression, it may be seen
as 'Calvinism's lower-class alter ego'.[4] If one knew, as a certainty,
that one was elected to be saved – and that this was God's will –
then it could follow that one would be saved whatever one did: the
'saints' might live henceforth outside 'the moral law'. It might
seem that this logic must lead on to scandalous conclusions. However, the antinomian teacher found ways of hedging around the
way to such conclusions by many thickets of apologetics. In the
main, these turned on Michael's theme of the inner law of conscience: 'what the Spirit within/Shall on the heart engrave'. The
elect might dispense with the moral law since they had a surer
guide in conscience; and if a 'saint' led a scandalous life, then this
was evidence that he or she was none of the elect. However, we
need enquire into this position little further, since it offered little
to William Blake. He was not troubled by Calvinist determinism,
and even the concealed pre-destinarianism which he detected in
Swedenborg gave him instant offence.

A second position commonly inveighed against in eighteenth-
century apologetics was, in the main, a position dreamed up by
main-line Protestant orthodoxy, much as Stalinist orthodoxy had

---

[2] Christopher Hill discusses Milton's proximity to antinomianism in *Milton and the English
Revolution* (1977), see esp. p. 106 and chapter 24.
[3] Barry, *The Only Refuge*, p. 113.
[4] Christopher Hill, *The World Turned Upside Down* (1972), p. 130.

always to position itself between a Right and a Left deviation. On the Right there stood an excessive belief in justification by works, or forms; on the Left there was Antinomianism, or an excessive belief in justification by faith, or free grace or pureness of heart, which led on to a carelessness towards all forms or works or observances and even to a light-heartedness towards sin, supported by over-confidence in the universality of divine mercy. Antinomians (in the eyes of the orthodox)–

Are *against* the law . . . Some are against it in *principle*, others in *practice*, and some in *both*. The name is most commonly applied to those who are, in pretence at least, mighty advocates of free grace; and object to the law as the *rule* of the good man's life.

Such persons might neglect observances, attend stage plays, music and dancing, and break the Sabbath; others might 'take liberty to sin, from the saving freedom, the abounding riches of divine grace'. And from this we pass to the ritual condemnation:

In a word, an Antinomian is a living libel on Christianity; a scandal to religion; a compound of iniquity and impudence; a nuisance, a very pest to society; an enemy to God, to man, and to himself; Christ's opponent, the devil's respondent. . .[5]

Thus the orthodox view. But the positions in fact avowed by the advocates of grace could be more cogent than this, and also more various. We will not examine these now, since, although we are moving closer to a possible influence upon Blake, we can move closer still. The third position attributed to Antinomians consists in carrying to an extreme the advocacy of grace, and bringing the gospel of Christ into direct *antagonism* to the 'covenant of deeds' or the 'moral law'. That is, in the view of critics, there is not just too much emphasis upon grace and faith, too little upon moral law: the two are seen as being radically opposed to each other. This is a meaning which observers increasingly assign to Antinomianism in the turbulent 1790s. They believe (a critic writes)

That the Law of Moses, commonly called the Moral Law, contained in the Ten Commandments, ought not to be preached as a rule of conduct to believers of the Gospel, but by so doing, you should bring them again under the Law as a Covenant of Works.[6]

---

[5] Anon., *Antinomianism Explained and Exploded; in a Letter to a Friend* (Coventry, n.d.), pp. 9, 15.

[6] 'A Friend to the Gospel of Christ', *A Looking-Glass for the Antinomians* (Shrewsbury, 1796), p. 10.

It is no longer a question, as with Milton's Michael, of the Law being 'imperfect' – perhaps a necessary schoolmaster to the unregenerate – nor a criticism of the Law's limitations: 'Law can discover sin, but not remove. . .' The Ten Commandments and the Gospel of Jesus stand directly opposed to each other: the first is a code of repression and prohibition, the second a gospel of forgiveness and love. The two might have flowed from the minds of opposing gods. And if this is married – and when such a doctrine has gathered social force it usually has been so married – to political radicalism and to the outlook of the oppressed, then the doctrine acquires a new force again. For the Moral Law is *their* Law, the law of 'God & his Priest & King/Who make up a heaven of our misery', while the Gospel is the affirmation, in the face of all the Schools and Orthodoxies, of the truths of the pure-in-heart and the oppressed.

We are now close enough to Blake to touch some of his lines. Which we will do again in a moment. But we will first delay over one issue which has, perhaps, served to confuse a little the question of the derivation of Blake's thought from the antinomian tradition. Very commonly, because of the weight of seventeenth-century precedent – as well as specific doctrinal signatures – Antinomianism has been discussed as a distinctively Calvinist heresy.[7] That is, the emphasis has been upon the doctrine of election carried through to the extremity that the elect *must* be saved, do what they may. This may be a proper emphasis until the 1630s, but when we come to the next decades the emphasis may change.[8] Not all Ranters necessarily held themselves to be elected 'saints', and Milton's Michael was scarcely a Calvinist divine. And when we move into the eighteenth century, any necessary connection between Calvinist doctrines of election and antinomian tenets can no longer be expected.

For Pauline premises, to which Luther gave emphasis, could lead to identical conclusions. Those with a nicely discriminating theological palate might classify these as 'solifidian' rather than antinomian.[9] The solifidian premise rested particularly upon Romans 3:

[7] See Peter Toon, *The Emergence of Hyper-Calvinism* (1967).

[8] Hill in *The World Turned Upside Down* tends to emphasise antinomianism's Calvinist character, whereas A.L. Morton in *The World of the Ranters* (1970), pp. 50–1, 72, 117, 129, gives more emphasis to Lutheran heresies. See also G. Huehns, *Antinomianism in English History* (1951), pp. 13–15, 40–3.

[9] F.L. Cross (ed.), *The Oxford Dictionary of the Christian Church* (Oxford, 1974).

For all have sinned, and come short of the glory of God;

Being justified freely by his grace through the redemption that is in Christ Jesus;

Whom God hath sent forth to be a propitiation through faith in his blood. . .

Therefore we conclude that a man is justified by faith without the deeds of the law. (Romans 3. 23–5, 28)

The doctrine of justification by faith invited the further doctrine of 'imputed righteousness', which was a contentious issue in the early Swedenborgian milieu, and which we will discuss later (pp. 162–4). The point now is that the zealous life of theological private enterprise which was thrown open by the English Civil Wars allowed hundreds of humble experimenters in doctrine to fashion eclectic systems, now drawing upon Calvin and now upon Luther, now upon Joachim of Fiore and now upon Boehme. These combined in the brief climax of the Ranters (1649–51), when antinomianism in one form or another assumed epidemic proportions.[10] In this moment, the doctrine of 'free grace', derivative from St Paul and Luther, seems to me to be more significant than the Calvinist doctrine of election. John Saltmarsh's *Free Grace: or the Flowing of Christs Blood to Sinners* (1645) had a profound influence on the Ranter movement that succeeded. The emphasis is upon, not election, but belief. The free grace of Christ's blood was shed for all mankind, and all the sins of believers were 'done away on the Crosse':

The Spirit of Christ sets a *beleever* as *free* from *Hell*, the *Law*, and *Bondage*, as if he was in *Heaven*, nor wants he anything to make him *so*, but to make him *believe* that he is so.

The Gospel is 'a *perfect law* of life and *righteousnesse*, of *grace* and *truth*; and therefore I wonder at any that should contend for the ministry of the *Law* or *Ten Commandments* under Moses'. In the next year Thomas Edwards in *Gangraena* was denouncing those who held,

---

[10] These questions have been obscured by J.C. Davis, *Fear, Myth and History: The Ranters and the Historians* (Cambridge, 1986). Davis constructs, for the purpose of his own arguments, a somewhat narrow definition of antinomianism (pp. 21–5), with heavy emphasis on the supposed 'practical' antinomianism of sexual libertinism, and inattention to theological variants: see my 'On the Rant', *London Review of Books*, 9 July 1987. Debate as to the existence of the Ranters, initiated by Davis, of course continues: see Christopher Hill, 'Abolishing the Ranters' in *A Nation of Change and Novelty* (1990); Symposium of Comments in *Past & Present*, forthcoming (1993).

That by Christs death, all the sins of all men in the world, Turks, Pagans, as well as Christians committed against the moral Law and the first covenant, are actually pardoned and forgiven, and this is the everlasting gospel.

It was as a preacher of 'free grace' that Laurence Clarkson – later to be called the 'Captain of the Rant' – first made his mark, and William Erbery, who was to become a leading Seeker, first caught the eye of Thomas Edwards when 'he declared himself for general Redemption, that no man was punished for Adam's sin, that Christ died for all. . .' James Nayler, who is often taken as the leader of the Ranting tendency in early Quakerism, defended also 'the universal free grace of God to all mankind'.

The teaching of 'free grace' need not necessarily lead on to antinomian conclusions. In Blake's London of the 1790s this teaching was vigorously revived by several groups: by William Huntington, and by Elhanan Winchester and the Universalists, who held that Christ's blood had removed from all the curse of eternal punishment (pp. 226–7): groups which refused, with equal vigour, the antinomian resolution. But logically the solifidian premise ('faith without the deeds of the law') could pass easily, as it had done with the Ranters, to an antinomian destination (crudely, faith *against* the law). One may observe, throughout the eighteenth century, preachers, sects and churches, struggling to find some doctrinal foothold half-way down this logical slope. The visionary or pietistic sect might impose (as the Moravians did) a severe discipline upon its own members, while keeping itself at a great distance from the legalism and forms of State and Church. Or a dual standard might be employed, by which the Moral Law (both ceremonial and real) was abrogated for those within the true faith, whereas for those *without* faith the Moral Law remained binding.[11] And if this position were chosen, then it need not be held that the faithful were predestined to be so, and hence were everlastingly secured from the pains of transgression. For a believer might always fall away from the faith, and hence fall within the rule of the Law once more.

Early Methodism had a surfeit of these problems, and nearly choked upon them. The doctrine of justification by faith – a moment of 'immediate and mysterious relationship of the individual soul with the Deity',[12] coming as the free gift of God in an

---

[11] See William Cudworth, *The Truth Defended* (1746).
[12] E. Halevy, *The Birth of Methodism in England* (Chicago, 1971), p. 33.

experience of conversion in the heart of the receptive sinner – both
brought the Wesleys and George Whitefield together, and then
flung them apart in Calvinist and Arminian directions. John Wesley's Arminian resolution (an 'eclecticism which logic may call
inadmissible')[13] denied predestination and denied also the irresistible power of God's free grace: the sinner must first be receptive
and prepared. Only 'he that believeth' shall be saved, but it
remained possible – and, as time went on, it proved to be only too
possible – that believers should 'backslide'. Hence, with increasing
and dismal emphasis, the doctrine of works could be brought to
supplement the doctrine of faith and grace, for works were both a
sign of continuing grace and an insurance against backsliding. But
the antinomian heresy continued to harass the early history of
Methodism. Whitefield's former fellow-preachers, William Cudworth and James Relly, might, in the view of observers, be called
'properly Antinomians', even though they themselves rejected the
'scandalous name'.[14] Cudworth, indeed, was well versed in the
work of seventeenth-century antinomian divines, and reprinted a
number of their tracts and sermons.[15] Cudworth and Relly
denounced their critics as 'Legalists'. In the view of a later observer, the Antinomians of the 1790s had largely been recruited from
those 'we commonly call Irregular Methodists'.[16] In the early years
of the next century, the Primitive Methodists were often referred
to as Ranters.

In this case the thrust of such Antinomianism as can be found
came from a Calvinist quarter – from those who seceded from
Whitefield: the notion of the abrogation of the law and the notion
of elected 'sainthood' tended to go together. This is true also of
another antinomian sect, the Muggletonians, whose beliefs we shall
interrogate later: their doctrine of 'the Two Seeds' was inexorably
predestinarian, although founded upon a materialist historical
explanation of alternative conceptions (pp. 75–6). This is true also

---

[13] Ibid., p. 50.
[14] See William Cudworth, *A Dialogue between a Preacher of Inherent Righteousness and a Preacher of God's Righteousness, Revealed from Faith to Faith* (1745); W. Mason, *Antinomian Heresy Exploded, in an Appeal to the Christian World* (n.d.); James Relly, *Anti-Christ Resisted, in a Reply to . . . W. Mason* (1761); William Hurd, *A New Universal History of the Religions, Rites, Ceremonies, and Customs of the Whole World* (Blackburn, 1799 edn), p. 767. On Relly, see also Jon Mee, *Dangerous Enthusiasm*, p. 160.
[15] W. Cudworth in *Christ Alone Exalted* (1747).
[16] W. Hurd, *New Universal History*, p. 641.

of such idiosyncratic little groups as a Church of Christ in Spitalfields, which surface from time to time in eighteenth-century
London, and which may perhaps be survivals from earlier
'Ranters'. This church held that all its members were justified in
Christ and their sins blotted out – 'so that they are now holy and
unblameable and unreprovable in the eye of his justice, and are
made the righteousness of God in him. . .' But, also, all such had
been elected and 'ordained to eternal life before the world began'.[17]

There is a disposition, then, for antinomian and Calvinist tenets
to be found as a couple. But this was not *necessarily* so. It was
possible to hold that Christ had abolished the Moral Law for all
mankind, and hence for sinners as well as saved: 'the whole work
of salvation was accomplished by Jesus Christ on the cross. Christ's
blood and our sins went away together. . .' All that then remained
for the sinner to do was to attain to faith or belief. So long as he
or she remained in a state of belief, the Moral Law had no force.[18]
It was just as possible for an Antinomian to play at the game of
equivocation as it was for John Wesley.

I have said that, in the third position sketched above, we are
close enough to William Blake to touch some of his lines. But this
is so only if we discard the expectation of any notion of election:

> Thus wept they in Beulah over the Four Regions of Albion
> But many doubted & despaird & imputed Sin & Righteousness
> To Individuals & not to States, and these slept in Ulro
>
> (E169)

These are the concluding lines of chapter 1 of *Jerusalem*. The
imputation of sin and righteousness to individuals entails the doctrine of election, or predestination, which was abhorrent to Blake.
The imputation of these to 'states' is Blake's own resolution. I
cannot say that this resolution is easily explained.

What must, however, be insisted upon is the ubiquity and
centrality of antinomian tenets to Blake's thinking, to his writing

[17] *Declaration of the Faith, and Practice of a Church of Christ, meeting in Black and Grey-Eagle Street,
Spitalfields; and Peter's yard in Castle Street, near Leicester Fields, and at the French Chapel in New
Hermitage-street, Wapping* (n.d., but bound in with British Library copy of W. Cudworth,
Christ Alone Exalted (1747)). For the 'French Prophets' who created a millenarian sensation
in London in the first decades of the eighteenth century, see D.P. Walker, *The Decline of
Hell* (1964), pp. 253–63; Halevy, *The Birth of Methodism*, pp. 52–3; Hillel Schwartz, *The
French Prophets* (Berkeley, 1980); J.F.C. Harrison, *The Second Coming: Popular Millenarianism,
1780–1850* (1979), pp. 25–9.
[18] Hurd, *New Universal History*, p. 638.

and to his painting. Throughout his work there will be found this radical disassociation and opposition between the Moral Law and that gospel of Christ which is known – as often in the antinomian tradition – as 'the Everlasting Gospel'. We will encounter this throughout this study, and I will be content now with a blunt set of assertions. The signatures of this antinomian sensibility will be found, not at two or three points only in Blake's work, but along the whole length of his work, at least from 1790 until his death. They are manifest in the *Songs*. *The Marriage of Heaven and Hell* is an antinomian squib thrown among Swedenborgians. In the early prophecies, Urizen is the author of the Moral Law; in the major prophetic books the argument between law and love, repression and regeneration, is intrinsic to their structure. In Blake's annotations to several authors – notably to Watson, Bacon and Thornton – there are unequivocal and unqualified antinomian affirmations. Such affirmations recur in the conversations of his last years, recorded by Crabb Robinson. (Some statements were, very probably, so explicit and so shocking in their heresy that Frederick Tatham felt it necessary to destroy them.)[19] These statements, first offered as the voice of the 'devil' in Plate 23 of *The Marriage of Heaven and Hell* (1790–3) – 'I tell you no virtue can exist without breaking these ten commandments . . . Jesus was all virtue, and acted from impulse, not from rules' – were re-worked once more, in affirmative terms, in the late, unpublished, *The Everlasting Gospel* (*c*.818):

> It was when Jesus said to Me,
> 'Thy Sins are all forgiven thee.'
> The Christian trumpets loud proclaim
> Thro' all the World in Jesus' name
> Mutual forgiveness of each Vice,
> And oped the Gates of Paradise.
> The Moral Virtues in Great fear
> Formed the Cross & Nails & Spear,
> And the Accuser standing by
> Cried out, 'Crucify! Crucify!. . .'   (E793)

I am not the first to comment on the pressure of this tradition

---

[19] Tatham may have destroyed some of Blake's manuscripts, under the conviction that Blake had been inspired by Satan! See G.E. Bentley, *Blake Records* (Oxford, 1969), pp. 417–18, and, for Tatham's comment on Blake's 'Extravagant and rebellious thoughts', see his 'Life of Blake', in *ibid.*, p. 530.

in Blake;[20] nor do I suppose that very much has been settled if we hang up his work on a hook marked 'antinomian' and think that then we have put it in place. Antinomianism, indeed, is not a place at all, but a way of breaking out from received wisdom and moralism, and entering upon new possibilities. The particular attack of Blake's thought and feeling is unique, and it cannot be understood without reference to adjacent ideas and symbols – although some of these (the mistrust of 'reason', the acceptance of 'energy' and of sexuality) have often come together in a cluster in the antinomian tradition. Moreover, the fact that these character-istic oppositions recur throughout Blake's mature work does not mean that they recur in the same way.

Even so, I am not saying nothing. I am arguing that these ideas are intrinsic and central to the structure of Blake's thought, and that they remain so, even when he passes from revolutionary enthu-siasm to more quietist conclusions, and equally when he is subject to very strong Deist and atheistic influences and when he has become reconciled to a (highly unorthodox and idiosyncratic) Christian faith. And I am arguing also that even those critics who have noted the antinomian influence have rarely noted its struc-tural centrality; and that, in general, extensive critical attention has been paid to quite secondary, or even trivial, influences upon Blake, while this major and continuing influence has remained little examined. And, finally, I am arguing that there are readers of Blake who still refuse to read what he plainly says, or who dismiss as a *jeu d'esprit* a statement as flat and as challenging as that Christ

> His Seventy Disciples sent
> Against Religion & Government   (E794)

For a certain kind of scholar, these two lines offer room for a textual commentary upon why (from what obscure source) Blake should have chosen the number *seventy*. If he looks at what is actually being *said* in those two lines, then it seems altogether too disturbing: it is either wrong, or mad, or it requires the rewriting of history. Blake requires the latter.

We cannot reduce Blake's thought and art to a few antinomian propositions. Within the field of possibility which these proposi-

---

[20] See, for example, Michael Ferber, *The Social Vision of William Blake* (Princeton, 1985), pp. 116–26, and Jon Mee, *Dangerous Enthusiasm*, pp. 57ff.

tions opened to him, a multitude of other themes are disclosed. But these themes are often governed, they are controlled and assigned their significance, by the antinomian verb. Yet, as we close in upon Blake, we find that it is necessary to disengage once more, and to interrogate a prior history of ideas. Because, however original Blake's use of the antinomian vocabulary may be, it is impossible to argue that he re-invented it *ab novo*. The terms employed – the Moral Law, the Everlasting Gospel, the New Jerusalem – are more specific and more radical than the mainstream Puritan tradition. We have therefore to enquire by what routes this tradition came down to Blake. This will help us to understand the terms which he employed, even if it cannot tell us what he did with those terms.

CHAPTER 3

The 'ranting' impulse

There is a robustness and a radical political attack – the direct equation of the Moral Law with State and Church – as well as a clustering of related themes in Blake's writing which takes us back instantly to the imagery and to the intellectual world of Diggers, Ranters, Behmenists, hermeticists and heresiarchs of the Interregnum. The resemblance was shown in A.L. Morton's *The Everlasting Gospel* (1958), and the reminiscences cannot fail to strike the reader in page after page of Morton's *The World of the Ranters* (1970) and Christopher Hill's *The World Turned Upside Down* (1972). What these authors and others have already recovered so expertly it is unnecessary for me to repeat. Here I will only offer a reminder as to certain of the ideas then in currency. If my selection appears to be arbitrary, it has been made with an eye, not to the understanding of the seventeenth century, but to anticipations of ideas which recur in the 1790s, either in Blake's own work or in Swedenborgian and adjacent circles.

Notoriously the apocalyptic vision bursts forth in each period of social disturbance. This is a time when not only the political world but also the worlds of intellect and value are turned upside down. Here we have the exuberant revolutionary milieu – egalitarians, the Family of Love, Fifth Monarchy Men, Ranters; here also we have the conjunction of the Behmenist and hermetic traditions with a radical social constituency; here, again, we have the inspired prophets and the pretenders to actual divinity.

Throughout this milieu there is an utter repudiation of the outward forms of religion (including, for some, the forms of marriage), and a counterposing to these of the inner light of faith, inspiration or prophecy. For the Digger leader, Winstanley, the God of magistrates, property-owners and the Church was 'the God Devil' (sometimes 'the right Devil'). When the soldiers of the New Model

Army sang their marching song, they identified their enemy with Antichrist or the Beast:

> For God begins to honour us,
> The Saintes are marching on;
> The sword is sharp, the arrows swift
> To destroy Babylon.
> Against the kingdome of the beast
> Wee witnesses do rise. . .

Throughout the 1640s the language of the battle of the godly against Antichrist spread out into every area of political and social, as well as spiritual, life.[1]

The defeat of the Leveller soldiers at Burford in 1649 served as a sharp check to the temporal political hopes of the more advanced democrats. Like a gymnast on a trampoline, the democratic faith which met its check at Burford, soared back into the air once more in 1649–51, somersaulting and displaying itself in the brief Ranter climax. For a moment the revolutionary spirit, which had met a set-back in realistic political objectives, leapt to even more outrageous heights of utopian ideals and visionary teachings. *The Power of Love* had already been a favourite theme of antinomian divines; it was advocated with force and with practical demonstration by Gerrard Winstanley; and the quiet and rational theorist of the Levellers, William Walwyn, was to write in 1649:

I, through God's goodnesse, had long before been established in that part of doctrine (called then, Antinomian) of free justification by Christ alone; and so my heart was at much more ease and freedom, than others, who were entangled with those yokes of bondage, unto which Sermons and Doctrines mixt of Law and Gospel, do subject distressed consciences.

And he declared himself to be 'not a preacher of the law, but of the gospell', the gospel of love.[2]

The abrogation of the Moral Law did not leave a vacuum, for Law was driven out by Love. This gospel (love against law) was sometimes known, by shorthand, as the Everlasting Gospel. In longhand, the notion of the everlasting gospel derived from the twelfth-century Calabrian abbot, Joachim of Fiore, and proposed three successive Ages or Commissions: the Age of Fear and

[1] *Thurloe State Papers*, III, p. 137. For the 'liberation of Dissent' see M. Watts, *The Dissenters* (Oxford, 1978; 1985), pp. 179–86.
[2] *The Power of Love* was written by Walwyn in 1643. The passage cited is from Walwyn's *Just Defence*, 1649, p. 8, see Morton, *World of the Ranters*, pp. 146–7.

Inheritance

Servitude, which ended with the birth of Christ, and which followers might see as the Age of the Old Testament and the Moral
Law; the Age of Faith and Filial Obedience (the Age of the New
Testament and the apostolic succession); and the Age of Spiritual
Liberty for the Children of God, in which the scriptures would
appear in a wholly new light – a New Age, now imminent, and
perhaps to be announced by new prophets or Commissions of the
Spirit.[3] We do not know by exactly which routes this teaching had
reached the antinomian divines (such as Tobias Crisp and John
Saltmarsh) – to be transmitted by them to the most flamboyant of
all the Ranters, Abiezer Coppe – but by the 1640s it often came
down through the misty and suggestive filter of Jacob Boehme,
with his successive Ages of the Nettle, the Rose and the Lily.[4]

Thus the notion of the Everlasting Gospel had, by the late 1640s,
become part of the available vocabulary of radical heresy. For
Winstanley, in 1648, the time was expected when the authority of
apostles and prophets would give way to the time when 'the Lord
himself, who is the everlasting Gospell, doth manifest himself to
rule in the flesh of sonnes and daughters'. Winstanley came to see
this New Age as an Age of Reason.[5] And many joined this imagery
of the New Age to that of 'the New Jerusalem', when Babylon (or
Rome) was finally destroyed, and – in the words of the Welsh
Seeker, William Erbery, 'after the fall of *Rome*, there shall be the
new *Jerusalem*, and then the Church shall be one, one street in that
city and no more'.[6]

The Ranters, soaring from the trampoline in 1649–51, carried
the gospel of love further than Winstanley, Walwyn or Erbury were
prepared to follow. Disclaiming 'digging-levelling and sword-
levelling', Coppe proclaimed in a torrent of rhetoric a gospel of
spiritual Levelling which is 'Universall Love . . . who is putting
down the mighty from their seats; and exalting them of low degree'.
Breaking from the constraints of a Puritan upbringing, some
Ranters were said to have found relief in obscenities, swearing,
grotesque inversions of sanctified themes and divine jests, the

[3] See Marjorie Reeves and Warwick Gould, *Joachim of Fiore and the Myth of the Eternal Evangel*
(Oxford, 1987). The authors, however, are severely critical of any notion of a direct line
of transmission of Joachimite doctrines to Boehme, the Ranters or to Blake. But what we
should be looking for is a characteristic rhetoric and the trope of the everlasting gospel.
[4] See Morton, *World of the Ranters*, pp. 126–7; Hill, *The World Turned Upside Down*, p. 118,
note 187.
[5] Morton, p. 127; Hill, pp. 118–19, 315–16.   [6] Morton, p. 129.

exhibition of nakedness and in sexual licence. This last, together with expressions of primitive communism, naturally attracted the attention of critics most of all. For Alexander Ross Ranters was 'a sort of beasts', and, for them, 'Christian liberty . . . consists in community of all things, and among the rest, of women; which they paint over with an expression called *the enjoyment of the fellow-creature*.'[7] Going beyond the old opposition, Moral Law/Gospel, they were held to believe that 'all the commandments of God, both in the Old and New Testaments, are the fruits of the curse'. Nor can all the stories of Ranter excesses be turned away as the lampoons of prurient critics: Laurence Clarkson, in his remarkably self-revelatory auto-critique, *The Lost Sheep Found*, described how he came to the conviction that 'none can be free from sin, till in purity it be acted as no sin. . .'; and when he was 'Captain of the Rant' in London, 'I had most of the principal women came to my lodging for knowledge' until 'at last it became a trade so common, that all the froth and scum broke forth into the height of this wickedness, yea began to be a publick reproach'.[8]

As so often in a moment of political confusion and extremist – and sometimes exhibitionist – excitement, the quieter and more persevering voices are drowned in the loud noises of the self-appointed prophets. And when these prophets apostasised, they were inclined to accuse all their fellows of excesses which in fact had been specialties of their own. We have seen this very often, and we go on seeing it still. Innumerable ears attended to the roar of those called Ranters and incorporated some of their tenets into more stubborn and less self-dramatising beliefs. This can be seen, for example, in the records of several small Baptist churches in East Anglia, whose members repeatedly in the 1650s 'spake many things which savoured of Rantism', such as that they 'did not desire to be in such bondage' as to observe 'outward, ceremonial and

---

[7] This 'yellowpress' on supposed Ranters is discussed by J.C. Davis, *Fear, Myth and History*, *passim*, and Morton, *World of the Ranters*, *passim*. See also N. Cohn, *Pursuit of the Millenin* (1957), Appendix. Alexander Ross, *A View of all Religions* originated in 1640 and went through several revised editions. J.C. Davis, p. 124, consulting a 1653 edition, says that Ross 'saw fit not to mention' the Ranters, and he adduces this as one more proof that the Ranters did not exist; but in the (undated) edition which I consulted they are given an uncomplimentary place at pp. 256–7, as cited: also 1655 edn, pp. 387–8.

[8] For Clarkson, or Claxton, see Morton, chapter 5; Barry Reay in Hill, Reay and Lamont, *The World of the Muggletonians* (1983), chapter 6. J.C. Davis, pp. 58–75, attempts to throw doubts on Clarkson's association with any actual Ranters, in an unpersuasive display of special pleading.

carnal ordinances'.[9] Among such notions were the denial that there
was such a thing as sin, or, in Bauthumley's words, 'sin is properly
the dark side of God which is a meere privation of light'; and that
Hell had no real existence save in 'an accusing Conscience which
is Hell. . .'[10] Most important, for our purposes, was a radical, quasi-
pantheist redefinition of the notion of God and of Christ. John
Holland, one of the most sober critics of the Ranters, affirmed that
'they maintain that God is essentially in every creature, and that
there is as much of God in one creature, as in another, though he
doth not manifest himself so much in one as in another'. This is
confirmed by Jacob Bauthumley's *The Light and Dark sides of God,
Or a plain and brief Discourse of The Light side (God, Heaven and Earth)
The dark side (Devill, Sin, and Hell)* (1650), which was perhaps Holland's source:

Nay, I see that God is in all Creatures, Man and Beast, Fish and Fowle,
and every green thing, from the highest Cedar to the Ivey on the wall;
and that God is the life and being of them all, and that God doth really
dwell, and if you will personally . . . in them all, and hath his Being no
where else out of the Creatures.[11]

This has been described, by the historian of the Ranters, as 'the
central Ranter doctrine, from which all else logically flows'.[12] But
what may flow from it may depend upon different exercises of logic.
A general dispersed pantheism may flow logically into mortalism
or even materialism, in which all life returns to a common source
as streams to a sea. Or, in a more literal and intense variant, the
essential presence of God is to be found only in men and women
(his presence in nature is felt only dimly); hence these *are* God,
and, in consequence, 'man cannot either know God, or beleeve in
God, or pray to God, but it is God in man that knoweth himself,
believes in himself and prayeth to himself'.[13] As Morton concludes,
the identification of God with man and with the natural universe
might have 'two apparently opposite consequences. It might lead
to a mysticism which found God in everyone: equally it might
lead to a virtual materialism which in practice dispensed with him
altogether.'[14] It might also, one must add, lead to strange con-

---

[9] Hill, *The World Turned Upside Down*, p. 184.
[10] Cohn, *Pursuit of the Millenin*, pp. 338–9.
[11] *Ibid.*, pp. 336–7. John Holland, *The Smoke of the Bottomless Pit* (1657), is cited in Morton, *World of the Ranters*, p. 73.
[12] Morton, p. 73.   [13] *Ibid.*, p. 73, citing Holland.   [14] *Ibid.*, p. 74.

sequences in the unbalanced mind, for whom the very notion of 'God' was inflated with the most powerful symbolism and invested with expectations of omnipotence: for if a humble believer decided that he *was* God, or had more of the essence of God within him than his crabbed and jealous neighbours, then he might easily conceive of himself as a prophet or a pretender to God's throne.

The Ranters did not conceive of themselves as a church or a congregation: they may have used instead the term 'my one flesh',[15] for they were in fact the flesh within which dwelt the spirit of God, they were 'fellow-creatures' in Christ. This is the cluster of ideas which most concerns us, and we need not delay over other ideas which were sometimes attendant: chiliastic notions of the Second Coming, or of the rule of the Saints, various competing notions of the Resurrection, or of the enhancement of sensual joys and sexual powers in Heaven. What should be added is the influence of Jacob Boehme, whose writing was being translated at this time, and whose influence upon the Ranters may be felt – as in Bauthumley's *Light and Dark sides of God* – in a somewhat-qualified dialectic of the co-existence within God of good and evil principles. God (in Coppe's words) is both 'a jealous God, and the Father of Mercies; in him (I say) the Lyon and the Lamb, Servant and Lord, Peace and War, Joy and Jealousie, Wrath and Love, etc. are reconciled and all complicated in Unity'.[16] And this, one must add, must have been a complicating unity indeed when God had his being only in 'my one flesh'.

For by 1651 the Ranters had fallen back upon the trampoline once more with a heavy thud. Their descent was hastened in 1650 by the Blasphemy Act, and the subsequent imprisonment of several of their supposed leaders. In the less exhilarating ambience of prison, these were swift to recant, showing a lack of fortitude which would have been despised by their Lollard and Puritan forebears. And then, in a final rebound, the tumbler of the radical spirit rose into the air once more.

This time it arose, not as Ranting, but as prophetic dogma and as sectarian organising zeal. In this moment there is a scatter of competing prophets, and the consolidation of sectarian doctrines: Quakers, Fifth Monarchists, Muggletonians. And here and there thinkers of more intellectual rigour (Erbery, Pordage) retired to

---

[15] Hill, *The World Turned Upside Down*, p. 165.   [16] Cited in Morton, p. 75.

meditate more coherent systems. It was this moment, rather than
the climax of the Ranters, which found ways of transmitting itself,
by way of Baptists, Quakers, Philadelphians, Behmenists, Muggletonians and others into the next century, although much was to
be softened and transformed in the transmission.

This moment can be seen as both an extension of Ranting into
new forms and as a reaction against Ranting: what was extended
was, in the same moment, limited and controlled. The reaction
was sometimes general, sometimes very specific. The first commission given by God to John Reeve and Ludowick Muggleton was
to visit the Ranting prophets, John Robins and Thomas Tany, and
pronounce upon them a sentence of eternal damnation. (Laurence
Clarkson was later to renounce his Ranter faith and join the
Muggletonians.) A more general form of reaction is to be seen in
the increasing withdrawal from temporal objectives and expectations, so that old tenets were redefined in a more spiritual or quietist sense. Not only George Fox but also John Reeve placed in the
forefront of their teaching the prohibition of the 'sword of steel'; it
is the portion of true Christians in this world (John Reeve said)
'to suffer all kind of wrong from all men, and to return mercy and
forgiveness. . .'[17] Millenarial expectations tended – except with the
Fifth Monarchists – to be indefinitely postponed, or to be redefined
in an 'internal' sense: the New Jerusalem was an image of spiritual
community, and was perhaps already in existence among the
faithful.

Robins and Tany were two of the most bizarre voices of the
Ranting climax. Both appear to have suffered delusions of personal
divinity. Robins was sometimes known as 'the Ranter's god' or
'the Shakers' god'; his wife announced that she was pregnant with
a Messiah; Robins, who claimed that he had risen from the dead,
started to enlist and train volunteers for a crusade to the Holy
Land. When Reeve (a former disciple) visited him in the New
Bridewell and uttered his sentence of damnation, Robins collapsed
and recanted. For years afterwards Muggleton was to claim this
as a victory over Antichrist, and to taunt the Quakers with being
led and guided by the spirit of Robins.[18] Tany is more interesting,

---

[17] *A Transcendent Spiritual Treatise*, sometimes attributed to John Reeve and Ludowick Muggleton, and sometimes to Reeve alone: chapter 3, 'Of the Unlawfulness for a Spiritual
Christian to war with a Sword of Steel'.
[18] Alexander Gordon, *The Origin of the Muggletonians* (1869), pp. 16–17, and the same author's
excellent entry on Robins in DNB. L. Muggleton, *Acts of the Witnesses of the Spirit* (1699:

and might, just possibly, be more relevant to Blake. For Muggleton, Tany was 'the Head of . . . the Atheistical Ranters and Quakers Principle'. A goldsmith in the Strand, he read some of Boehme's work, and, in 1650, announced that it had been revealed to him that he was 'a Jew of the tribe of Reuben' and that he must change his name to Theaurau John: he announced the return of the Jews to the Holy Land, and prepared to follow Robins with 'bow and spear'. As a necessary preparation, he circumcised himself. He was undismayed by Reeve's sentence of damnation, busied himself with other projects, claimed first the throne of England and then the throne of France, had an armed affray at the houses of parliament, and finally seems to have disappeared, perhaps in 1655, perhaps later, sailing in a home-made boat in the Channel, crying 'Ho, for the Holy Wars'.[19]

Tany, unlike Robins, left some writings behind: they are compounded of wilful eccentricity, delusion and passages of transparent intensity. His *Theauraujohn His Theousori Apokolipikal* (1651) was dedicated 'to the Army and the risen people in all Lands'. The soul of man is the divine breath of God 'inclosed within the circumference of the body': 'this is the Image of God in Man', the 'living life of our Spirit', which at death returns to a common fountain. 'Man is Christ, and Christ is God . . . both one, the product are we.'

Christ in the head is a lye, without being in the heart . . . Brethren, till ye be doers, ye are a lye, and . . . your Religion is of the devil; for ye name Jesus to effect another end, but love is Jesus acting, by a living distributing life, to his members.

To know Hell is truly to know Heaven, for 'Hell is a separation from happiness; Hell is the restraint from injoyment.' Tany was as curt with the authority of the Scriptures as he was with that of the churches: the New Testament 'is but a name of dead letters set together with much interweaving of man's invention'.[20] We also find some passages of Behmenist dialectic:

1764 edn), pp. 20–2, 45–8; *A Transcendent Spiritual Treatise*, chapter 2; Muggleton, *The Neck of the Quakers Broken* (1756 edn), pp. 16–17; Muggleton, *A Looking-Glass for George Fox* (1756 edn), pp. 98–9.

[19] Gordon, *The Origin of the Muggletonians*, pp. 18–19, and also his entry on Tany in DNB. Hill, *The World Turned Upside Down*, pp. 181–2; Hill, *Antichrist*, p. 115; Muggleton, *Acts of the Witnesses*, pp. 20, 43–5; *A Looking-Glass for George Fox*, p. 99.

[20] In 1654 Tany in Lambeth threw a bible, along with a saddle, pistols and sword, into a great bonfire, upon which 'the people were ready to stone him'.

Take notice there is two alls, a light all, and a dark all, and God but one
all to them two alls; Light and darkness to him are one . . . Love is that
great day that shall burn as an oven, for love is fire. . .

And we also find the Everlasting Gospel:

This is the everlasting Gospel that should be preached, which is God
dwelling with men, by a divine Evangelical living in them, they in it,
here lies the mystery. . .

The heart lives in God when God lives wholly in the heart:

Now here is the mystery. Thus God lives in us, he cannot live out of
us. . .

The essence creative in us is good, for 'tis God's image, but our dissenting
from that living life in us, causes the evil in us. . .

It is difficult to say how much of this came to Tany through the
Familist tradition, how much from Boehme ('God must become
man, man must become God . . . the earth must be turned to
heaven'[21]), how much from the general radical and Ranting milieu,
how much was his own variation upon all these themes. In a con-
tinuation of the same work, in 1653, the Everlasting Gospel was
defined simply as Love:

> Now know that can be no Gospel,
> That must be upheld by a humane Law;
> But it is the Lye in the whole earth:
> For the Gospel is Love, and then no Law. . .

Among much unloving invective against the established churches
('the *Bishops are gone*, and I Theauraujohn say, that the *Cleargy*
shall not long stand'), and more Kabbalistical, Hebraic and Arabic
juggling of terms, he returned often to this central theme, expressed
in what had become, by now, fairly commonplace antinomian
terms: those who are justified not by Works of the Law but by
faith 'are risen with Christ, they act in love', and 'love is the new
Jerusalem that is above':

God is love, and he that acteth in love, acteth in God, for them the spirit
hath taken that man or woman into itself.

These were Tany's most lucid tracts, and they are not as lucid
as they may appear in my extracts. Later he issued *Theauraujohn*

---

[21] Boehme, *The Signature of All Things*, cited in Hill, *Milton*, p. 312. Boehme also asserted
that 'God dwells in all Things'.

*High Priest to the Jewes his Disputive challenge to the Universities of Oxford
and Cambridge, and the whole Hirarch of Roms Clargical Priests* (1655).
In this he remarked that he had 'taken my Degrees' in the two
'Colleges' of Newgate and King's Bench: 'the Prisons were alwayes
the Prophets Schools, we read true Lectures in the empty walls'.
Neither Oxford nor Cambridge have been able to answer his disputive challenge yet.

I beg the impatient Blake reader to favour me with at least a
temporary suspension of disbelief. I am not simply rambling on,
wherever curiosity may lead me. I am engaged in a complex operation, teasing out strands which may lead on to other strands across
150 years. The Ranting strand leads directly into early Quakerism,
within which it was said that some former Ranters were swept up.
The degree to which Ranters and early Quakers shared common
attributes is another difficult question, and one which must be
handled with a certain delicacy to this day, since some part of the
evidence may appear to belie the sober testimony of George Fox.
But the interpenetration of Ranting and Quaker notions is incon-
trovertible.[22] I am interested not in continuing vagaries of exhibitionist and enthusiastic behaviour among early Friends, or the
ecstatic 'witchcraft-fits' (howling and groaning, foaming at the
mouth, speaking with 'tongues') which Muggleton was to make
much of in his polemics.[23] What is more significant is the continuity
of Ranting doctrine into Quakerism, a continuity which can be
easily overlooked because of the very evident Quaker reaction
against Ranting – a reaction, above all, against the Ranter excesses
in personal and sexual conduct – a reaction expressed in sobriety
of life, dress and manners.

The continuity is found, in part, in a common Behmenist influence;[24] and, with this, in the literalism with which many early
Friends held themselves to be vectors of the divine spirit. Reeve
and Muggleton were not guilty of hyperbole when they said that
the Quakers were still guided by the spirits of Robins and Tany:

The Quakers Principle is but the Ranters refined into a more civil Kind

---

[22] See Hill, *The World Turned Upside Down*, chapter 10; Morton, *World of the Ranters*, pp. 91–
2; Frank McGregor, 'Ranterism and the Development of Early Quakerism', *Journal of
Religious History* (Sydney, 1978), pp. 349–63.

[23] *A Looking-Glass for George Fox*, pp. 44–6.

[24] *Ibid.*, p. 10: 'I suppose *Jacob Behmont*'s Books were the chief Books that the Quakers
bought, for there is the Principle or Foundation of their Religion.'

of Life. For the Ranters were so grossly rude in their Lives, that spoiled their high Language, and made People weary of them; but the Quakers that were upon the Rant are the best able to maintain the Quakers Principles of Christ within them.[25]

For many early Quakers, God was 'an infinite Spirit, that fills Heaven and Earth, and all Places, and all things', whereas 'as touching Christ's Flesh, we are Bone of his Bone, and Flesh of his Flesh, and we have the Mind of Christ'.[26] However George Fox interpreted these beliefs, contemporary observers insisted that many Quakers held to them in the most literal sense. The believers, like the Ranters, were still 'my one flesh'. They say 'some of them are Christ, some God himself, and some equal with God, because they have the same spirit in them which is in God', 'Christ hath no other body but his church'. Some inveighed against all learning (the fruit of the Tree of the Knowledge of Good and Evil). They held that they were justified by their own inherent righteousness, and that 'many of them cannot sin'; that the more othodox churches were Antichristian; 'that Christ came to destroy all property; and that therefore all things ought to be common . . . and that one man ought not to have power over another'. Thus a critical observer in 1653.[27] And there is independent confirmation that some early Quakers held most of these tenets.[28]

In this selective account we have at length reached the year 1653. And there are still a dozen or more decades to traverse before we can come up to William Blake. Is there any reason to suppose that Blake was aware of this early moment of antinomianism, or that tenets and tropes could have been conveyed to him across these decades in any form? What possible vectors could have carried this tradition from 1650 to 1790?

[25] *Ibid.*, p. 55. Cf. Ephraim Pagitt, 'the *Ranter* is . . . much of the same make with our *Quakers* . . . only the *Ranter* is less severe'; and Baxter, 'Quakers . . . were but the Ranters turned from horrid Prophaneness and Blasphemy, to a Life of extreme Austerity on the other side. Their Doctrines were mostly the same with the Ranters': Morton, *World of the Ranters*, p. 91.
[26] Muggleton, *The Neck of the Quakers Broken*, pp. 9, 23.
[27] Alexander Ross, *A View of all Religions* (1653), pp. 252–7. This account continued to be reprinted in the eighteenth century, but subsequent editors added an Appendix, pp. 322–3, noting that 'considerable alterations' had taken place among the Quakers, who were now noted for 'probity and uprightness in their dealings', frugality, simplicity, &c.
[28] See Hill, *The World Turned Upside Down*, chapter 10; J.F. McGregor, 'Ranterism and the Development of Early Quakerism', *Journal of Religious History*, 9 (1977); Barry Reay, *The Quakers and the English Revolution* (1985), chapter 2.

CHAPTER 4

The polite witnesses

We are back once more in the argument indicated in my Introduction: Blake and *which* tradition? It is an extraordinarily complex argument, and very different answers have been offered, with great confidence. For convenience we may put the answers into three groups: (1) The strongest influence upon Blake comes from one major source – the Bible – but the Bible read in a particular way, influenced by Milton and by radical Dissent; (2) To this may be added suggestions of more specific vectors – the Moravians, Baptists, Philadelphians and Behmenists, the Rosicrucians and masons, and thence to the Swedenborgians – which it is argued claimed Blake's allegiance; (3) While the influence of the first two vectors is not discounted, it is suggested that the weight of influence upon Blake is literary and scholarly: that Blake's ideas and images were derived primarily from his reading: that he was an omnivorous reader in an extraordinarily diverse (and often obscure) range of classical, neo-Platonist, Kabbalistic, hermetic and Behmenist sources. Scholars have suggested either that Blake drew upon these influences eclectically, or that his work should be placed firmly within 'The Tradition' of neo-Platonic and hermetic thought (G.M. Harper, Kathleen Raine).[1]

The answers may shade into each other. But, in the end, there is a real divergence of emphasis between (1) and (3). To make the matter more difficult, one answer may be adequate for 1788–93 but less adequate for any time after 1793 (or 1800). For it is probable that Blake, in his later years, read widely in both classical

---

[1] G.M. Harper, *The Neoplatonism of William Blake* (Chapel Hill, N.C., 1961); Kathleen Raine, *Blake and Tradition* (Princeton, 1968), 2 vols. For the possible influence of the Cambridge Platonist, Henry More, see S. Foster Daman, *William Blake: his Philosophy and Symbols* (Gloucester, Mass., 1958).

and 'mystic' sources, and, as he did so, his field of reference enlarged and any kind of allusion is possible.

My own answer is compounded of (1) and (2), and I will propose a new possible vector coming through to Blake in his childhood. But when we come to the later prophetic books, then we must attend with respect to the influences suggested in (3).

The best way into this very complex argument may be to look at the strongest candidates offered as a line of transmission from the late seventeenth century to Blake: the Behmenists and Philadelphians. But a search for possible influences may take us back a great deal further: indeed to the Gnostic Christian heresy in the first and second centuries AD. In several of the Gnostic sects there were some quite startling pre-figurations of ideas and symbols which recur in Blake. Gnostic dualism which proposed a second God or demiurge as Creator of matter and the world could sometimes take the demiurge to be an evil power acting in hostility to the Supreme Power. The Naasenes and some of the Gnostic sect of Ophites venerated the serpent, and interpreted its role in the Fall as a benefaction, since it first raised human beings to higher knowledge. (This reverence for the serpent persisted in the later heresy of Manichaeism.) The Gnostic sect of Cainites (if they ever existed) held the God of the Old Testament to be an evil being, and Cain and Abel to be the 'offspring of antagonistic spiritual powers'.[2] We will find such ideas cropping up in Blake. Indeed, Crabb Robinson, a friend of the Romantic poets and a voluminous diarist, who recorded some fascinating conversations with Blake in his last years, instantly recognised some of his ideas as Gnostic. Blake had told him that 'Nature is the work of the Devil.' When Crabb Robinson objected (in the authority of Genesis) that 'God created the Heaven & the Earth . . . I was triumphantly told that this God was not Jehovah, but the Elohim, & the doctrine of the Gnostics repeated with sufficient consistency to silence one so unlearned as myself.'[3]

Nearly all of what the eighteenth century knew about Gnosticism came from hostile and heresy-hunting sources, such as Irenaeus, a bishop of Lyons in the second century.[4] Blake could have picked

[2] H.L. Mansel, *The Gnostic Heresies of the First and Second Centuries* (1875), pp. 96, 101–2.
[3] G.E. Bentley, *Blake Records*, p. 545.
[4] Giovanni Filoramo, *A History of Gnosticism* (Oxford, 1990), pp. 3–4. The discovery of

up some notion of Gnostic beliefs from several second-hand sources: even Gibbon gave a sketchy account of Gnostic dualism: 'in the system of the Gnostics, the Jehovah of Israel, the Creator of this lower world, was a rebellious, or at least an ignorant spirit'.[5] But it is unlikely that Blake would have directly consulted Gnostic 'sources', even such unreliable accounts as those of Irenaeus. For a historian of Gnosticism affirms that 'we see a veritable efflorescence of Gnostic mythology in Jacob Boehme'.[6] The influence of Boehme upon Blake is undoubted (and was acknowledged) and he could have derived any Gnostic notions through this source.[7]

Jacob Boehme (1575–1624) was a prosperous shoemaker from Gorlitz on the Bohemian border, who discussed mystic, Kabbalistic, Gnostic, alchemical (Paracelsian) and other unorthodox ideas in a circle of merchants, intellectuals, tradesmen and one or two noblemen, and who worked out his own theosophical system which he published in a succession of tracts in his last years. His reputation travelled rapidly to an England which was in a state of spiritual enquiry, and by the 1640s his ideas were already circulating among enthusiasts. The followers of Boehme were often known as 'Behmenists', but the case for a direct line of Behmenist transmission to Blake – a case sometimes suggested by those who propose a Great Tradition of Christian and neo-Platonist mysticism – is hazardous. I will rehearse the hypothesis briefly, since anyone who puts together the engaging account in Désirée Hirst (*Hidden Riches*)

Gnostic works in Coptic in a jar at Nag Hammadi in Egypt in 1945 has, of course, transformed subsequent understanding of Gnosticism.

[5] Edward Gibbon, *The Decline and Fall of the Roman Empire*, chapter XLVII (II). Secondary accounts of Gnosticism which were possibly available to Blake include Nathaniel Lardner's *History of Heretics* and *Credibility of the Gospel History* in *Works* (1788), J.L. von Mosheim, *An Ecclesiastical History, Ancient and Modern* (1765), and several works by his contemporary, Joseph Priestley, especially *An History of the Corruptions of Christianity* (Birmingham, 1782). See also Stuart Curran, 'Blake and the Gnostic Hyle', *Blake Studies*, Vol. 4 no. 2, Spring 1972. But note also the warning of G.E. Bentley: 'It is much easier to find parallels to Blakean myth in Boehme's system than in the fragmentary accounts of Gnosticism available to him': G.E. Bentley, 'William Blake and the Alchemical Philosophers', B.Litt. thesis, Oxford, 1954, p. 185. Unfortunately this thesis, which is the closest examination of the relation of Boehme's ideas to Blake's known to me, has never been published.

[6] G. Filoramo, *A History of Gnosticism*, p. xvi.

[7] In *The Marriage of Heaven and Hell* Blake wrote: 'Any man of mechanical talents may, from the writings of Paracelsus or Jacob Behmen, produce ten thousand volumes of equal value with Swedenborg's, and from those of Dante or Shakespeare an infinite number.' The evidence that Blake used William Law's edition of *The Works of Jacob Behmen* (1764, 1772 and 1781) comes from his late years, when he praised Freher's plates to Henry Crabb Robinson: see Bentley, *Blake Records*, p. 313 and note.

with works by D.P. Walker, Walton, Thune, Hutin and (with some caution) G.M. Harper and Kathleen Raine, can decipher it there.[8]

The story commences in the vortex of 'The World Turned Upside Down', when Behmenist influence was profound both upon some scholars and some Commonwealth sects. Dr John Pordage, ejected for Behmenist and other heresies from his living in 1654, returns to view in 1681, when Mrs Jane Lead, author of *The Everlasting Gospel Message*, adopts his teaching, publishes many volumes of visionary and trance-like writing, and becomes the centre of a small group of Philadelphians:

> From thy dark Cell now great Bohemine rise;
> Tutor to Sages; Mad to th' Worldly Wise.
> Wisdom's first distant Phosphor, to whose Sight
> Internal Nature's Ground, all naked bright
> Unveils, all Worlds appear, Heavens spread their Light. . .
>
> The Glorious Aera *Now, Now, Now* begins.
> *Now, Now* the Great Angelick Trumpet sings:
> A Now in ev'ry Blast, Love's *Everlasting Gospel* Rings.[9]

These ecstatic Philadelphians take us forward into the eighteenth century, when there is a brief moment of confluence and argument with the Camisards or 'French Prophets'. From this point we may find lesser and eccentric figures: Francis Lee, a disciple of Jane Lead, the advocate of an 'Enochian life on earth', 'a transcendentally exalted spiritual renovation and illumination';[10] Francis Okeley, at one time ministering to the Moravians, author of the *Dawnings of the Everlasting Gospel-Light* (1775); and Richard Clarke, a late exemplar of the tradition, a contemporary of Blake in London, much preoccupied with the symbolism of the 'New Jerusalem' and of *Revelation*.

Alongside, but standing a little apart from, this tradition we have the most articulate and cogent of the English eighteenth-century Behmenists, the Anglican clergyman, William Law (1686–1761). He is best known today for his evangelical influence upon John Wesley. But Law's nineteenth-century disciple, Christopher

---

[8] Désirée Hirst, *Hidden Riches: Traditional Symbolism from the Renaissance to Blake* (1964); D.P. Walker, *The Decline of Hell* (Chicago, 1964); Nils Thune, *The Behmenists and the Philadelphians* (Uppsala, 1948); S. Hutin, *Les Disciples Anglais de Jacob Boehme* (Paris, 1960); A.G. Debus, *The English Paracelsians* (1965). Also Francis Yates, *The Rosicrucian Enlightenment* (1972).

[9] Jane Lead, *A Fountain of Gardens*, 3 vols. (1696–1700), sig. E.2.

[10] Francis Lee, *Dissertations* (1752), p. 640.

Walton, saw him as having two aspects – the one 'Elias-like', or evangelical, the other 'Enochian' or prophetic. In his Enochian aspect Law's work runs closely parallel to the Philadelphians. Deism he saw as 'the religion of *human reason*, set up in opposition to the Gospel'. The laws of Moses were a matter of mere 'carnal ordinances', 'a temporary provisional Help'. '*Reasoning* instead of Faith brought about the first Fall', and–

To live by *Faith* is to be truly and fully in Covenant with God; to live by Reasoning, is to be merely and solely in compact with ourselves, with our own vanity and blindness.[11]

However oddly it assorts with his evangelical writings, there is a kind of spiritualised antinomian pressure in Enochian William Law.

These, then, may be traditions germane to Blake. From these the Swedenborgians were to make some early converts.[12] But, as so often, the evidence is elusive. We have no proof that Blake read any of them, although we can show the probability in certain cases. Such correspondence of this circle as survives in the late eighteenth century shows no known associates of Blake.[13] And if we look back to Mrs Jane Lead, early in the century, we can see some of the difficulties. Very certainly, Jane Lead, in her visionary writings, employs a vocabulary which seems to flash signals forward to Blake. The 'Everlasting Gospel' and the 'New Jerusalem' apart (which will be found in many different places), we also have references to the 'Pure Humanity of Christ' and to 'Christ's perfect Deity in his Eternal Humanity', to the Last Vintage and Harvest, to the 'secret gate' of the spirit, to 'states' and to 'golden chains', and (perhaps even more striking) recommendations to enter in 'to a Self-Annihilation'.[14]

Nor is this all. If we potter around in the writings of Lead, Pordage and Philadelphians we will stumble repeatedly upon 'Blakean' themes. To Jane Lead this world is 'under the government of that Great Monarch Reason, to whose Scepter all must

[11] William Law, *A Short but Sufficient Confutation of the Reverend Dr Warburton's Projected Defence of Christianity in his Divine Legation of Moses* ... (1757), pp. 63, 76–7; C. Walton, *Notes and Materials for a Biography of William Law* (1854), p. 522; Désirée Hirst, *Hidden Riches*, chapter 7.
[12] One was Thomas Hartley, author of *Paradise Restored: or a Testimony to the Doctrines of the Blessed Millenium* (1764).
[13] In Dr Williams's Library, MS 1.1.43 (Walton Papers).
[14] See, e.g., *A Fountain of Gardens*, p. 14; *Theosophical Transactions of the Philadelphian Society*, no. 1, 1697.

bow that live in the Sensitive Animal Life'.[15] This Monarch is
sometimes seen as a Serpent. The title of one of Pordage's works
was *The Angelickal World: or, a Treatise concerning the Angelical Principle,
with the Inhabitants thereof, and God in this Principle. The Dark Fire
World: or Treatise concerning the Hellish Principle, with the Inhabitants,
and Wonders, and God manifesting himself in this Principle.*[16] Jane Lead
is always speculating on the Seven Churches of Asia, and on four-
fold, or five- or six-fold, sensual, intellectual, visionary, prophetic
and mystical states. Pordage's circle also defined four degrees of
revelation: (1) Vison, (2) Illumination, (3) Transportation or
Translation, (4) Revelation; and as early as 1683 one was bitterly
attacking 'Natural Religion':

> The *Rational*, which the confounding Jesuit wold mak the *pure Religionist
> beleev* to be Mechanism (*the Diana of this inquisitiv Age*) and the whole
> Encyclopoede of Arts and Sciences but a brisk circulation of the Blood,
> and all thinking and reasoning Power a mere local motion, and that too
> tumultuous. . .[17]

(It will be seen that our author, like Tany before him and Thomas
Spence after him, was a spelling reformer.) 'There is no use of
Reason but in the Babylonish principle, and the kingdom of the
beast', wrote Pordage, referring to the authority of Boehme.[18] 'All
Formal Worships set up by Men, and constituted by Rational
Inventions, as a Shadow must pass away', prophesied Jane Lead.[19]
They would give way to the ministration of the Everlasting Gospel
'which is all Love, Grace, Mercy and Peace'.[20] And in the *Theosophical Transactions* of the Philadelphian Society – a journal conducted
for five numbers in 1697 – contributors sent in Paracelsian,
hermetic and Kabbalistic lucubrations replete with 'emanations'
and magic numbers, and sometimes uncomfortably close to the
machinery of Blake's prophetic books:

---

[15] *Ibid.*, p. 37.

[16] This is advertised in *A Fountain of Gardens*, but I have not found an English edition.
Several of Pordage's works were never published in England, but in Amsterdam, etc., in
German: see D.P. Walker, *The Decline of Hell*; Thune, *The Behmenists*, pp. 99–100. For
John Pordage and his son, Samuel, see Hill, *The Experience of Defeat*, chapter 8; and Hirst,
Hidden Riches, pp. 105–9, 168–72.

[17] J.P., M.D. (John Pordage), *Theologia Mystica* (1683), pp. 65–9, 98, 101–3. This curious
work is edited by J.L. (Jane Lead) and E.H. (Edward Hooker) and carries a vigorous
and witty 100-page introduction, perhaps from Hooker's pen.

[18] A Gentleman Retired from Business, *A Compendious View of the Grounds of the Teutonick
Philosophy* (1770), p. 41.

[19] Jane Lead, *The Tree of Faith; or the Tree of Life* (1696), p. 1.

[20] Lead, *A Fountain of Gardens*, p. 210.

Now by these manifold Emanations, and Circular Returns or Reverbera-
tions and Extractions from the dark Waters of Nature in the Abyss and
void Chaos; as by so many Coitions and Copulations of the Male with
the Female, were brought forth all the foresaid Circular Globes and
Worlds, fill'd with all Sorts of Creatures and Inhabitants; distinguish'd
into their several Sphears and Regions of Modified Light and Darkness,
Higher and Lower . . . the inferiour Female Nature always Breathing and
Aspiring upward, as with a Divine Lust, to be impregnated with the
Influence and Immanations of the Superiour Divine Male.[21]

As a result of all these divine copulations 'thus . . . have Good and
Evil grown up together, from one Original in the Beginning of
Creation'.

It is instructive to note parallels with Blake's ideas and symbolism. But exactly what instruction do these bring? We are reminded,
perhaps, that notions which scholars confidently attribute to
Blake's reading of Proclus, Fludd or Thomas Taylor, could equally
have come through reading of this kind. We are also prompted to
reflect that notions or symbols which appear to be grand or profound when presented as part of a 'Great Tradition' of hermetic
and neo-Platonist thought need not always be handled with such
reverence. Philadelphian and Behmenist thought has a significance
as a counter-Enlightenment impulse, as a reaction against the
mechanistic philosophy of the time, and hence as a potential
resource for alternative positions. But it can scarcely be argued
that it articulated such positions. Some part of the continuing 'Tradition' was little more than an arcane vocabulary and ecstatic
visionary rhetoric, in which circulated a repetitious symbolism of
matter/spirit. And some considerable part of the 'Tradition' was
claptrap (which also, now and then, was gathered up by Blake).

Moreover, we can make few attributions of influence with any
confidence. Let us take the state of Beulah, which Blake offers as
a moony paradise, sometimes a garden of repose, sometimes marriage or sexual love, sometimes as 'a place where Contrarieties are
equally True'. Scholars at first supposed Blake found the name in
a rather non-committal reference in Isaiah: then it was noted that
he could have found it also in *Pilgrim's Progress*, in a more suggestive
passage. To put these two together, one perceptive critic has
argued, is one of Blake's 'more clever pieces of symbolic align-

[21] *Theosophical Transactions* (Philadelphia Society, 1697), pp. 277, 289.

ment'.[22] How much more clever, then, to put these two together with Mrs Jane Lead's *A Fountain of Gardens* (1696):

Know then that there is a secret hidden Garden, within that Land called *Beulah*, in which grow all Physical Plants, which the River *Pison* doth Water. It is a temperate Climate, neither too Hot, nor too Cold: and the Sun never goeth down there. For there is no Night, but one perpetual Day in the borders of this Blessed and Beautiful Land. And here do grow all sorts of Herbs, that have such a vigorous Seed of Life in them, that their Life never doth fade. Here also groweth every Kind of Spicy Trees, which through the Exhaling Sun, through the rest of the Divine Plants, do produce a mighty Frangrancy; insomuch that none into this Place can come, but Seraphical Ones; who are used to this pure Climate. Here are hid within the Bowels of this Holy Ground, the Veins of pure Gold, with all Oriental Pretious Stones.[23]

But before we claim this as a third source, or *the* source, of Blake's Beulah, we have to ask how far the name was part of the common currency of eighteenth-century radical Dissent, as the name for a peaceful and fertile paradise. Certainly, it was well enough understood to Morgan John Rhees, a fervent Welsh Baptist, who, when he founded with utopian hopes a town in Western Pennsylvania in 1796, called it Beula.[24]

It is my impression that Beulah often came up in the rhetoric of eighteenth-century Dissenting circles (especially Baptist). We are dealing, not with a Great Tradition of a few scholars and mystics, but with several little traditions, some with literary attainments and some without, all of which employed a vocabulary of symbolism familiar to Blake.

Even attributions of influence from the scholarly tradition are exceedingly hazardous. Let us take the Philadelphians again. Behind them stood Boehme. Behind Boehme stood much else – influences from Paracelsus, the Kabbala, millenarial impulses, even gnosticism. But Boehme's influence came through to the Philadelphians by way of seventeenth-century translators and scholars, Ranters and Antinomians (in her youth Mrs Jane Lead had sat at

---

[22] John Beer, *Blake's Visionary Universe* (Manchester, 1969), p. 27. Also Northrop Frye, *Fearful Symmetry* (Princeton, 1947: Boston, 1962), *passim*: Paley, p. 130; Masashi Suzuki, ' "Architecture", "Foot", and "Beulah": Visionary Gate' in *Milton, English and English–American Literature*, No. 24, 1989 (Tokyo).

[23] Lead, *A Fountain of Gardens*, p. 105. Hirst also briefly notices this passage, *Hidden Riches*, pp. 303–4.

[24] See Gwyn A. Williams, 'Morgan John Rhees and his Beula', *Welsh History Review*, Vol. III, 1966–7, pp. 441–72.

the feet of Tobias Crisp, the antinomian divine[25]), and by way of
Dr John Pordage, an associate of the Commonwealth radicals and
visionaries. Blake may or may not have read Jane Lead or Pordage,
but fellow Swedenborgians, with whom he may have argued, certainly did (below, p. 43). Moreover, there is good evidence that
Swedenborg himself was influenced in his youth by the writings of
English Philadelphians, as these had filtered through to Sweden
by way of German pietism (pp. 133–4n). And, finally, the great
influence of Milton, who himself had been touched by the Ranting
and Behmenist milieu, worked continually upon Blake.[26] How are
we to say, with any confidence, how a given symbol, common to
all this tangled inheritance, ended up in Blake's mind?

Another way of approaching the problem is to ask the mundane
question: *could* Blake have read in the various sources discussed so
far? So far as I know, no scholar has yet identified any 'public' or
subscription library of which Blake was a member. But most of
such libraries would have been unlikely to hold stocks of 'mystic'
writings. If we look, rather, at what was available in recent editions, and at the skimpy evidence as to what was to be found in
private collections, the answer is remarkable. Blake *could* have
found in London, in the 1790s, copies of almost every work that
we have discussed. The scarcest and most inaccessible works will
have been those which Miss Raine cites as central to her notion of
The Tradition. If Blake consulted these, then he could only have
done so in editions published in the Civil War and Commonwealth
vortex: translations of *The Divine Pomander* of Hermes Trismegistus
(1650), of Agrippa's *Occult Philosophy* (1651), all the englished versions of Paracelsus, all the works of Thomas Vaughan, Fludd's
Mosaicall Philosophy (1659). And in whatever collections Blake
found these (if he did) he would be likely to have found them cheek
by jowl with the works of Antinomians, Ranters and Seekers, with
the works of such men as Crisp, Everard, Erbery, Webster, Bauthumley or Pordage. Miss Raine always gives us the transcendental
cheek and neglects to mention the antinomian and millenarian
jowl.

[25] Nils Thune, *The Behmeniste*, p. 70. For Tobias Crisp see Christopher Hill, *Religion and Politics in 17th Century England* (1986).
[26] The major discussion of this is in Hill, *Milton*. The claims once put forward for Boehme's direct influence on Milton – see Margaret L. Bailey, *Milton and Jakob Boehme* (New York, 1914) – tend now to be discounted by scholars, including Hill.

It is in fact the more radical seventeenth-century thought which seems to have been more readily available in Blake's time. Of the Antinomians and Ranters (and their milieu) works by Tobias Crisp were republished in 1791,[27] by John Saltmarsh in 1811 and 1814,[28] by John Simpson and John Eaton in 1747,[29] by Richard Coppin in 1763, 1764 and 1768,[30] by John Everard in 1757 and 1817[31] and by John Pordage in 1776.[32] Works of Boehme remained available in several editions.[33] Virtually all of the works of John Reeve and Ludowick Muggleton were kept in print throughout the century (p. 69).[34]

The extensive range of works from these traditions which could be gathered by an eighteenth-century collector is exemplified by the private library of John Byrom (1692–1763), now in the Cheetham's Library, Manchester. A similar library may have been in the possession of a contemporary and possible acquaintance of Blake's, Henry Peckitt. Peckitt, a retired apothecary, was an ardent Swedenborgian, the first President of the Theosophical Society in London, a student of Hebrew and Arabic, an antiquarian and astronomer (perhaps dabbling in astrology?). His library consisted of many thousands of volumes 'in every branch of science' and 'a rare collection of mystical books, to which he was known to be very partial'. In the 1780s he lived in Old Compton Street, Soho, five minutes' walk from Blake: we cannot show that the two men were acquainted, but if Blake ever attended meetings of the Theosophical Society or the Reverend Duché's gatherings at Lambeth, then they would have met.[35] Prior to his adhesion to the Sweden-

[27] *Christ Alone Exalted* (1791).

[28] *Free Grace* (1814). Saltmarsh's *Holy Discoveries and Flames* and *Sparkles of Glory* were republished by William Huntington in 1811.

[29] Reprinted by William Cudworth, in 1747, along with Crisp in a compilation, *Christ Alone Exalted*.

[30] *The Advancement of All Things in Christ* (1763); *A Blow at the Serpent* (1764); *Truth's Testimony* (1768). For Coppin, see Hill, *The World Turned Upside Down*, pp. 177–9 *et passim*; Hill, *The Experience of Defeat*, pp. 45–6; Davis, *Fear, Myth and History*, pp. 36–40. See also below, pp. 55–6.

[31] John Everard, *Some Gospel Treasures* (Germantown, 1757). A MS note in the British Library copy says that a London edition was also printed by 'I.O.' at the 'Bible and Heart', Little Britain. *The Rending of the Vail* (1817).

[32] Anon. [Pordage] *A Compendious View of the Grounds of the Teutonick Philosophy* (1776).

[33] See the bibliography in S. Hutin, *Les Disciples Anglais*.

[34] Gerard Winstanley may have disappeared from view, although not from that of Thomas Spence, who reprinted a tract in the Digger tradition, *A Plea for a Commonwealth*, 1659, in *Pigsmeat*, Vol. III (1795).

[35] See David V. Erdman, *William Blake: Prophet against Empire* (Princeton, 3rd edn, 1976), pp. 11–12, note 19.

borgians (*c.*1783), Peckitt was a follower of Boehme, Madame Guyon 'and others of that class'. In 1785 his library ('a full waggon-load') was utterly destroyed by fire, and only a few manuscripts survived.[36] Among these – and an indication of what may have been lost – was a rare Philadelphian manuscript[37] and a copy of Tany's *Theauraujohn His Theousori Apokolipikal* (1651). At the end of the manuscript, Peckitt has made a note: 'I, H.P., cannot rely upon this Mans declarations, as I do upon the honerable Emanuel Swedenborg's writings.'[38]

That books and manuscripts from these traditions were circulating in London in the 1780s and 1790s can be confirmed from other snatches of evidence. The Muggletonian church preserved its own archives, including late manuscripts by Laurence Clarkson (See Appendix 1). A Muggletonian family of painters, the Pickersgills, owned manuscripts by the Muggletonian, Thomas Tomkinson.[39] There was something of a revival of interest in Jane Lead. Three of her works, now in the British Library, carry the stamp of Philip de Loutherbourg the painter, an acquaintance of Blake, a member of the Theosophical Society in the 1780s and a follower of the millenarial prophet, Richard Brothers, in the 1790s.[40] The Swedenborgian, Benedict Chastanier, a friend of Henry Peckitt, was also well versed in Jane Lead's writings.[41] There is preserved in Dr Williams's Library some voluble correspondence from Mrs Pratt in 1791–2, a lady who repudiated the views of her Swedenborgian husband, and who was searching for inspiration in alternative visionary traditions. She found in William Erbery, the seventeenth-century Seeker, 'a very choice author'. 'I have read manuscripts

[36] H.L. Tafel, *Documents concerning the Life and Character of Emanuel Swedenborg* (1877), Vol. II, part 2, pp. 1191–2; Robert Hindmarsh, *Rise and Progress of the New Jerusalem Church* (1861), p. 15.
[37] 'A faithful account of the last Hours of Mrs Jane Lead, by one who was a witness of her dying words', MS in archives of Swedenborg Society, A/25. According to Hutin, *Les Disciples Anglais*, p. 256, note 49, there was no English edition of this account (by Francis Lee), and only a German edition (Amsterdam, 1705).
[38] Archives of Swedenborg Society, MS A/25. Another remarkable library of 'scarce valuable mystical and alchymical books' was collected by John Dennis, the publisher of the *New Jerusalem Magazine*: see James Lackington, *Memoirs* (1830), p. 212; G.E. Bentley, 'William Blake and the Alchemical Philosophers', p. 113.
[39] A note on Tomkinson MSS in the Muggletonian archive shows that these were bought by the Church from the Pickersgill family, *c.*1843.
[40] The following carry the stamp of P.J. de Loutherbourg: Jane Lead, *A Message to the Philadelphian Society* (1696); *The Signs of the Times* (1699) – stamped '1796' – and *A Fountain of Gardens* (1696).
[41] [B. Chastanier], *Tableau Analytique et Raisoné de la Doctrine Céleste de l'Église de la Nouvelle Jerusalem* (1786), p. 40.

and many (almost all) Hermetic books.' Her more specific references are to Mme Guyon, Bourignon, Poiret, Boehme, Roach and
Philadelphians. At length the seventh seal was opened to her and
(following in the tradition of Jane Lead) she had her own ecstatic
visions in 'the supercelestial life'. We will encounter her again.[42]

   The evidence is sketchy, but it is sufficient to show that the
books, private collections and some manuscripts were available at
that time, and in circles proximate to Blake. And yet, how far
should we be looking, in this literal way, for *books*? Or, indeed, for
these books? For there are difficulties, which some scholars pass
over too lightly, when we seek to 'derive' Blake in any direct way
from a Behmenist or Philadelphian tradition. Although Blake himself referred to Paracelsus with approval, the detectable influence
is only marginal; it may be felt, perhaps, behind some passages on
the 'poetic imagination', and in the notion of 'signatures' which
prepared Blake for Swedenborg's notion of 'correspondences': but
Blake dispensed with most of the astrological business and the
alchemical terminology of Paracelsus and Boehme. The English
Paracelsian, Robert Fludd, wrote largely and suggestively about
'the two contrarieties, or opposite natures' of which the whole
world and every creature is composed. Indeed, the essential unity
of contrary principles, light and darkness, is posed as the 'real and
onely foundation . . . of universall Philosophy and Theology'. But
a dialectic which came to influence Blake's whole stance – his
historical, moral and utopian thought – remains trapped with
Fludd, and also with Pordage and the Behmenist tradition generally, in an obscure and repetitious symbolism of creation and genesis. Why did God permit these co-existent contraries, Fludd once
asks. And his reply is a simple cop-out: 'It is too occult a Caball
to be explained by mortall capacity.' For enlightenment we must
wait till 'the seventh Seal shall be opened'.[43]

   And Boehme? Undoubtedly there is a significant direct influence
here. But is it an influence central to Blake's stance? Those who
wish to place Blake firmly in the 'Great Tradition' have hurried,
with averted eyes, past some warning-signs. Thus M. Serge Hutin,
a French scholar deeply versed in Behmenist thought, has published a study of the English disciples of Boehme. In his closely

---

[42] Dr Williams's Library, MS 1.1.43: Mrs Pratt to Henry Brooke, 17 July 1792, 25 August
    1792, 4 October 1792. See also below, pp. 138–9, and Hirst, *Hidden Riches*, pp. 260ff.
[43] Robert Fludd, *Mosaical Philosophy* (1659), pp. 143–4.

argued conclusions on Blake, he notes that his writings employ
the notions of 'correspondence', of the 'Grand Man' and of the
primordial unity of God and the universe, but shows that there is
nothing specifically Behmenist about any of these: they are current
in all occultism and theosophy, and in the cosmological speculations of the prophetic books 'it is absolutely impossible to discover
the least echo of Behmenist metaphysic'. Boehme's concept of contraries (he agrees) had influence on Blake, but Blake translates the
operation of the dialectic from metaphysical machinery to values:
he has appropriated it and metamorphosised it into 'a decided
antinomianism', a sort of 'gnostic antinomianism', original to
Blake, pushed to extremes from which Jacob Boehme would have
recoiled in horror. Blake, in Hutin's reading, was *no* disciple of
Boehme, was attached to *no* previous school, but used the works
of previous theosophists with complete independence of spirit.[44]

Despite Hutin's expertise, his argument is conducted at a level
of generalities, and we may not be satisfied that he is a sufficiently
close and perceptive critic of Blake to substantiate these conclusions. But another, complementary warning-sign was set up, in
1957, by Martin K. Nurmi in an excellent and close critical study
of *The Marriage of Heaven and Hell*. Here Nurmi does see evidence
that Blake was passing through a spiritual crisis 'in which intellectual affinity shifted from Swedenborg to Boehme'. But critical analysis of Blake's text gives us a complex and nuanced conclusion.
Blake was *not* 'a Behmenist'; in *The Marriage* he borrowed (perhaps
tried out?) some ideas from Boehme 'that he had not really assimilated and that he was never to assimilate'. Other ideas he made
'entirely his own', but 'no ideas enter Blake's thought unchanged'.
These changes were so considerable as, on occasion, to invert
Boehme's meaning, and to leave us with fragments of his vocabulary of symbolism turned to quite different ends. And it is interesting to note that Nurmi and Hutin, who were working independently of each other, arrive at very similar conclusions. Boehme's
contraries are 'primarily cosmosgenic principles . . . they explain
how creation came about more than they explain its present character'. 'Blake's contraries, on the other hand, describe the vital
nature of Human life, especially of ideal society. . .' 'The most
important application of the doctrine of contraries' with Blake 'is

[44] Hutin, *Les Disciples Anglais*, chapter 8, *passim*.

the social one'. Blake's crucial distinction between active contraries
and mere 'negations' owes nothing to Boehme. What Blake did
was to take over some parts of the symbolic machinery of 'The
Tradition' and turn it to his own purposes.

The distinction between contraries and negations, in Blake's opinion, is
a crucial one for the salvation of man. For to see the qualities of things
as vital, necessary contraries is to live in a Human world of vision and
imagination, whereas to see them as negations is to live in the fallen world
of materialism and repressive social, religious, and political laws, a world
in which the contraries are distorted and given the crude normative desig-
nations 'good' and 'evil'.[45]

To develop this theme I have had to run ahead of myself, and
to assume in the readers some knowledge of the points at issue.
But, short of a very long exposition, this is the only way. And it is
necessary to offer this compressed critique of certain current readings of Blake if we are to propose the need for an alternative one.
For Nurmi's critique implies – as Hutin's does more explicitly –
that Blake has wrested the Behmenite vocabulary back into a
markedly antinomian and millenarial tradition, for which Boehme
himself provides only fitful, ambiguous and obscure warrant. That
is, Blake's stance is very much closer to that of the seventeenth-
century sectaries whom I have discussed (themselves employing
some Behmenist language) than it is to the Philadelphians. This
is true, most evidently, in the loss of radical attack, in the failing
social content, of the theosophical tradition as it drifts (and sometimes burbles) down through the eighteenth century. The closer
we are to 1650, the closer we seem to be to Blake. The fierce
antinomian opposition between *our* faith and *their* reason becomes,
with the Philadelphians, an opposition between mundane materialist reason and supercelestial visionary mystery. It may be true
that Jane Lead was an inheritor of 'the Cromwell–Muggletonian–
fanatic days',[46] but as the old century gave way to the new so that
tradition was translated into an ecstatic and arcane quietism. The
Philadelphians explicitly declared, in 1697, that they 'are not for
turning the world upside down as some have Represented 'em'.[47]

[45] Martin K. Nurmi, *Blake's Marriage of Heaven and Hell* (1957; 1972 New York), esp. pp.
19–23, 30–7.
[46] As was suggested by William Law's nineteenth-century disciple, Christopher Walton,
Biography of William Law, p. 148.
[47] *The State of the Philadelphian Society* (1697), p. 9. See Thune, *The Behmeniste*, p. 95.

Jane Lead was prophetess of a new, universal, non-sectarian New
Jerusalem church; but, at the same time, the messengers of this
church were to be a 'Secret Blessed Society' since 'a Philadelphian
concealeth all things'.[48] And the New Jerusalem church is sometimes a 'state', and opening of 'the Soul-Centre', sometimes a
'time', when 'nothing but what is purely taught of God shall abide
or stand'.[49] William Law, a much sounder scholar of Boehme, was
irritated by their transports: the Philadelphians were 'great
readers, and well versed in the language of J. B. [Jacob Boehme],
and used to make eloquent discourses of the mystery in their meetings. Their only Thirst was after visions, openings and revelations &c. . .'[50]

Law was more true to some part of Boehme's thought, which he
sought to bring within some rational exegesis. But his thought
moves around the faith/reason, spirit/matter antimonies, and his
emphasis upon Faith, with its concomitants, the Spirit of Prayer,
Penitence, Self condemnation, Confession and Humility provides
an insight into the way in which he managed to combine the prophetic (or 'mystic') and evangelical characters. It is an emphasis at
the opposite pole to that of Blake, and there is scarcely any sense
in which Law inhabits the older antinomian tradition: as Désirée
Hirst notes, Law 'was quite out of sympathy with the radical attitude stemming from the seventeenth century Levellers and their
fellows'.[51]

So we might move on through the century. Behmenist scholarship
was a polite and retiring occupation. The antinomian pressure
comes, not from this quarter, but, as we have seen, more often
from Baptists, irregular Methodists, breakaway sects like that of
William Huntington. Only the last figure on that eighteenth-
century line, Richard Clarke, revives some of that radical impulse
which had first impelled John Pordage. We owe the rediscovery of
Clarke to Désirée Hirst, and she makes a strong case to show that
he 'was a man after Blake's own heart'.[52] Very certainly she shows
that Clarke, preaching and writing in London in Blake's time,
employed many of the terms of the traditional vocabulary, with

[48] Jane Lead, *The Messenger of Universal Peace* (1698), p. 69.
[49] *A Fountain of Gardens*, p. 5.
[50] Copy of William Law to Penny, 8 April 1747, Dr Williams's Library, Walton Papers, MS 1.1.43.
[51] Hirst, *Hidden Riches*, pp. 196–9.   [52] *Ibid.*, p. 253.

48   *Inheritance*

emanations and Elohim and the Everlasting Gospel and covering
cherubs and much else, and with much millenarial rhetoric from
Revelation. He is a figure who straddles (as Blake also does) the
scholarly tradition of Boehme, Law and Kabbalistic studies and
the radical language of popular Dissent. But, in making this strong
case, Hirst does not allow us to see quite how eccentric, and even
cranky, this unusual man was, with his obsessive and scholastic
concern with numbers, derivations and the abracadabra of millenarianism. Nor did Clarke share Blake's kind of radical stance. Antinomians he lampooned in conventional terms as sensualists.[53] In a
compassionate passage about the poor, written in 1772, he looked
forward to a millenarial day when 'a true community of the spirit
will open a community of temporal things'.[54] But after the French
Revolution, Clarke, by now in his seventies, signalled his sense of
alarm at the new ferment within humble London radical Dissent.
The American prophet of Universal Restoration, Elhanan Winchester, had been preaching in London:

Mr Winchester is very popular for the time; he has been here: in the
doctrine of the Millenium and Restoration we agree, but no further. I
expect no Jerusalem, no Temple, no city, no land, but that the Lord
creates, and not man; the new heavens and new earth, and the new city
of the living God, and his Lamb. He expects a third city of brick and
stone, the work of the hammer and axe; if it were even of pearls, it would
not answer; for all the stone must be *living*, have life in the *heavenly materiality* of the chrystalline sea, where all Babylon, the creation in Bondage,
must be dissolved, to pass into the liberty of the glory of the Sons of God,
the true Israel.[55]

The reply of Richard Watson, the Bishop of Llandaff, to Paine's
Age of Reason, which Blake annotated with such fury, Clarke com-
mended as a 'judicious book'.[56]

I am certainly willing to accept Clarke as a spiritual kinsman to
Blake, but his degree of relationship is not within the main line of
antinomian descent. As for one other contemporary of Blake's,
whose claims have been more strenuously pressed, Thomas Taylor
the Platonist, no case for kinship can be supported. Taylor, who

[53] *Ibid.*, p. 259.
[54] *Ibid.*, p. 253.
[55] Clarke to Brooke, May/June 1790, Dr Williams's Library, Walton Papers, MS 1.1.43.
Ferber, *The Social Vision of William Blake*, pp. 190–1, suggests the Universalists and Winchester as an influence on Blake, but see pp. 226–7 below.
[56] Richard Clarke, *Jesus the Nazarus, Addressed to the Jews, Deists, and Believers* (n.d.), p. xii.

courted the reputation in the 1790s of being 'the renowned Champion of Platonic Polytheism, the modern supporter of Greek science, and lawful heir of the Genius Learning & Truth of Aristotle & Plato',[57] stands at an opposite pole to Blake. In 1792, when we know Blake's political enthusiasms were at their warmest, Taylor published his sneering *A Vindication of the Rights of Brutes*. This mean-spirited jest, embellished with neo-Platonic learning, was a scholastic *reductio ad absurdam*: if women — *any* women — were to claim equality of rights, why not also dogs and birds? Regard, for example, the independent spirit now evinced by female servants—

Who so happily rival their mistresses in dress, that excepting a little awkwardness in their carriage, and roughness in their hands, occasioned by untwisting the wide-bespattering radii of the mop, and strenuously grasping the scrubbing-brush, there is no difference between my lady and her house-maid. We may therefore reasonably hope that this amazing rage for liberty will continually increase; that mankind will shortly abolish all government as an intolerable yoke; and that they will as universally join in *vindicating the rights of brutes* as in asserting the prerogatives of man.[58]

This was compounded, in the course of a leering discussion of masturbation, with a prurient sneer at Mary Wollstonecraft.[59] And if Taylor's commonplace sexual and class prejudice and anti-Radicalism will have placed him in an opposite corner to Blake in the 1790s, so his hostility to Christianity will have done so in later years. While G.M. Harper is entitled to argue that Blake's attitude to the classical inheritance was both changing and contradictory, his final resting-point was unambiguous: 'The Greek & Roman Classics is the Antichrist' (E656). No doubt Blake read some of Taylor's works. But the influence of these upon his prophetic writings has been greatly exaggerated, and in general turns upon allusions and symbolic machinery (much of which might equally well have been drawn from other sources). It could also be argued that some of the allusions and machinery are obscurantist and regrettable. In any case, Taylor touches at no point on Blake's central stance.

The argument of the last few pages has been highly compressed and necessarily assertive. I have argued that the polite literary

[57] Henry Crabb Robinson to William Pattison, 31 October 1798, Pattison MSS (in private hands).
[58] [Thomas Taylor], *A Vindication of the Rights of Brutes* (1792), pp. vi–vii.
[59] *Ibid.*, pp. 81–2.

tradition (Behmenists, Philadelphians, Neo-Platonists) appears to carry some of Blake's vocabulary (including symbolic vocabulary) but that it does not prepare us for his stance nor influence the structure of his thought and art. It is a characteristic of those critics who argue most strongly for the 'Great Tradition' that they avoid discussion of stance and structure and offer Blake's thought as fragments: there is discussion of discrete symbols and myths, particular literary allusions, all of which appear to refer to a body of thought *outside* Blake's writing. And when this thought is then reconstituted, with the help of Proclus, Boehme or Fludd, it turns out to be very distant from the meanings conveyed by Blake's own text.

Blake *plays*, in his prophetic writings, with some of these symbols and myths. I could myself wish that he played with them less. But he plays in distinctive ways. In his prose, even his visionary statements have a matter-of-fact quality, totally unlike theosophical visions. He has no time for speculations about the number of the Beast or for the scholasticism of the tradition. His New Jerusalem is neither situated in an 'angelickal world' between Mount Zion and the glassy sea,[60] nor is it about to descend in some millenarial consummation[61]: 'to Labour in Knowledge is to Build up Jerusalem, and to Despise Knowledge is to Despise Jerusalem & her Builders' (E230).

If Blake read any or all of these works, he read them in his own way. He employs an inherited vocabulary to make statements directly opposed to those authorised by the 'Tradition'. He appropriates old symbols and turns them to new purposes. This is true, most of all, in the prophetic writings, where the machinery of a traditional symbolism often arouses expectations in the learned reader which are directly at odds with Blake's meaning. As John Beer has noted:

Blake's imagination has usually been at work before his reminiscence reaches the printed page: this is no passive importation of a symbol from outside but an integration into a new pattern, carrying its own associations and functions.[62]

---

[60] A Gentleman Retired from Business [John Pordage], *A Compendious View of the Ground of the Teutonick Philosophy* (1770).

[61] For an example of this kind of claptrap, see Elhanan Winchester, *A Course of Lectures on the Prophesies that Remain to be Fulfilled* (1789), in four volumes.

[62] John Beer, *Blake's Humanism* (Manchester, 1968), p. 19.

To say this may be simply to insist upon Blake's genius and originality. But if we go behind the symbols and vocabulary to the stance and structure of his thought, we may still ask whether these were wholly original, or whether he owed some part of these to other traditions. And some answer may be found by considering the various traditions of Dissent.

CHAPTER 5

Radical dissent

Let us shift our attention from the literary tradition to the vocabulary and doctrine of little churches and sects.

With the defeat of Levellers, Diggers, Ranters, and with the subsequent Restoration, the rebellious tradition of antinomianism (as its historian has written) 'curved back from all its claims'.[1] The extreme sectaries were persecuted, and some took refuge in a deliberate esotericism – a tradition of secrecy germane to Blake in his later writings. The hopes which were dashed in this world were projected into an inner world of the spirit. Here the old rhetoric lived on, but the stance of the sect towards all temporal things might now be quietist.

It is difficult for a historian to trace the record of quietist faiths. Since they do not impinge upon social or political movements, their surviving evidences are sermons, tracts, hymns, occasional internal disputes. It is even more difficult when a group makes a mystique of secrecy, like the 'Secret Blessed Society' of the Philadelphians. At the end of the eighteenth century, Philadelphians may have still had some loosely organised existence, as lecturers or preachers who gave addresses to audiences of any denomination – a sort of tiny Fabian Society, attempting to permeate the churches from within.[2]

But, as J.F.C. Harrison suggests (*The Second Coming*), Behmenist, antinomian and millenarial beliefs may have been dispersed even more widely, in the discourse of a few professional men, tradesmen and farmers, and even 'the simple and illiterate sort'. Mystical experiences were claimed by men and women 'simple and low in the world', of several denominations; a letter of 1775 survives from Ralph Mather (subsequently to become a Swedenborgian

---

[1] G. Huehns, *Antinomianism in English History* (1951).
[2] W. Hurd, *New Universal History*, pp. 695–6.

missionary) in which he describes many such 'poor people' up and down the country who 'love J. Behme and Wm Law'.[3]

Most difficult to identify are those who continue to be described, from time to time, as 'Ranters'. Wesley continued to meet and to argue with such people.[4] But even in the 1650s Ranting scarcely had any central organisation. In the eighteenth century 'Ranting' was little more than a term of abuse – a description of wild enthusiasm – applied with little discrimination to petty sects, or to 'irregular' Methodists.

From time to time in London little churches may be glimpsed which might (in the eyes of opponents) fit this description, like a 'Church of Christ' in New Street in 1712,[5] or a group around a 'Millennium Press' in Spitalfields who were still predicting a 'Fifth Monarchy' in 1786.[6] In the earlier part of the century, disputes between humble sectaries could still draw audiences of hundreds, at such places as 'The Magpie' in the Borough, Southwark.[7] An important stimulus for the revival of mystic and millenarial thought came with the great Huguenot immigration to London in the years following upon the revocation of the Edict of Nantes (1685) – some of the skilled tradesmen in different crafts settling in the West End, the silk weavers more thickly in the East. The neighbourhood in which William Blake grew up (the parish of St James, Westminster) shows many foreign names, some, perhaps, of Huguenot descent. Fellow electors with his father in Broad Street in 1749 include James Serzes, the minister of a 'French or Dutch Church by St James'; Philip Tuesay, a coal-merchant, born in Normandy; Dr Fevat or Fivatt, a physician; Dr Guordiant, a surgeon; and Benjamin Cusheir, an undertaker.[8]

The strong network of French Protestant churches was not, of

[3] J.F.C. Harrison, *The Second Coming*, pp. 21–2.
[4] See, e.g., John Wesley's encounter with antinomians in Birmingham, *Journal*, 23 April 1746.
[5] R.D., *A Description of a Gospel Church* (1712), p. 85.
[6] *Reasons from Prophecy why the Second Coming of Christ and the Commencement of the Millennium is immediately to be expected* (Millennium Press, no. 40, the corner of Dorset St, Spitalfields, 1786).
[7] Joseph Smith, *A Descriptive Bibliography of Friends' Books* (1867), Vol. I, p. 933: William Henderson, 'Truth and Reason defended against *Error* and *Burning Envy*, in a PUBLIC DISPUTE, held at the *Magpie* . . . on the 16th and 18th days of *Dec.* 1728 between John Rawlinson, a *Muggletonian*, and William Henderson, a *Quaker*, in the presence of some Hundreds of People. . .' (copy in Friends' Library); *A Conference betwixt a Muggletonian and a Baptist* (London, 1739).
[8] Pollbook of 1749 election, Westminster Reference Library.

course, antinomian or millenarian in doctrine. But around these, especially in East London, there appear to have been tremors and breakaways. A more remarkable impulse came from the Camisards or 'French prophets', who in dramatic and sometimes hysterical scenes of revivalism, *circa* 1707–10, reinvigorated the rhetoric of New Jerusalem and made many English converts, some of whom continued the tradition of prophecy and trance for several more decades.[9] There was both argument and confluence between French prophets and Philadelphians: the Camisard faith was millenarial – man should regain the perfection of Adam in communion with God, and henceforth the Law would be 'writ in every Man's Heart, so that he should have no more need to enquire of his Neighbours, but that every Man should be Priest unto himself'.[10] As the old Huguenot churches in London declined, and as the second and third generation of immigrants merged into the discourse of their fellow Londoners, it is possible (the evidence is unclear) that the more heretical among them gave adhesion to existing English sects. The most intellectual leader of the Muggletonians in the 1730s was Arden Bonel – perhaps of Huguenot extraction.[11] When William Cudworth (above, p. 17) split off from the Methodists in the 1740s his new congregations ('The Hearers and Followers of the Apostles') took over the former French church in Black and Grey Eagle Street, Spitalfields, the former French chapel in New Hermitage Street, Wapping, and the former French chapel in Castle Street, Leicester Fields.[12] Maybe these places had simply fallen vacant, or maybe – as sometimes happened when meeting-houses passed from one sect or preacher to another – some of the congregation stayed on. The 'Church of Christ' in Spitalfields certainly has a millenarial feel about it. They believed in one God, who was Christ: 'the living and true God is known no where but in Jesus Christ . . . he is God manifest in the flesh'. Their doctrine fully endorsed an antinomian notation of Free Grace and

---

[9] See Hillel Schwartz, *The French Prophets*.

[10] Theophilus Evans, *The History of Modern Enthusiasm* (1757, 2nd edn), pp. 100–1. Cf. Blake '. . .henceforth every man may converse with God & be a King & Priest in his own house' (E605).

[11] In Dr Williams's Library, Caleb Fleming's copy of 'A.B.', *Observations on Some Articles of the Muggletonian Creed* (1735) is annotated: 'N.B. Mr Bonell was at ye head of these fanatics.' In Certificates of Denizatia (*Pubs. of the Huguenot Society*, Vol. xviii, 1911, ed. W.A. Shaw), there are: 2 March 1681, Peter Bonnel and family; 19 August 1688, Abraham Bounel or Bonnel and family.

[12] J.C. Whitebrooke, *William Cudworth and his Connexion* (1918).

the imputation of righteousness: 'God has made a deed of free gift and grant . . . which whosoever believeth, or receiveth by faith, the obedience and sufferings of Christ is imputed to them as verily as though they personally had accomplished the whole.'[13]

And what other sects lived on? It is difficult to know. A journalist in 1706 composed a kind of directory: Quakers, Muggletonians (a religion 'more talk'd of than known'), Millenaries, Sabbatarians or Seventh-Day Men, Thraskites, Adamists (whose meeting-place was 'Paradise' and whose devotions were made in nakedness), Seekers, Ranters (who condemned the Bible and called it ironically 'The Divine Legacy'), Brownists, Tryonists (vegetarians), the 'Church of the First-Born' (Behmenists), Salmonists, 'Heavenly-Father-Men' (whose whole emphasis was on Mercy) and 'Children of the New-Birth', much given to meditation and to 'Visions of Angels and Representations'. And others. The 'Sweet Singers of Israel' were 'very poetically given, turning all into Rhime, and singing all their Worship. They meet in an Ale-house and eat, drink and smoak . . . They hold that there is no Sin in them: that Eating and Drinking and Society is bles'd: That Death and Hell are a Terror only to those that fear it.' All sin is forgiven to believers, for Christ would save all by his Blood: 'the Employment of the Bles'd will be Singing of Praises to their Maker in the New Jerusalem'. There was also a 'Family of Love', described in conventionally sensational terms as holding 'a Community of Women' with sexual orgies in place of services, but who also (more soberly) maintained a stock for the poor, and believed that the soul was 'an Emanation of the Deity' which (at death) is lost 'in the Eternal Ocean of Beings': 'the greatest Sin is Doubting, or Want of Faith'.[14]

Is this just hearsay, with the seventeenth-century directories of heresy (Thomas Edwards's *Gangraena*, Alexander Ross's *Pansebia*) warmed up? It seems not: now heresies are identified, and new sects formed around old beliefs. Did all, or nearly all, of these sects die out soon after 1706? We do not know: some were probably transformed, by way of Camisards or irregular Methodists, into new sects, but others certainly lived on. Thus our author mentions the 'Copinists', who followed the associate of Ranters, Richard

---

[13] 'Declaration of the Faith, and Practice of a Church of Christ' (n.d.). See above, p. 18, and note 17.
[14] G.C. [Galton], *The Post-Boy Robb'd of his Mail* (1706), pp. 423–31.

Coppin.[15] These disbelieved in the Devil or in eternal Hell, and espoused the doctrine of Universal Restoration (a doctrine also held by Richard Clarke and Elhanan Winchester in the 1790s). Coppin had been close to some of the tenets of Thomas Tany (or Theauraujohn). Emphatically antinomian, he affirmed that the ministers of orthodox churches were 'evil angels, reserved under chains of darkness', and he distinguished between two opposed ministrations or 'contrarieties': that of the Law ('a ministration of wrath, death, the curse, hell, and condemnation') and that of the Gospel ('a ministration of love, joy, peace, life, light, heaven and salvation'). He was a firm advocate of the right of women to preach. His Universal Restoration would take in 'Heathens, Pagans, Turks, Jews, Infidels'. The true believer must pass successively through three 'states': a state of 'Nature', a state of the Kingdom of Jesus Christ in the flesh ('here man sees not God clearly but through a vail, and this vail is the flesh of Christ, which a Christian is not to stay in, but to pass through. . .'), and a state of the Kingdom of Jesus Christ in the spirit: 'Then will the creature, the Image of God, be reduced again into its original and divine Image.'[16] Firm evidence as to the continuity of a Coppinist sect (or group of believers) is provided by the republication of his works in the 1760s – James Relly, an 'irregular' Methodist (himself accused of antinomian heresy) complained that these publications were sold 'under my nose', and that members of his own congregation subscribed for the re-printing.[17] Philip de Loutherbourg had a copy of Coppin's *A Blow at the Serpent* (reprinted 1796) in his private library (along with the works of Jane Lead) in the 1790s.[18]

Another interesting directory of heresy was published by William Hurd at the end of the century. Once again, a good deal is hearsay, although Hurd did make some enquiries. His account suggests that the number of miniscule sects had by now diminished (but he probably did not enquire far into the East End, nor did he take notice of individual heretical preachers like William Huntington or Elhanan Winchester). There are important new arrivals in the eighteenth century: the Moravians, the Sandemanians, the

---

[15] For Coppin, see above, p. 42, note 30; A. Ross, *A View of all Religions*, p. 379; Richard Coppin, *Truth's Testimony* (1655; reprinted 1768), esp. pp. 58–65; *A Blow at the Serpent* (1796), *passim*; *The Advancement of All Things in Christ* (1763), p. 28.
[16] *Ibid.*, p. 58.
[17] See James Relly, *The Sadducees Detected and Refuted* (1764).
[18] Now in the British Library.

Hutchinsonians and Methodist breakaways. In each case one seems to glimpse some belief or practice which prompts a reminiscence of Blake. The Moravians were well established in London, at Nevile's Court, Fetter-lane and Chelsea; the suggestion has been made that they influenced Blake, through their antinomian emphasis upon regeneration by faith, and through the frankness of their sexual symbolism, which extended to a veneration of the genitals.[19] I do not find the suggestion convincing: regeneration by faith was common to all forms of revivalist enthusiasm (notably Methodism), Blake's employment of phallic symbolism might well have been influenced by other sources[20] or none, and there are other notable elements in Moravian symbolism (such as the obsession with the wounds of Christ) which are never to be found in Blake. The Moravian tradition seems to dilute the antinomian vocabulary; it lacks an 'intellectual' or doctrinal anti-intellectualism found in obscurer sects.

Such intellectual pretension was certainly not lacking among the Hutchinsonians. Their founder, John Hutchinson (1674–1737), offered an alternative, symbolic reading of the Scriptures, based upon an eccentric reading of Hebrew, and was a fierce opponent of Newtonianism and an even fiercer opponent of 'Natural Religion' ('The Religion of Satan'). His anti-Newtonian 'Mosaic' principles found some support in the universities, and has recently won sympathetic attention from historians of science. But Hutchinson himself would probably have been amazed to learn that he would have humble 'Hutchinsonian' followers meeting in London alehouses at the end of the century, traducing the words 'morality' and 'good works', and denouncing 'natural religion' in the name of grace.[21] Possibly Hutchinsonian arguments could have confirmed Blake in his hostility to Newton and mechanical materialism. Both this and the Moravian influence may merit further exploration.

More interesting may be Hurd's suggestion that antinomianism, in particular sectarian forms, had been pushed into oblivion by the rise of Methodism, but that it had subsequently regenerated itself from among 'irregular Methodists' and from the lapsed of other denominations. His account is worth quoting at length, since it

---

[19] See Jack Lindsay, *William Blake* (1978), pp. 275–6. See the sympathetic account of the Moravians in Hurd, *New Universal History*, pp. 643–68.

[20] Notably R.P. Knight, *An Account of the Remains of the Worship of Priapus* (1786).

[21] Hurd, p. 676.

carries the full comminatory tone of the times. Only two or three meetings were now (1788?) to be found in England. Antinomians professed a religion 'which does not inculcate morality'. They teach that 'men may sin as much as they please; because however God may hate sin, yet he takes pleasure in forgiving it.' They–

Discuss their religion in public houses. As morality is an unnecessary thing, and as holiness, say they, can be no evidence of faith, so some of them meet in a room in a public house every Sunday evening, having before them that much despised book the Bible. Each member pays for a pot of beer, which is drunk by the company in a social manner. Then a text of sacred scriptures is read, and every one in his turn is called to deliver his opinion concerning it. A great deal of jargon with no meaning ensues, and every thing is said that can possibly be thought of against holiness or good works. The sacred scriptures are debased to the worst purposes, namely, to set open the flood-gates of profaneness; and youth are corrupted under the prostituted name of religion. A few foolish, weak and insignificant persons attend these meetings . . . They do all they can to pervert the Scriptures, and to trample under foot every Divine institution.[22]

The relaxed, democratic structure of the meetings is of interest, with everyone in turn called on to speak – forerunner of a London Corresponding Society or adult education branch. But William Hurd was probably drawing only upon gossip. He had more patience in expounding the doctrines of Turks, Jews, Catholics, Moravians, Deists and the devotees of 'Numbo-Jumbo' than he showed with these antinomians.

So – all this (and much more that is lost) was around in William Blake's London. There had probably been, over the century, a geographical shift in the location of sectarian Dissent, from West to East and South London. Still, in the first half of the century, one finds support for the old sects among professional families and prosperous tradesmen in Westminster; at the end of the century, the sects survive in Spitalfields (with its strong Huguenot inheritance), Southwark or Islington, drawing support among weavers, artisans, and petty tradesmen. Westminster and Holborn are now the gathering-grounds for congregations which follow more fashionable and charismatic heretical preachers, or for brand-new sophisticated faiths like the Swedenborgian New Jerusalem Church.

---

[22] *Ibid.*, p. 641.

All share some part of a vocabulary (mystic, millenarian, antinomian) which prepares us for Blake. But all lack that 'firm outline' which Blake demanded – the colours run into each other. And we should add that a major carrier of this vocabulary was simply the central tradition of radical Dissent. Milton had brushed his shoulders against antinomian doctrines, and wherever he was honoured (as Blake honoured him) some part of this inheritance might be conveyed. And if we move from doctrine to rhetoric and stance, we find the radical anti-statist tradition very much alive, and vigorously assertive in the 1790s.

We sometimes forget the total intransigence with which the eighteenth-century Dissenter (Baptist or Sandemanian or even Unitarian) could repudiate all intercourse with the Stations and Powers of this world. All saw in the Whore of Babylon not only the Roman Church but also all Erastianism: the Anglican Church *a fortiori*, and from thence all compromise between the spiritual and temporal power.

We could pick up this tradition where we will, among dissenting congregations in London and the great towns. It erupted, here and there, in fervent Old Testament rhetoric during the French Wars. And in the 1790s it also had notable intellectual representatives: for example, it is strongly marked in that group of radical Unitarians and others – William Frend, Benjamin Flower, George Dyer, Estlin, Gilbert Wakefield – with whom young Coleridge was associated.

A characteristic device of such men is to be found in an inversion, sometimes brought to the edge of blasphemy, of orthodox doctrine. Thus Estlin, in a sermon of 1795, contrasted the true gospel of Jesus 'whose first, last lesson to the world was LOVE' with orthodox religion, 'an unwieldy, cumbrous dress which has been put on the fairest form that ever was exhibited in the world'. The prophecies in *Revelation* as to the rule of Anti-Christ were now fulfilled within contemporary religious orthodoxy: they refer 'to every assumed power of decreeing rites and ceremonies and authoritatively interfering in matters of faith', as well as to 'that general corruption of morals' which prevailed among the 'professors of christianity'. All this is 'anti-christian'.[23] So it was also to George Dyer, who offered, in a pamphlet of 1799, Christ the Jacobin opposed to the Caiaphas

[23] John Prior Estlin, *Evidences of Revealed Religion* (Bristol, 1796), pp. 13, 41, 57.

and Pilate of Church and State: 'Christ asserted at Jerusalem liberty of thought and liberty of speech', he was 'adjudged to death by the verdict of his own countrymen, as a seditious person, as a libeller against church and state'.[24] Gilbert Wakefield, attacking the apostate Bishop of Llandaff, had pointed the contrast more savagely. The established Church he described as–

An impious prostitution of the simplicity and sincerity of the Gospel . . . I regard your Archbishops, Bishops, Deans, Canons, Prebendaries, and all the muster-roll of ecclesiastical aristocracy as the despicable trumpery of priestcraft and superstition.

(One should note that the radical Dissenter could denounce 'priestcraft and kingcraft' in much the same terms as the Deist.) 'I see Religion employed as a State engine of despotism and murder by a set of men, who are worse than heathens and infidels in their lives.' Let *them*, he said (referring to the French War), 'fight the battles of their Baal and their Mammon'[25]:

I should entertain far better hopes of leading a French infidel to accept the pure religion of the scriptures, than a bigotted superstitious Churchman.[26]

We don't have to construe Blake into this context: he has placed himself within it. It was in the same year – and perhaps with an eye on the Wakefield trial – that he annotated the Bishop of Llandaff's *Apology for the Bible*: 'To defend the Bible in this year 1798 would cost a man his life. The Beast and the Whore rule without control.' But the Bible which Blake would defend is not, of course, that of Bishop Watson: 'Paine has not attacked Christianity. Watson has defended Antichrist.' *Both* Paine and the Bishops were wrong – 'The Bishops never saw the Everlasting Gospel any more than Tom Paine.' But Paine (in Blake's view) has much the best of the argument, since his polemics are directed, not at the Everlasting Gospel (which he does not understand) but at the Moral Law of Antichrist:

---

[24] G. Dyer, *Address on the Doctrine of Libels and the Office of Jurors* (1799), pp. 109–12. The occasion for this pamphlet was the defence of Gilbert Wakefield, himself imprisoned for seditious libel.

[25] Cf. G. Wakefield, *The Spirit of Christianity Compared with the Spirit of the Times in Great Britain* (1794), p. 24: 'The Worshippers of *Baal* have been always numerous, the servants of *Jehovah* and his *Christ* comparatively few.'

[26] G. Wakefield, *Reply to some parts of the Bishop of Llandaff's Address to the People of Great Britain* (2nd edn, 1798), esp. pp. 39–44. See also my 'Disenchantment or Default' in (eds. C.C. O'Brien and W.D. Vanech) (New York, 1969), pp. 164–7.

All Penal Laws court Transgression & therefore are cruelty & Murder.
The laws of the Jews were (both ceremonial & real) the basest & most
oppressive of human codes, & being like all other codes given under
pretence of divine command were what Christ pronounced them The
Abomination that maketh desolate, i.e. State Religion, which is the source
of all Cruelty. (E607)

(In his Preface 'To the Deists' in *Jerusalem* Blake made the same
charge: 'Every Religion that Preaches Vengeance for Sin is the
Religion of the Enemy & Avenger and not of the Forgiver of Sin,
and their God is Satan, Named by the Divine Name' (E199).)
Throughout these annotations – marginal notes written under the
stress of direct responses and without thought of any audience –
Blake oscillates between two uses of 'the Bible' which are directly
opposed. He writes as one 'who loves the Bible': 'The Perversions
of Christ's words & acts are attack'd by Paine & also the perversions of the Bible; Who dare defend either the Acts of Christ or
the Bible Unperverted?' At one point he cites the authority of 'the
Bible' against Bishop Watson's apologetics; on the next page he is
stung to fury by the Bishop's complacent endorsement of the
Bible's authority for the divine justice of massacring the
Canaanites:

To me, who believe the Bible & profess myself a Christian, a defence of
the Wickedness of the Israelites in murdering so many thousands under
pretence of a command from God is altogether Abominable & Blasphemous. (E603–4)

The 'Bible' is then divided between the Gospel and the 'Jewish
Imposture . . . the Jewish Scriptures, which are only an Example
of the wickedness & deceit of the Jews & were written as an
Example of the possibility of Human Beastliness in all its
branches'. The opposition between these two is pressed to its furthest possible extent: 'Christ died as an Unbeliever & if the Bishops
had their will so would Paine.' But this is not only a simple *inversion*
of 'the Bible'–

> The Vision of Christ that thou dost see
> Is my Vision's Greatest Enemy. . .
>
> Both read the Bible day & night,
> But thou read'st black where I read white. (E516)

Nor is it a simple opposition between the Old Testament and the New. For Blake accepts at will, not as literal truth but as a 'Poem of probable impossibilities' whatever parts of the Bible endorse his faith. Both Testaments provide 'Sentiments & Examples' and 'this sense of the Bible is equally true to all & equally plain to all'. The Bible becomes the book of Antichrist ('a State Trick') only at that point where the Mosaic Law is 'rent' from the Gospel, and this gospel is eternal because it exists within man's faith every day:

The Bible or Peculiar Word of God, Exclusive of Conscience or the Word of God Universal, is that Abomination, which, like the Jewish ceremonies, is for ever removed [i.e. by Christ's sacrifice] & henceforth every man may converse with God & be a King & Priest in his own house.

And Blake reached, in these annotations, exactly the same conclusion as did Gilbert Wakefield in the same year: 'It appears to me Now that Tom Paine is a better Christian than the Bishop' (E605, 609).

   This is writing which comes out of a tradition. It has a confidence, an assured reference, very different from the speculations of an eccentric or a solitary. It also assumes something like a radical constituency, an 'us' of 'the People' or of 'every man' as against the 'them' of the State, or of Bishops or of the servitors of 'the Beast and the Whore'. The antinomian argument does not drift off into transcendental essays on 'faith' versus 'works' but is pressed, always, to a political conclusion: 'Penal Laws', 'State Religion', 'a State Trick'. It is, as always, combative, even though at the last moment Blake shrinks from the combat: 'I have been commanded from Hell not to print this, as it is what our Enemies wish' (E601). But notice '*our* Enemies': this man does not feel himself to be alone. ('Let every Christian, as much as in him lies, engage himself openly & publicly before all the World in some Mental pursuit for the Building up of Jerusalem' (E230).) And, as always, the language is blunt, matter-of-fact, concrete: the wicked and the faithful, the Satanic Law and the Everlasting Gospel, are evoked as being locked in combat in the immediate arena, in the streets, churches and palaces of London, in a spiritual conflict which wears temporal disguises, but which is the more real for being spiritual.

   The tradition behind Blake had become obscure by the 1790s. Most educated men and women had long been engaged in rational theological exegetics, in linguistic or historical criticism of the

Scriptures, in debate on the great question as to the Trinity and Christ's divinity, in arguments about miracles or about ceremonial forms, or in bolder ventures into Deism or atheism. By 1810 Blake's views had become so strange in the polite culture that Henry Crabb Robinson could comment that 'his religious convictions had brought on him the credit of being an absolute lunatic'.[27] Many years later Blake's friend, the painter John Linnell wrote, perceptively, that Blake was 'a saint amongst the infidels & a heretic with the orthodox', and, less perceptively, that 'he said many things tending to the corruption of Xtian morals' and 'outraged all common sense & rationality'.[28] But at any point between the 1640s and the 1790s there were men and women in London who would instantly have understood (and shared) Blake's reference and stance. The French prophets (and many others) had held that 'every Man should be Priest unto himself' (above, p. 54). The Coppinists (and many others) had preached the radically opposed ministrations of the Gospel and the Law (above, p. 56). A multitude of radical Dissenters saw in Church and State the Whore and Beast. I need not go on. Blake still inhabits that tradition, giving to it an unusual intransigence and purity of expression, sometimes as affirmation ('The Kingdom of Heaven is the direct Negation of Earthly domination' (E619)), sometimes as Jacobinical imprecation ('The Prince of darkness is a Gentleman & not a Man he is a Lord Chancellor' (E612)), sometimes as blasphemy, irony or jest.

And yet . . . and yet . . . How far, in the end, does this take us? It tells us what Blake was *against*, something of his stance, something of the quality of his feeling. But does it disclose certain affirmatives, certain essential and uniting ideas, recurrent images which belong to the structure rather than the ambience of this thought? Perhaps it does. Yet I remain unsatisfied. We still have not found out by what route or routes this tradition came through to Blake.

There is throughout Blake's writings an intellectual confidence and assertiveness – as of, not sentiments but *doctrines*, long-pondered and then arduously restructured and made his own, which are not 'given' in any of these sources. Of course, Blake may, through reading, conversation, the sampling of different sectarian doctrines, have made his own unique construction. Undoubtedly

---

[27] Bentley, *Blake Records*, p. 448.   [28] *Ibid.*, p. 318.

this is a major part of the answer. But I will take my sense of dissatisfaction as a licence to probe once more, and for a last time, even more deeply into one particular and obscure circle in sectarian London. It may – I have lived with this thought for many years – be a false track altogether. But it will at least bring us into very much closer proximity with the minds and voices of one group of sectaries. And if it is then considered that I have suggested the wrong group, at least we will understand more about how such groups argued, thought and passed on their faith.

CHAPTER 6

A peculiar people

There is one direct line of continuity between the antinomianism of the Civil War sects and the London of the 1790s that can be firmly established. On 3 February 1652, after the defeat of Levellers and Diggers, God spoke to John Reeve and told him: 'I have chosen thee my last Messenger for a great Work unto this bloody unbelieving World.' Joining forces with his cousin, Ludowick Muggleton (Reeve was the Messenger and Muggleton was his 'mouth'), Reeve sought to rally a following among the remnants of the Ranters. The two prophets commenced their mission by quarrelling violently with Thomas Tany; they also visited John Robins, the self-proclaimed Son of God, then in prison under sentence of death, and discovered that he was in fact the Anti-Christ. They quarrelled also with the emergent Quakers, who were competing for support in very much the same post-Ranter circles: this quarrel Muggleton kept warm long after Reeve's early death (1658) and it was repaid with equal warmth from the Quaker side. In these controversies Reeve and Muggleton discovered that they had been endowed by God with a power of the tongue, not only to bestow on their followers eternal blessing and confirmation that they were indeed of the elect, but also to curse anyone who contradicted their doctrines and sentence them to eternal damnation. These powers were used to good effect on Robins and to less effect on the Quakers.[1]

Thus the Muggletonians arose within the whitest heats of the vortex around which Ranting, Quakerism, egalitarian, Behmenist and sexual liberationist notions turned. While they quarrelled most fiercely with their most proximate neighbours, as is the way of sects, a great deal of the imagery which turned in that vortex was gathered into their doctrine. Certainly they denounced Thomas

[1] See Christopher Hill, Barry Reay and William Lamont, *The World of the Muggletonians* (1983), esp. pp. 67–9.

65

Tany and repudiated Boehme: but an intense sectarian dispute is often the signal of an *affinity*, and while Muggletonian doctrine repudiated the dispersed pantheism of the Behmenist tradition, of the Ranters ('my one flesh'), and of Tany and the Quakers,[2] and replaced it by a literal belief in a singular God/Christ in the image of man, yet in other parts of the doctrine (the nature of Creation, the origin of evil, the notion of contrarieties) Muggletonianism was grafted upon Behmenist or Ranting stock.[3] And, as if to signal this, there was gathered into the Muggletonian church Laurence Claxton, or Clarkson, who had once been known as 'the Captain of the Rant'.

We might suppose, in Muggletonianism, our missing vector. For the sect did establish itself, and it survived for over three hundred years.[4] Muggleton outlived John Reeve by forty years, enlisting 'believers in the third commission', occasionally visiting the faithful (in Cambridgeshire, Staffordshire and Derbyshire, Essex, Kent), and conducting a copious correspondence. He did not seek out followers: the faith was to be diffused by the publication of the tracts of the two prophets and a few followers (Clarkson, Saddington, Tomkinson). Muggleton's funeral in 1698 was attended by 248 believers. It is probable that the church fluctuated around, or a little beneath, these numbers for the next hundred years. A count of male believers only, in 1803, showed one hundred in all England: thirty-five in London, twenty in Kent, twenty-one in Derbyshire, eleven in Norwich and the remainder diverse.[5] But the London church had recently suffered from splits and secessions, and the number of male Muggletonian believers, if heretics are taken into account, will certainly have been greater. Since women played a prominent part in the church, and since strong familial continuities can be observed, as children were inducted into the faith, we may safely double these figures.

Although its most prominent member at the commencement of the eighteenth century was a Staffordshire farmer and factor,

---

[2] *Ibid.*, pp. 47–8, 88.

[3] Muggleton argues with a correspondent influenced by Boehme in Reeve and Muggleton, *A Stream from the Tree of Life* (1758 edn), p. 33; he told another correspondent in 1661 that Boehme's 'philosophical light was above all men that does profess religion, until this commission of the Spirit came forth, which hath brought Jacob Behmen's light . . . down very low': *A Volume of Spiritual Epistles* (1820 edn), pp. 45–6; Alexander Gordon, *The Origins of the Muggletonians* (Liverpool, 1869), pp. 9–11, 19–20.

[4] See Appendix 1.

[5] Muggletonian archive.

Thomas Tomkinson, the Muggletonian church was really a London church. But for its first two hundred years it was a church without any chapel, conventicle, meeting-house or permanent home. Fiercely anti-clerical, the Muggletonians had no preachers or officers: an early attempt by Clarkson to establish himself as such ('Claxton, the onely Bishop, and true Messenger of our last Commission') was roughly brought to an end by Muggleton.[6] They met for discourse, readings and songs in each others' homes: and, ducking under the Conventicle Act, they took to meeting in public houses. Here they would hire a room for their meetings, drawing up an agreement with the publican to install a locked closet holding their books and records. To all intents and purposes they appeared as a private friendly or glee club; they sent out to the landlord for pots of beer, or for punch on their two annual ceremonial 'holidays';[7] the 'divine songs' which the members wrote were set to the popular tunes of the day ('Fanny blooming fair', 'Scots wha hae', 'Young Nancy one morn', 'The Bishop of Hereford and Robin Hood'), which no doubt disarmed the suspicions of the curious. (During the French Wars, when anti-Jacobin narks were on the look-out for seditious glee clubs, new divine songs were written to the airs of 'God save the King', 'Heart of Oak' and 'Rule, Britannia'). In 1692 we find a meeting at 'The Green Man', Holloway; in the mid-eighteenth century a 'Church of Christ' at 'The Blue Boar', Aldersgate Street; another in Barnaby Street, Southwark; then at 'The Gun', Islington, 'The Hampshire Hog' off Goswell Street, and moving from 'The Blue Boar' to 'The Nag's Head' in Aldersgate Street. This church was, like the other meeting of 'Antinomians' we have met with before (above, p. 58), 'The Little Vagabond' among the churches:

> Dear Mother Dear Mother the church is cold
> But the alehouse is healthy & pleasant & warm
> Besides I can tell where I am usd well
> Such usage in heaven makes all go to hell.[8]

[6] L. Claxton, *A Paradisical Dialogue betwixt Faith and Reason* (1660), p. 117. See also Reay on Clarkson in Hill, Reay and Lamont, *The World of the Muggletonians*. Also DNB (entry by Alexander Gordon) and A.L. Morton, *The World of the Ranters*, chapter 5.

[7] The holidays celebrated were 14, 15 and 16 February (to commemorate Reeve's receiving the commission from God), and 30 July (to commemorate Muggleton's release from gaol in 1677): G.C. Williamson, *Ludowick Muggleton* (1919), p. 38.

[8] This is the first version in Blake's notebook (N105). In the revised version as published in the *Songs* the last line became: 'The poor parsons with wind like a blown bladder swell.' As David Erdman notes (p. 274, note 13), this is a rare case of Blake bowdlerising one of his own poems.

There grew up early among Muggletonian believers a habit of secrecy. In the last decades of the seventeenth century they had their share of sufferings: the imprisonment and pillorying of Muggleton, fines and the seizure of goods for non-attendance at church, for refusal of parish office or of oaths of allegiance, or for blasphemy. But Muggleton advised the faithful to avoid confrontations, while Clarkson chided the Quakers for 'disturbing the peace': 'in things concerning this Government, give the Magistrates due honour. . .'[9] More painful than fines may have been ostracism and ridicule, and the accusations of obscenity and blasphemy which attached to the name. On occasion the ostracism or excommunication of the believer could take the most bitter forms: Mary Cundy, a widow in Orwell, Cambridgeshire, who died as an excommunicant, was buried in 1686 in a close next to the churchyard 'with the burial of an asse'.[10]

In self-defence, Muggletonians in the eighteenth century normally did not avow their faith publicly, unless they were directly asked. A believer wrote in 1786:

As we have no Outward Ordinances of Worship, nor bound to Meetings it is not in the power of all the Devils who govern the World to hinder our Meetings, which are, when we meet in the Streets, or in the Fields, or Change, in a House Public, or Private, or in a Vessel by Water, or on the Land, we can Mutually Edify one another.[11]

A journeyman shoemaker, migrating from London to Coventry in 1770 to find work, found himself surrounded by the suspicions of his fellow journeymen when he named his son 'Ludowick': 'Some people makes it a matter of wonder at my calling my boy after so odd a name as they stile it, and as they most of them are presbytarians, they whisper about concerning of what religion I am but canot find it out.' After some more brushes with his neighbours, 'I am Inform'd they have given me a new name, viz. Mr Odd Principle.'[12] Even some of the Muggletonian printing operations were conducted with great privacy: a master printer of the faith in Bristol wrote to the London church in 1786 offering to undertake work,

[9] L. Claxton, *The Quakers Downfall* (1659), p. 35.
[10] M. Spufford, *Contrasting Communities* (Cambridge, 1971), p. 27.
[11] Roger Gibson of New London (Connecticut) writing to the London Church: Muggletonian archive.
[12] Incomplete letter, no signature, from Coventry, 25 February 1770, to 'Loving Friend and Brother', in *ibid.*

which he promised that he could do in complete secrecy since he employed no journeymen.[13] If it was difficult to identify a Muggletonian two hundred years ago, we will find it more difficult to identify him today.

We can, however, identify some of the beliefs and practices of the church. One thing the London believers attended to with zeal and address: they succeeded in keeping in print the works of the prophets, and they even added a few new works to that number. Printing of the works of Reeve and Muggleton was going on in the 1680s and 1690s; in 1719; in the 1730s; and then, very vigorously, from 1751 to 1764, encompassing *all* the works of the prophets as well as some newly published letters – a remarkable achievement 'considering what a Handful we are, and how few of that Handful have Substance sufficient to support so great an Undertaking'.[14] The achievement did not go uncontested; Boyer Glover (the leading songwriter at that time)–

Objected against the presant subscription for printing, saying we had done sufficient already; and advised to let alone the Other for another genration, little showing his love to God or his Seed; nor Considering that Eternity is at the door, and men must be Instruments in the hand of God to fullfill his Will in divers Respects before all is finished, pertiqularly in publishing His Third Record, thereby sealing men up for that glorious yet dreadfull day.[15]

More reprinting was going on in the 1790s, and then a comprehensive programme of publication was undertaken by James and Isaac Frost (brass founders in Clerkenwell) in the 1820s. Of other publications, the most important were those of Thomas Tomkinson, published in 1695, and, posthumously, in 1721–4, 1729, 1757 and 1823.[16] The dates indicate the consistency and longevity of the enterprise, and they also are indicative of a loyal, if small, audience.

I do not intend here to recapitulate the writings of the founding prophets but rather to direct attention to some parts of the doctrine which can most clearly be seen to be alive in the eighteenth century.[17] In doing so I will attend to certain parts which suggest a possible 'fit' with William Blake. Reeve and Muggleton were seen

[13] W. Mathews, Bristol, 17 December 1786 to D. Shield: in *ibid*.
[14] Foreword by John Peat to *A Stream from the Tree of Life* (1758 edn).
[15] Unsigned and undated (but 1760s) to 'dear Friend' in Muggletonian archive.
[16] See DNB (by Alexander Gordon) for publications.
[17] An excellent summary of Reeve's doctrines is in Hill, Reay and Lamont, *The World of the Muggletonians*, pp. 74–91.

as Messengers of a Third Commission, prophets of a 'New Age'.
The first age (the age of the Law and of the Old Testament) was
signified by *water* (Urizen was 'prison'd on wat'ry shore'); the
second age (the age of the Gospel of Jesus and of the New
Testament) was signified by *blood* (one recalls the repeated motif
of *Vala* in which Luvah descends in blood); the third age (the age
of the Commission and of the prophetic writings of Reeve and
Muggleton) was the age of *spirit*. (This possibly Joachimite notion
of the 'commission' was certainly known to Blake, who told Crabb
Robinson, in connection with Irving, that 'they who are sent sometimes exceed their commission'.[18]) With the Third Commission,
the New Age has already commenced among the believers, with
all the attendant imagery of the coming of New Jerusalem. The
faithful sometimes thought of themselves as 'saints'[19] or as 'sealed'
with the conviction of their redemption: 'The regenerated Children
of Adam are the Church, & every believer's body is a Temple for
the living God.'[20]

Muggletonian doctrine concentrated upon three areas – the
problem of the first creation of matter and of the origin of evil;
Genesis and the Fall; and *Revelation*. Both God and Matter had
existed from eternity, as in Gnostic doctrine, God as an 'active
omnipotent Being', matter as an 'unactive Principle' – 'inert and
merely passive'. Matter was a necessary object for God to work
upon, for if there had been nothing but God's own essence from
eternity, 'then there was nothing for him to have Power over, or
to act upon, and then he must have continued alone to all Eternity'.
But while matter was 'in a Condition to be wrought upon as Clay
in the Hands of the Potter', nevertheless it possessed properties
different from those of God. Matter–

Was an unactive Principle from Eternity; and as it was not possible to
be hid from the active omnipotent Being, he by making it active rendered
it capable of producing Evil.[21]

[18] Bentley, *Blake Records*, p. 313.
[19] Thus Thomas Tomkinson, writing to a Friend in Ireland (1674), declares the 'effectual
faith is seen in His Saints by the cheerfulness of their countenances': Letters copied by
Frederick E. Noakes in Muggletonian archive.
[20] 'The Faith and Practice of the Muggletonians', 1 January 1870, in *ibid*.
[21] 'A.B.' (Arden Bonnell?), *The Principles of the Muggletonians Asserted* (1735), pp. 10–11. This
was a reply to a reasonably fair pamphlet by a critic, *Observations on Some Articles of the
Muggletonian Creed* (1735). Cf. a creed (undated but eighteenth century), 'I Believe God
the Creator of Heaven and Earth was a Spirital Body in the form of a man from all
Eternity, and that earth and water wher an Eternal Substance Distinct from the Creator.

This is an intellectually coherent view (more coherent, perhaps, than some conventional Christian apologetics), and it also brings us within hailing distance of neo-Platonist and Behmenist arguments. A similar resolution is implied in a comment of Blake's recorded by Crabb Robinson (who quizzed Blake more closely as to his theological beliefs than any other acquaintance of his last years): 'Asserted that the Devil is eternally created not by God – but by God's permission. And when I [made an] objection that permission implies power to prevent he did not seem to understand me.'[22]

Muggletonians also held to a version of Behmenist dialectic, and referred to 'God's manifesting himself by Contrarieties in Creation'.[23] But there seems to be a difficulty here. For the 'contrarieties' seem to be sometimes envisaged as an opposition between God/Nature, spirit/matter and Faith/Reason. 'The substance of earth and water were from eternity', and 'darkness, death or devil and hell lay secretly hid in that earth above this perishing Globe and in the sight of the Creator were eternally naked and bare'.[24] Creation would appear to mix, as in Manichaean doctrine, two opposing principles, one material (and evil) the other spiritual and divine. (Blake, in his last years, appears sometimes to have expressed such views: according to Crabb Robinson, 'He was continually expressing . . . his distinction between the natural & spiritual world. The natural world must be consumed.' And 'he denied that the natural world is any thing. It is all nothing and Satan's empire is the empire of nothing.'[25]) This gives us contraries, not in the Blakean sense of 'two contrary states', but as barren negations. Satan, for the Muggletonians, was the God of Reason, and–

> Reason's god is in all life,
> Human, brutal, vegetive,
> Which, at first, from nothing came,
> And must to nothing return again.[26]

(But notice also 'vegetive', so close to Blake's 'vegetate' and 'veget-

---

In wich Substance Lay Secretly hid the very root of Death and Darkness.' Muggletonian archive.
[22] Bentley, *Blake Records*, p. 318.
[23] *The Principles of the Muggletonians Asserted*, p. 21.
[24] MS at back of copies of Muggleton, 'Three Records' and 'Letter to James Whitehead' in Muggletonian archive.
[25] Bentley, *Blake Records*, pp. 312, 316.
[26] Richard Wynne in *Divine Songs of the Muggletonians* (1829), pp. 156–8.

ative', by which he describes the material, corporeal universe of sexual generation.)

In the argument of one Muggletonian apologist, God permitted 'the root of spiritual darkness' to manifest itself since without this contrast his divinity could not have been known:

> So all contraries are manifested by contraries, as
> darkness is not known but by light, nor light but
> by the darkness; neither would any man prize his
> friends if he never met with enemies. . .

> Since by contraries all things are made clear,
> Without contraries nothing can appear:
> So had not God a devil sent on earth,
> We had not known his glory and his birth. . .

> [And] had not God permitted us to fall,
> We had not known him, nor his power at all.[27]

But equally the contraries exist within man, as Reason and Faith, and it is the *nature* of Reason to 'fight and plunder and kill':

> Roar cursed Reason roar
> You can't disturb me more
> For wrongs receiv'd
> Thy cursed Serpent Tongue
> That with Revenge is hung
> Tis what thy Nature craves.[28]

Or, as Thomas Pickersgill, a Muggletonian painter (and contemporary of Blake) wrote in a private letter in 1803:

Every thing Acts according to its Nature, Reason Acts [h]is Nature, in Going to War, to fight and kill, with Sword and Guns killing One a Nother, Army against Army, Kingdom Against Kingdom, but it is not so with faith, for no True believer . . . can make use of aney Such Weapons of Warr . . . to Slay the Image of God, our Blessed Redeemer, because faith being of a Nother Nature, which is all love, and is that peacable Kingdom of God. . .[29]

The Muggletonian version of *Genesis* was arresting:

---

[27] John Brown, a Brother to the *Saints*, and a Friend to the *Elect*, *The Saint's Triumph, and the Devil's Downfall*, &c (Norwich, n.d.), pp. 8–9.

[28] Song by Margaret Thomas, Muggletonian archive.

[29] Thomas Pickersgill to Abraham Tregone, London, 1 December 1803, Muggletonian archive.

The *Tree* of which Eve eat, called the *Tree of the Knowledge of Good and Evil*, was her being overcome by the glorious Appearance of the Devil made in the form of an Angel of Light.[30]

This Devil (or Angel of Light) appeared in the form of a glorious Serpent, who copulated with Eve. Entering within Eve's womb the Serpent transmuted himself 'into Flesh, Blood and Bone' and the offspring of this intercourse was Cain, whereas Abel and his young brother Seth (in whose generation the Devil had no part) were the offspring of the divine principle in which God had created Adam. But from the moment of the Fall, Satan disappears from the rest of the cosmos, having dissolved himself in Eve's womb and perpetuated himself in Cain and Cain's seed and only there. Hence there was implanted within the human race, at the moment of the Fall, two contrary principles, diabolic and divine: the offspring of Cain and the offspring of Seth.

In 1675 John Saddington, a sugar factor, codified with clarity forty-eight Articles of Muggletonian faith. Since the doctrine of the Two Seeds is central to these beliefs, we will resume this from the relevant Articles:

XV

I do believe that the Tree of Knowledge of good and evil was that serpent angel which GOD cast out of heaven down to this earth for his rebellion. . .

XVII

I do believe that that outcast angel or serpent-tree of knowledge of good and evil did enter into the womb of Eve, and dissolve his spiritual body into seed, which seed died and quickened again in the womb of Eve.

XVIII

I do believe that Eve brought forth her first born the son of the devil, and very devil himself.

XIX

I do believe that there is no other devil but man and woman; since the first devil, that serpent angel devil, became seed in the womb of Eve, and clothed himself with flesh and bone.

XX

I do believe that Cain was not the son of Adam, though he was the son of Eve.

---

[30] *Observations on Some Articles of the Muggletonian Creed*, p. 8.

XXI

I do believe that the seed of the woman and the seed of the serpent are two distinct generations of men and women in this world.

XXII

I do believe that the seed of the woman is the generation of faithful people, which proceed from the loins of blessed Seth, who was the son of Adam, who was the son of God.

XXIII

I do believe that the seed of the serpent is the generation of unbelievers or reprobate men and women, which proceed from the loins of cursed Cain, the son of the devil, and the first lying and murdering devil that ever was.[31]

The Muggletonian doctrine of the Two Seeds might seem to be inexorably predestinarian. And so, in a general interpretation, it was:

A part of Mankind are the Spawn of the Devil, or the Produce and Offspring of a carnal Knowledge the Devil had of Eve: whilst others, viz, *themselves*, are only and truly the Seed of the Woman.[32]

This was the view of a critic (in 1735), but it is a fair representation of one emphasis. But, at the same time, Muggletonians did not overlook the fact that the human race was the product of millennia of miscegenation. Hence within each man or woman two contrary principles, Satanic and divine, were implanted, struggling for dominance over each other, although in a strict view it was predestined that one only should triumph. This allowed (as with most predestinarian faiths) some laxity of interpretation. On the one hand, it was possible for the faithful to regard themselves as 'saints': the faithful, wrote Tomkinson, had the 'seal of salvation stamped in their souls. . .'[33] And at the same time, all opponents of the faithful – including, of course, kings, magistrates, priests and Quakers – could be identified unequivocally as the seed or spawn of the devil. Henry Bonel, in 1763, wrote an unloving Muggletonian song addressed to 'hypocritical priests':

[31] John Saddington, *The Articles of True Faith, depending upon the Commission of the Spirit* (1830). Written in 1675, copies were circulated in manuscript in the eighteenth-century Church.
[32] *Observations on Some Articles of the Muggletonian Creed*, p. 7.
[33] See note 19, p. 70 above.

You who by long prayers do prey on the poor,
The bread and the substance of widows devour;
Of external righteousness make a fair show,
While nothing but praise and gain's in your view;
Ye vipers, ye serpents, ye seed of the devil,
How can you escape the last great day of evil?[34]

On the other hand, it was possible to view the spiritual struggles
of the uncommitted (or of backsliders) as an intense inner drama
in which the divine and Satanic principles wrestled with each other
for dominance. Humphry Broadbent, an early eighteenth-century
believer, in a letter to a straying member of the flock, expresses
this drama of pride and penitence locked in immortal combat:

It seems you through the Weakness and Luceferian Pride of thy Spirrit
for promises of Silver & Gold that Perrishes have let Satan, that is thy
unclean Spirrit of Reason, Captivate thy Seed of Faith . . . O! that the
Allmighty God if it be his Blessed Will may open your Eyes before it be
too late & that unpardonable Sin against the holy Ghost is Committed,
for you know that all Manner of Sins shall be forgiven but the Sin against
the Holy Ghost. . .

Since the Holy Ghost is the spirit presiding over the Third Commission of Reeve and Muggleton, this sin was defined as that of
repudiating the prophet's words and backsliding from the Commission of the Spirit. But Broadbent yet had hopes that God would
'restore the strayed Sheep to his fold' before that sin was
committed:

Now where your Treasure is, above in the Celistiall Heavens or below
on the Teristiall perishing Earth which must stoop to Deaths Infernall
Night, is best known to the Allmighty God & Your Selfe for to mee at
this time it seems dubious Which.[35]

Hence Muggletonians, like other predestinarian creeds, allowed
for both a determinist and voluntarist vocabulary: in the latter it
was 'Uncleane Reason, the Devill' that threatened always to 'captivate the Seed of Faith'. There are certainly times when Blake
also appears to play with the notion of the Two Seeds, or 'the two
natures which are in man'.[36] 'Men are born with a devil & an

---

[34] *Divine Songs of the Muggletonians*, p. 159.
[35] Muggletonian archive.
[36] Thomas Tomkinson, *A System of Religion* (1857), p. 92.

angel', he told Crabb Robinson, who added: 'but this he himself interpreted body & Soul'. And again: 'Every Man has a Devil in himself. And the conflict between his *Self* and God is perpetually carrying on.'[37] Nor is this simply neo-Platonist imagery, for genealogies of two seeds are offered in *Jerusalem*:

> Satan Cain Tubal Nimrod Pharoh Priam Bladud Belin
> Arthur Alfred the Norman Conqueror Richard John
> [*Edward Henry Elizabeth James Charles William George*] (*del.*)
> And all the Kings & Nobles of the Earth & all their Glories
> These are Created by Rahab & Tirzah in Ulro: but around
> These, to preserve them from Eternal Death Los Creates
> Adam Noah Abraham Moses Samuel David Ezekiel
> [*Pythagoras Socrates Euripides Virgil Dante Milton*] (*del.*)   (E226)

This version of the two seeds is turned to use to dramatise Blake's robust republican and aesthetic sympathies, but we commence in each case with the line of Satan/Cain and that of Adam/Seth as sanctioned by *Genesis*. An earlier reference in *Jerusalem* (E210–11) is more eccentric:

> I see the Maternal Line, I behold the Seed of the Woman!
> Cainah, & Ada & Zillah & Naamah Wife of Noah.
> Shuahs daughter & Tamar & Rahab the Canaanites. . .

– a line which ends with Mary: 'These are the Daughters of Vala, Mother of the Body of death.' This notion of a 'Maternal Line' could perhaps be sanctioned by the notion to be found among eighteenth-century Muggletonian believers that 'the Sons of Adam, who were called the Sons of God, intermixed in Marriage with the Daughters of Cain, who are called the Daughters of Man. . .'[38] The line, Cain–Adah and Zillah–Naamah is found in *Genesis* 4 verse 25 (Naamah is sister to Tubal-cain, the 'instructer of every artificer of brass and iron' (verse 22)), where will also be found (verse 25) authority for the line of divine seed by way of Seth. By what authority Blake married Naamah to Noah of the line of Seth (*Genesis* 5) I do not know.

That Blake played with the notion of the Two Seeds does not prove that he was indebted to Muggletonian doctrine. In a general metaphorical sense the notion of the line Satan/Cain leading on to the rulers and potentates of the earth turns up elsewhere in the

---

[37] Bentley, *Blake Records*, pp. 337, 547–8.
[38] *The Principles of the Muggletonians Asserted*, p. 18.

radical Christian tradition: a Digger pamphlet declared that 'Cain is still alive in all the Great Landlords'. 'Cain's brood', wrote Bunyan, were 'lord and rulers', while 'Abel and his generation have their necks under oppression'.[39] (But the *literal* notion of dual genealogies, which Blake employs, is perhaps specific to the Muggletonians.) In any case, as always, Blake does not *follow* doctrine but turns it to his own account.

I will post over that small interval between the Fall and the Annunciation. A more leisurely survey would show that Muggletonian doctrine laboured over episodes and images which also fascinated Blake, some of which were eccentric to the main concerns of Christian faith. Thus there was much attention to the cherubim with flaming swords guarding the Tree of Life (*Genesis* 3.24), identified by both Muggleton and Blake as Satanic guardians.[40] There is the same concern with the Seven Churches of Asia. Muggletonians were preoccupied with certain marginalia, such as the apocryphal Epistle of Jude and the 'Book of Enoch', which also caught the eye of Blake. But we will let these matters pass.

The story of Christ commences with the story of the Fall inverted. It was now God, and not the Serpent, who entered Mary's womb and dissolved into her conception. Eighteenth-century believers sometimes wrote creeds into their song-books or tracts. Here is one:

I believe in God the Man Christ Jeasus, in Glory who was a Spiritual Body from all Eternity Who by Virtue of his Godhead Power Entered into the narrow passage of the Blessed Virgin Mary's Womb And so Dissolved Himself into Seed and Nature as Clothed Himself with Flesh Blood and Bone as with a Garment; thereby made Capable to Suffer Death who made himself man, the Express Image of his Farther's Person And so became a Son to his own God power. He Absolutely poured out His Soul unto Death; and lay three Days Dead in the Womb of the Earth. . .[41]

(Such creeds, with their frank sexual symbolism, gave rise to accusations against Muggletonians of obscene blasphemy, and for this reason were not published.) It is important also that Muggle-

---

[39] Hill, *The World Turned Upside Down*, p. 117.
[40] See Muggleton, *A True Interpretation of the Eleventh Chapter of the Revelation of St John* (1662 and 1753), chapter xx; for Blake (and Boehme) see Raine, *Blake and Tradition*, i, pp. 329–32.
[41] MS creed in front of a copy of Muggleton, *A Transcendent Spiritual Treatise* (1822 edn) in Muggletonian archive.

tonian doctrine insisted upon the indivisibility of God, employing
the language of the Trinity only to describe differing manifestations
of the same indivisible divinity: 'I Believe God the Creator of
Heaven & Earth was a Spiritual Body in the form of a man from
all Eternity.'[42] It followed that when God 'transmuted' himself into
the infant Jesus in Mary's womb, there could then be no God in
heaven or in any other part of the cosmos – Christ, the man, was
not only divine, he was the *only* God. It followed also that between
the crucifixion and the resurrection there was no God either in
heaven or on earth: God had been killed. This must have been,
for believers, a logical, but daring and frightening, idea. In the
words of another eighteenth-century creed:

When Christ died the whole Godhead was absolutely Void of all Life
heat or Motion. Father son & Holy Ghost became Extinct in Death. The
whole Life of the Infinet power was Dead.[43]

This accentuated the dramatic sacrificial symbolism of the Cross:
God literally took on mortality and paid its penalty in order to
redeem the faithful. How he got *out* of this situation at the Resurrection was a fruitful source of dispute and dissension among subsequent believers.[44]

I want to put in a word here for the Muggletonians, who have
had a bad historical press, based often on little more than the
absurdity of the name. From a certain rational standpoint – the
single vision of literalism – all religious symbolism may appear as
absurd. The rational mind can do little more than stand outside
it and comment on its consistency or inconsistency. From this
standpoint I can see nothing more absurd in Muggletonian doctrine than in great and supposedly intellectually reputable faiths.
The story-line of *Genesis* is utterly absurd, and Muggletonians were
sometimes at pains to point out these absurdities to the orthodox:

What do you Quakers think the Tree of Knowledge of Good and Evil
was, and that Serpent that beguiled *Eve*? [Muggleton enquired with sar-

---

[42] Another creed (eighteenth century) in Muggletonian archive. Muggletonian references
to God were of a precise physical kind – in the form of an old man of about six feet
high – perhaps a figure not unlike Blake's Urizen.
[43] Muggletonian archive.
[44] In the literal version of the prophets God had the foresight to appoint vice-regents –
Moses and Elias (with whom Enoch was sometimes associated) to serve him *in absentia*
and to reclaim him from death; in the more intellectual creeds of eighteenth-century
believers, Christ was 'a Quickening Spirit', who, like grain in the earth, 'had Power to
quicken out of pale death again': Creed in Muggletonian archive.

casm]. Do you look upon it to be some Apple-tree, and the Serpent to be an ugly Snake? and so this Snake crept up the Tree, and got an Apple in his Mouth, and the Woman took the Apple out of the Snake's Mouth, and so eat of it, and gave her Husband to eat, and so brought themselves into this Misery, and all Mankind? Do you teach your Hearers this?

Or do the Quakers turn it into a mere allegory, 'so that nothing can be made of it, neither one Way nor other'?[45] And Tomkinson echoes this argument: 'The eating of an apple could not have contracted an hereditary evil, as is generally said by those who take this in the vulgar manner.'[46]

The Muggletonian doctrines of the Fall, the Two Seeds and the conception of Christ, combine literalism with a robust symbolic power. The dual impregnations of Eve and Mary give to the doctrine a certain symmetry, like a figure-of-eight, as well as intellectual consistency. And notoriously the notion of the unity of one God in the three persons of the Trinity has offered difficulties to the reason. If the Trinity is repudiated, and not merely juggled with, then we must either be led to an undivine Christ or to a Muggletonian transmutation of God into Christ. And such a translation, which follows well-authenticated natural processes, appears as no more irrational than the translation of wine and wafers into blood and flesh. I will suggest that – a few peripheral doctrines apart – Muggletonian beliefs were logical, powerful in their symbolic operation and have only been held to be 'ridiculous' because the Muggletonians were losers and because their faith was professed by 'poor enthusiasts' and not by scholars, bishops or successful evangelists.[47]

Muggletonianism also remained, throughout the eighteenth century, a faith in which believers exercised their intellectual faculties in doctrinal disputes. Hence it has a kinship with the intellectual traditions of Old Dissent rather than the raw or confessional emotionalism of Wesleyanism and the Evangelical revival. The disputes may appear as merely scholastic – do beasts partake in the Last Ascension?[48] – or even as a little sad. At a regular meeting of

[45] Muggleton, *A Looking-Glass for George Fox* (1761 edn), pp. 20–1.
[46] Thomas Tomkinson, *A System of Religion*, p. 93.
[47] On this (and most other matters) I am in agreement with Hill, Reay and Lamont, *The World of the Muggletonians*.
[48] The answer seems to have been 'no': see Arden Bonnell, 'A Reply to a Discourse on the Beasts Ascension Where What I formerly advanced in a Letter to Friends, against the Ascension of Beasts is further defended' (1736: MS in Muggletonian archive).

London believers in the 1760s there was a long discourse concerning the Ark:

> Whether all in it was in a spiritual Condition and eat No Food, seeing they did represant Heaven; or Whether they might not be a tipe of Heaven, notwithstanding eating or drinking, seeing they took of all Manner of Food into the Arke and it is not to be suposed the savage wild Creatures would stay to be fed by Noah after coming out of the ark, tho' Obedient to the purpose of God while in it. I shall not relate the divers Opinions as there was some on each side, but leave it to your own Judgement. . .[49]

Other issues were more significant. The doctrines were flexible enough to allow ulterior issues to be argued out in terms of its symbols. Thus the doctrine of the Two Seeds allowed for rival patriarchal and feminist emphases. Reeve and Muggleton, of course, transmitted a patriarchal orthodoxy. Sin, at the Fall, entered through the weakness of Eve, and this could happen only because Faith, in the person of Adam, was asleep, resting from his arduous toils in the Garden of Eden:

> So in the fall of Adam
> When reason Changed Condition
> Faith was asleep while he took flesh
> As says Reeves glorious Mission–

so runs a verse in a characteristically argumentative doctrinal song by James Miller (1745).[50] And Muggleton tended to invest the opposing genealogies of the Two Seeds with masculine prejudice: 'the Soul of Man doth partake of the Father's Nature, even the Seed and Nature of Faith', and so, presumably, the Seed and Nature of Reason (or the Satanic inheritance) partook of the nature of the mother.[51] According to this view, Mary's part in the conception of Christ was merely passive, as a receptacle or breeding-place for the divine seed; in neo-Platonic imagery Mary 'Clothed the Eternal spirit with a Body of flesh in her womb'.[52] So God 'Clothed Himself with Flesh Blood and Bone as with a Garment' (above, p. 77) and Mary was no more than a biological hostess to the divine donor. (It should be said, and sharply, that Blake, who is sometimes sup-

[49] *Ibid.*

[50] James Miller, 'A Spiritual Song on the two Seeds, or the Impossibility for Faith to Sinn', verse 30, MS 1772, in *ibid.*

[51] Muggleton, *The Answer to William Penn, Quaker* (n.d.), p. 82.

[52] MS eighteenth-century creed, in Muggletonian archive.

posed to have transcended gender prejudices, often was willing to employ anti-feminine imagery. That remarkable and powerful late addition to the *Songs of Experience*, 'To Tirzah', employs throughout the imagery of the feminine principle (the womb) clothing, enclosing and binding the spirit in a way which Muggletonians as well as neo-Platonists would have understood (see below, pp. 148–9). 'Christ', he told Crabb Robinson, 'took much after his Mother And in so far he was one of the worst of men.'[53]

But there were heretical Muggletonian voices who also held that Christ took somewhat after the mother, and that he was none the worse for that. Thomas Tomkinson, whose writings always contain much emphasis on the virtues of love and mercy, declared that we should say no ill of a woman, 'for though a woman was the inlet to sin, yet a woman was the outlet of sin, and the inlet of salvation':

And though the first woman compassed a man of death, hell and damnation; yet let not her after-seed by *Adam* speak ill of her: because they and her were blessed by a gracious promise of an after redemption, which was and is by this new created man compassed by a woman.[54]

Other believers pressed the argument in the eighteenth century. A paper survives which argues tenaciously (and clearly in the face of opposition) that in Mary's conception God's seed united with Eve's seed of Faith, 'and that God & man and all things that come forth of the womb receive life from the Femaile as well as the Maile'.[55] One senses that there was an active feminine presence in the tiny Muggletonian church;[56] many songs were written by women, and in the 1770s a dissident group (of both sexes) left the church under the leadership of Martha Collier, an aspirant visionary and prophetess.

One other perennial dispute had some significance. This was an attempt to break out of the severe closure imposed by Reeve and Muggleton's orthodoxy when, in their fierce opposition to the Ranters' pantheism and in their polemics against the claims of the early Quakers to divine visitation, they had repudiated any divine principle except in God/Christ. And yet the prophets were also

[53] Bentley, *Blake Records*, p. 548.
[54] Thomas Tomkinson, *The Harmony of the Three Commissions; or, None but Christ* (1882), pp. 52–3.
[55] Unsigned MS, n.d. but late eighteenth century, in Muggletonian archive.
[56] As also in the seventeenth-century church, see Hill, Reay and Lamont, p. 54.

responsible for implanting a contradiction in their teaching, in the doctrine of the Two Seeds. For if the Satanic principle existed nowhere in the cosmos except in the seed of Cain, might it not equally be argued that God existed nowhere but in the seed of Seth? And, again, if the founding prophets claimed divine inspiration, why might the same inspiration not come to their followers? Throughout the century believers wrestled with this, in controversies about the 'indwelling God' and 'immediate notice'.[57] The sanctified were anxious to claim at least some kinship with God: 'the same spirit that dwels in the father and in the son, the same dwels in the saints . . . and he that is joyned to Christ is one spirit, and not distinct nor seperate. . .'[58] In 1794 William Sedgwick, a leading believer, tried to find a formula to settle the dispute:

Christ is the Light that Lighteth Every man that Commeth in to the world yet none but God is Infinite. Notwithstanding tho' God the Creator virtuale [virtually] Dwells in all his Creatuers. Nothing is Capable of the Indwelling Infinite power But God alone. Why Because that wich Procedeth Cannot be Equal to that from wich it Procedeth any more than a Streem can be Equal with a Fountain. Even man in his Created Purity tho' of the very nature of the Divine Creator yet not Infinite Because it was in measuer only and so but finite. . .

In a postscript Sedgwick added that he flattered himself that if these few lines were impartially considered 'no faithfull man or woman whould Contend against it', but, in a second and more sober after-thought, he added that rather than contention should be perpetually upheld in the Church 'it whould be Best to Seperate'.[59] There were such separations, as there had been in the previous two decades, notably that of James Birch, a watch-motion maker, who claimed direct prophetic inspiration.[60] But, of course, the argument which Sedgwick attempted to resolve is one which reappears, in many forms, in quite different doctrines and churches. Sedgwick's contemporaries, the Swedenborgians of the

[57] Eighteenth- and nineteenth-century 'Reevonians' claimed that the denial of God's immediate notice' in human affairs was a doctrine introduced by Muggleton after Reeve's death: see W. Lamont, 'Ludowick Muggleton and "Immediate Notice"', in *ibid.*, chapter 5.

[58] Eighteenth-century MS (n.d.) of Edward Pallmer in Muggletonian archive.

[59] MS of William Sedgwick in *ibid.*

[60] For Birch see DNB (entry by Alexander Gordon) and Lamont, p. 127. Birch and W. Matthews declared themselves to be 'prophets' on the model of Reeve and Muggleton.

New Jerusalem church, were arguing it vigorously in the 1790s, in terms of 'the divine influx'.[61]

I hesitate to carry this discussion into the whole matter of *Revelation*, upon which Muggleton wrote two major commentaries and his followers wrote more. Surrounded by candlesticks, the Beast and its number, the Whore of Babylon and diverse commentaries on these, it would be foolhardy to suggest that Blake, in prophetic works or paintings, leaned more towards the Muggletonian than any other interpretation. In a few matters there may be some congruence. Muggletonians were mortalists or 'soul-sleepers'.[62] They rejected any body/soul dualism: Reeve declared 'the spirit is nothing at all without a body, and a body is nothing at all without a spirit: neither of them can live, or have a being, without the other'.[63] 'The soul of man is generated with its body,' repeated Saddington, 'therefore it liveth and dieth with the body, and is never parted from it.'[64] 'The soul is the author and cause of every action', wrote Tomkinson: 'It is that which acts and lives, thinks and perceives.' 'It is not possible to conceive, that the soul can be conscious of its existence, it cannot be sensible of itself if it center not in a body. . .'[65] Blake's 'voice of the Devil' in *The Marriage of Heaven and Hell* also exposed the error that 'Man has two real existing principles: Viz: a Body & a Soul'. 'Man has no Body distinct from his Soul; for that call'd Body is a portion of Soul in this age' (E34).

The soul, however, will be awakened dramatically from its sleep at the Last Judgement, since, although it perishes with the body like grain, there is 'an invisible principle or seed still remaining, which will spring forth'.[66] Muggletonians affirmed that all celestial creatures, including angels, were created in the form of males, but without the faculty of procreation: 'neither was there any Female created in the Celestial Heavens'.[67] As one ecstatic female believer sang:

---

[61] Muggletonians sometimes used the term 'the divine income': see, e.g., 'A copey of a Letter Origenaly written by James Birch to Joseph Coal and the Brethren in Wales' (1778) in Muggletonian archive.

[62] See Tomkinson, *A System of Religion*, p. 91.

[63] See James Hyde, 'The Muggletonians and the Document of 1729', *The New-Church Review* (Boston, Mass.), 7, 1990, pp. 215–27.

[64] John Saddington, *A Prospective Glass for Saints & Sinners* (1823), p. 104.

[65] Thomas Tomkinson, *A System of Religion*, pp. 57, 83–4.

[66] *Ibid.*, p. 120.

[67] Muggleton, *The Answer to William Penn, Quaker*, pp. 4–5.

> There is all such creatures as is here,
> But spiritual, like chrystal clear;
> All males, not made to generate,
> But live in divine happy state. . .[68]

At the Last Judgement the souls would spring forth in changed bodies; according to Tomkinson, the saints 'will have bodies, new, pure, and glorious', the reprobate will have dark spiritual bodies 'suitable to their evil nature and wicked lives',[69] but both (it would seem) translated into androgynous form.[70] Blake also employed on occasion the image of souls awakening from their graves (it was Mercy who 'changed Death into Sleep') (E30). And in the *Song* 'To Tirzah' he also borrowed, from some source, perhaps from Boehme, the notion of an androgynous resurrection:

> Whate'er is Born of Mortal Birth
> Must be consumed with the Earth
> To rise from Generation free. . .

And the engraving accompanying 'To Tirzah' is inscribed: 'It is Raised a Spiritual Body.'

I am uncertain as to how far it is helpful to define eighteenth-century Muggletonians as millenarians. They shared in the widespread Christian faith in a Second Coming, but had taken pains to distinguish themselves from Sectaries such as the Fifth Monarchists who believed in a literal reign of Christ on earth.[71] On the other hand, Christ's return was still expected, but only in heaven–

Those who expect a God here upon this earth, after any other manner than a personal Jesus, seated on a throne of eternal glory in the Heaven above, will never find him; and whoever looks for a God to come before the end of the world, or a God without a personal form, will find their hopes in vain.[72]

In the early years of the Church, while memories of the spiritual disturbance of the Commonwealth still kept alive expectations, the Last Judgement was sometimes felt as imminent: 'we that live now near the end of the world', wrote Tomkinson, 'are waiting for his

---

[68] Rebecca Batt, in *Divine Songs of the Muggletonians*, p. 140.
[69] Tomkinson, pp. 121–2.
[70] Reeve, *Sacred Remains* (n.d.), p. 90; Reeve and Muggleton, *Joyful News from Heaven* (n.d.), p. 56.
[71] 'Christ will come no more to reign upon this earth with his saints, as it is imagined by many. . .': Saddington, *The Articles of True Faith*, p. 19.
[72] Tomkinson, *A System of Religion*, p. 81.

second coming'.[73] As the years stretched out into decades, the expectations of the faithful seem to have been postponed. One eighteenth-century Creed runs–

I Believe The same Mighty God, the man Christ Jesus in Glory, will suddenly Appear In the Clouds of heaven to Judg Both the Quick and the Dead and to make an Everlasting Sepperation Between the Elect and the reprobate world. The One will Enter into Ever Lasting happyness & the Other in Endless & Everlasting Torments to all Eternety where will be weeping & Nashing of teeth for Evermore. Amen.[74]

But there is less suggestion that these satisfactory arrangements would be fulfilled at an early date. The groups which seceded with Birch and Martha Collier in the last decades of the century expressed a renewed millenarial fervour. But the orthodox believers were millenarians only in the quieter sense that 'a New Age' (the Third Age of the Spirit) had already commenced when John Reeve received his 'Commission' in 1652. Their songs and correspondence frequently employ the symbolism of the Last Vintage, the winepress of God, the threshing-floor of the barn and the separation of the wheat from the reprobate tares – 'when the Harvest is ripe and a General seperation shall take place and be divided the *Seed* of the Woman and the *Seed* of the Serpent which is now so entangled together...'[75] Then at last the elect should gain their new bodies of 'bright burning glory' and 'they shall all ascend together as one body, to meet their head, the Lord Jesus, in the air'.[76]

It is a silly enough picture, but it is one which many Christians in many churches have shared. It is also one which Blake turned to his own account repeatedly in his writings and his paintings.[77] I don't mean that Blake ever used these images in exactly the same way. Muggletonians offered them as literal accounts of events to be firmly expected; for Blake, 'the Last Judgment is not Fable or Allegory but Vision' (E544), and he added in a grumpy aside: 'A Last Judgment is Necessary because Fools flourish' (E551). But what is interesting, in the present context, is that Blake's visions repeatedly return to this vocabulary of symbolism. This is a

---

[73] *Ibid.*, p. 80.
[74] MS in Muggletonian archive.
[75] Letter (n.d.) from John Carwithon of Derby to the London church, in Muggletonian archive.
[76] Muggleton, *A Transcendent Spiritual Treatise*, chapter xiv.
[77] See David Bindman, *Blake as an Artist* (Oxford, 1977), chapter 19.

language, a set of signs, which he knows by heart, but which he employs as he pleases. And at certain points Blake's vocabulary has a markedly Muggletonian accent.

I will return to this in a moment. But first we may enquire a little further into the eighteenth-century Muggletonian Church. How did these doctrines fare in the keeping of a small sect which survived through decades of eighteenth-century Enlightenment? And here we encounter a paradox within a paradox. The old seventeenth-century sects which survived into the new century faced the choice of submission to the rationalism and civilising modes of the time, with an accompanying upwards drift in the social status of their following – and this was the trajectory of Old Dissent in general, including those old opponents of the Muggletonians, the Quakers; or else of maintaining their original doctrinal integrity (and a diminishing familial and perhaps plebeian following) by ever-fiercer resistance to rationalism, to the polite theology of biblical criticism and to accommodation with Newtonian physics, and by ever-stronger insistence upon the virtues of faith, grace and purity of heart. Such was the course followed by some minuscule (and threatened) sects, some Baptist congregations and by some of those swept up by Whitefield's and Wesley's early evangelism. The impulse – the return to grace – was often explicitly 'counter-enlightenment'; hemmed in in the first half of the century, this impulse eventually met with its reward in the last decades of the century, breaking out from its petty strongholds, sweeping across the counties and multiplying into thousands of little Bethels.

This 'counter-enlightenment' resistance may very certainly be seen in the Muggletonian Church. Where seventeenth-century antinomians, Familists or Seekers had laboured with sweat on their spiritual brows through forests of vivid imagery in the effort to bring some kind of logic or system into being, most eighteenth-century mystics and antinomians relaxed into anti-rational postures and gave up the struggle. No theme recurs more often in the Muggletonian songs than hostility to Reason, 'the right devil'. The faithful prided themselves on their rejection of the reasons of the enlightened. They pitted their faith against the 'serpent reasonings' of polite learning. In one song by Thomas Tomkinson–

> Love, what art thou that art divinely bent?
> And how cam'st thou into this continent?
> What is thy birth, and where can divines tell?
> Yes, but not such as in Cambridge do dwell.

Yet Cambridge schools know thy bare name of love
But not the nature that comes from above;
For tho' love there was born and born again.
Yet divine breath's not known by learned men. . .[78]

This active stance of resistance to the hegemony of the polite and reputable culture was enforced with a severe, even intellectual, severity. Education itself was no less than re-enacting the Fall, by eating of the Tree of the Knowledge of Good and Evil. In the front of one eighteenth-century song-book I find transcribed on the title-page (*c.*1777)–

By edducation most have been mislead
So they believe because they were so bred
The Priest continues what the Nurse began
And thus the Child imposes on the Man[79]

'There is no use in education', Blake told Crabb Robinson in 1825. 'I hold it wrong. It is the great sin. It is eating of the tree of the knowledge of good and evil. . .'[80]

Muggleton, a working tailor, had expressed particular hostility to the learned professions. His followers, in the main, were tradesmen, artisans and persons in humble circumstances. Among eighteenth-century Muggletonians I have found butchers, watch and clock-makers, a shoemaker, a painter, a musician, a printer, a master weaver, a ticket porter, a joiner, a tailor, a clerk, a pastry cook: believers are found in most parts of London, but more thickly in the City and East End (Leadenhall Street, Cripplegate, Mile End, Spitalfields, Moorfields, Whitechapel) than the South or West. Muggletonians had no priesthood or officers of any kind. They imposed few duties on each other. Perhaps the first was the accumulation of funds to keep the works of the Prophets in print. They succeeded in doing this; and from these tracts they won a few literate recruits. They were also sustained by strong traditions of familial loyalty.[81] They survived, with indomitable tenacity, the long years in the wilderness, and yet they had no share in the subsequent evangelical harvest.

This brings us to our second paradox. For the Muggletonians were not only anti-enlightenment: they were also anti-evangelical.

[78] *Divine Songs of the Muggletonians*, p. 372.
[79] At front of MS Song Book collected by John Peat, *c.*1777, in Muggletonian archive, Brit. Lib. Add. MSS 60211.
[80] Bentley, *Blake Records*, p. 540.
[81] Family continuities can be traced in the *Divine Songs* and Muggletonian archive.

For they had survived the rational bombardments of the century
by lying low and keeping their heads down. They were quietists
in the most elementary sense: they kept quiet. The fellowship of
the faithful was itself a little Zion:

> Who shall in Zion's joys abide
> Where Revelations softly glide
> The man whose faithfull heart and Tongue
> Ne're strove to do his Neighbour wrong
> Nor try'd with Infamy his name
> In Reason's Kingdom to defame
> Whilst lofty Cedars, scorcht with fire
> Who dare unto the Sun aspire
> Upon the humble rose, distills
> The Spicy dew of Zion's hills.[82]

This self-confident, introverted enthusiasm contributed to the
transmission, with singular purity, of the doctrines. But it left them
unequipped to evangelise. If they had found great numbers turning
towards them they would have been alarmed at the possibility of
Satan's seed entering among them. Small numbers at least brought
with them a sense of security, from which they could contemplate
with equanimity the oncoming downfall of their enemies:

> The fat-gutted priest will roar for assistance;
>   The lawyer may say, he did plea for a fee;
> But unto our God they have both shewn resistance,
>   They are damn'd without mercy to eternity.[83]

It is greatly heartening to think of a small circle of friends, united
in love, singing these lines in the midst of eighteenth-century
London – perhaps in a private room in 'The Gun' in Islington or
'The Blue Boar' in Aldersgate Street. But this would be the limit
of their formal expression. Their faith forbade them to attend any
formal public worship. They held no formal services, and their
meetings – apart from their two annual 'feasts' or 'holidays' – were
confined to readings from the works of the Prophets and the singing, *not* of hymns, but of 'divine songs' or 'songs of grateful praise'.
Even prayer they regarded as a 'mark of weakness' ('marks of
weakness, marks of woe').[84] Among believers (who often referred

---

[82] From lines by Margaret Thomas in MS Song Book, Brit. Lib. Add. MSS 60207.
[83] From a song by John Peat (mid-eighteenth century), in *Divine Songs*, p. 441.
[84] One of John Birch's heresies was to disparage songs in favour of prayer; but prayer
    presumed God's 'immediate notice', the Reevonian 'heresy' which Birch espoused. For

to each other, like Quakers, as Friends) the traditions of the
Church and of former believers were cherished:

> I know John Saddington, and Claxton both
> Were strong believers; and wrote things of worth;
> John Brown; and others glorious things have pen'd,
> But farr too short of my Renowned Friend,
> Brave Tomkinson, like to a Cedar tall
> In fair Libanus that o'er topped all.[85]

(Claxton also was remembered still, in 1760, for other qualities,
one believer writing of a quarrelsome friend: 'I believe Brother
Ned is a faithfull man but a little like Clackston, full of Sperituall
Pride.'[86]) As late as the 1790s oral anecdotes of the Prophets still
circulated.[87] Although the Church had not property, funds or regular minutes in the eighteenth century, the manuscripts of the
prophets, of Saddington, Tomkinson, Bonnell, and others, and of
humble believers were carefully preserved, either in closets
installed in the pubs where they met or in private hands.

It was a highly literate Church, but small enough for all its
internal affairs to be conducted by manuscript. Believers spent
many hours in copying the works of their forebears, in circulating
doctrinal polemics, in corresponding with provincial friends and
in transcribing letters from believers in distant places (Ireland,
Wales, North America). The songs, until the 1790s, were copied
by each believer – according to his or her own selection – into a
private song-book, and it was clearly a devout ambition of each
believer to add an acceptable song to the common stock.[88] Sick,
needy and aged believers were, from time to time, on an *ad hoc*

---

prayer, see also G.C. Williamson, *Ludowick Muggleton*, p. 30; Alexander Gordon, *Ancient and Modern Muggletonians* (Liverpool, 1870), p. 44.

[85] Early eighteenth-century MS verses, 'Elegy on Tomkinson's death, addressed to William Hall', in Muggletonian archive.

[86] John Wright to 'Loving Brother', complaining of Edward Fever's behaviour, MS, n.d. (*c.*1760), in *ibid*.

[87] 'I have been told by an ancient Believer who now sleeps that had it from one that lived in the prophet's day that it was common for the Believers to dispute one with another in the prophet's presence, and he would sit and hear them. . .': MS letter, Hudson to Mr Collier, n.d. (but *c.*1779), in *ibid*.

[88] A collection was made in 1711 called 'A Divine Garland of Spiritual Songs and Verses for the Consolation of the Seed of Faith, written by the Believers of the Communion of the Spirit'. This remained in MS and was copied (sometimes with additions) by the faithful. The first printed collection of *Songs of Gratefull Praise* was in 1790(?), a much-enlarged *Divine Songs of the Muggletonians* was published in 1829. The MS Song Books are now in Brit. Lib. Add. MSS 60207–60230.

basis, supported by their fellows. Muggletonians were opposed to capital punishment, and, like the Quakers, they were supposed to refuse tithes and oaths, and they certainly refused the use of arms. Thomas Pickersgill wrote to a believer who worked in Chatham docks in 1803: 'My dear friend, I understand . . . that you are in greate trobles, for the power of the Nation Wants you to take up Arms againts the Common Enemy, these are greate Trobles to a New born Saint. . .' No true believer could 'become a Slave to a Slave':

On my own part I would live on one penny worth of bread per day, and drink at the clear stream, before I would use such cursed weapons as Swords & Guns, cannot you git you living no where but at Chatham. . .[89]

In response to this moment of crisis a petition was drafted to the authorities: 'we being a peculiar people redeem'd by the Lord Jesus Christ our consciences are too tender to make use of the sword of steel to slay the Image of God with'.[90] 'If you Avenge you Murder the Divine Image', wrote Blake (E792):

> The Soldier armed with Sword & Gun
> Palsied strikes the Summers Sun. . .
>
> Nought can deform the Human Race
> Like to the Armours iron brace.   (E483)

I like these Muggletonians, but it is clear that they were not among history's winners. Nor did they wish to be. It was their business to preserve and to hand down the divine vision. By the mid-eighteenth century we can see that they were a recondite sect, whose beliefs appeared to outsiders as impenetrable and esoteric (if not obscene and blasphemous), whose closet and chest of manuscripts enclosed the sleeping energies of a half-forgotten spiritual and political vocabulary, and who were highly intellectual disciples of an anti-intellectual doctrine. Here at least we have identified one possible vector of seventeenth-century traditions, both Ranting and Behmenist, whose faith holds in suspension certain key ideas and critical images which should arrest the attention of the reader of William Blake.

I have been engaged, throughout the first part of this book, in an

---

[89] Pickersgill to Tregono, 1 December 1803, Muggletonian archive.
[90] In Muggletonian archive.

exceedingly difficult argument, and I am not wholly sure myself what this argument adduces. I have directed attention to the antinomian tradition, and have suggested a number of sources germane to Blake's thought. I have suggested more: that the Muggletonian Church preserved a vocabulary of symbolism, a whole cluster of signs and images, which recur – but in a new form and organisation, and in association with others – in Blake's poetry and painting. I will go further: of all the traditions touched upon, I know of none which consistently transmits so large a cluster of Blakean symbols.

This is a difficult and contestable point, and I shudder at the thought of the learning that would be required to establish it. What other sects were there, about which we know nothing and about which nothing will ever come to light? But I must argue that I have been directing attention not just to discrete symbols or tenets but to certain elements critical to the *structure* of Blake's thought and art. I will single out four such elements.

First, there is the specifically antinomian tradition, with its repudiation of the Moral Law. This will have been apparent throughout. The tenets of Reeve and Muggleton were close to those of Milton's Michael ('law can discover sin, but not remove'), with the additional predestinarian severity of the doctrine of the Two Seeds. The moral law is inscribed in human nature to enlighten and restrain corrupted Reason;[91] its origin was in the Fall (although Moses was the first explicitly to propound its prohibitions) and it entered in through the Serpent-Angel's 'Nature of Reason' and 'so by Generation the Law comes to be written in every Man's Heart'; 'man finds it there accusing of him, but knows not how it came written there'.[92] As such the Law has a certain serviceability, in constraining those – including magistrates and temporal powers – whose corrupted Reason would otherwise be under no restraint. It may even, on occasion, protect the saints from their persecutors. But 'though the law may sometimes hinder a sin, yet it can never root out sin . . . It changeth not the heart'.[93] Christ came to fulfil the law, with his blood displacing it with the gospel of love: 'the

[91] See *A Stream from the Tree of Life* (1758), p. 71; Muggleton, *A True Interpretation of the Eleventh Chapter of the Revelation of St John* (1753 edn), p. 100.
[92] Reeve and Muggleton, *Acts of the Witnesses* (1764 edn), p. 124; also Muggleton, *A Letter sent to Thomas Taylor, Quaker* (1756 edn), p. 96.
[93] Tomkinson, *Truth's Triumph*, p. 294.

law was given by Moses, and grace and truth by Jesus Christ'.[94]
'The moral law was written in the nature of reason, and so had
death written in it'; by 'fulfilling' the law Christ liberated the elect
from eternal damnation.[95] Believers 'are not under the law, but
under grace', and they are 'freed from the law of sin and death':

The law is not written in the seed of faith's nature at all, but in the seed
of reason's nature only. Therefore the seed of faith is not under the law,
but is above the law. . .[96]

Whosoever hath the divine light of faith in him, that man hath no need
of man's law to be his rule, but he is a law unto himself, and lives above
all laws of mortal men, and yet is obedient to all laws.[97]

Hence we are placed within the characteristic set of antinomian
oppositions. The Law is warlike and punitive, the Gospel is merciful and pacific.[98] Law and Gospel are sometimes seen as direct
contraries. The Moral Law was promulgated by Moses. 'I declare',
wrote Reeve, 'that the Law of Moses, both moral and ceremonial
. . . did belong to the Jews only.' The gospel of Jesus made 'all
Observations of the Law of Moses . . . of no Use for ever'.[99] (Blake
held that 'the laws of the Jews were (both ceremonial & real) the
basest & most oppressive of human codes' (above, p. 61).) Envy
is the leading principle of the Law (or Reason); Love the leading
principle of the Gospel – sometimes referred to among believers as
the 'everlasting gospel'.[100]

Love lieth down at Envy's Feet to be killed of him, and slayeth Envy by
its Patience and Meekness. . .

Love is generous, and pitiful; but Envy is covetous and cruel. . .[101]

The Two Seeds are impelled either by 'pure burning love' or 'a
fiery law of unbelieving burning envy'.[102] The first are in bondage,
the second in freedom: 'We who are believers are both free-born,
and free by redemption':[103]

[94] *A True Interpretation*, p. 11; also *A Stream*, p. 71.
[95] *Ibid.*, p. 108.   [96] *Ibid.*, p. 10.
[97] Tomkinson, p. 288.   [98] *A True Interpretation*, p. 228.
[99] Reeve, *Sacred Remains* (n.d., but 1706), p. 74.
[100] See, e.g., *Sacred Remains* (1706), p. 78.
[101] Reeve and Muggleton, *Joyful News from Heaven* (1658), pp. 37–8.
[102] Tomkinson, *Truth's Triumph*, p. 284.
[103] Saddington, *The Articles of True Faith*, p. 54.

The law of Moses and gospel of Jesus are contrary . . . The law and sin
are a cross couple, and a sad society, in that they gender to bondage,
whilst faith in the free-woman genders to peace.[104]

Finally, and in the vocabulary of Christian radicalism, the Law
belongs to the priests and potentates of the earth, the Gospel to
believers without temporal ambitions. 'The dragon, beast, and
false prophet, they by their council, power, and authority, did
invite all the kings of the earth . . . to fight against the Lord Jesus,
and the remnant of the seed of faith, who are the saints. . .'[105]
Against these powers the faithful may employ only spiritual
weapons: in a song of Thomas Tomkinson:

> Love is the fiery chariot sent from on high,
> Love mounts the saints into eternal joy,
> Love being such as I've described to be,
> Love I will love, and love, do thou love me.[106]

Against this image of the 'chariot of fire' is counterposed the
image of the Law as a 'flaming sword'. 'Those cherubims which
had the flaming sword which turned every way, to keep the way
of the Tree of Life' Muggleton declared to be of the same nature
as the Serpent, 'which had the same law of reason written in their
seed'. 'And this flaming sword . . . was that very law of reason
which . . . is called the moral law, or the law of Moses.'[107]

> When Satan first the black bow bent
> And the Moral Law from the Gospel rent
> He forgd the Law into a Sword
> And spilld the blood of mercys Lord.   (E200)

> I stood among my valleys of the south
> And saw a flame of fire, even as a Wheel
> Of fire surrounding all the heavens: it went
> From west to east, against the current of
> Creation, and devour'd all things in its loud
> Fury & thundering course round heaven & earth. . .

---

[104] Tomkinson, p. 289.
[105] *A True Interpretation*, p. 236.
[106] *Divine Songs of the Muggletonians*, p. 373.
[107] *A True Interpretation*, p. 56. The authority for this in Genesis 3, v.24: 'So he drove out the
man; and he placed at the east of the garden of Eden Cherubims, and a flaming sword
which turned every way, to keep the way of the Tree of Life.'

And I asked a Watcher & a Holy-One
Its Name; he answered: 'It is the Wheel of Religion.'
I wept & said: 'Is this the law of Jesus,
'This terrible devouring sword turning every way
He answer'd: 'Jesus died because he strove
'Against the current of this Wheel; its Name
'Is Caiaphas, the dark Preacher of Death,
'Of sin, of sorrow & of punishment:
'Opposing Nature! It is Natural Religion;
'But Jesus is the bright Preacher of Life
'Creating Nature from this fiery Law
'By self-denial & forgiveness of Sin. . .'   (E230)

As soon as we attend to such passages of Blake, we must see
that he is writing directly in this antinomian tradition, but also
that he is employing its terms in original and idiosyncratic ways
not sanctioned by any part of that tradition. The suggestion of
a Muggletonian derivation for Blake's vocabulary becomes more
persuasive if we attend to a second element in these doctrines,
the explicit and repetitive identification of 'Reason' as the Satanic
principle, the fruit of the Tree of the Knowledge of Good and Evil.

No theme recurs more in Muggletonian discourse. The angels
only are creatures of pure reason. Reason entered the human race
through the Fall and the seduction of Eve, and temporal reason is
always 'unclean' and 'corrupted'. Reason is 'the right devil',

That devil . . . that tempts men and women to all unrighteousness, it is
man's spirit of unclean reason and cursed imagination.[108]

'It was the Spirit of Reason in Man that always blasphemed and
fought against God, and persecuted and killed the Just and the
Righteous, because God would not accept of the Devil Reason's
Worship', wrote Muggleton, who had had some persecution from
reasonable magistrates himself. And, by way of illustration, he
discussed Pilate's 'reasons' for condemning Christ:

His Reason was, he thought better to keep the Favour of *Caesar*, and the
Honour of this World, than the Peace of his Conscience and Favour with
God; so his Reason and their Reason together delivered up the Just One
to be crucified by reasonable Men; for the Centurion, and those that
guarded him, were reasonable Men also. . .[109]

---

[108] See James Hyde, The Muggletonians.
[109] *A Looking-Glass for George Fox* (1756), pp. 62–3.

'Christ & his Apostles were Illiterate Men', wrote Blake: 'Caiaphas Pilate & Herod were Learned' (E657). 'Rational Truth is not the Truth of Christ, but of Pilate. It is the Tree of the Knowledge of Good & Evil' (E610).

If anything, the theme of Reason, the 'right devil', became more prominent in Muggletonian doctrine among believers in the eighteenth and nineteenth centuries, as they found their faith threatened on every side by rationalism. The reason got a remarkably bad press in their songs of the mid-eighteenth century. In one (by George Hermitage):

> Darkness long kept me fast bound,
> Sin and death my soul did wound,
> Reason's chains made me to groan;
> Freedom, freedom then unknown.[110]

In another (by William Miller), on the fate of the reprobate after the Last Judgement–

> Reason will here with reason lie,
> Howling to all eternity;
> A burning sand their bed will be,
> And dying, live eternally.[111]

Few themes recur with more consistency in the whole trajectory of Blake's work than Reason (often in association with the moral law) binding, constraining or corrupting life. It is suggested even in that fragment of juvenilia, 'Then She bore Pale desire' ('Reason once fairer than the light till foul in Knowledges dark Prison house' (E438)), and it is found still in those late works, 'The Gates of Paradise' ('Serpent Reasonings . . . of Good & Evil' (E265)) and the Laocoon inscriptions – where, however, Reason has become synonymous with the reasons of materialism: 'Money, which is the great Satan or Reason the Root of Good & Evil in the Accusation of Sin' (E272). Between these two points the values which Blake attributes to Reason change a good deal – Reason is the 'ratio of all we have already known' or 'the bound or outward circumference of energy' (E34) but with Urizen the repressive symbolism is enforced. In *Milton* and *Jerusalem* the 'spectre' is 'the reasoning power in every man', at enmity with poetry and imagination. Blake's note on 'A Vision of The Last Judgment' commences:

---

[110] *Divine Songs of the Muggletonians*, p. 18.   [111] *Ibid.*, p. 203.

The Last Judgment when all those are Cast away who trouble Religion
with Questions concerning Good & Evil or Eating of the Tree of those
Knowledges or Reasonings which hinder the Vision of God. . . (E544)

'Angels are happier than Men . . . because they are not always
Prying after Good & Evil in one Another & eating the Tree of
Knowledge for Satans Gratification' (E555).

These first two elements may be found in other sources than
Muggletonianism, although the specific identification of Reason
(rather than Pride or Lust or Disobedience) with the Serpent seems
to me to be rare.[112] But when we put these together with two other
elements, then the hypothesis of some Muggletonian influence
upon Blake becomes persuasive. The third element is to be found
in the unusual symbolism of the Fall, and of the Serpent-Angel's
actual copulation with Eve and transmutation into flesh and blood
in her womb.

Serpent-symbolism, of course, has a central place in Blake's
work: it is even more prominent in his visual art than in his poetry.
I will argue that it can be found in his poetry as early as in *An
Island in the Moon* (1784), in a song which is given to the Cynic:

> When old corruption first begun
> Adornd in yellow vest
> He committed on flesh a whoredom
> O what a wicked beast
>
> From them a callow babe did spring
> And old corruption smild
> To think his race should never end
> For now he had a child. . .   (E445)

If we take 'old corruption' as the Serpent-Angel appearing as an
'angel of light' ('Adorned in yellow vest') and the whoredom committed on flesh as his copulation with Eve, then this is Muggletonian symbolic machinery, and, in the race that 'should never end'
we have Cain and the Two Seeds. This imagery is manifestly present in 'I saw a chapel all of gold'

> I saw a serpent rise between
> The white pillars of the door
> And he forcd & forcd & forcd
> Down the golden hinges tore

---

[112] However, it is found in William Law: '*Reasoners* are of the Seed of the Serpent . . . to live
by Reason is to be a prey of the old serpent, eating dust with him, grovelling in the mire
of all earthly passions. . .': *A Short but Sufficient Confutation of the Reverend Doctor Warburton*
(1757), p. 66.

It is there in *America* (1793) where Orc:

> anon a serpent folding
> Around the pillars of Urthona, and round thy dark limbs
> On the Canadian wilds I fold. . .

> I see a serpent in Canada, who courts me to his love. (E50–1)

It returns again in the *Book of Urizen* (1794), 'When Enitharmon, sick, Felt a Worm within her womb:

> All day the worm lay on her bosom
> All night within her womb
> The worm lay till it grew to a serpent
> With dolourous hissings & poisons
> Round Enitharmon's loins folding. . .

(The child was named Orc.) It continues in the convoluted coup-lings of serpents and females in the prophetic books; and it takes a new and powerful form (both visually and in verse) in the image of the 'mortal coil' – a literal serpent coil – which Christ sheds on the cross, shedding thus one of his two natures.

One or another form of this symbolism repeatedly recurs in his graphic art and painting. It is found in 'The Temptation of Eve' (1799–1800) (Illus. 1). David Bindman has written:

Eve's position within the coil of the serpent is apparently unprecedented in European art and although her hand reaches upward it is not towards the apple in the mouth of the serpent; she appears to be preening herself at the serpent's flattery, and the sexual overtones are confirmed by her open nakedness and her failure to make the gesture of modesty associating the fatal act with the sense of shame. . .[113]

It is true, as Bindman points out, that Blake had Milton's authority for the gorgeous presence of the upright serpent:

> And towards Eve
> Address'd his way, not with indented wave
> Prone on the ground, as since, but on his rear,
> Circular base of rising foulds, that tour'd
> Fould above fould a surging maze, his Head
> Crested aloft, and Carbuncle his eyes;
> With burnished Neck of verdant Gold, erect
> Amidst his circling spires, that on the grass
> Floted redundant. . .

But Milton's serpent then conducts Eve, with many wily speeches, to another part of the Garden where the Tree is found. He neither

[113] Bindman, *Blake as an Artist*, p. 119.

seduces her nor himself offers her the apple. Bindman also suggests as 'unprecedented' the presence of the sleeping Adam with his spade on the ground behind Eve. But this also finds authority in Muggletonian doctrine, where, we recall, the Serpent could seduce Eve only because Faith was asleep (above, p. 80). Blake's Serpent is emphatically a Muggletonian 'Angel of Light' accomplishing a material seduction. To complicate matters further, a Muggletonian influence may have been felt upon Milton, just as the Miltonic influence is felt upon young Blake, whose 'old corruption' was 'adorned in yellow vest' after Milton's serpent 'with burnished Neck of verdant Gold'. Phallic symbol the serpent may be, and manifestly is, but we cannot avoid the additional Muggletonian identification.

I am talking about symbolic machinery, or vocabulary, not the realised effects. Even in the Cynic's song in *An Island*, Blake appropriates the vocabulary to a new purpose, passing on into a ludicrous polemic against 'Surgery'. The Serpent becomes an image of the material body, as later it sometimes becomes a symbol of Nature: 'the vast form of Nature, like a Serpent, roll'd between'. As machinery, however, the serpent often appears as ravishing the female, as in 'the chapel all of gold' (p. 171), or as giving rise to a monstrous conception, as in the *Book of Urizen*.

Eve is shown even more explicitly within the coital embrace of the serpent in 'Satan Exulting over Eve' (Illus. 2) as also in 'The Temptation and Fall of Eve' in the *Paradise Lost* series (Illus. 3), where the apple is transferred from mouth to mouth. In the extraordinary illustration to Job, 'Job's Evil Dreams', a Satanic God with cloven hoof points to the Mosaic Tables of the Law: once again he is entwined with a serpent (Illus. 4). The Satanic characters and mythical malevolent beasts in Blake's paintings nearly always have reptilian scales, most thickly around the genitals. The striking painting of 'Moses Erecting the Brazen Serpent' (Illus. 5) may carry a somewhat different symbolism: Blake was no admirer of Moses and one suspects that he was not following biblical authority (Numbers xxi, 6–9) but was taking the serpent as a symbol of the Moral Law. And Blake was delighted to borrow, probably from Stukeley, the image of organised religion as a 'serpent temple'.[114]

---

[114] W. Stukeley's *Stonehenge, a Temple Restored to the British Druids* (1740) and *Abury, a Temple of the British Druids* (1743) clearly had a strong influence upon Blake: see Jon Mee, *Dangerous Enthusiasm*, chapter 2: also Raine, *Blake and Tradition*, Vol. II, pp. 236–7.

But one cannot proclaim that Blake's symbols stand for one thing or for two things only. They are constantly shifting in emphasis and sometimes seem to 'mean' whatever Blake wishes at the time. Even the confident S. Foster Damon in his *Blake Dictionary* offers for serpent 'a number of overlapping meanings'. One is Hypocrisy, especially in priestly form. 'The Serpent also symbolizes the worship of Nature', as it is found on the title page of *Europe* (Illus. 6).[115] Further, the serpent may represent Nature herself: 'its coils represent its dull rounds and repetitions'.[116] One would not refuse any of these meanings, and other critics have other emphases. John Beer finds the serpent to be a symbol both of energy and of selfhood.[117] Morton Paley finds that it represents the 'energies of nature . . . and cyclical recurrence'.[118] Other uses suggest that the serpent may sometimes be Reason.[119] To complicate matters further serpent-entwined gods may be found in the iconography of Zoroastrianism and Mithraism, although it cannot be shown that Blake knew this.[120]

If we wish to examine the meaning with which Blake invests these symbols, then we cannot do it with a scatter-shot of examples: each examination must return to the context of the poems or paintings. The serpent may indeed sometimes symbolise the imprisoning selfhood, or may appear, as critics of the neo-Platonic persuasion have argued, as a symbol of constraining matter or Nature. In the famous print, 'Elohim Creating Adam' (Illus. 7) the material imprisonment of Creation is suggested by the giant worm or serpent coiled around Adam's leg. It must follow that Christ's sacrifice on the Cross expels this serpent-nature; in shuffling off the 'mortal coil' Christ resumes a spiritual uncorrupted body and

---

[115] David Erdman notes also that this serpent embodies 'energy, desire, phallic power, the fiery tongue': *The Illuminated Blake* (Oxford, 1975), p. 157.

[116] S. Foster Damon, *A Blake Dictionary* (1973 edn), pp. 365–6.

[117] John Beer, *Blake's Humanism* (Manchester, 1968), *passim*, and the same author in *Blake Newsletter*, Vol. 4, no. 4, Spring 1971, p. 145. Northrop Frye first emphasised that 'the serpent with its tail in its mouth is the perfect emblem of the Selfhood', but his analysis is confusing: *Fearful Symmetry* (Princeton, 1947), chapter 5.

[118] Morton D. Paley, *The Continuing City: William Blake's Jerusalem* (Oxford, 1983), p. 109. Blake himself claims the serpent as shut up in 'image of infinite/finite revolutions. . .'

[119] In different sketches for the title page of *Europe* Blake appears to associate the serpent, who fathers Orc upon Enitharmon, with the rational principle (emerging from the neck of Los) or with Moses–Urizen, riding upon the serpent's head and holding the tablets of the Moral Law: see Martin Butlin, *William Blake* (Tate Gallery, 1978), p. 54, figs. 70, 71: Erdman, *The Illuminated Blake*, p. 396.

[120] Mary Jackson, 'Blake and Zoroastrianism', *Blake: an Illustrated Quarterly*, Vol. 11, no. 2, 1977.

promises the same to the faithful. This is forcefully expressed in
'Michael Foretelling the Crucifixion' (Illus. 8), with the serpent's
head nailed to the Cross beneath Christ's feet. For this there is
authority also in *Paradise Lost* (Book XII), Christ's sacrifice in the
same moment removing the Law and redeeming man's sin:

> But to the Cross he nailes thy Enemies,
> The Law that is against thee, and the sins
> Of all mankinde, with him there crucifi'd,
> Never to hurt them more who rightly trust
> In this his satisfaction. . .

The image was familiar in the antinomian tradition (see above,
p. 11) and is found in at least one (somewhat less memorable)
Muggletonian song:

> The writings which against me stood,
>   It was God's law, I see;
> But God has shed his precious blood,
>   And slew the law in me;
> I see it nail'd upon a cross
>   When Christ was crucified;
> And now my soul is at no loss,
>   For God for me has died.[121]

Blake handled the same theme in verse with his usual robust
assertiveness:

> And thus with wrath he did subdue
> The Serpent Bulk of Natures dross
> Till he had naild it to the Cross
> He took on Sin in the Virgins Womb
> And put it off on the Cross & Tomb
> To be Worshiped by the Church of Rome   (E515)

Once again, the congruence in symbolic vocabulary and in antinomian tenets falls short of any proof of Muggletonian influence.
The myth of the Serpent, Samael, who had relations with Eve, from
which Cain was the offspring, can be found also in Kabbalistic
writings.[122] (But I do not think that these also carry the image of

---

[121] *Divine Songs of the Muggletonians*, p. 213.

[122] See A.E. Waite, *The Holy Kabbalah* (1902; 1965), p. 286. The Muggletonians had some
notion of these traditions: Tomkinson refers to 'the Hebrew doctors' and specifically to
'Menacham, a Jewish Rabbi' for the confirmation that the seed of the Serpent was
conveyed to Eve: *The Muggletonian Principles Prevailing* (1695; 1822), p. 45. A problem in
identifying Kabbalistic, like Gnostic, sources is that they may pass through so many

the serpent-nature entering thereafter into the human race).[123] In any case, it seems to me unreasonable to suppose that Blake would have taken so vivid and persuasive a symbolic cluster from seventeenth-century hermetic sources rather than from a sect whose members were his contemporaries in London, and whose publications were also contemporaneous. And the case for some Muggletonian influence becomes even stronger when we bring these three elements together with a fourth, and final, one: the unique image of God incarnated as Jesus Christ, and having no other existence save as Christ. This theme is as important as any which we have examined. But, when considered in relation to Blake, it cannot be discussed except in conjunction with the Swedenborgian notion of the 'divine image'. And since this must involve us in a change of symbolic machinery and a whole new *dramatis personæ* I will leave it to Part II.

It is time that I was a little more plain with my readers. Where is my argument tending? And, equally, where is it *not?*

First, I am not suggesting that we can reduce any part of Blake's art to the exposition of Muggletonian doctrine. (There are, in any case, parts of that doctrine, such as the rigid predestinarian notion of the Two Seeds, which he would have found to be abhorrent.) I am suggesting that he could have been situated in some way in relation to this tradition, which made available to him certain antinomian tenets and a remarkable and coherent cluster of symbols, which he then employed (along with others) much as a painter sets the paints on his palette to work. What he did with these symbols is another question again, but I find it helpful to identify the source of the pigments.

Second, I have been emphasising that this 'vocabulary' was readily available, in the publications and discourse of believers in Blake's London. We first encounter William Blake in a precise religious context as a signatory to a document of the Swedenborg-

intermediaries, pre-eminent among them Jacob Boehme: see Désirée Hirst, *Hidden Riches*, *passim*. Sheila Spector in 'Kabbalistic Sources – Blake's and his Critics'', *Blake: an Illustrated Quarterly*, Vol. 17, no. 3, Winter 1983–4, shows what (very imperfect) accounts of Kabbala could possibly have been available to Blake, but there is no evidence that he used these.

[123] The language of the Two Seeds was employed by Boehme and by George Fox (R. M. Jones, *Spiritual Reformers in the 16th and 17th Centuries* (1914), pp. 225–6) and also more widely: see Christopher Hill, *The English Bible and the Seventeenth-Century Revolution* (1993), pp. 239–42.

ian New Jerusalem Church in 1789. We will examine this context
in the next part. But it is relevant to note now that the similarity
of certain Muggletonian and Swedenborgian tenets was remarked
upon by observers at the time.[124] It would have been strange if
there had been no exchanges between the two groups of believers,
even if these had ended in mutual repudiation.[125] And that at least
one or two members of that early New Jerusalem milieu were
versed in Muggletonian sources is confirmed by the re-printing in a
Swedenborgian magazine of 1790 of some of Thomas Tomkinson's
writing (see below, p. 160).

    Third, I am not suggesting that William Blake was a member
of the Muggletonian Church. I did play half-heartedly with the
notion for some years. But I can now announce, as my only definitive finding, that at any time after 1780 he was not, for I have
examined the Church's records which are comprehensive enough
after this date to warrant confidence. Nor have I identified any
known friend of Blake's. Nor have I even identified any persons
who by neighbourhood, occupation or common interests might
seem to be likely acquaintances of Blake. Nor does it seem anything
but improbable that Blake would have rubbed shoulders with the
London believers who, at the end of the 1780s, an observer wrote
off (prematurely) as 'a set of jolly fellows, who drink their pot
and smoak their tobacco', meeting on Sunday evenings 'at obscure
public-houses in the out-parts of London, and converse about those
of their sect who have gone before them'.[126] We would expect to
find Blake, in the late 1770s or 1780s, in the more sophisticated
ambience suggested by *An Island in the Moon*, or in the polite proto-

[124] See W.H. Reid, *The Rise and Dissolution of the Infidel Societies in the Metropolis* (1800), p. 53:
'The principal article of this self-called *New* church . . . is just as *Old* as Muggleton and
Reeves; who, after the protectorship of Oliver, were the first who published, that the
whole godhead is circumscribed in the person of Jesus Christ, still retaining the human
form in heaven. . .'
[125] The Muggletonians formed an obsessively close and hostile relation with Swedenborgians, who replaced the Quakers as the prime object of their comminations, perhaps
because of a supposed identity in their doctrine that Christ is God. In 1845 a Mr
Robinson of Camberwell, writing to a believer in New York, described the Swedenborgians as 'one of the worst Spirits in opposition to Truth': 'they say that Christ was the
Almighty God, yet they deny his being the whole and alone God'. Copy of letter in
Muggletonian archive. See also Gordon, *Ancient and Modern Muggletonians*, p. 60.
[126] Hurd, *New Universal History*, pp. 669–71. Hurd was probably not going on much more
than gossip. He alleged that the Muggletonians had 'a very pernicious effect on the
morals of the people. It has induced many of them to become Deists and practical
Atheists.'

Swedenborgian meetings held by the Reverend Jacob Duche in Lambeth.[127] We can say with some confidence that Blake at this time was an adherent of no 'sect'; his annotations show a repugnance to 'sectaries', although a sympathy with 'poor enthusiasts'.

But, even so, this does not quite conclude the matter. For the interesting question may be, not what faith Blake subsequently adopted, but in what faith he was brought up as a child. The enquiry must then be extended backwards to the 1740s to 1760s, when Blake's parents were young and were establishing their household. The suggestion that 'Blake does not belong by birth to the established church, but to a dissenting sect' – although firmer than any of the numerous subsequent hypotheses – gives us too little to go on.[128] More interesting, perhaps, is Gilchrist's information that William's matter-of-fact elder brother, James (a hosier like their father), 'had his spiritual and visionary side too; would at times *talk Swedenborg*, talking of seeing Abraham and Moses' and to outsiders seemed, like his brother, to be 'a bit mad'.[129] This is confusing – not many Swedenborgians in London had visions of 'Abraham and Moses' – and to an outsider any strange symbolic vocabulary might have been put down to 'talking Swedenborg'. What it does suggest is that both brothers shared an inherited familial vocabulary which was arcane.

Much would become clear to us if William Blake had been born into a Muggletonian family. The Church was vigorous in the mid-century, winning new converts, actively publishing the prophets' works and writing many new songs. There was also a smaller group of believers, in a 'Church of Christ' known as Reevites or Reevonians. These appear to have followed the more radical and also less aggressive and less bullying writings of John Reeve, disavowing several of Muggleton's absurdities, and at the same time avowing their ability to converse with angels and have visions of the dead (a faculty which Muggleton repudiated).[130] But next to nothing is known of the Reevonians and I doubt whether anything ever will be known. As for the orthodox Muggletonian Church, no member-

---

[127] Erdman, *William Blake: Prophet against Empire*, p. 12, note 19; J.F.C. Harrison, *The Second Coming*, p. 72.

[128] Bentley, *William Blake*, p. 452, translating Crabb Robinson's essay in the *Vaterländisches Museum*, 1811.

[129] Alexander Gilchrist, *Life of William Blake* (1863; 1942), p. 48.

[130] See Lamont, 'Ludowick Muggleton and "Immediate Notice"'.

ship records survive for those decades, and among the surviving correspondents and song-writers no name of any Blake appears.

There does, however, appear the name of George Hermitage, two of whose songs – which are better than the usual run – turn up in the Muggletonian *Divine Songs* and in several manuscript song-books compiled around the mid-century. From several evidences – stylistic, the air to which one song was set – one may confidently assume that George Hermitage was writing songs for believers *circa* 1750.[131] And, back-tracking from this, I have found that William Blake's mother, who had been previously known as Catherine Harmitage should more properly be known as Hermitage. She was almost certainly the widow of Thomas Hermitage, hosier, of 28 Broad Street. Soon after her first husband's death she married James Blake, also a hosier, of Glasshouse Street, uniting the two businesses at her own address. Hermitage is not a common name (nor is Harmitage), but other Hermitages can be found in the registers of the same parish of St James's, Westminster, one of whom, named George, appears in 1742 as father to a baby. So we can at least establish that there was a George Hermitage, of an age to be Catherine's brother-in-law or other kin, living in the same Westminster parish. We cannot show that he was the same George who wrote Muggletonian songs, although the dates fit well enough. The evidence for all this is set out at more length in Appendix 2.

If Catherine Hermitage had Muggletonian kin – if she came herself from a Muggletonian family – then this would explain very satisfactorily the derivation of William Blake's antinomian vocabulary. If George the songwriter was kin to Thomas, then this is plausible, for, like all sectaries, Muggletonians were by preference endogamous – and Catherine, in choosing a second husband, might have looked for someone sympathetic to her faith as well as to a convenient business alliance. By one account, Blake composed some of his earliest illuminated songs to be hung up in his mother's chamber.[132] And in the same place, this whole vocabulary of signs, the robust antinomian beliefs, and the tradition of writing 'divine songs', could have entered his formative mind.

---

[131] Hermitage's songs were copied in several eighteenth-century song books (Muggletonian archive). 'Praises to my Maker's glory' was to the air 'Stella, darling of the Muses' (Mrs Pilkington).

[132] Bentley, p. 481.

We could suppose that William Blake in his childhood was made familiar with the structure of antinomian thought and the central images of *Genesis* and *Revelation* in a Muggletonian notation; that he turned sharply away from this in his 'teens, rejecting the know-all dogmatism of the sect, and its philistinism towards all the arts (except divine songs); read widely and entered the artistic world without restraint; took stock of works of the Enlightenment; was led back towards his origins by reading Boehme and Swedenborg; and then, in his early thirties (the years of the *Songs* and the *Marriage of Heaven and Hell*) composed a symbolic world for himself in which the robust tradition of artisan and tradesman antinomianism reasserted itself, not as literal doctrines, but as a fund of imaginative possibilities and as intellectual footholds for an anti-Enlightenment stance.

This is not a large 'finding'. We are not likely to find more, since if Blake's family *had* been Muggletonian, they would have kept this to themselves and made no open testimony. I will leave it with four verses from one of George Hermitage's songs:

> When I saw the Serpent's head
> In man bruised, my sorrows fled;
> CHRIST's ascension from the grave,
> Freedom, freedom, to me gave. . .
>
> Tell me not what reason saith;
> Reason has not light of faith;
> Reason doom'd to endless woe,
> Freedom, freedom cannot know.
>
> Though he long has claim'd the field,
> The last fight shall make him yield;
> Adam's sons shall then regain
> Freedom, freedom, lost through Cain. . .
>
> Brethren, now come join with me
> In praises for your liberty,
> Till we chaunt in heavenly bowers,
> Freedom, freedom, freedom's ours.[133]

It is at least a pleasant fiction to think of Blake's mother crooning that song to baby William on her lap.

[133] *Divine Songs of the Muggletonians*, p. 19.

CHAPTER 7

Anti-hegemony

This has been a long, and perhaps strange, way into William Blake. On one matter I am impenitent. Blake can't have dreamed up a whole vocabulary of symbolism, which touches at so many points the traditions which I have discussed, for himself *ab novo*. Nor can he have put it together like mosaic from his reading. Things don't happen like that. Nor can it have arisen just from a reading of the Bible, for this presupposes the Bible, and particular passages of *Genesis*, read *in a particular way*. The author of the Prefaces to *Jerusalem* and the 'Annotations to Watson', of *The Marriage of Heaven and Hell* and *The Everlasting Gospel*, was writing within a known tradition, using terms made familiar by seven or eight generations of London sectaries.

Certainly my argument does not stand or fall upon the Muggletonian hypothesis. What this does is to give the argument concretion and indicate one possible actual context. Whether or not Blake's family, or any of them, came from this particular church is not the critical question. There were other sects and other milieux, whose records may be irrecoverable. Coppinists and 'Sweet Singers of Israel' perhaps had meetings and discourses over doctrine of a similar kind, at least until the 1740s or 1750s. The astonishing survival of these Muggletonian records shows at least that such kinds of people were about, that their faith was strong and that the seventeenth-century antinomian traditions ran strongly through to Blake's time. He must have come from some such familial context.

By 1750 or 1760 it is probable that most of the petty sects reported as existing in 1706 no longer survived in their old forms. But the vocabulary survived, and it was continually in search of new vehicles for its expression. The sects had never been hermetically sealed against each other; part of the intellectual excitement of sectarianism (then, as now) had been found in the factional

1 *Eve Tempted by the Serpent.* Tempera, painted for Thomas Butts, *c.*1799–1800.

2   *Satan Exulting over Eve.* Pencil, pen and black ink and watercolour over colour print, 1795.

3 *The Temptation and Fall of Eve*, from Nine Illustrations to *Paradise Lost*. Pen and watercolour on paper, 1808.

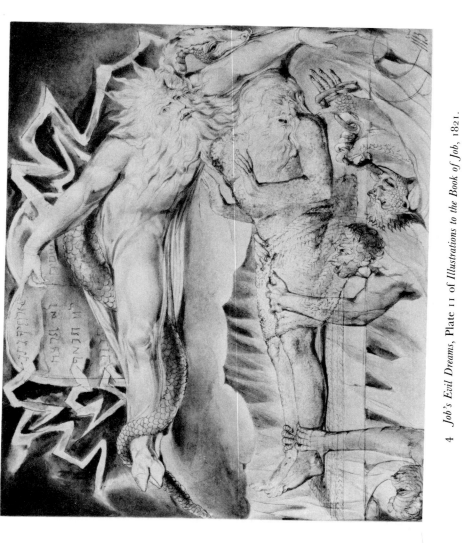

4 *Job's Evil Dreams*, Plate 11 of *Illustrations to the Book of Job*, 1821.

5　*Moses Erecting the Brazen Serpent.* Pen and watercolour on paper, *c.*1805.

6   Title page to *Europe*, 1794.

7   *Elohim Creating Adam*. Colour print finished in pen, from the Thomas Butts
    Collection, 1795.

8 *Michael Foretells the Crucifixion*, from Nine Illustrations to *Paradise Lost*. Pen and watercolour on paper, 1808.

9 *The Nativity.* Tempera on copper, from the Thomas Butts Collection, c.1799.

10 'The Garden of Love', from *Songs of Experience*, 1794.

11 'London', from *Songs of Experience*, c.1794.

12   *The Number of the Beast is 666*. Pen and watercolour, painted for Thomas Butts, *c*.1805.

13   *The Whore of Babylon*. Pen and watercolour, painted for Thomas Butts, c.1809.

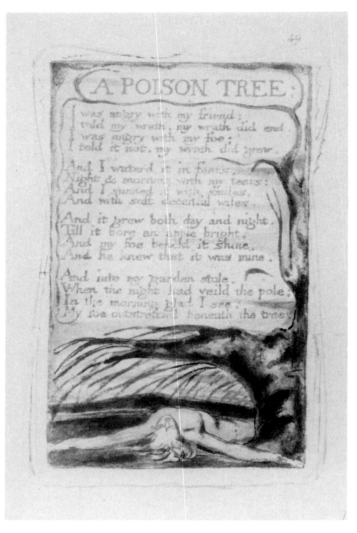

14   'A Poison Tree', from *Songs of Experience*, 1794.

15   *Malevolence*. Watercolour drawing, 1799.

16   Title page to *The Book of Urizen*, 1794.

17 *God Writing upon the Tables of the Covenant.* Pen and watercolour, painted for
Thomas Butts, *c.*1805.

18   *The Blasphemer*. Pen and watercolour, painted for Thomas Butts, *c.*1800.

19   *The Woman Taken in Adultery.* Pen and watercolour over traces of pencil on
      paper, painted for Thomas Butts, 1805.

20   *The Great Red Dragon and the Beast from the Sea.* Pen and ink with watercolour
      over graphite, painted for Thomas Butts, *c.*1803.

disputes between sects, the open debates, the struggle to convert each other's disciples. An earnest seeker might sample different sects, and move on from one to another. Such seekers were still to be found at the end of the century, like the earnest artisans, John Wright and William Bryan, who, in 1789, walked all the way to Avignon in search of spiritual revelation.[1] And the same fierce intellectual disputes continued. When the Reverend Richard Clarke came to the city in 1788 and preached universal redemption, 'the sectaries were ready to tear him out of the Pulpit; and one person called out when preaching at the Temple Church, "This man preaches false doctrine."'[2] We will do best to think of a sectarian and antinomian gathering-ground in London, where heretical tracts were cherished, where sects suffered secessions and new hierarchs arose, where Behmenists disputed with Universalists, and where seekers shopped around among preachers and little churches. If James Blake, Senior, can be shown to have been, at some moment, a Baptist or a Moravian, or if Catherine Hermitage was at one time a Muggletonian, this does not go to prove that they remained in these churches always. It is more relevant that we should see them within this general gathering-ground, with its intellectual and sometimes passionate concern for heretical doctrine. And it was from this same gathering-ground that some of the first members of the Swedenborgian New Jerusalem Church were to be drawn.

By the end of the eighteenth century this tradition of plebeian and tradesman Dissent had drifted a great distance away from the polite and rational religious culture – a culture which, with its uneasy memories of the Commonwealth, still feared 'enthusiasts'. And the derisory judgements which the learned and the accomplished then made upon these enthusiasts still imposes itself upon us today. We see them only as eccentrics or as survivors. At a casual glance it seems self-evident that those who turned their backs upon rational (and historical) biblical criticism, and who even ignored or traduced all the advancing findings of the natural sciences (as did the Philadelphians, Hutchinsonians and Muggletonians), must have been locked into a religiose fantasy-

---

[1] J.F.C. Harrison, *The Second Coming*, pp. 69–72. A brisk account of this episode is in Robert Southey, *Letters from England* (1807), Vol. III, chapter LXVIII.
[2] Dr Williams's Library, Walton Papers, MS 1.1.43, Langcake to Henry Brooks, 1 August 1790.

world; they are quaint historical fossils. Donald Davie, who has cast a casual and partial eye upon the 'antinomian and heretical sects' which '*effectively* influenced Blake', has concluded that 'as specifically *religious* insights, their ideas are beneath contempt'. And he asks whether we may not have, in Blake, 'a case of an imaginative genius born into a stratum of religious experience too shallow to sustain him'.[3]

In my view, the reply which Davie predicates, in the manner in which he proposes the question, is profoundly wrong, and this book is offering a different answer. But Davie is still asking a necessary and significant question.

I cannot see how an answer can be provided, by one who is not a Christian, at the level of arguments as to the rationality of particular religious beliefs. How are we to say which view is 'shallow': the doctrine of the Virgin Birth or the Muggletonian doctrine of God's transmutation in Mary's womb into Christ?

It might be more helpful to consider, not individual doctrines but the degree to which different traditions were capable of sustaining, in the vocabulary of their doctrines, a disciplined and consistent pursuit of knowledge and an enquiry into value, even when subsequent ages have come to the view that much of this vocabulary was erroneous. Where most kinds of positive knowledge are concerned (scientific, historical) then the answer would seem to be flatly on Davie's side: the mystical and antinomian sects were not only shallow, they adopted a counter-Enlightenment stance which was obscurantist. But where social or political assumptions or enquiries into value are at issue, then the answer must be very much more complex.

The danger is that we should confuse the reputability of beliefs, and the reputability of those who professed them, with depth or shallowness. I have already suggested, in discussing justification by faith, that the antinomian position was consciously anti-hegemonic. That is, if we accept the view that in most societies we can observe an intellectual as well as institutional hegemony, or dominant discourse, which imposes a structure of ideas and beliefs – deep assumptions as to social proprieties and economic process and as to the legitimacy of relations of property and power, a general 'common sense' as to what is possible and what is not, a

[3] Donald Davie, *A Gathered Church* (1978), p. 52.

limited horizon of moral norms and practical probabilities beyond which all must be blasphemous, seditious, insane or apocalyptic fantasy – a structure which serves to consolidate the existent social order, enforce its priorities, and which is itself enforced by rewards and penalties, by notions of 'reputability', and (in Blake's time) by liberal patronage or by its absence – if we accept this large mouthful, then we can see that these antinomian sects were hegemony's eighteenth-century opposition.[4] More than this, anti-nomianism's intellectual doctrines (the suspicion of 'reason', justi-fication by faith, hostility to the Moral Law) constituted in quietest periods a defence against the reigning hegemony, in more active periods a resource for an active critique not just of policies or personalities but of the deep assumptions of the social order.

And we can take this argument a little further. For what the antinomian or Muggletonian declaimed against as 'Reason' we might today prefer to define as 'Ideology', or as the compulsive constraints of the ruling 'discourse'. Antinomian doctrine was expressive of a profound distrust of the 'reasons' of the genteel and comfortable, and of ecclesiastical and academic institutions, not so much because they produced false knowledges but because they offered specious apologetics ('serpent reasonings') for a rotten social order based, in the last resort, on violence and material self-interest. In short, the antinomian stance was not against know-ledge but against the ideological assumptions which pretended to be knowledge and the ideological contamination of the rest.

I am bringing into emphasis a *resource* of antinomianism, a *stance* towards the polite culture, whose strength is most evident in the confidence which it gave to Blake. But this emphasis also enables us to put into a single place a sociological and an intellectual ana-lysis of this minority tradition. For in cultural or intellectual terms it is significant that antinomianism is an artisan or tradesman stance. Notations of class derived from the categories of an indus-trial society will always be anachronistic and misleading when brought to English eighteenth-century society. In between the basic polarity of the gentry and 'the industrious sort' or 'the labouring poor' there is an immense range of different social grada-tions and aspirations, but we are taken little further if we try to

---

[4] In my view John Barrell's persuasive argument as to the classical character of Blake's views of art and its function takes too little account of this anti-hegemonic stance: see *The Political Theory of Painting from Reynolds to Hazlitt* (Yale University Press, 1986), chapter 3.

categorise these as 'petit-bourgeois', or 'middle class'. For what
may define the consciousness of these groups more clearly will be
such factors as their degree of *dependency*; that is, their dependence
on or independence of the lines of interest, influence, preferment
and patronage which structured that society from top to bottom.
In so far as some – but by no means all – tradesmen and artisans
had a degree of occupational independence from interest and patronage somewhat greater than their more affluent neighbours who
were petty clergy, tutors, clerks in public office, soldiers or sailors,
attorneys and even (in some cases) journalists or artists, so it was
possible for a more robust, anti-Court, and sometimes republican,
consciousness to be nourished in this milieu.

And to this we must add a further cultural or intellectual definition of 'class'. Everything in the age of 'reason' and 'elegance'
served to emphasise the sharp distinctions between a polite and a
demotic culture. Dress, style, gesture, proprieties of speech, gram-
mar and even punctuation were resonant with the signs of class;
the polite culture was an elaborated code of social inclusion and
exclusion.[5] Classical learning and an accomplishment in the law
stood like difficult gates-of-entry into this culture: the grammarian
must show his expertise in derivations and constructions, the politician a familiarity with the models of Rome, the poet and artist a
fluency in classical mythology. These accomplishments both legit-
imated and masked the actualities of brute property and power,
interest and patronage. A grammatical or mythological solecism
marked an intruder down as an outsider.

Antinomianism, and in particular Muggletonianism, can be seen
as an extreme recourse open to the excluded. It challenged the
entire superstructure of learning and of moral and doctrinal teaching as ideology: the Reason of the Seed of the Serpent, now embodied in the temporal rulers of the earth. If we read this as a simple
opposition between reason and unreason (or blind faith) then this
is self-convicted irrationalism. But if we consider the *actual* assumptions of the 'Age of Reason' then the antinomian stance acquires
a new force, even a rationality. For it struck very precisely at critical positions of the hegemonic culture, the 'common sense' of
the ruling groups, which today can be seen to be intellectually un-
sound and sometimes to be no more than ideological apologetics.

---

[5] See Olivia Smith, *The Politics of Language 1791–1819* (Oxford, 1984).

In particular, the dominant mechanistic (environmentalist or associationist) psychology with its set of stepping-stones from self-interest to rational benevolence (whose evidence is useful works) is challenged by the antinomian doctrine of the unlawed impulses of faith and love. The increasingly remote and impersonal image of God, the Newtonian prime mover of 'Natural Religion', is challenged by the personal embodied image of God/Christ. The profoundly paternalist character of the dominant social thought and moral sensibility is curtly challenged by the antinomian vocabulary of the humble saints persecuted by the temporal powers. Above all, antinomianism offered a central challenge to the Moral Law in a society whose legitimating ideology was precisely that of Law. And when we recall that this same polite and rule-governed society multiplied new prohibitions and capital offences on every side, placing the altar of Tyburn at the centre of its institutions, can we decide so easily on which side 'reason' is to be found?

This may help us also to place Blake. Blake came, very firmly, from a background of London *tradesmen*. His father and mother were hosiers (although not, it seems, enrolled in the Guild), his wife was probably a tradesman's daughter, and the same social status was maintained throughout life by his younger brother, James, who was described by Gilchrist as 'an honest, unpretending shopkeeper in an old-world style'. Blake grew up in the strongest centre of tradesman and skilled artisan *independency* in the kingdom; both his father and his mother's first husband voted for the anti-Court candidate in the face of every resource of influence and courtly pressure in the dramatic election of 1749 (see Appendix 2); and we may at the least assume that an anti-Court propensity was implanted in him in childhood. When Erdman tells us that Blake's interest in the paintings of Mortimer, Barry and Fuseli 'had aligned him with the underdog in the art community' I suspect that he has placed the cart before the horse. Blake was already disposed to take their part because 'while Sr Joshua [Reynolds] was rolling in Riches' and while 'only Portrait Painting [was] applauded & rewarded by the Rich & Great' they were deprived of fame and patronage. Blake had been taught in childhood to place a critical distance between himself and the Rich and Great. And the distance was never closed. Annotating *The Works of Joshua Reynolds* he came upon a list of members of the Literary Club which included Reynolds, Dr Johnson, Edmund Burke, Sir John Hawkins, the Hon.

Topham Beauclerk and Dr Goldsmith, and he noted: 'Oliver Goldsmith never should have known such knaves' (E629). By the late
1780s and 1790s, when perhaps we may begin to use the term
'middle class' Blake found many of his friends and associates
among artists and intellectuals from a middle-class milieu. Even
so, his relations with gentry or clergy (William Hayley, Esq., the
Reverend Dr Trusler) remained exceedingly tetchy, watchful
against any controlling gesture of patronage, full of the susceptibil-
ities of one who doubted whether he should know such knaves.

   The difficulty is that, in today's received wisdom, tradesman or
shop-keeper is suggestive of conservatism and dependency: 'petty-
bourgeois' has become a term of commination. But in eighteenth-
century London the tradesmen were, exactly, where a robust, Wilk-
esite, radical independency was located. And if we suppose that
Blake's family were adherents at some time of an antinomian faith,
then this independency would have had an uncrackable doctrinal
defence, a profound cultural resource in faith, a presumption of
spiritual superiority over the Rich and Great. What most distingu-
ishes these pockets of radical Dissent among the trades is a stubborn lack of deference, both social and intellectual.

   This lack of deference is the veritable signature of William Blake.
It is true that the gifted tradesman's son found entrance into the
'republic' of artists – or into what, in today's jargon, may be seen
as an upwardly mobile profession – taking him away from the
stodgy station of his brother James. It is also true that the arts are
professions with their own long historical traditions, some – but
by no means all – of which are strongly resistant to deference.
Blake's chosen masters and friends – Barry, Flaxman, Fuseli – will
have confirmed him in his anti-deferential stance, his fury against
patronage, his desire for an enlightened 'public' and an open
market for artistic talent: 'Liberality! We want not Liberality We
want a Fair Price & Proportionate Value & a General Demand
for Art' (E626).

   But the stance itself, which extends far beyond the arts and into
matters of intellectual, political and religious judgement, has got
that kind of cultural confidence and hostility to genteel hegemony
which we have found in the sectarian traditions of radical Dissent.
There is the abrupt dismissal of Bacon's *Essays* as 'Good Advice
for Satans Kingdom'; 'the Wisdom of this World is Foolishness
with God' (E609). When Bacon comments suavely that 'triumphs,

masks, feasts, weddings, funerals, capital executions, and such shews . . . are not to be neglected', Blake notes: 'Bacon supposes that the Dragon Beast & Harlot are worthy of a Place in the New Jerusalem' (E616). The oppositions proposed are between Caesar and Christ, or between Jesus and 'the Prince of darkness' who 'is a Gentleman & not a Man he is a Lord Chancellor' (E612). What belongs to Caesar is power, riches and war, and an attendant ideology which masks, apologises for and rationalises power or 'Satans Kingdom'. Hence there follows a profound and critical suspicion of classical learning, of Greek or Roman models in philosophy, politics or art, which are the innermost defences and ornaments of the polite culture. 'Moral Precepts' [i.e. the Moral Law] 'belong to Plato & Seneca & Nero' (E608); Bacon's references to Sylla, Caesar and Augustus are dismissed with the comment, 'Roman Villains' (E618); and, in his last year, annotating Thornton: 'The Greek & Roman Classics is the Antichrist' (E656). Thornton's God 'is just such a Tyrant as Augustus Caesar & is not this Good & Learned & Wise & Classical' (E658). As for the hegemonic rhetoric of his society, in terms of Constitution and Law, the judgement is explicit: 'All Penal Laws court Transgression & therefore are cruelty & Murder' (E607). And 'Satans Kingdom' is seen as of one piece, as a *systematic* order: the power and the ideology must be taken together. Those intellectuals and artists who are corrupted by patronage or who act as apologists for the *status quo* are doubly damned, for it is art's divine mission to be eternally at war with this Kingdom. On the title page of Reynold's *Works*: 'This Man was Hired to Depress Art' (E624). Blake frequently falls back upon abuse of 'hirelings' or 'Cunning Hired Knaves':

The Enquiry in England is not whether a Man has Talents. & Genius But whether he is Passive & Polite & a Virtuous Ass: & obedient to Noblemens Opinions in Art & Science. If he is; he is a Good Man: if Not he must be Starved. (E632)

But this situation is maintained also by the ideological defences of polite rational philosophy. Reynold's assertions are grounded upon Bacon, Locke, Newton and Burke, for whose works Blake feels 'Contempt & Abhorrence' since 'they mock Inspiration & Vison' (E650). This is the old antinomian antimony, but faith has been replaced (although not always) by inspiration, imagination or the poetic genius. These are engaged in eternal war with Satan's Kingdom, and that war is on every front: material, ideological, artistic, political. When Malone, introducing Reynolds, refers to England's 'unparalleled state of wealth and prosperity' (in 1798!) and ridicules the 'seditious declamations' of reformers, Blake comments: 'This Whole Book was Written to Serve Political Purposes' (E630). And, nearly thirty years later, he wrote on the title page of Thornton's new translation of the Lord's Prayer, 'I look upon this as a Most Malignant & Artful attack upon the Kingdom of Jesus By the Classical Learned' (E656).

Not many antinomians delivered such shrewd and accurate blows against the ideological defences of their society as did Blake. They preferred, in the eighteenth century, to disengage from the combat and to nurture a somewhat spiritually complacent faith. But it is their confident stance, their robust contempt for the ruling ideology, which was transmitted to Blake. And if we follow any of Blake's annotations closely, we are left in little doubt as to who is shallow. Examine the 'Annotations to Watson'. Who is shallow? Blake, or the utterly self-satisfied and intellectually complacent bishop, with his justifications for genocide ('The Word of God is in perfect harmony with his work; crying or smiling infants are subjected to death in both') and his bland composure: 'Kings and priests . . . never, I believe, did you any harm.' That the antinomian tradition had limitations is apparent; yet 'shallow' can scarcely be the right word for a tradition nurtured so long and so tenaciously, or for one so close to the impulse of John Milton and John Bunyan. By the end of the century, certainly, it was becoming cranky, esoteric or a mere family habit. Blake, himself almost certainly a child of the tradition, let his whole intellectual and imaginative genius play upon its detritus, recomposed some of its elements in new and more challenging forms, and redirected it forward to us.

APPENDIX I

The Muggletonian archive

I had been trying to track down the Muggletonian archive for a few years, when a correspondence about Muggletonian doctrine commenced in the *Times Literary Supplement* (see 7 March, 11 April, 1975). An observant and accurate historian, the Unitarian minister, the Revd Alexander Gordon, was permitted to visit the Church's reading room in 1869, and he published two valuable lectures[1] in which he described his findings. He also contributed informed entries on a number of Muggletonians to the DNB.[2] The meeting room was then in 7 New Street, Bishopsgate, where all the Church's papers and properties were kept. (The site was close to Walnut Street Yard, the Prophet's birthplace.) The trail remained warm until 1939, when it ran out. In about 1919 the meeting room was moved to 74 Worship Street (also in Bishopsgate) where a believer was installed as caretaker.[3]

The *TLS* correspondence enabled me to mention my searches and to ask readers for information. In a few days I received a message from a friend that she had been contacted by a Mr Johnson, whose father-in-law, Mr Philip Noakes, was 'the last Muggletonian'. A meeting was arranged: Mr Noakes was cautious but courteous, and an invitation to his home at Matfield near Tunbridge Wells in Kent followed, where Mr and Mrs Noakes received

---

[1] Alexander Gordon, *The Origin of the Muggletonians* (1869); *Ancient and Modern Muggletonians* (1870).

[2] Gordon's DNB entries, in addition to Muggleton and Reeve, include Birch, Claxton, Alexander Delamaine, Boyer Glover, Saddington and Tomkinson. These were among 778 entries he contributed to the DNB. Gordon was Principal of the Unitarian College, Manchester, from 1889 to 1911; H. McLachlan, *Alexander Gordon* (Manchester, 1932): private communication from the Revd F. Kenworthy, Principal of the College, 22 June 1965.

[3] Information from the late Philip Noakes. No. 7 New Street was 'destroyed by enemy action' in the Second World War, private communication from the Secretary, Bentworth (New Street) Limited, 2 June 1965.

me with warm hospitality. Mrs Noakes (while sympathetic) was not herself a believer, and it seemed that Mr Noakes was indeed the last Muggletonian.

It was a strange situation. Nr Noakes himself was the last repository of a 300-year-old tradition. He conversed with me freely about Muggletonian practices and doctrine, which had been carried down to him with a clarity (and, indeed, coherence) which reproduced their seventeenth-century origin. Mr Noakes frequently said: 'We believe' – and yet one could not point to another believer. There was absolutely nothing of the fanatic or crank in his manner. He was always quiet and concise in his explanations, and I quickly formed a respect for him. On his part he seemed to be pleased that there was a revival of interest in the faith and he did everything he could to help me.

I found out that the Church's archives had been in the upper floor of the meeting room at 74 Worship St, with the now elderly believer as caretaker. This house was fire-bombed in 1940 or 1941, and the caretaker moved out. Mr Noakes, who was a fruit farmer in Kent, and was one of the Church's three trustees, drove up to Covent Garden with a load of apples, and packed into more than eighty apple boxes all the archives of the church. He took these back to his farm, where they were again threatened by a V-bomb, and eventually the boxes were placed in storage in a Tunbridge Wells furniture depository.

However, Mr Noakes had preserved some of the most interesting documents in his own home. These included three large guard books with papers and correspondence of the London Church: (1) late seventeenth century to mid-eighteenth; (2) mid-eighteenth to early nineteenth; and (3) subsequently. With extraordinary goodwill and trust, he allowed me to carry these off for a while, to study and xerox. There were also a number of notebooks in which Muggletonian documents had been carefully transcribed by Mr Noakes and his father.[4] (Unfortunately, once transcribed, the originals were destroyed.)

The apple boxes? I did not get a chance to see these until a later visit. Mr Noakes and I spent a long afternoon in the furniture depository, where a somewhat grumpy staff had dragged all eighty-plus into view in a dimly lit store-room. We started with no. 1. It was wholly made up of nineteenth-century paper-covered reprints

[4] See William Lamont, 'The Muggletonian Archive' in *The World of the Muggletonians*.

of the works of Muggleton and Reeve. And so, on and on, for eighty boxes. Eventually at boxes 80–82 we struck oil. Eighteenth-century bindings appeared, and manuscripts, as well as holograph song-books. I confess that the light was so bad that, when we came to the last box, with trembling fingers I lit a match. I was rewarded by finding in front of me a manuscript by Lawrence Claxton (Clarkson). We managed to get these last three boxes back to Mr Noakes's house and to inspect them at more leisure. It seemed that all the manuscripts which Alexander Gordon had seen in the 1860s had been preserved.

My concern, of course, was to guide the archive to a national library. But here we met with a difficulty. Muggletonians eschewed evangelism unless by the printed word. It was in print that the faith must be preserved, and through which conversions might be made. Mr Noakes was willing to let the archive pass to a library, but on condition that the library housed also all the Muggletonian reprints and circulated libraries in the English-speaking world offering to supply copies. This proved to be too large a commitment for any library which I approached to accept.

I then departed for a year to teach in the United States (1976–7). On my return I learned with dismay that Mr Noakes had been seriously ill with angina: he was anxious to lodge the archive in a suitable library and was willing to forego his previous conditions. We approached the British Library which – after a little hesitation – agreed to purchase the archive.

The hesitation was about title: did Mr Noakes have title to dispose of the Church's property? It seemed that possession was nine points of the law. No other surviving member of the London church (or any other) could be found. The Church was never an incorporated body. Philip Noakes (then over seventy) was the last survivor of three Church Trustees. He himself was the descendant of well-known Muggletonian families – Noakes and Frost – Joseph and Isaac Frost being particularly active in the Church in the early nineteenth century.[5]

---

[5] Outstandingly active in the Church's affairs in the first half of the nineteenth century – scrutinising the archive, editing *Divine Songs* – Joseph and Isaac Frost were brass founders in Clerkenwell. Isaac Frost published in 1846 *Two Systems of Astronomy*, a literal portrayal of Muggletonian cosmology – a handsome example of early colour plates. The Frosts were perhaps associated with an Elias Noakes (also a Muggletonian) in their business in the early nineteenth century. James Frost's daughter, Florence Frost, married Frederick Noakes, Philip Noakes's father (Conversations with Philip Noakes, 1977).

That is how the archive came, in January 1978, to the British Library. Mr Noakes died less than two years later, and over three hundred years of direct transmission of a unique faith came to an end.

From internal evidence it seems that in 1772 the Church collected together all manuscripts and letters, as well as books, available, and from that time forward held them as Church records and library, in locked closets in the public houses where they met. In 1831 the entire collection was scrutinised very carefully by two leading Church members, Joseph and Isaac Frost, and they wrote on the covers annotations. As a result of their scrutiny a few hitherto unpublished letters of Muggleton and Reeve were published as *Supplement to the Book of Letters* (1831). The archive eventually was preserved in the reading room in 7 New Street, opened in May 1869. This was where Alexander Gordon saw it.

The British Library has arranged the archive in eighty-nine volumes, Add. MSS 60168–60256, to which some supplementary volumes of transcribed correspondence will subsequently be added. The series is divided into five parts: Letters, Add. MSS 60168–60183; Treatises, Add. MSS 60184–60206; Verse, Add. MSS 60207–60230; Accounts, 60231–60245; Printed Works, 60246–60256. In the 'Letters' will be found the contents of the three guard books which Mr Noakes loaned to me, at 60168–60170. This includes general church correspondence, including some letters exchanged with believers in Ireland, Connecticut, &c; material concerning internal church disputes, including the splits occasioned by James Birch and Martha Collier; and copies of matters of church concern. In preparing this book for the press I have in general relied on the xeroxes in my possession, but the cautious scholar will find most of my quotations in Add. MSS 60168 and 60169.

The 'Treatises' are mostly copies of works by Muggleton, Reeve, Claxton, Tomkinson, Saddington, and others: several of the works of Tomkinson and Arden Bonnell are unpublished.

The 'Verse' is made up in the main of the manuscript songbooks copied by believers in the eighteenth century. A standardised collection, dating perhaps from 1711, was entitled 'A Divine Garland of Spiritual Songs': to this subsequent believers made their additions, or compiled new selections altogether. These manuscript collections were perhaps replaced by the printed *Songs of Grateful Praise*

(?1790) – I have not seen a copy[6] – which, however, included only twenty-one songs and was replaced in 1829 by the very much fuller *Divine Songs of the Muggletonians* (228 songs collected by the industrious Joseph and Isaac Frost, which leaned heavily on mid-eighteenth-century and subsequent songs, and dropped some of the earlier ones). The manuscript collections therefore remain significant.

The 'Accounts' are accounts and include lists of members.

The 'Printed Works' include a few MS annotations of interest.

As I go through my files concerning this matter I am surprised to be reminded as to how much time and labour were expended in inspecting, recording and guiding the archive to its haven, and the formidable volume of correspondence generated. But all is sweetened by the recollection of the kindness shown to me by Mr and Mrs Noakes. It was indeed a privilege to have been taken into the confidence of 'the Last Muggletonian'.

---

[6] Its existence is recorded by Gordon, *Ancient and Modern Muggletonians*, pp. 44–5, and Joseph Smith, *Bibliotheca Anti-Quakeriana* (1873), p. 320.

APPENDIX 2

William Blake's mother

According to Bentley's authoritative *Blake Records*[1] and other sources William Blake's father and mother were married in St George's chapel, Hanover Square, on 15 October 1752, as 'James Blake and Catherine Harmitage'. An inspection of the register disclosed that the entry was undoubtedly Hermitage, and not Harmitage. (Extensive searches in sundry Westminster registers and indexes in fact turned up no Harmitages.) Catherine was then about thirty and James twenty-nine.[2]

The chapel at St George's, Mayfair, was a notorious bucket-shop for marriages, and convenient for couples who did not want to tangle with the Church of England. No licence, publication of banns or consent of parents were required: 6,000 marriages were registered between 1749 and 1753, and a critic commented that it 'constructed a very bishopric of revenue' from the fees. The facilities were advertised in the papers: 'The Marriages (together with a Licence on a Five Shilling Stamp and Certificate) are carried on for a guinea, as usual' (*London Gazette*, 12 January 1749). The chapel was brought under Church control in 1753.[3] There is an unexplained cross beside the names of James and Catherine. All that one can say is that the chapel was a place where radical dissenters, outside the Church, might obtain a quick marriage.

Catherine comes into the record out of obscurity. In fact she was the widow of Thomas Hermitage of 28 Broad Street, near Golden Square.[4] The rates on this property had been paid by — Armitage

[1] G.E. Bentley, *Blake Records*, p. 2.
[2] *Ibid.*, p. 47. The name is correctly recorded as Hermitage in H.M. Margoliouth, 'William Blake's Family', *N&Q*, Vol. 192 (1947), pp. 380–1.
[3] Margoliouth; George Clinch, *Mayfair and Belgravia* (1892), pp. 56–8.
[4] This appears from the will of Thomas Armitage of the parish of St James, Westminster, haberdasher and hosier, drawn 23 July 1751 and proved 27 November 1751 in PRO. P.C.C. Wills. This leaves, after several legacies, the residue of his estate to his wife, Catherine Armitage.

from 1748 to 1753,[5] and in the fiercely contested Westminster election of 1749 the poll-book shows Thomas Hermitage, of Broad Street, hosier, voting for the anti-Court candidate.[6] (Blake's father, James Blake of Glasshouse St, hosier, voted on the same side in the same poll.) Thomas Hermitage's will was proved in November 1751. The marriage of Catherine with James Blake took place eleven months later. It was a fortunate uniting of two businesses. James Blake had only recently completed his apprenticeship. The newly married couple moved into Broad Street in 1753, and (if Catherine was already there and paying the rates) perhaps earlier.

Not much can be found out about the Hermitage family, despite extensive searches.[7] Several Hermitages can be found in the parish registers of St James's, Westminster, between 1720 and 1750. It will be recalled that a George Hermitage has two songs in the *Divine Songs of the Muggletonians*, probably from the 1730s or 1740s. Could George have been Thomas's kin? George and Susannah Hermitage appear as parents of a child (Elizabeth) in the parish register in November 1742. If Muggletonians favoured endogamy Catherine's first husband, and herself, might have been of the faith?

[5] Bentley, *Blake Records*, pp. 551–2.
[6] Both the printed pollbook and MS poll are in Westminster Reference Library: *A Copy of the Poll for a Citizen for the City and Liberty of Westminster* (1749) and (MS) WR/PP (1749).
[7] I must thank Jean Haynes for genealogical assistance.

PART II

Human images

Introductory

In this part I will discuss some aspects of Blake's work, and the context of that work, in the years 1788 to 1794. In 1788 William and Catherine Blake were living in Central London, at 28 Poland Street (Soho), but in 1790 they moved south of the river to Hercules Buildings, Lambeth, where they stayed until 1800. Blake was busy engraving and writing. He worked as an engraver for (among others) Joseph Johnson, the bookseller and leading publisher of Radical Dissenting authors. But he did not aim at publication in the usual ways. In 1788 he commenced his 'illuminated works', in the form of relief etchings, and only a few copies of each were sold, among his patrons, friends and acquaintance. Catherine helped in the work, especially the colouring: each copy is unique, and sometimes (as with the *Songs*) the pages are in a different sequence. In 1788 also the Blakes appear to have become closely interested in the Swedenborgian New Jerusalem Church, although they soon became alienated from it. This is a theme of chapters 8, 9 and 10. In 1789 the *Songs of Innocence* were engraved and published although after 1794 they were usually issued bound together with the *Songs of Experience*. After the French Revolution Blake was probably drawn more closely into the Radical Dissenting circles which warmly supported it. In 1790 or 1791 he commenced a long poem, in prophetic mode, on *The French Revolution*, to be published by Joseph Johnson, but only the first book survives, in a set of page proofs. It presumably went unpublished and the project was discontinued. Blake did not attempt to employ normal publishing channels again.

That is a bald summary of a very active and productive life. These were also times of great excitement in London with the accelerating events in France, with the passionate debates provoked by Thomas Paine's *The Rights of Man* (part one, 1791; part two, 1792), and with the formation and rapid growth of the popular reform societies, culminating in the failed attempt of the government to convict the leaders of the London Corresponding Society for high treason in 1794.

After the Blakes broke with the Swedenborgians – the break is dramatised by the satirical and polemical critique, *The Marriage of Heaven and Hell* (published in 1793 although commenced in 1790) – it is not easy to place them in any church or group. Perhaps the experience extinguished Blake's appetite for 'joining'? There were numerous illuminist and millenarial circles in London which he could have entered, but there is no evidence to associate him with any.[1] All such circles were either swept by revolutionary enthusiasm in 1789–92, or, like the Swedenborgians or the groups around William Huntington (above, pp. 6–8), were thrown into controversy by the events in France and by Paine's *Rights of Man*.

There can be no doubt that Blake shared these enthusiasms. Alexander Gilchrist, his first biographer, who had the direct testimony of several of Blake's surviving acquaintances, had no hesitation in describing him as an ardent republican:

Down to his latest days Blake always avowed himself a 'Liberty Boy', a faithful 'Son of Liberty'[2] . . . He courageously donned the famous symbol of liberty and equality – the bonnet-rouge – in open day, and philosophically walked the streets with the same on his head.[3]

Gilchrist reports that after the days of terror in Paris in September 1792 Blake 'never wore the red cap again'. That is possible. But there was no reversal in his republican enthusiasm. This is testified by his writings and his art, as any close study shows.[4] Even Blake's trial for sedition in Sussex in 1803–4, which is sometimes treated as a literary humour, was a serious matter. No doubt the evidence

---

[1] See Iain McCalman's excellent study, 'The Infidel as Prophet: William Reid and Blakean radicalism' in *Historicising Blake*. For illuminist circles, see Clarke Garrett, *Respectable Folly: Millenarians and the French Revolution in France and England* (Baltimore, 1975), and J.F.C. Harrison, *The Second Coming*.

[2] There was in fact a 'Sons of Liberty' with a brief existence as a secession from the London Corresponding Society: see *Selections from the Papers of the London Corresponding Society*, ed. Mary Thale (Cambridge, 1983), index under 'reform societies'. But this is perhaps to take Blake's claims too literally.

[3] Alexander Gilchrist, *The Life of William Blake* (1907 edn), pp. 95–6. Gilchrist's widow, Anne, staunchly repeated this in her entry on Blake in DNB (1902). As to the *bonnet-rouge*, the normally reliable Bentley (*Blake Records*, p. 40, note 3) says 'Gilchrist got the colour wrong' and says it should have been a white hat. But the white hat was a symbol borrowed from Henry Hunt in the post-war agitations.

[4] Notably, of course, David Erdman's brilliant study, *Blake: Prophet against Empire*.

against him was perjured, with respect to the actual indictment. But it could have found its source in village gossip as to Blake's indiscretions. A careful watch was kept in these years upon reformers, especially in coastal districts, and men were jailed for utterances similar to those of which Blake was accused.[5] Blake had to thank his influential friends, like his patron, William Hayley, his excellent defence barrister, Samuel Rose, and perhaps his reputation in the village as an amiable eccentric, for his acquittal.

Undoubtedly Blake belongs with the Jacobin tendency among English reformers. He straddled two social worlds: that of intellectuals and artists, and that of tradesmen and artisans. In the first world, he was occasionally present at Joseph Johnson's weekly dinner parties, where he will have met Paine, Fuseli (already his friend), possibly Dr Priestley, no doubt Mary Wollstonecraft.[6] Yet his name has not been recorded among the active members of this circle's reform organisation, the Society for Constitutional Information. In the second world, no barrier would have prevented Blake from joining a division of the London Corresponding Society. In surviving division lists, while tradesmen and artisans are most numerous, occasional 'gentlemen' are present, as well as engravers, surgeons, booksellers, &c. Yet there is no William Blake in the lists that survive.[7] A Lambeth Association (where the Blakes lived) even rose to the dignity of having assigned to it as government spy the botanic printer to His Majesty: no doubt with such a patron he could scarcely refuse the assignment. But again there is no mention of Blake.[8]

However, it is not the intention of the present study to review the political and social associations of Blake. This has already been done by other scholars. My intention, rather, is to follow the intellectual routes by which (through Blake) the antinomian tradition

[5] For the trial, see Bentley, *Blake Records*, pp. 122–48. And see, for example, PRO KB11.61, Indictments 41 Geo. III, Hil. Kent; a Dartford coachmaker for saying 'Damn the King, and those who wear his livery.'
[6] For a judicious assessment of Blake's relations with Johnson and with the 'Paine set', see Erdman, *Blake: Prophet against Empire*, pp. 153–62.
[7] This is supported by my own searches in the Public Record Office, among Privy Council, Treasury Solicitor's and Home Office papers, as well as the searches of other scholars.
[8] Frederick Polydore Nadder: information, based on TS and PC records, kindly supplied by Dr Günther Lottes. Thomas Spence was a member of this Association. Dr Lottes adds (in a private communication) that if Blake had been a member this would almost certainly have been recorded, since the Association engaged in some histrionic drilling and was watched closely by government.

came to a conjunction with the Enlightenment and in particular with Jacobin thought, argued with it, and gave rise to the unique Blakean mutation.

Blake's consistently radical and antinomian stance persisted within large fluctuations in his preoccupations, in his optimism or pessimism as to the outcome of the revolutionary struggles of his own time (in France or in England), in his optimism or pessimism as to his own art, and in his relation to Painite or deist (and atheist) thought. In this relationship Blake was more influenced by the blunt, activist, iconoclastic thought of the popular reformers than he was by the thought of the *philosophes*. He was attracted by the French revolutionary and atheist thinker, C.F. Volney (see below, pp. 199–202) and repelled by Gibbon; and it would not be difficult to show that he was equally attracted by Paine and repelled by the hero of the intellectuals, the polite philosophical anarchist, William Godwin. The moment of Blake's greatest poetic achievement belonged exactly to this moment of extraordinary conjunction, at the time of the French Revolution, when that part of Enlightenment thought, represented by the blunt, humane, ultra-radicalism of Paine and Volney collided with an older antinomian tradition, co-existed fraternally in Blake's heart and argued matters out inside his head. This is the theme of chapters 11 and 12 and indeed of the whole of Part II. William Blake, the antinomian caught in the Enlightenment, should be our central thesis. Once this is understood, the rest falls into place. Moreover, the antinomian inheritance was not just some old baggage which could be discarded once he was enlightened. For it enabled Blake to question and to resist the simplicities of mechanical materialism and Lockeian epistemology, in which the revolutionary impulse was to founder. For in shedding the prohibitives of the Moral Law, Blake held fast to the affirmative: Thou Shalt Love. It is because this affirmative remains an essential need and quest of our own time that William Blake still speaks with such power to us.

CHAPTER 8

The New Jerusalem church

Until now we have been engaged in a conjectural history of ideas. In this part we can commence on firm ground at last, in April 1789, when the names of W. and C. Blake appear in a document of the Swedenborgian New Jerusalem Church. Now at last we know where to find Blake, on the eve of the French Revolution, as a Swedenborgian.

But as soon as we tread on this ground it begins to quake beneath us. David Erdman, in a rollicking polemic in 1953, utterly demolished the 'legend' of Blake's early Swedenborgianism;[1] and so effectively was it demolished that, until recently, scholars were discouraged from looking into the matter much further.[2] (They have, of course, examined, sometimes obsessively, Swedenborg's own writings for influences, sources, themes, but that is a different matter.) And much of what Erdman established cannot be controverted. It is scarcely possible that Blake's father could have been 'a Swedenborgian', Blake could not have written the song, 'The Divine Image', in 1789 while sitting in a church which was not opened until 1799, nor could his father and brother have studied books which were not published until after their deaths. But if we replace this legend within a careful context, we still may make something of it.

What we know about Blake's intellectual evolution is very little. We have his fooling passage of poetic autobiography addressed to his friend Flaxman in 1800; three of Swedenborg's works annotated by Blake; the signatures of the Blakes on the New Church docu-

---

[1] 'Blake's Early Swedenborgianism: a twentieth-century Legend', *Comparative Literature*, 5 (1953), pp. 247–57.
[2] A notable exception is the helpful article by Morton D. Paley, ' "A New Heaven is Begun": Blake and Swedenborgianism', *Blake: an Illustrated Quarterly*, 1979, 12, no. 2, pp. 64–90.

ment at the General Conference, at Easter, 13–17 April 1789: and one or two scraps of reminiscence. For the rest we must interpret the poet's own writings.

When Blake offered an intellectual autobiography to his friend, the sculptor and painter John Flaxman, in 1800, his c.v. did not come to a climax with a doctorate and the publication of his first learned articles. It was that of a self-educated seeker after truth:

> Now my lot in the Heavens is this, Milton lov'd me in
>   childhood & shew'd me his face.
> Ezra came with Isaiah the Prophet, but Shakespeare in riper
>   years gave me his hand:
> Paracelsus & Behmen appear'd to me, terrors appear'd in the
>   Heavens above
> And in Hell beneath, & a mighty & awful change threatened the
>   Earth.
> The American War began. All its dark horrors passed before my
>   face
> Across the Atlantic to France. Then the French Revolution
>   commenc'd in thick clouds. . . (E680)

This should not be read too literally. We are not to suppose that a formal education (Milton, the Old Testament, Shakespeare, Paracelsus, Boehme) was completed before the American War began. (It is difficult to detect any influence of Paracelsus or Boehme in Blake's early *Poetical Sketches* (1783) or *An Island in the Moon* (1784).) The syntax and thrust of the verse, which hurries us on, with a comma, from Behmen to 'terrors' and thence to 'horrors', suggests a preoccupation with Paracelsus and Boehme coincident with the 'mighty & awful change' signified by the passage of the American into the French Revolution. Blake is describing a single experience, made up of both spiritual and corporeal events, rather than a sequence of steps in time. And Flaxman, a Swedenborgian 'receiver', could be expected to understand the 'correspondence' by which the intellectual and historical events emblemised and echoed each other.[3]

Three of Swedenborg's works were annotated by Blake, probably in 1788–90. The annotations show a distinct modification in Blake's response to Swedenborg. His annotations to *Heaven and Hell* (1784) are desultory and languid. His annotations to *Divine Love*

[3] It might, however, be significant that Blake in 1800, did not include Swedenborg in his list.

and Divine Wisdom (1788) suggest a thorough-going and sympathetic scrutiny, with Swedenborg's doctrines set against Blake's own already developed and strongly formed system. His annotations to the *Divine Providence* (1790) suggest ridicule or indignant rejection.[4] There is a suggestion of a rapid passage through the Swedenborgian influence, to which, however, in later years he may have returned.[5] In the same years he annotated Lavater's *Aphorisms on Man* (1789) in great detail.

Blake appears to have liked Lavater more than he liked Swedenborg, and where he most approved its 'true Christian philosophy' was at those points where Lavater emphasised humanity's 'divine' attributes. 'Man', Blake exclaimed at one point, 'is either the ark of God or a phantom of the earth and of the water' (E585). But he gave, for the time, the benefit of the doubt to Swedenborg. The Swedish seer moves through so many convolutions, so many correspondences and self-contradictions, that it was difficult for Blake to decide. When, shortly afterwards, he annotated his *Divine Providence* he had decided very firmly *against*: 'Cursed Folly', 'Lies & Priestcraft', 'Predestination'. If one part of man was the dispersal of the divine essence, how could his end be predestined? Moreover, Blake was watching like a hawk every reference to 'truth' and the 'understanding'. The Reason which Blake suspected had some affinity with what he was defining at the same time in *There is No Natural Religion* as 'natural or organic thoughts'. In opposition to Locke (and all that Blake was later to make him and Newton responsible for) Blake proposed that 'naturally' man 'is only a natural organ subject to Sense'; but 'none could have other than natural or organic thoughts if he had none but organic perceptions' (E1–3). Without divine spirit or 'poetic genius' in humanity, expressed in the affections and not in the understanding, man could never transcend his own material nature. Swedenborg's vaporous exegesis appeared at times to confirm Blake's view and won his approval: where the seer spoke of Divine Love in some higher part

[4] See Erdman, 'Blake's Early Swedenborgianism', pp. 139–46. Also Morton D. Paley, *Blake and Swedenborgianism*, pp. 17–21.
[5] Garth Wilkinson recorded that Blake's friend and patron, C.A. Tulk, was told by Blake that 'he had two different stages; one in which he liked Swedenborg's writings, and one in which he disliked them. The second was a state of pride in himself, and then they were distasteful to him. The first was a state of humility, in which he received and accepted Swedenborg'; James Spilling, 'Blake the Visionary', *New Church Magazine*, May 1887, p. 210.

of the hierarchy to Understanding, or where he said that it was impossible for man 'from a *merely natural* Idea' to 'comprehend that the Divine is every where', Blake underscored or wrote: 'Mark this.' But he was clearly thinking at the same time of recent disputes 'in the society', where some 'absurd' and 'perverse' members (moreover, 'mercenary & worldly' ones) were denying the possibility of visions and even asserting that 'love recieves influx through understand^g' (E596, 598).

What is apparent is that Blake has brought to both Lavater and Swedenborg an advanced and ordered system of thought. There is no conversion here: it is a strict examination. This system Blake had adopted, or evolved for himself, probably by 1788. But what about his fellow Swedenborgians? Admirers and receivers of Swedenborg had been corresponding and grouping in the 1780s. By the end of the decade several tendencies were evident. A strong tendency remained committed to working within the Church of England. A philosophically minded group gathered around the Revd Jacob Duché, and eventually evolved into the Theosophical Society, a group which Blake could have sometimes attended.[6] After failing to convince their colleagues who were dedicated to the permeation of the Established Church, Robert Hindmarsh and a group of supporters decided to go ahead and inaugurate a separatist New Jerusalem Church in May 1787.[7] This Church immediately began to enrol members. In December 1788 this group sent around 500 copies of a circular letter calling a first general conference of the New Church for the following April: the tone of the letter was welcoming:

Any person within the circle of your acquaintance, whom you know to be a Lover of the Truths contained in the Theological Writings of Emanuel Swedenborg, and friendly to the formation of a New Church . . . you are at Liberty also to invite.[8]

---

[6] Morton D. Paley, 'Blake and Swedenborgianism', p. 16; Charles Higham, 'The Reverend Jacob Duché, His Later Life and Ministry in England', *New Church Review*, 22 (1915); Robert Hindmarsh, *Rise and Progress of the New Jerusalem Church* (1861), pp. 40–1; Erdman, pp. 11–12, note 19; Clarke Garret, 'Swedenborg and the mystical enlightenment in late eighteenth-century England', *Journal of the History of Ideas*, 1984.

[7] Thomas Robinson, *A Remembrancer and Record* (Manchester, 1864), pp. 86–9. The Church was preceded by a 'Society for Promoting the Heavenly Doctrines of the New Jerusalem Church', meeting in the Middle Temple, from which a minority, led by Hindmarsh, seceded to form the New Church. This was formally named the 'New Church' in May 1788: *Minute Book of the Society* in New Church Library and Archives.

[8] Reprint of circular letter in Swedenborgian Society archive, H25.

What the attenders were called upon to endorse at the conference itself was somewhat stricter and more doctrinal than that. They were required to assent to thirty-two propositions, which included the repudiation of the Old Church, a renunciation of the Trinity (Jesus Christ is 'the only God') and various proposals as to the forms and conduct of the New Church.[9] These propositions were subscribed to by seventy-seven signatories, the attenders at the conference. There are then added eighteen further signatures, including those of W. and C. Blake. A comparison of the signatures with the Minutes of the Great Eastcheap church shows that the overwhelming majority of the seventy-seven were already admitted as church members (fifty-six or more), while not one of the subsequent eighteen had been so admitted, in the period May 1787 to April 1788. The Blakes therefore attended as sympathisers, not as members.[10] A subsequent circular letter to 'all lovers of Truth', transmitting the resolutions, claimed that there was 'not a single dissentient Voice among us'.[11] Thus we know that Blake, at Easter 1789, was willing to assent to a large mouthful of Swedenborgian doctrine.

To read through more than a few pages of Emmanuel Swedenborg's writings induces such mental tedium that few students of Blake succeed in conveying more than the same tedium in their commentaries. It is difficult to understand what a poet with an imagination so concrete could have made of a language which dissolves whatever it touches into abstractions. A more concentrated attention reveals that Blake was reading into Swedenborg opinions which he already held and which he seemed to glimpse through hazes which arose probably from similar Behmenist fires. What Swedenborg tried to do was to bring this extraordinary and contradictory group of ideas (some from Behmenist sources) within a polite and rationalised framework.[12]

---

[9] These thirty-two proposals are reproduced in the *Minutes of the First Seven Sessions of the New Church* (1885). See also Bentley, *William Blake*, pp. 35–7. However, a markedly different and doctrinally much stricter set of forty-two propositions is reproduced in P.F. Gosse, *Portefamille d'un Ancien Typographe* (Le Haye, 1824). These were perhaps sent out with the original circular letter?

[10] *Minutes.* If the Blakes formally joined the Church it will have been during the period when the pages have been cut out of the Minutes.

[11] Gosse. The circular was signed by Swedenborgian heavyweights – Augustus Nordenskjöld and C.B. Wadstrom (from Sweden), Henry Peckitt, Henry Servanté, Benedict Chastanier, J.A. Tulk, but not by Robert Hindmarsh.

[12] Swedenborg had not only read Boehme in his youth but also Pordage and Jane Lead; C.W. Schneider, *Nachricht von der so-genannten neuen Kirche, oder dem neuen Jerusalem* (Weimar,

The decline, simply in terms of literary exuberance, from the seventeenth-century antinomians is discouraging. The direct influence of these writings upon Blake was slight, except (as in *The Marriage of Heaven and Hell*) through opposition. At most he was confirmed in the mental style of thinking in 'correspondences' (but this, under other names, is of the very nature of poetry); he was encouraged to speak of objectifying his insights as visions or as conversations with spirits: and he was confirmed in a mode which enabled him to read the Bible as myth or as parable. Indeed, this was singled out for particular note at the beginning of an account of the principal doctrines of the New Church. Swedenborg—

points out an intire and singular way of reconciling the apparent contradictions in scripture, by distinguishing between two kinds of truth, namely, genuine and apparent. He maintains that the holy scripture, as well as every thing in nature, is resolvable into one or other of these two kinds of truth. Thus, when it is said, that the sun rises or sets, this is only an apparent truth, as the genuine truth is, that the earth revolves around its own axis[13] . . . Just so (says Swedenborg) it is with the Scriptures . . . Thus, when it is said, that God is angry, and revengeful, that he punishes and casts into hell, we are to understand that it is man who brings punishment on himself, and casts himself into hell. . .[14]

If the Blakes were prepared to indicate support for the New Church in 1789, this signified not only a general support for Swedenborg's writings but also a commitment to working with fellow Swedenborgians in promoting a new church. We have perhaps paid too much attention to the writings, too little to their interpreters and to the notion of such a 'church'. The old seer had spent his last months in England, where he had died at his lodgings in 1785.[15] In addition to Swedenborg's published works which were steadily undergoing translation into English, the seer had left a heap of manuscripts, and these included a 'spiritual diary' in Latin, a copy of which was brought from Sweden by C.B. Wadstrom in 1787 and left in the hands of a disciple named Benedict Chastanier,

1789), pp. 26–8. I am indebted to Dr Hans Medick for a sight of this rare item. In addition, according to Walton, Swedenborg had read Reeve and Muggleton, as well as William Law; C. Walton, *Notes and Materials for a Biography of William Law*, p. 158. See also anon. [B. Chastanier], *Tableau Analytique et Raisoné de la Doctrine Céléste de L'Eglise de la Nouvelle Jerusalem* (1786), p. 40n.

[13] Blake inverts this in *Milton*, 1 (E126, lines 15–16).

[14] *New-Jerusalem Magazine* (1790), pp. 102–3.

[15] Anon., *Remarks on the Assertions of the Author of the Memoirs of Jacobinism respecting the Character of Swedenborg* (Philadelphia, 1800), p. 11.

a French surgeon who had emigrated to England in 1763 and who formed a centre of international communication.[16]

The Church was a gathering-ground for a miscellany of seekers after mystic experiences, Behmenists, Philadelphians, Rosicrucians, masons, enthusiasts for mesmerism and magnetism, and after the initial euphoria of the founding conference, different tendencies at once revealed themselves. What was going on in these early years has been seriously obscured in orthodox Swedenborgian apologetics, especially those which derive from Robert Hindmarsh, who was intent upon presenting an apostolic succession descending from his own mysterious derivation of the power to ordain priests as a result of a lottery. Indeed, the closer one gets to the actual record the more Hindmarsh's *Rise and Progress of the New Jerusalem Church* appears to merit as much and as little credence as Stalin's *Short History of the CPSU(B)*. If there had been a Trotsky in that small congregation in 1789 – if Blake had been that Trotsky – his name would certainly have been expunged from the record. Indeed, the critical pages for the critical period (May 1789 to April 1790) were cut out of the Minute Book of the Society (or Church) meeting in Great Eastcheap. The annual conferences continued (a federal occasion) but in 1792 two rival sets of Minutes of the conference were issued, and in 1793 rival conferences were held.[17]

The most forceful evangelist for the New Church was undoubtedly Robert Hindmarsh, the son of a Methodist minister, James, who also joined the work. A printer, he kept himself busy in both spiritual and corporeal ways. In the apt characterisation of Swedenborg's biographer, William White, 'to him the New Jeru-

---

[16] The spiritual diary was also known as 'Memorabilia', and Chastanier translated a few 'memorable relations' from it for the Swedenborgian journals; see below, p. 141: James Hyde, *A Bibliography of the Works of Emmanuel Swedenborg* (1906), pp. 118–19. Chastanier gives a few biographical reminiscences in an eccentric pamphlet, *A Word of Advice to a Benighted World* (1795). I am grateful to the Royal Library of Stockholm for the sight of a copy, and to Professor Morton Paley for obtaining this for me. The *Prospectus* for the *New-Jerusalem Magazine* (British Library press-mark, 823c1(3)), to be edited by Henry Servanté and Chastanier claims that one of the editors 'is the Possessor of all the Original Manuscripts of Emmanuel Swedenborg, now in Stockholm', and that he had established the legal right to these copies. See also James Hyde, 'Chastanier and the Illuminati of Avignon', *New-Church Review* (Boston, Mass.), 14, 1907, pp. 181–205.

[17] Swedenborgian scholars corrected much of the record subsequently in their journals and other publications, drawn upon below. The most substantial independent study of the early church is Peter J. Lineham, 'The English Swedenborgians, 1770–1840' (University of Sussex, Ph.D. thesis, 1978). Also Alexander J. Morley, 'The Politics of Prophecy: William Blake's early Swedenborgianism' (Queen's University, Ontario, M.A. dissertation, 1991).

salem was no mystic city, but a sort of New Clerkenwell. It was a shop for the sale of theological notions warranted fresh from Heaven.'[18]

The Church at Great Eastcheap grew rapidly. At least one hundred members were admitted (by the unanimous voice of the members) up to the point in April 1789 when the Minutes are torn out. One knows from other sources that the members included a few gentry, among them J.A. Tulk, the father of Blake's patron, C.A. Tulk, former ministers of other persuasions (like James Hindmarsh) and surgeons and professional men. In a few cases the Minutes give occupations of new members – two booksellers, two tobacconists, a carver and gilder, chemist, cooper, druggist, enameller, letter carrier, musical instrument maker, shoemaker, smith, watchmaker, and often also their wives. As Robert Southey was to note, 'Few or none of the congregation belonged to the lower classes, they seemed to be chiefly respectable tradesmen.'[19] Over the door of the Church's rented premises in Great Eastcheap was posted the words 'Nunc Licet' (It is now allowable). This presumably was founded upon Swedenborg's claim (adopted as article thirty-three on the foundation of the New Church)–

That now it is allowable to enter intellectually into the Mysteries of Faith, contrary to the ruling Maxim in the Old Church, that the Understanding is to be kept bound under Obedience to Faith.[20]

What happened next is remarkably obscure. (This is where the pages of the Minutes have gone.) There was a thundering row and probably two or three different rows. First sex and then the French Revolution reared their ugly heads. After many solemn meetings, the Church 'withdrew herself' from six members, and these six included Robert Hindmarsh himself, as well as the French emigré and long-standing receiver, Henry Servanté, and two prominent Swedish enthusiasts, Augustus Nordenskjöld and C.B. Wadstrom.[21] One issue turned upon authorised and unauthorised ver-

[18] William White, *Emmanuel Swedenborg* (1867), Vol. II, p. 612.
[19] Robert Southey, ('Don Manuel Alvarez Espriella'), *Letters from England* (1814), Vol. III, p. 113.
[20] P. F. Gosse, *Portefamille*, article 33. The authorities cited are Swedenborg's *True Christian Religion*, Nos. 185 & 508. The *New-Jerusalem Magazine* (1789) carried 'NUNC LICET' on its first page, and (number 2) surrounded the words in a circlet of roses.
[21] Carl T. Odhner, *Robert Hindmarsh* (Philadelphia, 1895), p. 26, drawing upon the recollections of an early Church member, the Revd Manoah Sibley, *An Address to the Society of the New Church meeting in Friar Street, near Ludgate Hill, London* (1839).

sions of the prophet's *Conjugal Love*. The authorised version of this swimmy vision of Swedenborg's, which did not appear until 1794, could not have offended the strictest Elder of the Kirk. But there had been much discussion and piecemeal publication in the previous five years. Chastanier's earlier versions had an imagery more explicit and more sexy: some passages inserted in the *New Magazine of Knowledge Concerning Heaven and Hell* (1791) described the nakedness of angels who 'in bed . . . lie copulated as they were created, and thus they sleep. . .' These passages (Chastanier commented) and the explicit sexuality of heaven gave 'offence'.[22]

The offence had been severe. For this and previous publications and debates had been the apparent occasion for the Church withdrawing itself from six leading members. I say 'apparent' because the official record of any organisation is usually the smoke and not the fire: people seize on an issue and formulate rules and resolutions as a pretext for fighting out ulterior (but often unstated) issues. Some subsequent accounts suggest that what were at issue were not theological views but sexual practices. When a version of Swedenborg's *The Delights of Wisdom respecting Conjugal Love* was published in 1790[23] it was felt necessary to preface it with cautions against 'that dangerous and Anti-Christian Doctrine of a plurality of wives, which has lately been propagated. . .' A Church veteran recalled, sixty years later, that there was advocacy of the views that bachelors might take mistresses, and those receivers with 'disharmonious' marriages whose wives rejected the New Age might dismiss their wives and take concubines. 'I forget', this aged member wrote, 'whether or not the wife was to have the same privilege.'[24] This is a familiar area of male amnesia. But our loyal veteran, Mr Hawkins, promptly continued to reassure the faithful: 'I do not recollect any case where the notion was acted on.' However, other veterans were around to question his account. Dr Bateman, who had been doctor to both Hindmarsh and Sibley, reaffirmed that 'some of the early receivers' viewed Swedenborg's doctrines 'from an unchaste ground', and Elihu Rich affirmed that it was 'well known' to members that the matter had not stopped

---

[22] Vol. II, pp. 193–6, 248. A note in the Swedenborgian Society's copy of the *New Magazine* identifies the translator of the offending passage as J.A. Tulk.

[23] This was a publication of the London Universal Society, for which see below. A copy is bound in with the *New-Jerusalem Magazine*, as a supplement, Brit. Lib. press-mark C110d.7.

[24] John Isaac Hawkins in *New Church Repository* (NY), 1853, pp. 143–4.

short at theory: such sexual evils 'really existed at a period a little later'.[25] Indeed, Augustus Nordenskjöld, the author of an ambitious plan for the establishment of the New Jerusalem – a plan which made much of these unusual doctrines on marriage[26] – was himself accused of '*unchaste* conduct during his stay in Manchester . . . such as no New Churchman could overlook'.[27] Manoah Sibley, one of the first New Church ministers, went so far as to recall, forty years later, that in 1789 'the floodgates of immorality were in danger of being thrown open'.[28]

The supposed 'heresy' was in fact no heresy, for Swedenborg at one time or another advocated most of these views and, indeed, was an arrant male chauvinist. He condoned fornication by those who 'cannot as yet enter into marriage, and, from their passion for the sex, cannot moderate their desires', so long as they 'limit the vague love of the sex to one mistress'. But not with a virgin nor a married woman, and with no promise of marriage. He did endorse separation from a wife who was a non-receiver, and engaging 'a woman in her stead as a bed associate'. And Mr Hawkins's uncertainty can be clearly answered. This indulgence was granted only to men, 'but *not under any circumstances* is a corresponding indulgence granted to women'. The reason (explained Swedenborg) is that 'with men is the love of the sex in general, but with women the love *of one of the sex*'. 'The male sex', as is well known, 'has stimulations which actually kindle and inflame, but which is not the case with the female sex.' In short, some men might be 'driven so strongly by the inborn *amor sexus* they cannot contain themselves'.[29]

The chance survival of a few letters affords us a glimpse into the other side of such a situation of marital disharmony. Mary Pratt was an earnest Philadelphian and mystic seeker, and in January 1792 she was writing to her spiritual adviser, Thomas Langcake,

My husband is a strenuous follower of the visionary Swedenborg, and as the writings of the Baron militate against the pure doctrine and experience

[25] Dr Henry Bateman, *ibid.*, pp. 144–5; Elihu Rich, *ibid.*, p. 542.
[26] For Nordenskjöld's plan, see Morton Paley, *Blake and Swedenborgianism*, pp. 22–4. In general Paley and Peter Lineham, *The English Swedenborgians*, have excellent accounts of these early disputes.
[27] R.L. Tafel, *Documents concerning The Life and Character of Emmanuel Swedenborg* (1877), Vol. II, p. 807.
[28] C.T. Odhner, *Robert Hindmarsh*, p. 26.
[29] Tafel, Vol. II, pp. 1299–1304; W. White, *Emmanuel Swedenborg* (2nd edn, 1868), pp. 559–62; Odhner, *Robert Hindmarsh*, pp. 27–30.

of God manifested in the flesh, I have no fellowship with my partner in religion; nay I have been most cruelly treated by him, for my progress in the supercelestial life.

Mr Pratt, a builder and a relative of Lord Camden, can be identified as a contributor to the *Magazine of Knowledge concerning Heaven and Hell* under the guise of 'Ignoramus'. That the vibrations of this marriage were not wholly harmonious may be inferred if we scan the lucubrations of Ignoramus on 'the Lord's Maternal Humanity'–

The Lord was absolutely born as another man, being born of a woman, consequently inherited every evil and false hereditarily from his mother . . . His conception being from the Father, the being, the esse, the life of the Lord was Jehovah; but the recipient human form was from Mary, therefore his soul being Jehovah, could not possibly have the least shadow of evil; but in the humanity he received from Mary, was the recipient form of every evil then existing. . .[30]

Such profoundly anti-feminine views (which were indeed those of Swedenborg also and which perhaps influenced Blake's strange poem 'To Tirzah' (see below, p. 149)) may have contributed towards his wife, Mary's, search for solace not only in 'the supercelestial life' but also in communion with a certain 'Mr X':

I love and esteem Mr X; indeed he is the only person I have any fellowship with; and although our experience differs, yet he is pressing after the prize in earnest, through many difficulties both inward and outward.[31]

Scholars have with good reason tried to puzzle out where the Blakes may have been during these disputes in the early Church. It might seem that Swedenborg's teachings, and Nordenskjöld's plan, gave some licence to the old antinomian heresy of 'free love'. And in any event, Blake, who had recently annotated Lavater: 'They suppose that Womans Love is Sin, in consequence all the Loves and Graces with them are Sin', and who, in two years' time, was to write the *Visions of the Daughters of Albion*, with its explicit scenes of 'happy copulation', might seem to be on the side of the sexual liberation party. And there is even an oral tradition which

---

[30] Vol. II, p. 311. Ignoramus is identified as Pratt in pencil on the end-paper to my own copy (Vol. I) of the *Magazine*.

[31] Dr Williams's Library, MS 1.1.43. Mary Pratt added (14 October 1792) 'I have a persecuting husband and an infamous son, who is allowed plenty of money, while I am dealt with like Hagar the Ismailite – kept without a shilling.'

suggests that Blake meditated the taking of a concubine, to Catherine's distress.[32]

But it may not be so simple, and I suspect that the Blakes took neither side in the dispute. For as soon as the 'heretics' were excluded it would seem that dissension broke out among themselves. Some met in August 1789 to form a new society, 'The Universal Society for Promotion of the New Jerusalem Church'. This society was clearly prosecuting the old dispute. Its first resolution declared that –

the Truths contained in the Treatise of Conjugal Love . . . ought to be regarded . . . as the chief Jewel, support and Basis of the New Church, the fundamental Love of all Celestial, Spiritual and Natural Love. . .

These truths must be 'fully received' before any Society could be formed on genuine principles. But this 'chief Jewel' (it seems) was to be understood only in its spiritual sense, for members of the Society were also strictly instructed to keep the Ten Commandments. The Society also promised a speedy and accurate translation of the Treatise on Conjugal Love.[33]

The Secretary of the Universal Society was Henry Servanté, with J.A. Tulk, Chastanier and the two Swedish enthusiasts, Nordenskjöld and Wadstrom in support. The latter two were chiefly responsible for committing the Society to a rather grand project which no doubt had an influence on Blake's imagination: the plan to establish 'a Free Community on the Coast of Africa, on the Principles of the New Church'.[34] This plan was pursued with energy, the King was petitioned for his support and protection, Sierra Leone was selected, and in 1791 Nordenskjöld died pursuing rumours of an African Swedenborgian following.[35]

It is important to note that Robert Hindmarsh was not of the Universal Society. His objective remained, steadily, the recapture of the original Society at Great Eastcheap. This is emphasised by the fact that 1790 saw the publication of two Swedenborgian journals in London. The first, *The New-Jerusalem Magazine*, was the

---

[32] Mona Wilson, *The Life of William Blake* (1971 edn), p. 72.
[33] Constitution of 'the Universal London Society for Promotion of the New-Jerusalem Church', Swedenborg Society archive, H24.
[34] *Ibid.*, resolutions 12 and 13.
[35] See Paley, 'Blake and Swedenborgianism', Appendix A.

organ of the Universal Society. It ran for only six monthly numbers, from January to June, when it folded for lack of support.[36]
Its editor was Servanté, J.A. Tulk its part-owner, and Chastanier
passed on to the journal some unpublished passages from
Swedenborg. Against this threat to his hegemony, Hindmarsh
exerted his full energies as official Printer, not only to Swedenborg
but also to His Royal Highness the Prince of Wales. Expending
100 guineas in advertising, and issuing 50,000 handbills, he
launched *The New Magazine of Knowledge Concerning Heaven and Hell*,
in March 1790. This ran until October 1791, in twenty numbers,
and Hindmarsh was the sole editor.[37] When Servanté's journal
collapsed, a somewhat irritable Chastanier returned to Hindmarsh's correspondence columns.

Where in all this do we find the Blakes? There are no substantial
clues. But we can at least show that Blake was probably reading
both of these journals. I have a number of instances of this, which
it would be tedious to set forth in detail. We must be content now
with a blunt demonstration.

The New-Jerusalem Magazine. The magazine published in its first
two numbers five 'memorable relations', translated from a manuscript copy 'transmitted to us from Sweden'. The translation was
presumably Chastanier's. In the first memorable fancy a 'satan'
suddenly appears:

All Satans are merely natural, and can reason acutely, but from the
fallacies of the senses; for which reason they see falses as truths . . . This
Satan, when he came in view, appeared at first with a white living face,
afterwards with a dead pale face, and, lastly, with a black infernal face.

It would seem that Blake had this in mind, and was mocking it,
in his last 'memorable fancy' in *The Marriage of Heaven and Hell*
where an Angel is challenged by a Devil: 'The Angel hearing this
became almost blue but mastering himself grew yellow, & at last
white pink & smiling. . .' (Plate 23, E42). The reversal is a characteristic trick of Blake's as is the reversal of devils and angels.
Swedenborg's memorable fancy was not republished for fifty

---

[36] One thousand copies monthly were printed, but only half were sold, and fewer paid for:
New-Jerusalem Magazine, p. 255.
[37] Hindmarsh, *Rise and Progress*, pp. 108–9. When the *New Magazine* ended it was followed
by a *New-Jerusalem Journal* – also a Hindmarsh production – in 1792.

years.[38] I think it is clear enough that Blake was reading this journal.

The New Magazine of Knowledge Concerning Heaven and Hell. The example here is not so conclusive, since alternative sources can be found. But if Blake was reading it he cannot have overlooked the publication in the first three numbers, in three instalments, of J.P. Foersch's 'Natural History of the BOHON-UPAS, or POISON-TREE of the Island of JAVA'. This grisly account concluded that the Poison Tree may be called 'the *Tree of Death*, originating in *Hell*'. It is not likely to have contributed anything to Blake except the title of his 'Song of Experience'.[39] More convincing evidence might be found in the general discourse of the magazine, which touched on so many of Blake's preoccupations.

Meanwhile, apart from publishing, what else was Hindmarsh doing? He was not the man to suffer tamely the humiliation of being expelled from a Church which he had founded. Defeated on a matter of spiritual doctrine, he found a corporeal means of redress. He went to the landlord of the Church's premises in Great Eastcheap, and talked him into making him the sole tenant. He then descended on the astonished congregation and announced that they must either accept his doctrines and his form of church government or leave. Most of them left, in May 1792, and found a new temporary abode for New Jerusalem in Store Street, Tottenham Court Road.[40] Soon after the torn-out pages of the Eastcheap Minute Book resume, Hindmarsh was back there with a slender and disciplined congregation.

The dissensions, on this occasion, although they turned upon formal questions of church government, had a political dimension. None of the leading church members who survived to later years to write the history of the Church were of a radical or revolutionary persuasion. Chastanier who, on other counts, might have been close to Blake's positions, could only see (in 1792) that France was distracted by 'a spirit of mad philosophy'.[41] But clearly some

[38] Chastanier also called the memorable relations Swedenborg's 'Spiritual Diary'. For the complicated bibliography, see R.L. Tafel, *Emmanuel Swedenborg*, Vol. II, pp. 807–8, 1002; James Hyde, *A Bibliography*, pp. 118–19; *New-Church Review*, 1907, p. 441.

[39] Blake changed the title to 'A Poison Tree' from the advanced draft in the notebooks where it was 'Christian Forbearance'. *The Notebook of William Blake* (Oxford, 1973), ed. David V. Erdman, p. 114 reversed.

[40] Thomas Robinson, *A Remembrancer*, pp. 95–6, 113; Walter Wilson, *History and Antiquities of Dissenting Churches*, pp. 170–1.

[41] *New-Jerusalem Journal*, 1792, Vol. I, pp. 367–70.

members of the Great Eastcheap flock were touched by the democratic upsurge of those years. Matters came to a crisis, not in
terms of political issues, but on questions of Church discipline and
government. One point is overwhelmingly clear: Robert Hindmarsh himself was an ultra-conservative, desperately trying to
bring the movement under discipline and hierarchical control. He
advocated an episcopal (indeed papal) form of government, with
the power to ordain priests derivative from his own supposed
authority.[42] Somehow or other he managed to dominate the Second
Annual (federal) Conference of the Church in 1790, but his authority was rejected at the Third Annual Conference in April 1791.
This conference accepted several priests already ordained, but
insisted that in future no priests should be ordained without the
recommendation of the society to which they belonged and the
approbation of the General Conference. Hindmarsh and his clique
of self-appointed priests insisted that the power of ordination
should remain with them. In opposition to this, a resolution was
passed to put the clergy 'on an equal footing' with the laity.
Whether ministers would be allowed salaries was questioned.[43]

Hindmarsh returned to the offensive at the Fourth Annual Conference (1792), proposing an elaborate priestly form of government,
with 'one visible Official Head' (himself or his father) rather than
'the Votes of the People at large'. Hindmarsh's opposition to more
democratic forms of Church government was explicitly political:
he observed the duty incumbent upon all in the 'present critical
moment, when the Principles of Infidelity and Democracy was
Spreading abroad' to stand forward for the Constitution and
Order.[44] And he read to the conference a declaration of solemn
disapprobation of republican or democratical principles. It was his
big throw and he lost: the conference rejected his proposals. But
the Printer to the Prince of Wales was not so easily to be beaten.
He printed a rival version of the conference Minutes, enlarging

[42] On the Church's foundation leading members drew lots for the power to ordain: Robert
Hindmarsh drew a ticket mysteriously marked 'Ordain'. Subsequently he placed his
name at the head of documents and added: '*Ordained by the Divine Auspices of the Lord*',
Thomas Robinson, pp. 137–8. For Hindmarsh's version, see his *Rise and Progress*, pp. 69–
71.
[43] *Ibid.*, pp. 95–8; *Minutes of the First Seven Sessions of the General Conference of the New Church*
(1885).
[44] On the revolutionary sympathies of some early Swedenborgians, see Lineham, *The English
Swedenborgians*, pp. 268–82. C.F. Nordenskjöld translated Paine's *Rights of Man* into
Swedish.

upon his own position. He repeated his objection to the appointment of ministers 'by popular Elections'. Authority is the Lord's,
and is delegated to Kings and Ministers, who 'represent the Lord,
and not the People'. Appointment to offices in Church or State 'by
the popular Voice is so much like . . . atheistical Doctrine', and it
was 'absurdity to say that the Sheep have the Right and Power of
chusing and dismissing their Shepherd'. In 1793 there were rival
annual conferences: the Fifth (meeting in Birmingham) and a rump
meeting in London under Hindmarsh. Thereafter no more conferences were held until 1897, although Hindmarsh continued for
several years to meet with a small group of devotees to his episcopalian regime.[45]

Thus the founding five years of the Church were full of dissension. And we still have not placed Blake within this. Perhaps the
nearest we may get to a comment on the whole episode, as the
permissive 'Nunc Licet' gave way to Hindmarsh's priesthood, is
in the Song of Experience, 'The Garden of Love':

> I went to the Garden of Love,
> And saw what I never had seen:
> A chapel was built in the midst,
> Where I used to play on the green.
>
> And the gates of this Chapel were shut,
> And Thou shalt not. writ over the the door;
> So I turn'd to the Garden of Love,
> That so many sweet flowers bore,
>
> And I saw it was filled with graves,
> And tomb-stones where flowers should be:
> And Priests in black gowns, were walking their rounds,
> And binding with briars, my joys & desires.   (E26)

One possible link with Blake is suggested by a strange half-
serious, half-satirical proof of 1791.[46] 'Sons of Liberty, Children of
the Free-born Woman!' this commences and it offers a supposed

---

[45] Robinson, pp. 109, 115; *Minutes*, pp. 4, 7; Hindmarsh, *Rise and Progress*, pp. 145–8. On
the conservative evolution of the New Church in the 1790s, see also John Howard, 'An
Audience for *The Marriage of Heaven and Hell*', *Blake Studies*, Vol. III, no. 1, Fall 1970,
which shows that the Church placed an increasingly heavy emphasis on the decalogue:
i.e. the Moral Law.

[46] *Emmanuel Swedenborg's New-Year's Gift to his Readers for 1791*. This has been ascribed to
Benedict Chastanier: see Hyde, 'Benedict Chastanier and the Illuminati of Avignon', p.
205.

letter from the seer, indicting the fallacies of contemporary New-Churchmen, including that of 'the accursed doctrine of Predestination . . . the Cockatrice's egg'. This, of course, was also Blake's complaint in his indignant annotations to Swedenborg's *Divine Providence*. In a 'postscript' Swedenborg is made to give an enthusiastic description of 'the Lord's True Christian Church'. The Church's true members will be–

conspicuously distinguishable from all the rest of men, by their true and unaffected brotherly love, most tender regards and affections towards each other, as well indeed as by their most unbounded benevolence towards all their fellow-creatures of any nation, country, people, and language, religion, sect, or party whatsoever, and by their most indefatigable zeal in doing good to all God's creatures. Oh what a Society that will be!

Or as Blake had it more laconically, in his annotations to *Divine Love and Divine Wisdom*, 'The Whole of the New Church is in the Active Life & not in Ceremonies at all' (E595). There are other touches which suggest a Blakean association: a reference to a 'Real Devil' which cannot become an 'Angel of Light, agreeably to the system of Jacob Behmen, George Welling, Law, and most of the Hermetic Philosophers'.[47] And there is an editorial comment in which the author castigates those sects which 'fall into that unpardonable Babylonish Error, of thinking none can be saved but those who wear its own livery' and who 'naturally dwindle into that most antichristian principle of cordially hating whosoever . . . do not . . . precisely think as they do'.[48] This conforms to Blake's known dislike of 'Sectaries' (E582).

These inferences might place Blake in alliance with Chastanier, formerly of the Universal Society. But the evidence is inconclusive. And to press the suggestion too far is to lose the revolutionary and antinomian force of Blake's critique of Swedenborgianism. We have to find some other way of breaking open this problem. And the best point of entry may be with the 'divine humanity'.

---

[47] *Ibid.*, p. 27. This prompts the speculation that the author (Chastanier) might have been a possible original of the Angel in the *Marriage of Heaven and Hell* 'who is now become a Devil [and] is my particular friend; we often read the Bible together in its infernal or diabolical sense which the world shall have if they behave well'. (E43).

[48] *Ibid.*, p. 31.

CHAPTER 9

'The Divine Image'

'The Divine Image', in my view, is the axle upon which the *Songs of Innocence* turn, just as 'The Human Abstract' is the axle for the *Songs of Experience*. It is often supposed to be a profoundly Swedenborgian song, and this is what we must examine. It is certainly true that the 'Divine Human' was at the centre of Swedenborgian discourse at that time; indeed, it might be said to be the signature of the New Jerusalem church. When Robert Southey visited a congregation, he found that—

Christ is his *divine*, or in his *glorified human*, was repeatedly addressed as the only God; and the preacher laboured to show that the profane were those who worshipped three Gods. . .[1]

In shorthand the doctrine was CHRIST IS GOD, and Robert Hindmarsh was astounded to find these words chalked by unknown hands on walls in and for miles round London in the early 1780s.[2]

The doctrine of Swedenborgian receivers was set forth as the first to be recorded in a 'Compendious View of the principal Doctrines of the New Church':

Contrary to Unitarians who deny, and to Trinitarians who hold, a Trinity of persons in the Godhead, they maintain, that there is a Divine Trinity in the person of Jesus Christ, consisting of Father, Son, and Holy Ghost, just like the human Trinity in every individual man, of soul, body, and operation. . .

That Jehovah God himself came down from heaven, and assumed human nature for the purpose of removing hell from man, of restoring the heavens to order, and of preparing the way for a new church upon earth; and that herein consists the true nature of redemption, which was effected solely by the omnipotence of the Lord's Divine Humanity.[3]

[1] Southey, *Letters from England*, Vol. III, p. 113.   [2] Hindmarsh, *Rise and Progress*, p. 13.
[3] *New Magazine of Knowledge concerning Heaven and Hell*, Vol. I, pp. 16–18.

The Liturgy of the Church required that the Minister announce to the assembly that they were gathered to 'glorify his DIVINE HUMANITY'.[4]

The 'divine humanity' lay in the assumption by an omnipotent God of human nature in Christ's person. This was done, not by splitting into a Trinity, but by God infusing His own life into Christ, through the 'divine influx'. The doctrine created difficulties for early receivers. The Reverend Joseph Proud, a General Baptist Minister in Norwich who was converted to the New Church, later recalled his troubles when a Swedenborgian introduced him to 'the doctrine of the LORD as the only God in His divine Humanity':

I could very well agree to the Lord as being the *only God*, but when he mentioned a *divine humanity* I warmly opposed him and reply'd, 'what is divine cannot be *human*, nor what is *Human*, be *divine*'.[5]

Correspondents returned to the theme in the New Church magazines. Correspondents from Keighley affirmed–

That there is a Trinity in the Lord, namely, the Divinity, the Divine Humanity, and the Divine Proceeding . . . [but] a divine Trinity may be considered to exist in one person, and so to be one God; but not in three persons.[6]

The Reverend Proud, fully converted, explained the doctrine in a discourse in a newly opened New Jerusalem temple in Birmingham to which he ministered. God was '*in one person only*':

As to his essential divinity, he is the Father – as to his divine humanity, he is the Son – and as to his divine operation, he is the Holy Spirit. . .

He took on–

our nature; in that nature subdued the powers of hell, redeemed mankind, and made salvation possible to all; . . . he glorified that humanity, made it divine, united it with his own essential divinity, and is therefore *God and man in one divine person*.[7]

With the bringing of the divine together in one person, it is not surprising that the Unitarians viewed the Swedenborgians as competitors. Joseph Priestley addressed letters to members of the

---

[4] *Liturgy of the New Church* (printed and sold by R. Hindmarsh, 1791).
[5] 'Memoirs of Joseph Proud', MSS in Swedenborg Society Conference Library, 1822, pp. 7–8.
[6] *New Magazine of Knowledge*, Vol. II, p. 237.
[7] J. Proud, *The Fundamental Doctrines of the New Jerusalem* (Birmingham, 1792), p. 15.

New Church, urging them to adopt the Unitarian solution and to acknowledge Christ as a man 'but that God was with him, and acted by him'. A ding-dong exchange ensued.[8] In the course of this some apologetics turned upon the contrasting sexual derivation of the divine human. Swedenborg affirmed that 'human nature cannot be transmuted into the Divine Essence, neither commixed therewith'. Therefore a distinction must be maintained in Christ's genesis between the 'human nature from the mother' and the Divine Essence from the divine influx, or from the Father (i.e. the male principle which infused his soul).[9] What Mary supplied was 'a covering, called the maternal human, or a body like our own, so that the divine human (which was eternal and infinite) dwells in the maternal human, which was finite. . .' At the resurrection Christ cast off all materiality, the maternal human. 'Hence the God we worship, is not the material human of this world, but he that ever was, is, and ever will be, the invisible *I am*. . .'[10]

Correspondents in the *New Magazine* joined the same discussion, and it is difficult not to feel that the Virgin Mary was subjected to some male animosity. A distinction is laboured between the divine principle (always male) and the *humanum maternum* or in Swedenborg's phrase the *humanum infirmum*, 'the unfixed, unsteady, infirm humanity' (from the mother).[11] 'Ignoramus', whom we have already met (above, p. 139), explained that 'by putting off the humanity from the mother, is evidently meant the conquering and expelling the evil, and by putting on the humanity from the father, is bringing the first principles of human nature, or the divine human, into the ultimates. . .'[12] Another correspondent concluded that Christ's conception (or infusion) was 'manifested in the lowest parts of human nature, and the infirm body derived from the Virgin was tainted with hereditary evil. . .'[13] Hence it must be decisively put off. Chastanier returned to the columns with yet another passage from Swedenborg from his store of manuscripts.

---

[8] Joseph Priestley, *Letters to the Members of the New Jerusalem Church* (Birmingham, 1791), p. 31; J. Proud, *A Candid and Impartial Reply to the Reverend Dr Priestley's Letters* (Birmingham, 1791); R. Hindmarsh, 'Letters to Dr Priestley', *Analytical Review*, 11, Appendix, p. 517, 14, pp. 190–3; J. Bellamy, *Jesus Christ the Only God* (1792), a reply to Priestley.

[9] Bellamy, p. 51, citing Swedenborg, *Arcana Coelestia*, 2655–2659.

[10] Bellamy, Letter II.

[11] Benedict Chastanier, 'On the Lord's Humanity', *New Magazine*, 2, pp. 305–9. See also 2, pp. 266–8.

[12] *Ibid.*, 2, p. 313.   [13] *Ibid.*, 2, p. 314: 'M.B.G.'

From this it appeared that on the cross 'the Lord, from the divine in himself, wholly expelled the evil which he derived from his mother. . .'[14] 'Ignoramus' returned to the attack in the *Magazine*'s final number, making a clear distinction between the Lord's masculine and feminine souls: 'there was not an evil or a false that ever existed in the world, but what the Lord inherited from the mother as to the recipient form in the feminine soul'.[15]

All this helps one to understand the late addition to the *Songs of Experience*, 'To Tirzah', which some critics have found 'obscure':[16]

> Whate'er is Born of Mortal Birth,
> Must be consumed with the Earth
> To rise from Generation free;
> Then what have I to do with thee?
>
> The Sexes sprung from Shame & Pride
> Blow'd in the morn: in evening died
> But Mercy changd Death into Sleep;
> The Sexes rose to work & weep.
>
> Thou Mother of my Mortal part
> With cruelty didst mould my Heart,
> And with false self-decieving tears,
> Didst bind my Nostrils Eyes & Ears.
>
> Didst close my Tongue in senseless clay
> And me to Mortal Life betray:
> The Death of Jesus set me free,
> Then what have I to do with thee?

This, if we set aside the enigmatic second verse, might be an expression of orthodox Swedenborgian doctrine, even according to 'Ignoramus'. The *maternum humanum* supplies only a covering to clothe the divine spirit, and Blake recalls the words of Jesus to Mary (John 2:4): 'Woman, what have I to do with thee?' To this he adds a wider mythic dimension, in the name 'Tirzah', perhaps taken from *Revelation* 1.11, the name of a city which is rival and opponent to Jerusalem and which becomes for Blake an emblem of 'worldly authority and . . . materialistic thought'.[17] The poem

[14] *Ibid.*, 2, pp. 374–6.   [15] *Ibid.*, 2, pp. 442–4.
[16] As did Sir Geoffrey Keynes in his notes to the reproduction of the *Songs* (Oxford, 1967), p. 154.
[17] David W. Lindsay, *Blake: Songs of Innocence and Experience* (Atlantic Highlands, N.J., 1989), pp. 82–3.

was not added until 1805, and perhaps later, and hence belongs
to a period in which Blake may have been becoming reconciled to
Swedenborgianism.[18] And in *Jerusalem* he wrote:

> A Vegetated Christ & a Virgin Eve, are the Hermaphroditic
> Blasphemy, by his Maternal Birth he is that Evil One
> And his Maternal Humanity must be put off Eternally (E247)

However, let us return to 1789. All this debate about the 'divine
human' does rather little to prepare us for Blake's beautiful poem,
'The Divine Image':

> To Mercy Pity Peace and Love
> All pray in their distress:
> And to these virtues of delight
> Return their thankfulness.
>
> For Mercy Pity Peace and Love,
> Is God, our father dear:
> And Mercy Pity Peace and Love,
> Is Man his child and care.
>
> For Mercy has a human heart
> Pity, a human face:
> And Love, the human form divine,
> And Peace, the human dress.
>
> Then every man, of every clime,
> That prays in his distress,
> Prays to the human form divine
> Love Mercy Pity Peace.
>
> And all must love the human form,
> In heathen, turk, or jew.
> Where Mercy, Love & Pity dwell
> There God is dwelling too.

It is a pity to argue about so transparent a poem, but this must
be done. Mr F.W. Bateson, in common with other critics, found it
to be 'a thoroughly Swedenborgian poem',[19] and Kathleen Raine
has concurred: 'There could be no more simple and orthodox state-

---

[18] Alicia Ostriker, *William Blake, The Complete Poems* (Harmondsworth, 1977), p. 889, says
that poem cannot be earlier than 1803; Erdman (E722) suggests mid-1805 or later. Blake
told Crabb Robinson in 1826 that Christ 'took much after his Mother And in so far he
was one of the worst of Men'.

[19] F.W. Bateson, *Selected Poems of William Blake* (1957).

ment of the central doctrine of the New Church.'[20] It may therefore seem surprising that the poem, immediately, in its first verse, commences with a refutation of Swedenborg. For Swedenborg had argued in *Divine Love and Divine Wisdom*:

With Respect to God, it is not possible that he can love and be reciprocally beloved by others, in whom there is . . . any Thing Divine; for if there was . . . any Thing Divine in them, then it would not be beloved by others, but it would love itself. . .

Blake, who was then in his most sympathetic state towards the seer, challenged this with 'False': 'Take it so or the contrary it comes to the same for if a thing loves it is infinite' (E593). The first verse of 'The Divine Image' could not be more explicit in its rejection of Swedenborg's doctrine, and the verses which follow consolidate this. The poem resumes 'the central doctrine of the New Church' in no way.

One can illustrate this by the means of contrast. An early convert to the New Church, whom we have met already, was the Revd Joseph Proud, aged forty-five, who had already served for some twenty-five years as minister of the General Baptists. Converted dramatically to the new faith, he had a little reputation as a poet,[21] and – shortly after visiting London from Norwich in 1789 – he was urged to prepare a volume of original hymns for the use of the public worship of the New Church.[22] He did this with expedition, writing a modest contribution of three hundred hymns in the intervals between breaking the news to his Norwich flock that he was about to leave them to become one of the first Ministers of the New Church (in Birmingham). One of his first efforts was, exactly, 'On Divine Humanity',[23] from which these verses are taken:

[20] Raine, *Blake and Tradition*, I, p. 20. Also Raine, 'The Human Face of God', in *Blake and Swedenborg*, ed. Harvey F. Bellin and Darrell Ruhl (Swedenborg Foundation, N.Y., 1985), pp. 88–90. Miss Raine is strongly committed to the view that there could not possibly have been any humanist influence on Blake and therefore reads 'The Divine Image' as 'deep eschatological mystery'.
[21] His dreadful poem announcing his conversion, *Jehovah's Mercy made Known to all Mankind in these Last Days* was published in 1789 by Hindmarsh. I do not think that all mankind read it. The Old Church could not have received worse references: it was *'sunk, vastated, fallen'*, 'polluted' and 'to Whoredome, gross Adultery is given'.
[22] (Ed. E. Madeley), Revd Joseph Proud, *The Aged Minister's Last Legacy* (1854), p. xi; MS 'Memoir of Joseph Proud', pp. 15–16; at the General Conference, 5 April 1790, Proud announced that he had already written many hymns: *Minutes*, pp. 8–9.
[23] This hymn was singled out for special publication in the *New Magazine*, Vol. I, p. 288 (August 1790).

> ... Lord, we come to thee,
>   And bow before thy throne;
> In thy Divine Humanity,
>   Thou art our God alone.
>
> Thy esse none can see,
>   That is beyond our sight;
> But thy Divine Humanity
>   Is seen in heavenly light.
>
> Thou art the only God,
>   The *only Man* art thou;
> And only thee our souls adore,
>   At thy bles'd feet we bow.
>
> In essence thou art one,
>   And one in person too;
> Tho' in thy essence seen by none,
>   Thy person we may view. . .

In another hymn, on the same theme, we have these verses:

> But thou art God & God alone,
>   In thy Humanity;
> Before thee, Lord, no God was known,
>   Nor shall be after thee.
>
> Thy human nature is divine,
>   Divine is human too;
> Here God and Man in one combine,
>   And not three Gods, nor two.

One begins to suspect, from a certain barren shuttling of paradoxes, that the doctrine at this point created headaches for the pastor and perhaps dissension among the flock. And this can be confirmed by two lines from a further hymn:

> Why should we fear to say or sing,
>   Our God is Man alone. . .

But the Dutch courage of Mr Proud is immediately covered by an evasive footnote: 'By man alone, understand that God is the only man, strictly speaking, as all mankind are men from him and not in themselves. . .'[24]

[24] Joseph Proud, *Hymns and Spiritual Songs for the Use of the Lord's New Church* (2nd edn, 1791), pp. 142, 219–21. The first edition, in 500 copies, was published in 1790.

Let us now return to Blake's poem, and attempt the painful exercise of reading it with Mr Proud's alternative still in our mind. The instant contrast is between the deference of Proud and the egalitarian humanism of Blake.[25] Without any outrage or rupture of logical or poetic structure, with the greatest quietness, we move from the acceptable (although not to Swedenborg) statement of the first verse to the heresy of the last three. There is indeed some difference in matter between Blake and Proud. Blake passes by altogether the doctrinal issue of the Trinity. And there is an absence in him of that obeisance before 'thy throne' ('Thee we adore, eternal Lord/In thy Humanity') which distances God once more ('beyond our sight'), so that the notion of God's humanity comes through not as authentic but as a metaphysical conjuring trick. 'Thy esse none can see/That is beyond our sight' – but Blake's divine esse can be seen, in human virtues, and only seen there.[26] This is what Blake's song is about, and what it is saying is not so much around the theme of 'divine humanity' as of human divinity: the poem is called 'The Divine Image'. And hence if man worships – but Blake does not use this word, he uses prayers of distress, thankfulness and love – he must worship these qualities as he finds them in himself. Blake is breaking both with the paternalist image of God which (whether a vengeful Father or an all-knowing First Cause or, as with Mr Proud, a somewhat muddled but benevolent gentleman) occupied a position of critical importance within all eighteenth-century ideology, and he was breaking also – and as I think explicitly – with the abasement before 'Jehovah God in his GLORIFIED HUMANITY' as it was demanded by the Confessional of the New Church as expressed in its *Liturgy* (another Hindmarsh product):

Most merciful Lord Jesus, who in thy DIVINE HUMANITY art the Only God of Heaven and Earth, the supreme Governor of the Universe, and before whom the whole Angelic Host fall prostrate in profound Humiliation, permit us thy sinful Creatures, Worms of the Earth, to approach thy heavenly Majesty. . .[27]

---

[25] See Heather Glen, *Vision and Disenchantment: Blake's 'Songs' and Wordsworth's Lyrical Ballads* (Cambridge, 1983), pp. 151–6.
[26] In the Hindmarsh version of the *Liturgy* it is stated in a footnote that 'the Faces of Jehovah' in Holy Scripture signify 'the Love, Mercy, Peace and Goodness of the Lord'.
[27] An *Order of Worship* was drawn up as early as January 1788; Hindmarsh, p. 60. The Liturgy was named for revision at the second Annual Conference, April 1790: *Minutes*.

Blake at all times kept his distance from the Swedenborgian doctrine of the 'divine humanity'. The problem of immanence and transcendence, identity and essence, was being worked at in different ways in the early New Church milieu. A contributor to the *New Magazine of Knowledge Concerning Heaven and Hell* tried to explain it by offering a Swedenborgian version of the Lord's Prayer:

Our Father,	O infinite eternal esse,
Who art in the heavens	Manifested in the heavens
Hallowed be thy name	Whom we adore in the existence of thy Divine Humanity
Thy Kingdom come,	Let the divine influx of wisdom
Thy will be done	And love,
As in heaven	Flowing from thee through thy new heavens
So also upon earth.	Be received with a pure affection by each member of thy New Church.
Give us this day	Give us according to our various states of want
Our daily bread. . .	That true nourishment of our souls, that will be our increasing spiritual support to eternity. . .[28]

Nor was this contributor ('Ignoramus' once more) unusual in finding exceptional difficulty in selecting proper spiritual correspondences for such corporeal terms as 'earth' and 'bread'. The characteristic movement is away from the concrete image, whereas Blake leads us back to 'heart', 'face', 'form' and 'dress'. And it is Swedenborg's own writings which are responsible for this evasive movement. 'What Person of Sound Reason', he had asked in the *Divine Love and Wisdom*, 'doth not perceive that the Divine is not divisible?' If he should say–

that it is possible there may be several infinities, Uncreates, Omnipotents and Gods, provided they have the same Essence, and that thereby there is one and the same Essence but one and the same Identity?

This passage had bothered Blake (then in his most sympathetic state towards Swedenborg) a great deal. His annotation runs:

Answer   Essence is not Identity but from Essence proceeds Identity &

---

[28] Vol. II, p. 352. Another dreadful version of the Lord's Prayer appeared in the *Order of Worship* in which 'give us this day our daily bread' is given as 'a suitable supply from thy divine human give us momentarily, according to our state of reception'.

from one Essence may proceed many Identities as from one Affection
may proceed. many thoughts
Surely this is an oversight.

That there is but one Omnipotent Uncreate & God I agree but that there
is but one Infinite I do not. for if all but God is not Infinite they shall
come to an End which God forbid.

If the Essence was the same *as the* Identity there could be but one Identity.
which is false
Heaven would upon this plan be but a Clock but one & the same Essence
is therefore Essence & not Identity. (E593)

A consideration of this important note would take us back to
Behmenist and Muggletonian notions of eternity and creation (see
above, p. 70). But in its immediate relevance it bears upon the
problem of the 'divine humanity'. Blake prefers an image which
allows 'many identities' to proceed from one 'essence', just as many
thoughts may proceed from one 'affection': this allows him to think
of the divine essence both as 'one & the same Essence' and also
as that essence expressed in the many identities of men, while still
remaining essentially divine.

Swedenborg offered texts which were both diaphonous and contradictory, and which allowed several positions to be held. Thus
(1) – as endorsed in the principles of the New Church – it was
limited to the doctrine of God taking on mortal form in Jesus and
thus *assuming* divine humanity. As Proud warbled, 'thy esse none
can see' but 'thy Divine Humanity/Is seen in heavenly light.' But
(2) an extension of this could be proposed, in that God makes
himself known to man through heavenly inspiration, working upon
his affections (rather than upon his understanding) and hence his
'esse' enters into man as 'love'. A constant Swedenborgian image
is of the sun as the source of the influx of love, and of man's
spirit as the reflector or recipient of this influx. That part of man
enlightened by love shares in the divine esse and is in that sense
itself divine. Thus Miss Raine cites Swedenborg's *True Christian
Religion*:

A man is an organ of life, and God alone is life: God infuses his life into
the organ and all its parts; and God grants man a sense that the life in
himself is as it were his own.[29]

---

[29] Raine, *Blake and Tradition*, Vol. I, p. 18.

And she concludes that Blake is 'preaching the doctrine of the New Church'. But Blake's song doesn't sound like this. He sounds as if he is saying something much blunter: there is nothing in 'The Divine Image' about God 'infusing' or 'granting' to man 'a sense' of life being 'as it were' his own. I can't find the words 'as it were' anywhere in the Blake *Concordance*. It sounds as if Blake is saying exactly what he says in *The Marriage of Heaven and Hell*: 'God only Acts & Is, in existing Beings or Men' (E39). And that, too, can be read in two different ways: that God, as some disembodied esse, only finds embodiment in existing beings or men: or that there is no God anywhere else. I suspect that Blake fluctuated between contrary states, perhaps emphasising in 1789 the first, the second in 1791–3 and at some time thereafter returning to the first.[30]

In any case, we have a clear idea of how Blake came to his poem. In 1789 when annotating the humanist, Lavater, he was delighted with certain passages. When he fell upon 'He who *hates the wisest and best of men, hates the Father of men; for, where is the Father of men to be seen but in the most perfect of his children?*' he struck out both of the 'hates' and inserted above them 'loves' and underlined the italicised phrase, adding: 'this is true worship'.[31] When Lavater wrote that 'art is nothing but the highest sagacity and exertion of human nature; *and what nature will he honour who honours not the human?*' he underlined again, and noted 'human nature is the image of God'. And, immediately above, Lavater had written: '*He, who adored an impersonal God, has none; and, without guide or rudder, launches on an immense abyss that first absorbs his powers, and next himself.*' Blake underscored the whole passage, and exclaimed: 'Most superlatively beautiful & most affectionatly Holy & pure would to God that all men would consider it' (E586). This prepares us for the annotation to Swedenborg's *Divine Love and Wisdom*, probably in the next year, especially section 11 where the seer comments that the Africans 'entertain an Idea of God as of a Man, and say that no one can have any other Idea of God'. Blake notes approvingly: 'Think of a white cloud. as being holy you cannot love it but think of a holy man within the cloud love springs up in your thoughts. for to

---

[30] As late as 1820 Blake annotated Berkeley: *Siris*: 'God is Man & exists in us & we in him.'

[31] Blake returns to this in *The Marriage of Heaven and Hell*, Plates 22–3 (E42): 'The worship of God is. Honouring his gifts in other men each according to his genius. and loving the greatest men best, those who envy or calumniate great men hate God. for there is no other God.'

think of holiness distinct from man is impossible to the affections. Thought alone can make monsters, but the affections cannot' (E592–3).

There is, of course, a pre-history to all this. The eighteenth century, as is notorious, saw a general movement among the enlightened dissenters through Arianism to Socinianism towards the resting-place of Unitarianism, which entailed the denial of the Trinity and of Christ's divinity. This was one way to a humanist Christ. But the Muggletonians, the Philadelphians and what there was of an articulate antinomian tradition, took, with variants, a different path. Positing only one God, they might see him in the pantheist tradition, as dispersed through all life, or, as did the Muggletonians, as assuming Himself, in the infant Christ, full mortality. Thus Reeve:

There is no other God but the Man Jesus . . . the eternal God, the Man of Glory, who is a distinct God in the Person of a Man . . . Therefore . . . they cannot take the Sword of Steel to slay their Brother, because they know that Man is the Image of God.[32]

Thus also Thomas Tomkinson, some of whose gentle and slightly rationalised versions of the Muggletonian faith were published posthumously. He speaks of God 'begetting himself into a Son . . . God sent forth HIMSELF to be made of a Woman, to redeem us from the Curse of the Law. . .'[33] Both the pantheist and the embodiment-of-God-as-Christ versions were found among eighteenth-century Muggletonians, and they sometimes co-existed in the same mind. I find in a letter of a believer, William Sedgwick, in 1794 the old tension between the two being held:

Christ is the Light that Lighteth Every man that Commeth into the world yet none but God is Infinite. Notwithstanding tho God the Creater virtuale Dwells in all his Creatures. Nothing is Capable of the Indwelling Infinite power But God alone . . . Even man in his Created Purety tho of the very nature of the Divine Creator yet not Infinite. . .

The argument is close to the discourse preoccupying the New Church, but the emphasis – and where the Muggletonians differed sharply from the Swedenborgians – lay upon Christ's concentrated divinity:

---

[32] John Reeve, *Sacred Remains* (n.d.), p. 83.
[33] *A System of Religion*, first published in 1729 from manuscripts found among Tomkinson's papers after his death, pp. 22–3.

The Eternal God Left his glorious kingdom Came Down & Enterd The Blessed virgin Mary's whomb. There Desolved his Spritual Body in to seed and Natuer & Quickend into a body of flesh Blood & Bone Like unto man in all Respects (Sins Only Excepted). . .[34]

Man is the 'Image of God' and he is also the 'ark' or 'tabernacle' of God: and God is Christ. The image of Christ is always that of the sun or of blinding light: as Richard Pickersgill, the Muggletonian painter, wrote in 1803, in heaven 'we shall behold the bright burning Glorious person'.[35] It is such a bright burning glorious infant that Blake shows us in his remarkable (and unprecedented) Nativity, with Christ springing from Mary's womb into the hands of St Elizabeth, with St John the Baptist (also an infant) looking on (Illus. 9). David Bindman finds this treatment to be 'unique in European art': the 'moment of birth is represented as a heavenly burst of radiance'.[36]

> And thine the Human Face & thine
>   The Human Hands & Feet & Breath
> Entering thro' the Gates of Birth
>   And passing thro' the Gates of Death.   (E171)

The pantheist view, which proposed God as some quantum of divine energy dispersed through all life, but more especially in the spiritual nature of men and women, and the notion of God as Christ, are difficult to combine, and perhaps intellectually impossible. Or the difficulty may only be in reconciling these two alternative versions of the same vision. I suggest that, in his later years when he had rejected deism, Blake was often preoccupied with the problem of reconciling, through imagery or myth, these seemingly contradictory visions. Perhaps we have it in *Vala*:

Then those in Great Eternity met in the Council of God As one Man, for contracting their Exalted Senses They behold Multitude or Expanding they behold as one As One Man all the Universal family & that One man They call Jesus the Christ, & they in him & he in them Live in Perfect harmony. . . (E306)

Or in his *Descriptions of the Last Judgement*:

. . . I have seen [those States] in my Imagination when distant they appear as One Man but as you approach they appear Multitudes of Nations . . . I have seen when at a distance Multitudes of Men in Har-

---

[34] British Library, Muggletonian archive.   [35] *Ibid.*
[36] Bindman, *Blake as an Artist*, pp. 121–2.

mony appear like a single Infant sometimes in the Arms of a Female (this represented the Church). (E546)

And we have it also in the splendid exchange with Crabb Robinson in December 1825:

On my asking in what light he viewed the great question concerning the Divinity of Jesus Christ, he said; '*He is the only God.*' But then he added – 'And so am I and so are you.'[37]

Crabb Robinson was floored by that, and so in a way are we, although we rejoice at Blake's triumph and have a swift sense of some revealed truth. But what we may actually be sensing is a creative contradiction. Blake is refusing to renounce 'Mercy's lord' or to reduce the gospel to the level of rational historical explanation;[38] but equally he is refusing to sublimate Jesus or his gospel into an abstraction, to tease out from this some bodiless fiction and call this 'God', or to humiliate himself before a divine essence in which all men share. The reply breaks at a bound from the net of the theological disputes of his time, between Arian, Socinian, Unitarian or Deist positions. It conveys a truth of a poetic kind, expressive of a certain equipoise and tension of values, appropriate to lyrical expression. And expressed thus, neither Urizen nor Crabb Robinson could answer it.

Obscurities can arise in the later prophetic books, not just because Blake was managing his art badly, but because he was attempting to reconcile doctrines that could not be logically reconciled. The books plunge into obscurity at exactly those points (of which the problem of the unity and the dispersal of the godhead is one) where Blake was involved in actual doctrinal or philosophical contradictions.

But a contradiction in thought, which derives from an acute tension of contrasting values, neither of which can be abandoned, can be wholly creative. If we will neither deny Christ's divinity nor elevate it above that of mortal creation which shares in the same divine essence, then we have an intense and mystic humanism. If God exists in Men and nowhere else, then the whole cosmic conflict between darkness and light, things corporeal and spiritual, must be enacted within oneself and one's fellow men and nowhere

---

[37] Bentley, *Blake Records*, p. 310.
[38] In later years he said that Swedenborg 'was wrong in endeavouring to explain to the *rational* faculty what the reason cannot comprehend', *ibid.*, p. 312.

else. This meant above all – and this was perhaps the greatest offence of such an heresy in the eyes of a more vengeful Christian tradition – breaking with any sense of personal conviction in original sin. There had been a Fall and a dispersal of the godhead; the godly nature of man now struggled to repair the breach and return to universal harmony, the family of love, Jerusalem. Were man to be called an abject and sinful worm would be (from this standpoint) to blaspheme against the godhead within him. 'Every thing has as much right to Eternal Life as God who is the Servant of Man.'[39]

I cannot see that either Lavater or Swedenborg offers to us the vocabulary or the imagery of 'The Divine Image'. Blake's annotations to them indicate not discovery but recognition and assent, or correction and exposition, of tenets already held. It is a poem which with purity and lucidity holds in tension and reconciles the two positions we have been exploring. From the first verse – and how much is won in the first verse – we are drawn into an ascending circle of mutuality. It was therefore with a delighted shock of recognition that I came across in the *New Magazine of Knowledge Concerning Heaven and Hell*, inserted without preliminaries or explanation, a long extract from Thomas Tomkinson's *A System of Religion*: 'That God ever was, is, and will be, in the Form of a Man':

Can righteousness and holiness act forth themselves without a body? Or do you ever read, that righteousness and holiness were ever acted forth, in, or by any other form but the form of a man? When God said, *Be ye holy as I am holy*: what! must the souls run out of the bodies to be like him? If they did, they would be nothing. Where would mercy and justice, meekness and humility, be found? There could be no such virtues known, or have being, were they not found to center in a body.[40]

Here are our virtues of delight, and here is our human embodiment of the divine. It provides a clearer (and more Blakean) introduction to 'The Divine Image' than does Swedenborg. It is a tantalising piece of evidence. No other theological authority, apart from Swedenborg and contemporary readers of the review, appeared in

---

[39] Blake's 'Annotations to Thornton', *c.*1827 (E658).

[40] The extract leads Vol. I, no. 6 of the *New Magazine* (August 1790), pp. 243–7. It is taken, with some cutting but no alterations, from Tomkinson's *A System of Religion*, chapter 2. The Swedenborgians continued to show an interest in Tomkinson: see James Hyde, 'The Muggletonians and the Document of 1729', *The New-Church Review* (Boston, Mass.), 7, 1900, pp. 215–27.

the two volumes of the magazine. Whose hand brought it to the editor's attention? At least we have evidence that there was one person in that early New Church milieu conversant with Muggletonian writings. 'The Divine Image' might even be called a Tomkinsonian song.

CHAPTER 10

From innocence to experience

There were other contentious issues in the early New Church which may have concerned William Blake. For we have overlooked so far another of the principal doctrines of the church:

That the imputation of the merits and righteousness of Christ is a thing as absurd and impossible, as it would be to impute to any man the work of creation; for the merits and righteousness of Christ consist in redemption, which is as much the work of a divine and omnipotent Being, as creation itself. They maintain, however, that the imputation, which really takes place, is an imputation of good and evil; and that this is according to a man's life.[1]

Alongside this went a rejection of the doctrine of 'justification by faith alone' and of 'the notion of pardon obtained by a vicarious sacrifice or atonement' rather than repentance and reform.[2] These doctrines were associated with Calvinism, and perhaps with Calvinist antinomianism. An observer in 1788 singled out the doctrine of the imputation of the righteousness of Christ as a central doctrine of antinomians, who believe that they have no inherent righteousness, since 'the whole work of man's salvation was accomplished by Jesus Christ on the cross. Christ's blood and our sins went away together. . .' Hence works are unnecessary: belief is all that is required. 'Our righteousness is nothing but the imputation of the righteousness of Christ. A believer has no holiness in himself but in Christ only.'[3]

Thus the doctrines appear to be intended to wall out antinomianism.[4] And the church certainly had the authority of

---

[1] *New Magazine*, Vol. 1, p. 18. Also *New-Jerusalem Magazine*, p. 104.
[2] *Ibid.*   [3] W. Hurd, *New Universal History*, pp. 640–1.
[4] See 'Z.Z.', 'Thoughts on Imputed Righteousness', *New Magazine*, Vol. 1, p. 295, taking issue especially with Tobias Crisp, *Christ Alone Exalted*, which had been republished in 1791.

162

Swedenborg, who in *The True Christian Religion* (1781, chapter XI) denounced imputation.[5] And yet the New Church's emphasis upon the matter has a look as if to repel a heresy in its midst. And there had been one very notable poetic expression inclining towards this heresy. In Book III of *Paradise Lost* Milton's Christ intercedes for man 'as a sacrifice/Glad to be offer'd' and God accepts:

> His [Adam's] crime makes guiltie all his Sons, thy merit
> Imputed shall absolve them who renounce
> Thir own both righteous and unrighteous deeds,
> And live in thee transplanted, and from thee
> Receive new life.

This doctrine has two sides. First, it is of Christ's sacrifice and atonement (or ransom) for man before God. Second, the emphasis is more upon Christ's forgiveness of man and his intercession with God on man's behalf. As we have seen, the first aspect of the doctrine had been repudiated by Swedenborg and also by the New Church. And in this Blake almost certainly agreed. Many years later Crabb Robinson recorded: 'Speaking of the Atonement in the ordinary Calvinist sense, he said: "It is a horrible doctrine: If another pay your debt, I do not forgive it." '[6] 'But the language of 'ransom' and of man's 'redemption' by Christ's sacrifice endured within New Church apologetics,[7] and was confused only by the question of God's dual identity: if he was Christ, how did he intercede with himself?[8] Very certainly the New Church ascribed to God/Christ the role of delivering man from evil. As one of the church's principal doctrines recited:

That Jehovah God himself came down from heaven, and assumed human nature for the purpose of removing hell from man, of restoring the heavens to order, and of preparing the way for a new church upon earth; and that herein consists the true nature of redemption, which was effected solely by the omnipotence of the Lord's Divine Humanity.[9]

But this redemption 'did not consist in the passion of the cross' but was a regeneration effected more slowly by the repentance and

---

[5] See also *New-Jerusalem Magazine*, pp. 141–2.   [6] Bentley, *Blake Records*, p. 548.
[7] Yet only as translated into its 'internal' sense' Thus 'redemption by the *blood of Christ* means redemption by *divine truth* proceeding from the Lord.' &c: *New Magazine*, I, p. 320.
[8] An apologist explained that 'the true meaning of *atonement* or *expiation* is the removal of evils from man, and not the appeasing of Wrath in God, who is essential love and mercy; and ... the removal of evil is effected solely by the Lord's Divine Humanity. . .': *ibid.*, 2, pp. 133–4.   [9] *Ibid.*, I, p. 18.

works of redeemed man.[10] Blake had no time for the language of
Christ's intercession with a wrathful God: 'Forgiveness of Sin is
only at the Judgment Seat of Jesus the Saviour where the Accuser
is cast out' (E555). And he often insisted upon using the language
of God and of Christ, but as opposed principles.[11]

Returning to Milton, whom Blake so greatly admired, we find
him presenting Christ in *Paradise Lost* (Book XI, lines 32–6) as
pleading with his unforgiving Father:

> . . . let mee
> Interpret for him, mee his Advocate
> And propitiation, all his works on mee
> Good or not good ingraft, my Merit those
> Shall perfet, and for these my Death shall pay.

Mankind redeemed will be 'Made one with mee as I with thee am
one.' And in Book XII (line 290ff.) Milton moves much closer to
the antinomian doctrine of justification by faith alone: 'Law can
discover sin, but not remove':

> Some bloud more precious must be paid for Man,
> Just for unjust, that in such righteousness
> To them by Faith imputed, they may finde
> Justification towards God, and peace
> Of Conscience, which the Law by Ceremonies
> Cannot appease, nor Man the moral part
> Perform, and not performing cannot live.
> So Law appears imperfet, and but giv'n
> With purpose to resign them in full time
> Up to a better Cov'nant. . .

Christ, by fulfilling the full rigour of the Moral Law, appeases
'high Justice' (lines 400ff.):

> The Law of God exact he shall fulfill
> Both by obedience and by love, though love
> Alone fulfill the Law. . .
> Proclaiming Life to all who shall believe
> In his redemption, and that his obedience
> Imputed becomes theirs by Faith, his merits
> To save them, not thir own, though legal works.

[10] *Ibid.*, 2, p. 333.
[11] 'He spoke of the Old Testament as if it were the evil element', recorded Crabb Robinson:
Bentley, p. 548.

For this he shall live hated, be blasphem'd,
Seis'd on by force, judg'd, and to death condemnd
A shameful and accurst, naild to the Cross
By his own Nation, slaine for bringing Life;
But to the Cross he nailes thy Enemies,
The Law that is against thee, and the sins
Of all mankinde, with him there crucifi'd. . .

Thus Milton, Blake's mentor, gave outstanding expression to doctrines which the New Church repudiated. We cannot say exactly how Blake responded to this repudiation. His whole-hearted emphasis was not upon intercession or imputation but on Christ as a figure of forgiveness. As he was to write later in the *Everlasting Gospel* (1818): 'What then did Christ inculcate. Forgiveness of Sins   This alone is the Gospel & this is the Life & Immortality brought to light by Jesus': (E792)

It was when Jesus said to Me
Thy sins are all forgiven thee
The Christian trumpets loud proclaim
Thro all the World in Jesus name
Mutual forgiveness of each Vice
And oped the Gates of Paradise
The Moral Virtues in Great fear
Formed the Cross & Nails & Spear
And the Accuser standing by
Cried out Crucify Crucify   (E793)

He also took over with vigour the symbolism of Christ's feet nailed to the cross and also to the serpent's head, which represented his sinful and mortal part, shed at the crucifixion:

And thus with wrath he did subdue
The Serpent Bulk of Natures dross
Till he had naild it to the Cross
He took on Sin in the Virgins Womb
And put it off on the Cross & Tomb
To be Worshipd by the Church of Rome   (E515)

(It will be noted how this symbolism also takes in the 'Tirzah' theme: above, p. 149.) Blake also selected this theme for one of his illustrations to *Paradise Lost*. In David Bindman's words, he 'shows the Crucified Christ resting upon the bodies of Sin and Death, with the nail in His foot piercing the head of the Serpent' (see Illus.

8).[12] But is the female beneath the cross the discarded *maternum humanum*? (see above, pp. 148–9).

It will be noted that Blake's strongest statements of the pre-eminent virtues of Christ's forgiveness appear very often linked to the repudiation of the Moral Law: that is, with a markedly antino-mian inflexion. And this would have been anathema to the ruling powers in the New Church. We cannot with certainty say that Blake held these views in 1789–90 (his New Church days) although they are clearly present a year or two later in *The Marriage of Heaven and Hell*: 'Jesus was all virtue, and acted from impulse. not from rules' (E42). And there is evidence that antinomian heresy troubled the New Church in its early years. The *New Magazine* carried a contribution in September 1790 censuring 'the notion of *imputed righteousness* which prevails at this day with too many. They think that they can do nothing for themselves, therefore Christ must do all.' They discount 'repentance, self-examination, and continued watchfulness [as] legal doctrines for the carnal and unconverted':

Observe, too often, their bitter tempers, spiritual pride, and uncharitable censures; and yet these things trouble them not, because they are *justified freely without the work of the moral law*.[13]

Joseph Proud (who was very much of Hindmarsh's party in the 1790s) was haranguing his Birmingham congregation in 1791 against the 'falses' of imputed righteousness and justification by faith. It was 'generally believed' that the Lord came to abrogate or set aside the moral law. 'They say it is a *legal bondage*, a *covenant of works*, and in itself *impracticable*.' They say that Christ 'fulfilled every iota of that law on *our account*, and in *our stead*'. They accuse their critics (and accuse Proud himself?) of being 'a pharisee and a workmonger', and declare 'we are not under the law, but under grace'. And Proud added, perceptively, this is to suppose two Gods, with different natures: one of wrath, the other of mercy.[14]

Blake did not circle around the doctrines of 'imputation' and 'justification by faith', since his routes to truth were impulsive and imaginative, and not doctrinal. But it is clear that the New Church – or at least the Hindmarsh faction which effectively con-trolled the press – was censoring positions for which he had strong

---

[12] Bindman, *Blake as an Artist*, p. 189.   [13] Vol. I, p. 295.
[14] J. Proud, *Twenty Sermons on the Doctrines and Truths of the Lord's New Church* (Birmingham, 1792), pp. 93–6.

sympathy. And the evolution of the Church's forms was in the same direction. We have noted already Hindmarsh's efforts to introduce episcopalian forms of government (see p. 143). In the Liturgy of the church (1791) were introduced prayers for the king, royal family, both Houses of Parliament and all magistrates. More remarkably, in the evening service a prayer was introduced for the bishops, priests and ministers of the old Church.[15] The Reverend Proud was especially anxious to impress his loyalty on the Birmingham populace. During the 'Priestley Riots' in 1791 (Proud recorded proudly):

Two or three times the mob came to destroy our Temple, upon a supposition that we were against Church & King, as the unitarians were supposed to be, & the last time the Mob came by thousands, with wood under their arms, to burn our Temple. I rush'd in among the Crowd, to the Ring Leaders, explained to them that we had no connection with Dr Priestley or that Party, & that we wish'd no ill to the Church, or to the King, & putting a guinea or two into their hands . . . they went away, with '*Huzza to the New Jerusalem for ever.*'[16]

Proud became 'the model clerical priest' of Hindmarsh's order, preaching with an inner purple silken vest, outer garment of fine white linen and golden girdle.[17] Servanté, in a private letter, wrote that Proud, Sibley and Hodson were 'tinctured with some of the old Papal leaven of priestly supremacy'. James Hindmarsh, the father of Robert Hindmarsh, after his ordination at Eastcheap 'justly obtained the nick-name of Bishop of *Babylon*'.[18]

Let us resume what we know of the New Church episode, and what we may reasonably surmise. The first year or two of the Church were clouded with dissension. For the Blakes the entire Swedenborgian moment was fraught with conflict, but was nevertheless of profound significance. We cannot clearly identify Blake with any of the conflicting groups, but again and again we seem to glimpse his face, obliquely situated to a particular argument. There is his recognition of a body of visionary writing undoubtedly carrying some of the old Behmenist imagery. There is identification

---

[15] *Liturgy of the New Church* (4th edition, printed and sold by R. Hindmarsh, 1791), pp. 42, 56–7.

[16] Proud's MS 'Memoirs', p. 27.

[17] Robinson, *A Remembrancer*, p. 141. To be fair to Proud, this dress was recommended by the Annual Conference in 1791; *Minutes*. Robinson states that Proud was the only one to wear it.

[18] *Monthly Observer*, 1858, pp. 280–1, quoting Servanté to Glen, 19 October 1806.

not only with certain beliefs (Christ is man) but also with the very notion of a New Church of regenerated humankind. There is also some shared jargon of correspondences (chariot for doctrine, Edom for what is natural, dragon for the 'falses' of religion). The influence was deep, and, with *The Marriage of Heaven and Hell*, productive of polemic. It would also seem that Blake's antinomian tenets were resisted from the start by the orthodox within the Church.

If this is so, then 1789–90 will have been a profoundly unhappy experience – one of exalted enthusiasm followed by disenchantment and rejection. And the experience will have been the more cutting if we conjecture also that the *Songs of Innocence* were Blake's own offering to the life of the New Church. The *Songs* (apart from three which were drafted in 1784) were written at a time (1789 and perhaps into 1790) when we know that Blake was most closely interested in the church. The story that Blake wrote 'The Divine Image' in 'the New Jerusalem Church, Hatton Garden' has been quite properly dismissed, since that 'temple' was not opened until 1797.[19] However, the source of the story is a strong one: Charles Augustus Tulk, who said that he had been told this by Blake, was the son of J.A. Tulk, an attender at the Theosophical Society and a founder member (an active one) of the New Church. C.A. Tulk was born in 1786, only three years before 'The Divine Image' was written, and became in later years a close Swedenborgian sympathiser and a steady patron and friend of Blake's.[20] The temple in Hatton Gardens is the one which he will have remembered from his childhood, and if told by Blake that he had written the song in the New Church he could well have passed on the story with that addition.[21] Blake could have written 'The Divine Image' in the new church, albeit in Great Eastcheap and not in Hatton Gardens. And indeed the impulse of the church might have been behind the conception of a group of poems around the theme of 'innocence'.

[19] James Spilling, 'William Blake, Artist and Poet', *New Church Magazine*, June 1887, p. 254, demolished in Erdman, 'Blake's Early Swedenborgianism'.

[20] Raymond Deck, 'New Light on C.A. Tulk', *Studies in Romanticism*, 16, 1977, no. 2. J.A. Tulk was probably the author of 'A Layman', *A Letter Containing a Few Plain Observations, addressed to the Unbiased Members of the New Church* (n.d. but 1807?), which complained of the 'absurdity' of attempting to 'create a New Clergy', an opinion which Blake might have shared.

[21] The story in fact came by way of another Swedenborgian, J. Garth Wilkinson. For Wilkinson's enthusiastic promotion of Blake's *Songs*, see Geoffrey Keynes, 'Blake, Tulk and Garth Wilkinson', *The Library*, 4th ser., 26, 1945, and Deck, *New Light*, pp. 115–16.

In any case, we know that the early members of the church were anxious to have songs and were looking around for them. We have seen that shortly after he visited London in 1789 Joseph Proud was requested to compose a volume of hymns for the use of the New Church (above, p. 151). This was on the 'understanding that I had a turn for poetry'. 'In about three months . . . I presented them with a volume of better than 300: they were approved of, & 500 copies immediately printed.'[22] If Mr Proud could have made an offering of three hundred hymns in three months, Blake (who can never have liked Mr Proud very much) may have been stimulated to a little quiet competition. Moreover, we have evidence that the members of the church were actively concerned about the matter of songs, and that it may have been controversial. When Proud informed the 1790 Annual Conference that his hymns were ready, much satisfaction was expressed, but–

It was the unanimous request . . . that the Hymns may consist of Praises and Glorifications only, and not of Prayer and Supplication; as singing implies an *Elevation* of Mind, which is suited to an Act of *Praise*, but apparently inconsistent with the *Humiliation* requisite in Prayer.[23]

This sounds like a polite expostulation. If this was a triumph for a liberal tendency it was reversed at the next Annual Conference (1791), which was firmly controlled by Hindmarsh. This went to the trouble of rescinding even such a resolution, while forms of prayer and expressions of abject humiliation were being introduced into the *Order of Worship* and the *Liturgy* (see above, p. 153).

All these points of controversy – hymns, forms, humility – related to the central question: what was the life of the New Church to consist in? Blake's view, while he remained an enthusiast, was unequivocal: 'The Whole of the New Church is in the Active Life & not in Ceremonies at all' (E595). But the active life could include songs. It is surely more than a coincidence that Blake should have

---

[22] Proud, MS 'Memoirs', pp. 14–16. The dating of this is unclear. The hymns may have been written, discussed and approved in 1789, but not published until 1790. See also Proud, *The Aged Minister's Last Legacy*, p. xi.

[23] *Minutes*. Perhaps in response Proud claimed (falsely) that he had avoided 'whatever is *petitioning*, or *prayer wise*' as well as 'every Subject that is *improper for Praise, Thanksgiving, and Glorification*': *Hymns and Spiritual Songs for the Use of the Lord's New Church (2nd edn, 1791), Preface* v. But he continued the argument in a sermon, 'Humility Recommended', published the next year in *Twenty Sermons*. Blake repeatedly expressed his hostility to self-abasement and humiliation, as in the *Everlasting Gospel*, 'God wants not Man to Humble himself/This is the trick of the ancient Elf' (E511).

written the *Songs of Innocence* at exactly the same time that the New Church was calling for songs? What kind of songs, if one was determined to exclude all ceremonial, humiliation, prayer and obeisance before a paternal image of God, lessons of reward and eternal punishment, and, at the same time, the 'natural religion' of a deist First Cause? The songs must either be such as 'The Divine Image', or else songs of the primary affections (through whom alone the divine 'influx' of love could come, as in 'The Little Black Boy') – songs of innocence. And Swedenborg could have afforded to Blake a further suggestion, in the course of various lucubrations on the state of little children in heaven, which could have allowed Blake to proceed to his *Songs* while still having within his mind (as yet not fully realised, for the 'experience' was to take forms which he did not expect) a simultaneous notion of innocence's limitations and the need for complementary and contrary songs of experience:

Innocence is the receptacle of all heavenly good things, and therefore the innocence of little children is the place and ground of all their affections for good and truth, and consists in a resigned submission to the government of the Lord, and a renunciation of man's own will . . . but the innocence of little children is not genuine innocence because void of wisdom; for genuine innocence is wisdom. . .[24]

And so the *Songs* could have evolved: some on the primary affections and sympathies, some showing 'resigned submission' and renunciation of will, others glimpses of human *potentia*.[25]

This kind of offering was not what Hindmarsh, Proud and their supporters (like 'Ignoramus') wanted for the New Church. Already we have seen them at work to establish ceremonial, to ordain a priesthood, to expel democracy and to establish ritual forms: the Tree of Mystery was actually growing before Blake's eyes. The New Church, it turned out, was almost immediately to endorse half the forms and more than half of the ritualistic vocabulary (of prayer and humiliation before God) of the Old, and to become a refuge for genteel, well-heeled, *bien-pensant* spirits with an inclina-

---

[24] 'An Account of Infants or Little Children in Heaven', *New Magazine*, Vol. 1 (May 1790), p. 111. The date is too late to have directly influenced the *Songs*. But no doubt this was one of Chastanier's translations from his hoard of MSS, and it could have been circulated before publication or have been read at a private gathering. Or Swedenborg (who repeated himself copiously) may well have written this elsewhere.

[25] See Glen, *Vision and Disenchantment*, chapter 4.

tion towards artistic and visionary experience. This was the prohibitive chapel which Blake found in the midst of 'The Garden of Love', and the submissive self-abasement which he treated ironically in the *Experience* plate (see Illus. 10) of that song.

As the opposition (expelled from Great Eastcheap) fell away in disillusion, the New Church took a marked lurch to the political right, and this at a time when the radical Dissent of Price and of Priestley, under the influence of the French Revolution, was moving rapidly in the opposite direction. The Blakes went spinning off into whatever world they had come from, not (it would seem) as members of a breakaway Swedenborgian sect but with a more radical sense of disenchantment and disgust. It had been, if anything, a confirmation that 'the Active Life' perishes within 'Ceremonies'. It was no doubt after he had walked past Great Eastcheap that Blake wrote in his notebook the savage companion poem to 'The Garden of Love':

> I saw a chapel all of gold
> That none did dare to enter in
> And many weeping stood without
> Weeping mourning worshipping
>
> I saw a serpent rise between
> The white pillars of the door
> And he forcd & forcd & forcd
> Down the golden hinges tore
>
> And along the pavement sweet
> Set with pearls & rubies bright
> All his slimy length he drew
> Till upon the altar white
>
> Vomiting his poison out
> On the bread & on the wine
> So I turned into a sty
> And laid me down among the swine

The journey from the 'Garden of Love' to the sty was the journey from Innocence to Experience. Experience did not cancel out Innocence, for if innocence had been polluted by the serpent, it remained in its purity as emblematic of human potential. The sty, of course, was that of advanced radicalism (later Jacobinism) and Deism: the sty of Tom Paine, Joel Barlow, Joseph Johnson the dissenting publisher and his circle, and Mary Wollstonecraft, whose *Original Stories* for children Johnson engaged Blake to illustrate in 1791. There need be no doubt about 'the swine'. Burke's epochal and blundering vulgarity, 'the swinish multitude' was proudly and truculently adopted by the radicals as the titles of periodicals and pamphlets show – *Pig's Meat, Rights of Swine, Hog's Wash*, with contributions by 'Old Hubert' and 'Porker'. And at the same time the Hindmarsh-controlled *New-Jerusalem Journal* was denouncing–

Those who herd together like swine in *mobelo-equality*, aiming at republicanism, from which the worst infernals in hell are preserved by the pure mercy of the Lord.[26]

The exact route which Blake followed on this journey we do not know. An important staging-post was the joyfully satirical rejection of Swedenborgianism in *The Marriage of Heaven and Hell*, a work which was commenced in 1790 and completed in 1792–3 and which preceded the completed *Songs of Experience*. This includes (at Plate 23) one of his most explicit statements of antinomianism. In this 'Memorable Fancy' the Devil says:

The worship of God is: Honouring his gifts in other man each according to his genius: and loving the greatest men best, those who envy or calumniate great men hate God, for there is no other God.
The Angel hearing this became almost blue but mastering himself grew yellow, & at last white pink & smiling, and then replied,
Thou Idolater, is not God One? & is not he visible in Jesus Christ? and has not Jesus Christ given his sanction to the law of ten commandments and are not all other men fools, sinners, & nothings?
The Devil answer'd; bray a fool in a morter with wheat, yet shall not his folly be beaten out of him: if Jesus Christ is the greatest man, you ought to love him in the greatest degree; now hear how he has given his sanction to the law of ten commandments: did he not mock at the sabbath, and so mock the sabbaths God? murder those who were murderd because of him? turn away the law from the woman taken in adultery? steal the labor of others to support him? bear false witness when he omitted making a defence before Pilate? covet when he pray'd for his disciples, and when he bid them shake off the dust of their feet against such as refused to lodge them? I tell you no virtue can exist without breaking these ten commandments. (E42)

Against the argument that this is not Blake's voice but a provocat-

[26] *New-Jerusalem Journal*, 1792, p. 433.

ive voice reading Swedenborg in an 'infernal' sense – itself a jest upon Swedenborg's 'internal' sense – it should be recalled that he was to rework many of the same themes some years later and in his own voice in 'The Everlasting Gospel'.

The best way to follow Blake's route is to go direct to the *Songs*. Whether or not Blake had always envisaged some 'experience' poems as complementary to 'innocence', between 1789 and 1794, with the succession of French Revolutionary events and with the Painite excitement in London, experience had taken on an altogether more dramatic form. *Innocence*, and *Experience* were engraved and bound together, with the sub-title, 'Showing the Two Contrary States of the Human Soul'. What is evident at once is the quite new emphasis upon, and indeed validation of, 'energy',[27] – an energy often identified with revolution – as well as, both in the *Experience* songs and in *The Marriage of Heaven and Hell*, the emphatic turn to a dialectic of 'contraries', which – while present in Swedenborgianism – undoubtedly indicates that Blake was vigorously renewing his earlier interest in Behmenist (and perhaps Muggletonian) thought. Together with these important emphases there is also an explicitness in social and political criticism ('Holy Thursday', 'The Chimney Sweeper', 'The Garden of Love', 'London') which aligns the *Experience* songs with the advanced radicalism of the times.

'London' is not clearly paired with any song in *Innocence*, unless one takes as its contrary the rural song of play, repose and fulfilment, 'The Echoing Green'. Let us, then, examine it in its own right.

---

[27] See Morton D. Paley, *Energy and Imagination: A Study of the Development of Blake's Thought* (Oxford, 1970).

CHAPTER II

'London'

'London' is among the most lucid and instantly available of the
Songs of Experience. 'The poem', John Beer writes, 'is perhaps the
least controversial of all Blake's works', and 'no knowledge of his
personal vision is necessary to assist the understanding'.[1] I agree
with this: the poem does not require an interpreter since the images
are self-sufficient within the terms of the poem's own development.
Every reader can, without the help of a critic, see London simultaneously as Blake's own city, as an image of the state of English
society and as an image of the human condition. So far from requir-
ing a knowledge of Blake's personal vision it is one of those foundation poems upon which our knowledge of that vision can be built.
A close reading may confirm, but is likely to add very little to,
what a responsive reader had already experienced.

But since the poem is found in draft in Blake's notebook we are
unusually well placed to examine it not only as product but in its
process of creation. Here is the finished poem:

> I wander thro' each charter'd street,
> Near where the charter'd Thames does flow.
> And mark in every face I meet
> Marks of weakness, marks of woe.
>
> In every cry of every Man,
> In every Infants cry of fear,
> In every voice: in every ban,
> The mind-forg'd manacles I hear
>
> How the Chimney-sweepers cry
> Every blackning Church appalls,
> And the hapless Soldiers sigh,
> Runs in blood down Palace walls

[1] John Beer, *Blake's Humanism* (Manchester, 1968), p. 75.

But most thro' midnight streets I hear
How the youthful Harlots curse
Blasts the new-born Infants tear
And blights with plagues the Marriage hearse   (E26–7)

In Blake's draft the first verse was originally thus:

I wander thro each dirty street
Near where the dirty Thames does flow
And see in every face I meet
Marks of weakness marks of woe[2]

The first important change is from 'dirty' to 'charter'd'. Another
fragment in the notebook helps to define this alteration:

Why should I care for the men of thames
Or the cheating waves of charter'd streams
Or shrink at the little blasts of fear
That the hireling blows into my ear

Tho born on the cheating banks of Thames
Tho his waters bathed my infant limbs
The Ohio shall wash his stains from me
I was born a slave but I go to be free[3]

Thus 'charter'd' arose in Blake's mind in association with 'cheating' and with the 'little blasts of fear' of the 'hireling'. The second
association is an obvious political allusion. To reformers the corrupt political system was a refuge for hirelings: indeed, Dr Johnson
had defined in his dictionary a 'pension' as 'In England it is generally understood to mean pay given to a state hireling for treason
to his country.' David Erdman is undoubtedly right that the 'little
blasts of fear' suggest the proclamations, the Paine-burnings and
the political repressions of the State and of Reeves' Association for
Preserving Liberty and Property against Republicans and Levellers
which dominated the year in which these poems were written.[4] In

[2] *The Notebook of William Blake*, ed. David V. Erdman (Oxford, 1973), p. 109; hereafter
cited as N.
[3] N113. The obliterated title of this fragment has been recovered by David Erdman as
'Thames'.
[4] See David Erdman, *Blake: Prophet against Empire*, which fully argues these points on pp.
272–9. These poems were 'forged in the heat of the Year One of Equality (September
1792 to 1793) and tempered in the "grey-brow'd snows" of Antijacobin alarms and
proclamations'. See also A. Mitchell, 'The Association Movement of 1792–3', *Historical
Journal*, 4: 1 (1961), 56–77; E.P. Thompson, *The Making of the English Working Class*
(Harmondsworth, 1968), pp. 115–26; D.E. Ginter, 'The Loyalist Association Movement,
1792–3', *Historical Journal*, 4: 2 (1966), 179–90.

the revised version of 'Thames' Blake introduces the paradox which was continually to be in the mouths of radicals and factory reformers in the next fifty years: the slavery of the English poor. And he points also ('I was born a slave but I go to be free') to the first wave of emigration of reformers from the attention of Church-and-King mobs or hirelings.

But 'charter'd' is more particularly associated with 'cheating'. It is clearly a word to be associated with commerce: one might think of the Chartered Companies which, increasingly drained of function, were bastions of privilege within the government of the city. Or, again, one might think of the monopolistic privileges of the East India Company, whose ships were so prominent in the commerce of the Thames, which applied in 1793 for twenty-years' renewal of its charter, and which was under bitter attack in the reformers' press.[5]

But 'charter'd' is, for Blake, a stronger and more complex word than that, which he endows with more generalised symbolic power. It has the feel of a word which Blake has recently discovered, as, years later, he was to 'discover' the word 'golden' (which, nevertheless, he had been using for years). He is savouring it, weighing its poetic possibilities in his hand. It is in no sense a 'new' word, but he has found a way to use it with a new ironic inversion. For the word is standing at an intellectual and political cross-roads. On the one hand, it was a stale counter of the customary libertarian

---

[5] 'The cheating waves of charter'd streams' and 'the cheating banks of Thames' should prompt one to think carefully of this as the source which first gave to Blake this use of 'charter'd'. The fullest attack from a Painite source on the East India Company did not appear until 1794: see the editorial articles in four successive numbers of Daniel Isaac Eaton's *Politics for the People*, 2: 8–11: 'The East India Charter Considered'. These constituted a full-blooded attack on the Company's commercial and military imperialism ('if it be deemed expedient to *murder* half the inhabitants of India, and *rob* the remainder, surely it is not requisite to call it *governing* them?') which carried to their furthest point criticisms of the Company to be found in the reforming and Foxite press of 1792–3. No social historian can be surprised to find the banks of the Thames described as 'cheating' in the eighteenth century: every kind of fraud and racket, big, small and indifferent, flourished around the docks. The association of the banks of Thames with commerce was already traditional when Samuel Johnson renewed it in his 'London' (1738), especially lines 20–30. Johnson's attitude is already ambiguous: 'Britannia's glories' ('The guard of commerce, and the dread of Spain') are invoked retrospectively, in conventional terms: but on Thames-side already 'all are slaves to gold,/Where looks are merchandise, and smiles are sold'. Erdman argues that the 'golden London' and 'silver Thames' of Blake's 'King Edward the Third' have already assimilated this conventional contrast in the form of irony: see Erdman, pp. 80–1.

rhetoric of the polite culture. Blake himself had used it in much this way in his early 'King Edward the Third':

> Let Liberty, the charter'd right of Englishmen,
> Won by our fathers in many a glorious field,
> Enerve my soldiers; let Liberty
> Blaze in each countenance, and fire the battle.
> The enemy fight in chains, invisible chains, but heavy;
> Their minds are fetter'd; then how can they be free?[6]

It would be only boring to accumulate endless examples from eighteenth-century constitutional rhetoric or poetry of the use of chartered rights, chartered liberties, magna carta: the word is at the centre of Whig ideology.

There is, however, an obvious point to be made about this tedious usage of 'charter'. A charter of liberty is, simultaneously, a denial of these liberties to others. A charter is something given or ceded; it is bestowed upon some group by some authority; it is not claimed as of right. And the liberties (or privileges) granted to this guild, company, corporation or even nation *exclude* others from the enjoyment of these liberties. A charter is, in its nature, exclusive.

We are at a cross-roads because it is exactly this exclusive and granted quality of liberties which was under challenge; and it was under challenge from the claim to universal rights. The point becomes clear when we contrast Burke's *Reflections* and Paine's *Rights of Man*. Although Burke was every inch a rhetorician he had no taste for stale rhetoric, and he used the word 'charter' lightly in the *Reflections*. 'Our oldest reformation', he wrote, 'is that of Magna Charta':

From Magna Charta to the Declaration of Right it has been the uniform policy of our constitution to claim and assert our liberties as an *entailed inheritance* derived to us from our forefathers, and to be transmitted to our posterity. . .
We have an inheritable crown, an inheritable peerage, and a House of Commons and a people inheriting privileges, franchises, and liberties from a long line of ancestors.

Burke was concerned explicitly to define this chartered, heritable set of liberties and privileges (exclusive in the sense that it is 'an

---

[6] E415. If we take the intention of this fragment to be ironic, then Blake was already regarding the word as suspect rhetoric.

estate specially belonging to the people of this kingdom') as against
any general uncircumscribed notion of 'the rights of man'. It is in
vain, he wrote, to talk to these democratists:

of the practice of their ancestors, the fundamental laws of their country
. . . They have wrought underground a mine that will blow up, at one
grand explosion, all examples of antiquity, all precedents, charters, and
acts of parliament. They have 'the rights of men'. Against these there can
be no prescription. . .

Liberty, for Burke, must have its 'gallery of portraits, its monu-
mental inscriptions, its records, evidences, and titles'. The imagery,
as so often, is that of the great house of the landed gentry, with its
walks and statuary, its galleries and muniments' room.

For Burke, then, 'charter' and 'charter'd', while not over-
laboured, remain among the best of good words. But not for Paine:
'I am contending for the rights of the *living*, and against their being
willed away, and controuled and contracted for, by the manuscript
assumed authority of the dead.' A charter implied not a freedom
but monopoly: 'Every chartered town is an aristocratical monopoly
in itself, and the qualifications of electors proceeds out of those
chartered monopolies. Is this freedom? Is this what Mr Burke
means by a constitution?' It was in the incorporated towns, with
their charters, that the Test and Corporation Acts against Dissenters operated with most effect. Hence (Paine argued – and economic historians have often agreed with him) the vitality of the
commerce of un-incorporated towns like Manchester, Birmingham
and Sheffield. The Dissenters (he wrote), 'withdrew from the persecution of the chartered towns, where test laws more particularly
operate, and established a sort of asylum for themselves in those
places . . . But the case is now changing. France and America
bid all comers welcome, and initiate them into all the rights of
citizenship.'

This is (for Paine) the first offence of 'chartered': it implies exclusion and limitation. Its second offence was in its imputation that
anyone had the right to *grant* freedoms or privileges to other men:
'If we begin with William of Normandy, we find that the government of England was originally a tyranny, founded on an invasion
and conquest of the country . . . Magna Carta . . . was no more
than compelling the government to renounce a part of its assump-

tions.' Both these offences were criticised in a central passage which I argue lay somewhere in Blake's mind when he selected the word:

It is a perversion of terms to say that a charter gives rights. It operates by a contrary effect – that of taking rights away. Rights are inherently in all the inhabitants; but charters, by annulling those rights in the majority, leave the right, by exclusion, in the hands of a few . . . The only persons on whom they operate are the persons whom they exclude . . . Therefore, all charters have no other than an indirect negative operation.

Charters, he continued, 'are sources of endless contentions in the places where they exist, and they lessen the common rights of national society'. The charters of corporate towns might, he suggested, have arisen because of garrison service: 'Their refusing or granting admission to strangers, which has produced the custom of *giving, selling and buying freedom*, has more of the nature of garrison authority than civil government' (my emphasis).

Blake by now had come to share much of Paine's political outlook, although he did not share his faith in the beneficence of commerce. He thus chose 'charter'd' out of the biggest political argument that was agitating Britain in 1791–3, and he chose it with that irony which inverted the rhetoric of Burke and asserted the definitions of 'exclusion', the annulling of rights, 'negative operation' and 'giving, selling and buying freedom'. The adjectival form – charter'd – enforces the direct commercial allusion: 'the organisation of a city in terms of trade'.[7]

The other emendation to the first verse is trivial: in the third line 'And see in every face I meet' is altered to 'And mark. . .' And yet, is it as trivial as it seems? For we already have, in the fourth line, 'Marks of weakness marks of woe'. Thus Blake has chosen, with deliberation, the triple beat of 'mark'. And we respond to this, whether we are conscious of the nature of the response or whether the words beat upon us in subliminal ways: even in these biblically illiterate days we have all heard of 'the mark of the Beast'. Some of Blake's central images – his trees, and clouds, and caves, and serpents, and roots – have such a universal presence in mythology and literature that one may spend half a lifetime in the game of hunt-the-source. And sometimes the hunting is fruitful, provided that we remember always that the source (or its echo in Blake's

[7] Raymond Williams, *The Country and the City* (1973), p. 148.

mind) is not the same thing as what he makes of it in his own art. Miss Kathleen Raine, a Diana among hunters, has found this:

The opening lines of *London* suggest very strongly Vergil's account of the damned in Hades:

> Nor Death itself can wholly wash their Stains;
> But long-contracted Filth ev'n in the Soul remains.
> The Reliques of inveterate Vice they wear;
> And spots of Sin obscene in ev'ry Face appear.[8]

The suggestion need not be excluded; this echo, with others, could have been in Blake's mind. But if so, *what does Blake do with it?* For Blake's poem evokes pity and forgiveness – the cries, the 'hapless Soldiers sigh', 'weakness' and 'woe' – and not the self-righteous eviction to Hades of 'long-contracted Filth', 'inveterate Vice' and 'spots of Sin obscene'. Moreover, in the amendment from 'And see' to 'And mark', Blake (or the speaker of his poem) closes the gap between the censorious observer and the faces which are observed, assimilating both within a common predicament: the marker himself appears to be marked or even to be mark*ing*.[9]

But 'mark' undoubtedly came through to the reader with a much stronger, biblical resonance. The immediate allusion called to mind will most probably have been 'the mark of the Beast', as in Revelation xiii.16–17:

And he causeth all, both small and great, rich and poor, free and bond, to receive a mark in their right hand, or in their foreheads:
And that no man might buy or sell, save he that had the mark, or the name of the Beast, or the number of his name.

The mark of the Beast would seem, like 'charter'd', to have something to do with the buying and selling of human values.

This question is incapable of any final proof. The suggestion has been made[10] that Blake's allusion is not to Revelation but to Ezekiel ix.4: 'And the Lord said unto him, Go through the midst of the city, through the midst of Jerusalem, and set a mark upon the foreheads of the men that sigh and that cry for all the abominations

---

[8] Kathleen Raine, Vol. I, pp. 24–5 (citing Dryden's *Aeneid* VI. 998–1001).
[9] Heather Glen has noted that 'the sense of an inevitable and imprisoning relationship between the "facts" he sees and the way in which he sees is reinforced by the use of "mark" as both verb and object'. See 'The Poet in Society: Blake and Wordsworth on London', *Literature and History* 3 (March 1976).
[10] Among others, by Harold Bloom and David Erdman, and, with a different emphasis, by Heather Glen.

that be done in the midst thereof.' The man who is ordered to go
through the city has 'a writer's inkhorn by his side'. This seems at
first to fit the poem closely: in 'London' a writer goes through the
city of abominations and listens to 'sighs' and 'cries'. But even a
literal reading does not fit the poem's meaning. For Blake – or the
'I' of his poem – is not setting marks on foreheads, he is observing
them; and the marks are those of weakness and of woe, not of
lamentations over abominations. Moreover, in Ezekiel's vision the
Lord then orders armed men to go through the city and to 'slay
utterly old and young, both maids and little children, and women:
but come not near any man upon whom is the mark. . .' Thus those
who are marked are set apart and saved. Neither the intention nor
the tone of Blake's poem coincides with Ezekiel's unedifying vision.
Nor are we entitled to conflate the allusions to Revelation and to
Ezekiel with some gesture towards an ulterior 'ambivalence' in
which Blake has assimilated the damned to the elect. For if one
point is incontestable about this poem it is that *every* man is marked:
all share this human condition: whereas with Ezekiel it is the great
*un*marked majority who are to be put to the sword. Such a confla-
tion offers temptations to a critic but it would destroy the poem
by introducing into its heart a direct contradiction of intention and
of feeling. Ambiguities of this dimension are not fruitful multipliers
of meaning.

There is, further, the question of what response the word 'mark'
is most likely to have called up among Blake's contemporaries. I
must assert that the allusions called first to mind will have been
either to the 'mark of Cain' (Genesis iv.15)[11] or to the 'mark of the
Beast' in Revelation. And the more radical the audience, the more

---

[11] This suggestion has been pressed by Stan Smith, 'Some Responses to Heather Glen's
"The Poet in Society"', *Literature and History* 4 (Autumn 1976). The 'mark of Cain' in
Genesis was sometimes assimilated in theological exegesis to the mark of the Beast. The
Lord curses Cain and condemns him to be a fugitive and a vagabond. Cain complains
that he will be killed as an outlaw, and the Lord replies: 'Whosoever slayeth Cain,
vengeance shall be taken on him sevenfold. And the Lord set a mark upon Cain, lest any
finding him should kill him.' Whether the Lord did this as an act of forgiveness or as a
protraction of the punishment of ostracism and outlawry (as anthropologists would argue)
is a matter of interpretation. Stan Smith certainly carries the Lord's intentions very much
too far when he takes the mark as a sign of 'election'. But he is surely right to argue that
the poem can carry *this* ambivalence (men are 'both agents and patients, culprits and
victims'), since in Blake's Christian dialectic the mark of Cain could stand simultaneously
as a sign of sin and as a sign of its forgiveness. See Blake's chapter title to the 'Genesis'
fragment: 'Chapter iv How Generation & Death took possession of the Natural Man &
of the Forgiveness of Sins written upon the Murderers Forehead' (E667).

preoccupied it will have been with the second. For generations radical Dissent had sermonised and pamphleteered against the Beast (Antichrist) who has had servitors 'which worshipped his image' (Revelation xvi.2): social radicalism equated these with userers, with the rich, with those successful in buying and selling. And interpreters of Revelation always fastened with fascination upon the enigmatic verse (xiii.18): 'Let him that hath understanding count the number of the Beast: for it is the number of a man' (see Illus. 12). Such interest in millennial interpretation became rife once more in the 1790s;[12] it turned above all on these chapters of Revelation with their recurrent images of the Beast and of the destruction of Babylon, and the humble were able to turn to their own account the imprecations against kings, false prophets and the rich with which these chapters are rife. We hardly need to argue that Blake, like most radical Dissenters of his time, had saturated his imagination with the imagery of Revelation: chapter xiv (the Son of Man with the sickle, and the Last Vintage) is implanted in the structure of *Vala* and of *Jerusalem*.

These considerations, which are ones of cultural context rather than of superficial verbal similarities, lead me to reject the suggested allusion to Ezekiel. What Blake's contemporaries were arguing about in the 1790s was the rule of Antichrist and the hope of the millennium: the mark seen in 'every face' is the mark of the Beast, a mark explicitly associated with commercialism. And if we require conclusive evidence that Blake was thinking, in 'London', of Revelation, he has given us this evidence himself, with unusual explicitness. For the illumination to the poem[13] appears to be an independent, but complementary, conception; and for this reason I feel entitled to discuss the poem also as an independent concep-

[12] See, e.g., Thompson, pp. 127–9, 420–6, and sources cited there; and Morton D. Paley, 'William Blake, the Prince of the Hebrews, and the Women Clothed with the Sun', in Morton D. Paley and Michael Phillips (eds.), *William Blake: Essays in Honour of Sir Geoffrey Keynes* (Oxford, 1973). Swedenborgians were much concerned with interpretation of Revelation; and the verses which I have cited ('no man might buy or sell, save he that had the mark . . . of the beast') were discussed in the *New Magazine of Knowledge Concerning Heaven and Hell*, 1 (July 1790), 209–11. When Blake's acquaintance Stedman heard the news, on 6 April 1792, that Gustavus III, the King of Sweden, had been assassinated, his mind turned in the same direction: 'despotism dies away. Witness France, whose King may be compared to the beast in Revelation, whose number is 666, and LUDOVICUS added together makes the same. One, Sutherland, lately shot himself before King George . . . Such are the times': *The Journal of John Gabriel Stedman 1744–1797*, ed. Stanbury Thompson (1962), pp. 340–1; I am indebted to Michael Phillips for this reference.
[13] See Illus. 11.

tion and within its own terms. The illumination (if I am pressed to confess my own view) adds nothing essential to the poem, but comments upon the same theme in different terms. Nor are we even certain how the poem and the illumination are united, nor why they complement each other, until we turn to *Jerusalem*, Book 4 (E241):

> I see London blind & age-bent begging thro the Streets
> Of Babylon, led by child, his tears run down his beard

In both the poem and the illumination, London's streets appear as those of Babylon of Revelation; but in the illumination it is London himself who is wandering through them.[14]

In the second verse the important change is from 'german forg'd links' to 'mind-forg'd manacles'. The reference was, of course, to the Hanoverian monarchy, and perhaps to the expectation that Hanoverian troops would be used against British reformers.[15] The change to 'mind-forg'd' both generalises and also places us again in that universe of Blakean symbolism in which we must turn from one poem to another for cumulative elucidation. In this case we have already noted that the image of the mind as 'fettered' by the invisible chains of its own unfreedom had appealed to Blake in his youthful 'King Edward the Third'. The development of the image is shown in another fragment in the notebook, 'How to know Love from Deceit':

> Love to faults is always blind
> Always is to joy inclind
> Lawless wingd & unconfind
> And breaks all chains from every mind

[14] One further suggestion may be offered about the mark of the Beast. The Muggletonians afford yet one more possible resonance of 'mark'. In Swedenborgian exegesis the 'mark of the Beast' was sometimes taken to signify the solifidian doctrine of justification by faith without works. But Blake can scarcely have been using 'mark' in this way, since this was precisely his own, antinomian, 'heresy'. The Muggletonians, however, offer a very different interpretation. In their meetings prayer was rejected, as a 'mark of weakness', and Muggleton wrote:

The mark of the beast is this, when a head magistrate or chief council in a nation or kingdom, shall set up . . . a set form of worship, he or they having no commission from God so to do, and shall cause the people by their power and authority . . . to worship after this manner of worship that is set up by authority, as this beast did. . .

Hence to receive the mark of the Beast signifies 'to worship the image set up' by established authority. L. Muggleton, *A True Interpretation of . . . the Whole Book of the Revelation of St John* (1808), pp. 174–5. This appears to take us very much closer to the universe of Blakean symbolism than do the Swedenborgian glosses.

[15] See Erdman, pp. 277–8.

> Deceit to secresy confind
> Lawful cautious & refind
> To every thing but interest blind
> And forges fetters for the mind

The 'mind-forg'd manacles', then, are those of deceit, self-interest, absence of love, of law, repression and hypocrisy.[16] They are stronger and harder to break than the manacles of the German king and his mercenaries, since they bind the minds not only of the oppressors but also of the oppressed; moreover, they are self-forged. How then are we to read 'ban'? F.W. Bateson, a confident critic, tells us 'in every execration or curse (*not* in every prohibition)'.[17] I can't share his confidence: one must be prepared for seventeen types of ambiguity in Blake, and, in any case, the distinction between a curse and a prohibition is not a large one. The 'bans' may be execrations, but the mind may be encouraged to move through further associations, from the banns before marriage, the prohibitive and possessive ethic constraining 'lawless' love (' "Thou Shalt Not" writ over the door'), to the bans of Church and State against the publications and activities of the followers of Tom Paine.[18] All these associations are gathered into the central one of a code of morality which constricts, denies, prohibits and punishes.

The third verse commenced in the notebook as:

> But most the chimney sweepers cry
> Blackens oer the churches walls

This second line was then changed to:

> Every blackning church appalls

The effect is one of concentration. Pertinacious critics have been able to invert most of Blake's meanings, and readers have even found to suppose that these two lines (in their final form) are a comment upon the awakening social conscience of the churches

---

[16] Blake was also thinking of priestcraft, as we know from 'The Human Abstract'. Nancy Bogen suggests (*Notes and Queries*, new series, 15: 1 (January 1968)) that he may have been reading Gilbert Imlay's *Topographical Description* (London, 1792): on the Ohio (where the Thames-born slave will go to be free) Imlay found freedom from priestcraft which elsewhere 'seems to have forged fetters for the human mind'. But the poem itself carries this suggestion only in so far as the manacles immediately precede the 'blackning Church'. Fetters and manacles were anyway part of a very general currency of imagery: see, e.g., Erdman, p. 129, n. 35.

[17] F.W. Bateson, *Selected Poems of William Blake* (1957), p. 126.

[18] See E.D. Hirsch, *Innocence and Experience* (New Haven, 1964), p. 264.

under the influence of the evangelical revival: the churches are appalled by the plight of the chimney-sweeping boys.[19] The meaning, of course, is the opposite; and on this point the notebook entitles us to have confidence. In the first version the churches are clearly shown as passive, while the cry of the chimney-sweepers attaches itself, with the smoke of commerce, to their walls. By revising the line Blake has simply tightened up the strings of his indignation by another notch. He has packed the meaning of 'The Chimney Sweeper' of the *Songs of Experience* (whose father and mother 'are both gone up to the church' to 'praise God & his Priest & King,/Who make up a heaven of our misery') into a single line, the adjective 'blackning' visually attaching to the Church complicity in the brutal exploitation of young childhood along with the wider consequences of the smoke of expanding commerce. 'Appalls' is used in a transitive sense familiar in Blake's time – not as 'is appalled by' but as puts to shame, puts in fear, challenges, indicts, in the same way as the dying sigh of the soldier indicts (and also threatens, with an apocalyptic image)[20] the Palace.[21] 'An ancient Proverb' in the notebook gives the three elements of a curse upon England:

[19] For an example of this confusion, see D.G. Gillham, *Blake's Contrary States* (Cambridge, 1966), p. 12: 'The Church is horrified at the evil of the sweeper's condition, but it is helpless to do much about it. . .'

[20] On this point, see Erdman, pp. 278–9. The British reformers of the 1790s were, of course, at pains to stress the identity of interests of the soldiers and the people: and also to expose military injustices, flogging, forcible recruitment ('crimping'), etc.

[21] Many examples could be given of this transitive use of 'appal': see also the OED and the last line of 'Holy Thursday' in *Experience*. Thus William Frend, who shared something of Blake's ultra-radical Christian values, wrote: 'Oh! that I had the warning voice of an ancient prophet, that I might penetrate into the innermost recesses of palaces, and appal the haranguers of senates!' Frend's 'appal' means 'throw into consternation', 'warn', 'shock'. The phrase was used in the appendix to William Frend, *Peace and Union Recommended* (St Ives, 1792): this pamphlet occasioned the celebrated case of Frend's trial before the Vice-Chancellor and his expulsion from Cambridge: see Frida Knight, *University Rebel* (1971), esp. chapter 8. The pamphlet was on sale by mid-February 1793 (William Frend, *Account of the Proceedings. . .* (Cambridge, 1793), p. 72), and the appendix caused especial outrage among loyalists, and by the first week in May the University had opened its proceedings against Frend. From the juxtaposition of ancient prophet, palaces and appal, and from the fact that Blake and Frend shared friends and sympathies (see Erdman, pp. 158–9), one could argue that Blake's line could carry an echo of this celebrated case. But this is highly unlikely: Erdman gives a terminal date for inscribing the *Experience* drafts in the notebook as October 1792 (N7) – although 'appalls' was introduced as a revision, perhaps subsequently. But it is unnecessary to argue for such direct influence. What we are really finding is a vocabulary and stock of images common to a particular group or a particular intellectual tradition, in this case that of radical Dissent. It is helpful to identify these groups and traditions, since they both place Blake and help us to unlock his meanings: but as to the actual 'source' we must maintain a steady scepticism.

> Remove away that blackning church
> Remove away that marriage hearse
> Remove away that [place: *del.*] man of blood
> You'll quite remove the ancient curse.[22]

Church, marriage and monarchy: but if he had left it at 'place',
then it could have been Tyburn (or Newgate), the place of public
execution – the altar of the 'Moral & Self-Righteous Law' of Babylon and Cruel Og, in the centre of London, whose public rituals
Blake may have witnessed.

The poem, in its first version, was to end at this point, at 'Runs
in blood down Palace walls'. But Blake was not yet satisfied: he
returned, and worked through three versions of a fourth, concluding verse, squeezing it in between other drafts already on the page.
One attempt reads:

> But most thro wintry streets I hear
> How the midnight harlots curse
> Blasts the new born infants tear
> And smites with plagues the marriage hearse.

Bateson tells us that 'the images are sometimes interpreted as a
reference to venereal disease. But this is to read Blake too literally.
The diseases that descend upon the infant and the newly married
couple are apocalyptic horrors similar to the blood that runs down
the palace walls.'[23]

It may be nice to think so. But the blood of the soldier is for
real, as well as apocalyptic, and so is the venereal disease that
blinds the new-born infant and which plagues the marriage hearse.
We need not go outside the poem to document the increased discussion of such disease in the early 1790s,[24] nor, to turn the coin over,
the indictment by Mary Wollstonecraft and her circle of marriage
without love as prostitution. The poem makes the point very literally. Blake was often a very literal-minded man.

Another fragment in the notebook is closely related to this con-

[22] N107.
[23] Bateson, *Selected Poems*, p. 126. See also the more elaborate (and unhelpful) argument of
Harold Bloom, *Blake's Apocalypse: A Study in Poetic Argument* (Ithaca, 1963), pp. 141–2,
which also discounts the clear meaning of the third line.
[24] As, for example, the long review of Jesse Foot, *A Complete Treatise on the Origin, Theory,
and Cure of the Lues Venerea etc.* (1792 – but based on lectures read in Dean Street, Soho,
in 1790 and 1791) in *Analytical Review*, 12 (April 1792), 399, and 13 (July 1792), 261. See
also the discussion in Grant C. Roti and Donald L. Kent, 'The Last Stanza of Blake's
London', *Blake: an Illustrated Quarterly*, 11: 1 (Summer 1977).

clusion: a verse intended as the conclusion to 'The Human Abstract' (or so it would seem) but not used in its final version. It does not, in fact, relate directly to the imagery of 'The Human Abstract' and we may suppose that Blake, when he realised this, saw also how he could transpose the concept to make a conclusion to 'London':

> There souls of men are bought & sold
> And milk fed infancy for gold
> And youth to slaughter houses led
> And [maidens: *del.*] beauty for a bit of bread.[25]

This enables us to see, once more, that 'London' is a literal poem and it is also an apocalyptic one; or we may say that it is a poem whose moral realism is so searching that it is raised to the intensity of apocalyptic vision. For the poem is not, of course, a terrible cumulative *catalogue* of unrelated abuses and suffering. It is organised in two ways. First, and most simply, it is organised about the street-cries of London. In the first verse, we are placed with Blake (if we are entitled – as I think we are – to take him as the wandering observer) and we 'see' with his eyes. But in the second, third and fourth verses we are *hearing*, and the passage from sight to sound has an effect of reducing the sense of distance or of the alienation of the observer from his object of the first verse, and of immersing us within the human condition through which he walks. We *see* one thing at a time, as distinct moments of perception, although, by the end of the first verse, these perceptions become cumulative and repetitive ('in every face . . . marks . . . marks'). We *hear* many things simultaneously. Literally, we hear the eerie, almost animal cadence of the street-cries (and although we may now be forgetting them, if we were to be transported somehow to eighteenth-century London, these cries would be our first and most astonishing impression), the cries of the children, the 'weep', 'weep' of the chimney-sweeps, and, led on by these, we hear the more symbolic sounds of 'bans', 'manacles' and the soldier's 'sigh'. This second verse is all sounds and it moves through an acceleration of generalisation towards the third. If 'charter'd' is repeated, and if 'marks' falls with a triple beat, 'every' falls upon us no less than seven times: a single incidence in the first verse prepares for five uses in the second and a single incidence in the third ties it into

[25] N107.

the developing structure. 'Cry' also falls three times, carrying us from the second verse to the first line of the third. But in the third verse there is a thickening of sensual perception. Until this point we have seen and heard, but now we 'sense', through the sounds (the 'cry' and the 'sigh'), the activities that these indicate: the efforts of the chimney-sweep, the blackening walls of the churches, the blood of the soldier. We are not detached from this predicament; if anything, this impression of 'hearing' giving way to 'sensing' immerses us even more deeply within it.

We have been wandering, with Blake, into an ever more dense immersion. But the opening of the fourth verse ('But most thro' midnight streets I hear') appears to set us a little apart from this once more. 'I hear' takes us back from ourselves to Blake who is a little apart from the scene and listening. Nothing in the earlier verses had prepared us for the darkness of 'midnight streets', unless perhaps the 'blackning Church': what had been suggested before was the activity of the day-time streets, the street-cries, the occasions of commerce. The verse is not knitted in tidily to the rest at the level of literal organisation: the 'Marriage hearse' is a conceit more abstract than any other in the poem, apart from 'mind-forg'd manacles'. Since we know that he had intended at first to end the poem with three verses,[26] should we say that the final verse was an afterthought tacked on after the original images had ceased to beat in his mind – imperfectly soldered to the main body and still betraying signs of a separate origin?

It is a fair question. Blake, like other poets, had afterthoughts and made revisions which were unwise. And if we were to stop short at this literal or technical organisation of the poem we could make a case against its final verse. But we must attend also to a second, symbolic, level of organisation. The immersion in sights and sounds is of a kind which forces one to generalise from London to 'the human condition'. The point is self-evident ('In every cry of every Man'). But this kind of statement, of which a certain school of commentators on Blake is over-fond, takes us only a little way, and a great deal less far than is sometimes knowingly implied. For 'the human condition', unless further qualified or disclosed, is nothing but a kind of metaphysical full stop. Or, worse than that, it is a bundle of solecisms about mortality and defeated aspiration.

---

[26] This is emphasised by the fact that it was the first line of verse 3 which (in the notebook draft) was to begin with 'But most. . .'; 'But most the chimney sweepers cry'.

But 'the human condition' is what poets make poetry *out of*, not what they end up with. This poem is about a *particular* human condition, which acquires, through the selection of the simplest and most archetypal examples (man, infant soldier, palace, harlot), a generalised resonance; it expresses an attitude *towards* that condition; and it offers a unitary analysis as to its character.

Two comments may be made on the attitude disclosed by Blake towards his own material. First, it is often noted that 'London' is one of the *Songs of Experience* which carries 'the voice of honest indignation'. This is true. The voice can be heard from the first 'charter'd'; it rises to full strength in the third and final verses (appalls, runs in blood, blasts, blights). But it is equally true that this voice is held in equilibrium with the voice of compassion. This is clear from the first introduction of 'mark'. If we have here (and the triple insistence enforces conviction) the 'mark of the Beast', Blake would have been entitled to pour down upon these worshippers at the shrine of false gods the full vials of his wrath:

And there followed another angel, saying, Babylon is fallen, is fallen, that great city, because she made all nations drink of the wine of the wrath of her fornication.

And the third angel followed them, saying with a loud voice, If any man worship the beast and his image, and receive his mark in his forehead, or in his hand,

The same shall drink of the wine of the wrath of God, which is poured out without mixture into the cup of his indignation; and he shall be tormented with fire and brimstone in the presence of the holy angels, and in the presence of the Lamb:

And the smoke of their torment ascendeth up for ever and ever: and they have no rest day nor night, who worship the Beast and his image, and whosoever receiveth the mark of his name.[27]

But Blake indicates 'weakness' and 'woe', and the slow rhythm of the line, checked at mid-point, suggests contemplation and pity rather than wrath. Nor is this note of grave compassion ever lost: it continues in the cries, the fear, the tear: even the soldier is 'hapless'. If 'London' is that part of that human condition which may be equally described as 'Hell', it is not a hell to which only the damned are confined, while the saved may contemplate their tor-

[27] Revelation xiv. 8–11. These verses immediately precede those in which the Son of Man appears with 'in his hand a sharp sickle', and which lead on to 'the great winepress of the wrath of God' (xiv. 14–20) – that vision of the last vintage which worked in Blake's imagination.

ments; nor is this Virgil's 'Hades'. This is a city of Everyman; nor do we feel, in our increasing immersion, that we – or Blake himself – are observers from without. These are not so much our fellow-damned as our fellow-sufferers.

The second comment upon Blake's attitude is this: his treatment of the city departs from a strong literary convention. To establish this point fully would take us further outside the poem than I mean to go. But one way of handling the city, both in itself and as an exemplar of the human condition, derived from classical (especially Juvenalian) satire; and in this it is the city's turbulence, its theatre of changing human passions, its fractured, accidental and episodic life, its swift succession of discrete images of human vice, guile or helplessness, which provided the staple of the convention. Samuel Johnson's 'London' was the place where at one corner a 'fell attorney prowls for prey' and at the next a 'female atheist talks you dead'. And the convention was, in some part, a countryman's convention, in some part a class convention – generally both: a country gentleman's convention. From whichever aspect, plebeian London was seen from outside as a spectacle. Wordsworth was still able to draw upon this convention – although with significant shifts of emphasis – in *The Prelude*.[28]

Blake's 'London' is not seen from without as spectacle. It is seen, or suffered, from within, by a Londoner. And what is unusual about *this* image of the-human-condition-as-hell is that it offers the city as a unitary experience and not as a theatre of discrete episodes. For this to be so, there must be an ulterior symbolic organisation behind the literal organisation of this street-cry following upon that. And this symbolic organisation should now, after this lengthy discussion, have become fully disclosed. The tone of compassion falls upon those who are in hell, the sufferers; but the tone of indignation falls upon the institutions of repression – mind-forg'd manacles, blackning Church, Palace, Marriage hearse. And the symbolic organisation is within the clearly conceived and developing logic of market relations. Blake does not only list symptoms: within the developing imagery which unites the poem he also discloses their cause. From the first introduction of 'charter'd' he never loses hold of the image of buying and selling although these words themselves are never used. 'Charter'd' both grants from on

---

[28] See Williams, *Country and City*, chapter 14, and Glen, 'The Poet in Society'.

high and licenses and it limits and excludes; if we recall Paine it
is a 'selling and buying' of freedom. What are bought and sold in
'London' are not only goods and services but human values, affections and vitalities. From freedom we move (with 'mark') to a race
marked by buying and selling, the worshippers of the Beast and
his image. Then we move through these values in ascendant scale:
goods are bought and sold (street-cries), childhood (the
chimney-sweep), human life (the soldier) and, in the final verse,
youth, beauty and love, the source of life, is bought and sold in
the figure of the diseased harlot who, herself, is only the other side
of the 'Marriage hearse'.[29] In a series of literal, unified images of
great power Blake compresses an indictment of the acquisitive
ethic, endorsed by the institutions of State, which divides man from
man, brings him into mental and moral bondage, destroys the
sources of joy and brings, as its consequence, blindness and death.

It is now evident why the final verse is no afterthought but
appeared to Blake as the necessary conclusion to the poem. The
fragment left over from 'The Human Abstract'

> There souls of men are bought & sold
> And milk fed infancy for gold
> And youth to slaughter houses led
> And beauty for a bit of bread

is a synopsis of the argument in 'London'. As it stands it remains
as an argument, a series of assertions which would only persuade
those already persuaded. But it provided, in its last line, the image
of the harlot, whose love is bought and sold, which was necessary
to complete 'London' and make that poem 'shut like a box'. And
the harlot not only provides a culminating symbol of the reification
of values, she is also a point of junction with the parallel imagery
of religious mystification and oppression: for if this is Babylon,
then the harlot is Babylon's whore who brought about the city's

---

[29] With 'Marriage hearse' we are at the point of junction with another universe of imagery
which critics of the 'neo-Platonist' persuasion emphasise to the exclusion of all other
aspects of Blake's thought. In this universe, for the spirit to assume mortal dress is a
form of death or sleep: hence sexual generation generates death: hence (these would
argue) 'Marriage hearse'. There are times when Blake uses images in this way, although
often with more equivocation, inversion or idiosyncrasy than this kind of criticism suggests. This is not, however, one of these times. The poem is not concerned with lamenting
the constrictions of the spirit within its material 'coffin' but with the 'plagues' which
'blight' sexual love and generation.

fall 'because she made all nations drink of the wine of the wrath of her fornication'. For English radical Dissent in the eighteenth century, the whore of Babylon (see Illus. 13) was not only the 'scarlet woman' of Rome, but also *all* Erastianism, all compromise between things spiritual and the temporal powers of the State, and hence, very specifically, that extraordinary Erastian formation, the Church of England. One recalls Blake's annotations to Bishop Watson (throughout), and his polemic against 'The Abomination that maketh desolate. i.e. State Religion which is the Source of all Cruelty' (E607). Hence the harlot is able to unite in a single nexus the imagery of market relations and the imagery of ideological domination by the agency of a State Church, prostituted to the occasions of temporal power.

To tie the poem up in this way was, perhaps, to add to its pessimism. To end with the blood on the Palace walls might suggest an apocalyptic consummation, a revolutionary overthrow. To end with the diseased infant is to implant life within a cycle of defeat. And yet the poem doesn't *sound* defeated, in part because the tone of compassion or of indignation offers a challenge to the logic of its 'argument',[30] in part because the logic of the symbolic analysis of market relations proposes, at the same time, if not an alternative, at least the challenge that (in compassion and in indignation) this alternative could be found.

In any case, these pages of mine have been teasing out meanings from one poem of sixteen lines. And Blake's larger meanings lie in groupings of poems, in contraries and in cumulative insights into differing states. 'London' is not about the human condition but about a particular condition or state, and a way of seeing this. This state must be set against other states, both of experience and of innocence. Thus we must place 'London' alongside 'The Human Abstract', which shows the generation of the prohibitive Tree of Mystery, whose fruit continually regenerates man's Fall: and in this conjunction 'London' (when seen as hell) shows the condition of the Fallen who lie within the empire of property, self-interest, State religion and Mystery. And when the poem is replaced within the context of the *Songs* it is easier to see the fraternal but trans-

---

[30] See F.R. Leavis, 'Justifying One's Valuation of Blake', in Paley and Phillips, *Essays*, p. 80: 'the effect of the poetry [of the *Songs*] is very far from inducing an acceptance of human defeat. One can testify that the poet himself is not frightened, and, further, that there is no malevolence, no anti-human animus, no reductive bent, in his realism. . .'

formed relationship which Blake's thought at this time bears to Painite radicalism and to the deist and rationalist critique of orthodox religion. 'London' is informed throughout by the antinomian contempt for the Moral Law and the institutions of State, including monarchy and marriage, just as are 'The Garden of Love' and 'The Chimney Sweeper'. With great emphasis it is coming to conclusions very close to those of Paine and his circle. A conjunction between the old antinomian tradition and Jacobinism is taking place.

But while Blake is accepting a part of the Painite argument he is also turning it to a new account. For while 'London' is a poem which a Jacobinical Londoner might have responded to and accepted, it is scarcely one which he could have written. The average supporter of the London Corresponding Society would not have written 'mind-forg'd' (since the manacles would have been seen as wholly exterior, imposed by oppressive priestcraft and kingcraft); and the voice of indignation would probably have drowned the voice of compassion, since most Painites would have found it difficult to accept Blake's vision of humankind as being simultaneously oppressed (although by very much the same forces as those described by Paine) and in a self-victimised or Fallen state. One might seem to contradict the other. And behind this would lie ulterior differences both as to the 'cause' of this human condition and also as to its 'remedy'.

For Blake had always been decisively alienated from the mechanical materialist epistemology and psychology which he saw as derived from Newton and Locke. And he did not for a moment shed his suspicion of radicalism's indebtedness to this materialism, with its prime explanatory principle of self-love. We shall return to this. So that if Blake found congenial the Painite denunciation of the repressive institutions of State and Church, it did not follow that humanity's redemption from this state could be effected by a political reorganisation of these institutions alone. There must be some utopian leap, some human rebirth, from Mystery to renewed imaginative life. 'London' must still be made over anew as the New Jerusalem. And we can't take a full view of even this poem without recalling that Blake did not always see London in this way; it was not always to be seen as Babylon or as the city of destruction in the Apocalypse. There were other times when he saw it as the city of lost innocence:

> The fields from Islington to Marybone,
> To Primrose Hill and Saint Johns Wood:
> Were builded over with pillars of gold,
> And there Jerusalems pillars stood.
>
>   . . .
>
> The Jews-harp-house & the Green Man;
> The Ponds where Boys to bathe delight;
> The Fields of Cows by Willans farm:
> Shine in Jerusalems pleasant sight.

And it could also be the millennial city, of that time when the moral and self-righteous law should be overthrown, and the Multitude return to Unity:

> In my Exchanges every Land
> Shall walk, & mine in every Land,
> Mutual shall build Jerusalem:
> Both heart in heart & hand in hand.   (E170, 172)

CHAPTER 12

'The Human Abstract'

If 'London' shows the conjunction between Blake's antinomian tradition and Painite radicalism – and also the incompatibility of the two – then 'The Human Abstract' shows the conjunction with and also the incompatibility between antinomianism and deism. But before we examine the poem we should look more carefully at ways in which deism influenced Blake. (I am taking it that deism stopped short of atheism and, while rejecting with various degrees of emphasis Christianity and church organisation, still maintained a belief in a First Cause and a divine plan. That was the position where Paine stopped, while Volney probably went on to atheism.)

Blake was to preface the third chapter of *Jerusalem* with an address to the deists, who are identified somewhat loosely with the preachers of 'Natural Morality or Natural Religion'. Voltaire, Rousseau, Gibbon and Hume are singled out for mention (E198– 9). In this Blake was rehearsing his unwavering commitment to his earliest illuminated plates, 'THERE is NO Natural Religion' and 'ALL RELIGIONS are ONE' (1788). These manifestos include an unqualified rejection of any epistemology derived from sense perception as well as any religion derived from natural evidences: 'if it were not for the Poetic or Prophetic character the Philo-sophic & Experimental would soon be at the ratio of all things, & stand still unable to do other than repeat the same dull round over again' (E1). Against 'natural' or materialist epistemology Blake asserted the power of the Poetic Genius or Imagination, and the presence of innate ideas: 'Man is Born Like a Garden ready Planted & Sown':

Innate Ideas are in Every Man, Born with him: they are truly Himself. The Man who says that we have No Innate Ideas must be a Fool & Knave. (Annotations to Reynolds: E637)

His comminations were most commonly directed against Bacon,
Locke and Newton, who

> Deny a Conscience in Man & the Communion of Saints & Angels
> Contemning the Divine Vision & Fruition, Worshiping the Deus
> Of the Heathen, The God of This World, & the Goddess Nature
> Mystery Babylon the Great, the Druid Dragon & hidden
>   Harlot. . .   (*Jerusalem*: E251)

But on occasion other names are added to the trio:

>   . . . this Newtonian Phantasm
> This Voltaire & Rousseau: this Hume & Gibbon & Bolingbroke
> This Natural Religion! this impossible absurdity
>   (*Milton*: E140)

Successive Blake scholars have helpfully explored the reasons for
Blake's antipathy to most of these, especially to Newton and
Locke.[1] But the influence of Gibbon has received less attention.
We should make the imaginative effort to read the argument of
Gibbon in Chapter xx of *Decline and Fall of the Roman Empire* as an
antinomian or radical Dissenter would have read it. Here, surely,
was a feast for the eyes of those long prepared to believe that all
State Religion was the Anti-Christ? Constantine (Gibbon leaves
the reader in no doubt) embraced Christianity for reasons of State:
he was persuaded that the faith 'would inculcate the practice of
private and public virtue' – an end which should recommend itself
to any 'prudent magistrate':

The passive and unresisting obedience which bows under the yoke of
authority or even of oppression must have appeared in the eyes of an
absolute monarch the most conspicuous and useful of the evangelical
virtues. . .

The reigning emperor (Constantine) 'though he had usurped the
sceptre by treason and murder, immediately assumed the sacred
character of vice-regent of the Deity'. Moreover, Gibbon saw Constantine's progress towards Christianity as being in inverse ratio
to his progress towards morality:

He pursued the great object of his ambition through the dark and bloody
paths of war and policy . . . As he gradually advanced in the knowledge
of truth, he proportionally declined in the practice of virtue.

The year in which he convened the Council of Nice was polluted

---

[1] See D. Ault, *Visionary Physics: Blake's Response to Newton* (New York, 1974). Also Edward
Larrissy, *William Blake* (Oxford, 1985), pp. 70–3.

by the murder of his eldest son. Moreover, the establishment of the faith as imperial orthodoxy was accompanied by the degeneration of that faith: 'the piercing eye of ambition and avarice soon discovered that the profession of Christianity might contribute to the interest of the present, as well as of a future, life. The hopes of wealth and honours, the example of an emperor, his exhortations, his irresistible smiles, diffused conviction among the venal and obsequious crowds which usually fill the apartments of a palace.'

The clearest response can be seen in Blake's later work:

> The strongest poison ever known
> Came from Caesar's laurel crown. . .

Or we find it in his Address 'To the Deists' and in the verses which immediately follow. For his most concise expression of antinomian doctrine is followed immediately by an explicit reference to Gibbon's work:

> When Satan first the black bow bent
> And the Moral Law from the Gospel rent
> He forgd the Law into a Sword
> And spilld the blood of Mercys Lord.
>
> Titus! Constantine! Charlemaine!
> O Voltaire! Rousseau! Gibbon! Vain
> Your Grecian Mocks & Roman Sword
> Against this image of his Lord!   (E200)

The reference is to Chapter XLIX in the final volume published in 1788, in which Gibbon describes the donation of Charlemagne which established the temporal dominion of the Papacy, a donation endorsed by the forged 'donation' of Constantine: 'the world beheld for the first time a Christian bishop invested with the prerogatives of a temporal prince'. But if Blake could have found in every chapter of Gibbon evidence to illustrate the opposition of the 'moral law' to the 'everlasting gospel' he would (*and for the same reasons*) have been repelled in every chapter by Gibbon's tone. For Gibbon could, and by the same arguments, justify the donation of Charlemagne and the persecution by the imperial State of the early Christians. Of the first:

In this transaction, the ambition and avarice of the popes has been severely condemned. Perhaps the humility of a Christian priest should have rejected an earthly kingdom ... I will not absolve the pope from

the reproach of treachery and falsehood. But in the rigid interpretation
of the laws, every one may accept, without injury, whatever his benefactor
can bestow without injustice.

Of the second, 'the ecclesiastical writers of the fourth or fifth centuries ascribed to the magistrates of Rome in previous centuries
the same degree of implacable and unrelenting zeal which filled
their own breasts against the heretics or idolators of their own
times'. But

. . .the greatest part of those magistrates who exercised in the provinces
the authority of the emperor . . . and to whose hands alone the jurisdiction
of life and death was intrusted, behaved like men of polished manners
and liberal educations, who respected the rules of justice, and who were
conversant with the precepts of philosophy. (Ch. xvi)

Thus the 'Grecian mocks & Roman sword', the urbane sentiments
of the defenders of property and order which Blake was to see,
under whatever religious forms, as 'natural religion'. As he was
to write in the address 'To the Deists' which prefaced the 'Grey
Monk':

Those who Martyr others or who cause War are Deists, but never can
be Forgivers of Sin. The Glory of Christianity is, To Conquer by Forgiveness. All the Destruction therefore, in Christian Europe has arisen from
Deism, which is Natural Religion. (E199)

Thus in 1804. The influence of Gibbon upon Blake has been an
argumentative one: he has ended up by accepting Gibbon's history,
while redefining State Christianity as polity and self-interest and
therefore as 'deism'. But in 1792, and perhaps for some years thereafter, Blake had been subjected to influences of a quite different
order. Undoubtedly Blake was deeply interested in researches into
comparative religion and mythology, which had been enlarging for
the previous century.[2] This came sometimes from deist, sometimes
from more orthodox Christian sources, and by the 1780s and 1790s
such exercises had become a commonplace of intellectual discourse. By exactly which routes this body of knowledge and of
speculation came to Blake is unclear. He certainly had a quirky
interest in Druidism,[3] was fascinated by Stukeley's identification of
Stonehenge as the 'serpent temple', probably knew Richard Payne

---

[2] See Frank E. Manuel, *The Eighteenth Century Confronts the Gods* (Boston, Mass., 1959), and
(for Blake) Jon Mee, *Dangerous Enthusiasm*, chapter 3.
[3] See *ibid.*, chapter 2.

Knight's *A Discourse on the Worship of Priapus* (1786) and also the recent translation of the *Bhagavad-Gita*,[4] and he could (but need not) have consulted Jacob Bryant's *A New System: Or an Analysis of Ancient Mythology* (3 vols., 1774–6).[5] However, I wish to press the claims of another candidate, C.F. Volney.[6]

Volney's *Ruins* belonged decisively, not to an academic, but to a revolutionary tradition: he pressed always his arguments to conclusions both republican and hostile to State Religion. Once published in English it was enthusiastically taken up by London radicals; extracts were circulated as fly-sheets;[7] and by the mid-1790s every advanced member of the London Corresponding Society could have bought a tiny cheap edition to carry around in his pocket.[8] It was a book more positive and challenging, and perhaps as influential, in English radical history as Paine's *Age of Reason*, which it preceded by several years. And it is by no means a trivial book. It is an essay in comparative mythology in a form (a 'vision') congenial to Blake. Volney had had the chance of seeing some part of Dupuis' twelve-volume *Religion Universelle, ou L'Origine de Tous les Cultes*,[9] whose standpoint is succinctly expressed in the preface: 'For me, the Gods are children of men; and I think, with Hesiod, that the earth has made Heaven.' In a sense Volney offered a 'trailer' for Dupuis in his *The Ruins; or a Survey of the Revolutions of Empire*, published in Paris in 1791, but a passionate, polemical trailer. Where Dupuis emphasised the emergence of all religions from a common Mithraic origin (in Sun-worship), Volney proposed a succession of naturalistic explanations, in which human needs or natural experiences were objectified in deities, thence

---

[4] *The Bhagrat-Geeta, or Dialogues of Kreeshna and Arjoon*, trans. Charles Wilkins (1785). See also Morton D. Paley, *Energy and the Imagination*, p. 139.

[5] Northrop Frye, p. 173, doubts whether Blake read this. Jerome J. McGann shows that Blake and Bryant held different views of ancient mythology: 'The Idea of an Indeterminate Text', *Studies in Romanticism*, 25, no. 8, Fall 1986, esp. pp. 312–14, and he offers Alexander Geddes, *Prospectus of a New Translation of the Holy Bible* (1786) as another influence upon Blake. Jon Mee recovers more about Geddes in *Dangerous Enthusiasm*, chapter 4, and (on Bryant) pp. 132–3.

[6] See Brian Rigby's helpful essay, 'Volney's Rationalist Apocalypse', in Francis Barker *et al.* (eds.), *1789: Reading Writing Revolution* (University of Essex, 1982). Jon Mee pays close attention to Volney's possible influence upon Blake: *Dangerous Enthusiasm*, esp. pp. 138–42.

[7] The confrontation between the 'distinguished class' and the 'people' was circulating as a fly-sheet perhaps as early as December 1792: in PRO, HO 42.23 fo. 631 (my thanks to James Epstein). See also *The Making of the English Working Class*, pp. 107–8.

[8] My own copy of this edition has no date.

[9] Frank Manuel has a helpful chapter on Dupuis, but does not mention Volney.

abstracted from their original impulse, and exploited as serviceable mysteries by priestcraft and by privileged orders. The text is lucid and utterly innocent of Gibbon's 'Grecian mocks'; the footnotes, with tantalising information as to the symbolism or doctrines of a score of different religions and cults, would have whetted Blake's appetite – and perhaps contributed to the dramatis personae of the prophetic books. Moreover, the narrative of the book carries the reader forward on a wave of enthusiasm, not to a politic wisdom of the world, but to the vision of a 'New Age' in which men will shed their warring religions and attain brotherhood in clear-eyed self-knowledge. Mystery, priestcraft and kingcraft will fall together. For Volney's message was also revolutionary: the error of the Declaration of Rights was that Liberty was allowed to precede Equality. Equality must be the basis upon which Liberty is founded.

The argument of Plate 11 of the *Marriage of Heaven and Hell* is close to the argument of Volney:

The ancient Poets animated all sensible objects with Gods or Geniuses, calling them by the names and adorning them with the properties of woods, rivers, mountains, lakes, cities, nations, and whatever their enlarged & numerous senses could perceive.

And particularly they studied the genius of each city & country. placing it under its mental deity.

Till a system was formed, which some took advantage of & enslav'd the vulgar by attempting to realize or abstract the mental deities from their object; thus began Priesthood.

Choosing forms of worship from poetic tales.

And at length they pronounced that the Gods had ordered such things.

Thus men forgot that All deities reside in the human breast.

In certain chapters of *The Ruins* it is difficult *not* to encounter these ideas. Thus in Chapter XXII on the 'Origin and Genealogy of Religious Ideas', Volney describes how man in his 'original state' 'animated with his understanding and his passions the great agents of nature . . . and substituting a fantastic to a real world, he constituted for himself beings of opinion, to the terror of his mind and the torment of his race':

Thus the ideas of God and religion sprung, like all others, from physical objects, and were in the understanding of man, the produce of his sensations, his wants, the circumstances of his life. . .

Hence the Divinity 'was originally as various and manifold as the forms under which he seemed to act; each being was a power, a genius. . .' (XXII, sect. 1) The idea in Blake's second paragraph (the 'genius of each city & country' placed 'under its mental deity') is implicit throughout Volney's argument, although never expressed quite as explicitly as this.[10]

The third paragraph is crucial: here Blake argues that thus 'a system was formed' which some made use of to enslave the vulgar 'by attempting *to realize or abstract the mental deities from their object*; thus began Priesthood' (my emphasis). Again, this idea is central to the structure of Volney's argument: in Chapter XXII, section 3, Volney describes how there were established 'in the very bosom of states sacrilegious corporations of hypocritical and deceitful men who arrogated to themselves every kind of power; and priests . . . instituted under the name of religion, an empire of mystery, which to this very hour has proved ruinous to the nations of mankind'.[11] The attributes of God (Volney argues) are '*abstractions* of the knowledge of nature' (my emphasis), 'the idea of whose conduct is suggested by the experience of a despotic government' (Ch. XXII):

Thus the Deity, after having been originally considered as the sensible and various actions of meteors and the elements . . . became at last *a chimerical and abstract being*: a scholastic subtlety of substance without form, of body without figure; a true delirium of the mind beyond the power of reason at all to comprehend. (Ch. XXII, section 8, my emphasis)

Volney's *Ruins*, after its appearance in Paris in 1791, quickly came to English notice. It has sometimes been supposed that Blake could not have seen it while writing *The Marriage of Heaven and Hell*, and this is a difficult textual question. It is generally agreed that the Marriage may have been started in 1790 and concluded, with the 'Song of Liberty', in 1793, and most of the work is attributed to the earlier part of this span, 1790 to 1791. And David Erdman,

---

[10] Thus XXII, sect. 3: 'every family, every nation, in the spirit of its worship adopted a particular star or constellation for its patron . . . the names of the animal stars having . . . been conferred on nations, countries, mountains, and rivers, those objects were also taken for gods. . .' The 'medley of geographical, historical, and mythological beings' which thus arose is central to Volney's argument and the theme of, e.g., Chapter XXI, 'The Problem of Religious Contradiction'.

[11] See also Chapter XXIII, 'The End of All Religion the Same', with its denunciation of priesthood: 'they had invented ceremonies of worship to attract the reverence of the people, calling themselves the mediators and interpreters of the Gods with the sole view of assuming all his power [cf. Blake; "And at length they pronounced that the Gods had orderd such things"] . . . always aiming at influence, for their own exclusive advantage. . .'

using the signature of a change in the mode in which Blake engraved his 'g', puts Plate 11 in the earlier part.[12] But at the same time the dating of the English translation of Volney is frequently mistaken – sometimes as late as 1795. However, a long review of the French edition appeared in Johnson's *Analytical Review* in January 1792, with extensive extracts.[13] The review concluded 'we understand that a translation of this work is in the press'.[14] And the translation was indeed published before the end of 1792, by Joseph Johnson, the publisher who was at that time employing Blake as an engraver.[15] It cannot be shown conclusively that Blake could or could not have seen an English version of Volney before writing Plate Eleven; and indeed as a visitor to Johnson's shop he could have seen manuscript or proof versions of the book before its due publication date.

But if Blake is drawing upon Volney (as seems probable) he is not merely repeating Volney.[16] He has assimilated his concepts, while giving to them a novel and characteristic twist. First, Blake's argument is extraordinarily compact: he has made the argument wholly his own. Second, Blake has introduced a new agent, unexamined in Volney's account – 'the ancient Poets'. For Volney's account stems from the limitations of the understanding of primitive men, whereas Blake sees the myth-making faculties of the 'ancient Poets' as deliberate and creative ('particularly they studied. . .'). Priesthood – a system to enslave the vulgar – by abstracting mental deities from their object makes 'poetic tales' into 'forms of worship': the Moral Law. This seemingly small reorganisation of Volney's sequence has profound consequences; since for Volney, the 'New Age' dawns with the over-throw of Priesthood and of Mystery, and the New Age is the Age of Reason; but for Blake, while it dawns in exactly the same way, it is the age in which the 'true man', the Eternal Man of Poetic Genius, reasserts his humanity. Third, Blake, in his own argument, has rejected certain of Volney's assumptions, and in particular two: (1) that all

---

[12] D.V. Erdman, 'Dating Blake's Script: the "g" hypothesis', *Blake Newsletter*, June 1969.

[13] *Analytical Review*, Vol. XII, pp. 26–38.

[14] But it was not listed as published until the second half of 1792: *ibid.*, Vol. XIV, p. 331. It was reviewed in the *Critical Review*, December 1792.

[15] The 1792 volume is scarce, and the only copy I know is in the collection of the Library Company of Philadelphia. My thanks to Professor Leslie Chard and Camilla Townsend for help in locating it.

[16] As Rigby affirms (above, p. 199, note 6), Volney's is a 'rationalist apocalpyse' and, as both Marilyn Butler and Jon Mee also point out, Blake will have repudiated this deification of Reason: Butler, pp. 44–5, and Mee, pp. 138–40.

the past achievements of human civilisation (and, it is implied, the greater achievements of the future) have been founded on enlightened self-interest or on 'self love . . . the parent of all that genius has effected';[17] (2) 'that man receives no ideas but through the medium of his senses'.[18] The first principle directly contradicted 'The Divine Image'; the second Blake had been at pains to refute in his illuminated plates of 1788. The plate 'ALL RELIGIONS are ONE' ('The Voice of one crying in the Wilderness') had declared, as its fifth principle, 'The Religions of all Nations are derived from each Nation's different reception of the Poetic Genius which is every where call'd the Spirit of Prophecy': and he had concluded that the source of all religions is 'the true Man . . . he being the Poetic Genius' (E1–3).

Thus Blake's particular, and intellectually structured antinomian development had prepared him to meet the moment of deist or atheist thought represented by Volney's *Ruins* in an affirmative way: but it had also prepared him to reorganise this thought: 'Thus men forgot that All deities reside in the human breast.' For Plate 11 in the *Marriage* is only a temporary resting-point before the full statement of 'The Human Abstract':[19]

> Pity would be no more,
> If we did not make somebody Poor:
> And Mercy no more could be,
> If all were as happy as we;
>
> And mutual fear brings peace;
> Till the selfish loves increase.
> Then Cruelty knits a snare,
> And spreads his baits with care.
>
> He sits down with holy fears,
> And waters the ground with tears:
> Then Humility takes its root
> Underneath its foot.

[17] See esp. Ch. VII.
[18] See esp. Ch. XXII.
[19] The argument of this chapter – the deist–antinomian conjunction and quarrel – need not stand or fall on the hypothesis of Volney's influence. Many of his ideas were already around – e.g., R.P. Knight, p. 176: 'men naturally attribute their own passions and inclinations to the objects of their adoration; and as God made Man in his own image, so Man returns the favour, and makes God in his' – while others Blake was quite capable of thinking out for himself. But the hypothesis of Volney neatly illustrates the question at issue.

Soon spreads the dismal shade
Of Mystery over his head;
And the Catterpillar and Fly,
Feed on the Mystery.

And it bears the fruit of Deceit,
Ruddy and sweet to eat;
And the Raven his nest has made
In its thickest shade.

And Gods of the earth and sea,
Sought thro' Nature to find this Tree
But their search was all in vain:
There grows one in the Human Brain.

That this poem is intended as a direct 'contrary' to 'The Divine Image' is manifest: the title of the Notebook draft is 'The Human Image', and the poem, in its first six lines, picks up, ironically, 'Pity', 'Mercy', 'peace' and 'loves'. And if 'The Divine Image' is the hinge upon which the *Innocence* songs turns, we should expect to find a similar significance for *Experience* in this. But it is difficult to see how any reader could find 'The Human Abstract' to be a 'satire' upon the former poem.[20] It represents, as clearly as any of the 'paired' songs, a 'contrary state', neither one of which need cancel or satirise the other: and in the most simplified terms, the one is about the source of 'good', the other about the source and the origin of 'evil'. Nor is it a plain opposite, a mere negation of the first. Blake had tried this, in the early (but rejected) contrary, *A* (as opposed to *The*) 'Divine Image':

Cruelty has a Human Heart
And Jealousy a Human Face
Terror, the Human Form Divine
And Secrecy, the Human Dress

The Human Dress, is forged Iron
The Human Form, a fiery Forge.
The Human Face, a Furnace seal'd
The Human Heart, its hungry Gorge.

This is a straight negative: but, even so, not one which must cancel out the earlier poem. The source of 'evil' is human, but the human

[20] E.D. Hirsch suggests this in his (usually helpful) *Innocence and Experience* (Yale, 1964), pp. 265–70.

form remains 'divine' since this 'evil' is projected as 'A Divine Image' of a jealous wrathful God (or Satan). Vice is self-consuming, 'hell' is the furnace of this self-consumption.[21]

But such a negation dissatisfied Blake. It states a contrary, but it offers no explanation for it. Page 107 of The Notebook shows him making two false starts before finding his way into 'The Human Image'–

> How came pride in Man
> From Mary it began
> How Contempt & Scorn

This was scratched out and followed with another opening:

> What a world is Man
> His Earth

–deleted again. Since we can be sure that 'pride' was for Blake, at this time, a virtue, the first opening suggests a poem contrasting the origin of 'The Divine Image' in Mary and of a 'human image' of 'contempt and scorn' for man's own divine humanity within man's own false consciousness. No one should ever attempt to re-write Blake, but one can suggest that he was leading on to some such contrast as:

> How Contempt & Scorn
> From Reason it was Born

But such an opposition (Mary/Reason) was a false opposition, and, moreover, one that Blake in 1792 would have thought too easily to be taken in a comforting way by orthodox Christians like Mr Pratt. The next beginning ('What a World is Man/His Earth') suggests that he was trying for an image which would suggest the common soil of both the 'divine' and the 'human', and that the image of the tree had already been decided upon. But why should the same human soil nurture two opposing trees? It was at this point that the final organisation of the poem presented itself to him. It looks as if he then wrote an advanced draft straight through.

---

[21] There is no cancelling-out of concepts here: Thomas Tomkinson who might have provided a 'text' for 'The Divine Image' (above, p. 160) also provides the contrary text: the devil 'is no where to be found but in Man': *A System of Religion*, 1729, p. 35. Thus also Reeve: 'thy Body shall be thy Hell, and thy Spirit shall be thy Devil that shall torment thee to Eternity'. Thus also Blake on Lavater: 'hell is the being shut up in the possession of corporeal desires. . .' (E579).

In one sense the poem starts, somewhat cryptically, with a conclusion written into the commencement:

> Pity could be no more
> If there was nobody poor—

And then, to emphasise the meaning, he struck out the second line and wrote above it the final version:

> If we did not make somebody poor

The thought returns directly to the already-completed 'The Clod & the Pebble': one kind of 'love'—

> . . . for another gives its ease,
> And builds a Heaven in Hells despair.

The other kind—

> . . . seeketh only Self to please,
> To bind another to its delight;
> Joys in anothers loss of ease,
> And builds a Hell in Heavens despite.

But the clod and the pebble simply offer to each other contrary states. And Blake's actual point of entry was given to him by the notebook poem (never used in the *Songs*) 'I heard an Angel singing':

> I heard an Angel singing
> When the day was springing
> Mercy Pity Peace
> Is the worlds release
>
> Thus he sang all day
> Over the new mown hay
> Till the sun went down
> And haycocks looked brown
>
> I heard a Devil curse
> Over the heath & the furze
> Mercy could be no more
> If there was nobody poor
>
> And pity no more could be
> If all were as happy as we
> At his curse the sun went down
> And the heavens gave a frown

Down pourd the heavy rain
Over the new reapd grain
And Miseries increase
Is Mercy Pity Peace.

Blake had tinkered a good deal with the final verse, and, in one variant, the final couplet had been:

And by distress increase
Mercy Pity Peace   (N114)

The thought is the same as that in *Jerusalem*, Chapter 2, where 'the Oppressors of Albion in every City & Village. . .'–

. . . compell the Poor to live upon a crust of bread by soft mild
    arts:
They reduce the Man to want: then give with pomp & ceremony.
The praise of Jehovah is chaunted from lips of hunger & thirst.
                                    (E191)

This 'Angel' is not just a hypocrite: Mercy, Pity, Peace *could* be 'the worlds release': about these 'virtues of delight' Blake was never cynical. And this 'Devil' is not a devil of energy or of antinomian wisdom (as in *The Marriage of Heaven and Hell*): he is a real devil and no doubt Gibbon would have found him to be a man 'of polished manners and liberal education . . . conversant with the precepts of philosophy'. (The recurrent and central experience behind this, of dearth and high prices – real or manipulated – followed belatedly by a little inadequate display of benevolence and charity, need not be documented.) The poem is about class society, and in an area central to the eighteenth century: the 'paternalist' conscience of an agrarian capitalist class.

So all this was tipped in to the first quatrain of 'The Human Abstract': we start with a class society, and this is emphasised by the revision of the second line – we make others poor. The 'peace' of class society is founded only on an equilibrium of 'mutual fear', within which the 'selfish loves' increase. But this self-love only increases: it has been present from the start and is, in a sense, the unexplained source from which the whole process of the poem is generated. What is interesting is that while much of the rest of the poem follows Volney's analysis of process, Blake insists upon turning upside-down the central value of Volney's deism by which self-love, if duly enlightened, will generate all civilised values. But

while Blake emphatically rejects this, he takes from Volney something of the very notion of class antagonism. For in a crucial chapter of *The Ruins* (often to be republished as a leaflet by subsequent
reformers) Volney has a vision of an immense assembly (in-
distinctly located in France) in which the people and the privileged
class separate from each other and question each other's creden-
tials. On the one hand, there is an immense concourse of
'labourers, artisans, tradesmen, and every profession useful to society'; on the other hand a much smaller group of 'priests, courtiers,
public accountants . . . &c'. The people regard the privileged class
with astonishment: 'We toil, and you enjoy; we produce, and you
dissipate; wealth flows from us, and you absorb it.' One can never
be certain when dealing with ideas and images so widely dispersed,
but Volney's vision appears to contribute to Blake's Plate 16 in
The Marriage of Heaven and Hell: 'These two classes of men [the
"Prolific" and the "Devourer"] are always upon earth, & they
should be enemies; whoever tries to reconcile them seeks to destroy
existence.'[22]

Perhaps Blake was seeking to put more into the first quatrain of
'The Human Abstract' than four lines could bear. By contrast, the
next four quatrains have a leisurely development. The Tree of
Mystery grows slowly, and it grows very much as Volney had
argued and as Blake had agreed in Plate 11 of *The Marriage*. In
chapter xii of *The Ruins*, Volney and the mysterious 'Genius' who
is enlightening him have a distant global vision of desperate human
warfare (Russian, Mussulman, Tartar) in which all parties call
upon the aid of divine power for their cause. At length the 'Genius'
can contain himself no longer and bursts out:

Hear these men, and you would imagine that God is a being capricious
and mutable; that now he loves, and now he hates . . . that he spreads
snares for men, and delights in the fatal effects of imprudence . . . that
he . . . is to be appeased only by servility like a savage tyrant. I now
completely understand *what is the deceit of mankind, who have pretended that
God made man in his own image, and who have really made God in theirs*; who
have ascribed to him their weakness, their errors, and their vices; and
. . . surprised at the contradictory nature of their own assertions, have
attempted to cloak it with hypocritical humility, and the pretended impot-

---

[22] Volney, Ch. xv, 'The New Age'; Blake, E39. Blake again uses Volney's vision, but departs
from his conclusion, in: 'But the Prolific would cease to be Prolific unless the Devourer
as a sea recieved the excess of his delights.'

ence of human reason, calling the delirium of their own understanding the sacred mysteries of heaven. (My emphasis)

Here we have the 'snares', the 'hypocritical humility', the inversion of the values of 'Christian Forbearance' (as Blake first entitled the Song of Experience, 'A Poison Tree') so that they are seen to be the chains of oppression imposed by an interested priesthood. The Tree of Mystery is certainly that of priestcraft and of State Religion: the Caterpillar and Fly are certainly priestly parasites:[23] and the Raven has the same precise areas of definition combined with imprecise, evocative symbolism: he may be Rome, or the Genius of Mystery, or Death, or Bishop Watson of Llandaff, or God hiding in the Tree waiting for Adam to eat the fruit, or the Prophet of a Prohibitive, Negating Moral Law (as he is in the 'Song of Liberty')[24] – and, more probably, he is intended to suggest all of these at once. The 'fruit of Deceit' was being more exactly defined in another of Blake's (unused) notebook drafts, 'How to know Love from Deceit'. As opposed to joyous and unconfined 'Love', which 'breaks all chains from every mind' Deceit is confined to 'secresy': it is first thought of as 'Modest prudish & confind' and then revised to 'Lawful cautious & refind':

> To every thing but interest blind
> And forges fetters for the mind.   (N106–7)

This poem provides the essential link which binds 'The Human Abstract' into 'London', with its 'mind-forg'd manacles'. But with the 'fruit of Deceit' we are also linked to 'A Poison Tree', and we have further joined the symbolism of the Tree of Mystery with that of the Fall. That kind of critic who is given to collapsing into a kind of academic supercelestial blur whenever confronted with the antique symbolism of the Fall, the Creation or the Resurrection, tends to abandon Blake's poem at this point and go off into a

---

[23] Cf. Proverb of Hell: 'As the catterpiller chooses the fairest leaves to lay her eggs on, so the priest lays his curse on the fairest joys.' But it requires very little reading in the pamphlets of radicalism and Dissent in the 1790s to find caterpillars and flies abounding: or, indeed, Trees of Mystery: for example, Henry Yorke, *Thoughts on Civil Government* (1794), 'The Clergy have planted their power in the fertile soil of Superstition, which has been watered and manured by the Ignorance, Poverty, and Fears of Men.'

[24] 'Let the Priests of the Raven of dawn, no longer in deadly black. with hoarse note curse the sons of joy ... Nor pale religious letchery call that virginity, that wishes but acts not!' E44. Once again, a sampling of pamphlet and sermon material of the 1790s provides a profusion of reference: it is not necessary to trace such universal symbols back to neo-Platonist or to hermetic sources.

different (and irrelevant) essay in exegesis, in which the 'naturalism' of the poem's development is denied, and in which every 'snare', 'tear', 'shade' or priestly parasite is squeezed for the last drop of possible mythic association. Plainly reversing the actual movement of the poem, in which the Tree of Mystery grows up out of self-interest in class society, we must translate it into some Christian orthodoxy in which the Fall (the 'fruit of Deceit') is read back into the commencement. And nothing has bothered this kind of critic more than the symbolism of trees.

Blake's poem (we recall) concludes:

> The Gods of the earth and sea,
> Sought thro' Nature to find this Tree
> But their search was all in vain:
> There grows one in the Human Brain.

Aha! says this kind of critic. If the Tree of Mystery doesn't grow in 'Nature' then we can't accept the poem's apparent naturalistic development: all that must be the symbolism of something altogether more mystic and Otherwards. And the confusion is compounded by the supposition that Blake was at the same time making a scholarly in-joke about the Upas Tree, a 'mysterious poison plant which appeared constantly in the literature of his time' but which 'no one stated that he himself had actually seen'.[25]

As it happens, Blake had, as we have seen (above, p. 142), recently read a very detailed and naturalistic account, purportedly at first hand from a Dutch traveller and medical man, of the Upas

[25] John Beer, *Blake's Humanism*, p. 73. I don't intend to suggest that Mr Beer is the kind of critic at whom I've been making faces. If an example must be given, I have to say that I find Miss Raine's chapter on 'The Ancient Trees' (*Blake and Tradition*, II, pp. 32–52) one of the least helpful and most confusing sections of a book which (along with other confusions and irrelevancies) offers genuine insights and discoveries.

[26] N.P. Foerfch's 'Natural History of the Bohon-Upas, or Poison Tree of the Island of Java' had been serialised in the *New Magazine of Heaven and Hell*, 1790. The author claimed to have interviewed condemned criminals who had been offered the alternative of execution or of obtaining the poison of the tree, and who had succeeded in doing the latter. But the failure rate was very high. The tree lay in the midst of ten or more miles of barren land, in which all life was polluted by its miasmas: even birds, crossing this territory, fell dead from the sky. A criminal might succeed in obtaining the poison only if he had the good fortune, during two or three days of difficult journey over ground littered by skeletons, of having the wind blowing always away from the tree. The tree itself was growing in a solitary state, except for some little trees or suckers around it. Along with much other circumstantial detail, Dr Foerfch claimed to have witnessed state executions effected by this poison, and to have experimented on his own account on domestic animals. The Swedenborgian magazine published the account to demonstrate the 'intimate connection

Tree in Java.[26] But neither the Tree of Mystery in 'The Human Abstract' nor 'A Poison Tree' owe very much to this Upas Tree: Blake's trees both bear poisoned fruit, whereas the virulence of the Upas Tree lies in its bark and in its effluvia.[27] It is best with these to regard each tree as *a tree for that poem*, defined in its own terms.

But for a Tree of Mystery Blake didn't have to rely upon texts from Paracelsus or Boehme: he could have taken them from ten hundred places in previous literature, or from the common vocabulary of radical Dissent, or from Gibbon's accounts of the sacred groves of the ancient Germans,[28] or from accounts of Druid rites,[29] or from his own shaping imagination or, indeed, from Volney, who has several trees, as well as dragons, serpents, Orphic eggs, Mithraic caves, ravens and lions, in his text and notes.

What he could have taken less easily, except from antinomian or rationalist sources, was the notion of a tree of *mystery*, coincident with priesthood. I have suggested already (above, pp. 200–1) that when composing Plate 11 in *The Marriage* he may have been conversant with this notion in Volney. A separate caste of astronomers &c arose, which 'assumed to themselves exclusive privileges', and under their authority:

subsisting between the spiritual and natural worlds': Dr Foerfch provided evidence that 'the influences of Hell are as visible in the vegetable productions of certain parts of this globe' as in wild beasts. The Poison-Tree of Java may be called 'the *Tree of Death*, originating in *Hell*'. I don't think the Upas Tree played a very important part in Blake's imagination, but Foerfch offered a wonderful bunch of images. His tree turns up in a deleted line of the Notebook poem on Fayette, 'Let the Brothels of Paris be opened' (N99):

> But our good Queen quite grows to the ground
> There is just such a tree at Java found (*del.*)
> And a great many suckers grow all around

It is interesting also that the plate of 'A Poison Tree' in *Songs of Experience* (see Illus. 14) shows *not* an apple-tree (as in the poem) but a tree in a barren landscape which conforms very much to the mental image called up in my own mind by reading Dr Foerfch: a dead criminal, who has failed to get the poison, lies beneath the tree. For various attributions of the Upas Tree imagery in Blake, see Geoffrey Grigson, *The Harp of Aelus* (1948), ch. v; John Adlard, *The Sports of Cruelty* (1972), p. 45; Glen, p. 193.

[27] Foerfch's account of the Upas Tree may have contributed more to, e.g., the imagery of the Tree of Mystery in *Vala*, Night vɪɪa.

[28] Chapter ɪx: 'The only temples in Germany were dark and ancient groves . . . Their secret doom, the imagined residence of an invisible power, by presenting no distinct object of fear or worship, impressed the mind with a still deeper sense of religious horror; and the priests . . . had been taught by experience the use of every artifice that could preserve and fortify impressions so well suited to their own interest.'

[29] See Jon Mee, *Dangerous Enthusiasm*, pp. 7, 97–103.

. . . the progress of knowledge, it is true, was hastened, but by the mystery that accompanied it, the people, plunged daily in the thickest darkness, became more superstitious and more slavish. . .

From this caste came priesthoods who 'instituted under the name of religion, *an empire of mystery*. . .' (XXII, sect. 3, my emphasis). And what Blake is doing, in the final quatrain of 'The Human Abstract', is both to appropriate deist analysis and to reorganise it in exactly the same way as he had done in Plate 11 of *The Marriage*.

Let us place this quatrain side by side with the conclusion to that passage:

Till a system was formed, which some took advantage of & enslav'd the vulgar by attempting to realize or abstract the mental deities from their object; thus began Priesthood.
Choosing forms of worship from poetic tales.
And at length they pronounced that the Gods had ordered such things.
Thus men forgot that All deities reside in the human breast.

An inattentive reading leads some to suppose that the final line is saying much the same as the final line of the poem: 'There grows one in the Human Brain.' This leads us to a somewhat complacent rationalist orthodoxy, that 'good' and 'evil' both arise from man, without much further explanation of process. And Blake, when he writes that 'the Gods of the earth and sea' sought in vain through Nature for this Tree, is then making only a whimsical joke.

True, Blake *is* making that sort of joke, but it has a finer edge of irony. For 'the human breast' and 'the Human Brain' are not the same thing. Men forgot that all deities reside in the breast; the poetic genius of the 'true man' (and in this respect Blake is still not far distant from the Swedenborgians) achieves its insights in the first place through the *affections*. Nor was this poetic capacity to attribute qualities and to animate these into deities in any sense (until abused) a faculty encouraging mystery; if the Gods were imaginary, the truths of imagination were always more real to Blake than the natural observations of the senses; or, in a more contemporary definition, Blake considered that human creativity was grounded upon his poetic, mythogenic faculties, and that man lives in a world of his own creation (our 'culture') and not in 'nature'. Hence the old, poetically imagined Gods 'animated' by man from 'the earth and sea' had a perfect right to go on their rather ironic search for this new Tree. But these Gods do not (*pace* Miss Raine and her disciples) discover that the Tree of Mystery is yet one more (rather dreary and repetitive) symbol of 'nature' or of 'matter'. It is exactly in 'Nature' that they *can't* find the Tree. It grows in the human brain (and not breast). And hence the care which Blake put into revising the poem's title. In 'The Divine Image' we are given in fact an image of actual human virtue; in 'The Human Abstract' we are given an image of an imaginary God of deceit and mystery. But Blake means to insist that this God is created, not by the poetic faculty of imagination, but by the abstracting faculties of the reason. If he had not thought this through for himself, the notion of abstraction as barren and self-deluding could have come to him from many sources.[30] But he could certainly have been reminded of this propensity at several points in Volney: 'that God whose attributes are abstractions of the knowledge of nature' (Ch. xxii); 'the Deity . . . became at last a chimerical and abstract being: a scholastic subtlety of substance without form' (xxii, sect. 8); and:

. . .the understanding, at liberty to disengage itself from the wants of nature, must have risen to the complicated art of comparing ideas, digesting reasonings, and seizing upon abstract similitudes. (Ch. xxii)

We can now resume our argument. Blake had been habituated, whether in his Swedenborgian phase or before, to the way of thinking in 'correspondences' and in inversions. He took from the deists, and perhaps from Volney in particular, an enormous amount: in the case under examination he has taken a full-blown naturalistic analysis of the process by which religious mystery and priestcraft grow up. But, in the very moment of taking it, he has twisted it in such a way that it remains ambiguous. The twist is of two kinds: Volney (and mechanistic psychology generally, however sophistic-ated, from Hartley through Priestley to Bentham or Godwin) still saw 'self-love', in whatever form, as the basic sociological motor, for good or ill. Once self-love had been enlightened by philosophy, and mystery had been dispersed, men would see that brotherhood and equality were in their evident interest. But Blake, even in his most revolutionary temper, did not think that this kind of equation

[30] D.G. Gillham, *Blake's Contrary States*, p. 65, usefully recalls the introduction to Berkeley's *Principles of Human Knowledge*: 'the fine and subtile net of abstract ideas, which has so miserably perplexed and entangled the minds of men'.

would be easy. Indeed, he may have doubted this most of all at
those times when he was most sanguine about revolutionary possibilities: for brotherhood was (for him) not a matter of interest
but of love. Hence while Volney starts his analysis with self-love
giving rise to primitive societies and to civilised values (and only
subsequently becoming entangled with mystery) Blake commences
his at a point where self-love has already alienated man from man
in class society, and mystery arises from the increase of 'selfish
loves'. The second twist lies in the description of the process of
this alienation. For in Volney the process by which men have fash-
ioned the false consciousness of religious mystery is described,
repeatedly, as a 'chain of ideas' or 'a chain of reasoning'.[31] It is
scarcely possible not to see the ironic glint which must have come
into Blake's eye. For he was familiar with the imagery of other
kinds of 'fetters', 'links' and 'chains'. And in 'The Human
Abstract' (one notices) the process of maturing false consciousness
is not that of rationality but of mystification and alienating values:
'mutual fear', 'Cruelty', 'holy fears', 'Humility' and 'Deceit' which,
we recall, is itself 'to every thing but interest blind/And chains &
fetters every mind' (N106). And yet the source of Blake's chain of
values is 'in the Human Brain'. What the reason does is to
rationalise ('spreads his baits with care'), legitimate and ultimately
mystify, self-interest; moreover, in 'the fruit of Deceit', it perpetuates itself. Reason, if based on self-love produces its opposite,
Mystery.

It must follow from this that if we look forward to a 'remedy',
to man's liberation from false consciousness, we must expect to
find different answers in Volney and in Blake. As indeed we do.
Volney's vision, as we have seen, is a 'New Age' of triumphant
rationality; in the light of a new self-knowledge mystery (and the
resultant alienation of nation from nation) will be dispersed; 'the
people' simply dismiss the 'privileged class' and its priestly apologists as unnecessary parasites. Blake does not offer his 'New Age'
in the *Songs of Experience*, although it is clear (from the 'Introduction' and from 'Earth's Answer') that if it should come it must be
an affirmation not of reason but of wrath and love. He had suggested it a little more plainly in the 'Song of Liberty' at the end of
The Marriage, and it is clear enough from this that any vision of his

---

[31] See, e.g., Ch. XXII, sect. 1 and sect. 8.

would be likely to take prophetic and apocalyptic form: the 'son of fire'—

Spurning the clouds written with curses, stamps the stony law to dust,
loosing the eternal horses from the dens of night, crying
Empire is no more! and now the lion & wolf shall cease. (E44)

But the new Jerusalem cannot be seen only as the driving out of self-love by affirmative love: it must also be seen as the reappropri-ation by man of his own humanity, by expelling the abstract, quantitative, ratiocinative power (Locke's reason founded upon the senses), and by reassuming the imaginative or poetic genius of the ancients who had 'animated' the first Gods of the earth and sea.

Blake was not concerned to argue with Volney or the deists whether these Gods were 'imaginary' or not. He was happy, at least until 1795, to co-exist with atheists and deists (of the Volney, but not of the Gibbon or Godwin stamp). But Blake's point, even in 1792–3, was different. The human world was a world of culture; 'imaginary' or not, anything created in the world of culture *was real*. The deists, with a mechanical and naturalistic psychology, placed an excessive emphasis upon material interest, whereas Blake, while appropriating some of their arguments, placed a full emphasis upon affective and imaginative 'culture' – an emphasis which became after 1795, as events in the world around him became increasingly confusing, discouraging or ominous, more and more extreme and idiosyncratic. With no alternative psychology to hand he set himself the impossible labours of the prophetic books, seeking to construct a syncretic mythology which would reorganise the myths of all past culture into a new structure. For once animated by the imagination, once released into culture and myth, those old Gods went on eternally, unless they were slain by the imagination or hammered by it into new forms and myths. As he grew older he became increasingly provoked by any levity towards the creatures of imagination. As he told Crabb Robinson, when he came across the lines in *The Excursion*:

> Jehovah – with his thunder, and the choir
> Of shouting Angels, and the empyreal thrones,
> I pass them, unalarmed. . .

they made him ill for weeks with a bowel complaint. But earlier, in *Jerusalem*, we can detect that old argument with the deists rum-bling on:

And this is the manner of the Sons of Albion in their strength
They take the Two Contraries which are called Qualities, with
    which
Every Substance is clothed, they name them Good & Evil
From them they make an Abstract, which is a Negation
Not only of the Substance from which it is derived
A murderer of its own Body: but also a murderer
Of every Divine Member: it is the Reasoning Power
An Abstract objecting power, that Negatives every thing
This is the Spectre of Man: the Holy Reasoning Power,
And in its Holiness is closed the Abomination of Desolation

Therefore Los stands in London building Golgonooza
Compelling his Spectre to labours mighty; trembling in fear
The Sceptre weeps, but Los unmovd by tears or threats remains

'I must Create a System, or be enslav'd by another Mans
'I will not Reason & Compare: my business is to Create'

                                                        (E151)

If Blake in these prophetic books moved away from deism, and
ultimately into sharp antagonism to rationalism in the assertion of
his own 'everlasting gospel', it is not very helpful to argue that he
was moving towards (or back to) anything recognisable as Christianity, orthodox or heterodox. For if he had been doing so he
would have had no need to labour at the creation of his own mythic
system. And he pursues unremittingly, through all the shifting
emanations of his curiously static and repetitive narratives, the
problem of man's self-alienation from his own true imaginative
identity, and of his aspiration to the ultimate New Age or Jerusalem which is co-terminous with the overthrow of Mystery and the
reassumption of undivided humanity. Thus, in the First Book of
Milton, Los announces the 'Last Vintage' in terms reminiscent of
the Enlightenment:

And Los stood & cried to the Labourers of the Vintage in voice of
    awe:
'Fellow Labourers! The Great Vintage & Harvest is now upon
    Earth
'The whole extent of the Globe is explored: Every scatterd Atom
'Of Human Intellect now is flocking to the sound of the Trumpet.
'All the Wisdom which was hidden in caves & dens from ancient
'Time; is now sought out from Animal & Vegetable & Mineral
'The Awakener is come. outstretch'd over Europe! the Vision of
    God is fulfilled

'The Ancient Man upon the Rock of Albion Awakes,
'He listens to the sounds of War astonishd & ashamed;
'He sees his Children mock at Faith and deny Providence.'

(E120–1)

The vision is fulfilled, the awakening has come: but it signals not
the Age of Reason but the necessary dispersal of Mystery before
the re-awakening of the faith of the Ancient Man. And so, after
winding our way through eight nights of *Vala*, we come, in Night
the Ninth, to the ultimate triumphant irony. It is Urizen himself,
who, in such a voice as Volney's, cries: 'Times are Ended!', and
who prepares for the final Vintage and threshing of the nations.
The same reasoning power which abstracted mental deities from
their object and which created Mystery has now pierced through
Mystery, understood its own limitations, and is ready to destroy
its own creations. Once rid of the fear of death and the hope of
immortality, humankind sheds its alienation from nature. Once rid
of self-mystification, humankind reassumes imaginative existence:

> The Expanding Eyes of Man behold the depths of wondrous
>   worlds
> One Earth one sea beneath nor Erring Globes wander but Stars
> Of fire rise up nightly from the Ocean & one Sun
> Each morning like a New born Man issues with songs & joy
> Calling the Plowman to his Labour & the Shepherd to his rest
> He walks upon the Eternal Mountains raising his heavenly voice,
> Conversing with the Animal forms of wisdom night & day
> That risen from the Sea of fire renewd walk oer the Earth. . .

(E391)

But this renewed life of imagination and faith is certainly not one to
be comprised in any Christian – or, for that matter, neo-Platonist –
doctrine:

> Attempting to be more than Man We become less said Luvah
> As he arose from the bright feast drunk with the wine of ages
> His crown of thorns fell from his head he hung his living Lyre
> Behind the seat of the Eternal Man & took his way. . .

(E388)

This is later: but the old deist–antinomian discussion is still
being argued out. And Luvah (who is sometimes Christ) may allow
us to return, finally, to the question of Blake's trees. For the Tree
which the Gods sought in the final verse of 'The Human Abstract'
is certainly the Tree of Mystery, but it may also be allowed to
suggest the Cross upon which the Christ of the gospel of forgiveness

(or the human virtues of 'The Divine Image') was crucified. It is, anyway, the same tree. And the tree in 'A Poison Tree', while naturalistic in its symbolic evolution, may also be allowed to suggest the Fall,[32] just as the fruit of the Tree of Mystery, which is 'ruddy and sweet to eat' suggests the same. And both Trees must be central to *Songs of Experience* which are, exactly, songs of the 'wisdom' gained by man when he lost innocence through the Fall. But Blake's notion of the Fall is very different from any warranted by Christian doctrine or by Miss Raine's 'Tradition'. For we can now see how three of the *Songs* are intimately related. 'A Poison Tree' (if we read it in the sense that 'I' could be God and his 'foe' could be Adam) shows 'a very Cruel Being' spreading a deliberate bait before man. In the Tree of Mystery of 'The Human Abstract' we see the triumph of the prohibitive God of the Moral Law, the fruit of whose Tree continually entices man to the perpetual renewal of his own Fall. The Fall from innocence into this kind of experience – the moralising of contrary 'Qualities' or impulses into an 'Abstract' of Good and Evil – extends outwards throughout the *Songs of Experience* and pollutes both parental and sexual love. 'Thou shalt not' is writ over the door, and 'Priests in black gowns' are binding 'my joys & desires'. But we can also relate this to 'London'. For if 'The Human Abstract' shows the generation of the prohibitive Tree of Mystery whose fruit continually regenerates man's Fall, so 'London' (seen as hell) shows the condition of the Fallen, who

---

[32] Miss Raine (II, pp. 38–9) helpfully draws attention to two passages of Boehme, which imply a criticism of God for deliberately planting within the Garden of Eden a tree 'pleasant to the eye and to be desired' within which was hidden 'the Wrath of the Anger of God'. Boehme asks 'Reason says, *Why* did God suffer this Tree to grow, seeing Man should not eat of it? Did he not bring it forth for the *Fall* of Man? And must it not needs be the *Cause* of Man's Destruction?' In the same way Blake hid his unspoken wrath within his tree and 'sunned it with smiles', encouraging his foe to his own destruction. If we wish to read the 'I' of the poem as God, and the 'foe' as Adam in the Garden of Eden, then we must say that Blake (if he read Boehme's rhetorical question) answered 'yes, God did deliberately plan and cause Adam's destruction, and in a deceitful way'. Such a conclusion is perfectly consonant with Blake's explicit statement in later life: 'Thinking as I do that the Creator of this world is a very Cruel Being & being a Worshipper of Christ I cannot help saying the Son O how unlike the Father. First God Almighty comes with a Thump on the Head. Then Jesus Christ comes with a balm to heal it.' This 'Thump' is fairly clearly the contrivance of the Fall, since this sentence immediately follows upon: 'Angels are happier than Men & Devils because they are not always Prying after Good & Evil in one Another & eating the Tree of Knowledge for Satans Gratification' (*A Vision of the Last Judgement*, E555). Thus if we accept Miss Raine's helpful suggestion, it helps us to the view that the God who planted the tree and who threw Adam out of Eden was in fact Satan – a view which neither Miss Raine nor Boehme would endorse.

lie within the empire of property, self-interest, state religion and Mystery.

For 'London' bears exactly the same kind of fraternal but transformed relationship to Painite political radicalism as 'The Human Abstract' bears to deism or atheism. In these songs Blake is not quarrelling with either: he is both accepting their thought and turning it to a new account. Blake is not likely to have changed his view very markedly between writing these poems and 1799, when he wrote to Dr Trusler. Blake had been commissioned by Trusler to prepare a design of 'Malevolence' (see Illus. 15):

A Father, taking leave of his Wife & Child, Is watch'd by Two Fiends incarnate, with intention that when his back is turned they will murder the mother & her infant. If this is not Malevolence with a vengeance, I have never seen it on Earth. . .

Trusler rejected the design. Blake's 'Fancy' did not 'accord . . . with my Intentions': he had different views on 'Moral Painting' which should 'follow the Nature' of 'This World'. In reply Blake sought to defend his design against 'a mistaken' criticism,

which is, That I have supposed Malevolence without a Cause. Is not Merit in one a Cause of Envy in another, & Serenity & Happiness & Beauty a Cause of Malevolence? But Want of Money & the Distress of A Thief can never be alledged as the Cause of his Thieving, for many honest people endure greater hardships with Fortitude. We must therefore seek the Cause elsewhere than in want of Money, for that is the Miser's passion, not the Thief's.[33]

We have noted that 'The Human Abstract' appears to emerge with the 'Cause' unexplained, and prior to the poem, just as Dr Trusler complained of his Malevolence. Or, rather, the 'cause' lies in class-society, in which contraries have become polarised, and the pity of one feeds on the misery of the other. It is in this context that 'the selfish loves increase'. But self-love on its own, in its 'innocent' state, is not the ultimate cause of 'sin'. It is a 'contrary' to affirmative love, 'necessary to Human existence'. 'From these contraries spring what the religious call Good & Evil.' In *Jerusalem* the cause is described in a metaphysical sense, as a matter of

[33] *The Letters of William Blake*, ed. Geoffrey Keynes (1968), pp. 28–31. Blake's point is not, of course, that money doesn't matter: he probably already saw it as double-sided, as in the 'Laocoon' (E272), where Money is both 'The Great Satan' and 'the lifes blood of Poor Families'.

naming, of moralising, of thinking about necessary contraries in an abstract way:

> They take the Two Contraries which are called Qualities, with
>   which
> Every Substance is clothed, they name them Good & Evil
> From them they make an Abstract, which is a Negation
> Not only of the Substance from which it is derived
> A murderer of its own Body: but also a murderer
> Of every Divine Member: it is the Reasoning Power. . .
>
> (E151)

This is so close to 'The Human Abstract' that one easily over-looks the fact that it is itself more abstract and indefinite than the earlier poem. What Blake is saying in the *Songs* (and also commun-icating with much greater poetic immediacy) is that one does not need to find a Cause for primary human impulses or instincts: both love and self-love exist beyond any question of Cause, and are necessary to human existence. Such impulses or instincts cannot be rationalised or moralised. They become 'innocent' or Fallen according to context, and the societal context is exactly that in which the contentment of one is the misery of another. It is this context which pollutes innocence, generates negations and turns contraries into opposites: 'Prisons are built with stones of Law, Brothels with bricks of Religion', and 'Bring out number weight & measure in a year of dearth.' It is within the context of 'dearth' and of social antagonism that the 'selfish loves increase': and it is in exactly the same soil that Empire and Mystery take root.

This is why the structural analysis which was offered of the symbolism of 'London' is important. The cause of man's Fall into this hell is, at one and the same time, its context in the clearly articulated imagery of the buying and selling of infancy, affections, life and love.[34] Commercialism, class society, activates contraries and turns them into self-bound antagonism: 'Is not Merit in one a Cause of Envy in another. . .?' 'The Human Abstract' shows Mystery arising from this soil, while 'London', in its symbolic structural organisation, shows the soil itself. To simplify (if we return to Dr Trusler) an environmentalist psychology following the Nature of 'This World' – let us say the sophisticated pain–pleasure

[34] We recall that the notebook lines 'There souls of men are bought & sold' which gave Blake his idea for the final verse of 'London' were at first intended as a final verse to 'The Human Abstract' – see above, p. 187.

associationism of Godwin – would have supposed that Want of Money 'caused' theft, and that if thieves had more money the cause would cease. Blake did not think so since he might have found the 'cause' in envy or self-love plus a context in which the wealth of one man inflamed the envy of another. At a less simple level, Blake insists that the Fall is made up of primary impulses (which, being primary and 'necessary', it is pointless or mystifying to describe as 'good' and 'evil') operating within a particular context which we could describe as class-culture. And it follows (although this is not argued in the *Songs*) that the abolition of this culture, by revolution, will not abolish the impulses. And all within that culture, oppressors and oppressed, bear its 'marks of weakness' and its 'mind forg'd manacles'.

Hence Blake, however close he is to the Painites, will not dispense with 'The Divine Image' or the 'Everlasting Gospel'. Just as with deism or atheism, he can agree with the analysis but still require, at the end of it, a utopian leap. The Fall is not cancelled out by abolishing the context, even if that context *is* the Fall. For humankind can't live context-less and a new context will grow up. There must be some Redemption, the creation of a new context in which not the 'selfish loves' but brotherhood will increase. But Blake could see no way to derive such an affirmation of love from naturalistic psychology, which was, at its very root, derivative from self-interest. Hence he must, even when in his most 'Jacobin' and revolutionary temper, hold fast to the Everlasting Gospel of his older antinomian faith. To create the New Jerusalem something must be brought in from outside the rationalist system, and that something could only be found in the non-rational image of Jesus, in the affirmatives of Mercy, Pity, Peace and Love.

CHAPTER 13

Conclusion

At this point we might recall the earlier arguments in this study. For if, as I have suggested, Blake had been deeply influenced by the tradition defined as Muggletonian, no symbolism would have imprinted itself more upon his mind than that of the Tree and of the Fall as being the emblem not of disobedience nor of sexuality but of the Knowledge of Good and Evil: 'That devil . . . that tempts men and women to all unrighteousness, it is man's spirit of unclean reason, and cursed imagination.' Thus Reeve and Muggleton (above, p. 94), and thus also Thomas Tomkinson: 'the tree of knowledge was not a natural tree; if it had, it could not have operated such venom in all mankind. . .' It must therefore have been the 'devil', or 'reason', a character very close to Blake's 'Human Abstract'.[1] In one sense, this Tree was taken to stand for Knowledge, and in the subsequent Muggletonian tradition could either encourage mere obscurantism, or could support a defence of the imagination and the affections against the 'reason' of the polite culture of a ruling-class. In another sense, the Tree was taken to stand for the Knowledge of Good and Evil: that is, the Moral Law of tablets and commandments as opposed to the gospel of forgiveness of sins, moralism as opposed to love, or, as Muggleton had it in his onslaught on George Fox, the Reason of Pilate which 'delivered up the Just One to be crucified by reasonable Men. . .'[2] And this same Muggletonian symbolism of Tree and Fall also (in the doctrine of man's 'two natures') offered a dramatic forecast of the inversions of *The Marriage of Heaven and Hell*, for 'the *Tree* of which Eve eat, called the *Tree of Knowledge of Good and Evil*, was her being overcome by the glorious Appearance the Devil made in the form of an Angel of Light. . .'[3] Hence the devil, seducing Eve

[1] *Truth's Triumph* (1823), p. 101.
[2] *A Looking-Glass for George Fox* (1656), p. 62. [3] *Observations*, 1735, p. 8.

and transmuting himself in her womb, enters human nature (through Cain), and manifests himself in the abstracting and moralising faculties of 'reason'.[4]

And even if we dispense with a Muggletonian hypothesis, much the same symbolism could have come by way of Boehme. Thus:

> Natural Reason without the Light of God seeth only to natural Image-likeness, . . . and frameth in itself the Divine Being or Essence, as if that were just such a Thing. From whence is come Strife amongst the Learned in Reason, & so that Men strive & dispute about God . . . where each of them holdeth his Imagination for Divine & will have his own Image which he hath framed in the Imagination of his Reason to be honoured for God: whereas yet it is only a natural Image of Reason.[5]

Thus just as Tomkinson's notion of virtues found only in men prepares us for 'The Divine Image' so the Muggletonian or Behmenist Tree prepares us for both 'The Human Abstract' and 'A Poison Tree'. In suggesting this I am not suggesting that Blake, in this or in any other case, took a symbol or a doctrine ready-made and used it in its original meaning. Just as he could borrow from, but transform, Volney, so he took this symbolism of Tree and Serpent and turned it to new uses. Moreover, we should never expect to find Blake employing a symbol consistently, in *exactly* the same way: we should rather think of his central symbols as a point of junction at which alternative, but closely related, meanings coincide. Thus he is using the same Tree in later life in alternative ways. In 'A Vision of the Last Judgement' (1810) the 'Tree of Knowledge' is one of officious moralising – 'always Prying after Good & Evil in one Another'; in 'For the Sexes: the Gates of Paradise' (*c.*1818) it was 'Rational Truth Root of Evil & Good'; in his conversation with Crabb Robinson it was Education (above, p. 87); in the late 'Laocoon' the symbol comprises still that emphasis upon man's self-division and self-alienation arising from self-love in class society with which 'The Human Abstract' commences:

> Good & Evil are
> Riches & Poverty a Tree of Mystery
> propagating Generation& Death

But Blake is now becoming wilful and somewhat cranky: a

---

[4] *Ibid.*, p. 10; *Principles*, 1735, p. 16; Tomkinson, *A System of Religion*, 1729, pp. 36–7, 87ff.
[5] Jacob Behmen, *Works* (1754), IV, pp. 167–8.

symbol can mean whatever he decides it means at any moment.
'SCIENCE' is also 'the Tree of DEATH'. 'ART is the Tree of LIFE.'
Jesus and his apostles and disciples 'were all Artists'. 'The whole
Business of Man Is The Arts & All Things Common' (i.e. in the
simultaneous destruction of both 'Science' and of 'Riches &
Poverty'). 'The outward Ceremony is Antichrist': so also is Science.
'HEBREW ART is called SIN by the Deist SCIENCE.' And
'Money, which is The Great Satan or Reason the Root of Good &
Evil In The Accusation of Sin' (E270–2). In the even later Annota-
tions to Thornton still more meanings are swept in: 'The Greek &
Roman Classics is the Antichrist.' 'Christ & his Apostles were
Illiterate Men . . . Caiphas Pilate & Herod were Learned.'[6]

It is splendid knockabout stuff. It is more than that – each
insight probes, inverts, checks us in our tracks, turns the polite
world of culture around. Such aphorisms remind us that Blake
remained something of a revolutionary to the end. And also something of a Muggletonian. But we would be wrong to sit down and
try to knit all these into a system: in doing so we are performing
the tasks of Urizen and seeking to impose a boundary or 'ratio'
upon the insights. These insights are all interrelated, certainly;
they cross and inter-cross, and arise from a common nexus. But
they are never worked through again with the rigour employed in
the *Songs*. And the nexus from which they arise is not one of systematic philosophy nor of a particular intellectual or metaphysical
'tradition'. It is a nexus of attitude, stance, attack – the stance of
the radical anti-hegemony of the antinomian tradition.

This, finally, explains one contradiction which baffles Blake
studies. Where one scholar, adopting a biographical approach, can
demonstrate evolution (perhaps not always of an ascendant kind)
in Blake's thought, another scholar can, with equal force, demonstrate consistency and fixity of symbol and of meaning. I have
suggested that the consistency is founded upon an unbroken
sequence of preoccupation and of symbolism which stems from
antinomianism. This endures through Swedenborgian and deist
influences: and persists through the Lambeth Books to the major
prophetic works to the end of Blake's life. The signatures of this
consistency are to be found in a stance rejecting the polite culture;
in such evidences as the symbolism of the Tree, which may fluctu-

[6] Cf. Muggleton's *A Looking-Glass for George Fox*, cited above, p. 94.

ate through Reason to the Moral Law to Mystery to Education to Money to Science, and the more obscure symbolism of the Serpent; and in the affirmation of the 'Everlasting Gospel': 'The Gospel is Forgiveness of Sins & has No Moral Precepts these belong to Plato & Seneca & Nero' (E608).

Few themes return more consistently than his hostility to the Moral Law. It is rehearsed frequently in the Lambeth Books, for example in *The Book of Urizen* (1794) (see Illus. 16) where Urizen writes in 'the Book/Of eternal brass'–

> One curse, one weight, one measure
> One King, one God, one Law.   (E71)

(Many critics find this Book to be Blake's ironic version of the Book of Genesis for his 'Bible of Hell'). The theme is found repeatedly in Blake's paintings and illuminations. His patron, Thomas Butts, was evidently sympathetic to the theme,[7] and it was for Butts that Blake painted 'God Writing upon the Tables of the Covenant' (Illus. 17), 'The Blasphemer' (Illus. 18) and 'The Woman Taken in Adultery' (Illus. 19), as well as 'The Beast of Revelation' (Illus. 20). The theme is present in *Milton* and *Vala* and ever-present in his last prophetic book, *Jerusalem*, as when Albion is shown in chapter 2–

> Cold snows drifted around him: ice coverd his loins around
> He sat by Tyburns brook, and underneath his heel, shot up!
> A deadly Tree, he nam'd it Moral Virtue, and the Law
> Of God who dwells in Chaos hidden from the human sight.
>   (E172)

But–

> No individual can keep these Laws, for they are death
> To every energy of man, and forbid the springs of life. . .

The same theme recurs in the prologue to *For the Sexes: the Gates of Paradise* (1818 or earlier):

> Jehovahs fingers wrote the Law
> Then Wept! then rose in Zeal & Awe
> And the Dead Corpse from Sinais heat
> Buried beneath his Mercy Seat.
> O Christians, Christians! tell me Why
> You rear it on your Altars high.   (E256)

---

[7] Butts was a chief clerk in the office of the Commissary General of Musters: see G.E. Bentley, 'Thomas Butts, White Collar Maecenae', *PMLA*, 71, pp. 1052–66. He was rumoured to be a Swedenborgian, but nothing definite is known of his religion.

This remains the dominant trope throughout *The Everlasting Gospel* (*c*.1818): thus when the women taken in adultery is brought before Jesus—

> He laid His hand on Moses Law
> The Ancient Heavens in Silent Awe
> Writ with Curses from Pole to Pole
> All away began to roll   (E512)

And when in his very last year (1827) at the age of seventy Blake annotated with fury Dr Thornton's *New Translation of the Lord's Prayer*, it was still the submissive obeisance to 'law' which drew his savage commentary:

Lawful Bread Bought with Lawful Money & a Lawful heaven seen thro' a Lawful Telescope by means of Lawful Window Light   The Holy Ghost [& whatever] cannot be Taxed is Unlawful & Witchcraft.
Spirits are Lawful but not Ghosts especially Royal Gin is Lawful Spirit No Smuggling real British Spirit & Truth (E658)

As always Blake's visionary spiritualism combines with a combative polemic against the 'Beast' of the State.

Blake was not a hurrah-revolutionary, as he is sometimes represented, nor was he a premature practitioner of Marxist dialectic.[8] But he was not isolated in his employment of the vocabulary of the 'New Jerusalem'. In the millenarian effervescence in London throughout the 1790s and into the next decade, this vocabulary was ever-present.[9] Not only Richard Brothers and Joanna Southcott were fully involved in the rhetoric,[10] but many other minor prophets and pamphleteers like William Huntington.[11] The Universalists, who emerged in the Swedenborgian nexus, were saturated with the vocabulary of the millennium, and might possibly have caught Blake's notice.[12] Their prophet, Elhanan Winchester, republished in 1792 a translation of Siegvolk's *The Everlasting*

[8] See David Punter, 'Blake, Marxism and Dialectic', *Literature and History*, No. 6, Autumn 1977.
[9] See Morton D. Paley, *The Continuing City: William Blake's Jerusalem* (Oxford, 1986), chapter 3.
[10] M. D. Paley, 'William Blake, The Prince of the Hebrews, and The Woman Clothed with the Sun'; J.F.C. Harrison, Part II, pp. 80–5.
[11] See, e.g., W. Huntington, *Key to the Hieroglyphical Print of the Church of God in her Fivefold State including the Holy Jerusalem*, &c (1808).
[12] There is, however, no evidence that Blake was interested in the (very loose and sloppy) Universalists or in Winchester, and I find Michael Ferber's description of Blake as a 'Holy Ghost Universalist' (*The Social Vision of William Blake*, pp. 190–1) to be misleading.

Gospel, and by 1794 the Universalists had their own hymn-book in which the New Jerusalem was announced:

> Its jasper walls so great and high,
> How glorious to behold!
> Four-square doth this great city lie.
> Its streets are purest gold.

And Winchester himself had published in the previous year a poem in twelve books, of which Book ix described the Millennium:

> Our sons shall be as plants grown up in youth,
> Beautiful, cheerful, gay, strong, innocent,
> Pleasant, wise, affable, sensible, good.
> Our daughters like to precious corner-stones,
> Polish'd, as if for palaces design'd.
> Fair, lovely, gentle, kind, polite, sincere,
> Virtuous, modest, humble, prudent, meek,
> Form'd to delight and cultivate mankind.[13]

Even the epic-prophetic mode appears to have been sufficiently familiar to a light-hearted London audience for it to have been adopted as an acceptable form of satire.[14]

To cite such anaemic comparisons as those of Winchester is to draw attention not to the typicality but to the untypicality of Blake. Among Winchester's prophecies were the personal coming of Christ; the resurrection of the saints; the conversion of the Jews; a final great war after which Satan was to be bound in the abyss for 1,000 years; then the millennium; then Satan loosed again and again overthrown; then the New Jerusalem and a general restoration.[15] All this was to happen independently of human agency, whereas Blake's 'Jerusalem' was to be built by strenuous intellectual, imaginative and artistic labours: 'to Labour in Knowledge is to Build up Jerusalem' (E230). The essential utopian leap for Blake was to brotherhood, the return to universal man. It is possible to trace in Blake's thought a lingering gnostic myth, by which an

---

[13] E. Winchester, *The Universalists Hymn Book* (1794); E. Winchester, *The Process and Empire of Christ* (1793). It is fair to state that W. Blake does *not* appear in the list of subscribers to the latter.

[14] See *The Revelation in Six Chapters* (1805), Brit. Lib. T1123(1), a jest, in messianic form, upon the supporters of Sir Francis Burdett; e.g., 'The Daughters of Albion waved their snow-white handkerchiefs/They joined in the shout of the populace, and exclaimed, "Francis for Ever!"'

[15] Elhanan Winchester, *A Course of Lectures on the Prophecies that Remain to be Fulfilled* (1789).

original Unity fell into division and ever since has sought to return
to the One once more:[16]

> . . . Man subsists by Brotherhood & Universal Love
> We fall on one anothers necks more closely we embrace
> Not for ourselves but for the Eternal family we live
> Man liveth not by Self alone but in his brothers face
> Each shall behold the Eternal Father & love & joy abound
>
> (E387)

Blake did not achieve any full synthesis of the antinomian and
the rationalist. How could he, since the antinomian premised a
non-rational affirmative? There was, rather, an incandescence in
his art in which the incompatible traditions met – tried to marry –
argued as contraries – were held in a polarised tension. If one
may be wrong to look for a coherent intellectual system, there are
certainly constellations of related attitudes and images – connected
insights – but at the moment when we attempt a rational exegesis
we are imposing bounds on these insights. Certainly there are
places where Blake denies the values of rationality, but one can
also see why, to preserve the 'divine vision', he had to do so. For
within the prevailing naturalistic psychology of the time there was
no way to derive, no place into which to insert, the central antinomian affirmatives of *Thou Shalt*: Thou Shalt Love, or Thou Shalt
Forgive. Blake's unique image of Christ, simultaneously humanist
and antinomian ('Jesus was all virtue and acted from impulse, not
from rules') could be, in the available philosophy, derived only
from the inspiration of a 'madman'. It is exactly the absence of
such an affirmative in the complacent doctrine of 'benevolence' to
be found in the Godwinian circle which alienated Wordsworth and
Coleridge. One might add that these affirmatives cannot be easily
derived from materialist thought today. That is why every realis-
ation of these values (such as Blake's) is a plank in the floor upon
which the future must walk.

The busy perfectionists and benevolent rationalists of 1791–6
nearly all ended up, by the later 1800s, as disenchanted men.
Human nature, they decided, had let them down and proved stubborn in resistance to enlightenment. But William Blake, by denying
even in the *Songs of Experience* a supreme societal value to rational-

---

[16] See Ferber's helpful chapter on brotherhood in *The Social Vision of William Blake*; and, on
Gnostic and neo-Platonist myths of Unity, M.H. Abrams, *Natural Supernaturalism* (New
York, 1971), pp. 143–63.

ity, did not suffer from the same kind of disenchantment. His vision had been not into the rational government *of* man but into the liberation of an unrealised potential, an alternative nature, within man: a nature masked by circumstance, repressed by the Moral Law, concealed by Mystery and self-defeated by the other nature of 'self-love'. It was the intensity of this vision, which derived from sources far older than the Enlightenment, which made it impossible for Blake to fall into the courses of apostasy. When he drew apart from the deists and when the revolutionary fires burned low in the early 1800s, Blake had his own way of 'keeping the divine vision in time of trouble'. This way had been prepared long before by the Ranters and the Diggers in their defeat, who had retired from activist strife to Gerard Winstanley's 'kingdom within, which moth and rust does not corrupt'. And so Blake also took the characteristic antinomian retreat into more esoteric ways, handing on to the initiates 'The Everlasting Gospel'. There is obscurity and perhaps even some oddity in this. But there is never the least sign of submission to 'Satan's Kingdom'. Never, on any page of Blake, is there the least complicity with the kingdom of the Beast.

Index